THE FRONTIERS OF PUBLIC LAW

This major collection contains selected papers from the third Public Law Conference, an international conference hosted by the University of Melbourne in July 2018. The collection includes contributions by leading academics and senior judges from across the common law world, including Australia, Canada, New Zealand, the United Kingdom and the United States. The collection explores the frontiers of public law, examining cutting-edge issues at the intersection of public law and other fields. The collection addresses four principal frontiers: public law and international law; public law and Indigenous peoples; public law and other domestic fields, specifically criminal law and private law; and public law and public administration. In common with the two books from the previous Public Law Conferences, this collection offers authoritative insights into the most important issues emerging in public law, and is essential reading for those working in the field.

The Frontiers of Public Law

Edited by
Jason NE Varuhas
and
Shona Wilson Stark

·HART·
OXFORD · LONDON · NEW YORK · NEW DELHI · SYDNEY

HART PUBLISHING

Bloomsbury Publishing Plc

Kemp House, Chawley Park, Cumnor Hill, Oxford, OX2 9PH, UK

1385 Broadway, New York, NY 10018, USA

29 Earlsfort Terrace, Dublin 2, Ireland

HART PUBLISHING, the Hart/Stag logo, BLOOMSBURY and the Diana logo are trademarks of Bloomsbury Publishing Plc

First published in Great Britain 2019

First published in hardback, 2019
Paperback edition, 2021

Copyright © The Editors and Contributors severally 2019

The Editors and Contributors have asserted their right under the Copyright, Designs and Patents Act 1988 to be identified as Authors of this work.

All rights reserved. No part of this publication may be reproduced or transmitted in any form or by any means, electronic or mechanical, including photocopying, recording, or any information storage or retrieval system, without prior permission in writing from the publishers.

While every care has been taken to ensure the accuracy of this work, no responsibility for loss or damage occasioned to any person acting or refraining from action as a result of any statement in it can be accepted by the authors, editors or publishers.

All UK Government legislation and other public sector information used in the work is Crown Copyright ©. All House of Lords and House of Commons information used in the work is Parliamentary Copyright ©. This information is reused under the terms of the Open Government Licence v3.0 (http://www.nationalarchives.gov.uk/doc/open-government-licence/version/3) except where otherwise stated.

All Eur-lex material used in the work is © European Union, http://eur-lex.europa.eu/, 1998–2021.

A catalogue record for this book is available from the British Library.

Library of Congress Cataloging-in-Publication Data

Names: Public Law Conference (3rd : 2018 : Melbourne, Vic.) | Varuhas, Jason, editor. | Stark, Shona Wilson, editor.

Title: The frontiers of public law / [edited by] Jason N.E. Varuhas, Shona Wilson Stark.

Description: Chicago : Hart Publishing, an imprint of Bloomsbury Publishing, 2019. | Includes bibliographical references and index.

Identifiers: LCCN 2019034062 (print) | LCCN 2019034063 (ebook) | ISBN 9781509930371 (hardback) | ISBN 9781509930388 (Epub)

Subjects: LCSH: Public law—Congresses.

Classification: LCC K3150.A6 P835 2018 (print) | LCC K3150.A6 (ebook) | DDC 342—dc23

LC record available at https://lccn.loc.gov/2019034062

LC ebook record available at https://lccn.loc.gov/2019034063

ISBN: HB: 978-1-50993-037-1
PB: 978-1-50995-356-1
ePDF: 978-1-50993-039-5
ePub: 978-1-50993-038-8

Typeset by Compuscript Ltd, Shannon

To find out more about our authors and books visit www.bloomsbury.com. Here you will find extracts, author information, details of forthcoming events and the option to sign up for our newsletters.

CONTENTS

List of Contributors vii

1. *Introduction: The Frontiers of Public Law* 1
   Jason NE Varuhas and Shona Wilson Stark

PART 1
PUBLIC LAW AND INTERNATIONAL LAW

2. *Global Constitutionalism: Myth and Reality* 19
   Cheryl Saunders

3. *Frontiers of Global Administrative Law in the 2020s* 41
   Benedict Kingsbury

4. *International Law and National Security Policy-making:
   The Case of the PPG* 71
   Laura A Dickinson

5. *Public Law in the UK after Brexit* 91
   Jack Beatson and Emma Foubister

PART 2
PUBLIC LAW AND INDIGENOUS PEOPLES

6. *Indigenous Rights, Judges and Judicial Review in New Zealand* 123
   Matthew SR Palmer

7. *Coming to Terms with Communal, Land-related Decision-making by Aboriginal
   and/or Torres Strait Islander Peoples in a Public Law Context* 157
   Debbie Mortimer

8. *Representing Jurisdiction: Decolonising Administrative Law in a Multijural State* 177
   Mary Liston

9. *From the Heart: The Indigenous Challenge to Australian Public Law* 205
   Kirsty Gover

10. *Public Law, Legitimacy and Indigenous Aspirations* 227
    Harry Hobbs

11. *Places as Persons: Creating a New Framework for Māori-Crown Relations* 255
    Andrew Geddis and Jacinta Ruru

PART 3
PUBLIC LAW, CRIMINAL LAW AND PRIVATE LAW

12. *Changing Boundaries: Crime, Punishment and Public Law* 277
    David Feldman

13. *Discretionary Power and Consistency: Is the Sentencing Discretion Different?* 297
    Chris Maxwell

14. *Public and Private Law: A Redundant Divide* 315
    Carol Harlow

15. *The 'Contracting State' and the Public/Private Divide* 335
    ACL Davies

16. *Public and Private Boundaries of Administrative Law* 353
    Margaret Allars

PART 4
PUBLIC LAW AND PUBLIC ADMINISTRATION

17. *The Nature and Bounds of Executive Power: Keeping Pace with Change* 387
    KM Hayne

18. *Peering into the Black Box of Executive Power: Cabinet Manuals, Secrecy and the Identification of Convention* 399
    Anne Twomey

19. *Fomenting Authoritarianism Through Rules About Rulemaking* 429
    Kathryn E Kovacs

20. *Non-fettering, Legitimate Expectations and Consistency of Policy: Separate Compartments or Single Principle?* 443
    Shona Wilson Stark

21. *The In-between Space of Administrative Justice: Reconciling Norms at the Front Lines of Social Assistance Agencies* 471
    Jennifer Raso

22. *A 'Culture of Justification'? Police Interpretation and Application of the Human Rights Act 1998* 499
    Richard Martin

Index 523

LIST OF CONTRIBUTORS

Margaret Allars is Professor of Law at the University of Sydney.

Sir Jack Beatson is a former Lord Justice of the Court of Appeal of England and Wales.

ACL Davies is Professor of Law and Public Policy at the University of Oxford.

Laura A Dickinson is the Oswald Symister Colclough Research Professor of Law at the George Washington University.

David Feldman is Emeritus Rouse Ball Professor of English Law at the University of Cambridge, and Emeritus Fellow of Downing College, Cambridge.

Emma Foubister is a Barrister at Matrix Chambers.

Andrew Geddis is Professor of Law at the University of Otago.

Kirsty Gover is Professor of Law at the University of Melbourne.

Carol Harlow is Emerita Professor of Law at the London School of Economics and Political Science.

KM Hayne is a former Justice of the High Court of Australia.

Harry Hobbs is a Lecturer at the Faculty of Law, University of Technology Sydney.

Benedict Kingsbury is Murry and Ida Becker Professor of Law at New York University.

Kathryn E Kovacs is Professor of Law at Rutgers Law School, The State University of New Jersey.

Mary Liston is an Assistant Professor at the Peter A Allard School of Law, University of British Columbia.

Richard Martin is a Fellow in the Department of Law, London School of Economics and Political Science.

Chris Maxwell is the President of the Victorian Court of Appeal.

Debbie Mortimer is a Judge of the Federal Court of Australia.

Matthew SR Palmer is a Judge of the High Court of New Zealand.

Jennifer Raso is an Assistant Professor at the Faculty of Law, University of Alberta.

Jacinta Ruru is Professor of Law at the University of Otago.

Cheryl Saunders is Laureate Professor Emeritus at the University of Melbourne.

Shona Wilson Stark is a University Lecturer in Public Law at the Law Faculty, University of Cambridge, and an Official Fellow of Girton College, Cambridge.

Anne Twomey is Professor of Constitutional Law at the University of Sydney.

Jason NE Varuhas is Professor of Law at the University of Melbourne.

1
Introduction: The Frontiers of Public Law

JASON NE VARUHAS AND SHONA WILSON STARK*

This collection originates from the third biennial Public Law Conference, entitled 'The Frontiers of Public Law', a major international conference held at Melbourne Law School in July 2018, co-organised by the University of Melbourne and the University of Cambridge. We acknowledge the Wurundjeri people of the Kulin Nation as the Traditional Owners of the land on which the Conference took place.

The 2018 Conference was the third in an ongoing biennial series of major international conferences, following on from the first two Public Law Conferences, both held in Cambridge, in 2014 and 2016 respectively. This collection is the third book in an ongoing series, following on from those collections derived from the first two Conferences: *Public Law Adjudication in Common Law Systems: Process and Substance*,[1] and *The Unity of Public Law? Doctrinal, Theoretical and Comparative Perspectives*.[2]

The motivation for the conference series is to provide a leading international forum for public lawyers from a broad range of jurisdictions to discuss and debate the most important public law issues facing common law systems; and through this enterprise to foster a community of public lawyers drawn from multiple jurisdictions and from the academy, judiciary, legal practice and government. From the time of founding the series it was always the intention of the convenors that following the second Cambridge Conference the series would move to different parts of the common law world. The Melbourne Conference, from which this collection derives, was the first such conference to be held outside the United Kingdom (UK). Moving the conference carries forward the goals of the series, bringing in a wider range of perspectives and participants from different jurisdictions, and focusing attention on public law issues pertinent to different countries and regions. As is evident from the content of this collection, as well as addressing cutting-edge issues that arise across the common law world, the Melbourne Conference also focused attention on a set of public law issues that had not so far been a central focus of the conference series, and which are of particular significance in Australia. Specifically, it was of fundamental importance that public law issues relating to Indigenous peoples

---

* We are grateful to Kirsty Gover and Cheryl Saunders for comments on this chapter.
[1] J Bell, M Elliott, JNE Varuhas and P Murray (eds), *Public Law Adjudication in Common Law Systems: Process and Substance* (Oxford, Hart Publishing, 2016).
[2] M Elliott, JNE Varuhas and SW Stark (eds), *The Unity of Public Law? Doctrinal, Theoretical and Comparative Perspectives* (Oxford, Hart Publishing, 2018).

should be a core concern of the Conference and collection, especially in the light of recent landmark developments in Australia, including the Uluru Statement from the Heart and moves towards a treaty with Indigenous peoples in the State of Victoria, and given the importance of these issues for other common law settler states, including New Zealand and Canada. The Conference included plenary and parallel sessions addressing this topic within single jurisdictions and from a comparative perspective. The topic will again be one of a number of important themes to be explored at the fourth biennial Public Law Conference, to take place in Ottawa in June 2020, co-organised by the Universities of Ottawa, Melbourne and Cambridge. The Ottawa Conference will be the first conference in the Public Law series to take place in North America.

The conference series, now established as the leading regular forum for the scholarly discussion of public law in the common law world, continues to grow and develop. The Melbourne Conference saw the largest number of attendees of any conference in the series, with 250 delegates in attendance from 125 institutions, drawn from 20 countries. It also saw the largest response to our general call for papers, and largest conference programme, with 80 papers presented in just over two days. It is particularly pleasing that the Melbourne Conference attracted the largest number of judges, officials and legal practitioners of any of the conferences in the series, with these groups accounting for approximately half of all delegates, which produced an exciting and stimulating environment for exchange of ideas between those within the academy and those working outside universities. All legal analysis can be enriched by engagement among academic public lawyers and those in practice, in government and on the bench, each group bringing different perspectives to bear in the light of their different experiences. The Conference opened with a panel comprising Kenneth Hayne, formerly of the High Court of Australia, and Lord Mance, then Deputy President of the UK Supreme Court, who considered the frontiers of judicial and executive power. The keynote plenary session featured Professor Cheryl Saunders, of Melbourne Law School, and Professor Benedict Kingsbury, of New York University School of Law, who considered the rise of global constitutional and administrative law.

In common with the previous collections, this book brings together leading academics and judges, as well as a stellar group of early career scholars, drawn from across the common law world, to discuss and debate issues at the cutting-edge of public law. The essays identify, analyse and provide solutions to a range of novel issues of great importance at the border of public law and other fields, many of these issues so far having been unrecognised or under-explored, despite their significance. The chapters will be an invaluable reference point for public lawyers seeking to understand these emergent issues at public law's frontiers, and are likely to lead thinking on these topics and set the parameters for future debate and discussion. Importantly, the issues addressed herein implicate not only public law but variously international law, the law relating to Indigenous peoples, private law, criminal law and the practice of public administration. As such, the essays will be of importance to those working in these fields. As is discussed in the next section, many of the most important legal issues arising within and across common law jurisdictions implicate more than one field, and therefore call for thinking across the traditional categories around which legal thought and legal practice have been organised.

I. The Frontiers of Public Law

The theme of this collection, which follows the theme of the Melbourne Conference, is 'The Frontiers of Public Law'. The book builds on the intellectual foundations set by the previous collections. The first collection, published in 2016, interrogated a supposed boundary that runs through public law, between process and substance or, perhaps more accurately, multiple boundaries between process and substance within public law. If the first book focused on an important distinction within public law, the second book, published in 2018, examined the extent to which public law is or is not a unified field or discipline, considered from the perspectives of doctrine, theory and comparative law. This included consideration of multiple boundaries within public law, and consideration of public law across jurisdictional boundaries. This book, on the frontiers of public law, moves from looking at questions squarely *within* public law, to examining *intersections* between public law and other fields (albeit the essays have significant ramifications for public law itself, as discussed further below). The term 'frontiers' was preferred to 'boundaries' in order to encourage exploration not only of the constraints on or limits of public law, but also of the possibilities for legal development and legal thought at public law's outer edges. The chapters address four frontiers: public law and international law; public law and the law relating to Indigenous peoples; public law and other fields of domestic law, including criminal law and private law; and public law and public administration.

One important prompt for the 'frontiers' theme is that public lawyers have tended to focus on matters at the perceived 'centre' of, or within the 'mainstream' of, public law, with the vast majority of scholarly writing preoccupied with a relatively small set of well-known topics, such as the legitimacy of judicial strike-down powers, dialogue under bills of rights, deference, statutory interpretation and so on, the terms of debate for each topic being well established, with scholarship in regard to each becoming increasingly specialised and detailed, concomitant with the increasing specialisation of the legal academy. The topics are no doubt important, thus why they have garnered such attention, but at a certain point the law of diminishing returns must invariably cut in. What has been far less explored is public law's outer edges. Yet it is at the outer edges of a field or discipline that one often learns the most about the nature of that field or discipline. This is because at the outer edges certain matters, taken for granted at the (perceived) centre of the field, are brought squarely into focus and tested. These include the fundamental question of whether there is a distinct field of public law at all and, if so, in what way it differs materially from other fields. Often, as one explores the edges of public law, one identifies topics of such significance that they should be a core concern of public law inquiry and/or should not be considered distinct from the field of public law. For example, there must be a serious question whether any public law issue in a settler state can be examined in isolation from a consideration of how the issue impacts on Indigenous peoples. In other words, Indigenous laws, rights and culture should be at the very heart of public law thinking and scholarship, including in scholarship on those established public law topics considered above, such as dialogue and interpretation, as chapters in this collection demonstrate.

Certain matters of fundamental importance, including matters that are of increasing prominence, such as contracting by government, the rise of soft law techniques, the phenomena of global administrative and constitutional law, the role of the judge in criminal law proceedings and the regulation of Indigenous property rights, simply cannot be addressed without the input of public lawyers, and equally cannot be addressed solely through the application of public law tools. These matters implicate international law, criminal law, private law, the law relating to Indigenous peoples, and the discipline of public administration. One aim of the collection is to draw out this complexity, and the multi-dimensional nature of emerging legal problems. A further aim is to encourage conversation on these topics among specialists in public law, specialists in the other fields and those with knowledge across fields. In turn the chapters provide an incisive and well-rounded set of insights into the selected topics, interrogating these topics in a way that recognises their complexity and multi-dimensional nature.

An important and interesting question raised by the chapters is the extent to which there are discernible boundaries or frontiers between public law and the other fields. It is difficult to provide a single answer to what is a 'big' question, and in a sense the question is one posed for readers, to draw their own conclusions, in light of the rich material presented in the chapters.

Nonetheless, there is at least one golden thread running through the contributions to this collection. As certain phenomena, which are the subject of legal regulation, tend to greater complexity – government, public administration, politics, social life, technology, economy, the international order and so on – there are significant ramifications for public law practice and thought. In particular, the law must of necessity adapt to comprehend and effectively regulate this changed reality, which in turn often has the consequence of challenging, and possibly breaking down, established legal categories or boundaries. In turn there is greater fluidity between fields previously considered distinct, such as public law/international law, public law/Indigenous law, public law/private law, public law/criminal law, and public law/public administration. Of course, the path of legal development may not necessarily be smooth. Indeed, legal change is likely to be messy, uneven and stuttering, as longstanding concepts and categories prove resilient to varying degrees. From a comparative perspective it is important to observe that new lines are likely to be drawn differently in different jurisdictions, depending on local contextual features.

Turning first to the division between domestic and international law, for a long time there has been much consideration of the influence of international law on the domestic order, but as the division between the two has worn thin, we increasingly see ideas drawn from the domestic sphere ebbing into the international domain, such as constitutionalism and administrative law, and indeed more generally there has been a reassertion of the domestic and the local, which in turn challenges the universalising tendencies of international law. Moreover, the international realm has itself become increasingly complex, making its intersection with an increasingly pluralistic domestic order far from uniform.

The increased recognition that the law ought to specifically protect the interests of Indigenous peoples, has contributed to the increased plurality of common law legal systems. This may be because Indigenous legal norms are read into or inform the general law of the state. It may be because a settler legal system creates new norms specifically to address the interests of Indigenous peoples, such as variants of fiduciary obligation, duties to consult, Indigenous legal rights or new institutional structures. Or it may be because the distinctiveness of claims seeking to protect Indigenous rights or interests adds a new dimension to existing fields, such as the law of judicial review. Furthermore, a normative concern to recognise and protect the interests and culture of Indigenous peoples cuts across established legal categories; it is a concern relevant to public law, property, tort, equity, succession, contract and so on. Indeed, it is difficult to think of a legal field where the normative concern is not relevant. Because this normative concern cuts across established categories, it also operates to challenge and break down those categories. So, for example, 'private' ideas of personhood, property and rights are put to 'public' ends, such as safeguarding sites of cultural importance, and at the same time give legal recognition and effect to important aspects of Indigenous culture such as Indigenous conceptions of nature. Treaties with Indigenous peoples defy categorisations of purely public, private or international. Thus, as the normative concern to recognise and protect Indigenous interests gains force and momentum, it will likely operate to reshape or break down traditional modes of thought and categorisation.

Modes of government have become increasingly pluralistic and sophisticated, with governments mobilising new tools such as soft law (with corresponding developments in the international sphere). In the case of soft law, its legal regulation challenges existing public law categories, posing questions as to whether old categories should adapt or new ones be created, and draws public law and judges deeper into the domain of public administration (raising the question of whether judicial control is the best form of control). Indeed soft law tools such as policies, which are creatures of public administration, may be co-opted as judicial tools of legal regulation, collapsing any discernible division between law and administration.[3] Another technique, government by contract, challenges intuitively familiar categories of public and private, administrative law and contract law. Indeed it is increasingly difficult to differentiate an autonomous public sphere from an autonomous private sphere in the world, the two being increasingly intermingled, with the consequence that any distinction between public law and private law will struggle to provide a workable basis for organising legal thought or the legal system. In turn, concepts are likely to float more freely between formerly distinct fields, and satisfactory and workable solutions to contemporary problems are unlikely to be found by applying the lens of solely public law or private law, administrative law or contract law, and so on.

II. Structure and Chapters

The book is in four Parts. The chapters in each Part address a particular frontier of public law: public law and international law (Part 1); public law and the law relating to Indigenous peoples (Part 2); public law and other domestic fields of law, specifically criminal law and private law (Part 3); and public law and public administration (Part 4). While this structure has been adopted for organisational purposes, there are multifarious interconnections between the chapters in different Parts, so that the divisions are porous rather than impermeable. The different Parts should be read as being in conversation with one another.

Part 1: Public Law and International Law

Part 1 considers new and emergent issues at the intersection of public law and international law. A common thread is the influence of the domestic on the international. The following

---

[3] See M Elliott and JNE Varuhas, *Administrative Law*, 5th edn (Oxford, Oxford University Press, 2017) 181–85.

are a particular focus: (i) ideas and concepts associated with domestic public law, such as constitutionalism and administrative law, gaining traction in the global sphere, and also the resilience of domestic law and politics in the face of globalisation; (ii) new governmental techniques prevalent in domestic public administration, such as soft law, being increasingly mobilised in the context of international law and relations; and (iii) the impact of domestic politics on the supranational or international stage, and the 'feedback effects' this has on domestic public law.

In regard to (i), Cheryl Saunders (chapter 2) explores the phenomenon of global constitutionalism, examining from the perspective of domestic constitutions the apparent gap between certain claims made in relation to global constitutionalism and realities on the ground. The chapter scopes the field, disaggregating different strands of global constitutionalism. The heart of the chapter is a detailed consideration of two foundational dimensions of constitutional law, constitution-making and change, and constitutional adjudication, in order to gauge the effects of globalising forces domestically. The studies reveal a mixed picture, including the considerable resilience of domestic constitutional law and theory, despite the global context in which they operate, but also scope for better responses to issues raised by that global context within the domestic public law order.

Moving from constitutional to administrative law, Benedict Kingsbury (chapter 3), a founder of the field of global administrative law (GAL), considers the field's frontiers as it moves into the 2020s. The chapter offers an account of GAL as a set of mechanisms, principles and practices that promote or otherwise affect the accountability of global administrative bodies. It charts the piecemeal and incremental development of GAL within a plurality of contexts in the global space, and with variable normative content. Kingsbury considers concepts and methods central to understanding of the field, including 'law', 'administration', 'distributed administration' and 'private governance'. Importantly, the chapter explains the interdependence of GAL and changes in global political, economic and social orders, examining reasons for the rise of GAL and its prospects going forward in a context of shifting responses to globalisation that increasingly strain, negate and remake international ordering.

In regard to (ii), Laura Dickinson (chapter 4) identifies and analyses the United States' (US) use of 'legalised' policy to govern its approach globally to counter-terror operations outside traditional theatres of war. Such policies cut across multiple boundaries, including law and policy, domestic and international law, and different areas of both domestic and international law. Dickinson explains the different and overlapping international legal paradigms that might govern counter-terror operations. In contrast to many of its allies, the US has, as a matter of international law, adopted the international humanitarian law approach, which imposes less onerous constraints than alternative paradigms, such as international human rights law. However, by adoption of legalised policy, the US has imposed additional restrictions on its operations beyond the legal baseline set by international humanitarian law. Dickinson considers the advantages and disadvantages of such use of policy from the perspectives of the US Executive Branch and the Human Rights Community.

In regard to (iii), Jack Beatson and Emma Foubister (chapter 5) consider the potential impact of Brexit on the future trajectory of UK public law. How will the UK's decision to leave the EU feed back into UK constitutional and administrative law? The authors focus on two issues. First, how will Brexit affect the scope and grounds of judicial review? Despite the obvious influence on the UK system of EU legal norms and methods such as proportionality, the authors argue that the ebbing out of EU law will not halt the rise of a jurisprudence of fundamental rights and proportionality, as proportionality is a 'common law construct' and there is a 'sound doctrinal basis' for the common law to recognise rights in appropriate cases. Second, how will Brexit affect relationships between different branches of government, particularly in the wake of the *Miller* case?[4] The authors consider the broader ramifications of that decision are not yet clear, but the courts will continue to play an 'important and legitimate role' in dealing with difficult constitutional questions, including in connection with the concept of 'constitutional' statutes.

Part 2: Public Law and Indigenous Peoples

Part 2 considers the interface between public law and the law relating to Indigenous peoples, principally within the settler states of Australia, Canada and New Zealand. A commonality among the chapters is that they consider different *modes* of recognising and protecting Indigenous rights, interests, law and culture, while also emphasising the importance of recognising and responding to the distinctiveness of the Indigenous context in which law and legal institutions exist and operate. The first three chapters are focused principally on judicial protection within public law proceedings, in which context statute can play an important framing role. The next two chapters consider political and institutional mechanisms for protecting Indigenous rights, and affording Indigenous peoples a voice in matters that affect them. The final chapter considers a novel mode of protection of places of cultural significance to Indigenous peoples.

The first three chapters, focused on judicial protection, demonstrate that it is not possible within settler states to have a complete understanding of fields of public law, such as administrative law, without an appreciation of the emerging and dynamic strand of authorities relating to Indigenous rights and decision-making, which render established public law fields increasingly pluralistic and have the potential to recalibrate those fields in significant ways.

Matthew Palmer's chapter (chapter 6) asks how the judicial branch contributes to protection of Indigenous rights in New Zealand, a constitutional system in which rights are protected principally through politics. Palmer examines the answer in two ways. First, even in such a constitutional system, constitutional dialogue provides a role for the judiciary in shaping constitutional protection of Indigenous rights, a role that only requires the judiciary to perform its conventional function of using reason to apply law to specific facts. Through performance of this role, and dynamic interactions between the judicial and political branches, courts have contributed significantly to the meaning and legal status of the Treaty of Waitangi. Second, Palmer offers a comprehensive account of judicial review cases that have invoked the Treaty, including where the Treaty is referred to in statute, as a primary case study of the judiciary developing law and engaging in dialogue in relation to Indigenous claims. He finds review to be a significant vehicle for protection of Indigenous rights, and that the case law exhibits a blurring of review grounds and indicates Treaty principles have been developed to mirror the substantive law of judicial review.

---

[4] *R (Miller) v Secretary of State for Exiting the European Union* [2018] AC 61.

Debbie Mortimer's chapter (chapter 7) examines a set of complex and fundamental, yet so far under-explored, issues that have arisen within judicial review claims concerning statutory provision for communal decision-making by Aboriginal and Torres Strait Island Peoples in relation to land. In relation to certain dealings with or decisions that affect Indigenous rights and interests in land, legislation imposes certain requirements. These include the requirement of a group decision, such as the giving of consent or authorisation, which is the product of a communal decision-making process by Indigenous people in accordance with traditional law or customs, or a process agreed by the group. Through detailed examination of two legislative examples, both recently the subject of significant judgments, Mortimer identifies and analyses several important issues for the courts raised by these decision-making requirements. These include recognition that public law principles are here being applied in a distinctive context, and the need for courts to come to terms with these differences, including the importance, reflected in the statutory schemes, of empowering Indigenous peoples; questions over whether majority decision-making is an appropriate 'default' position in this context; and questions over how courts receive evidence as to decisions reached by Indigenous peoples.

Whereas public law issues relating to Indigenous peoples have generally been considered through the prism of constitutional law in Canada, Mary Liston's chapter (chapter 8) shifts the conversation to administrative law, shedding light on an under-explored yet significant emergent body of 'Aboriginal administrative law'. In a case study of administrative law and Indigenous 'local governance law', Liston considers case law on judicial review of both electoral processes to appoint Indigenous decision-makers and those decision-makers' subsequent decisions. She examines the proper definition of 'jurisdictions' in various contexts – the jurisdiction of the Indigenous authority, the reviewing court and the Canadian state itself. This study raises questions over whether certain jurisprudential boundaries are useful to 'protect Indigenous legal orders', or are 'unhelpful barriers' that 'obstruct proper recognition of Indigenous decision-makers'. Ultimately, Liston argues for the 'decolonisation' of administrative law. The sui generis nature of Indigenous decision-makers must be recognised, with implications for deference, statutory interpretation, procedural fairness, substantive review and remedies.

The next two chapters move from a principal focus on judicial modes of protection to consider the design of political and legal institutions, underpinned by a concern to ensure recognition and voice for Indigenous peoples. These are matters of great moment for all jurisdictions with Indigenous populations, and these issues are currently at the forefront of legal, political and popular consciousness in Australia in light of the Uluru Statement from the Heart.

Kirsty Gover's chapter (chapter 9) addresses the 2017 Uluru Statement from the Heart, an expression of Indigenous sovereignty and charter for constitutional reform to empower Aboriginal peoples, which has permeated legal and political discourse in Australia. Gover examines the potential for the Uluru proposals for 'Voice, Treaty, Truth' to transform Australian public law and augment its democratic processes. She compares the proposals to developments in New Zealand and Canada, finding them modest, reasonable and vitally necessary given the deficiencies of the Australian constitutional order with respect to Indigenous peoples. In contrast to those jurisdictions, Australia lacks recognition of a distinctive constitutional relationship between settler peoples and Indigenous peoples, and between their respective representatives and governments. In turn, the identification in Australian law of Indigenous peoples as primarily members of a given race leaves them peculiarly vulnerable to discriminatory measures. Lacking recognition of a distinctive relationship, Australian public law has not developed the tools that other jurisdictions have to require governments to consult Indigenous peoples about decisions affecting them. The Uluru proposals would go some way to remedying these significant deficits.

Harry Hobbs (chapter 10) examines the tensions involved in designing Indigenous decision-making institutions connected to or embedded within the public law apparatus of the state. While such institutions are increasingly prevalent and proposals for such institutions increasingly gain traction across settler states, there is an inherent tension between the concerns of Indigenous peoples that such institutions reflect their own ontologies and values, and concerns of the dominant community, who may wish to accommodate these institutions within pre-existing public law frameworks, with the result that Indigenous claims may be subordinated beneath state rationality. Hobbs seeks, by reference to the notion of legitimacy, to identify indicia of institutional design likely to ensure public law remains flexible and substantively accommodative of diverse normative orders. He presents a case study to demonstrate the opportunities and challenges inherent in accommodating Indigenous institutions within state structures. He applies his analytical framework to the now-abolished Aboriginal and Torres Strait Islander Commission, an Indigenous representative body, with a view to distilling insights for the future, given coalescence of Indigenous aspirations behind the Uluru proposals, which include a proposal for a national representative body.

The final chapter in Part 2, by Andrew Geddis and Jacinta Ruru (chapter 11), explores a novel and innovative set of legal developments in New Zealand that defy any neat categorisation. Through legislation, two places of cultural significance to Māori – Te Urewera National Park and the 300-kilometre Whanganui River – have been conferred with legal personhood, while future legislation is envisaged in relation to a third place, Mount Taranaki. By these reforms places gain independent legal existence and are possessed of rights that may be asserted in legal proceedings. As Geddis and Ruru observe, they are no longer 'things' over which human beings exercise dominion, but rather 'persons' with which humans have a relationship. Importantly, these developments afford recognition to the way in which Māori conceive of and relate to the places in issue, which involves a cosmological view of people as part of nature, not separate from it. Geddis and Ruru explain the reasons why the New Zealand Parliament adopted the 'legal personhood' model, and go on to explore the two existing legislative regimes, including the commonalities and differences between them, concluding that the developments are 'constitutional' in nature, and also raise significant constitutional questions, including how and where these new legal persons sit within constitutional structures.

Part 3: Public Law, Criminal Law and Private Law

The chapters in Part 3 consider issues at the intersection of public law and other doctrinal fields of municipal law, specifically criminal law and private law. The chapters identify and analyse a series of legal issues that are of fundamental importance today and which are not capable of full and complete understanding without thinking across traditional doctrinal boundaries. Divisions such as criminal law/public law and private law/public law may be unhelpful distractions and unduly constrain the legal imagination.[5] Rather than invoking a binary division between fields, workable and principled solutions are more likely to arise from a legal approach that acknowledges and endogenises the complexity and multi-dimensional nature of contemporary legal issues.

Turning first to criminal law, David Feldman (chapter 12) charts how public law principles have 'flowed' into criminal justice, examining legal issues relating to the police, prosecutorial discretion and prisons. He highlights the 1960s–1970s as the crucial turning point at which deference towards such institutions began to wane. Politicians, academics, inquiries, pressure groups and other phenomena contributed to increased scrutiny of authority, and several scandals led to a view that the police were 'out of control'. Increased access to justice through legal aid, combined with an increase in solicitors, barristers and judges concerned with such issues, enabled greater scrutiny of criminal justice issues. Such developments can be situated alongside the judicial review revolution of the 1960s. But legislative interventions increased accountability in a way which '[l]itigation could not have achieved'. Ultimately, '[c]onstitutionalising criminal justice' required collaboration between the legal and political worlds – a collaboration Feldman worries is not as close today.

Chris Maxwell (chapter 13) addresses the consistency of sentencing decisions. He critiques the apparent 'special character' of sentencing discretion in Australia, and the prevailing notion of 'individualised justice' in Australian criminal law. According to orthodoxy, Australian judges ought to enjoy maximal freedom when making sentencing decisions, unaided by 'inappropriate intrusions' such as sentencing guidelines. By contrast, Maxwell argues that sentencing decisions 'as a species of public power' should instead enjoy the 'full rigour' of the public law principle of equal treatment. Rather than sentencing guidelines being viewed with suspicion, they should instead be seen as 'indispensable' aids to achieving consistency – the value of which Maxwell expounds in his chapter. Crucially, the chapter reminds us that a 'structured discretion is not a fettered discretion'. This holds for sentencing decisions as it does more generally, including in relation to discretions regulated by administrative law – consistency in administrative law being a focus of several chapters in Part 4.

Turning from criminal to private law, the final three chapters in this Part, as well as addressing the public law–private law division, have synergies with and lead naturally into the chapters in the next Part, in that they directly address legal responses to new and increasingly prevalent modes of government, including the use of contract, digital decision-making and non-statutory powers.

Carol Harlow's chapter (chapter 14) revisits the topic of her seminal 1980 article, '"Public" Law and "Private" Law: Definition without Distinction'.[5] The sequel examines the public–private division in the light of those developments, including fundamental shifts in government, economy and society, that have occurred in the 40 years since. Harlow's argument is not that the distinction should never be drawn. Rather, where the boundary falls in given cases is contestable: the boundary should fluctuate, and any distinction should be based on functional and substantive reasoning. The chapter (i) identifies doctrinal pressure points where questions over the divide have played out; (ii) considers developments that have threatened public law, and public law's response, including the rise of the 'hands

---

[5] C Harlow, '"Public" Law and "Private" Law: Definition without Distinction' (1980) 43 MLR 241.

off' state and subsequently, the 'new regulatory state'; and (iii) charts the emergence of the global and digital era in which public law must now function, arguing that public law, rather than having no further role, has to extend its frontiers so that its control functions can be exercised in the global space in which the parameters of public and private are fluid and constantly changing.

Anne Davies's chapter (chapter 15) records that while governments have always used contract to purchase goods and services, over the latter part of the twentieth century there was a marked quantitative and qualitative increase in this activity in many countries, including the UK. The phenomenon has been analysed by mainstream public lawyers principally through the lens of the 'public/private divide'. From this perspective, the central question was whether private contractors performing public services were subject to judicial review and, later, human rights review. In turn, this discussion contributed to a deeper enquiry about the extent and nature of any differences between public and private law, because the significance of the boundary question is much reduced if the two bodies of law are not that dissimilar. Davies's chapter is dedicated to arguing that while this set of issues is undoubtedly important, it has been something of a distraction from the real problem in this area, which is that public law does not have the right tools to ensure that the government and its contractors are accountable for the proper use of public funds and the effective delivery of public services.

Margaret Allars' chapter (chapter 16) offers a comprehensive doctrinal account of the scope of application of administrative law principles, which demonstrates that the terrain of administrative law extends beyond the boundary of judicial review. The chapter examines the scope of judicial review, considering whether it is settled that exercises of statutory power are invariably justiciable, and the extent to which non-statutory power is justiciable, reflecting on the concept of a 'public law element' as a potential marker of the limits of review, but ultimately considering it an unhelpful distraction. The chapter goes on to consider the potential for judicial review of 'common law capacities' of the executive branch, including the power to enter contracts, as well as the possibility of reviewing a non-statutory decision-maker, possibly with regulatory functions pursuant to a contract with government. The chapter then considers the scope for applying administrative law standards, outside of judicial review, specifically to domestic bodies established under contract, and – pursuant to a fast-developing body of law – to other types of contractual decision-makers.

Part 4: Public Law and Public Administration

The chapters in this Part examine various intersections between public law and public administration. Following on from the previous Part, a number of chapters examine issues raised by and legal responses to the increasing array of techniques utilised by government and public agencies, including use of contract, exercise of non-statutory executive power, executive rule-making, use of soft law instruments such as policy guidance, and reliance on convention. The last two chapters utilise empirical methods to examine intersections between public law and public administration viewed from within administrative agencies; the results are valuable for what they reveal of administrative engagement with legal norms, but also because they ought to inform the approach to legal regulation of public administration, including through judicial review. Ultimately, the chapters in this Part reinforce the deep interconnectedness and inherent interdependence of public law and public administration, to the point that it may, on occasion, be difficult to distinguish the two phenomena.

Kenneth Hayne's chapter (chapter 17) considers whether public law doctrines have kept pace with changes in the ways executive power is used, focusing on the political branches' looking to the market economy as the model for providing public services, principally through contracting with private entities for provision of such services. Hayne first considers how these sorts of dealings intersect with accepted notions of government structures and the law of judicial review. The chapter then goes on to directly address the nature and extent of executive power, interrogating the basis of executive powers to contract, and examining the political and financial consequences of government contracting. He ends with reflections on whether lawyers have too often examined these arrangements solely through the lens of contract, and whether, when viewed through a public law lens, legal norms have kept up with change or been too confined by pre-existing habits of thought.

Anne Twomey's chapter (chapter 18) examines constitutional conventions pertaining to prerogative powers, with a specific focus on the 'tension between secrecy and transparency'. Public access to archival documents and via freedom of information legislation is revealed to be patchy through case studies such as the saga surrounding Prince Charles's so-called 'black spider letters'. The rise of Cabinet Manuals is examined, and useful comparisons are drawn between the UK, Canada, Australia and New Zealand. Cabinet Manuals' utility as tools of transparency is, however, questioned. Their partisan recording of conventions threatens to 'distort' rather than clarify, and hence must be supplemented by access to underlying documents, so that the Manuals themselves may be scrutinised. Twomey explains how a balance must be struck between the advantages of convention's flexibility and the resulting lack of clarity as to its scope. Her work importantly aims to crack open the 'black box of secrecy' in order to maximise clarity and minimise constitutional crises caused by misunderstandings.

Kathryn Kovacs (chapter 19) writes on the topical issue of presidential power in the US. Her chapter offers a useful history of the Administrative Procedure Act (APA) and outlines how agency rulemaking in the US 'has become increasingly difficult' through a mixture of Congressional, Presidential and judicial requirements. Such difficulties, combined with the atrophying of Congressional policymaking, have led to the President filling the 'power vacuum'. Kovacs outlines the problems with this increased Presidential function, such as insulation from judicial review. She argues that the judicially-created 'rules about rulemaking' are particularly problematic for various reasons, including their conflict with both precedent and the ethos of the APA. She emphasises that fidelity to the APA is particularly important given its 'deep deliberation' during 'an epic legislative battle'. The eventual compromise embodied by the APA 'mandates respect from the courts', which is not currently being shown.

Shona Wilson Stark's chapter (chapter 20) addresses the increasing need to find the right combination of flexibility and consistency in administrative law. In order to address this issue, she considers the relationships between the different grounds of judicial review of non-fettering, legitimate expectations and consistency of policy. She argues that the emergent consistency ground of review is of a piece with 'a long history of consistency' in English administrative law, and that its emergence may clarify the proper limits of the hitherto messy legitimate expectations doctrine. Contrary to suggestions elsewhere that these two relatively new grounds of review are in tension with the well-established non-fettering principle, Stark argues that all three grounds of review are needed for clear jurisprudence, as well as to send a clearer message to decision-makers. In so doing, we can strike the right balance between flexibility and consistency in order to have 'the best of both worlds'.

The consistency thread continues to run through chapter 21. Jennifer Raso shifts our focus from the usual perspective of legislative and judicial constraints on administrative action, to the structuring of discretion within administrative agencies themselves. Her empirical research into the behaviour of caseworkers in the 'Ontario Works' social assistance programme is particularly important because few caseworker decisions are judicially reviewed. Their interpretations of the programme are therefore 'practically, if not formally, "the law"'. Building on Jerry Mashaw's 'internal' theory of administrative justice, Raso found that Ontario Works caseworkers mapped – in almost equal numbers – onto a 'professional identity spectrum' between 'pro-client social workers' and 'black and white efficiency engineers'. Caseworkers therefore differ between responding to an individual's 'unique needs' or attempting to ensure consistency 'en masse', as well as to whether they are more likely to bend or adhere to the rules. The two categories, however, were not as rigidly observed as previous studies may have suggested, because all caseworkers engaged in a process of balancing competing programme norms that in fact may allow for closer internal regulation than judicial review would provide.

Richard Martin's chapter (chapter 22) presents the results of his study of the Police Service of Northern Ireland's (PSNI's) interpretation and application of the Human Rights Act 1998 (HRA 1998). He helps us to 'extend our gaze' beyond judges as the 'interpreters and appliers of the HRA 1998', reminding us that the 'culture of justification' the 1998 Act attempts to foster can only be achieved by other administrators performing an interpretive function too. His research 'shines a rare light' on the PSNI's approach to policing public order in Northern Ireland. Revealing that approach is extremely useful in considering the question of how deferential the courts should be when checking the Convention-compatibility of police exercises of powers. Particularly interesting is the role of the PSNI's in-house lawyer, whose advice the police declare 'takes precedence' over the case law. Given that lawyers who become 'embedded' in such positions may 'use their legal expertise to secure, rather than challenge, organisational goals', such observations are potentially alarming. More positively, Martin concludes that the PSNI commanders use human rights 'to reason their way to a decision, not merely to rationalise it to appeal to oversight bodies'.

III. Acknowledgements

In organising the conference on which this collection is based, and preparing this volume for publication, we have received assistance and support from a number of people and institutions.

We are particularly grateful to Mark Elliott. He was a co-convenor of the 2014 and 2016 Conferences, and involved in the planning stages of the 2018 conference. We wish to acknowledge his significant contributions to organisation of the Conferences, and the establishment of the conference series. We have greatly benefited from his involvement as one the leading public lawyers in the common law world, his tireless work ethic and his intellectual generosity. We are delighted that Mark will remain involved in the conference series as a member of the Conference Advisory Board.

We owe a special debt of gratitude to Phapit Triratpan, who was the conference assistant for the 2018 Public Law Conference. She provided significant administrative support for the year and a half leading up to the Conference, led the team of student assistants during the Conference and provided editorial assistance with the preparation of this book. We have greatly valued working with her, and appreciate the hard work she put into this endeavour. During her involvement in the conference she was a JD student at Melbourne Law School, and she is now working as a practising lawyer at a leading firm in Melbourne.

We are grateful to Anna Dziedzic, a doctoral student at Melbourne Law School, who also provided invaluable editorial assistance with the preparation of the manuscript. We thank the group of Melbourne Law School JD and doctoral students who served as assistants at the Conference: Grace Borg, Anne Carter, Laura Kuhn, William Phillips, Charlie Schaffer, Carlos Arturo Villagran Sandoval, Geordie Wilson and William Zhou. We also thank Aftab Hussain, Administrator of the Centre for Comparative Constitutional Studies at Melbourne Law School, who provided administrative support in the lead-up to and during the Conference.

We wish to acknowledge the support we received from the many people at Melbourne Law School with whom we worked on the Conference, and grant funding received from the Law School's International Collaboration Fund. We are especially grateful for the strong support of Carolyn Evans and Pip Nicholson, in their capacities as successive Deans of the Law School. We also wish to thank Cheryl Saunders, whose advice and continuous strong support and enthusiasm for this endeavour we have greatly valued. We have also appreciated the advice of the members of the Conference Advisory Board. The members of the Board for the 2018 Conference were: Mark Aronson (UNSW), John Bell (Cambridge), Mark Elliott (Cambridge), David Feldman (Cambridge), Carol Harlow (LSE), Richard Hart (founder, Hart Publishing), Cora Hoexter (Witwatersrand), Janet McLean (Auckland), Lord Reed (UK Supreme Court), Cheryl Saunders (Melbourne), Adrienne Stone (Melbourne) and Robert Thomas (Manchester).

We are grateful to Hart Publishing, the exclusive sponsor of the 2018 Public Law Conference, and of the Public Law series of conferences, for its ongoing commitment to, and support of, the conference series. The conference series is very much a collaboration with Hart Publishing, which has been heavily involved with the series since its inception, having been the exclusive sponsor of each conference in the series and having published each of the edited collections associated with the series. We have greatly benefited from the more general support and advice of those at Hart in planning the conference series and preparing this volume. In particular we have greatly appreciated the support of Hart's Editorial Director and General Manager, Sinead Maloney. We were delighted that Sinead was able to attend the Melbourne Conference and address the delegates on the first morning of the Conference. We also wish to thank the production team at Hart who worked on this book, including Kate Whetter, Linda Staniford and Richard Cox, and Catherine Minahan, for her characteristically meticulous copy-editing of the book manuscript.

The Public Law series continues to maintain its strong commitment to supporting and promoting the work of early career scholars. The 2018 Conference included dedicated doctoral panels, an innovation first introduced at the 2016 Conference, and the panels were once again a tremendous success and a highlight of the Conference. More generally, we were delighted to receive an overwhelming response from doctoral students from across the world to our call for papers. The Richard Hart Prize for the best paper delivered by an early career scholar was first established and awarded at the 2016 Conference, and was offered again at the 2018 Conference. We are very grateful to Richard Hart, founder of Hart Publishing, who had a significant role in establishing the conference series, for his continued support of the Prize. The 2018 winner was Anna Dziedzic, a doctoral student at Melbourne Law School, for her paper entitled, 'Constitutional Adjudication by Foreign Judges and the Boundaries of the Judicial Role in Pacific Constitutional Systems'. We are very grateful to the members of the judging panel: Richard Hart, Carol Harlow (LSE), Lord Mance (former Deputy President of the UK Supreme Court) and Cheryl Saunders (Melbourne Law School). The Prize will be offered again in 2020.

Lastly, we wish to thank artist Ande K Terare. We are delighted that his Aboriginal artwork *River Bed* appears on the cover of this book, and we acknowledge his generosity in asking that the licence fee be donated to The Royal Children's Hospital Melbourne. The original artwork is displayed in the foyer of Melbourne Law School.

More information on the 2018 Public Law Conference, including video-recordings of the plenary sessions at the 2018 Conference, can be found at the conference website: https://law.unimelb.edu.au/public-law-conference.

PART 1

Public Law and International Law

2

Global Constitutionalism: Myth and Reality

CHERYL SAUNDERS

I. Introduction

Theories of global constitutionalism make a series of claims about the consequences of globalisation for constitutional arrangements across the world, both within and above the level of the state. Collectively, they make global constitutionalism one of the most challenging, complex and, occasionally, frustrating segments of the fields of domestic public law and public international law.[1] For this purpose, globalisation comprises myriad manifestations of the interdependence of states and peoples across state borders that appear to have implications for public law. These have been catalysts for theories to explain what has happened, to justify, celebrate or decry the changes, and to make predictions for the future. At the same time, however, domestic public law has continued, if not unaltered, then at least without the degree of change that debates on global constitutionalism might suggest. There is something of a disjunction, between the high theory of global constitutionalism, some of the global practices it reflects and realities on the ground. This may be because global constitutionalism is, to use Anne Peters' term, 'descriptively false'.[2] Alternatively, or in addition, it may be because domestic public law has not kept up with the demands of global developments.

This chapter explores the apparent gap between theory and reality from the standpoint of domestic constitutions, considered globally. This perspective is less usual, but necessary for a rounded understanding of global constitutionalism. I argue that while many of the more extravagant claims for global constitutionalism miss their mark, globalisation nevertheless places pressures on national systems of government to which domestic constitutions could respond more effectively. To these ends, section II sketches some of the main claims of global constitutionalism as they affect domestic constitutions and explores the challenges that top-down theories of global constitutionalism face, from the standpoint of domestic constitutionalism. Sections III and IV are the heart of the argument that I seek to make. These sections, respectively, draw on constitution-making and change and constitutional interpretation and adjudication, as two foundational dimensions of constitutional law, to explore global constitutionalism at the domestic level more closely. Both sections reveal a

---

[1] For a convenient overview of different perspectives on this vast field, see A Peters, 'Global Constitutionalism' in MT Gibbons (ed), *The Encyclopedia of Political Thought* (Malden, John Wiley and Sons Ltd, 2015).
[2] ibid.

mixed picture: considerable resilience on the part of domestic constitutional law and theory, despite the global context, which nevertheless continues to throw up challenges that demand a better response from domestic public law. Section IV outlines a series of conclusions for the theory, form and operation of domestic constitutions in an interdependent world.

II. Scoping the Field

Global constitutionalism is a compendious term for a range of different claims about the impact of globalisation on constitutional ordering in the world of the twenty-first century. At least three strands of thought can be identified. One dominant set of ideas focuses on the emergence of constitutional forms and practices at the international level or in institutionalised regional groupings of states.[3] This aspect of the field might also be described as the constitutionalisation of international law.[4] A second, somewhat different strand of thought points to the framework of typically soft law and practice within which state and non-state actors exercise considerable transnational authority. This strand examines the advantages of subjecting such actors more effectively to principles of a broadly constitutional kind and the limitations of individual state action for this purpose.[5] This sub-set of the field also can be characterised as global administrative law.[6] As the terminology of constitutionalism suggests, the interest in both these strands is in the extent to which familiar features of liberal constitutionalism, as it has evolved within states, are or can be replicated on an international or transnational plane. These features include at least the rule of law, sufficiently broadly conceived to encompass limited and accountable government and the protection of human rights.[7] Some of the literature is descriptive and analytical.[8] Some is functional in the sense of teasing out what constitutionalisation needs to achieve, in order to accomplish its goals.[9] Much of the rest is prescriptive or conceptual, identifying new ways of thinking about international, regional or transnational organisation and the directions in which, ideally, each should evolve.[10]

A third strand of the field of global constitutionalism focuses on the implications of regional or international developments for national constitutions, with particular reference to the relationship between national constitutional orders and legal orders above the level of the state. National constitutions may be understood generically for this purpose to comprise

---

[3] JB Auby, 'Global Constitutionalism and Normative Hierarchies' in M Belov (ed), *Global Constitutionalism and its Challenges to Westphalian Constitutional Law* (Oxford, Hart Publishing, 2018).

[4] J Klabbers, A Peters and G Ulfstein, *The Constitutionalization of International Law* (Oxford, Oxford University Press, 2009).

[5] Auby, 'Global Constitutionalism and Normative Hierarchies' (n 3); G Teubner, *Constitutional Fragments: Societal Constitutionalism and Globalization* (Oxford, Oxford University Press, 2012).

[6] N Krisch and B Kingsbury, 'Introduction: Global Governance and Global Administrative Law in the International Legal Order' (2006) 17 *European Journal of International Law* 1.

[7] Peters, 'Global Constitutionalism' (n 1).

[8] Auby, 'Global Constitutionalism and Normative Hierarchies' (n 3).

[9] J Dunoff and J Trachtman, 'A Functional Approach to International Constitutionalization' in J Dunoff and J Trachtman (eds), *Ruling the World? Constitutionalism, International Law and Global Governance* (Cambridge, Cambridge University Press, 2009).

[10] Auby, 'Global Constitutionalism and Normative Hierarchies' (n 3).

the body of fundamental, usually legal, norms that empower and limit the institutions of government for a state, and which structure key relations between a state and its people, from whom the constitution derives its authority. The significance of a constitution draws on the concept of a state itself, as a formally sovereign entity, equal with others, bounded by a territory within which government is provided for a people. There is nothing in the sparse normative foundations for statehood to suggest that government must take any particular form.[11] Indeed, constitutional arrangements have varied considerably between the states of the world and continue to do so. The claims of global constitutionalism nevertheless are that the role, status and function of state constitutions now are changed, possibly in fundamental ways. Globalisation variously is said to have driven convergence;[12] created interdependence; limited the effectiveness of constitutions; supplemented them with external sources of law and practice; and shifted the locus of legitimacy, or at least caused it to be shared.[13] At its height, in conditions of globalisation, national constitutions are seen as components of a 'compound constitutional system', supplemented by international law.[14]

The first and third strands of global constitutionalism are connected. Perceptions of the diminution of the role of state constitutions naturally focus attention on what can be achieved above the level of the state and create demands for at least some of the features of constitutionalism to be replicated there. Conversely, expansion of the authority of international or regional orders, at the expense of national constitutions, may be legitimised through association with constitutional principles of some kind. Much of the energy of global constitutionalism is directed to considering the extent to which this can be achieved and how. As matters presently stand, it may be plausible that the international sphere could gradually consolidate a form of the rule of law, observe a form of separation of powers and acknowledge the primacy of human rights. There is still a long way to go in each case, however, and democratic legitimacy always is likely to be a step too far.[15] Recognition of the strengths and weaknesses of what can be achieved consistently with constitutional principle at each level of government therefore has encouraged more muted visions of what is normatively desirable, involving 'close symbiosis' between the domestic and international spheres.[16]

The claims of global constitutionalism are driven by a range of phenomena that characterise the world of the twenty-first century. A host of global realities demand collaboration between states to manage transnational activity and to deal with shared problems of which pandemic diseases, global warming and international terrorism are only a few examples. Acceptance of a common humanity, valuing individual worth, underpins international protection of human rights and international interest in conditions within states that fail to comply with human rights standards. Flows of conditional aid from richer to poorer

---

[11] Such as it is: J D'Aspremont, *International Law as a Belief System* (Cambridge, Cambridge University Press, 2018) 79–86.
[12] C Saunders, 'Towards a Global Constitutional Gene Pool' (2009) 4 *National Taiwan University Law Review* 3, 21–22.
[13] V Perju, 'Double Sovereignty in Europe? A Critique of Habermas' Defense of the Nation-state' (2018) 53 *Texas International Law Journal* 49.
[14] A Peters, 'The Globalization of State Constitutions' in JE Nijman and A Nollkaemper (eds), *New Perspectives on the Divide between National and International Law* (Oxford, Oxford University Press, 2007).
[15] Klabbers, Peters and Ulfstein, *The Constitutionalization of International Law* (n 4) 330–32.
[16] N Walker, 'The Shaping of Global Law' (2017) 8 *Transnational Legal Theory* 360, 367.

states, sparked by altruism and self-interest, seek to stimulate development and alleviate poverty, with varying degrees of success. These developments in turn have prompted and been prompted by a dramatic increase in the range and penetration of international law and institutions. Regionalism has emerged as a new layer of governance, both in the form of integration for which the European Union remains a paradigm and for the specific purpose of human rights protection. The ease of mobility of people, goods, services and capital, which also characterises the current phase of globalisation, has mixed peoples, diffused citizenship ties and created economic interdependence, with concomitant challenges for national governance.[17] The communications revolution offers almost instant transmission of information around the world, including information of a constitutional kind.

These familiar developments are merely the most obvious vehicles through which globalisation may have constitutional effects. Geopolitical movement is part of the story as well. The international institutions created at the end of World War II limited freedom of state action and created an organised capacity for collective action for the preservation of peace and for other common purposes.[18] The end of the Cold War in the 1990s proved a catalyst for constitutional change around the world; an extraordinary phase of constitutional renewal that witnessed considerable cross-fertilisation of constitutional ideas and provided the occasion for new forms of international influence.[19] The end of the constraints that the dynamics of the Cold War imposed, as superpower rivalry propped up authoritarian regimes in various parts of the globe, helps to explain the incidence of intrastate conflict across the decades of twenty-first century, often with cross-border actors and effects, attracting the authority of international institutions.[20] Triumphalism about the victory of liberal constitutionalism, as another product of this period, fuelled expectations about the directions that all constitutions ultimately would and should take, legitimising external influence to that end.[21]

The impact of forms of globalisation on constitutional ordering at different levels is by no means new. Theories, institutions, principles and practices of a constitutional kind, including the very conception of a written constitution representing fundamental law, have moved across state borders for centuries. The long age of colonisation was another period during which the governing arrangements of communities in all regions of the world were dramatically reshaped by or in reaction to imperial powers, whose own constitutional arrangements necessarily also adapted to deal with their new responsibilities. These earlier phases of globalisation were critical in setting the patterns of constitutional government that can be seen across the world of the twenty-first century. The current phase is at least equally important, however. It is broad, deep and pervasive, with distinctive features of its own.

---

[17] M Tushnet, 'The Inevitable Globalization of Constitutional Law' (2009) 49 *Virginia Journal of International Law* 985.
[18] Arguably, these developments had earlier roots: OA Hathaway and SJ Shapiro, *The Internationalists: How a Radical Plan to Outlaw War Remade the World* (New York, Simon & Schuster, 2017).
[19] A Ladley, *Constitution-Building after Conflict: External Support to a Sovereign Process* (Stockholm, International Institute for Democracy and Electoral Assistance, 2011) 8.
[20] K Dupuy et al, *Trends in Armed Conflict, 1946–2016* (Zurich, EZH Zurich Centre for Security Studies, 2017), available at http://www.css.ethz.ch/en/services/digital-library/articles/article.html/a7992888-34fc-44e6-8176-2fcb3aada995/pdf.
[21] L Zucca, 'Two Conceptions of Global Constitutional Order' (2018) *King's College London Law School Research Paper No 2018-22*, available at https://ssrn.com/abstract=3188161.

Even so, as matters presently stand, it is difficult to derive from the realities of globalisation a coherent theory of global constitutionalism with universal application. This difficulty has various causes, four of which are considered here.

One concerns the nature of international law itself, as a building block for claims of global constitutionalism. International law famously is fragmented between its principal regimes, giving them uneven effect.[22] Different key actors have different conceptions of what international law requires and how it should be understood.[23] There are gaps between international legal norms and their domestic implementation, notwithstanding the development of techniques for more effective enforcement, which also are fragmented between regimes.[24] These difficulties are less marked in schemes for regional integration, of which the European Union is an exemplar, to which entry is regulated by constitutional-type standards and which can more readily achieve coherence and consistency.[25] Even here, however, as the history of the European Union shows, there are problems of enforcement as states push against ostensibly shared constitutional standards without significant intervention by the group as a whole.[26] Also relevant for present purposes is the use of the margin of appreciation and other techniques by the European Court of Human Rights, to make allowance for national differences in interpreting and applying the European Convention on Human Rights.[27]

Second, it may be too early to gauge the depth of the impact of globalisation on state constitutional arrangements. Superficial similarities between constitutional systems can be observed and quantified. They show significant convergence of norms and institutional arrangements along broadly liberal democratic lines, among many states and between states and international legal standards.[28] Superficial similarity may mask underlying variations on common constitutional themes, however, which may provide bases for further divergence over time.[29] And, by definition, each national constitution operates in a distinctive context, of which history and current circumstances are part. These have not been harmonised by globalisation. In these circumstances, while it may be possible, it seems unlikely that domestic constitutional norms and standards adopted in consequence of globalisation will become sufficiently internalised over time to result in globally consistent patterns of constitutional behaviour. The prospects of such an outcome are further dimmed by the

---

[22] 'Fragmentation of International Law: Difficulties arising from the Diversification and Expansion of International Law' (2006) II(2) *Yearbook of the International Law Commission* 175.

[23] A Roberts, *Is International Law International?* (Oxford, Oxford University Press, 2017).

[24] Y Shany, 'The Universality of Human Rights: Pragmatism Meets Idealism' (2018) *Hebrew University of Jerusalem Legal Research Paper No 29*, available at https://ssrn.com/abstract=3217779.

[25] Consolidated Version of the Treaty on European Union [2012] OJ C326/13, Arts 2, 49; S Bartole, 'The Role and Contribution of the Venice Commission to the EU Integration Process and the EU Neighbourhood Policy' (2017) *Venice Commission* CDL-UDT(2011)017, available at https://www.venice.coe.int/webforms/documents/default.aspx?pdffile=CDL-UDT(2011)017-e.

[26] Hungary and Poland have been cases in point. Such problems may stem even from the time of admission, however: P Rezler, 'The Copenhagen Criteria: Are they Helping or Hurting the European Union?' (2011) 14 *Touro International Law Review* 390.

[27] J Gerards, 'Margin of Appreciation and Incrementalism in the Case Law of the European Court of Human Rights' (2018) 18 *Human Rights Law Review* 495.

[28] DS Law and M Versteeg, 'The Evolution and Ideology of Global Constitutionalism' (2011) 99 *California Law Review* 1163.

[29] C Saunders, 'Theoretical Underpinnings of Separation of Powers' in G Jacobsohn and M Schor (eds), *Comparative Constitutional Theory* (Cheltenham, Edward Elgar Publishing, 2018).

influence of global competitors to liberal democracy in, for example, China and Russia; the mixed success of liberal democratic transplants; and reactions against the imposition of liberal democratic norms by way of globalisation that have characterised the second decade of the twenty-first century.

Third, on any view, globalisation is so patchy in the nature and effect of its impact on the national constitutions of the world that generalisation is bound either to overstate or understate the case. At least two lines of cleavage between states make the point.

One such dividing line lies between states in the global north and those in the global south. Many of the latter receive aid and other forms of international assistance, which comes with conditions, sometimes of a broadly constitutional kind, including at the point of constitution-making. States in the global south also are more likely to be sites of intrastate conflict or other destabilising forces, attracting the possibility of international intervention in some form. Globalisation potentially affects the constitutional arrangements of these states to a much greater degree than those of states in the global north.

A different line of cleavage, also relevant to the impact of global constitutionalism, lies between states that are members of regional integration arrangements, regional human rights bodies or other forms of transnational association and those that are not. To complicate the calculations further, all these arrangements vary in depth and effectiveness, leading to differences in their impact between regions as well.[30] Much of the literature on global constitutionalism is generated from Europe, where the modalities of the European Union and institutions of the Council of Europe have ensured the deep interpenetration of regional and domestic constitutional law, throwing up a range of genuinely novel constitutional problems, attributable to this form of globalisation.[31] States in Latin America and Africa also are members of regional organisations of various kinds, with some, although lesser constitutional impact.[32] Large parts of the world, however, are parties to no institutionalised regional arrangements with constitutional relevance. The vast regions of Asia, the Pacific and Oceania are the principal cases in point. In these parts of the world, many of the claims made for the current phase of global constitutionalism have no real resonance and, indeed, are likely to be resisted, for reasons attributable to experiences of global constitutionalism in the past.

Other lines of cleavage complicate generalisation as well: between states that accept the direct effect of international law on domestic law, including domestic constitutional law and those that do not;[33] between states that have engaged in major constitution-making projects during the current phase of globalisation and those with constitutions that have continued, substantially unchanged;[34] between weak or fragile states and states with a well-established sense of statehood, whatever their economic circumstances;[35] between states with clout in international decision-making, including as permanent members of the Security Council, and those without it. Reflection on this matrix of differences makes it possible to understand

---

[30] M Wiebusch, *The Role of Regional Organizations in the Protection of Constitutionalism* (Stockholm, International Institute for Democracy and Electoral Assistance, 2016).
[31] From a huge literature see, eg, D Grimm, *Sovereignty* (New York, Columbia University Press, 2015) 87–98.
[32] Wiebusch, *The Role of Regional Organizations* (n 29).
[33] Compare, for example, Guatemala and Australia in this regard.
[34] Compare South Africa and the United States.
[35] Compare Timor Leste and Sri Lanka.

why global constitutionalism has taken such a hold on the imagination without adequately representing global constitutional experience, at least some of which is antagonistic to any such movement.[36]

A fourth reason for the difficulty of assessing the reach and depth of global constitutionalism is that the situation is not static.

On the one hand, the evidence of interdependence is increasing and, with it, the need for collective action. Climate change is one catalyst. Another is the extraordinary flow of refugees around the world, placing pressure on the management of national borders and prompting political unrest. Refugee flows are likely only to increase with global warming, augmenting the already pronounced diversity of state populations and the potential for conflict within and between states.[37]

On the other hand, there is evidence everywhere of reaction against supra-national and international arrangements that impact on constitutional autonomy and other key areas of national decision-making. Ironically, the global spread of such reactions suggests another form of globalisation at work, as information, ideas and, perhaps, strategies transcend national boundaries. The referendum vote in favour of the withdrawal of the United Kingdom from the European Union is only one, admittedly extreme, example that might be cited.[38] The newly explicit focus on the national interest in the United States is an influential other marked by, for example, withdrawal from the Trans-Pacific Partnership and projected withdrawal from the Paris Agreement on climate change.[39] At least some of these reactions against globalisation may be deplored, as illustrations of xenophobia, intolerance and manipulation of public opinion by autocratic leaders seeking to augment their own power. Others, however, reflect disillusionment with the harsh economic effects of neoliberalism, the challenge of making liberal democracy work effectively in states where it has only shallow roots or a preference for retaining authority at the level of the state over which, whatever its faults, citizens perceive at least the potential for control. It is feasible that there will be a counter-backlash in due course, favouring transnational collaboration and global standards for democracy and human rights. There are grounds on which to suspect, however, that there is unlikely to be a return to the business of global constitutionalism as usual, whatever this is assumed to have been. The past holds lessons for the manner in which authority is calibrated within states, between states and transnational orders, and within transnational orders themselves, to maximise the contribution of all levels of government. Identifying these lessons and responding creatively to them is one of the major challenges of our time.

---

[36] M Koskenniemi, 'Less is More: Legal Imagination in Context: Introduction' (2018) 31 *Leiden Journal of International Law* 469.

[37] In 2018 the United Nations High Commissioner for Refugees (UNHCR) estimated that there were 25.4 million refugees in the world and 3.1 million asylum seekers, in addition to 40 million internally displaced persons: see UNHCR, 'Figures at a Glance' (2018), available at http://www.unhcr.org/en-au/figures-at-a-glance.html.

[38] N Walker, *Brexit Timeline: Events Leading to the UK's Exit from the European Union* (House of Commons Briefing Paper No 7960, 22 March 2019). The example admittedly is weakened by the difficulty of 'Brexit', which at the time of writing has not yet occurred.

[39] Presidential Memorandum Regarding Withdrawal of the United States from the Trans-Pacific Partnership Negotiations and Agreement, 23 January 2017, available at https://www.whitehouse.gov/presidential-actions/presidential-memorandum-regarding-withdrawalunited-states-trans-pacific-partnership-negotiations-agreement/; Depositary Notification, United Nations, 8 August 2017, available at https://treaties.un.org/doc/Publication/CN/2017/CN.464.2017-Eng.pdf.

The rise of new world powers, and in particular China, makes the future directions of global constitutionalism even less clear. China has long since offered an alternative to the liberal constitutional paradigm, which has its attraction for some parts of the world. Formally, at least, China eschews direct interference in the constitutional affairs of others, making it an attractive international partner for states in the global south, on this score at least.[40] China is a major player on the world stage, a permanent member of the Security Council and a formidable presence in international fora. In these circumstances, reference to the preferences of the 'international community' is more ambiguous than ever, at least in contested contexts.[41]

Equally significantly, China is taking steps to pursue what may prove to be a transnational community of its own, albeit of a very different kind, with different implications for states involved in it. The Belt and Road Initiative involves not only major investment in infrastructure development through bilateral arrangements between China and the 70 or more states to which this initiative extends, but also, potentially, a new community of interest, in which China has considerable influence, supported by new arrangements for international dispute resolution and other steps to encourage a meeting of hearts and minds.[42] This development is sufficiently significant to prompt early speculation about the emergence of a new form of world order.[43] This possibility adds further to the complexity of speculating about what the future of global constitutionalism might hold.

Whatever the future holds, speculation about global constitutionalism does not presently detract from the significance of the concept, form and operation of state constitutions. At least some things seem clear for the foreseeable future. Absent a cataclysm of some kind, there will continue to be states, however imperfect; they will continue to have constitutions; and constitutions will continue to matter for the ways in which states operate. At the same time, however, myriad world problems will continue to require collective action. Some values will continue to be shared by the peoples of the world united by, at least, a common humanity. Ideas, people, resources and trade will continue to move across state borders, with varying degrees of freedom, challenging the untrammelled de facto authority of individual states and, sometimes, their de jure authority. The premises on which at least some of the literature on global constitutionalism is based are correct, in the sense that globalisation creates many challenges with which individual states cannot adequately deal and many opportunities of which they can usefully take advantage.

Not all action to respond to the challenges of globalisation can or should take place at the supra-national and international levels, however, with the consequences for domestic constitutions that some theories of globalisation claim. I argue that state constitutions themselves could do more to recognise particular challenges of globalisation and to structure the actions of their respective states in responding to them. As foreshadowed earlier, sections III and IV of this chapter focus on two aspects of state constitutional law and practice that have

---

[40] R Aidoo and S Hess, 'Non-interference 2.0: China's Evolving Foreign Policy Towards a Changing Africa' (2015) 44 *Journal of Current Chinese Affairs* 107.

[41] United Nations, 'Secretary-General examines "Meaning of International Community" in address to DPI/NGO conference', Press release SG/SM/7133, 15 September 1999, available at https://www.un.org/press/en/1999/19990915.sgsm7133.doc.html.

[42] J Chaisse and M Matsushita, 'China's "Belt and Road" Initiative: Mapping the World Trade Normative and Strategic Implications' (2018) 52 *Journal of World Trade* 163.

[43] Zucca, 'Two Conceptions of Global Constitutional Order' (n 21).

been catalysts for theories of global constitutionalism: the making of constitutions and their interpretation over time. In each case, this part of the chapter seeks not only to identify whether and, if so, how global constitutionalism presently is reflected in state constitutional theory, law and practice, from the top down, but also to explore the potential for state constitutions to concern themselves more effectively with the challenges that globalisation presents, from the bottom up.

III. Constitution-making and Change

A. Top Down

The often-protracted moment of constitution-making, defined to include major constitutional change, generates many of the claims about global constitutionalism, the practices associated with it and the questions to which it gives rise.

The spate of constitution-making that has characterised the last 30 years or so has affected the constitutions of well over half the states of the world.[44] Many, although not all, of these constitution-making projects have encountered significant degrees of external influence, to use a relatively neutral term.[45] External influence comes in many forms.[46] At one end of the spectrum it is, effectively, determinative. Bosnia-Herzegovina and Kosovo are extreme examples in modern times where Constitutions were, in substance, externally imposed.[47] Other cases come close, however, albeit in different ways. One is the Constitution adopted by Iraq, under United States' influence, in the wake of the occupation.[48] Another may be Syria, as a range of international actors vie for authority over the terms of a new Constitution and the conditions under which it will be made.[49] While the relationship is more nuanced and consensual, the European Union also holds considerable sway over the shaping of the Constitutions of applicant states.[50] Some cases of United Nations involvement lie come close to determinative influence as well: the United Nations administration of Timor Leste during the constitution-making phase is one example;[51] United Nations Security Council resolutions that prescribe constitutional process or substance for states in or emerging from conflict are another.[52]

Not all external influence is so prescriptive. Most constitution-making in states in the global south nevertheless attracts a welter of external assistance in some form, under the

---

[44] Ladley, *Constitution-Building after Conflict* (n 19).
[45] ibid.
[46] Z Al-Ali, 'Constitutional Drafting and External Influence' in T Ginsburg and R Dixon (eds), *Comparative Constitutional Law* (Cheltenham, Edward Elgar Publishing, 2011).
[47] ibid 82–84.
[48] P Dann and Z Al-Ali, 'The Internationalized *Pouvoir Constituant*: Constitution-Making under External Influence in Iraq, Sudan and East Timor' (2006) 10 *Max Planck Yearbook of United Nations Law* 423.
[49] N Norberg, 'A Primer on Syria's Constitutional Committee' *Lawfare* (22 December 2018), available at https://www.lawfareblog.com/primer-syrias-constitutional-committee.
[50] Bartole, 'The Role and Contribution of the Venice Commission' (n 25).
[51] Dann and Al-Ali, 'The Internationalized *Pouvoir Constituant*' (n 48).
[52] S Wheatley, 'The Security Council, Democratic Legitimacy and Regime Change in Iraq' (2006) 17 *European Journal of International Law* 531.

auspices of the United Nations Development Programme or other United Nations agencies, and non-government, national and international organisations that support peace, human rights, democracy or development.[53] Ostensibly, assistance of this kind is provided pursuant to invitation, although donors can be insistent. Constitution-making processes in Nepal, Myanmar, Tuvalu, Yemen and Somalia are only a few of many examples that might be given.

External influence on constitution-making is not new. The constitutions of the world were constructed through mixing local initiatives and preferences with ideas, principles and institutions adopted and adapted from elsewhere. Constitutions have been externally imposed, in varying degrees, by victors or other hegemonic powers from Napoleon, through colonial times, to actions of the United States and its allies in the wake of World War II. In theory, at least, under the terms of the United Nations Charter, the days of imposing constitutions through conquest and colonialism are over.[54] The Charter, however, has set up a new dynamic, through its empowerment of international action in the face of threats to global peace and security.[55] Most intrastate conflict has potential for spillover effects, formally empowering the United Nations and member states acting under its auspices to intervene in ways that may have implications for a final constitutional settlement. This link between peace-making and constitution-making sets up a dilemma for both to which I shall return.

External influence on constitution-making, in the conditions of globalisation that characterise the early twenty-first century, affects both the processes of constitution-making and the substance of the constitutions that are made. Formally, international actors accept the need for constitution-making projects to be 'nationally owned and led'.[56] At the same time, however, they press for the adoption of international standards.[57] These include, for example, public participation in constitution-making in ways that reflect the diversity of the society, including gender diversity; the incorporation of international human rights norms into the constitutional text; and the adoption of institutional arrangements that provide a framework for democracy, the rule of law, separation of powers and, in appropriate cases, power-sharing. Other features that may be pressed as well, in the name of 'international best practice', include foundations for proportionality reasoning, specialist rather than generalist constitutional courts and provision for independent institutions, created at arm's-length from politics.

It can readily be seen how these developments encourage claims of convergence and prompt questions about whether constitutional legitimacy now depends on international approval, in whole or in part. In many respects, moreover, these claims are well-founded and the questions justifiable. The outcomes of external involvement should not be overstated, however. Some constitution-making supported by external assistance conspicuously fails.[58] There is often a gap between form and practice, once the Constitution is made and

---

[53] C Saunders, 'International Involvement in Constitution Making' in D Landau and H Lerner (eds), *Elgar Handbook on Comparative Constitution Making* (Cheltenham, Edward Elgar Publishing, 2019).
[54] Hathaway and Shapiro, *The Internationalists* (n 18) xviii–xix. Russian action in the Ukraine, in both the Crimea and the Donbass, is a reminder that, in this context as well, theory does not always reflect practice.
[55] Charter of the United Nations, ch VII.
[56] United Nations, *Guidance Note of the Secretary-General: United Nations Assistance to Constitution-making Processes* (2009).
[57] ibid.
[58] Somalia and South Sudan are cases in point, at the time of writing.

needs to be put into effect by domestic actors, to whom the task of implementation primarily falls.[59] Even formal compliance with international expectations typically falls short in some respects.[60] The modalities and effectiveness of public participation are variable, and indeed there is ongoing debate about whether and when it is a good idea or not.[61] International human rights norms are selectively included in constitutions, but in terms adapted to local preferences and within frameworks, including limitations clauses, that affect their operation in practice.[62]

More particularly, however, for present purposes, it is remarkable how little effect these apparently significant developments on the global plane have had on state constitutional law and the theories that underpin it. Not all constitutional traditions have a developed theory of constituent power, but in states for which constituent power founds constitutional legitimacy, the theory continues to prevail.[63] Elsewhere, the looser notion of popular sovereignty as the source of authority for the constitution as a form of social contract remains dominant, subject to some peripheral if important questions, to which the answers vary, about whether the diaspora should be included or not.[64] Logically problematic as these theories are, they underpin constitutionalism, offering a justification for constitutional supremacy, insisting on the primacy of the people vis-à-vis the institutions of the state, and providing a focal point for the mythology on which constitutions, at least in part, depend, which in turn fuels habits of compliance.[65] Alternative theories, based on observations about coordination, which are more plausible but do not have the same cachet, in any event also offer a state-centred approach.[66] Paradoxically, perhaps, the emphasis on actual rather than virtual public participation in twenty-first-century constitution-making, some of which is attributable to external influence, although some also reflects a natural extension of democracy, has reinforced state-centred theories of constitutional legitimacy.

State actors subscribe to these theories and sometimes rely on them to push back against external involvement. The peoples of states broadly subscribe to them too, even when external intervention is more welcome. And international actors, notwithstanding the influence that they seek to wield, formally subscribe to state-centred theories of constitutional legitimacy as well, routinely describing constitution-making as a 'national sovereign process'.[67]

---

[59] Amnesty International 'Government of Nepal must act Diligently to Implement Rights Provisions under the Constitution' (12 October 2018), available at https://www.amnesty.org/en/documents/asa31/9243/2018/en/.
[60] ibid.
[61] D Landau, 'Democratic Erosion and Constitution-Making Moments' (2017) 2 *UC Journal of International, Transnational and Comparative Law* 87, 105–07.
[62] M Versteeg, 'Law versus Norms: The Impact of Human Rights Treaties on National Bills of Rights' (2015) 171 *Journal of Institutional and Theoretical Economics* 87.
[63] M Loughlin and N Walker (eds), *The Paradox of Constituent Power and Constitutional Form* (Oxford, Oxford University Press, 2008).
[64] C Saunders, 'The Concept of Representation: A Study in Similarity and Difference' in H Krunke et al (eds), *Rettens magt – Magtens Ret: Fetskrift til Henning Koch* (Copenhagen, Jurist-og Økonomforbundet, 2014).
[65] For critique see, eg, R Hardin, 'Why a Constitution?' in DJ Galligan and M Versteeg (eds), *Social and Political Foundations of Constitutions* (Cambridge, Cambridge University Press, 2013).
[66] ibid.
[67] United Nations, *Guidance Note* (n 56).

B. Bottom Up

Section III.A sought to show that there is a disjunction between the beliefs and practices of constitutional law and some of the claims of global constitutionalism, as they operate top down. It suggested that there also is a disjunction between the beliefs and practices of constitutional law and the extent of external influence on constitution-making in at least some states. The status quo is unsatisfactory. External influence is opaque and its modalities complex. In consequence, the various forms of external involvement are inadequately understood, much less theorised at the domestic level. The current state of play offers no framework of principle within which external involvement can be managed and forms of accountability assured. There is developing interest in tackling at least some of these issues from the standpoint of international law and practice.[68] My present purpose, however, is to suggest that responses are possible from the standpoint of constitutional law as well.

External involvement in domestic constitution-making gives rise to at least three sets of problems for which constitutional theory, doctrine and practice could provide better answers.

The first is the core problem of bringing external influence into line with constitutional theory and practice in order both to understand it and, in some cases, to control it. To this end, theory should acknowledge the influence of external context on the exercise of constitution-making authority. This could, in turn, assist constitution-making practice to more explicitly weigh the implications of external factors for the decisions to be made, managing them where management is feasible.

This approach requires attention to be paid to the outward, as well as to the inward, face of constitutions; that is, to the role of constitutions in the exercise of the external, as well as the internal, authority of the state.[69] Constitutions always have been made with an eye to the rest of the world. This is not just a point about borrowing principles, practices and ideas, although this too has always been rife. Part of the very function of a constitution is to constitute a people vis-à-vis the rest of the world, not only conceptually, in providing a framework within which people become citizens of a polity, but actually, in distinguishing the people of one state from the people of another.[70] In similar vein, constitutions often serve to delineate territory as well.

More generally still, however, constitutions always have been tempered by international conditions, as they bear upon the state.[71] Sometimes these are so weighty as to be almost irresistible: the making of the Constitution of Japan during the post-War occupation is an example.[72] Sometimes international conditions are merely factors to be taken into account

---

[68] The 2009 Guidance Note of the Secretary-General of the United Nations on *United Nations Assistance to Constitution-making Processes* is one, early example. See also, more recently, United Nations Development Programme, *UNDP Guidance Note on Constitution-Making Support* (New York, United Nations Development Programme, 2014).

[69] N Walker, 'Sovereignty and Beyond: The Double Edge of External Constitutionalism' (2018) 57 *Virginia Journal of International Law* 799.

[70] E Benvenisti and M Versteeg, 'The External Dimensions of Constitutions' (2018) 57 *Virginia Journal of International Law* 515.

[71] C Hahm and SH Kim, *Making 'We the People': Constitutional Founding in Postwar Japan and South Korea*, (Oxford, Oxford University Press, 2015).

[72] ibid.

in designing a constitution-making process and determining constitutional substance. The almost palpable relevance of neighbouring India to decisions taken in Nepal, in response both to demands for federalism in the plains areas and to concerns about foreign influence on Nepalese politics through mixed marriages, is one of many examples that might be given.[73] Sometimes international influence is dependent entirely on the discretion of the recipient state, at least in theory: the welter of offers of international assistance received by any developing state with a significant constitution-making project is an obvious illustration.

All of these factors, however, are merely part of the context within which constitutional choices are made. Context is external as well as internal. Both shape what is possible and desirable and determine domestic choices. Even in the case of Japan, ostensibly an 'imposed constitution', local preference occupied whatever space it could find.[74] Domestic theories of constitutional legitimacy are not necessarily disturbed by this analysis. On the contrary, they are strengthened, by recognising reality.

The second problem, which is related, concerns the meaning of 'national ownership' in application to constitution-making. The primacy of national ownership is formally acknowledged in United Nations' guidance on constitution-making and other documents.[75] One obvious meaning of the term in this context is local ownership, in contradistinction to international or foreign ownership of some kind. National ownership in this sense typically is assumed by domestic decision-makers unless, at least, it is challenged by foreign intervention. Understood in this way, considerations of national ownership identify a boundary that international actors should not cross. From a practical perspective, this concept of national ownership must be relevant to constitutional implementation as well.

An alternative meaning of the term, however, which also derives some support from the context in which it typically appears, is that national ownership requires, as well or instead, a domestic constitution-making process to be 'national' in the sense of broad-based and inclusive. The combination of the two, however, involves a degree of circularity. National ownership precludes foreign ownership, but only if the constitution-making process complies with international standards for inclusion which themselves, to complicate matters further, are contested, both generally and in particular cases.

The circle could be squared by addressing the matter in domestic constitutional theory and practice. All domestic theories of constitutional legitimacy assume that there is something that distinguishes constitution-making from ordinary politics, which justifies the claim that the constitution is higher law, typically by recourse to the authority of the 'people' in some form. In the conditions of the twenty-first century, there is no need for the involvement of the people to be entirely virtual. The actual involvement of a wide cross-section of people, in ways that reflect the diversity of the population, now is a practical possibility. This does not mean that there is a template for the manner and timing of popular involvement that is transferable between states. What is useful and appropriate will vary, with factors that include the heterogeneity and dispersal of the population; security, including cybersecurity; and constitutional tradition. The point is, however, that decisions about what is

---

[73] 'India tries to shape Nepal's new Constitution' *Worldview* (6 October 2015), available at https://worldview.stratfor.com/article/india-tries-shape-nepals-new-constitution.
[74] Hahm and Kim, *Making 'We the People'* (n 71).
[75] United Nations, *Guidance Note* (n 56) Guiding Principle 3.

required to found a claim that the constitution represents a solemn compact that reflects the authority of the people should be an integral part of a domestic process of constitution-making, required by theory and supported by practice. The timing, extent and manner of public involvement, with its implications for the legitimacy of the constitution, must be able to be justified by reference to the circumstances of the state, by state actors on whom responsibility rests.

A third problem concerns the often-vexed relationship between peace agreements and national constitutions. International involvement is an inevitable feature of peace processes to resolve inter-state conflict, and is a familiar feature even when a conflict is largely confined to the territory of a single state. International actors, including neighbours, may be contributors to the conflict, guarantors of peace, or acting under the auspices of the responsibility of the United Nations to secure international peace and security. The interface with constitutions arises where, as often is the case, a peace agreement includes commitments that require constitutional change.[76] A host of questions is presented by this circumstance, some of which revolve, again, around problems of national ownership, which may be even more acute in this context, given the nature of international involvement.[77] The novel question raised by this scenario, however, is the difficulty of giving commitments about governance, initially made in a peace agreement and typically with international involvement, domestic constitutional status and form.[78] The parties to the two processes may be different; different views may be taken about the suitability of particular commitments at the constitutional stage; the necessary majorities may not be forthcoming to make a new constitution or to amend an existing one; proposals enshrined in a constitution that emanated from a peace agreement may encounter problems in judicial review; and proposals that are formally incorporated in constitutional form may be watered down over time.

This is a problem with no simple answers. Despite creative attempts to find solutions within the framework of international law, moreover, it is a problem that needs to be resolved within a framework of national constitutional theory, doctrine and practice, where the tools for legal and political enforcement lie.[79] The problem is avoided if peace can be secured without specific constitutional commitments for the future. Where this is not possible, as often is the case, the difficulty of securing implementation should be anticipated during peace-making, as far as this is possible, in the design of the peace process and the substance of the undertakings. At the constitution-making stage, solutions may lie in the elaboration of a concept of a post-conflict constitution, as a sub-type of the more familiar category of transformative constitutions.[80] Post-conflict constitutionalism could assist both with the making of a constitution and its implementation in law and practice, by according priority to the values of reconciliation and peaceful and dignified co-existence, in ways that also enable the constitutional settlement to evolve over time.

---

[76] C Bell, 'Peace Agreements: Their Nature and Legal Status' (2006) 100 *American Journal of International Law* 373.
[77] Dann and Al-Ali, 'The Internationalized *Pouvoir Constituant*' (n 48).
[78] Bell, 'Peace Agreements' (n 76).
[79] C Bell, 'Peace Settlements and International Law: From *Lex Pacificatoria* to *Jus Post Bellum*' in N White and C Henderson (eds), *Research Handbook on International Conflict and Security Law* (Cheltenham, Edward Elgar Publishing, 2013).
[80] M Hailbronner, 'Transformative Constitutionalism: Not Only in the Global South' (2017) 65 *American Journal of Comparative Law* 527.

IV. Interpretation and Adjudication

A. Top Down

Judicial review to interpret and apply constitutional provisions also is affected by aspects of globalisation in ways that give rise to claims about global constitutionalism and that have implications for domestic constitutional theory and practice.

At least three sets of developments demonstrate the impact of globalisation on judicial review. One is the emergence of a plethora of transnational organisations through which constitutional judges meet, physically or virtually, to discuss common challenges and to share expertise. The Association of Asian Constitutional Courts and Equivalent Institutions (AACC) is one of the more formalised of many examples.[81] Another is the willingness of the courts of many, although not all, states to refer to the constitutional experience of others in resolving constitutional cases. The extent of this phenomenon became apparent in the extensive literature generated by controversy over the practice in the Supreme Court of the United States in the first decade of the twenty-first century.[82] Cross-fertilisation of ideas in the course of constitutional adjudication has become increasingly practicable with the instant availability of so much case law on-line, including, sometimes, in English translation. In a few courts the practice is systematised by, for example, hiring clerks from other jurisdictions[83] or providing research services on foreign law for the use of judges.[84] This practice has a parallel in the increasing references to international law by domestic courts, now expressly authorised in some new constitutions.[85] Yet another manifestation of globalisation that is relevant for present purposes is the establishment of supra-national courts, regional human rights courts and other transnational adjudicative bodies, with inevitable impact, formal or informal, on the jurisprudence of the constitutional courts of participating states. In an associated development, regional and international human rights norms typically protect a right to impartial adjudication and thus, at least in principle, judicial independence, in both operation and design.[86]

Not all of this is new, at least in common law jurisdictions. Conferences to bring together judges and lawyers from Commonwealth countries have been held since at least 1955;[87] reference to the decisions of others has been a common practice in most jurisdictions;[88] for a long time, the Privy Council performed a role as a transnational court for former British colonies, and it continues to do so for some.[89] In a sense, these practices reflect an

---

[81] Association of Asian Constitutional Courts and Equivalent Institutions, available at http://aacc-asia.org/.
[82] C Saunders, 'Judicial Engagement with Comparative Law' in T Ginsburg and R Dixon (eds), *Comparative Constitutional Law* (Cheltenham, Edward Elgar Publishing, 2011) 571.
[83] eg Constitutional Court of South Africa, see at https://www.concourt.org.za/index.php/law-researchers/about-law-clerks; Supreme Court of Israel, at https://supreme.court.gov.il/sites/en/Documents/Foreign%20Clerkships%20at%20the%20Supreme%20court.pdf.
[84] eg the Constitutional Research Institute associated with the Constitutional Court of Korea, see at http://ri.ccourt.go.kr/eng/ccourt/research/publications.html).
[85] eg the Constitution of the Republic of South Africa, s 39(1)(b).
[86] eg the protection of the right to a fair trial in Art 6 of the European Convention on Human Rights.
[87] RG Henderson, 'The Third Commonwealth and Empire Law Conference' (1966) *Australian Bar Gazette* 4.
[88] Saunders, 'Judicial Engagement' (n 82).
[89] I Richardson, 'The Privy Council as the Final Court for the British Empire' (2012) 43 *Victoria University of Wellington Law Review* 103.

earlier phase of globalisation, now internalised as an element of common law method. The impact on adjudication of the present phase of globalisation is broader, deeper and more pervasive, however, spanning legal traditions. It can readily be seen how it provides a catalyst for convergence and some support for the claim that national constitutions no longer represent an exclusive source for norms of a constitutional kind that apply in a state. Striking illustrations include the spread of proportionality, as a principle or as a methodology for determining compliance with rights provisions;[90] the apparent popularity of the doctrine of unconstitutional constitutional amendment, merging the Indian basic structure doctrine, itself a transplant, with concepts derived from theories of constituent power;[91] and the institutional adjustments in member states required for compliance with the right to a fair trial under Article 6 of the European Convention on Human Rights.[92]

Again, however, care should be taken not to overstate the consequences of globalisation for constitutional adjudication or to overdraw their implications for theory and practice. Not all courts with a constitutional jurisdiction are affected by globalisation to the same extent or in the same way. Notably, in Asia and the Pacific there are no regional courts, significantly less formal commitment to international human rights instruments[93] and significantly less membership of the International Criminal Court.[94] The retreat from globalisation is particularly marked in relation to adjudication in all regions of the world, as states either withdraw from transnational commitments[95] or fail to give them full effect.[96] Everywhere, distinctive differences in constitutional law theory and doctrine remain, despite the pressures for convergence. In some respects, in common law states, divergence is increasing, as the once apparently unified common law diversifies through the decisions of domestic courts, interpreting their respective domestic constitutions.[97]

The explanation is not hard to find: the ultimate point of reference for domestic courts with a constitutional jurisdiction is the Constitution of the state, the values and principles that underpin it and the domestic jurisprudence built around it. Domestic courts derive their authority and legitimacy from their respective constitutions and operate within the milieu of the state, in a sometimes-precarious symbiotic relationship with the other organs of state. Europe is, or at least was, a possible exception, where the depth of regional integration stimulated theories of constitutional pluralism.[98] On one view, however, these also

---

[90] A Stone Sweet, 'Proportionality Balancing and Global Constitutionalism' (2008) 47 *Columbia Journal of Transnational Law* 68.

[91] Y Roznai, *Unconstitutional Constitutional Amendments* (Oxford, Oxford University Press, 2017).

[92] European Court of Human Rights, *Guide on Article 6 of the Convention on Human Rights* (2018), available at https://www.echr.coe.int/Documents/Guide_Art_6_ENG.pdf.

[93] See United Nations Office of the High Commissioner for Human Rights, *Status of Ratification Interactive Dashboard*, available at http://indicators.ohchr.org/.

[94] H Takemura, 'The Asian Region and the International Criminal Court' in Y Nakanishi (ed), *Contemporary Issues in Human Rights Law: Europe and Asia* (Singapore, Springer, 2018).

[95] Examples include the withdrawal of Burundi and the Philippines from the Rome Statute, which founds the International Criminal Court.

[96] On the phenomenon of resistance generally, see the symposium on 'Resistance to International Courts' (2018) 14 *International Journal of Law in Context*, Special Issue 2.

[97] C Saunders, 'Common law Public Law: Some Comparative Reflections' in J Bell et al (eds), *Public Law Adjudication in Common Law Systems* (Hart Publishing, Oxford, 2015) 353.

[98] L Pierdominici, 'The Theory of EU Constitutional Pluralism: A Crisis in a Crisis?' (2017) 9 *Perspectives on Federalism* 120.

demonstrated the continuing pull of state constitutional authority, which may yet prevail, although the jury is still out.[99] Other aspects of the European experience reflect similar dynamics, including the current and increasing focus on both subsidiarity and the margin of appreciation in relations between the national courts of member states and the European Court of Human Rights.[100] Elsewhere in the world, the challenges faced by regional courts are more formidable still, as accounts of resistance testify, in both Africa and the Americas.[101]

Similar observations may be made about the citation of foreign judgments. Where the practice is used, it contributes to constitutional reasoning in a variety of ways.[102] But no court regards foreign case law as binding. Rather, national courts draw insights from foreign experience for the interpretation and application of their own constitution, in their own context, adapting foreign experience or rejecting it as they consider fit. The authority of regional or international law has a different logic and is more compelling for reasons of both practice and principle, but even here there are variable patterns of judicial response. Different courts use different methodologies when faced with arguments drawn from foreign or international law, with an eye to an understanding of their own authority and to reasons for judgment that will be accepted as persuasive.[103] Some kind of comparative method is generally in evidence, however. This helps to explain, for example, the variations in formulations of proportionality,[104] rejections of the doctrine of unconstitutional constitutional amendment[105] and differences in conceptions of what freedom of speech involves.[106]

These observations go to those aspects of constitutional adjudication in current conditions of globalisation that concern the relationship between national courts and adjudicatory bodies outside state borders: a variable and fluctuating body of principle and practice, necessarily affected by context, about which generalisation is plausible only at a high level of abstraction. One of the many challenges for the future is to take stock of experience with such relationships to date so as to craft any adjustments that might maximise the strengths that national and transnational adjudicatory bodies each bring to securing the benefits of effective constitutionalism.

---

[99] A Hofmann, 'Resistance against the Court of Justice of the European Union' (2018) 14 *International Journal of Law in Context* 258.

[100] JM Sauve, 'The Role of the National Authorities', seminar on *Subsidiarity: A Two-Sided Coin?*, European Court of Human Rights (30 January 2015), available at https://www.echr.coe.int/Documents/Speech_20150130_Seminar_JMSauv%C3%A9_ENG.pdf.

[101] T Daly and M Wiebusch, 'The African Court on Human and Peoples' Rights: Mapping Resistance Against a Young Court' (2018) 14 *International Law in Context* 294; DA Gonzalez-Salzberg, 'Do States Comply with the Compulsory Judgments of the Inter-American Court of Human Rights? An Empirical Study of Compliance with 330 Measures of Reparation' (2014) *Revista do Instituto Brasileiro de Direitos Humanos* 13.

[102] A Jakab, A Dyevre and G Izcovich (eds), *Comparative Constitutional Reasoning* (Cambridge, Cambridge University Press, 2017).

[103] ibid.

[104] D Grimm, 'Proportionality in Canadian and German Constitutional Jurisprudence' (2007) 57 *Toronto Law Journal* 383.

[105] Roznai, *Unconstitutional Constitutional Amendments* (n 91).

[106] A Stone, 'The Comparative Constitutional Law of Freedom of Expression' in T Ginsburg and R Dixon (eds), *Research Handbook in Comparative Constitutional Law* (Cheltenham, Edward Elgar Publishing, 2010).

B. Bottom Up

My present purpose, however, is different. As with the earlier treatment of constitution-making, the inquiry here is whether there are particular challenges presented by globalisation with which constitutional courts can or could deal, consistently with their role in the domestic constitutional order, in a manifestation of global constitutionalism of a different kind.

There are likely to be many such examples, in many jurisdictions. The decision of the Supreme Court of the United Kingdom in *Miller* is one.[107] The Court was presented with a novel problem, raised by a distinctive form of regional integration, to which it gave a novel answer, founded on the premise that European Union law has become a 'source' of United Kingdom law, even though originally given effect by a statute of the United Kingdom.[108] On that premise, for the majority, a formal decision to give notice to leave the European Union required the authority of Parliament and could not be effected by the executive alone, in the exercise of the prerogative, on which reliance usually is placed in dealing with treaties. The critique of the decision is understandable, given previous law and practice.[109] The decision can be understood, however, as a rejection of the adequacy of the pre-globalisation dichotomy between the exercise of internal and external sovereignty, in the face of the depth of British integration in the European Union, creating what was, on one view, a hybrid regime.[110] The response of the majority of the Court effectively took this changed reality into account in a way that involved a development of constitutional law in response to globalisation, which nevertheless could be accommodated within the framework of the British Constitution.

For the remainder of this section, I give two other examples, from Australian experience, of the many diverse ways in which courts, operating within a domestic constitutional framework, might be faced with challenges that derive from globalisation, with which they need to deal. In some cases, an appropriate response may require adaptation of established principles and doctrines.

The first draws on a series of decisions of the High Court of Australia interpreting and applying a section of the Constitution that disqualifies Australians who also are subjects or citizens 'of a foreign power' from membership of the Commonwealth Parliament (section 44(i)). The section came into effect in 1901, in very different conditions of globalisation, when Australians were subjects of a Crown whose realms spanned a quarter of the world, in terms of both territory and population, and at a time when dual allegiance was a rarity, as either subject or citizen. Over the intervening period, national citizenship became the norm, including in Australia; and multiple citizenship became accepted by an increasing number of states, also including Australia,[111] where almost half the number of Australian

---

[107] *R (Miller) v Secretary of State for Exiting the European Union* [2018] AC 61.
[108] ibid [65], [80]; European Communities Act 1972.
[109] M Elliott, 'The Supreme Court's Judgment in *Miller*: In Search of Constitutional Principle' (2017) 76 *Cambridge Law Journal* 257.
[110] If anything, this perception has been further strengthened by the difficulties encountered in extricating the United Kingdom from the European Union over the ensuing period: D Baranger, 'Brexit as a Constitutional Decision: An Interpretation' (2018) 21 *Jus Politicum*, available at http://juspoliticum.com/article/Brexit-as-a-Constitutional-Decision-An-Interpretation-1241.html.
[111] PJ Spiro, 'Dual Citizenship as a Human Right' (2010) 8 *International Journal of Constitutional Law* 111.

citizens is estimated to have another citizenship as well.[112] There is little, if any, international coordination of the conditions on which citizenship is gained or lost, the incidents of citizenship and the treatment of multiple citizenship. Citizenship of another country may be acquired inadvertently, by a change in legislation of that country or a new interpretation of constitutional guarantees. States have different procedures for renunciation of citizenship, and in some states renunciation is not possible at all.[113]

The rise in the incidence, legality and modality of acquisition of multiple citizenships is a manifestation of the current phase of globalisation. It was only a matter of time, in these circumstances, before the provision in section 44(i) took its toll. Over the course of 2017–18, it caused 15 sitting Members of the Commonwealth Parliament to lose their seats through judicial process or voluntary resignation, and significantly destabilised the Parliament itself. The problem is likely to continue, despite a tightening of vetting procedures. Equally significantly, it can be assumed that many Australians with multiple citizenships are deterred from standing for election to the Commonwealth Parliament in these circumstances.

The relevant point for present purposes concerns the response of the High Court, when called upon to resolve questions about the validity of elections, acting as the Court of Disputed Returns.[114] The Court might have reacted by interpreting the section as restrictively as possible, so as to minimise its effects, in acknowledgement of the changed global context. This option was not taken, for a combination of reasons that included the relative specificity of the constitutional text and the impact of previous decisions on its meaning in a judicial culture in which the ties of precedent are strong, although not unbreakable.[115] With one important exception, the Court's response instead was to give the section a literal interpretation, leaving to the political process the task of amending the section, if there were sufficient popular support.

The exception is directed to the possibility that section 44(i) might disqualify some Australians with another citizenship that could not be renounced under the law of the other state or that could be renounced only under onerous conditions. In response to that possibility, the Court identified a 'constitutional imperative' underlying section 44(i), that 'an Australian citizen not be prevented by foreign law from participation in representative government where it can be demonstrated that the person has taken all steps that are reasonably required by the foreign law to renounce his or her foreign citizenship'.[116] This imperative has no foundation in constitutional text, although arguably it might be supported by what Australians term constitutional structure.[117] It is a doctrine prompted by conditions created by globalisation, which serves to protect the integrity of the Australian constitutional system.

---

[112] Joint Standing Committee on Electoral Matters, *Excluded: The Impact of section 44 on Australian Democracy* (Canberra, AGPS, 2018) paras 3.63–3.64.
[113] On comparative citizenship generally, see J Shaw (ed), *Citizenship and Constitutional Law* (Cheltenham, Edward Elgar Publishing, 2018).
[114] *Re Canavan* (2017) 349 ALR 534, [13]; *Re Gallagher* [2018] HCA 17.
[115] *Sykes v Cleary* (1992) 176 CLR 77.
[116] *Re Canavan* (n 114) [13]; *Re Gallagher* (n 114) [11], [23]–[26], [43], [51], [57].
[117] For critique, see A Twomey, '*Re Gallagher*: Inconsistency, Imperatives and Irremediable Impediments', AUSPUBLAW (28 May 2018), available at https://auspublaw.org/2018/05/re-gallagher-inconsistency-imperatives-and-irremediable-impediments/.

The second example is quite different, in both context and outcome. It also serves to show, however, the novel challenges raised by globalisation for national constitutional systems and the potential for courts to meet those challenges by adapting existing doctrine to take globalisation into account.

The case in question is *M68/2015 v Minister for Immigration and Border Protection* (*M68*).[118] The background stems from the response of successive Australian governments to the latest waves of people seeking to come to Australia by sea, seeking refuge from conditions elsewhere in the world that threaten their lives and their families, pursuant to the 1951 Refugee Convention, in another manifestation of globalisation. Unauthorised arrival of asylum seekers in Australia by boat became highly controversial. Deterrence was seen by both sides of politics as a prize that offered significant electoral advantage. A succession of political strategies to this end ultimately resulted in the establishment of 'regional processing centres' in the smaller, neighbouring countries of Nauru and Papua New Guinea, which are dependent on Australian aid and to which asylum seekers, intercepted at sea, were involuntarily sent, pursuant to bilateral agreements between Australia and its two neighbours. The policy framework was generated by Australia; transport to and from the centres was handled by Australia; the entire exercise was funded by Australia; the centres were managed by Australian contractors; and ongoing decisions about the running of the centres were made through joint arrangements in which Australia was, at least, an equal partner.[119]

In *M68*, a detainee on Nauru challenged the validity of Australia's involvement in these arrangements on several grounds, one of which invoked the Constitution. Due to the particularities of the Australian Constitution, the most obviously available constitutional ground involved an argument that people were detained in custody, without judicial process, in a manner that contravened the constitutional separation of judicial power, on the basis of a doctrine first enunciated in *Chu Kheng Lim v Minister for Immigration* (*Lim*).[120] The argument failed, and the validity of the Commonwealth's actions were upheld. For the plurality, the detention was effected through 'the independent exercise of sovereign legislative and executive power' by Nauru; the Commonwealth 'could not compel or authorise Nauru' to take such actions; and the principle in *Lim* was not attracted, notwithstanding the 'causal connection' between the Commonwealth's actions and the plaintiff's detention.[121] Despite the intricacies of the Court's jurisprudence on when immigration detention is 'punitive' and when it is not, Commonwealth authorities would have been subject to at least some constitutional limits had they implemented this policy onshore.[122] Offshore, however, they were subject to no constitutional limitations of this kind at all. The possibility of an alternative approach was demonstrated by the dissenting reasons of Gordon J; a detailed and forensic dissection of the legal framework governing the relations between Commonwealth actors on the one hand and Nauru and the contractors on the other, leading her to conclude that 'as a matter of substance the Commonwealth detained the plaintiff'.[123] She also would have

---

[118] *M68/2015 v Minister for Immigration and Border Protection* (2016) 257 CLR 42.
[119] These arrangements are outlined in detail in the reasons of Gordon J in *M68*, ibid [266] et seq.
[120] *Chu Kheng Lim v Minister for Immigration, Local Government and Ethnic Affairs* (1992) 176 CLR 1.
[121] ibid [39].
[122] M Foster, 'Separation of Judicial Power' in C Saunders and A Stone, *The Oxford Handbook of the Australian Constitution* (Oxford, Oxford University Press, 2018).
[123] *M68* (n 118) [352].

applied the doctrine in *Lim* to hold that, in these circumstances, the separation of judicial power was infringed in a way that did not fall within any established exception and did not justify the crafting of yet another exception that would 'allow the detention of an alien, by the Commonwealth, in a foreign state'.[124]

M68 is instructive as an illustration of the ways in which practices associated with globalisation threaten some of the most basic constitutional principles and inhibit the constitutional accountability of state actors. The reasons of Justice Gordon also show how the challenge might be met, through acknowledging the realities of the global context, in determining the applicable doctrine. *M68* was a difficult case for a Court with a narrow conception of judicial power, a tendency to focus on form rather than substance, and very little jurisprudence involving review either of decisions reached in collaboration with other states or of decisions effected through contract. These difficulties need to be overcome, however, in the interests of Australian constitutionalism. In the face of political intransigence, where legal questions are raised on which significant individual interests depend, they must be resolved by domestic courts. Of course, a court may resolve the question against the applicant, applying existing doctrine, as was done in *M68*. The point for consideration here is whether globalisation sometimes presents new conditions to which a court can appropriately respond, adapting existing doctrine to an emerging need.

V. Conclusions

At the end of the second decade of the twenty-first century, the future of global constitutionalism at the regional or international levels, or in the relationship between these levels and national constitutions, is hard to predict. The phenomena that underpin it have always been patchy in their incidence and operation, and there is no sign of change in this regard. There has always been a disjunct, which continues, between the discourse of global constitutionalism, some of the practices associated with it and realities on the ground. There are clear signs of pushback, reasserting state authority and state interests, not always in edifying form but on grounds that deserve attention. Geopolitical developments point to the emergence of new hegemons, with different ideas about the global order, which may create new challenges and shape new trajectories for global constitutionalism.

At the same time, however, there is a greater need than ever for global cooperation in relation to an ever-widening range of significant issues. A thick network of norms and institutions now exists at the international and some regional levels, performing useful functions, shaping ideas, moderating and mediating transnational action. Acceptance that the people of the world share a common and equal humanity, which is one of the great achievements of the twentieth century, may still have a long way to go to become a reality but nevertheless encourages action on a global scale. The erosion of national barriers is given further impetus by the extraordinary physical movement of people, in all walks of life and for a multitude of purposes, and by the continuing advances of information technology. All these factors suggest that globalisation is an ongoing condition and that systematisation of norms and institutions, across state borders, is likely to continue to be a goal. The present hiatus may,

---

[124] ibid [401].

in time, prove to have been a useful point to take stock in this regard, to reflect on insights from the past as bases for new approaches to global constitutionalism in the future.

At least some of the literature on global constitutionalism emphasises the erosion of the authority and relevance of national constitutions. By contrast, this chapter builds on the assumption that, eroded or not, state constitutions are critical tools for establishing, maintaining and developing constitutionalism, including democratic governance, in the only sphere on which either has been made effective so far. This reality alone makes state constitutions worth preserving and enhancing to the extent of their capabilities. In adopting this focus, I do not ignore the deficiencies in the will and/or capacities of the relevant actors in many states to govern in the interests of their people. These are broader problems, demanding complex solutions, which are beyond the scope of this chapter. In relation to both, however, I suggest that there may be something to be gained from expecting states to perform the functions for which they exist and insisting on the responsibility of leaders to act in the public interest and to account for their actions to their people.

Globalisation affects national constitutions in ways beyond those that are familiar in the literature on global constitutionalism. In the interests of maximising the effectiveness of national constitutions in current conditions, this chapter argues that domestic constitutional theory, doctrine and practice need to better reflect the reality of the global context in which states and their constitutions operate. What this might involve is explored primarily through the lens of constitution-making and constitutional adjudication. It is not necessary to rehearse the conclusions reached. The point should be made, however, that they would collectively assist to overcome a range of problems of a constitutional kind to which globalisation gives rise, in ways that would preserve and enhance the values that constitutionalism is designed to serve.

It would be appropriate for constitutional text itself to provide a base for these developments. The modalities of globalisation highlight the need for constitutions to make better provision for the exercise of the external sovereignty of the state in its relations with others so as, for example, to identify the authorised parameters of particular types of transnational arrangements, to provide a framework within which state actors can be held to account, to promote compliance with constitutional standards and to clarify the status of regional and international norms. Some constitutions already do this more explicitly than others. The constitutions of common law states typically are particularly deficient in this regard, for reasons that historically can be explained by the evolutionary character of progress towards constitutional monarchy and the convenient malleability of the prerogative. For this reason, if no other, the issues canvassed in this chapter can be said to lie at the 'frontiers' of public law. There is plenty of world experience on which to draw and lessons to be learnt from the effects of constitutional silence in relation to the exercise of external sovereignty. Exactly what constitutions might provide in this regard is unlikely to be susceptible to standardisation. Rather, in each case it should reflect the geographical and geopolitical position of the state in the world, the challenges it faces and the preferences of its people.

3

Frontiers of Global Administrative Law in the 2020s

BENEDICT KINGSBURY*

Global administrative law (GAL) has many pertinent antecedents,[1] but the framing and labelling of what is now regarded as GAL began with academic initiatives in the early 2000s.[2] In 2005 it was proposed that there was emerging a body of GAL, defined as comprising

> the mechanisms, principles, practices, and supporting social understandings that promote or otherwise affect the accountability of global administrative bodies, in particular by ensuring they meet adequate standards of transparency, participation, reasoned decision, and legality, and by providing effective review of the rules and decisions they make.[3]

The initial approach was explicitly a normative intervention: although mindful of pathologies in GAL, it asserted the broad desirability of seeking to render the rule-making and decision-making of these global regulatory bodies accountable and responsive to the diverse publics significantly affected by their decisions.[4] The aim of this chapter – written for a general readership more than as a specialist contribution to the scholarly debates on GAL – is to consider how GAL now stands in relation to some of the major conceptual and

---

* The author is deeply grateful to Professor Richard Stewart, and to Professor Nico Krisch and Dr Megan Donaldson, with whom he has collaborated in much work in this area.

[1] Some are crisply canvassed in C Bories, 'Historie des Phénomènes Administratifs au-delà de la Sphere Étatique: Tâtonnements et Hesitations du Droit et/ou de la Doctrine' in C Bories (ed), *Un Droit Administratif Global?* (Paris, Pedone, 2012). See also J Klabbers, 'The Emergence of Functionalism in International Institutional Law: Colonial Inspirations' (2014) 24 *European Journal of International Law* 645; J Klabbers, 'The Transformation of International Organizations Law' (2015) 26 *European Journal of International Law* 9 (particularly on Paul Reinsch and Frank Sayre).

[2] S Cassese, 'Administrative Law without the State? The Challenge of Global Regulation' (2005) 37 *New York University Journal of International Law and Politics* 663; B Kingsbury, N Krisch and RB Stewart, 'The Emergence of Global Administrative Law' (2005) 68(3–4) *Law and Contemporary Problems* 15. On the power and problems of this labelling, S Marks, 'Naming Global Administrative Law' (2005) 37 *New York University Journal of International Law and Politics* 995.

[3] Kingsbury, Krisch and Stewart, 'The Emergence of Global Administrative Law' (n 2) 17.

[4] Whether GAL mechanisms prove to be mere window-dressing, helping to give a gloss of legitimacy to what are in essence unjust arrangements, or instead prove to provide useful tools for the voices and interests of the relatively powerless and the disregarded, depends in part on struggles that occur case by case. Progressive advocates have made effective use of GAL mechanisms within some regulatory programmes, but have been thwarted or not engaged at all in many others.

contextual issues that might be thought likely to affect the nature and even the viability of this 2000s project in the 2020s.[5]

It will begin, in section I, by introducing the range of practices with which GAL has been concerned. In section II it first notes the contexts in which ideas about, and the practice of, GAL obtained some valence and rapid uptake in the period c 1990–c 2015, and then turns to some major contextual shifts that, from about 2015 onward, have seemed to alter the landscape for GAL quite dramatically. Building on this, section III examines some conceptual issues bearing on the nature and viability of GAL. Section IV takes a single set of GAL proceedings against a private global sports governance institution relating to eligibility to compete in the female category in elite athletics, to illustrate reasons for the continued and likely expanded role of GAL in the 2020s in some areas of private governance. Section V concludes.

I. The Practices Informing GAL's Development as an Analytic Field

The academic projects that have helped constitute GAL as a field of scholarship and research are by their nature interventions, aimed at encouraging practices to be viewed in a particular way. These interventions generate categories and ideas of a theoretical nature, but in a close interrogation with practice. In this case, practice pre-exists the theory, but the analytic and theoretical work may have some influence on practice over time. What constitutes the practice that is the subject matter of GAL?[6]

GAL scholarship tends to start with fragments of practice, rather than with grander ideas of global constitutional structures or values or fundamental unifying legal instruments. It brings together practices from the level of specific regulatory regimes and sectors, examining the deployment and gradual but uneven spread of GAL practices of transparency, participation, reason giving and review among different regulatory regimes. Given the current highly disaggregated state of global administration and governance, this approach has important analytic strengths. Further, a sufficient number of incremental steps in the development of GAL practices may have tipping points or other systemic effects, with the result that GAL's normative logic and mechanisms may come to be widely regarded as exemplary or even obligatory for global regulatory administrations, at least in some important fields.[7]

The development and spread of GAL practices and norms have not been accomplished through any overall plan or system. They are the product of accumulated discrete decisions by the different generative actors in different institutional settings, responding to the

---

[5] A few of the many thoughtful academic responses to the original project – which overall have expressed interest, puzzlement, scholarly debate and scepticism all in good measure – will be considered in this chapter.

[6] This section, and a few other paragraphs, draw with thanks from a paper (published in Spanish) jointly authored with Richard Stewart, which appears in the B Kingsbury and RB Stewart, *Hacia el Derecho Administrativo Global: Fundamentos, Principios y Ámbito de Aplicación* (Seville, Global Law Press-Editorial Depeche Global, 2016) 57.

[7] E Fromageau, *La Théorie des Institutions du Droit Administratif Global* (Brussels, Bruylant, 2016).

need to channel and discipline the exercise of administrative power occurring in certain recurring structural modes. These actors include not only domestic and international courts and tribunals but also other global regulatory bodies, domestic regulatory authorities, institutional entrepreneurs of various stripes, business firms, non-governmental organisations (NGOs), and private and public/private networks of actors.

Private actors enlist GAL to promote their regulatory agendas. Pharmaceutical companies successfully pushed for extensive GAL procedures in the 1994 Agreement on Trade-Related Aspects of Intellectual Property Rights (TRIPS) and the 2016/18 Trans-Pacific Partnership (TPP) agreements, in order to heighten intellectual property protections for their products and to constrain governments and certain competitors.[8] Environmental advocates promoted adoption of obligations on states to comply with demanding GAL standards, and some international supervision of these, in the Aarhus Convention to advance environmental goals.[9] Courts and tribunals, and international investment arbitral bodies, review the legality of global administrative decisions and norms (including those of their distributed domestic components) as a condition of their validity and, in some cases, their enforcement. In other cases, a domestic agency or another global regulatory body, in deciding whether or not to recognise or validate a global regulator's decisions or norms, may give weight to whether or not it followed GAL practices in decision-making. In still other cases, private actors are deciding whether to conform to the decision or norm in order to enhance their reputations, become credible partners in business or other transactions or ventures, or otherwise further their interests. In all of these contexts, the extent to which the global regulator has followed GAL practices of transparency, participation, reason giving and opportunity for review in making decisions is often a substantial and in some cases a controlling factor in the decision of the validating or recipient authority or actor on whether or not to validate, recognise or conform to the decision or norm in question.

Transparency, participation, reason giving and review can help global regulatory bodies solve regulatory coordination and cooperation games by enhancing the quality of their rules and their responsiveness to the interests and concerns of the rule users and other constituencies, generating support for the regime. At the implementation stage, these procedures, especially when coupled with review, can promote accurate and consistent execution of the rules by both internal and distributed administrations, as illustrated by regimes as diverse as the World Trade Organization (WTO), the Aarhus Convention and the global sports anti-doping regime.[10] GAL procedures, however, involve costs and delays, may limit negotiation flexibility and have other drawbacks in specific regulatory fields, for example in security, where transparency may defeat regulatory efficacy.

---

[8] RC Dreyfuss, 'Fostering Dynamic Innovation, Development and Trade: Intellectual Property as a Case Study in Global Administrative Law' in H Corder (ed), *Global Administrative Law: Innovation and Development* (Cape Town, Juta, 2009); L Helfer, 'Pharmaceutical Patents and the Human Right to Health' in TC Halliday and G Shaffer (eds), *Transnational Legal Orders* (Cambridge, Cambridge University Press, 2015); P Mertenskötter and RB Stewart, 'Remote Control: TPP's Administrative Law Requirements' in B Kingsbury et al (eds), *Megaregulation Contested: Global Economic Governance After TPP* (Oxford, Oxford University Press, 2019).

[9] Convention on Access to Information, Public Participation in Decision-making and Access to Justice in Environmental Matters (Aarhus, 25 June 1998) (entered into force 30 October 2001) 2161 UNTS 447.

[10] For materials on these regimes, see S Cassese et al (eds), *Global Administrative Law: The Casebook*, 3rd edn (Rome, IRPA, 2012).

The need and justification for the GAL quartet of mechanisms, or for some of them, depends upon the type of regulatory regime, including its objectives and 'business plan', its members and structure, its distributed administration (explained in section III.C) and other contextual variables. The mechanisms may not be needed, and their use may actually be counterproductive. For example, formal structures of participation, reason giving and review may be unnecessary and indeed counterproductive in regulatory regimes that resolve coordination games through technical standards to align the behaviours of market actors in a given sector, at least where distributional issues and externalities are modest.[11] There may be far greater need for the mechanisms in the case of many regimes to solve cooperation games that involve significant distributional consequences and require measures to prevent free riding, or in programmes that may impose serious deprivations on individuals or groups.

In some contexts, both functional and normative logics combine to favour use of GAL procedures – they advance the regime's mission, for example transparency, participation, reason giving and review may improve regulatory decisions that command broad support, and may also serve goals such as accountability and responsiveness to the disregarded. In other cases, for example in programmes to combat illicit activities, the two logics have conflicting implications for GAL. Pervasive tensions operate between transparency and decision-making according to public reason, epistemic authority and negotiated resolution of differences as modes for regulatory decision-making. Moreover, there are many dimensions to transparency, different forms of participation, variants in reason-giving requirements and numerous different mechanisms to provide review.

The precise types of GAL mechanisms capable of advancing functional and normative goals in particular circumstances require careful examination and specification. Global regimes' use of GAL mechanisms will depend largely on assessments by an organisation and its most important members of their costs and benefits relative to those of other available governance tools. Constructivist factors may also play a significant role. The wide use of GAL in regulatory bodies founded by NGOs based in the North Atlantic region in the 1990s and 2000s illustrates their enthusiasm for mechanisms and styles of governance that had worked well for them in Europe and North America. But NGOs in Europe and elsewhere have increasingly come to voice doubts about the actual effects of neutral-seeming transparency and public participation provisions, at least in the context of market-oriented regulatory regimes such as the Transatlantic Trade and Investment Partnership (TTIP), critiquing them as licences for business to lobby and as magnifying the returns to wealth. The GAL ethos or ideology has long been criticised by people connected with developing countries on the ground that the promise of participation is illusory; civil society groups, particularly in developing countries, do not have the organisational capacities and resources to make effective use of GAL mechanisms and are badly outmatched by business interests.

In sum, the institutional method for the development of GAL is decentralised, incremental, cumulative, variable as to the details and overall embrace of GAL, continually open

---

[11] As a study in progress by Orfeas Chasapis-Tassinis demonstrates, much of the work of the International Swaps and Derivatives Association (ISDA) falls into this category, but some of its work imposes major externalities on non-members.

to adjustment and revision, and subject to cycles of contestation and rejection along with embrace and reform. This piecewise approach, while it in part echoes the style of common law legal systems, is here inflected by the sheer multiplicity of jurisgenerative bodies and participants or critics throughout the global administrative space. Insofar as various global regulators adopt GAL practices, and gradually internalise GAL norms, this is for highly diverse reasons. These reasons include, most obviously, the desire to obtain validation, recognition, and acceptance of their decisions and norms by relevant validating or recipient authorities or actors. The various different global regulatory bodies operating in different sectors and fields of regulation accordingly become subject (albeit very unevenly) to GAL norms developed and applied by international tribunals, by domestic courts, and by other global regulatory bodies and domestic authorities on whose cooperation they depend. Or global regulatory organisations may impose GAL practices on some of their own components to address internal management objectives and promote institutional and programmatic coherence. Or they may adopt such practices to garner demand for adherence to their norms from businesses or individual consumers concerned to follow or support socially and environmentally responsible practices and products, or to meet criticism and enhance their public reputation. Domestic administrations that function as the distributed element of global regulatory regimes are subject to GAL norms applied by the global regulatory bodies of which they are a part, by international tribunals and arbitral bodies, and by their own domestic courts. Widespread practices of voluntary, uneven or idiosyncratic adoption of GAL norms, and unsanctioned deviance from them, naturally raise issues regarding the legal status of these norms.

II. GAL and Changes in Global Political, Economic and Social Orders

The regulatory terrain of standard-setting and decision-making, and the evaluation of GAL, is integrally connected with, but not necessarily synchronous with, changing patterns in global and sub-global orders.

A. The Period Prior to 2015

From a North Atlantic perspective, a familiar narration of the advent of modern global regulatory governance – up until a sharper turn around 2015 – runs as follows. Legal-administrative structures began to be created and used actively to address beyond-the-state practical problems of coordination and expertise-building from the 1850s, so that the category of international administrative unions was flourishing along with globalisation by 1910, and a new, more formal juridification and programmatic ambition was added on top of this in the League of Nations era but largely failed. This latter initiative was tried anew in inter-governmental structures from 1945 with greater endurance.

On top of this structure of treaties and formal inter-governmental organisations was layered from about 1990 a growing set of inter-state courts, including some providing direct access for private parties. Contemporaneously from 1990, in a period of United States

(US) dominance buttressed by support from most North Atlantic powers, there occurred an increase in active military interventionism and in imperial-type governance structures based on coalitions of the more-or-less willing,[12] accompanied by some sidestepping, or undisguised assertions, of hierarchy within formally inter-state structures. This US–NATO–OECD dominance was countered quietly by some soft balancing, and non-state violence, and eventually in more overt inter-state initiatives both by rival organisations (such as the Shanghai Communiqué Organisation) and by resistance from emerging powers within existing institutions (as in the WTO). A parallel development was the growth of intergovernmental networks of domestic regulatory officials operating in specific fields (banking regulation, pharmaceutical testing, anti-money laundering, etc) to coordinate regulation without the encumbrances of treaty arrangements. Initiated by the US with leading European nations and, often, Japan, these coalitions sooner or later provided for participation by others. Also characteristic of this period was growth in private standard-setting, transnational NGO and corporate norm production, and systems of regulatory discipline. The label 'global governance' became prevalent in this period, applied by some to this whole congeries, and by others to the more liberal or North Atlantic-palatable aspects.

However, further new global inter-state institutional juridification and judicialisation came to a near halt after 2000. In part it was blocked by inter-governmental politics – including by BRICS (Brazil, Russia, India, China and South Africa) contestation and US neo-conservatism – and in part it was undermined by democratic-legitimacy objections and ponderous or even sclerotic multilateral processes. Energy and attention were diverted into other forms of global regulatory governance, including the proliferation of intergovernmental networks and the still largely unblocked possibilities of global hybrid and private governance, in which North Atlantic values and techniques still had space to predominate.[13] These values were articulated and pursued in the languages and techniques of law, but rather than inter-state public international law, hybrid and private governance were characterised by newer combinations of law or law-like forms. Attempts were made to marry these again with inter-state public international law forms, as in the Paris Climate Agreement of 2015, or the 12-state TPP as finalised in 2015–16. Contemporaneously and partly in response, the European Union (EU) pushed for the EU–US TTIP, China initiated the Asian Infrastructure Investment Bank, following broadly the established institutional script for multilateral development banks, and inter-governmental institutionalisation continued in Africa and (albeit with strong political divisions among different groups of states) in Latin America.

B. Reasons for the Rise of GAL

Five elements that in different ways prompted interest in, and uptake of, GAL in the period 1990–2015 may be summarised as follows.

---

[12] A Rodiles, *Coalitions of the Willing and International Law* (Cambridge, Cambridge University Press, 2018).

[13] AM Fejerskov, *The Gates Foundation's Rise to Power: Private Authority in Global Politics* (New York, Routledge, 2018); J Pauwelyn, R Wessel and J Wouters (eds), *Informal International Lawmaking* (Oxford, Oxford University Press, 2012); A Berman et al (eds), *Informal International Lawmaking: Case Studies* (The Hague, Torkel Opsahl, 2012).

i. Burgeoning of International Institutions

GAL offered one response to the dramatic post-Cold War growth in the number and reach of formal and informal international institutions exercising governance power with uncertain legitimacy.[14] Some sought through deployment of GAL to make these institutions more efficient, more effective or more accurate in accomplishing their burgeoning tasks. Others were primarily concerned that these institutions exercised power without – and at times circumvented or undercut – the rule of law and accountability structures embedded in national democracy and human rights;[15] or that the operations of these institutions were deformalised and skewed against developing countries and their interests.[16]

ii. Securitisation

GAL was invoked as an ameliorating response to (and equally as a legitimation of) the securitisation of transnational structures that followed the 9/11 attacks. This is exemplified in the classic GAL loci of cases related to freezing of assets under United Nations (UN) Security Council regimes against financing of terrorism, symbolised by *Kadi* I & II,[17] and various reforms of process within the UN Security Council, including the creation and remit of an

---

[14] If there was significant and growing regulatory authority or governance power located in institutions outside the territorial state, or if policies were being set in inter-governmental or even private transnational settings with major implications for governance within the state, then (it was argued) there was a strong case for fashioning a body of law that might fulfil functions roughly equivalent to those performed by administrative law within the state. See L Casini, 'The Expansion of the Material Scope of Global Law' in S Cassese (ed), *Research Handbook on Global Administrative Law* (Northampton, Edward Elgar, 2016); S Battini, 'The Proliferation of Global Regulatory Regimes' in S Cassese (ed), *Research Handbook on Global Administrative Law* (Northampton, Edward Elgar, 2016); G della Cananea, *Due Process of Law Beyond the State* (Oxford, Oxford University Press, 2016).

[15] F Kratochwil, *The Status of Law in World Society* (Cambridge: Cambridge University Press, 2014) 177–99; G Teubner, 'Quod Omnes Tangit: Transnational Constitutions Without Democracy' (2018) 45 *Journal of Law and Society* S5.

[16] For Chimni, the amelioration of international institutions has been GAL's major focus, hence GAL 'only offers a partial approach to international law, focused as it is primarily on addressing democratic deficit in the functioning of international bodies': BS Chimni, *International law and World Order* (Cambridge, Cambridge University Press, 2017) 4. His own forward-looking project, which he calls an 'Integrated Materialist Approach to International Law', specifies nine self-imposed requirements, including that it 'should seek to promote democratic modes of global governance. It would envisage the restructuring of regional and international institutions to address the problem of democratic deficit through inter alia promoting deliberative and participatory democracy and adherence to global administrative law': ibid 549. The long-serving South African Finance Minister, Trevor Manuel, while in office visited a GAL conference in 2008 to proclaim that 'Global Administrative Law is an idea whose time has come': TA Manuel, 'Opening Address' in H Corder (ed), *Global Administrative Law: Innovation and Development* (Cape Town, Juta, 2009) xix. He explained that his own experience representing South Africa in the Financial Action Task Force, the G20 (which he chaired), the IMF, the World Bank and other bodies led him to conclude 'we have to find solutions to poor decision-making structures and to find resonance for a body of applicable law … a legal system that is trusted and tested, that aligns the responsibilities at both a global and sovereign level, and a system capable of compelling the commitment of states in the interest of the global good. Such a legal system is, of course, this whole nascent and visionary branch of philosophy you have elected to call Global Administrative Law': xvi–xvii.

[17] Case T-315/01 *Kadi v Council of the European Union* [2005] ECR II-3659 (*Kadi I*); C-402/05 P, C-415/05 P *Kadi v Council of the European Union* [2008] ECR I-6351 (*Kadi II*).

ombudsperson in regard to some of these matters. Another cluster of GAL *causes célèbres* address accountability for actions of UN peacekeepers or for UN-authorised military operations.[18]

iii. Economic Governance

GAL concepts and mechanisms have been prominent both as a tool of international economic governance[19] and as a means of refining or curbing some elements of its international institutional operation.[20] The WTO *Shrimp-Turtle* case became a GAL classic not only because of the Appellate Body's extensive review, using GAL criteria, of the sufficiency of the US Government's administrative and review processes in prohibiting imports of shrimp from the complaining countries, but also because the Appellate Body exercised an institutional governance function in crafting (and supervising) some legal space for environmental goals in the trade regime when the member states had been unable to reach political agreement on that.[21] Invocation of GAL became more prominent – as instrument and as critique – with the expansion of such economic governance after the 2008–09 financial crisis.[22] GAL was invoked as a ground for critique of institutions ranging from the G7 and the International Monetary Fund (IMF), to credit ratings agencies and ISDA. Arguments to deploy GAL principles and mechanisms to increase transparency and accountability were made, and quite often adopted, in many such institutions.

iv. Post-Washington Consensus

GAL was a key feature in the instantiation of the shift from North Atlantic-led neoliberalism toward a post-Washington Consensus agenda.[23] Insofar as GAL principles and

---

[18] On *Kadi* and on the introduction by UN peacekeepers of cholera to Haiti, see D Hovell, 'Due Process in the United Nations' (2016) 110 *American Journal of International Law* 1.

[19] RB Stewart and MR Sanchez Badin, 'The World Trade Organization: Multiple Dimensions of Global Administrative Law' (2011) 9 *International Journal of Constitutional Law* 556.

[20] For example in pushbacks against investor-state arbitration: G Van Harten and M Loughlin, 'Investment Treaty Arbitration as a Species of Global Administrative Law' (2006) 17 *European Journal of International Law* 121; J Alvarez, 'Is Investor-State Arbitration Public?' (2016) 7 *Journal of International Dispute Settlement* 534; C Henckels, 'Protecting Regulatory Autonomy through Greater Precision in Investment Treaties: The TPP, CETA & TTIP' (2016) 19 *Journal of International Economic Law* 27; A Kawharu and L Nottage, 'The Curious Case of ISDS Arbitration Involving Australia and New Zealand' (2018) 44 *University of Western Australia Law Review* 32.

[21] Shrimp Turtle I (United States – Import Prohibition of Certain Shrimp and Shrimp Products), WTO Appellate Body WT/DS58/AB/R (1998). See BS Chimni, 'Cooption and Resistance: Two Faces of Global Administrative Law' (2005) 37 *New York University Journal of International Law and Politics* 799.

[22] In this context, the critical scholar Kanishka Jayasuriya refers to the institution-constitutive acts and substantive output of rules and decisions of such institutions as being GAL (rather than to the more procedural aspects of GAL): 'In one sense, the common element of both 9/11 and the current [2008–09 financial] crisis lies in the ushering-in of a global state of emergency; and in a distinct form of international emergency regulation and standards – very much in the form of a global administrative law – that reframes the jurisdictional practices that have shaped national constitutional formations. The economic crisis, like 9/11, was a global state of emergency that may lead to the emergence of new jurisdiction of governance layered onto the domains of national and international law. With the current crisis, we are back to the idea of global administrative law, and here too as in the 9/11 crisis, new forms of state power have been created that allow actors to bypass "national" constitutional and administrative structures.' J Sprague, 'Statecraft in the Global Financial Crisis: An Interview with Kanishka Jayasuriya' (2010) 3 *Journal of Critical Globalisation Studies* 127, 131–32.

[23] Kratochwil summarised this neatly: '[In the 1990s] the neo-classical orthodoxy that had informed the Washington consensus moved towards a "post Washington Consensus". The latter contained some new policies

mechanisms became normal accoutrements of post-Washington Consensus institutional forms and prescriptions, they have tended to be replicated in processes of emulation, and used to provide some openings for critique. In some cases, they have come to be cabined or bypassed as more powerful interests reassert themselves, including by shifting between institutions or by resorting to informal arrangements or direct external governance by unilateral national action.

v. In-Country Reform

Some groups in developing countries saw GAL as a means to nudge policies and institutions in their own countries onto some other preferred global track, or onto a different and often locally-adapted (perhaps locally-constructed) path.[24]

C. Post-2015

By about 2015, the ideology – as well as many specific practices – of 'global governance' had become the subject of some intense political and technical criticism. Governmental and public mistrust was reflected in the extreme rarity of any national politician anywhere in the world championing 'global governance' as a desirable objective. In many places 'global governance' had by 2015 become strongly and pejoratively associated with some or other of: the pursuit of US interests and techniques of US regulatory domination and self-exemption; vindication of North Atlantic preferences and styles; the rule of experts and technocracies, and a new post-bureaucrat class of polyglot, post-national and comprador highly-educated 'participants' including NGO and multi-stakeholder policy entrepreneurs allied to super-rich corporate owners and agenda-driving philanthropists and political insiders; the endurance of severe poverty and the rise and rise of global and societal inequality; circumvention of democratic state structures; deliberate strategies of fragmentation and displacement of issues away from forums where small states have power; facilitation of greenwashing and other techniques of corporate evasion; failure to reach much into China or other major counter-powers; and relative overall ineffectiveness in relation to the most serious global risks and problems.

---

such as poverty abatement, greater accountability of governments and international organizations, the promotion of the "rule of law," and the adoption of "best practices" developed by experts in informal networks, sometimes even with the participation of members of civil society. Everything seemed to fit like a hand in a glove: accountability could be strengthened, participation enhanced, welfare augmented (as waste and corruption could be cut), and law – even though thoroughly "deformalized" and largely cut off from its traditional sources – could provide the discursive "space" within which we could pursue the necessary global collective goods.' Kratochwil, *The Status of Law in World Society* (n 15) 169.

[24] N Dubash and B Morgan (eds), *The Rise of the Regulatory State of the South* (Oxford, Oxford University Press, 2013) includes substantial theoretical discussion as well as infrastructure case studies. Cases in other fields are presented in depth in E Fox and M Trebilcock (eds), *The Design of Competition Law Institutions: Global Norms, Local Choices* (Oxford: Oxford University Press, 2013); RC Dreyfuss and CA Rodríguez-Garavito (eds), *Balancing Wealth and Health: The Battle over Intellectual Property and Access to Medicines in Latin America* (Oxford, Oxford University Press, 2014). See also RF Urueña, 'Global Administrative Law and the Global South' in S Cassese (ed), *Research Handbook on Global Administrative Law* (Cheltenham, Edward Elgar, 2016).

Popular cynicism or indifference were accompanied by active resistance to particular visible or symbolic markers of 'global governance' at work. Donald Trump campaigned successfully in 2016 on opposition to TPP and a whole set of other trade agreements. His administration energetically extracted the US from commitments to the Paris Climate Agreement of 2015, the United Nations Educational, Scientific and Cultural Organization, and the Arms Trade Treaty. It largely opposed investor-state dispute settlement during the North American Free Trade Agreement renegotiations, so that its role in the 2018 Canada–Mexico–US Agreement (USMCA) is much diminished; the US acted assertively against any glimmers of International Criminal Court action directed to the US; and (in continuation of Obama-era approaches) it obstructed the WTO Appellate Body's replenishment.[25] President Bolsonaro, inaugurated as President of Brazil in early 2019, employed similar rhetoric on some international issues (including the Paris Climate Agreement). Within the EU, nationalist (and in some cases populist) leaders in several countries took sceptical positions on what had previously been received ideas about the European project.

By the 2020s, the 1990s-era vision and subsequent drivers toward GAL had by no means entirely dissolved, and many existing institutions continued to have GAL practices and norms embedded in them, but some of the earlier drivers had certainly abated or been overshadowed. In world terms they had become less generative. The styles and registers of national politics in many countries have changed significantly from those that spilled over into 1990s global governance. In the era of Presidents Putin, Trump and Xi, and of Prime Minister Modi, the pursuit of international politics through multilateral and legally-framed international institutional initiatives is hardly a prevalent governance strategy. More fundamentally, transnational regulatory governance strategies are now shaped in different places, often addressing newer technological forms or players, and the articulate political interest in international legal construction as a means for innovating in these situations is very limited in many major countries (though certainly not all).[26]

D. The Future

Five sets of such macro-contextual conditions and considerations seem noteworthy in informing the next phases of scholarship with regard to GAL. These five sets by no means exhaust the range, and may not be what is most relevant and important. Moreover, they are likely to interact together, and also to interact with significant vestiges of the earlier impetus, in relation to GAL and to determining its future influence.

i. Managing Globalisation while Opposing Global Governance

The first set is about the political management of globalisation in different places – globalisation's economic dislocations and security concerns, its cultural implications, and its

---

[25] J Goldsmith and ST Mercer, 'International Law and Institutions in the Trump Era' (2018) 61 *German Yearbook of International Law* (forthcoming).
[26] A Hurrell, 'Beyond the BRICS: Power, Pluralism, and the Future of Global Order' (2018) 32 *Ethics & International Affairs* 89.

effects on political autonomy and legal self-government. Every state is striving to manage the opportunities and threats of globalisation and technological disruption, experimenting at times with different development models (eg 'the new developmental state') and struggling to maintain particular varieties of capitalism under external pressures. Yet public suspicions of 'global governance' as a means of management are great (other than a baseline acceptance of the UN and some of its longstanding agencies). Few national politicians mention 'global governance' except to excoriate it (China is a major exception, but there the term is used with a different valence, carrying a confidence that the states (certainly China) will be able to maintain control of policy-making).[27] For many of them, the drive is to cabin globalisation and return to an accent on national autonomy and control of the borders. Whereas the protests of the 1990s (such as those in 1993–95 in India against TRIPS, and those in Seattle in 1999 against the WTO and G7) were couched roughly as *anti*-globalisation,[28] by the late 2010s and 2020s a more affirmative *de*-globalisation movement was in progress, as a significant political agenda if not an economic reality. Insofar as GAL has been an artifact of globalisation, the retreat of the tide could potentially leave it a stranded construction from an earlier era. In practice, however, so long as international institutions endure, GAL may be significant in precisely the venues where populist and nationalist projects (including their legalist and autonomy-promoting dimensions) are both pursued and contested.[29]

ii. Power Shifts

The second set of macro-contextual conditions and considerations is more of an agitated mix of changes in societal distributions and demographics, changes in the means and forms of wealth, power, dominance and risk, and shifts in the world-affecting (or geopolitical) distribution and balances of power and vulnerability. The global distribution of state power has tipped toward rising powers in Asia. China is evolving toward a match for the US and embarking on its own ordering projects (such as Belt and Road), and many Asian economies are increasing in their international weight.[30] Global tectonic friction as well as regional positioning have followed as these new realities are felt. Africa's fast-growing and fast-urbanising young populations hold and seek many new possibilities.[31] Intra-polity social and economic inequality has risen and risen, as in some places has discontent, with associated alienation and weakening of old democracies, and growing appeal of authoritarian (or populist) government or techniques. The 1990s North Atlantic dominance that facilitated 'law and global governance' projects like GAL is most unlikely to be renewed,

---

[27] L Chan, P Lee and G Chan, 'Rethinking Global Governance: A China Model in the Making?' (2008) 14 *Contemporary Politics* 3; J Zeng, 'Chinese Views of Global Economic Governance' (2019) 40 *Third World Quarterly* 578.
[28] R Howse, 'The Globalization Debate – A Mid-Decade Perspective' in S Cassese (ed), *Research Handbook on Global Administrative Law* (Cheltenham, Edward Elgar, 2016).
[29] C Bob, *Rights as Weapons: Instruments of Conflict, Tools of Power* (Princeton, NJ, Princeton University Press, 2019).
[30] C Cai, *The Rise of China and International Law* (Oxford, Oxford University Press, 2019).
[31] JT Gathii, *African Regional Trade Agreements as Legal Regimes* (Cambridge, Cambridge University Press, 2011); D Bach, *Regionalism in Africa: Genealogies, Institutions and Trans-State Networks* (London, Routledge, 2017).

but its institutional and programmatic edifices (like GAL) still stand, and are to some extent being repurposed or (re)appropriated for the more uncertain new conditions.

iii. Private Ordering

While private ordering has long been a major feature of much transnational governance, the obstructed environment of intergovernmental governance innovation has made more room for private structures and intensified demand for them.[32] Whether and how GAL applies in private ordering arrangements – or at their numerous interfaces with public power – involves debated but unresolved conceptual problems, as well as a raft of practical questions about the suitability or frailty of particular mechanisms for enforcement. Some private ordering is organised for the closed production of 'club goods' for members, taking little procedural account of non-member interests, while other forms are polyarchic, using multi-stakeholder models with sophisticated GAL mechanisms.[33] The ecosystem of private ordering has shifted with the sharp restriction in many countries on transnational NGOs and foreign funding.[34] International economic law increasingly protects foreign for-profit investment but not foreign non-profit activities. Most private ordering is dependent on state blessing or more active support – or on state promises of non-interference – and state and private are not too sharply separated in many places. The political-institutional consequences of all of this for GAL play out every day in nearly every space.

iv. Digitisation

The fourth set of macro-contextual conditions and considerations concerns the digitisation of society, the capacities of Artificial Intelligence, the arrival of more granular and self-enforcing (algorithmically coded) law,[35] and the implications for transparency, participation, reason-giving, review (including adjudication), forms of contestation and the nature of the administrative output.[36] United States-model and China-model governance forms contend with one another in the digital economy – where Facebook and other companies have created their own surrogate GAL-type terminology – and soon probably in space as US-style private sector ventures increasingly define standards and affect third parties and other states. GAL scholars have obtained only limited purchase in addressing outputs that have regulatory effects but deliberately do not have the form of standard regulatory instruments, including recommended best practices, ranked indicators of performance on one or

---

[32] MP Vandenbergh and JM Gilligan, *Beyond Politics: The Private Governance Response to Climate Change* (Cambridge, Cambridge University Press, 2017).

[33] P Schleifer, 'Varieties of Multi-Stakeholder Governance: Selecting Legitimation Strategies in Transnational Sustainability Politics' (2019) 16 *Globalization* 50.

[34] D Rutzen, 'Aid Barriers and the Rise of Philanthropic Protectionism' (2015) 17 *International Journal of Not-for-Profit Law* 1; E Bornstein, 'The Report: A Strategy and Nonprofit Public Good' (2019) 10 *Humanity: An International Journal of Human Rights, Humanitarianism, and Development* 109.

[35] C Busch and A de Franceschi, 'Granular Legal Norms: Big Data and the Personalization of Private Law' in V Mak, E Tjong Tjin Tai and A Berlee (eds), *Research Handbook in Data Science and Law* (Northampton, Edward Elgar, 2018).

[36] R Brownsword, E Scotford and K Yeung (eds), *The Oxford Handbook of Law, Regulation and Technology* (Oxford, Oxford University Press, 2019).

more criteria, models (such as climate risk and macroeconomic forecasting models), lists (such as no-fly lists) and algorithms.[37] The global regulation of the regulatory output of Silicon Valley corporations is ephemeral,[38] and often jurisdictionally fragmented or misaligned with the technology and its effects. One approach is to refocus this as the regulation of digital infrastructure and its physical and human actants, dependents, constructors and maintainers.[39]

v. Concepts

The final set of macro-contextual conditions and considerations is conceptual. Topics that received considerable attention in the first decade or so of GAL scholarship included fundamental conceptual matters: What does it mean to use the concept of 'law' in GAL, and are the analytical proponents of GAL justified in referring to this as law? What is the concept of 'administration' and can it be defined with sufficient precision? Does the 'global' moniker have enough meaning, and does it do any more than put a veneer of legitimacy over massive differences in power, influence and life-chances? These are bound to be perennial questions. Yet the reasons for asking them, and the terms and significance of debates about them, are likely to change as the contextual shifts already mentioned come to have larger impact. This chapter turns now to some of these conceptual questions.

III. GAL Concepts and Methods

A. Administration and Administrative Action

Central to the whole idea of GAL is that 'administration' is a relevant, usable and useful category for legal analysis relating to governance beyond a single state. The 2005 framing of the emergence of a body of global administrative law focused on the accountability of global *administrative* bodies (and in particular on transparency, participation, reasoned decision, legality and effective review).[40] By 'global administrative bodies' was meant

> formal intergovernmental regulatory bodies, informal intergovernmental regulatory networks and coordination arrangements, national regulatory bodies operating with reference to an international intergovernmental regime, hybrid public-private regulatory bodies, and some private regulatory bodies exercising transnational governance functions of particular public significance.[41]

---

[37] KE Davis, A Fisher, B Kingsbury and SE Merry (eds), *Governance by Indicators* (Oxford, Oxford University Press, 2012); SE Merry, KE Davis and B Kingsbury (eds), *The Quiet Power of Indicators* (Cambridge, Cambridge University Press, 2015); F Johns, 'Data, Detection, and the Redistribution of the Sensible in International Law' (2017) 111 *American Journal of International Law* 57.
[38] K Klonick, 'The New Governors: The People, Rules, and Processes Governing Online Speech' (2018) 131 *Harvard Law Review* 1598; ME Walsh, 'Facebook Plans to Create a Judicial-like Body to Address Controversial Speech' (1 May 2019) *American Bar Association Journal* (online).
[39] This is the direction of the New York University (NYU) Law School Institute for International Law and Justice's InfraReg research project, available at iilj.org/infrareg. This work is linked also to NYU Law School's Guarini Global Law and Tech initiative, available at guariniglobal.org.
[40] Kingsbury, Krisch and Stewart, 'The Emergence of Global Administrative Law' (n 2) 17.
[41] ibid.

The range of bodies encompassed was thus highly heterogeneous. To focus on the entities provides legal purchase that a simple focus on the action does not. It is essential, however, not to confine legal analysis to each entity in isolation from others. The terms of inter-entity relations must also be part of legal analysis. This creates difficult problems of plural authority, protection of different voices and different rights achieved not by any one entity but by combination, and mismatches of jurisdiction.[42] One sub-set of these questions will be addressed in section III.C with reference to distributed administration.

GAL is about the exercise of power on a quotidian basis. Much of the action studied is politically obscure, even unnoticed. Insofar as GAL is about power of these kinds, the forms of regulatory governance it addresses continue to flow as deep currents even while political storms create choppy seas above. The focus on entities and administration may thus prove in the 2020s to have more vitality than grander political forms.

The understanding of what was potentially within the domain of 'administrative' law in the GAL framing literature was and remains a capacious one – recognisable to those familiar with common law jurisdictions, but much broader than what is ordinarily regarded as 'administrative law' in many civil law countries.[43]

The potential 'administrative' matter within the field of GAL extends across:

(1) The institutional design, and legal constitution, of the global administrative body (a public entity, or a private entity with public implications, other than a state)
(2) The norms and decisions produced by that entity, including norms and decisions that have as their addressees, or otherwise materially affect:
    - other such public entities
    - states and agencies of a particular state
    - individuals and other private actors.
(3) Procedural norms for the conduct of those public entities in relation to their rules and decisions, including arrangements for review, transparency, reason-giving, participation requirements, legal accountability and liability.[44]

These three categories may be separated analytically. In simplified terms, they represent input, output and process dimensions. The (input-side) legal constitution and institutional rules of a global administrative body may be 'law' for that body – and for its members and even for others – depending on the powers and intentions of the authors of its constitutive instruments and the views taken in the institution's own practice and in responses to this. There may be delegation to the institution – by a *pouvoir constituent* – or there may not (some institutions are primordial). The institution may be confined by the terms of a mandate, or not.

The (output-side) norms and decisions issued by the entity may themselves be law, if it has such powers and status and is treated that way, or they may not. If they are transitive,

---

[42] N Roughan, *Authorities: Conflicts, Cooperation, and Transnational Legal Theory* (Oxford, Oxford University Press, 2013); E Benvenisti, *The Law of Global Governance* (The Hague, Hague Academy of International Law, 2014).
[43] This observation is rightly made by Paul Craig (endorsing the wider approach) in P Craig, *UK, EU and Global Administrative Law: Foundations and Challenges* (Cambridge, Cambridge University Press, 2015) 629–32.
[44] B Kingsbury, 'The Concept of "Law" in Global Administrative Law' (2009) 20 *European Journal of International Law* 23, 34. This approach draws from D Dyzenhaus, 'Accountability and the Concept of (Global) Administrative Law' [2009] *Acta Juridica* 3.

or could potentially be made so, there are stronger grounds for treating them as law – does a structure exist, or might one be conceivable, in which someone could revisit this administrative action or call to account those engaging in it? Would that review entail the use of GAL standards as normative guides for evaluation? This applies also to output that affects other entities, and helps structure inter-entity relations. Thus much of the output of these global administrative bodies could be characterised as 'administrative action' (to which GAL might apply): rulemaking, administrative adjudication between competing interests, and other forms of regulatory and administrative decision and management.[45]

Finally, process norms of GAL are focused on how the entity operates and how it produces output. This is the core focus of GAL. Principles and mechanisms applying to govern how an entity operates and produces output, could themselves be law even if the output itself is not law, and even if the entity is not itself legally constituted.

It is proposed that considerations of publicness may be introduced through this process layer.[46]

An important theoretical rejoinder to this whole focus of GAL on administration reprises a long-standing view that 'administration' must be distinguished from 'law'.[47] One way of putting this is reminiscent of Hans Kelsen: no doubt these bodies do many things that might be termed administration, but it is not law-governed except to the extent that there are constitutive rules of the relevant entity which it must follow. If there are process norms that flow across from one issue silo to another, these procedural norms might be simply meta-management principles.[48] A related suspicion of GAL is that it is simply a lawyerly version of managerialism, and moreover one that deformalises and even denatures law by using the language of law and rights but in an entirely managerial context.[49] A similar argument is now made about Facebook and other digital platform companies.[50]

---

[45] This avowedly broad approach to legally-cognisable administrative action was influenced by common law sensibilities; other national systems of administrative law are framed with reference to much narrower understandings of administrative action: cf L Hilton, 'Rethinking Global Administrative Law: Formulating a Working Definition of "Global Administrative Action"' (LLM Research Paper, Victoria University of Wellington, 2015) examining New Zealand, South African and US administrative law.
[46] Kingsbury, 'The Concept of "Law" in Global Administrative Law' (n 44); B Kingsbury, 'International Law an Inter-Public Law' in HS Richardson and MS Williams (eds), *Nomos XLIX: Moral Universalism and Pluralism* (New York, New York University Press, 2009); B Kingsbury and M Donaldson, 'From Bilateralism to Publicness in International Law' in U Fastenrath et al (eds), *Essays in Honour of Bruno Simma* (Oxford, Oxford University Press, 2011).
[47] C Möllers, 'Constitutional Foundations of Global Administration' in S Cassese (ed), *Research Handbook on Global Administrative Law* (Cheltenham, Edward Elgar, 2016) 107–28.
[48] Much of the practice 'is too far removed from the self-conscious application of legal procedures to pass as instance of a legal process ... The problem that arises for the GAL project is that owing to its practical ambition it is inclined to describe processes which do not give rise to legally binding acts as though they were constituted by administrative law, while these very same processes can equally plausibly also be described as mere instances of permissible conduct.' A Somek, 'The Concept of "Law" in Global Administrative Law: A Reply to Benedict Kingsbury' (2009) 20 *European Journal of International Law* 985, 987.
[49] A related concern, as Jason Varuhas has suggested (personal communication), is that attribution of 'law' to managerial practices leads to the legal formalisation of *administration*, and to associated problems such as ossification and lack of flexibility.
[50] T Shadmy, 'The New Social Contract: Facebook's Community and Our Rights' (2019) 37 *Boston University International Law Journal* (forthcoming); N Sheffi, 'The Fast to the Furious' in D McKee, F Makela and T Scassa (eds), *Law and the 'Sharing Economy': Regulating Online Market Platforms* (Ottawa, University of Ottawa Press, 2018) (about Airbnb).

This is probably not a debate that is soluble in theoretical terms, as the claims are in part contingent and empirical. A feature of the GAL approach is that it introduces law and legal criteria, including values immanent in law or carried by well-trained lawyers; and it links otherwise disparate areas of practice through the unifying idea of a complexly-differentiated global administrative space. One potential contribution of GAL is in helping to overcome problems of disregard. Other potential contributions include the recognition and protection of rights and promoting democratic governance practices. In the churned political conditions of the 2020s it does not seem that any other promising strategy is really displaced by GAL, nor that other strategies are so much more likely to contribute to such goals that they should be prioritised instead.

B. Does GAL Really Involve 'Law'?

The claim made in 2005 was that GAL was (then) 'emerging'. Could this claim still be made in the 2020s? In the ordinary rhythm of human secular affairs, this seems rather a lengthy emergence. Neil Walker's charitable reading of scholars' championing almost every type of global law is that this indefinite temporality is intrinsic to the specific circumstances and character of the 'global law' enterprise. He thus looks not for the arrival of global law, but for intimations of it (intimations here meaning both informative announcements and unspoken indications).[51] No doubt this is sage counsel. The consolidation (or formal arrival) of fully-fledged GAL, if it occurs, is likely to be discernible more in retrospect – the changes in practice and normativity are not millenarian but quotidian, dispersed, uneven, gradual and not unidirectional.

If the claims for GAL are somewhat airy about time and embodiment, is there anything special about the nature of the claim(s) that might be made to 'law'? Liam Murphy puts neatly the problematique as regards GAL:

> To pursue … the question of what distinguishes the legal from other normative orders, and perhaps to justify raising it in the first place, we can consider the case of emerging law. The most important and interesting discussion in contemporary international legal theory concerns what is usually referred to as 'global governance'. … [T]he rough idea is to highlight the impact made by international organizations on the policy options of states and the lives of people globally. It is important that while these institutions may be the creatures of treaties and so too of international law in the classical sense, that is just one possibility. They may also be informal club-like arrangements between states' executive branches, hybrid public/private institutions or even fully private institutions. The political issue raised by this aspect of globalization is that there is a global institutional sphere of great impact that is not necessarily subject to the control of states and so potentially lacks even so much accountability as customary and treaty law may have … [The claim of] the global administrative law model … is that accountability for the effects of the actions of these multifarious international organizations requires compliance with such norms as transparency, consultation, participation, rationality and review. In the absence of more robust democratic accountability, compliance with these norms of process would obviously be a good thing. But the

---

[51] N Walker, *Intimations of Global Law* (Cambridge, Cambridge University Press, 2014). Whether it is convincing to submerge different sets of ideas and practices into a unifying idea of 'global law' (let alone 'post-national law') is a different matter.

proposal is that a global administrative law is emerging, and my question is what exactly this means in a context where conventional jurisprudence currently recognizes no such law.[52]

Legal philosophy canvases numerous criteria that might be relevant. Some of the requirements Lon Fuller identified as qualities of legality are clearly necessary,[53] but their external manifestation alone is not sufficient for the existence of law.[54] Specific institutions (legislatures, courts) are highly germane in that their presence and effective operation are strong indicia of the presence of law, but they are not strictly necessary for law. Clearly a basic social acceptance and efficacy is a *sine qua non* for the epithet 'law' in the kinds of circumstances with which legal philosophers have generally been concerned, although violation or disregard of law cannot in itself negate the existence of law (as law must be understood normatively, not simply behaviourally). Liam Murphy articulates one view in arguing that the claim to law is the claim to a

> kind of normative order that would appropriately (where feasible) include some rules designed to encourage compliance and that it would be right and proper for the authorities (if there are any) to enforce the norms coercively in the ordinary course of events. We have in mind a normative order whose rules are generally taken to be, and are presented as being, appropriately enforced – if feasible and done in accordance with rules of that very order. That is one main difference law makes, one value that it adds. And that is why, I venture, you would want a global administrative law if you are concerned about the impact of unaccountable global institutions on our lives, rather than just international organization ethics.[55]

This view is Dworkinian in focusing on law as justification for enforcement action (although Murphy's approach does not limit that to coercion). Other views focus on law as providing reasons (perhaps exclusionary reasons) for action (or forbearance), with legal reasons having particular qualities and significance. Another view of law, particularly apposite to infrastructure and to digital platforms, focuses on the relationship of law to affordances. Under each of these views, the presence of, or aspiration toward, particular qualities or effects or a particular kind of order helps explicate the 'law' element that is built into claims about GAL. This claim about law within the articulation of GAL does not mean that 'global administrative law' must be a freestanding form of law, unmoored from other forms of law.[56] An argument has been made that GAL might be built up from lots of fragments

---

[52] L Murphy, 'Law Beyond the State: Some Philosophical Questions' (2017) 28 *European Journal of International Law* 203, 222 and 224.

[53] L Fuller, *The Morality of Law* (New Haven, CT, Yale University Press, 1969), refers in particular to generality, promulgation, prohibition of retroactive laws, clarity, non-contradiction within or among laws, prohibition of laws requiring the impossible, constancy of the law through time, and congruence between official action and declared rule. These principles form a central basis for efforts to distinguish law from non-law in the interactional account of international law developed by J Brunnée and SJ Toope, *Legitimacy and Legality in International Law* (Cambridge, Cambridge University Press, 2010).

[54] A slightly different critique is of non-systematic thinking and conceptual fuzziness in GAL. See, eg, the introductory chapter in C Möllers, A Voßkuhle and C Walter (eds), *Internationales Verwaltungsrecht* (Tübingen, Mohr Siebeck, 2007).

[55] Murphy, 'Law Beyond the State' (n 52) 225–26.

[56] This has some echoes of Dicey's objection to the whole idea of introducing 'administrative law' into English law – state officials were for legal purposes just like everybody else, and subject to the general laws (eg liability for torts against private persons). That debate is succinctly reprised by Jason Varuhas: JNE Varuhas, 'Taxonomy and Public Law' in M Elliott, JNE Varuhas and SW Stark (eds), *The Unity of Public Law?* (Oxford, Hart Publishing, 2018).

of law in different practice sectors – these are sectors in which there exist law-like conduct and claims, an internal sense of obligation toward these norms, and a shared view among relevant officials in the practice sector on what constitutes law and what they will recognise as law in their sector (a rule of recognition).[57] Others have argued against this approach, asserting that it promotes fragmentation, dis-connecting one micro-sector from another, and in doing so is likely to impair the possibilities of law's being actually efficacious and accepted as truly law anywhere.[58] Scholars have variously urged that the legal elements are better understood as part of an international public law,[59] or as part of traditional public international law,[60] or perhaps (for some portions) as part of a private international law of global governance. Standard resources (whether formal sources of applicable law, or bodies of material used analogically) drawn upon in propositions about the global administrative norms that govern the foundation, governance structures, competence and decision-making procedures of the various global regulatory bodies are found in national public law, private law, private international law and public international law; these also supply some standard techniques of interpretation and legal evaluation.[61]

The critique that argues that what is called GAL would be better evaluated as international law, says that the broadly-accepted authority-claims and universality of international law, and consequently the terms of its relations to other orders (such as national law in different places), are an important resource of humanity (which GAL is most unlikely to replicate) and should be nurtured and utilised rather than fragmented.[62] As a statement of the ultimate objective, this seems correct.[63] It does not in itself answer the questions whether this is attainable in the world as it is now or could become, and if so, what are the best paths to pursue to get there. The enduring commitment of all governments and many other institutions to the basic principles of public international legal order has

---

[57] Kingsbury, 'The Concept of "Law" in Global Administrative Law' (n 44).
[58] This is the view taken in L Murphy, *What Makes Law* (New York, Cambridge University Press, 2014) 170; it is not addressed in Murphy, 'Law Beyond the State' (n 52).
[59] A von Bogdandy, 'General Principles of International Public Authority: Sketching a Research Field' (2008) 9 *German Law Journal* 1909, esp 1920.
[60] M Forteau, 'Le Droit Administratif Global, Signe d'une Evolution des Techniques du Droit International?' in C Bories (ed), *Un Droit Administratif Global?* (Paris, Pedone, 2012).
[61] See the remarks of Alain Pellet (interviewed with Benedict Kingsbury) in C Bories, 'Views on the Development of a Global Administrative Law' in C Bories (ed), *Un Droit Administratif Global?* (Paris, Pedone, 2012).
[62] Cf Murphy, *What Makes Law* (n 58); Murphy, 'Law Beyond the State' (n 52). A different claim is that international law is in any case no longer confined to the narrow inter-state forms and sources by which some GAL writing has stylised it, and has the practical resources to address many of the issues and entities addressed by GAL: see remarks of Alain Pellet, 'Views' (n 61); JM Thouvenin, 'Conclusions Generales' in Bories (ed), *Un Droit Administrative Global?* (n 61).
[63] É Fromageau, 'The Concept of Positive Law in Global Administrative Law: A Glance at the Manhattan and Italian Schools' (2015) *E-Publica* [online], 121, 127–29, makes this exegesis: 'Kingsbury's conception of positive international law is thus state-centered and sourced in the will and consent of states (or jus inter gentes), and GAL is not a part of it. The reasons underpinning this exclusion relate essentially to the need to retain a "unified view of an international legal system". One may wonder that if GAL is not part of positive international law, part of international law "as it is", is it positive law at all? … [I]n Kingsbury's concept of GAL, the purpose of GAL was never to be positive law. It is rather meant to be a factor of change, a "valuable way forward", aiming to reform a positive law that is not performing a listed number of functions. In this context, Kingsbury's "ideal positive law" seems rather to be what he describes as an "inter-public law", as the law between public entities. By including states as public entities in this model, Kingsbury reunites the two sides of his dual positivism. Inter-states relations are then integrated in the wider context of public entities relations.'

survived notwithstanding other significant shifts in context and style. Simultaneously and separately, however, significant legal normativity exists in key transnational organisational and contracting forms of capitalism,[64] in transactional ordering led by governments, and in private sector or private–public forms ranging from global sports bodies and the Internet Corporation for Assigned Names and Numbers (ICANN) to State-Owned Enterprises and Sovereign Wealth Funds, many of which also interact with numerous other entities in complex inter-entity relations and sectoral standard-setting and governance.[65] The engagement of GAL through these multiple entry points into major forms of legal normativity seems indispensable both to the management of these forms of power and to the uptake of GAL.

Whether the embrace of claims to law made for GAL can be regarded as adhering to the requirements conventionally associated with legal 'positivism' has been a matter of intense debate. It has been suggested that the kinds of norms and values associated with GAL can be, and are being, operationalised through a requirement of 'publicness' – a requirement that law be made by taking account of the entire relevant public and that law speak to that entire public.[66] It has been proposed that such a requirement could be part of the rule of recognition applied in relation to claims to be law within the ambit of GAL – a kind of 'inclusive legal positivism'.[67] Even scholars sympathetic to the substance of this publicness requirement, however, have baulked at the argument that an approach to law that introduces a content-dependent requirement to the specification of law can properly be regarded as positivist.[68] However, in situations where there is no state or national juridical society whose law and practices about law are determinative in relation to some transnational legal practice, and where there is no other clearly and strongly constituted legal power, it might be thought that the adoption of a rule of recognition is a matter for participants. And they can include a view of what law means within that, which enables them to include elements they consider to be immanent in law. As a practical matter this is usually not the case within a state, as the coercive power and political legitimacy of the sovereign can in effect exclude a relatively free choice as to what the rule of recognition is – there already is one. But transnational governance contexts are often much more amorphous, with rather little ability to compel, and an authority that may be fragmented and quite tenuous.

---

[64] K Pistor, *The Code of Capital: How the Law Creates Wealth and Inequality* (Princeton, NJ, Princeton University Press, 2019); G Hadfield, *Rules for a Flat World* (Oxford, Oxford University Press, 2017); G Mallard and J Sgard (eds), *Contractual Knowledge: One Hundred Years of Legal Experimentation in Global Markets* (Cambridge, Cambridge University Press, 2016); KW Abbott, D Levi-Faur and D Snidal (eds), *Regulatory Intermediaries in the Age of Governance* (Special issue of *The Annals of the American Academy of Political and Social Sciences*, vol 670, 2017); J Black, '"Says Who?" Liquid Authority and Interpretive Control in Transnational Regulatory Regimes' (2017) 9 *Transnational Legal Theory* 286.
[65] M Young (ed), *Regime Interaction in International Law* (Cambridge, Cambridge University Press, 2012); N Roughan and A Halpin (eds), *In Pursuit of Pluralist Jurisprudence* (Cambridge, Cambridge University Press, 2017).
[66] B Kingsbury and M Donaldson, 'From Bilateralism to Publicness in International Law' in U Fastenrath et al (eds), *From Bilateralism to Community Interest: Essays in Honour of Bruno Simma* (Oxford, Oxford University Press, 2011) 79, drawing on work of Jeremy Waldron. The term 'publicness' is seldom used in common law systems, nor until recently in international law. Its meaning and value are strongly contested. However, space constraints make it impossible to enter into this important debate here.
[67] Kingsbury, 'The Concept of "Law" in Global Administrative Law' (n 44).
[68] Craig, *UK, EU and Global Administrative Law* (n 43), arguing that GAL may correctly be characterised as law, but only under a non-positivist account of law.

C. Distributed Administration

The roles and real operation of GAL procedures can only be understood and evaluated in relation to different regulatory bodies' missions and governance structures,[69] their regulatory logic (eg coordination versus cooperation games), their regulatory environment, their business model and strategies, the relevant inter-institutional relations (regulatory cooperation versus competition), and their niche in global institutional ecology. Frequently, however, they must be studied not in isolation but in intricate networks or clusters. It is quite common for rules and decisions to be adopted by one body but implemented by numerous entirely separate bodies, then challenged in a third body, at the suit of persons who had had little or no involvement in the earlier rule-making and decision-making but were centrally affected. The *Dutee Chand* and *Caster Semenya* cases in the Court of Arbitration for Sport, discussed in section III.D, exemplify this pattern. Reflection on such cases also illustrates the frequent impossibility of effectively analysing and influencing global regulatory governance without taking account of the relations between entities. This section considers just one specific and particularly neglected instantiation of this, the important phenomenon of distributed administration.[70]

One key element in relation to many global governance institutions is the structure of the pertinent distributed administration. 'Distributed administration' is the term used to encompass the other institutions (often very local or specialised institutions) through whose efforts the rules, decisions and other normative acts adopted in a global regulatory institution actually come to take effect (often in adapted or attenuated form) on the ground. These other institutions may also provide monitoring, accreditation, information, proposals for localised adjustments, funding, expertise, personnel or other inputs to the further work of the global regulatory institution in a continuous iterative or reflexive process. It is thus vital to study the distributed administrations of global regulatory institutions in close detail. Legal scholarship has tended to neglect this need and focus overly on the central global institutions.

Although the term 'distributed administration' is one introduced by the GAL literature, it refers to an old and simple notion. The obvious and mundane-seeming idea in relation to inter-state global regulatory institutions is that they frequently depend on national (state) governments, including national regulatory agencies, to take the rule-making, decision-making, and implementation and enforcement steps necessary for an agreed international regulatory scheme to actually have operational effect. This 'distributed administration' structure has echoes of what in the 1930s Georges Scelle termed '*deboublement fonctionnel*',

---

[69] Similar points are often made with regard to certain national administrative law systems. De Smith observed with regard to English (and Commonwealth) law, 'Administrative law is not a homogeneous body of jurisprudence, but is rather an agglomeration of diverse and complex branches of law [such as public health, housing, etc] and judicial review in each individual branch of administrative law has tended to develop in a distinctive manner' (SA De Smith, 'Wrongs and Remedies in Administrative Law' (1952) 15 *MLR* 189, 189). A similar view about French administrative law was articulated by J Rivero, 'Existe-t-il un critère du droit administratif?' (1953) 59 *Revue du droit public et de la science politique en France et à l'étranger* 279.

[70] The analysis of distributed administration here draws freely on B Kingsbury, 'Three Models of "Distributed Administration": Canopy, Baobab, and Symbiote' (2015) 13 *International Journal of Constitutional Law* 478. It will be further developed and systematised in a book to be edited by Benedict Kingsbury and Richard B Stewart on global private and hybrid governance (in preparation).

where national agencies take on, in addition to the functions they were established for in national administration, a second overlapping set of functions as the administering agents of an international law rule.[71]

That older account has been somewhat reinforced by two features of modern practice in international regulatory bodies established by states. First, in many international regulatory network institutions, key national regulatory agencies are represented directly (rather than through the Foreign Ministry), so the standards set by the international bodies are likely closely to reflect the views and priorities of at least some of the major national agencies, and national agencies generally are more likely to have some degree of ownership of and commitment to these standards. Second, many national regulatory agencies have been created or re-engineered in accordance not with the demands of national politics but with 'global scripts'. The regulatory practices they follow are inspired by, and receive credence and validation from, currents of ideas and practices that flow through global networks of professionals and through transnational business and civil society connections.

In practice, however, the agent/principal relationship of national regulatory institutions to international institutions in many cases may be rather attenuated or unreliable (and in the case of the most powerful states, the global body may operate as their agent). This attenuation is exactly what is called for by much national normative political theory, particularly democratic or sovereignty-oriented theories, as well as being an inherent consequence of design and structure. National agencies are constituted under national law, accountable to the national executive or legislative branch, in many cases dependent on the national government for resources and senior appointments, and dependent on national constituencies for political support in exercising regulatory powers. Moreover, in a large state, the primary interactions of national regulatory bodies may be with other regulatory bodies in the same state, rather than with foreign counterparts or with international bodies. Even in developing countries where the regulatory agencies have been designed and constituted in accordance with practices abroad (such as the creation of independent regulatory agencies to supervise privatised enterprises in sectors such as telecommunications, electricity, medicines or water supply), the actual operation of the agencies may take on a distinctly local or national style and prioritisation.

A special case of purpose-built distributed administration, however, is where an inter-governmental body and its most powerful members effectively press each state to establish and operate a specific form of national agency, facilitate supply of technical assistance and even financial support to help it operate, and aggressively monitor and report on the performance of the national agency and associated national government activities. A strong version of this is the Financial Action Task Force (FATF), which, in tandem with its multi-country regional affiliates, effectively requires each country (whether a member or non-member) to have a Financial Intelligence Unit (FIU), and it assesses (with site visits and peer review) and reports on each country's performance in relation to a set of detailed standards. The national FIUs in turn tend to share the basic orientations and regulatory priorities of the FATF, and seek to impose these through national regulations on banks, casinos, auction houses and other entities required to report suspicious financial transactions and to take special measures in relation to certain customers.

---

[71] G Scelle, *Précis de Droit des Gens: Principes et systématique* (Paris, Sirey, 1934) 10–12.

Distributed administration through national government bodies has considerable potential, as well as some hazards, as a means for improving quality and effectiveness in governance beyond the state. The local administrative site can be a focal point for contestation and resistance to global regulatory norms, as civil society actors ally with domestic authorities to evade or block implementation and enforcement. Entrenched political and economic interests, for example, may resist WTO norms, including GAL norms, for promoting market access by foreign firms. Alternatively, NGOs in a number of Latin American countries, in some cases allied with local pharmaceutical companies and national agencies, have resisted application of global patent protection standards to essential medicines.[72] Reliance by global regulators on domestic administrations also readily accommodates pluralism, local flexibility, and the use of experimentalist governance forms to enable innovation and (where the appropriate global networking structures are in place) sharing of results and learning among different national agencies, with the possibility then of revision of standards and of processes such as certification and accreditation.

Private and hybrid global regulatory bodies typically rely on various types of distributed administrations other than national government entities; in a few cases, regulatory bodies established by states may do so as well. These distributed administrations may be separated into two categories: territorially-defined functional entities (examples of which are given in the next paragraph) or non-territorial functionally-defined entities (discussed in the paragraph following). Each of these categories may be further divided into member entities, endorsed or accredited non-member entities, and separately existing entities.

Some global private and hybrid institutions have territorially-defined national member bodies that participate in the international institution and also, in their national activities, give effect to its standards and decisions. Thus the International Olympic Committee provides for one (and only one) National Olympic Committee in each country, and the International Organization for Standardization (an immensely important body in setting product, process and interoperability standards in use worldwide) has in each country one (and only one) National Member Body. Endorsed or accredited but non-member territorial bodies include the Global Fund to Fight Malaria, Tuberculosis and HIV AIDS (a major global health-funding body), whose system requires one (and only one) Country Coordinating Mechanism in each country as a precondition for funding activities in that country. The World Anti-Doping Code structure requires a national anti-doping agency in each country, with some oversight from the World Anti-Doping Agency and subject to the jurisdiction of the Court of Arbitration for Sport.

Global regulatory institutions with membership that is functionally defined and not territorially structured are prevalent in issue areas with transnational or global business structures, relatively free flow of goods, services, money and information, and civil society or social entrepreneurial groups with transnational organisation or focus. These bodies (and others) may use functional, non-territorial distributed administration entities, whether non-profit or for profit, providing, for example, accreditation, validation, verification, certification, audit and related services to promote implementation and compliance with the

---

[72] Dreyfuss and Rodríguez-Garavito (eds), *Balancing Wealth and Health* (n 24).

global regulatory norms. International regulatory programmes established by states may also use such entities. One such structure is the Clean Development Mechanism (CDM), established by the United Nations Framework Convention on Climate Change Conference of the Parties and administered by the CDM Executive Board. The CDM delegates power to private certifying companies, whose funding and profit depend in turn on the fee paid to them by the entities whose projects they certify. These companies are thus engaged in applying, interpreting and verifying compliance with the standards, including proposing new methodologies, which the CDM may then adopt. The ICANN similarly began with a primarily functional rather than territorial structuring, and administration by functional entities such as top-level domain name registries. But the increasing role of governments, territorially-defined governmental Internet regulation and nationally-characterised registries reflect global struggles as to whether the Internet will be regulated on a national basis or primarily on a functional basis.

Stronger global regulatory institutions seek to exercise some degree of discipline and control over less powerful entities forming part of their distributed administration systems. International sports bodies (such as FIFA – the Fédération Internationale de Football Association) require that the national government not interfere with the relevant national sports body, and they also require that the leadership, rules and decisions of each such body be established in accordance with both its own constitution and with standards set by the global institution. This can prevent political interference; but it can also result in sheltering a corruptly-governed national entity from discipline by domestic governments. The global sports regulatory bodies enjoy immense leverage because of their ability to exclude the national team, and players or clubs registered through the national system, from all international competitions and from sharing in revenues from webcasting and broadcasting agreements. This leverage operates, however, as cassation power – the global institution can refuse to approve a national entity, but it cannot easily itself restructure or remake that entity or name leaders to it, so that while coups and flagrant abuses can be reversed, chronic mismanagement, unproven corruption and mediocrity are all difficult to combat.

Supervision of non-member entities in distributed administration is possible where the entity is accredited by the global institution, as the threat of non-renewal provides leverage. The Forest Stewardship Council (a private multi-stakeholder global body that sets standards for sustainable forestry and issues certificates and labels for products from such forests) established its own specialist body, Accreditation Services International, to administer its accreditation system for validators and verifiers, and that body is now also used by other global regulatory institutions. The CDM Executive Board also has an elaborate system of certification of designated operating entities, but the relatively low market value of carbon credits is likely increasingly to impose cost constraints on the rigour of this supervision. In each case, effective supervision and control by the global institution of the distributed administration entities depends on leverage. That is, leverage based on asymmetric dependence (enhanced where the global institution is effectively a monopoly or dominant and non-substitutable supplier of under-supplied goods sought by the entities), and deployment by the global institution of cost-effective means of monitoring, assessment and approval or sanctioning of performance. Global institutions lacking these attributes of leverage are unlikely to operate a tightly disciplined system of distributed administration.

Further, from the perspective of principal–agent models, entities with multiple principals spurring them in different directions are unlikely to be faithful agents of any one principal. This is a structural feature of many forms of distributed administration in global regulatory programmes. Local territorial entities, for example, are typically expected to answer to local constituencies, indeed to be embedded in the national polity, as well as the global institution. Where certifying entities are financed by the firms whose performance they certify, they may be more responsive to their interests than those of the global regulator.

In the most extreme cases, the principal–agent relation may be reversed; the distributed administration may be bigger and much more powerful financially and politically than the global institution, and may come to dominate it.

IV. Private Governance

The interaction between private governance and state power is pervasive and fundamental.[73] Partly this stems from: the dominance of states in the capacity for forcible action and coercive taxation; the dependence of most property rights and many organisational forms on state law; the centrality of states in most economies; the interests of states in significant markets and flows; and the interests of major market players in invoking state power in certain circumstances. Few major markets are sustained without regulation, and states (whether acting individually or in coordination) are major suppliers of territorial and some extra-territorial regulation.

This is the background in which the private governance of global elite sport has developed. Just as states have proved indispensable for sports governance in several key areas, at the same time as sports bodies also need to hold states at arm's length on other issues, so too is there in global sports bodies both attraction to and repulsion of GAL principles and some binding GAL rules and mechanisms. On some issues, GAL is recognised to be essential as a means to head off intervention by state governments, or by national or regional courts interested in assuring human rights protections or upholding other public values and interests.

Independent review mechanisms where athletes can challenge decisions of sports governance bodies have increasingly been adopted to provide a managed and somewhat limited system of rights protection. The Court of Arbitration for Sport (CAS) is an intra-regime reviewing body, directed in part at the efficient functioning of the regime of which it is designated as a component – but following decisions of the Swiss Federal Tribunal, it maintains formal independence from the sports administrative bodies it reviews. In the background are other international and domestic courts and tribunals that might well assert the right and capacity episodically to review decisions of global sports bodies, particularly when implemented by their distributed administrations. The structural problem posed by trans-systemic activities involving fundamental rights or public interests is inescapable: how to combine or trade off the great advantages of cross-system coherence with the strongly felt imperatives of the forum's (or the local) legal order. Where this is not neatly solved by acceptable legislation, national or regional courts and tribunals forced to weigh in on the issue often look for procedural pathways. Comity, deference, proportionality and private

---

[73] EF Lambin and T Thorlakson, 'Sustainability Standards: Interactions between Private Actors, Civil Society, and Governance' (2018) 43 *Annual Review of Environment and Resources* 369.

international law doctrines such as public policy, the revenue rule and mandatory rules are among the many familiar techniques. A special kind of challenge for national public law, however, is how to treat global private orders applying to numerous individuals as a precondition for participation in a vocation, such as that of elite sport.

The case brought by Dutee Chand to CAS proved an important episode in the long struggles of the International Association of Athletics Federations (IAAF) to draft a rule specifying and limiting eligibility of athletes to compete in women's athletics events.[74] A longstanding practice is to separate women's events from men's events, in a simple binary structure. Under the IAAF's 2011 Regulation, only people characterised by pertinent national law as male could compete in men's events, and only people characterised by national law as female could compete in women's events. However, among people meeting this latter criterion, the 2011 Regulation disbarred from eligibility women with a level of naturally-occurring testosterone higher than a specified concentration. This hyperandrogenism regulation was the basis – in a crudely approximated way – for a 2014 decision by relevant sports authorities in India to exclude Dutee Chand from elite competition, both national and international.

Under contracts Dutee Chand (like all elite athletes) had been required to sign in order to take part in top-level athletics, recourse against any such decisions of the IAAF or the Athletics Federation of India (AFI) was to CAS in Switzerland.[75] The IAAF defended its regulation, but not aggressively, having for several years been well aware that making rules in this space was fraught, and that whatever approach it adopted was unlikely to prove compelling and durable with both social attitudes and scientific research changing rapidly. The Indian authorities by this time were backing Dutee Chand despite their previous conduct in declaring her ineligible (and mishandling the whole process with her). There was thus general relief that the matter could be handed over to CAS – and CAS and the parties seemed to understand its institutional role in that light, appointing an arbitral panel chosen carefully for the task.[76] This panel was equipped to – and did – act more boldly and with

---

[74] *Dutee Chand v IAAF and AFI*, Court of Arbitration for Sport, Interim Award of 24 July 2015.
[75] Dutee Chand did not try to challenge the 2014 AFI decision excluding her from competition in the Indian courts. Had she done so, she would likely also have challenged the Sports Authority of India (SAI), a government entity that was directly involved in her exclusion but not subject to CAS jurisdiction. The administrative law basis, and quite possibly also the constitutional law basis, of her case would have been strong. The Indian courts would then have had to consider whether an overall policy of deferring to international sports bodies about sports rules, or more specifically the damage done to the obvious value of having a globally uniform rule on which athletes were eligible to compete (as at international events they would be competing with one another), should weigh (and if so, how much) on the other side of a human rights-based claim that an Indian national detrimentally affected by actions in India of a state agency (and a private agency under state oversight) ought to be able to vindicate her rights under Indian law. (This is somewhat comparable to the ECJ's approach in *Kadi II* (n 17).) The court might also have had to consider the effects of a clause (if there was one) in her athletics contract requiring all challenges to go to the CAS and excluding recourse to national courts. (And a privity issue – since the SAI is unlikely to be party to that contract.) Instead, the AFI allowed itself to be brought into the arbitration – along with the IAAF – even though this meant the laws of Monaco were part of the applicable law, and even though the arbitration clause did not necessarily reach the AFI. The SAI was clearly not bound by the arbitral award – but seems to have decided to align its conduct with the award. In effect, all parties were delegating to CAS the de facto authority (overlapping its de jure authority) to resolve the whole matter.
[76] The ad hoc arbitral panel chosen comprised Justice Annabelle Bennett, a very experienced judge of the Federal Court of Australia (President), Richard McLaren (a Canadian, and a very prominent and experienced figure in sports arbitration and energetically committed to anti-doping and anti-corruption) and Hans Nater (a well-known Swiss lawyer with much experience in commercial and sports law arbitration).

more of a public law sensibility than has been common in CAS cases. The panel determined that the Regulation discriminated between two different groups of women, and that as there was prima face discrimination, the burden of justifying it shifted to the IAAF. This burden was not met, as there was not enough evidence that the Hyperandrogenism Regulations as written

> were necessary and proportionate to pursue the legitimate objective of organizing competitive female athletics to ensure fairness in athletic competition. Specifically, the IAAF has not provided sufficient scientific evidence about the quantitative relationship between enhanced testosterone levels and improved athletic performance in hyperandrogenic athletes.[77]

The operation of the rule was therefore suspended for two years, and Dutee Chand, who had already been accorded temporary eligibility by the panel early in the proceedings, became eligible during the suspension.

In 2018, the IAAF adopted a new rule that would exclude only runners at distances longer than Dutee Chand's sprint events, so her eligibility was effectively accepted, although the new rule was then challenged in CAS by Caster Semenya, a well-known South African athlete who was affected by it. Her application was rejected in April 2019 – with much hesitation – by a differently constituted CAS Tribunal with overlapping membership to that which decided the *Dutee Chand* case.[78] The *Caster Semenya* tribunal concluded, by majority, that the more important flaws that had led to the earlier IAAF rule's being suspended had been overcome in the 2018 rule. As regards some of the distances covered it had doubts, however, and in effect it left open the possibility of further review as new evidence became available.[79] Caster Semenya challenged the CAS Award in the Swiss Federal Tribunal, which in July 2019 ended a temporary stay in implementation of the 2018 IAAF Regulation pending its own consideration of the Award, as it doubted the challenge would succeed.

This was classic administrative law: rule-making by one body, reviewed by another, focused on the evidentiary record, discrimination, justification and proportionality. The process was a kind of dialogue between the regulator and the review body. In both cases the athlete affected was present in person and participated (with language a barrier, however, for Dutee Chand), and many other interested persons (including other elite female athletes) found ways to make their voices heard in the review. The entire review process was almost indispensable for the IAAF as a means to obtain some legitimacy for the rule that eventually entered into force. Puzzlingly, however, while CAS focused in detail on the rule as drafted,

---

[77] *Dutee Chand v IAAF and AFI*, Court of Arbitration for Sport, Interim Award of 24 July 2015, para 547.

[78] The Chair of both Panels was Judge Annabelle Bennett. Dr Hans Nater was appointed by the IAAF in both cases. Whereas Dutee Chand appointed Richard McLaren, Caster Semenya appointed Judge Hugh Fraser, a nomination supported by Athletics South Africa (ASA). Hugh Fraser, who competed as a track athlete in the 1976 Olympics, had retired after a long career as a judge of the Ontario Court of Justice. ASA had objected to, and challenged, the appointment in the *Semenya* case of any members of the *Dutee Chand* panel, but the Board of the International Council of Arbitration for Sport rejected these challenges.

[79] *Caster Semenya and Athletics South Africa v IAAF*, Court of Arbitration for Sport, Award of 30 April 2019, dismissing (by majority) requests for arbitration. At paras 606–624 the tribunal expressed doubts about the adequacy of evidence with regard to performance in 1500m and mile races; and also about the possible unfairness for DSD athletes taking medication to reduce endogenous testosterone below the prescribed level, if changes in their training regimes or other situations resulted in fluctuations above that level that they could not reasonably be expected to control.

and on the evidence in support of it (a rationality requirement), very little attention seems to have been given to the IAAF's rule-making process, either for the rule Duteee Chand challenged, or for the modified rule issued in 2018 and challenged by Caster Semenya. The consultation process used by the IAAF was not trumpeted – and there does not seem to have been any notice and comment structure. The CAS review process was demanding in its application of a proportionality standard in substantive review, but also rather limited with regard to rule-making process, in that it did not indicate (let alone de facto prescribe) for the IAAF what process it would have to follow in its rule-making. This may be contrasted to other review bodies, such as the WTO Appellate Body's statements about standard-setting processes (for Codex Alimentarius[80] and other bodies) in *Sardines*,[81] or the WTO Technical Barriers to Trade (TBT) Committee's prescriptions on the same matter.[82]

V. Conclusion

At its zenith in the post-Cold War 1990s, global regulatory governance was a new articulation of global order, dependent on and layered over the existing political-realist and liberal-institutionalist models, and grappling in distinctive ways with core considerations of power, value conflicts and inequality. That period of North Atlantic pre-eminence and global regulatory governance, which combined American global predominance with European confidence in its post-national legal and economic integration project, was fleeting and is long over. It has left an important politico-legal and institutional residuum; and some aspects of North Atlantic leadership and the 1990s–2000s global regulatory governance project retain a continuing vitality. However, many other locales and forces have substantial effects in contesting, and in shaping, the prevailing contours of global political and social order, the terms in which it is enunciated (beyond the vital fundamentals articulated in the UN Charter), and the major influences on and in it. As has been true in the past, global order in its more demanding or aspirational dimensions is once again multivalent, contested and uncertain. This chapter has reflected on the nature, roles and limits of global administrative law in a period in which the UN Charter order and the subsisting North Atlantic global governance legacy co-exist with re-assertive nationalism and even deglobalisation in the North Atlantic region, a power shift away from that region, new ordering forms such as the Chinese infrastructure-based Belt and Road Initiative, and a tilt in US practice toward transactional governance and against institutionalised governance and multilateral treaties.

---

[80] The Codex Alimentarius is a collection of standards, guidelines and codes of practice concerning food. These are adopted by the Codex Alimentarius Commission, a body with 188 member states and over 220 observer organisations. The Commission was established jointly by the UN Food and Agriculture Organization and the World Health Organization and has operated since 1963.
[81] *European Communities – Trade Description of Sardines*, WTO DS231, Appellate Body Report, 26 September 2002.
[82] WTO, TBT Committee, Decision of the Committee on Principles for the Development of International Standards, Guides and Recommendations with relation to Articles 2, 5 and Annex 3 of the Agreement, G/TBT/9, 13 November 2000.

Headwinds, crosswinds and choppy seas now characterise the inter-state environment in which GAL precariously operates. Yet states and their leaders have strong reasons to undertake intergovernmental governance initiatives, including to reinvigorate economic activity at times of stagnation, manage geopolitical issues and defend their own interests, in matters such as: anti-terrorism preoccupations; migration and infectious diseases crises; partly-coordinated state-centered efforts to use criminal law to combat illicit activities such as illegal drugs, illegal fishing, human trafficking and intellectual property violations; rising inter-state military-security tensions; struggles over climate/energy policy; and growing restiveness associated with human vulnerability, inequality and disrespect. Moreover, the already-existing governance structures have largely been maintained rather than abolished or superseded. While inter-governmental creation of new global legal institutions or major governance agreements was largely frozen from 2016 in the absence of US support, the leaders of most other states are well aware that cooperative international regulatory governance can enhance the effectiveness of their regulatory programmes, increasing the welfare of their members and, often, some broader constituencies as well. States establish and support global regulatory regimes in order to build markets, redress market failures, promote security and otherwise advance the welfare of their citizens under conditions of global interdependence where purely domestic action would fall short. This was the logic (certainly contested) of the Comprehensive and Progressive Agreement for Trans-Pacific Partnership, and of Japan's Abe-era steps toward a greater leadership role.[83] A similar logic drives the creation of many private and hybrid regulatory bodies.

Global regulatory governance in multiple forms accordingly seems certain to endure, and to deepen in some areas while retracting in others. Whether it features significant elements of GAL depends in part on whether inter-state patterns tip heavily toward the transactional (and non-institutional) or veer toward legal governance through institutions. This is a major question for world political ordering in relation both to the US and to China. For other states, however, the pursuit of institutionalised governance may become part of a strategy to balance against transactional and hub-and-spoke models in which their interests fare poorly as against those of much more powerful counterparts. In any case, private governance in institutionalised forms is likely to grow in importance, at least in the subject areas and with the forms acceptable to major open-but-authoritarian state systems.[84] It thus remains imperative both to understand the roles of legal and organisational as well as political features in governance, and to assess them as targets of bitter critique and as potential sources of normative value.

Insofar as global administrative law is a functional response to 'the emergence of global governance and the corresponding need to regulate it',[85] the practice of GAL may be expected to continue. Explaining GAL in these politico-economic terms suggests a basic capitalist logic: that the key drivers are the maximisation by each actor of achievement of its own (self-defined) interests within the constraints of the prevailing constellation of power.

---

[83] B Kingsbury et al (eds), *Megaregulation Contested: Global Economic Governance After TPP* (Oxford, Oxford University Press, 2019).

[84] D Guttman et al, 'Environmental Governance in China: Interactions between the State and "Nonstate Actors"' (2018) 220 *Journal of Environmental Management* 126.

[85] Benvenisti, *The Law of Global Governance* (n 42) 25.

But global order is almost equally concerned with identities and values – including values conflicts and cultural diversity – and with the implications of humiliation and powerlessness and dramatic but shifting gradients of power.

A multiplicity of normative justifications for developing accountability and responsiveness has received some support: achieving the substantive objects of the institution(s); securing rights and rule of law; overcoming improper disregard of the various affected publics and persons; mitigating injustice or promoting substantive justice; nudging the welfare and distributional consequences of the global regulatory bodies' decisions.[86] To some degree GAL has been viable because it has been possible to agree on some procedural standards even without agreement on the normative justifications for them. A second source of support for GAL is the wide recognition that it is and needs to be defeasible. In particular settings (not all settings), some or all components of GAL may be counter-productive; embrace of GAL principles and mechanisms is likely to produce losers as well as winners; the winners are likely to be those who are already powerful or wealthy; and the whole GAL enterprise may do more to legitimate the unjust than it does to promote substantive justice. Even from such viewpoints, however, GAL provides valuable lenses from which to critique existing institutional arrangements and demand reform.

The academic proponents of GAL have not generally been suspected of charting a decisive political course at the outset – indeed the absence of a clear political direction on such normative matters, or of a weighty moral keel to keep the vessel upright and on course, was one of the charges levelled in some of the early critiques of GAL. (Another was that the proceduralist terminology and globally-inclusive rhetoric of GAL masked its likely course – variously supposed to be liberal diversionism from fundamental injustices,[87] neo-liberal corporate-capitalist domination, the shoring up of American power and legalised influence, or a Western ideology for defence against the rise of the rest.) At a time of plurality of power as well as style, culture and interest, the open-textured and somewhat indistinct political valence of GAL may prove a vital source of buoyancy, as much larger forces that express in shifting responses to globalisation increasingly strain, negate and remake international ordering in the 2020s.

---

[86] RB Stewart, 'The Normative Dimensions and Performance of Global Administrative Law' (2015) 13 *International Journal of Constitutional Law* 499; M Savino, 'What if Global Administrative Law is a Normative Project?' (2015) 13 *International Journal of Constitutional Law* 492.

[87] J Linarelli, M Salomon and M Sornarajah, *The Misery of International Law: Confrontations with Injustice in the Global Economy* (Oxford, Oxford University Press, 2018).

4

International Law and National Security Policy-making: The Case of the PPG

LAURA A DICKINSON

When the United States killed Al Qaeda leader and United States (US) citizen Anwar Al-Awlaki in a 2011 drone strike in Yemen,[1] a heated debate erupted in the US and elsewhere about the possible legal basis for the strike.[2] In addition to significant questions about whether the US Constitution permitted such lethal action against a US citizen overseas, lawyers and policymakers both inside and outside the US Government disagreed about whether the action violated international law. At the heart of this discussion was a profound disagreement regarding which body of international law even applied to the operation. Global counter-terror operations have, in the years since the September 2001 attacks on the US, stretched the boundaries of armed conflict and its applicable law.[3] Accordingly, was the anti-terrorism drone strike to be analysed based on international human rights law (IHRL), which typically governs during peacetime, or instead based on the *jus in bello* (the law of armed conflict (LOAC), also known as international humanitarian law (IHL))? The difference matters, because although this body of law imposes important restrictions on the use of force, it is in general more permissive than IHRL.

Subsequent to 2011, the US has essentially adopted the legal position that the war on terror is ongoing and the scope of the battlefield is broad. From this perspective IHL/LOAC applies globally to US counter-terror operations, at least as to certain terrorist groups such as Al Qaeda.[4] Many US allies, by contrast, have adopted a more confined view of the scope

---

[1] See M Mazetti, E Schmitt and RF Worth, 'Two Year Manhunt Led to Killing of Awlaki in Yemen' *New York Times* (30 September 2011), available at https://www.nytimes.com/2011/10/01/world/middleeast/anwar-al-awlaki-is-killed-in-yemen.html.

[2] See, eg, C Savage, 'Secret US Memo Made Legal Case to Kill a Citizen' *New York Times* (8 October 2011), available at https://www.nytimes.com/2011/10/09/world/middleeast/secret-us-memo-made-legal-case-to-kill-a-citizen.html.

[3] See generally R Brooks, *How Everything Became War and the Military Became Everything* (New York, Simon & Schuster, 2016); C Savage, *Power Wars: The Relentless Rise of Presidential Power and Secrecy* (New York, Little, Brown and Company, 2015).

[4] See, eg, Office of the White House, *Report on the Legal and Policy Frameworks Guiding the United States' Use of Military Force and Related National Security Operations* (2016) (hereinafter 'Frameworks Report').

of IHL/LOAC. They have maintained that IHL/LOAC does not necessarily apply globally to operations against terrorists such as Al Qaeda, instead adopting a more fact-specific analysis of whether an armed conflict is occurring in the particular geographic location where operations are contemplated. If an armed conflict is not occurring according to their analysis, the generally higher standards of IHRL applicable to the use of force and detention would be applicable.[5]

This conflict in legal approach is potentially quite significant. Many of the countries that adopt the more confined view of IHL/LOAC, such as the United Kingdom (UK), France, Germany and Canada, partner with the US in counter-terror operations. Thus, different views regarding the applicable legal regime could potentially present numerous so-called 'interoperability' challenges that could make it more difficult for these allies to cooperate with the US.[6] It could, for example, affect intelligence-sharing and other aspects of military operations, because '[s]tates may not wish to participate, or perhaps more likely, be known to participate, in such information provision if the actions taken on the basis of that information conflict with their understandings of IHL or human rights law'.[7]

Enter what I would call 'legalised' policies. In the face of these conflicting interpretations of applicable international law, the US has crafted a number of national security policies that have imposed rules and standards that are more restrictive than the legal minimum, but they have done so as a matter of *policy* rather than as an interpretation of *international law requirements*. They are policies that national governments adopt to set forth how they will conduct themselves on the international stage and do not have any legal status on the international plane. However, although they are merely policies at the international level, they are often quite legalistic. They are written in a way that requires legal analysis and legalistic judgements, because they impose rules and standards that must be interpreted. Indeed, many of them impose legal obligations as a matter of domestic law. Yet, because they are framed as policies, they allow the US Government to formally retain its interpretation of the scope of IHL/LOAC.

These policies also highlight the permeability of the boundaries between and among multiple fields of law: different domains of international law, such as IHL/LOAC and IHRL, international law and domestic law, domestic criminal law and administrative law, and indeed the boundary between law itself and policy. Accordingly, this chapter explores key issues at the frontiers of law, and in particular it delves into the question of how policies in the national security domain may bridge or even obscure these frontiers and boundaries.

As a case study, this chapter focuses on one such legalistic policy, the Presidential Policy Guidance on the Use of Force Outside the United States and Areas of Active Hostilities (PPG).[8] Adopted during the Obama Administration, this policy reportedly has been retained in the Trump Administration, though some of its elements have been altered.[9]

---

[5] See, eg, K Watkin, *Fighting at the Legal Boundaries: Controlling the Use of Force in Contemporary Conflict* (New York, Oxford University Press, 2016).
[6] See L Wexler, 'International Humanitarian Law Divergence' (2015) 42 *Pepperdine Law Review* 549, 563–67.
[7] ibid 573.
[8] Presidential Policy Guidance, 'Procedures for Approving Direct Action Against Terrorist Targets Located Outside the United States and Areas of Active Hostilities' (22 May 2013) (redacted) (hereinafter 'PPG'), available at https://perma.cc/S6JE-5YNS.
[9] See section II.A.

First, I describe the conflicting and sometimes overlapping international legal regimes that could apply to the use of force in this context, creating disputes about the appropriate legal standard and setting the scene for the use of policy as a way of responding to the disagreements. Then, I analyse the example of the PPG and show how it attempts to paper over the disputes to create a workable approach, without actually resolving the conflict of legal regimes as a matter of law. Finally, I highlight some of the implications of adopting such legalistic policies in the face of conflicting legal interpretations.

I. Conflicting and Overlapping Legal Paradigms Regarding the Use of Force

Military operations against terrorists globally since the 11 September 2001 attacks on the US have presented complex questions about the scope of applicable legal paradigms and have stretched the boundaries of those paradigms. Lawyers, policymakers and scholarly commentators often disagree about which paradigm should apply to a given situation, as well as about the scope of each legal paradigm and its relationship to other paradigms. One of the most difficult questions is what legal regime should govern extraterritorial operations against terrorists beyond traditional battlefields such as Afghanistan, Iraq and Syria.

One approach is to treat terrorists outside these traditional battlefields largely as criminals and to deploy the law enforcement model for tracking, capturing, prosecuting and, in certain limited circumstances, killing terrorists. Within this model, the framework of IHRL would generally apply. In contrast, if terrorists are viewed as fighting a global war, then the battlefield itself is potentially global, and the largely less-restrictive IHL/LOAC regime would apply. It should also be noted that these legal regimes are not necessarily mutually exclusive and that there are as many views on how they intersect as on which regime governs in a particular context. Not surprisingly, states and commentators have taken different positions regarding when, where and in what circumstances human rights or IHL/LOAC regimes should apply and how they overlap.[10]

These differences matter. The question of which legal regime (or combination) applies has consequences for decisions related to (i) whether to capture or kill a terrorism suspect; (ii) the rules applicable to targeted killings; (iii) the level of acceptable civilian casualties; (iv) the process by which detentions may be carried out; and (v) the appropriate procedures and personnel to conduct operations.

A. The Strict Law-enforcement Model

A strict law-enforcement approach to extraterritorial terrorism operations outside of traditional battlefields would generally fall within the framework of IHRL. According to this approach, IHRL governs crucial decisions about the tracking, capture and disposition of

---

[10] See, eg, Watkin, *Fighting at the Legal Boundaries* (n 5) 267–326.

terrorist targets outside a country's territory. In many circumstances this legal regime is more restrictive than the legal rules imposed by the alternative IHL/LOAC paradigm, which generally allows more leeway for the conduct of military operations.[11]

For example, IHRL generally requires capturing a terrorist suspect, if at all possible, rather than using lethal force. Authorities would be required to make a decision about the feasibility of capture. They could not proceed to other, potentially lethal, options unless they first determined that capture was not possible.

In addition, even if capture were deemed infeasible, IHRL sets a high bar for targeting a terrorism suspect with lethal force. In particular, IHRL generally restricts the use of lethal force to situations in which the suspect poses an imminent threat. Thus, before targeting the suspect, authorities would be required to make a determination regarding the imminence of the threat, and if the imminence threshold could not be reached, lethal force would be off the table.

International human rights law further requires assessment of the impact of any use of force on civilians who might, for example, be in the vicinity of the terrorist target. In general, IHRL limits the use of force to circumstances in which it is a last resort.[12] Thus, even if authorities were to conclude that the target posed a continuing, imminent threat, their hands would nonetheless be tied if they assessed that too many civilians would be injured or killed in a use-of-force operation.

Application of IHRL also has important consequences for any decision to detain a terrorism suspect. If authorities decided to detain such a suspect, IHRL would mandate that the detention conform to rigorous standards, including minimum standards for the conditions of detention, as well as due process requirements regarding access to a lawyer, charges to be filed before an independent court within a specific period of time, notice of such charges to the detainee and so on. There is some disagreement about the precise obligations that apply to the treatment of detainees within an armed conflict,[13] but, as discussed in section I.B, there is general agreement that IHL/LOAC does not require the same due process standards as IHRL.

Finally, if IHRL governs, that body of law may restrict the type of personnel who are permitted to conduct operations, as well as dictate procedures that they must follow. For example, in many contexts, IHRL may require civilian, rather than military, personnel to conduct operations.[14] And IHRL may dictate specific procedures to be followed in order to assess operations in advance, as well as to investigate and evaluate them afterwards.

---

[11] For an overview of this paradigm, see, eg, S Breau, M Aronson and R Joyce, *Discussion Paper 2: Drone Attacks, International Law, and the Recording of Civilian Casualties* (Oxford Research Group, 2011); ME O'Connell, Testimony, *Lawful Use of Drones, Hearing: Rise of the Drones II: Examining the Legality of Unmanned Targeting* (US Congress, 28 April 2010); Watkin, *Fighting at the Legal Boundaries* (n 5).

[12] See, eg, L Blank, 'Defining the Battlefield in Contemporary Conflict and Counterterrorism: Understanding the Parameters of the Zone of Combat' (2010) 39 *Georgia Journal of International and Comparative Law* 1, 14–15.

[13] For a fuller discussion of different approaches to extraterritorial military detention, see LA Dickinson, 'Administrative Law Values and National Security Functions: Military Detention in the United States and the United Kingdom' in P Cane, E Ip, H Hoffman and P Lindseth (eds), *Oxford Handbook on Comparative Administrative Law* (Oxford, Oxford University Press, forthcoming).

[14] See, eg, *McCann and Others v United Kingdom* (1996) 21 EHRR 97.

B. The International Humanitarian Law/Law of Armed Conflict Model

International humanitarian law, also known as the law of armed conflict (IHL/LOAC), provides a far more permissive framework for counter-terrorism operations than the law-enforcement/human rights model. The precise rules differ depending on the type of armed conflict – either international or non-international. Because contemporary counter-terrorism operations do not generally entail international armed conflicts between and among states, this chapter will focus on the rules of non-international armed conflicts (NIACs).

To begin with, under IHL/LOAC, there is generally no obligation to capture, rather than kill, a legitimate target taking part in hostilities, assuming that the armed forces conducting the strike follow the fundamental principles of IHL/LOAC. These principles include, for example, distinction, proportionality, military necessity and feasible precautions. The principle of distinction mandates that only military objects or certain types of individuals may be targeted for attack. Civilians, for example, may not be targeted.[15]

To be sure, there is considerable disagreement about how individuals are classified. For example, if an individual is taking a direct part in hostilities, he or she may be targeted for such time as he or she is doing so. And states and other entities sometimes disagree about what counts as taking a direct part in hostilities.[16] In addition, the US has maintained that, separate from what counts as taking part in hostilities, mere membership in a particular armed group, such as specific terrorist organisations, renders one subject to attack.[17] Other states have disagreed with such a broad classification, asserting instead that the only relevant question in a NIAC is whether the individual is actually taking a direct part in hostilities.[18]

Even apart from the 'capture versus kill' decision, IHL/LOAC also provides a very different approach to the use of lethal force than IHRL. For example, IHL/LOAC does not require armed forces to assess the imminence of a threat before deploying lethal force. Rather, the key issues would be whether the fundamental principles of IHL/LOAC, as discussed previously, had been satisfied. In addition to the distinction analysis already described, the armed forces would need to determine whether military necessity justified the attack, whether any precautions were feasible (such as dropping leaflets or providing other warnings in the area of attack), and whether the attack would be proportionate. In practice, the extent of these assessments might differ depending on the circumstances of the attack, for example whether the attack is 'deliberate' (pursuant to an operation planned in advance over an extended period) or 'dynamic' (pursuant to an operation that takes place in the midst of unfolding events on the ground).[19] And these assessments are quite meaningful. Yet, regardless of the

---

[15] For the US view on these principles, see Frameworks Report (n 4).
[16] See eg N Bhuta and H Liu, 'Targeted Killing, Unmanned Aerial Vehicles and EU Policy' Global Governance Program 1, 4–5 (March 2013), available at http://cadmus.eui.eu/bitstream/handle/1814/27737/2013-1-Policy%20Brief_RSCAS_GGP.PDF?sequence=1.
[17] ibid 29.
[18] See, eg, *Public Committee Against Torture v Israel*, Supreme Court of Israel, HCJ 769/02 (2006). Under this framework, membership in a group, and the role an individual plays within that group, might be relevant to determine whether that individual is performing a 'continuous combat function'.
[19] JM O'Connor (General Counsel, Department of Defense), 'Applying the Law of Targeting to the Modern Battlefield', Remarks at the New York University School of Law (28 November 2016), available at https://perma.cc/X7H2-2DLA.

nuances, the key point is that IHL/LOAC generally does not restrict the use of lethal force to the extent of IHRL.

Under IHL/LOAC, the assessment of harm to third-party civilians in any attack also differs from the assessment dictated by IHRL. Military authorities applying the principle of proportionality, for example, would evaluate whether an attack is expected to cause incidental loss of civilian life, injury to civilians, damage to civilian objects, or a combination thereof, to a degree that would be excessive in relation to the concrete and direct military advantage anticipated. This calculus, while significant, is much less restrictive than the corresponding obligation under IHRL to limit harm to civilians in all circumstances.

Detention obligations would also differ under IHL/LOAC from those under IHRL. For example, IHL/LOAC contains extensive rules for the treatment of prisoners of war (POWS) in international armed conflicts. To be sure, states' IHL/LOAC obligations with regard to security detainees in *non*-international armed conflicts are somewhat ambiguous because such detainees do not qualify as POWs. Yet even assuming fairly substantive obligations regarding treatment and process – for example to establish the status of detainees – the standards under IHL/LOAC and IHRL differ quite fundamentally.[20] In particular, IHL/LOAC permits detention for the duration of hostilities and does not necessarily mandate that detainees be charged with, and prosecuted for, a crime within a particular time frame, or even at all.

Finally, IHL/LOAC obligates states to follow certain legal procedures, but they do not match the procedural obligations of IHRL.[21] For example, IHL/LOAC imposes an obligation to investigate allegations of violations that amount to war crimes, but does not mandate the same level of investigation as IHRL.[22]

C. Contrasting Approaches

The US and other allied nations have in many circumstances embraced contrasting legal paradigms when they have engaged in extraterritorial counter-terror operations outside traditional battlefields. In general, the US has adopted the IHL/LOAC framework, also sometimes dubbed the 'conduct of hostilities approach', and has maintained that IHL/LOAC applies globally to operations against specific terrorist groups. By contrast, many European allies and Canada take the position that the conduct of hostilities approach must be more geographically constrained and that the law enforcement/human rights paradigm applies, even as to Al Qaeda and members of ISIS, if they are outside specific territorial locations.

i. United States

The US has essentially adopted the view that IHL/LOAC applies globally to certain categories of terrorist groups, such as Al Qaeda, some Al Qaeda affiliates and ISIS. Probably the

---

[20] For a more detailed treatment of this issue, see Dickinson, 'Administrative Law Values and National Security Functions: Military Detention in the United States and the United Kingdom' (n 13).

[21] See MN Schmitt, 'Investigating Violations of International Law in Armed Conflict' (2011) 2 *Harvard National Security Journal* 31.

[22] See ibid.

clearest articulation of this approach can be found in a report issued during the last days of the Obama Administration, the 2016 *Report on Legal and Policy Frameworks Guiding the United States Use of Military Force and Related National Security Operations*, often termed the 'Frameworks Report'.[23] The Frameworks Report synthesises a variety of prior public statements by top US officials and assertions in public documents. It reflects the views of the entire US Executive Branch. Although the Trump Administration may have changed some of the policies discussed in the document, the new Administration does not seem to have deviated from the legal frameworks the Report maps out[24] and has even issued a follow-up report that largely embraces the approach of the prior Obama Administration Report.[25]

In particular, the Frameworks Report stresses that the US applies a conduct of hostilities model to extraterritorial counter-terror operations. Although the US has said that it will apply *ad bellum* constraints to the initiation of operations in other countries, once it has surmounted the *ad bellum* hurdle, it views its operations as governed by IHL/LOAC rather than the more restrictive IHRL. For example, the Frameworks Report notes that, 'in armed conflicts with non-State actors that are prone to shifting operations from country to country, the United States does not view its ability to use military force against a non-State actor with which it is engaged in an ongoing armed conflict as limited to "hot" battlefields'.[26] The Report treats groups such as Al Qaeda and ISIS as enemy forces within this ongoing global armed conflict.

In addition to the broad geographic scope of the conduct of hostilities, and thus the applicability of IHL/LOAC, the US has taken an expansive approach to the temporal scope of the armed conflict. Thus, it has asserted that the armed conflict against terrorist groups will only end when 'the United States will degrade and dismantle the operational capacity and supporting networks of terrorist organizations like al-Qa'ida to such an extent that they will have been effectively destroyed and will no longer be able to attempt or launch a strategic attack against the United States'.[27] Only at that point will there 'no longer be an ongoing armed conflict between the United States and those forces'. Moreover, the Report notes that once it has made an *ad bellum* calculation with respect to such a group, 'it is not necessary as a matter of international law to reassess whether an armed attack is occurring or imminent prior to every subsequent action taken against that group, provided that hostilities have not ended'.[28]

---

[23] Frameworks Report (n 4).

[24] See C Savage and E Schmitt, 'Trump Poised to Drop Some Limits on Drone Strikes and Commando Raids' *New York Times* (21 September 2017), available at https://www.nytimes.com/2017/09/21/us/politics/trump-drone-strikes-commando-raids-rules.html; C Savage and E Schmitt, 'Trump Eases Combat Rules in Somalia Intended to Protect Civilians' *New York Times* (30 March 2017), available at https://www.nytimes.com/2017/03/30/world/africa/trump-is-said-to-ease-combat-rules-in-somalia-designed-to-protect-civilians.html; see also C Fonzone and L Hartig, 'The More Things Stay the Same: Why the Trump Administration's Counterterrorism Strategy is Surprisingly Conventional and What It Means for the Future' *Just Security* (13 November 2018), available at https://perma.cc/7YRP-DQ5L.

[25] Office of the White House, *Report on the Legal and Policy Frameworks Guiding the United States' Use of Military Force and Related National Security Operations* (2018) (hereinafter 'Trump Administration follow-up Frameworks Report'), available at https://www.lawfareblog.com/document-white-house-legal-and-policy-frameworks-use-military-force.

[26] Frameworks Report (n 4) 11.

[27] ibid 12.

[28] ibid.

ii. Alternative Approach of Some Leading US Allies

Many leading US allies have taken a much narrower view of the scope of hostilities against terrorist groups. As a result, they have embraced a more constrained approach to the scope of IHL/LOAC and instead have applied a law enforcement paradigm, which often entails the application of IHRL, to extraterritorial operations against such groups.

One of the leading accounts of these competing paradigms can be found in a recent book by Ken Watkin, who formerly served as Canada's top military lawyer. Watkin notes that many in the international community limit their application of the IHL/LOAC paradigm to traditional armed conflict zones.[29] While governments have been reluctant to clearly articulate their positions on this issue, many states have indicated their support for a narrow view of the scope of IHL/LOAC.[30] For such countries, the range of a NIAC against terrorist organisations is confined to the geographic boundaries of the territory in which the armed conflict is most obviously occurring. Therefore, IHL/LOAC targeting would be permissible only in a territorial battlefield.[31]

Outside these zones, such states follow a law-enforcement paradigm that generally entails implementation of IHRL (although the precise scope of specific IHRL obligations will depend upon the extraterritorial application of those obligations). Terrorist acts outside these zones generally are viewed as fitting within appropriate criminal justice responses.[32] In addition, under this paradigm, states typically view each terrorist act as a single crime, rather than as a series of acts connected to one another.

Many of these states also view the scope of the armed conflict as more limited temporally than does the US. They do not necessarily agree that the armed conflict against a non-state actor ends only when that non-state actor is 'unable to launch a strategic attack'.[33] Such language in the Frameworks Report goes beyond existing statements about the end of hostilities under IHL/LOAC in international courts and tribunals.

iii. Ambiguity and Overlap

The conflict between the legal paradigms discussed so far may not always be quite as sharp as it may seem at first blush. It is important to acknowledge that the precise rules within each of the paradigms described are often contested, and may in some contexts be stretched to resemble one another. In addition, the conduct of hostilities and law-enforcement paradigms are not necessarily mutually exclusive and may overlap in some circumstances. Furthermore, both paradigms intersect with the *jus ad bellum* framework, including self-defence. As a result, the conflict between the conduct of hostilities and law-enforcement approaches may not always be a stark one.

International human rights law, for example, is somewhat in flux when addressing counter-terrorism issues, depending on the context. The European Court of Human Rights, one of the leading judicial bodies to interpret IHRL within the broad swath of Council of

---

[29] Watkin, *Fighting at the Legal Boundaries* (n 5) ch 8.5.
[30] See Bhuta and Liu (n 16) 4.
[31] Watkin, *Fighting at the Legal Boundaries* (n 5) ch 8.5.
[32] ibid 294.
[33] Frameworks Report (n 4) 12.

Europe countries, has in recent opinions given states such as Russia a fair degree of latitude to conduct counter-terror operations. In such decisions, it has interpreted human rights obligations such as those related to the use of lethal force somewhat flexibly. For example, in the *Finogenov* decision,[34] the Court addressed a heavy-handed Russian operation to rescue civilians from a terrorist attack on a Moscow theatre in 2002. During the rescue, Russian authorities used military-like tactics and deployed a mysterious gas that killed hundreds of people. Although the Court faulted Russia for insufficient accountability and transparency, it took a relatively lenient approach to the underlying question of substantive rights-infringement.

Similarly, the precise content of some IHL/LOAC obligations remains somewhat uncertain, particularly in NIACs, where the treaty law is less developed. The Geneva Conventions address NIACs primarily only in Common Article 3, and although Additional Protocol II pertains to NIACs, not all states have ratified it. Furthermore, the status of customary international law as it applies to NIACs is contested and ambiguous. States have not helped matters because they have not generally provided much clarification regarding whether the practices they undertake in NIACs are followed as a matter of legal obligation. The recent *Department of Defense Law of War Manual*, for example, which runs to more than a thousand pages, devotes only one scant chapter to NIACs.[35]

In addition to ambiguity regarding the content of norms, there is also considerable debate about the extent to which the legal paradigms overlap and, if so, how they intersect. Within an armed conflict, under the doctrine of *lex specialis*, is IHRL completely inapplicable? Does it govern some situations not directly related to the armed conflict, for example when foreign militaries engage in policing or humanitarian operations? Or does it govern in some situations related to the armed conflict, such as the interrogation of detainees, and not others? Or might it inform the interpretation of standards within IHL/LOAC? There is a multitude of views about these topics. Watkin notes that it is 'no longer practically possible in the post 9–11 period to rely on traditional exclusionary views of the law or provide relatively simple answers based on the "black-letter" law of the 1949 Geneva Conventions governing inter-state conflict'.[36] He observes that 'the "counterterrorism" operating environment is simply too complex to permit such a simple, even static response'.[37]

An added wrinkle is the intersection of self-defence principles under the *jus ad bellum* with either or both legal paradigms. The US has asserted that it will apply fundamental *jus ad bellum* principles to the initiation of its use of force against non-state actors. Accordingly, the US recognises three circumstances in which it may use force on the territory of another state: (i) a UN Security Council resolution; (ii) consent of the state; (iii) individual or collective self-defence, including actions against non-state actors on the territory of a non-consenting state when the state is unwilling or unable to address the threat.[38] The US also takes a relatively broad approach to defining the kinds of 'imminent' armed attacks that justify self-defence. Other states may adopt different approaches to the right of

---

[34] *Finogenov v Russia*, 2011-VI Eur Ct HR Rep 365.
[35] US Office of General Counsel Department of Defense, *Department of Defense Law of War Manual* (12 June 2015, updated December 2016) ch 17, available at https://perma.cc/J6H3-PQ6T.
[36] Watkin, *Fighting at the Legal Boundaries* (n 5) 272.
[37] ibid.
[38] Frameworks Report (n 4) 8.

self-defence in the *jus ad bellum* (for example adopting a narrower view of imminence)[39] and the intersection of the *jus ad bellum* with IHL/LOAC and IHRL.

Nevertheless, despite these various nuances, it is clear that the IHL/LOAC and the IHRL approaches are competing paradigms that have concrete consequences. The bottom line in all of this debate is that fundamentally the US has adopted a very different approach from its allies on these questions. Indeed, the Frameworks Report acknowledges these differences and notes that allies meet regularly to address the operational consequences of this disagreement.[40]

II. The Role of Legalised Policy: The Case of the PPG

Although, as discussed, the US has essentially embraced a global conduct of hostilities paradigm with respect to the international law regime governing its activities against certain terrorist organisations, the US has nonetheless *as a matter of policy* at the international level imposed certain additional restrictions on its operations. These restrictions consist of rules that are more demanding than the minimum legal requirements the US has said it is obligated to follow under international law. The UK has also sometimes adopted such restrictions.[41]

Historically, states have regularly adopted such restrictions in the form of rules of engagement, which are military rules specific to a particular armed conflict that may exceed the minimum obligations imposed under IHL/LOAC. But the pressures of contemporary armed conflicts, marked by protracted NIACs with terrorist organisations, have sparked many new circumstances in which states have adopted such policies. Probably the most prominent recent example is the targeting policy formulated during the Obama Administration entitled the Presidential Policy Guidance on Procedures for Approving Direct Action Against Terrorist Targets Located Outside the United States and Areas of Active Hostilities (PPG). Other instances include US policies on civilian casualty monitoring, reporting and investigation, as well as the periodic review process for Guantanamo detainees, among others.[42] This chapter focuses on the PPG.

A. The PPG Framework

The PPG provides a detailed framework for using force against terrorists outside territories described as 'areas of active hostilities'.[43] The term 'areas of active hostilities' does not correspond to any accepted legal category within IHL/LOAC, a point that has sparked some controversy, in part because it has enabled the US Executive Branch to determine unilaterally which territories qualify.[44] The phrase 'outside areas of active hostilities' has

---

[39] See, eg, N Bhuta and H Liu, 'Targeted Killing' (n 30) 3.
[40] ibid 14.
[41] See UK Joint Committee on Human Rights, 'The Government's Policy on the Use of Drones for Targeted Killing', HL 141/HC 574 (27 April 2016) available at https://perma.cc/78KR-Q293.
[42] See, eg, Dickinson, 'Administrative Law Values and National Security Functions: Military Detention in the United States and the United Kingdom' (n 13).
[43] See PPG (n 8) 3.
[44] See, eg, JC Daskal, 'The Geography of the Battlefield: A Framework for Detention and Targeting Outside the "Hot" Conflict Zone' (2013) 161 *University of Pennsylvania Law Review* 1165.

been understood, however, to refer to territories outside zones that virtually all states would agree are sites of armed conflict within existing IHL/LOAC tests for armed conflict. In the Frameworks Report, the US identified the specific places that it deemed at the time to be 'areas of active hostilities'. As of December 2016, the date of the Frameworks Report, those areas included Afghanistan, Iraq, Syria, designated areas in Libya, and US actions to defend US or partner interests outside the terrorism context, such as the 2016 US military strikes on radar facilities in Houthi-controlled territory in Yemen.

Outside these 'areas of active hostilities', the PPG provides a detailed set of substantive and procedural rules for direct action against terrorist targets, including the use of lethal force and capture. In particular, with respect to substantive rules, the PPG requires that lethal force can only be used against a target that poses a continuing, imminent threat to US persons. In addition, the PPG mandates that before lethal action can be taken, a determination has to be made that there is (i) near certainty that the terrorist target is present and that non-combatants will not be injured or killed; (ii) 'an assessment that capture [is] not feasible at the time of the operation'; (iii) 'an assessment that the relevant governmental authorities in the country where action is contemplated' are unable or unwilling to 'effectively address the threat'; and (iv) 'an assessment that no other reasonable alternatives [exist] to effectively address the threat to US persons'.[45]

In addition to these substantive rules, the PPG also imposes rigorous procedural requirements. For example, the PPG mandates that certain individuals or entities have to approve operations. In most cases involving the use of lethal force, senior Executive Branch officials are required to approve the operation.

The Trump Administration has reportedly retained some, but not all, of these requirements.[46] The new Administration has not released a report of comparable transparency outlining its policy, although a recent report acknowledges that the Administration does in fact have such a policy.[47] Newspaper accounts indicate that the Trump Administration expanded the zones designated as areas of 'active hostilities' to include Somalia.[48] With respect to the substantive rules, the new Administration reportedly dispensed with the rule that a terrorist target must pose a continuing, imminent threat to US persons and interests and that there must be a near certainty that the terrorist target is present – instead adopting a 'reasonable certainty' test.[49] But, according to newspaper accounts, the Trump Administration retained other elements found in the PPG, such as the requirement that there must be 'near certainty' that civilians will not be harmed before lethal force may be used.[50] Furthermore, with respect to the procedural elements, the Trump Administration reportedly has permitted decision-making to take place at lower levels of command.[51]

---

[45] ibid.
[46] See, eg, Savage and Schmitt, 'Trump Poised to Drop Some Limits on Drone Strikes and Commando Raids' (n 24).
[47] Trump Administration Follow-up Frameworks Report (n 25) 3 ('The United States continues, as a matter of policy, to apply heightened targeting standards that are more protective of civilians than are required under the law of armed conflict.').
[48] See, eg, Savage and Schmitt, 'Trump Eases Combat Rules in Somalia Intended to Protect Civilians' (n 24).
[49] See D Eviatar, 'Breaking the Silence on Civilian Casualties from U.S. Air Strikes in Somalia' *Just Security* (20 March 2019), available at https://perma.cc/PK8U-A9UP.
[50] See Savage and Schmitt, 'Trump Poised to Drop Some Limits on Drone Strikes and Commando Raids' (n 24); 'Donald Trump's Shadow War' *Politico* (9 May 2018), available at https://perma.cc/RU7Y-9XK6.
[51] See Savage and Schmitt, 'Trump Poised to Drop Some Limits on Drone Strikes and Commando Raids' (n 24); 'Donald Trump's Shadow War' (n 50).

B. A Legalistic Policy Exceeding the Minimum Standards of IHL/LOAC

The PPG – and its Trump Administration successor – represent a distinctive type of policy, one that is legalistic in nature. Moreover, these policies, even in the watered-down Trump Administration version, exceed the minimum requirements of IHL/LOAC and more closely resemble the framework imposed by IHRL.

The legalistic aspect of these policies is evident in both their substantive and their procedural elements. To begin with, as a substantive matter, the policy is based on specific rules, one of the hallmarks of legalism. Moreover, the substantive rules contain legalistic terms that appear to require legal interpretation and that at least resemble legal terms found in international law texts. Thus, as a procedural matter, the implementation of the policies seems to demand a role for lawyers, even if that role may be implicit. Indeed, it would be difficult for agency and military officials to comply with these policies without requiring legal advice from military and civilian lawyers within the Executive Branch bureaucracy.

Furthermore, the elements of the PPG, and to a lesser extent the Trump Administration successor policy, move in the direction of IHRL. For example, under the PPG, US authorities are required to determine that a terrorist target poses a 'continuing, imminent threat' to US persons and interests before approving the use of lethal force. This standard far exceeds the targeting standards of IHL/LOAC outlined in section I. Rather, it more closely resembles the standard typically mandated by IHRL, that authorities may not deploy lethal force except when harm is 'imminent'. Similarly, the PPG and Trump Administration successor policy more closely approximate international human rights standards for assessing civilian harm because the policy mandates that there must be 'near certainty' that no civilians will be harmed before lethal action may be taken. The IHL/LOAC proportionality rule does not even come close to requiring such certainty, but rather accepts the grim reality that civilian casualties are lawful within an armed conflict if expected casualties are proportionate to expected military advantage. Thus, as a matter of policy, the US has adopted restrictive rules – both in the PPG and in the Trump Administration successor policy – that are more akin to IHRL standards than to the IHL/LOAC standards that the US continues to insist are the appropriate legal rules in this context.

III. Implications of a Policy Approach

What are the implications of addressing these ambiguities, gaps and disputes in international law with policies, and in particular legalised policies? The advantages and disadvantages vary considerably depending on one's position and perspective. For example, an advantage for the US Executive Branch might be viewed as a disadvantage from the perspective of non-governmental organisations (NGOs) championing the cause of human rights. In addition, the governments of different countries may perceive the advantages and disadvantages in an altogether different light. What is clear, however, is that the adoption of legalised policies such as the PPG has consequences. Here, I will map them out from two somewhat contrasting perspectives: the US Executive Branch and the human rights community. I recognise that neither perspective is itself monolithic, but it may be helpful to understand how legalistic policies may look from these two vantage points.

A. The US Executive Branch – Advantages of Policy Solutions

From the perspective of US Executive Branch officials, it may be advantageous to embrace a legal paradigm that sets fewer minimum requirements and then to adopt legalistic policies such as the PPG that exceed these minimum legal requirements. In the face of ambiguity about the scope of international law and the choice of the appropriate legal paradigm, this approach offers an attractive path forward for a variety of reasons.

i. Policy is Flexible

To begin with, policy is flexible. When Executive Branch officials assert only a minimalist view of legal requirements but then exceed those requirements as a matter of policy, officials maintain room to manoeuvre. In this sense, such an approach reflects a kind of pragmatism. It can be fine-tuned and calibrated to specific circumstances, and it preserves discretion for the Executive Branch, which may be particularly important in the counter-terrorism context. Because the Government is not formally bound to the standards under international law, the Executive Branch can change the standards by issuing new policies.

This flexibility was likely an important consideration in adopting the PPG. Some might see the framework of IHRL as overly formalist and impractical in many circumstances applied to targeting terrorists extraterritorially. Watkin sums up this position quite forcefully, observing that that the strictures of a purist IHRL approach to counter-terrorism present the spectre of a 'security black hole'.[52] If governments must satisfy all the requirements of IHRL, including showing in virtually every circumstance that a threat is imminent before using lethal force, it may be difficult to act quickly enough to effectively counter that threat. The more minimalist rules of IHL/LOAC do not require imminence assessments before lethal force may be used. A state that embraces a policy such as the PPG retains the discretion to choose standards that resemble IHRL when it is feasible to do so. But because the policy does not impose legal restraints at the international level, a state that has adopted such a policy may also deviate from the standards in the policy if circumstances dictate.[53] The state thus preserves scope for a range of action, while still emphasising its commitment to follow international law.

ii. Policy can Bridge Gaps in Legal Interpretation Among States

A policy approach can also serve as a bridge between different interpretations of international law held by different states. When one state believes that IHL/LOAC governs extraterritorial counter-terror operations even outside traditional battlefields and another asserts that the more demanding IHRL applies, a policy that mirrors human rights law can minimise the impact of these contrasting views. If the state that adheres to the more permissive rules of

---

[52] Watkin, *Fighting at the Legal Boundaries* (n 5) 300.
[53] Some elements of these policies may find their way into domestic law in the form of legislation or Executive Order, or they may effectively function as administrative law. For a discussion of these issues in the detention context, and an argument that US and UK extraterritorial military detention policies have evolved into a kind of administrative law, see Dickinson, 'Administrative Law Values and National Security Functions: Military Detention in the United States and the United Kingdom' (n 13).

IHL/LOAC implements practices that exceed those minimum rules, the practical impact of this state's contrasting legal approach will diminish. The conflict over legal paradigms thus may disappear as a practical matter, at least at the operational level.

One could make the case that the PPG served precisely this role. As already discussed, the PPG brought the US closer – in practice – to the approach of many allies, international organisations and civil society groups that take a more constrained view of the scope of armed conflicts with terrorist groups. The standards for direct action specified in the PPG, including for targeted killing and capture, approximate the rules of IHRL outside areas designated as 'areas of active hostilities'. To be sure, these standards do not fully equal the stringent requirements of IHRL, and the terms of each do not fully map onto one another. And, furthermore, the Trump Administration successor policy moves back in the other direction, expanding the gap in approaches. But nonetheless, this policy still exceeds the minimum requirements of IHL/LOAC and thus still comes closer to an IHRL framework than a purely minimalist application of IHL/LOAC. Even under the Trump Administration approach, outside areas of active hostilities the US military reportedly still may not use lethal force unless there is a near certainty that civilians will not be killed. Thus, even though US allies may still disagree with the US view of the appropriate legal paradigm for such operations, there are fewer practical disagreements with regard to the specific actions the US actually undertakes during counter-terrorism operations.

The PPG, and to a slightly lesser extent the Trump Administration successor policy, also potentially reduces conflicts with the territorial states where the US is taking direct action. By requiring US actors to ensure there is a near certainty that civilians will not be harmed during a direct action, the PPG and the Trump Administration policy both minimise the extent to which host states may object to such action on their territory.

By bridging these types of differences among states, legalised policies such as the PPG can reduce interoperability concerns of multilateral operations. Such interoperability needs could arise when, for example, the US allies must consider whether to share intelligence that could be used in a US targeting operation. Indeed, the *Frameworks Report* acknowledges that differences in legal interpretation among states can bring challenges to such operations.[54] The report notes that the US regularly consults with allies to find pragmatic solutions in such situations – to find a way to work together. The PPG and the Trump Administration successor policy can help with this effort.

iii. Policy Provides a Path to Resolve Differences of Legal Interpretation Within a Government

Finally, a legalistic policy has the potential to bridge differences *within* a government. Executive Branch officials may themselves disagree about the applicable legal framework for a particular operation or type of operation. When such disputes arise, a legalistic policy can smooth over such differences. It may be easier in many cases to achieve consensus to adopt such a policy than to resolve the dispute with a definitive decision about what legal regime applies.

---

[54] Frameworks Report (n 4) 14.

The PPG may be an example of this kind of bridge. The precise history of the PPG is not known, due to the sensitivity of the national security context in which it arose. Accounts now public of debates within the Obama Administration at the time, however, indicate that top administration lawyers were locked in heated discussions regarding contrasting paradigms under international law and the use of force, as well as the interpretation of the rules within those paradigms.[55]

Against the backdrop of hard-fought contests over legal meaning, a policy approach such as the PPG certainly seems attractive. Rather than hashing out freighted differences over legal restrictions on US action, Executive Branch officials crafting policy solutions can avoid such differences altogether. The choice of a legal paradigm, particularly a restrictive one, has enormous consequences for a state that hews faithfully to its international legal commitments. Policies such as the PPG circumvent this issue while advancing the underlying values of the human rights paradigm. For Executive Branch officials opposed to the human rights paradigm, the policy preserves the legal discretion of the US. For Executive Branch officials who believe the human rights principles are important, the policy enables them to implement those principles in a pragmatic way. In this sense, such a policy is a win-win.

B. US Executive Branch – Disadvantages of Policy

For the reasons described, policies such as the PPG bring distinct advantages for the Executive Branch. But even from a purely Executive Branch perspective, such policies carry some disadvantages as well. Indeed, some of the benefits previously discussed have as their flip side some negative consequences.

i. *Policy Approaches Can Impede the Resolution of Legal Differences Among States and the Development of the Law*

Even as they serve a bridging function among states, policy approaches may slow or impede the resolution of legal differences among such states. Such policies to some extent mask the legal dimensions of a problem and can interfere with the development of the law. For example, a state that only chooses to bind itself as a matter of policy might still want *other* states to similarly bind themselves, but it loses its ability to insist on such compliance if the issue is only treated as a matter of policy, not law. Therefore, it may be in the state's interest to advance a view of the law that would bind others to standards the state itself is following, if only due to its policy.

Yet the adoption of a policy impedes the development of clear legal rules regarding state obligations under customary international law, which requires both state practice and a sense of legal obligation.[56] To be sure, there is a robust debate about the type of evidence that would establish such legal obligation or indeed sufficient state practice to amount to

---

[55] See Savage, *Power Wars* (n 3) 233–52.
[56] See Statute of the International Court of Justice (26 June 1945) 59 Stat 1055; 33 UNTS 933, Art 38.

customary international law.[57] But regardless, if adopted as mere policy, the practice of a state will not include a sense of legal obligation. Therefore, it will not support the development of customary international law, even though it may be in the state's interests for other states to be bound to respect rules the state already follows in practice.

The PPG offers an example of a policy that, while potentially easing interoperability concerns among states with different legal views, masks the legal dimensions of the problem and potentially slows the development of customary international law. The PPG and to a lesser degree the Trump Administration successor policy puts the US more on the same page – as a matter of practice – as those states that adopt a law-enforcement approach to extraterritorial counter-terrorism operations. But in doing so, it obscures the differences among states about the appropriate international law paradigm that governs the extraterritorial use of force in such operations. The policy itself does not refer to specific legal categories. Although the standards in the PPG resemble the categories of IHRL, these standards do not match those categories exactly. Indeed, the policy does not refer to IHRL at all. Thus, the policy does not in any sense explicitly acknowledge the conflict in legal paradigms. Accordingly, with respect to extraterritorial direct action outside of 'hot' battlefields, the policy does nothing to advance greater harmonisation of divergent legal perspectives – in the direction either of the more restrictive IHRL or of the more minimalist IHL/LOAC approach.

The PPG also does not contribute to the development of customary international law in this area. Because the US has embraced its practices pursuant to the PPG as a matter of policy – not as actions taken due to a sense of legal obligation – it would be difficult to cite the PPG as evidence to support the development of customary international law. One might argue that, to the extent that the policy is law at the domestic level, actions taken pursuant to the PPG should count as actions taken pursuant to a sense of legal obligation. Yet the notion that domestic legal obligations of this nature could satisfy the *opinio juris* element of customary international law is not widely accepted. Thus, operations conducted within the framework of the PPG would not do much to establish customary international law. Accordingly, the US could not rely on the PPG in the future to push other states to follow its approach as a matter of customary international law.

ii. *Policy Can Impede the Resolution of Different Legal Interpretations Within a Government*

As discussed, policy approaches can paper over differences in legal interpretation internally within a state. That also means, however, that the adoption of such policies can block the resolution of such legal issues within the government. Policy allows for a pragmatic path forward without forcing a decision to be made on the underlying legal question. But as a consequence, the policy decision can lead to inconsistency. Even within the administration that has adopted the policy, it does not provide as reliable a basis for coordinated action as a firm legal interpretation. A policy path can also lead to long-term inconsistency because it does not bind future administrations in the same way that legal interpretations do, given

---

[57] See, eg, JL Goldsmith and EA Posner, 'Further Thoughts on Customary International Law' (2001) 23 *Michigan Journal of International Law* 191.

that policies are more easily changed.[58] Although of course even a legal interpretation can be revisited by a future administration, the process for doing so is far more difficult than simply changing a policy.

In the case of the PPG, the policy approach has led to just this sort of malleability. It did not resolve what may have been internal differences in legal views about extraterritorial direct action against terrorists. And as discussed, one of the first initiatives the Trump Administration reportedly took was to revise the PPG, even as it retained some of the policy's elements. Moreover, it is possible that the Trump Administration or future administrations could make further changes to the policy.

iii. The Adoption of Policies Can be Misconstrued as the Development of Customary International Law

Finally, the implementation of a legalistic policy may also spark confusion about whether the policy is evidence of customary international law. As already discussed, the adoption of a policy should not technically establish customary international law because the states that embrace such policies are not doing so out of a sense of legal obligation. Nonetheless a variety of actors in the international community – including some states, international organisations or NGOs – may draw attention to a policy and assert that it is evidence of customary international law. Even if the state adopting the policy would stand on strong legal ground in rejecting such assertions, these types of statements require Executive Branch time and attention. From an Executive Branch perspective, legalistic policies therefore carry the risk that other entities will misconstrue the legal dimension of state actions according to the policies.

This risk has arguably been borne out to some degree with respect to the PPG. Some entities have suggested that the PPG reflects legal, rather than policy, rules.[59] To be sure, Executive Branch officials could mitigate this risk by repeatedly and transparently asserting that they are acting pursuant to policy. Indeed, if every time states adopt such policies an effort is made to infer that customary international law has been created, states might stop adopting more restrictive policies altogether and might instead retreat to a more minimalist approach.

C. The Human Rights Community

The advantages and disadvantages of legalistic policies depend in part on perspective. The Executive Branch perspective discussed previously is likely to differ from perspectives within the human rights community. To be sure, neither the US Executive Branch nor

---

[58] Of course, there might be domestic administrative law constraints on changes in legal interpretations and policies, but those constraints are beyond the scope of this chapter. For further discussion of the domestic law implications of using policy in the detention context, see Dickinson, 'Administrative Law Values and National Security Functions: Military Detention in the United States and the United Kingdom' (n 13).

[59] AA Haque, 'Targeted Killing Under Trump: Law, Policy, and Legal Risk' *Just Security* (10 February 2017), available at https://perma.cc/GR72-EWSY.

the human rights community is uniform. In particular, the human rights community is quite diverse, and it includes a variety of actors and entities from around the world. But in general, the concerns of the Executive Branch will not match those in the human rights community.

i. Advantages

From a human rights perspective, government adoption of more human rights-protecting policies is a mixed bag. On the one hand, such policies have the practical impact of making the state more compliant with human rights norms in its day-to-day counter-terrorism operations. And, to the extent that such policies are made public, they provide NGOs a standard they can use to hold the Government to account. This is a big plus from a human rights perspective, and it is possible that if the human rights community had pushed for a full-throated legal interpretation, the effort would have failed. Thus, one might see the adoption of legalistic policies as an important, pragmatic human rights victory with very real positive consequences on the ground. Moreover, even though administrations can in theory change such policies, they often turn out to be remarkably durable in practice.

In the case of the PPG, the human rights-protecting standards it imposed were a real win for the human rights community. Under the PPG, as a matter of policy, the US agreed to adhere to human rights values in the use of force extraterritorially. Furthermore, it is significant that some of the policy remains, even in the Trump Administration. (Although the Trump Administration's lack of transparency about the content of its targeting policy has reduced some of the benefits described previously, the transparent publication of the prior Obama Administration policy at least gives the NGO community the opportunity to ask about it and track the evolution of successor policies). The PPG is therefore evidence that a published policy decision can be sticky and lead to path dependence, even if not to the same extent as a legal determination.

ii. Disadvantages

On the other hand, as discussed, the adoption of legalistic policies can slow the development of the law. Thus, if a state opts to make policy rather than embrace a human rights-oriented view of the law, human rights groups may view this choice as a cop-out. And, as previously noted, a policy is more vulnerable to subsequent reinterpretation or case-by-case backsliding than a legal interpretation would be. Finally, unlike international legal commitments, such policies cannot be enforced in supranational courts, though it is possible that they could be enforced as a matter of domestic administrative or constitutional law.

With respect to the PPG, a fair case can be made that the Obama Administration missed an opportunity to articulate a more human rights-oriented approach to counter-terrorism. By adopting a legalistic policy, it failed to articulate legal limitations beyond the minimum rules of IHL/LOAC with respect to extraterritorial counter-terrorism operations outside of armed conflict. This failure has made it easier for the subsequent administration to reverse course. Of course, from a human rights perspective, adoption of the policy was still far preferable to a minimalist IHL/LOAC legal interpretation, so adoption of a potentially sticky policy was certainly better than no human rights regarding action at all.

D. Other Considerations: The Role for Lawyers

Policy presents one final issue worth noting. From a human rights perspective, one might be worried that rules adopted as a matter of policy rather than legal obligation might diminish the role of lawyers in decision-making regarding counter-terrorism operations. In general, decreasing the role of lawyers might give military officers a freer hand to make determinations that might be less human rights-regarding. However, because the policies I have described are sufficiently legalistic, they actually still require a role for lawyers in interpreting them. Thus, it is not clear that the role of lawyers actually diminishes. Indeed it may be that lawyers are needed *more*, because the interaction of the underlying IHL/LOAC and the policy may actually make the rules more complicated to parse. Of course, one could also view the role of lawyers as a problem, because legal vetting can delay the deployment of military operations, tie the military's hands, or lead to over-cautious decision-making.

In the case of the PPG and most likely its successor Trump Administration policy, both military and civilian lawyers must engage at a variety of levels to assess the implementation of the policy. The role for lawyers imposes a greater complexity on operations and could in theory slow them down. Whether that is good or bad depends on whether you focus on the potential human rights value in increased deliberation, or whether you think military operations will be unnecessarily delayed by needless red tape.

IV. Conclusion

The story of the PPG highlights that one of the critical frontiers of law is the boundary between law and policy in the domain of extraterritorial counter-terror operations. Although scholars and human rights observers who work in this domain tend to focus on legal rules, it turns out that Executive Branch policies can be a crucial aspect of compliance with the values underlying international legal regimes. Even if they do not accept certain international legal regimes as binding at the international level, governments may nonetheless embed legal categories within such policies.

And such policies may have important advantages, both for governments that seek consensus with other countries and within their own national security bureaucracy, as well as for human rights advocates who seek greater practical human rights compliance on a day-to-day level. Indeed, governments may be more willing to adopt robust human rights policies for many of their activities if they do not feel that doing so will bind them in all circumstances as a matter of law. On the other hand, when governments adopt policies, they miss important opportunities to clarify international law and incorporate core legal standards more forcefully into their military operations.

Thus, the decision whether to adopt policies rather than legal rules is a key issue for further study, and the advantages and disadvantages of policies versus legal interpretations are a fruitful area for continued investigation and debate. Comparative analysis may also reveal differences in decision-making processes in this area from country to country. Finally, it will be important to see the extent to which voluntary policies harden into customary law over time.

In any event, given that global counter-terrorism operations are likely to continue for the foreseeable future, those interested in charting the path of international law compliance must pay attention not only to the formal categories of international law, but also to the way different governments finesse those categories through the use of policy. Indeed, sometimes those policies may actually be more important in determining actual state practice on the ground than the official international law doctrines. Further, as a normative matter, scholars, NGOs and others must consider the advantages and disadvantages of a policy-oriented approach to international law compliance.

5
Public Law in the UK after Brexit

JACK BEATSON AND EMMA FOUBISTER

I. The Scope of the Inquiry

The implications of Brexit for constitutional and administrative law raise a large number of significant issues. They include the post-Brexit constitutional structure of the rules governing the relationship between the different parts of the state: questions about the 'devolved' administrations and the UK Government. They also include the rules and constitutional practices concerning the different branches of the state: questions about the roles of the legislature, executive and the courts. The implications for the rule of law and the role of United Kingdom (UK) courts in relation to European Union (EU) law in a post-Brexit world fall into this category. The third group of issues concerns the grounds and scope of judicial review.

It would be impossible to do justice to the complexity of all of these issues within the scope of this chapter. This chapter does not address the complex questions resulting from the provisions in the European Union (Withdrawal) Act 2018 (the 'Withdrawal Act 2018') about the repatriation of much EU law applicable before 'exit day' as 'retained EU law', and the powers it grants to Ministers to amend that law by secondary legislation to correct 'deficiencies' in it arising from the UK's withdrawal, although it briefly refers to the challenge by the UK Government to devolved legislation and to the Supreme Court's decision in December 2018. Its concern is mainly with two overlapping questions of a more general nature.

The first is what impact Brexit is likely to have on the grounds and scope of judicial review. The second, addressed perhaps more speculatively, concerns implications for the respective roles and relationships of the UK's legislature, executive and the courts in the light of the decision of the Supreme Court in *R (Miller) v Secretary of State for Exiting the European Union*,[1] the UK's most significant constitutional case for many years.[2]

II. The Implications of Brexit for the Grounds of Judicial Review

The traditional grounds of judicial review have altered over the past 30–40 years, under the influence of the principle of proportionality as applied under both EU law

---

[1] *R (Miller) v Secretary of State for Exiting the European Union* [2018] AC 61.
[2] There are other candidates: see, eg, *Liversidge v Anderson* [1942] AC 206; *Ridge v Baldwin* [1964] AC 40; *Anisminic v FCC* [1969] 2 AC 147; *A v Secretary of State for the Home Department* [2005] 2 AC 68 (the 'Belmarsh' case on the detention without trial of non-nationals who could not be deported from the UK, although the resonance of most of these was principally with the legal community rather than with the public in general).

and the jurisprudence of the European Convention on Human Rights (ECHR), and the development of fundamental rights in the EU Charter of Fundamental Rights ('the Charter').

A. Impact of Brexit on Proportionality

i. The Principle of Proportionality

There is no uniform formulation of the principle of proportionality and it is applied differently under EU law, the ECHR and domestic common law.[3] Proportionality has become a general principle of EU law[4] and is enshrined in Article 5(4) of the Treaty on European Union (TEU). The way in which the principle of proportionality is applied in EU law depends to a significant extent on the context,[5] but it broadly involves two questions. First, whether the measure in question is suitable or appropriate to achieve the objective pursued; and, second, whether the measure is necessary to achieve that objective, or whether it could be attained by a less onerous method.[6] While there is some debate as to whether there is a third question, namely what has sometimes been referred to as proportionality *stricto sensu*, the court usually omits the question unless it is argued by the parties.[7]

Under the ECHR, and particularly in the Strasbourg Court, the approach to proportionality is more broad-brush. The European Court of Human Rights (ECtHR) relies on proportionality as a mechanism for striking a 'fair balance' between the demands of the general interest of the community and the protection of an individual's fundamental rights.[8]

The approach to proportionality domestically under the Human Rights Act 1998 (HRA 1998) has not generally mirrored that of the Strasbourg Court.[9] The common law has developed a more structured approach. The question depends on an exacting analysis of the factual case advanced in defence of the measure, in order to determine: (i) whether its objective is sufficiently important to justify the limitation of a fundamental right; (ii) whether it is rationally connected to the objective; (iii) whether a less intrusive measure could have been used; and (iv) whether, having regard to these matters and to the severity of the consequences, a fair balance has been struck between the rights of the individual and the interests of the community.[10] This approach is widely endorsed, particularly in the context of fundamental rights in domestic law.[11]

---

[3] Unless otherwise stated, references to proportionality are to the general concept, rather than to any specific formulation.
[4] See *R v Minister for Agriculture, Fisheries and Food, ex parte FEDESA* [1990] ECR I-4023, [13].
[5] *R (Lumsdon) v Legal Services Board* [2016] AC 697, [23].
[6] ibid [33].
[7] ibid.
[8] See, eg, *Sporrong & Lonnroth v Sweden* (1982) 5 EHRR 35.
[9] *Bank Mellat v HM Treasury (No 2)* [2014] AC 700, [72] (Lord Reed).
[10] Lord Sumption (ibid [20]) described this as the culmination of the classic formulation in *de Freitas v Permanent Secretary of Ministry of Agriculture, Fisheries, Lands and Housing* [1999] 1 AC 69, which was applied in *R (Daly) v Secretary of State for the Home Department* [2001] 2 AC 532, [27], *Huang v Secretary of State for the Home Department* [2007] 2 AC 167, [19] and *R (Aguilar Quila) v Secretary of State for the Home Department* [2012] 1 AC 621, [45].
[11] See *R (Tigere) v Secretary of State for Business, Innovation and Skills* [2015] 1 WLR 3820, [33] (Baroness Hale) and the cases cited there.

ii. The Development of Proportionality

There has been much judicial and academic discussion[12] about the extent to which proportionality has altered rationality review or become a freestanding ground of judicial review, which does not require resolution here. In our view, while there has been no decision overturning the proposition[13] that proportionality is not a general ground of review at common law and the Supreme Court has not yet performed *Wednesbury*'s 'burial rites',[14] proportionality has undoubtedly altered rationality review in the context of fundamental rights, and beyond.

The influence of proportionality on the grounds of judicial review started slowly, with judges initially reluctant to apply it outside the strict confines of EU law or the ECHR. In *R v Secretary of State for the Home Department, ex parte Brind*,[15] a majority of the House of Lords[16] refused to apply a proportionality test when assessing the legality at common law of directives restricting freedom of expression. Lord Ackner and Lord Lowry ruled out proportionality until Parliament incorporated the Convention into domestic law,[17] but Lord Bridge and Lord Roskill did not rule out the development of proportionality in a more suitable case.[18] Lord Templeman went further, applying a formulation of the proportionality test proposed by the appellants, and stated that 'any restriction of the right to freedom of expression requires to be justified and that nothing less than an important competing public interest will be sufficient to justify it'.[19]

In *R v Ministry of Defence, ex parte Smith*[20] Lord Bingham endorsed the proposition that '[t]he more substantial the interference with human rights, the more the court will require by way of justification before it is satisfied that the decision is reasonable'.[21] This sliding-scale approach reflects the balancing of competing interests under a proportionality analysis.

The courts began to acknowledge that the principle of proportionality could apply in contexts where neither EU law nor the ECHR was at issue. In *R (Q) v Secretary of State for the Home Department*,[22] the House of Lords suggested that the proposition in *Smith* was not confined to the rights set out in the ECHR. Lord Phillips took a more intrusive approach to rights assessment, indicating a change in the common law grounds of judicial review to accommodate an approach akin to proportionality.[23]

In *R (Alconbury) v Secretary of State for the Environment, Transport and the Regions*,[24] Lord Slynn made one of the earliest judicial calls for wider adoption of the principle of

---

[12] See, eg, M Taggart, 'Proportionality, Deference, *Wednesbury*' [2008] *NZLR* 423; P Craig, 'Proportionality, Rationality and Review' [2010] *NZLR* 265; T Hickman, 'Problems for Proportionality' [2010] *NZLR* 303; J King, 'Proportionality: A Halfway House' [2010] *NZLR* 327; J Goodwin, 'The Last Defence of *Wednesbury*' [2012] *PL* 445; R Williams, 'Structuring Substantive Review' [2017] *PL* 99.
[13] *R (Association of British Civilian Internees: Far East Region) v Secretary of State for Defence* [2003] QB 1397.
[14] ibid [35].
[15] *R v Secretary of State for the Home Department, ex parte Brind* [1991] 1 AC 696.
[16] ibid (Lord Templeman dissenting).
[17] ibid 762–63, 766–67.
[18] ibid 749, 751.
[19] ibid 748–49.
[20] *R v Ministry of Defence, ex parte Smith* [1996] QB 517.
[21] ibid [554].
[22] *R (Q) v Secretary of State for the Home Department* [2004] QB 36.
[23] ibid [112].
[24] *R (Alconbury) v Secretary of State for the Environment, Transport and the Regions* [2003] 2 AC 295.

proportionality.[25] Although his dictum was not adopted by the other judges, it encapsulates the growing role of proportionality and its influence on traditional review.

In a number of cases, the courts have expanded the scope of rationality review, albeit often without acknowledgement, so as to incorporate into the common law significant aspects of the principle of proportionality. In *Kennedy v Information Commissioner*,[26] Lord Mance concluded that there would be no real difference between the nature and outcome of scrutiny required under common law and under Article 10 ECHR.[27] Lord Mance endorsed Paul Craig's conclusion[28] that 'both reasonableness review and proportionality involve considerations of weight and balance, with the intensity of the scrutiny and the weight to be given to any primary decision maker's view depending on the context'.[29] He highlighted the advantage of the structure of proportionality and its use in directing attention to factors, such as 'suitability or appropriateness, necessity and the balance or imbalance of benefits and disadvantages'.[30] He considered that there 'seems no reason why such factors should not be relevant in judicial review even outside the scope of Convention and EU law'.[31]

There has been a growing tendency to rely on the common law or to equate protections under the ECHR or EU law with domestic principles.[32] In *Pham v Secretary of State for the Home Department*,[33] the Supreme Court dismissed a challenge to the withdrawal of the claimant's citizenship by the UK, which also entailed a loss of EU citizenship. In dismissing the appeal, the Court did not assess the proportionality of the measure by reference to EU law but considered that the nature, strictness or outcome of such a review would be unlikely to differ according to whether it was conducted under domestic principles or proportionality under EU law. Lord Sumption observed that the courts have applied the proportionality test in a progressively large range of contexts in relation to EU and ECHR issues.[34] However, he noted that English law has moved towards 'a concept which is in significant respects similar, and over the last three decades has been influenced by European jurisprudence even in areas of law lying beyond the domains of EU and international human rights law'.[35]

Lord Reed considered that the application of a test of reasonableness may yield the same outcome as the application of a test of proportionality.[36] In cases involving important rights outside of those under the HRA 1998, the courts have adopted an 'approach amounting in substance to a requirement of proportionality',[37] and 'where Parliament authorises

---

[25] ibid [51].
[26] *Kennedy v Information Commissioner* [2015] AC 455.
[27] ibid [51].
[28] P Craig, 'The Nature of Reasonableness Review' (2013) 66 *CLP* 131.
[29] *Kennedy* (n 26) [54] (Lord Mance).
[30] ibid.
[31] ibid.
[32] See also *R (on the application of Rotherham MBC) v Secretary of State for Business, Innovation and Skills* [2015] UKSC 6. Lord Carnwath (dissenting) (at [174]) cited Lord Mance in *Kennedy* (n 26) as authority for the proposition that issues of unequal treatment and proportionality may play a part in that assessment in both European and domestic law. He (at [187]) considered that it mattered not whether expressed as an issue of unequal treatment or lack of proportionality under European law, or irrationality under domestic law, the decision was manifestly inappropriate under EU and domestic principles.
[33] *Pham v Secretary of State for the Home Department* [2015] 1 WLR 1591.
[34] ibid [104].
[35] ibid [105].
[36] ibid [116].
[37] ibid [118].

significant interferences with important legal rights, the courts may interpret ... a requirement of proportionality'.[38]

In *R (Keyu) v Secretary of State for Foreign and Commonwealth Affairs*,[39] Lord Neuberger observed that a nine-judge panel would be required to determine whether the time had come to perform *Wednesbury's* burial rites, as the implications would be 'profound in constitutional terms and very wide in applicable scope'.[40] However, *Kennedy* and *Pham* demonstrate that the 'domestic law may already be moving away to some extent from the irrationality test in some cases'.[41]

Lord Kerr questioned the constitutional importance of the change[42] and observed that the difference between a rationality challenge and one based on proportionality is not as stark as often portrayed.[43] Conventionally, proportionality is most frequently considered when a fundamental right is at stake,[44] and Lord Kerr questioned the feasibility of applying proportionality in the same way where the decision did not involve a right.[45] He envisaged a more loosely structured proportionality challenge where a fundamental right is not involved.[46]

The Supreme Court has applied a proportionality approach to the protection of common law rights of a 'constitutional' or 'fundamental' nature, without explicitly invoking the ECHR or EU law.[47] In *R (on the application of UNISON) v Lord Chancellor*,[48] the second ground upon which the Supreme Court found the Employment Tribunals and the Employment Appeal Tribunal Fees Order 2013 (SI 2013/1893) to be unlawful was that the degree of intrusion went further than was justified by its objectives. Lord Reed set out the common law right of access to justice,[49] observing that even where primary legislation authorises the imposition of an intrusion on the right of access to justice, the degree of intrusion must not be greater than is justified by the objectives which the measure is intended to serve.[50] Lord Reed observed the analogy between that principle and the principle of proportionality under the ECHR, which did not apply in *UNISON*.[51] He nevertheless considered that the case law of the Strasbourg Court on the right of access to justice was relevant to the development of the common law and it 'will be considered in the context of the case based on EU law, on which it also has a bearing'.[52] Lord Reed concluded that the application of the proportionality principle in Strasbourg was 'consistent with the principle of domestic law that such rights may be curtailed only to the extent reasonably necessary to meet the ends

---

[38] ibid [119].
[39] *R (Keyu) v Secretary of State for Foreign and Commonwealth Affairs* [2016] AC 1355.
[40] ibid [131]–[132].
[41] ibid [133].
[42] ibid [271].
[43] ibid [273].
[44] ibid [279].
[45] ibid [281].
[46] ibid [282].
[47] Our focus in this chapter is on individual rights that the courts have recognised as 'fundamental' and which are to be treated as such by the common law. See, eg, *Watkins v Secretary of State for the Home Office* [2006] 2 AC 395, [61] (Lord Rodger).
[48] *R (on the application of UNISON) v Lord Chancellor* [2017] 3 WLR 409.
[49] ibid [66]–[85].
[50] ibid [88].
[51] ibid [89].
[52] ibid.

which justify the curtailment'.[53] He then went on to consider proportionality under both ECHR and EU law, before concluding that the fees were disproportionate.[54] This analysis, though not explicitly based on the principle of proportionality, was plainly influenced by both the ECHR and EU concepts of the principle.[55]

Proportionality also has a role in several other areas. A number of authorities refer to a notion of unfair balance, with occasional references to proportionality. In *R v Barnsley MBC, ex parte Hook*, Lord Denning described the punishment as 'altogether excessive and out of proportion to the occasion'.[56] In *R v Secretary of State for the Home Department, ex parte Benwell*, Hodson J considered that 'in an extreme case an administrative or quasi-administrative penalty can be attacked on the ground that it was so disproportionate to the offence as to be perverse'.[57]

The notion of proportionality has also been introduced into the common law on legitimate expectations. In *Nadarajah v Secretary of State for the Home Department*, Laws LJ considered that the requirement of good administration was a legal standard which takes its place alongside ECHR rights.[58] The principle would be 'undermined if the law did not insist that any failure or refusal to comply is objectively justified as a proportionate measure in the circumstances'.[59] This is a further example of the role of proportionality outside the strict confines of the ECHR or EU law.

Where fundamental rights are at stake, proportionality has become relevant even outside the context of judicial review. *Zaw Lin v Commissioner of Police of the Metropolis*[60] involved an appeal under the Data Protection Act 1998 (DPA 1998), but Green J nonetheless applied a proportionality test in considering an individual's right to access to data. The claimants relied on an EU directive and the ECHR to 'stiffen the sinews of the Court in the application of any necessity or proportionality weighing exercise'.[61] However, Green J did not consider that there was a need to do so, as not much turned upon an invocation of broader principles of EU or Convention law. He observed that

> the common law leads inexorably to a purposive construction of section 29 DPA 1998 which permits of intensive scrutiny of *all* relevant interests arising and which injects a proportionality exercise into the weighing process. The common law takes account of context and adjusts accordingly.[62]

He considered it 'perfectly plain from both *Kennedy* and *Pham* that the common law, EU law and the Convention can walk side by side when protecting rights'.[63]

It is therefore clear that proportionality, as applied under ECHR and EU law, has altered the traditional grounds of review. First, there are a number of contexts in which rationality

---

[53] ibid [110].
[54] ibid [110]–[117].
[55] ibid [99]–[102].
[56] *R v Barnsley MBC, ex parte Hook* [1976] 1 WLR 1052, 1057.
[57] *R v Secretary of State for the Home Department, ex parte Benwell* [1985] QB 554, 569.
[58] *Nadarajah v Secretary of State for the Home Department* [2005] EWCA Civ 1363, [68].
[59] ibid.
[60] *Zaw Lin v Commissioner of Police of the Metropolis* [2015] EWHC 2484 (QB).
[61] ibid [47].
[62] ibid [49].
[63] ibid [51].

review mirrors the key elements of a proportionality analysis. The influence of the principle of proportionality has meant that *Wednesbury* principles will be applied with greater flexibility, with a greater focus on context.[64] It may be that this influence and the greater sensitivity to context are the reasons for the survival of *Wednesbury* rationality review. Second, in the context of fundamental rights, including rights at common law, the courts use proportionality as a structured tool to assess the justification for any interference. Third, legislation interfering with rights is read as implicitly subject to the principle of proportionality. Fourth, the direction of travel suggests that in future the Supreme Court may find that proportionality is a freestanding ground of judicial review in non-EU or HRA 1998 cases, or it will at least reconsider the question.

iii. Doctrinal Basis of the Principle of Proportionality

To determine the future role of proportionality it is necessary to consider its doctrinal basis. If proportionality stemmed solely from EU law, it could be of limited relevance post-Brexit, albeit it would still apply to HRA 1998 cases. Sir Philip Sales has argued that there are strong reasons of principle against the recognition of proportionality as a freestanding ground of judicial review, outside the context of the ECHR or EU law.[65] He considers that a shift from rationality to proportionality would be a substantive change in legal doctrine imposed by the judges without warrant from Parliament, and that the rule of law ought to prevent the courts from adopting an unduly free approach in changing the common law.

However, in our view, the doctrinal basis of proportionality as a common law construct affords its development legitimacy. While an assessment of whether the shift from rationality to proportionality amounts to a change in substantive law is outside the scope of this chapter, the gradual development outlined above does not represent an unduly free approach to the development of the common law.

Our domestic common law has evolved and drawn inspiration from a range of sources beyond EU law and the case law of the ECtHR to which we have referred. These were reviewed by Lord Reed in *Bank Mellat*.[66] He observed that the origins of proportionality are in German administrative law, from which it was adopted in the case law of the Court of Justice of the European Union (CJEU) and the ECtHR. From there, it moved to Canada and spread to a number of other common law jurisdictions.[67] The four-stage approach adopted domestically 'derived from case law under Commonwealth constitutions and Bills of Rights, including in particular the Canadian Charter of Fundamental Rights and Freedoms of 1982'.[68] The origins of the domestic approach lie in the three-limb test set out by Lord Clyde in *de Freitas v Permanent Secretary of Ministry of Agriculture, Fisheries, Lands and Housing*.[69] This was a Privy Council case concerned with fundamental rights under the

---

[64] See also *Gage v Scottish Ministers* [2015] CSOH 174, [39]; *R (Crompton) v Police and Crime Commissioner for South Yorkshire* [2018] 1 WLR 131, [89].
[65] P Sales, 'Rationality, Proportionality and the Development of the Law' (2013) 129 *LQR* 223.
[66] *Bank Mellat* (n 9) [68]–[76].
[67] ibid [68]. Other references to the Canadian approach include *R v DPP, ex parte Kebilene* [2000] 2 AC 326, [386] (Lord Hope).
[68] *Bank Mellat* (n 9) [72].
[69] *de Freitas* (n 10).

constitution of Antigua and Barbuda, and the dictum drew on South African, Canadian and Zimbabwean authority.[70] The House of Lords in *Huang v Secretary of State for the Home Department*[71] derived its approach to proportionality from the judgment of Dickson CJ in *R v Oakes*,[72] adding the further element of the need to balance the interests of society with those of individuals and groups.[73]

Proportionality is therefore not a unique concept developed under EU law. The domestic formulation represents a synthesis of the principles derived from the German Supreme Court and other civil jurisdictions, and the case law under Commonwealth constitutions and Bills of Rights. Proportionality has become a common law concept, and it does not have its origins in a text such as the ECHR. It developed as a general principle in EU law before being enshrined in Article 5(4) of the TEU. Accordingly, proportionality is capable of being applied to common law rights and used more widely in domestic judicial review.

In our view, the fact that the most direct influence on domestic law has been the application of the proportionality principle in EU law and the jurisprudence of the ECtHR does not mean that it cannot be of continued use domestically when EU law no longer applies or in cases in which the ECHR is not applicable.

iv. The Future of Proportionality Post-Brexit

It is likely that much EU legislation, and the principles developed under it, will be re-enacted as UK legislation. Those statutes that incorporate an element of proportionality will continue to do so, and the principle is likely to retain a more general role.

In respect of judicial review, we do not consider it likely that the courts will reduce the impact or reverse the evolution of proportionality. First, the doctrinal basis for the development of proportionality means it can legitimately continue to be applied outside the HRA 1998 and EU law. The UK has developed its own approach to proportionality that is distinct from the approach applied in Strasbourg or Luxembourg. It is plainly not dependent upon guidance from the case law of either the ECtHR or the CJEU.

Second, for the immediate future, it seems likely that the UK will remain a signatory to the ECHR. This means that the ECHR, and proportionality analysis under the HRA 1998, will continue to apply in those cases and to influence the common law approach to judicial review.

Third, the courts' increasing suggestions that they might be willing to apply a proportionality test outside EU and ECHR law indicates that it is gaining independent influence. In our view, it is likely that in an appropriate case the Supreme Court will consider whether proportionality should be a freestanding ground of judicial review. A shift from rationality to proportionality, whether as an additional ground or as a total replacement, would not, in our view, undermine the rule of law. It is capable of being a legitimate next step in the development of the grounds of judicial review. We do not consider it likely that Brexit, and the removal of the influence of EU law, will reverse this development.

---

[70] See the Zimbabwean case of *Nyambirai v National Social Security Authority* [1996] 1 LRC 64. Gubbay CJ (at [75]) drew on South African and Canadian case law.
[71] *Huang* (n 10) [19] (Lord Bingham).
[72] *R v Oakes* [1986] 1 SCR 103.
[73] *Huang* (n 10) [73].

Fourth, the courts have demonstrated an increasingly robust approach to rights protection. *Miller's* case, which we consider in more detail in section III.A, is a particularly noteworthy example of the courts' willingness to protect rights. This is likely to continue post-Brexit, particularly if concrete rights are lost under the Charter (see further discussion in the following section). To the extent that proportionality involves a more intense scrutiny of the issues at stake, particularly in the rights context, courts are likely to see an even greater role for it in defending common law rights.

B. Impact of Brexit on Rights

i. Loss of Rights under the Charter

Section 5(4) of the Withdrawal Act 2018 provides that the Charter is not part of domestic law on or after exit day. Fundamental rights that exist irrespective of the Charter are unaffected, and references to the Charter in any case law are, so far as necessary, to be read as references to corresponding retained fundamental rights (section 5(5)). A full discussion of the future of common law rights of a 'constitutional' or 'fundamental' nature is beyond the scope of this chapter. Our focus here is primarily on the narrow category of rights protected by the Charter, but not the ECHR or the common law.[74] For example, the Charter protects the right to protection of personal data;[75] the freestanding right to equality of treatment;[76] and the right to an effective remedy.[77]

ii. The Origins of Common Law Rights of a 'Constitutional' or 'Fundamental' Nature

Common law rights of a 'constitutional' or 'fundamental' nature existed before their explicit recognition as such in written human rights instruments. English lawyers contributed to the drafting of the ECHR, undoubtedly drawing inspiration from rights that originated in the common law. In *R (Daly) v Secretary of State for the Home Department*,[78] Lord Cooke observed that 'some rights are inherent and fundamental to democratic civilised society. Conventions, constitutions, bills of rights and the like respond by recognising rather than creating them'.[79]

The right of access to a court is probably the most deeply entrenched of the common law rights of a constitutional nature, and has been the impetus for the development of other such rights.[80] Other rights, however, developed in different ways. For example, the tort of

---

[74] See also the references to common law constitutional rights in the section on constitutional statutory provisions, section III.C.
[75] Charter, Art 8.
[76] Charter, Arts 20 and 21.
[77] Charter, Art 47.
[78] *Daly* (n 10).
[79] ibid [30]. See also *A v Her Majesty's Treasury* [2008] 3 All ER 361, [33] (Collins J); *Osborn v Parole Board* [2014] AC 1115, [55]–[57].
[80] J Beatson et al, *Human Rights: Judicial Protection in the United Kingdom* (London, Sweet & Maxwell, 2008) para 1–22; R Clayton, 'The Empire Strikes Back: Common Law Rights and the Human Rights Act' [2015] PL 3.

false imprisonment and the writ of *habeas corpus* effectively prohibited slavery,[81] and the right to life was protected by the common law offences of murder and manslaughter. From this basis, the common law evolved and came to explicitly recognise many constitutional and fundamental rights.[82] Other common law rights include the right to privacy in certain circumstances[83] and the right to a jury trial.[84]

iii. The Continuing Development of 'Constitutional' or 'Fundamental' Common Law Rights

Even with the entry into force of the HRA 1998 and the increased role of EU law in rights protection, common law rights have retained significance. Although, initially, the courts may to some extent have overlooked the continuing vigour of common law rights and values of a 'constitutional' or 'fundamental' nature, this is no longer the case. The Supreme Court has demonstrated an increased willingness to afford robust rights protection at common law.[85] In *Kennedy*, Lord Mance criticised undue reliance on the ECHR over common law rights, observing that domestic law should be the natural starting point in any dispute.[86] He noted that 'in some areas, the common law may go further than the Convention, and in some contexts it may also be inspired by the Convention rights and jurisprudence', and recognised that in time 'a synthesis may emerge'.[87] Lord Toulson agreed, stating '[w]hat we now term human rights law and public law has developed through our common law over a long period of time ... It needs to be emphasised that it was not the purpose of the Human Rights Act that the common law should become an ossuary.'[88]

It is our view that the courts would continue to protect common law rights were the Charter and the ECHR no longer to have effect. The question for present purposes, however, is the extent of the rights protected. Some of the rights that may be lost under the Charter are novel and have not had explicit common law recognition. It is therefore necessary to consider whether the common law could legitimately develop to encompass those rights, or whether those rights will necessarily be lost post-Brexit.

See *Re Boaler* [1915] 1 KB 21; *Chester v Bateson* [1920] 1 KB 829; *Bremer Vulkan Schiffbau und Maschinenfabrik v South India Shipping Corp Ltd* [1981] AC 909.

[81] *R v Knowles, ex parte Somersett* (1772) 20 State Tr 1.

[82] H Woolf et al, *De Smith's Judicial Review*, 8th edn (London, Sweet & Maxwell, 2018) has catalogued the following common law rights: access to a judicial remedy; the right to life; the liberty of the person; the doing of justice in public; the right to a fair hearing; the prohibition on the retrospective imposition of criminal penalty; freedom of expression; the rights of access to legal advice and to communicate confidentially with a legal advisor under the seal of legal professional privilege; limitations on searches of premises and seizure of documents; prohibition on the use of evidence obtained by torture; that a British citizen has a fundamental right to live in, or return to, that part of the Queen's territory of which he is a citizen; the deprivation of property rights without compensation; the privilege against self-incrimination; a duty on the state to provide subsistence to asylum seekers; and freedom of movement within the UK.

[83] *Morris v Beardsmore* [1981] AC 446, 464 (Lord Scarman).

[84] *Attorney-General v Gouriet* [1978] AC 435, 499.

[85] See, eg, *Osborn* (n 79); *R (Guardian News Media Ltd) v City of Westminster Magistrates' Court* [2013] QB 618; *Kennedy v Charity Commission* (n 26); *A v BBC* [2015] AC 588.

[86] *Kennedy* (n 26).

[87] ibid [46].

[88] ibid [133]. See also his judgment in *R (Guardian News and Media)* (n 85). See further *R (Calver) v Adjudication Panel of Wales* [2012] EWHC 1172 (Admin) [21], [40]-[44], [85].

iv. Legitimacy of Development of Common Law Rights Inspired by the Charter

At present, it is unclear what the precise role of the Charter will be post-Brexit. As the Charter will no longer apply in the same way, the legitimacy of the common law that has developed around it may be called into question. We consider that in continuing to apply common law rights the courts can legitimately draw on the Charter and the ECHR, and the repealing of the Charter, or the ECHR, should not reverse or preclude developments at common law.

First, fundamental rights have a special constitutional significance and the courts have a unique role in protecting them. Although there must be sensitivity to the respective roles of the courts and the legislature, it would be wrong to suggest that the development of doctrine in this area should be a purely legislative matter. Second, the ECHR and the Charter were not designed to replace common law rights, and have continued to exist alongside them. The HRA 1998 envisaged the development of a new form of common law by reference to the text of the ECHR; a legislative instrument. Third, while the teleological reasoning in EU and ECHR jurisprudence has influenced domestic jurisprudence, the common law itself has always developed as a 'living instrument'.

Therefore, in appropriate cases where it is clear that the common law has evolved to encompass new rights inspired by the Charter, we consider there to be a sound doctrinal basis for the courts to continue to recognise and further develop those rights post-Brexit.

v. Case Study: The Right to an Effective Remedy

Since the triggering of Article 50, the courts have demonstrated an increased willingness to rely on EU law-inspired common law rights. An important example is the principle of effectiveness, enshrined in Article 47 of the Charter. In *R (on the application of UNISON)*, the EU principles of effectiveness and of effective judicial protection made up a fundamental part of the reasoning leading to the Supreme Court's quashing of the Employment Tribunals and the Employment Appeal Tribunal Fees Order 2013.[89] Lord Reed observed that these principles have been enshrined in Articles 2 and 13 of the ECHR and Article 47 of the Charter[90] and any restrictions must be proportionate.[91] In applying Article 47, it was necessary to consider the Strasbourg jurisprudence, which emphasises 'the protection of rights which are not theoretical and illusory, but practical and effective'.[92] Lord Reed considered that this approach was 'consistent with the recognition in domestic law that the impact of restrictions must be considered in the real world'.[93]

In our view, Lord Reed's harmonisation of the approach in Luxembourg, Strasbourg and domestically demonstrates a willingness to show that the principle is capable of applying at common law independently of EU law.[94] The Supreme Court in *UNISON* arguably

---

[89] *UNISON* (n 48) [107]–[119], [121].
[90] ibid [106].
[91] ibid [107].
[92] ibid [109].
[93] ibid.
[94] Mark Elliott described the case as illuminating 'the common law's potential as a guarantor of basic rights' in M Elliott, 'The Rule of Law and Access to Justice: Some Home Truths' (2018) 77 *CLJ* 5, 5–8.

went beyond what was required under ECHR and EU law. The domestic law approach involved formulation of a specific principle, namely that fees cannot effectively prevent some persons from having access to justice. This means that fees always have to be set at a level that people can afford; proportionality cannot provide the Government with a defence or justification. In our view, the Supreme Court legitimately drew inspiration from Article 47 and, for the reasons outlined, may continue to do so at common law, independently of the Charter.

III. The Implications More Generally for the Constitutional Law of the UK

A. Overview

The prism for considering this is *R (Miller) v Secretary of State for Exiting the European Union*.[95] The Supreme Court of the United Kingdom held (by a majority of 8:3)[96] that the UK Government could not use the prerogative to serve notice of the UK's intention to leave the EU under Article 50(2) TEU. Legislation was required. The Court also held (unanimously) that there was no legal requirement for the UK Government to obtain the consent of the devolved legislatures in Scotland, Northern Ireland and Wales before serving such notice under Article 50(2). Two months after the decision the European Union (Notification of Withdrawal) Act 2017 was passed.

Miller's case is thus about high constitutional issues; the respective roles and responsibilities of the Westminster Parliament, the UK Government and the devolved legislatures and administrations, and the nature of the court's role in such matters. Mark Elliott pithily summarised it as engaging 'the axiomatic judicial function of determining disputes about how constitutional authority is allocated'.[97] Michael Dougan considers that the real significance of the decision lies in 'setting the "constitutional tone" for what comes next – the mood music ... for how the institutions of state should understand their roles and each others' roles in the far reaching processes to follow'.[98] Assessing that significance is a speculative exercise. But the starting point is to summarise the reasoning of the eight justices who gave a single majority judgment and the three who dissented. The next stage is to consider what impact the decision has on the constitutional environment and the debate between those who would give primacy to 'the legal constitution',[99] those who would give primacy

---

[95] *Miller* (n 1). See the extensive commentaries on the case in D Clarry (ed), *The UK Supreme Court Yearbook*, Vol 8: *2016–2017 Legal Year* (London, Appellate Press, 2018) 206–377.

[96] The majority were: Lord Neuberger, Baroness Hale, and Lords Mance, Kerr, Clarke, Wilson, Sumption and Hodge. The dissenters were Lord Reed and Lords Carnwath and Hughes, who agreed with him but gave separate judgments of their own, in Lord Carnwath's case from what he described as a slightly different legal perspective.

[97] M Elliott, 'The Supreme Court's Judgment in *Miller*: In Search of Constitutional Principle' (2017) 76 *CLJ* 257, 258.

[98] M Dougan, 'The UK's Institutional Balance of Power After Leaving the EU' in DJ Galligan (ed), *Constitution in Crisis: The New Putney Debates* (London, IB Tauris, 2017) 122.

[99] See, eg, TR Hickman, 'In Defence of the Legal Constitution' (2005) 55 *University of Toronto Law Journal* 981, although this is, in fact, an example of a much more nuanced approach.

to 'the political constitution'[100] and those who consider that neither law nor politics has primacy in the constitution of the UK in any simple fashion.[101] Does the decision have anything more general to say on the way the respective spheres of legislative and executive power are to be understood in the UK and the role of the courts? What impact will the decision have on the increased role of the courts in the continued development of the common law grounds of judicial review?

B. The Decision in *Miller's* Case

The issue was whether parliamentary authorisation was needed before the UK served notice to the EU of its decision to withdraw from the EU. Lord Hughes, one of the dissentients, identified the key question as centring on two well-understood constitutional rules, which appeared to point in opposite directions in the circumstances of that case. Rule 1 is that the executive cannot change law made by an Act of Parliament, nor the common law; and rule 2 is that 'the making and unmaking of treaties is a matter of foreign relations within the competence of the government'.[102] He accepted that this way of putting it carried a risk of over-simplifying the question. Provided this is recognised, we agree that it is a useful way of identifying the central question.

The majority's conclusion that rule 1 applied turned on their view that the European Communities Act 1972 (ECA 1972) is a statute of a constitutional character[103] authorising a dynamic process by which the substantive reality is that EU law became a direct, independent and overriding direct source of UK domestic law.[104] As the Divisional Court had stated, '[o]nly Parliament could create the necessary changes in national law to allow EU law to have the effect at the level of domestic law which the treaties required'.[105] The required effect achieved by the ECA 1972 was to confer rights on UK citizens/residents, including directly applicable and effective rights under EU law that would cease to have effect on withdrawal.[106]

Although section 2 of the ECA 1972 envisages domestic law and therefore the rights of UK citizens changing as EU law varies, the majority held that it does not envisage those rights changing as a result of Ministers' unilaterally deciding the UK should withdraw from the EU Treaties.[107] Withdrawal from the EU 'involves unilateral action by the relevant constitutional bodies [in the UK] which affects a fundamental change in the constitutional arrangements of the [UK]'.[108] The majority stated that they could not 'accept that a major

---

[100] eg JAG Griffith, 'The Political Constitution' (1979) 42 *MLR* 1; A Tomkins, 'In Defence of the Political Constitution' (2002) 22 *OJLS* 157; K Ewing, 'The Resilience of the Political Constitution' (2013) 14 *German Law Journal* 2111.
[101] eg Sir P Sales, 'Legalism in Constitutional Law: Judging in a Democracy', Neill Lecture (26 January 2018); A Tomkins, 'What's Left of the Political Constitution?' (2013) 14 *German Law Journal* 2275.
[102] *Miller* (n 1) [277].
[103] ibid [67]. No judge in the Supreme Court used the term 'constitutional statute', although Lord Carnwath (at [269]) cited a passage from Helen Mountfield QC's written submissions that uses it.
[104] ibid [60], [61], [65], [67], [80], [87].
[105] *R (Miller) v Secretary of State for Exiting the European Union* [2017] 1 All ER 158, [42].
[106] *Miller* (n 1) [70].
[107] ibid [83]. See also [70], [77].
[108] ibid [78]. See also *Miller* (n 105) [92]–[94].

change to UK constitutional arrangements can be achieved by ministers alone [and that it] must be effected in the only way that the UK constitution recognises, namely by Parliamentary legislation'.[109]

It was in that way that they set the boundaries on what the executive was constitutionally empowered to do by the exercise of the prerogative powers at the international level. It could not remove or change either domestic law or a source of domestic law. Accordingly, the executive could not exercise a prerogative power to frustrate the purpose of the ECA 1972 by emptying it of content or preventing its effectual operation.[110] But legislation that alters the domestic constitutional status of EU institutions or EU law is not constrained by the need to be consistent with EU law 'because of the principle of parliamentary sovereignty which is ... fundamental to the [UK's] constitutional arrangements, and EU law can only enjoy a status in domestic law which that principle allows'.[111] Accordingly, 'it will have that status only for so long as the 1972 Act continues to apply, and that, of course, can only be a matter for Parliament'.[112]

The minority's conclusion that rule 2 applied turned on their view that EU law was not an independent source of UK domestic law: it followed from the UK's dualist approach to international law that EU law is only a source of UK law because the ECA 1972 made it so.[113] The 1972 Act gave effect to EU law on a 'conditional basis', and where Parliament granted rights on the express or implied basis that they will expire in certain circumstances, no further legislation is required if those circumstances arise. If 'those circumstances comprise the UK's withdrawal from a treaty, the rights are not revoked by the Crown's exercise of prerogative powers: they are revoked by the operation of the Act of Parliament [here the ECA 1972] itself'.[114] Parliament had required statutes for other changes concerning the EU.[115] The ECA 1972, however, contained no express limitation on prerogative power or language from which it could be concluded that the necessary implication of the Act was that the prerogative to serve notice withdrawing from the EU had been removed or restricted.

We recognise the force of the arguments and the power of the dissenting judgments in *Miller*, in particular that of Lord Reed.[116] Notwithstanding that force and the contestability

---

[109] *Miller* (n 1) [82].
[110] ibid [51].
[111] ibid [67].
[112] ibid.
[113] ibid [228] (Lord Reed). See also [216] and [225], following Lord Mance in *Pham* (n 33) [80]. See also Lord Reed in *R (Buckinghamshire CC Council) v Secretary of State for Transport* [2014] 1 WLR 324, [79].
[114] *Miller* (n 1) [219] (Lord Reed), and note also [177], [185], [196]–[197], [202], [221].
[115] European Parliamentary Elections Act 1978, s 6; European Union Act 2008, s 5; European Union Act 2011, ss 2 and 4.
[116] See, eg, the views of J Finnis, 'Brexit and the Balance of Our Constitution' Policy Exchange/Judicial Power Project (2016), available at https://policyexchange.org.uk/judicial-power-project-john-finnis-on-brexit-and-the-balance-of-our-constitution, which were cited to the court: see *Miller* (n 1) [65]). See also R Ekins, 'Constitutional Practice and Principle in the Article 50 Litigation' (2017) 133 *LQR* 347; M Elliott, 'On Why, as a Matter of Law, Triggering Article 50 Does Not Require Parliament to Legislate' Public Law for Everyone (2016), available at https://publiclawforeveryone.com/2016/06/30/brexit-on-why-as-a-matter-of-law-triggering-article-50-does-not-require-parliament-to-legislate; M Elliott, 'Analysis: The Supreme Court's Judgment in *Miller*' Public Law for Everyone (2017), available at https://publiclawforeveryone.com/2017/01/25/analysis-the-supreme-courts-judgment-in-miller/; Elliott, 'The Supreme Court's Judgment in *Miller*' (n 97); T Endicott, 'Parliament and the Prerogative' Judicial Power Project (2016), available at www.judicialpowerproject.org.uk/timothy-endicott-parliament-and-the-prerogative-from-the-case-of-proclamations-to-miller/; T Endicott, 'This Ancient, Secretive Royal Prerogative' UK Constitutional Law Association (2016), available at https://ukconstitutionallaw.

of the arguments on both sides, the discussion does not seek to reopen those questions. The law was settled by the 8:3 majority and there are also powerful arguments supporting the majority.[117] But the extent to which the reasoning of the majority is open to legitimate criticism or lacks resilience is likely to affect the ultimate reach of the decision.

We also note that the Court was unanimous in rejecting the argument that the ECA 1972 had altered the UK's rule of recognition, the rule that identifies the sources of law in the UK's legal system and ultimately validates all other rules, or that the rule of recognition would be varied by its repeal.[118] We note that this aspect of the majority's decision has been criticised by those who support the decision itself, as well as by those who do not. For Paul Craig and Robert Craig, supporters, this is because the rule of recognition is inherently dynamic. They, and Mark Elliott, a critic, see at least tension between regarding EU law as a new, direct and independent source of domestic UK law and yet rejecting the argument that the rule of recognition has been altered.[119] The solution might lie in regarding the majority as stating only that, while modifying the doctrine of implied repeal, the ECA 1972 did not change the 'supreme rule' putting parliamentary sovereignty at the top of the hierarchy of the UK constitution.[120] Alternatively, it might lie in seeing them as implicitly accepting that, while statute cannot, in itself, alter the rule of recognition, it 'can act as a catalyst for a shift in the social acceptance on which the rule of recognition depends', and that happened in the years after the enactment of the 1972 Act.[121]

C. The Impact of *Miller's* Case on the UK's Constitutional Environment

Miller's case concerned the three constitutional actors at the UK level – the legislature, the executive and the courts – and the devolved legislatures. The statement by the majority quoted in section III.B, that they could not accept that a major change to UK constitutional arrangements can be achieved by Ministers alone and must be made 'in the only way that the UK constitution recognises, namely by Parliamentary legislation', suggests that the impact of the case may be widespread and profound.[122] Taking the UK level first, several commentators have considered the extent to which the decision will have the effect of enhancing the role of Parliament and the significance of parliamentary sovereignty. To the extent that this is so, can such court-led enhancement be put together with what has been said to be the

---

org/2016/11/11/timothy-endicott-this-ancient-secretive-royal-prerogative/; T Endicott, 'Lord Reed's dissent in Gina Miller's Case and the Principles of our Constitution' in Clarry (ed), *The UK Supreme Court Yearbook* (n 95) 259; G Phillipson, 'A Dive into Deep Constitutional Waters: Article 50, the Prerogative and Parliament' (2016) 79 MLR 1064.

[117] R Craig, 'A Simple Application of the Frustration Principle: Prerogative, Statute and *Miller*' [2017] PL 25; P Craig, '*Miller*, Structural Constitutional Review and the Limits of Prerogative Power' [2017] PL 48.

[118] *Miller* (n 1) [60] (Majority); Lord Reed (with whom Lord Carnwath and Lord Hughes agreed) at [224] and [227].

[119] Craig, 'A Simple Application of the Frustration Principle' (n 117) 45–46; Craig, '*Miller*, Structural Constitutional Review' (n 117) 64–65; Elliott, 'The Supreme Court's Judgment in *Miller*' (n 97) 270–72.

[120] Craig, 'A Simple Application of the Frustration Principle' (n 117) 45–46.

[121] Craig, '*Miller*, Structural Constitutional Review' (n 117) 65.

[122] *Miller* (n 1) [82].

greater confidence and authority of parliamentary Select Committees to argue that this will assist in achieving a more balanced constitution?

Tony Wright, former chair of the Public Administration Committee and the House of Commons Reform Committee, has partly attributed that increased confidence and authority to the fact that, in the House of Commons, the chairs and members are now elected by members rather than appointed by the whips, and to an increase in their public profile.[123] But Hannah White's 2015 study for the Institute for Government states that it is not clear whether that increased public profile has led to an increase in their impact on government.[124] Accordingly, in the short term one should not expect too much from parliamentary Select Committees in achieving a more balanced constitution.

The most recent study, by Lucy Atkinson in 2017 for the Constitution Society, concluded that government now accepts a certain level of constructive criticism from committees, particularly in areas of political contention and controversy, and that committees today are much bolder in their scrutiny. But she also stated that the powers afforded to committees are still limited, and the impact of their work is frequently undermined by inadequate or tardy government responses. Reliance on government cooperation ensures that Select Committees remain the 'underdogs'.[125]

The introduction to Lucy Atkinson's study, by Andrew Kennon, Clerk of Committees in the House of Commons from 2011 to 2016, states that, with a minority government and the complexity of Brexit, it is possible to imagine, on individual issues, that evidence-based reports from cross-party committees may form the basis of compromises which frontbenchers are unable to broker themselves but are happy to accept.[126] It may be that, even on Brexit issues where the disagreements are strong and cross party lines, this assessment is optimistic. In any event, it is a scenario that is only imaginable with a minority government, which has not been the norm under the UK's 'first past the post' electoral system.

i. The Courts and the Relationship between the Executive and the UK Parliament

Extrapolating from *Miller's* case more generally about the relationship between the executive and the UK Parliament will be difficult. This is because of the way the Supreme Court emphasised the constitutional nature of the ECA 1972 and the extent to which it integrated EU law into UK domestic law, and the way EU law became a direct and independent source of UK domestic law.[127] Under it, EU law was not to be compared with delegated legislation. The ECA 1972 'operates as a partial transfer of law-making powers, or an assignment

---

[123] Tony Wright's foreword to Hannah White's study for the Institute for Government, *Select Committees under Scrutiny: The Impact of Parliamentary Committee Inquiries on Government* (June 2015). P Dunleavy and D Muir, 'Parliament Bounces Back – How Select Committees have Become a Power in the Land' British Politics and Policy (18 July 2013), available at http://blogs.lse.ac.uk/politicsandpolicy/parliament-bounces-back-how-select-committees-have-become-a-power-in-the-land/, see the difference lying in increased media profile and do not comment on substantive achievements.
[124] White, *Select Committees under Scrutiny* (n 123) 1.
[125] L Atkinson, *House of Commons Select Committees and the UK Constitution* (The Constitution Society, 2017) 6–7, 46, 68.
[126] ibid 5.
[127] See section III.B and *Miller* (n 1) [61], [65], [69]–[70].

of legislative competences, by the UK Parliament to the EU law-making institutions (so long as Parliament wills it)'.[128] It is significant that the majority judgment stated that the provisions of the 1972 Act were 'unique in their legislative and constitutional implications' and that the statute grafted 'a dynamic, international source of law ... onto, and above, the well-established existing sources of domestic law: Parliament and the courts'.[129]

Paul Craig has stated that *Miller* is authority for limiting prerogative power (a) where the exercise of such power would impinge on a 'constitutional statute', and (b) where the exercise of prerogative power impacts on (legal) rights.[130] Its wider significance will thus depend on what statutory provisions are regarded as 'constitutional', and on the approach of the courts when considering whether the exercise of the prerogative affects (legal) rights.

ii. Constitutional Statutory Provisions

We appear to have moved beyond a Diceyan purely descriptive use of the term 'constitutional statutes',[131] but are in the early stages of understanding the basis of categorising statutes and statutory provisions in this way. We start with the particularly helpful analysis of the *Miller* Divisional Court, with which the majority in the Supreme Court agreed. The Divisional Court stated[132] that it was particularly important to construe the ECA 1972 against background constitutional principles because, particularly where those background principles are strong, there is a presumption that Parliament intended to legislate in conformity with them and not to undermine them, and thus to exclude the usual doctrine of implied repeal by later inconsistent legislation. The Divisional Court, in a phrase resonant of the principle of legality in *Ex parte Pierson* and *Ex parte Simms*,[133] referred to this as 'casual implied repeal'.[134] The stronger the constitutional principle, the stronger the presumption. The effect of this approach is, as Farrah Ahmed and Adam Perry have stated, to give 'the statutory parts of the constitution ... the same degree of protection as the common law parts receive under the principle of legality'.[135] In the context of *Miller's* case, the two relevant constitutional principles were the principles that there is no power to vary the law of the land by the exercise of the prerogative, and that the Crown's prerogative power in the conduct of foreign relations operates only on the international plane and has no effect in domestic law.

The crucial question of which statutes are constitutional has also been considered in other contexts. In *R (Brynmawr Foundation School Governors) v Welsh Ministers*,[136] the court considered the relationship between the provisions in a statute described as constitutional, the Government of Wales Act 2006, which defined the areas of the Welsh Assembly's legislative competence but without specific provisions either including or excluding education and training, and a specific (and potentially conflicting) provision in the earlier School

---

[128] *Miller* (n 1) [68].
[129] ibid [90].
[130] Craig, '*Miller*, Structural Constitutional Review' (n 117) 51, 68, 83.
[131] AV Dicey, *An Introduction to the Study of the Law of the Constitution*, 8th edn (London, Macmillan, 1915) 37.
[132] *Miller* (n 105) [82] et seq (Lord Thomas CJ, Sir Terence Etherton MR and Sales LJ).
[133] *R v Secretary of State for the Home Department, ex parte Pierson* [1998] AC 539, 573–75; *R v Secretary of State for the Home Department, ex parte Simms* [2000] 2 AC 115, 131.
[134] *Miller* (n 105) [88].
[135] F Ahmed and A Perry, 'Constitutional Statutes' (2017) 37 *OJLS* 461, 462.
[136] *R (Brynmawr Foundation School Governors) v Welsh Ministers* [2011] EWHC 519 (Admin). See the discussion by Ahmed and Perry, 'Constitutional Statutes' (n 135) 463–64, 473–74, 477–78.

Standards and Framework Act 1998. The court took account of the constitutional status of the 2006 Act in deciding that the principle presuming consistency between specific provisions in an earlier statute and general provisions in a later one did not apply, and concluding that the provisions defining legislative competence in the 2006 Act were not in effect to be 'read down' because of the 1998 Act.[137]

The starting point of all recent discussion regarding which statutes will be regarded as 'constitutional' and which principle will be used to determine this question is the influential judgment of Laws LJ in the Divisional Court in *Thoburn v Sunderland CC* in 2003.[138] Laws LJ appeared to regard the ECA 1972 as a constitutional statute because it incorporated rights on a large scale, gave domestic effect to EU law and had profound effects on many dimensions of our daily lives. In essence, he therefore so regarded it because of its scope and constitutional scale. But he also stated that 'ordinary' and 'constitutional' statutes should be distinguished on a principled basis. He considered that:

> [A] constitutional statute is one which (a) conditions the legal relationship between citizen and State in some general, overarching manner, or (b) enlarges or diminishes the scope of what we would now regard as fundamental constitutional rights. (a) and (b) are of necessity closely related: it is difficult to think of an instance of (a) that is not also an instance of (b). The special status of constitutional statutes follows the special status of constitutional rights. Examples are the Magna Carta, the Bill of Rights 1689, the Act of Union, the Reform Acts which distributed and enlarged the franchise, the HRA, the Scotland Act 1998 and the Government of Wales Act 1998. The ECA clearly belongs in this family. It incorporated the whole corpus of substantive Community rights and obligations, and gave overriding domestic effect to the judicial and administrative machinery of Community law. It may be there has never been a statute having such profound effects on so many dimensions of our daily lives. The ECA is, by force of the common law, a constitutional statute.[139]

The Divisional Court in *Miller's* case refers to the 'profound' changes made by the ECA 1972.[140] The majority in the Supreme Court, which did not use the term 'constitutional statute', refer to the fact that the ECA 1972 made EU law a new independent source of domestic law and to the fundamentality of its changes to the UK's constitutional arrangements, and of the changes to those arrangements that will result from withdrawing from the EU.[141] These references suggest that the approach of both courts was broadly similar to that of Laws LJ. They, however, gave little further guidance on this point. Mark Elliott's criticism of the approach of the majority in the Supreme Court as 'novel' is unfair in the light of *Thoburn's* case, but his criticism of it as imprecise has force.[142]

Is there guidance in other cases? *R (Buckinghamshire CC) v Secretary of State for Transport* ('the HS2 case') concerned the relationship of two statutes which have been stated to be 'constitutional': the ECA 1972 and the Bill of Rights 1689. Lord Neuberger and Lord Mance stated:

> The United Kingdom has no written constitution, but we have a number of constitutional instruments. They include Magna Carta, the Petition of Right 1628, the Bill of Rights and (in Scotland)

---

[137] *R (Brynmawr Foundation School Governors) v Welsh Ministers* (n 136) [87].
[138] *Thoburn v Sunderland CC* [2003] QB 151, [60]–[64].
[139] ibid [62].
[140] *Miller* (n 105) [4], [87], [93]. Para [88] refers to the consequences of so classifying a statute.
[141] ibid [62]–[68].
[142] Elliott, 'The Supreme Court's Judgment in *Miller*: In Search of Constitutional Principle' (n 97) 258, 264–68.

the Claim of Rights Act 1689, the Act of Settlement 1701 and the Act of Union 1707. The European Communities Act 1972, the Human Rights Act 1998 and the Constitutional Reform Act 2005 may now be added to this list. The common law itself also recognises certain principles as fundamental to the rule of law. It is, putting the point at its lowest, certainly arguable (and it is for United Kingdom law and courts to determine) that there may be fundamental principles, whether contained in other Constitutional instruments or recognised at common law, of which Parliament when it enacted the European Communities Act 1972 did not either contemplate or authorise the abrogation.[143]

This acknowledges that the historic statute (the Bill of Rights), recognised as constitutional, survived the enactment of the later statute (the ECA 1972) so recognised. But it does not identify any principle for determining which statutes are constitutional or contain fundamental principles. This issue has now been considered in two useful articles, which make the point that what is needed is an indicative definition not a list.[144]

The limited utility of lists is graphically illustrated by the fact that Laws LJ does not refer to the Northern Irish legislation in *Thoburn's* case, and the devolution legislation to which he did refer is not included in the more recent list in the HS2 case. This in itself provides support for the doubts that have been expressed as to whether there is a principled way of distinguishing between 'constitutional' and other legislation.

David Feldman considers that the linkage of 'constitutional' status to fundamental rights is problematic for three reasons.[145] First, Laws LJ would only accord such status to rights regarded as 'fundamental' 'by force of the common law', as opposed to statute. Second, it is under-inclusive because it does not comfortably include statutes concerned with institutions of the state and their interrelationship rather than those concerned with the relationship of the citizen and the state. Ahmed and Perry consider that this is its main problem.[146] Third, in including legislation concerned with the relationship between the citizen and the state the linkage may be over-inclusive. Feldman observes that most legislation is concerned with that relationship, although some not 'in a general overarching way'.[147] He prefers an approach that concentrates 'on the contribution of Acts, subordinate legislation, and individual provisions or groups of provisions to establishing institutions of the state, defining their roles and authority, and regulating their relationship with each other'.[148] He considers that 'the key function of a constitution is ... to constitute the state and its institutions and confer functions, powers and duties on them'.[149] But others have observed that this is also over-inclusive because, as Sir Philip Sales has stated, 'it is unlikely to be the case that full constitutional force can or should be given to every provision in a particular statute, even if it can be said in a general way that the statute is of constitutional importance'.[150] Ahmed and

---

[143] *R (Buckinghamshire CC Council) v Secretary of State for Transport* (n 113) [207] (Baroness Hale and Lords Kerr, Sumption and Carnwath agreeing).
[144] D Feldman, 'The Nature and Significance of "Constitutional" Legislation' (2013) 129 *LQR* 343; Ahmed and Perry, 'Constitutional Statutes' (n 135).
[145] Feldman, 'The Nature and Significance of "Constitutional" Legislation' (n 144) 345–48.
[146] Ahmed and Perry, 'Constitutional Statutes' (n 135) 466.
[147] Feldman, 'The Nature and Significance of "Constitutional" Legislation' (n 144) 348.
[148] ibid 357.
[149] ibid 350.
[150] P Sales, 'Rights and Fundamental Rights in English Law' (2016) 75 *CLJ* 86, 100. See also Ahmed and Perry, 'Constitutional Statutes' (n 135) 466.

Perry advocate a test based on two elements. The first (similar to Feldman's) is whether the statute or part of it creates or regulates a state institution. The second is that the statute or the relevant part of it substantially influences what other state institutions may do.[151]

It is also to be noted that the jumping-off point for Laws LJ's recognition of a category of 'constitutional' statutes was the recognition by the common law of rights 'which should properly be classified as constitutional or fundamental'. But this may in itself be controversial. For example, Brice Dickson has rejected the notion that the UK Supreme Court has recognised the concept of constitutional rights within the common law.[152] While the notion of 'constitutional' common law rights may well be contentious, many common law rights are so important or integral to the constitutional structure of the UK that they can properly be afforded special protection. The extent to which common law rights can be described as 'constitutional' or 'fundamental' is unclear. Common law rights that can be equated with those contained in the ECHR have been described as 'constitutional'.[153] While the right to vote or the right to preserve the confidentiality of legal correspondence are likely to be 'constitutional', and the right not to suffer misfeasance in public office may not be, it may be difficult to precisely define the boundaries in between in a principled manner.[154]

In substance *Miller's* case simply adopted Laws LJ's approach to the question of which statutes are 'constitutional' statutes. We do not, for instance, know whether provisions in statutes that do not wholly fall into the 'constitutional' category can qualify as 'constitutional provisions' and get similar protection, as advocated by Feldman. Although the search for a principle to identify those that do implies some normative criteria, Ahmed and Perry recognise that there are also difficulties with criteria based on the extent of its institutional influence. Moreover, a test for identifying whether a right or principle is constitutional which can appear parasitic on an international convention to which the UK is a party may be thought to be a fragile basis for creating a purely domestic set of constitutional rights.[155] Assessing whether a statutory provision is 'constitutional' in the sense of having protection from implied repeal involves difficult and value-laden judgments.

Sir Philip Sales has suggested that 'the courts should only identify a fundamental right or interest for the purposes of the principle of legality if it is plausible to infer that Parliament as a collective body itself recognises such a right or interest'.[156] He considers that, in the long run, the most defensible concept of domestic fundamental rights is one that aims to identify common background understandings of both courts and the legislature.[157] Although more promising, the first two of the tools he mentions – inferring constitutional force from the circumstances in which a particular piece of legislation was passed, or the prominence it is given in constitutional debate[158] – are also relatively open-textured. For these reasons,

---

[151] Ahmed and Perry, 'Constitutional Statutes' (n 135) 471.
[152] B Dickson, *Human Rights and the United Kingdom Supreme Court* (Oxford, Oxford University Press, 2013) ch 2.
[153] See, eg, *R v Lord Chancellor, ex parte Lightfoot* [2000] QB 597, [609].
[154] See *Watkins v Secretary of State for the Home Office* (n 47) [25] (Lord Bingham).
[155] See the concerns of P Sales and R Ekins, 'Rights-Consistent Interpretation and the Human Rights Act 1998' (2011) 127 *LQR* 217, 227 ff about analogies from the operation of the HRA 1998.
[156] Sales, 'Rights and Fundamental Rights in English Law' (n 150) 99.
[157] ibid 108.
[158] ibid 100.

the category remains an undeveloped one, and one has to be cautious about predicting the wider significance of this aspect of *Miller's* case. There is, however, force in Paul Craig's suggestion that 'a statute worthy of the denomination constitutional should not be rendered devoid of effect through recourse to the prerogative'.[159] Whether that can be the effect in any given case will in turn depend on whether the exercise of the prerogative is seen as affecting legal rights.

iii. When Does the Exercise of the Prerogative Affect (Legal) Rights?

The majority in *Miller's* case[160] identified two categories of case where the exercise of the prerogative may have domestic legal consequences. They are: (a) 'where it is inherent in the prerogative power that its exercise will affect the legal rights or duties of others';[161] and (b) where 'the effect of an exercise of prerogative powers is to change the facts to which the law applies'.[162] It was acknowledged that the latter does not change the law, only the extent of its application.[163]

Legal rights cannot be affected where statute covers the area of the prerogative because of the principle in *Attorney-General v de Keyser's Royal Hotel*[164] that in such a case the prerogative is displaced and cannot be exercised. Such cases apart, does the approach of the majority in *Miller* indicate a greater willingness to widen the category in which the exercise of the prerogative will be regarded as affecting legal rights, that is, a more rights-based background position, at least in relation to fundamental rights? Their willingness to look behind the ECA 1972, which they accepted was 'in one sense' the source of EU law, and their broad approach to the principle that, even where statute does not cover the area of the prerogative, the prerogative may not be used to frustrate the purpose of a statute[165] suggests that it does. One of the crucial elements of the dissenting judgments was that such widening is not legitimate and should not be done.

We have referred to Brice Dickson's rejection of the notion that the Supreme Court has recognised the concept of constitutional rights within the common law. It should also be noted that Sir Philip Sales, relying inter alia on the decision of the House of Lords in *Watkins v Secretary of State for the Home Office*,[166] rejects the idea that the court's control over the 'common law' prerogative powers of the Crown is based on controlling fundamental rights by analogy to the control of statutory and prerogative powers.[167] He argues that such powers cannot be characterised as having the status of positive law rights of individuals, and that

---

[159] Craig, 'Miller, Structural Constitutional Review' (n 117) 70.
[160] *Miller* (n 1) [52]–[53].
[161] The example given is that it is inherent in the prerogative power of the Crown to decide on the terms of service of its servants that those terms can be altered so as to remove rights: *Council for Civil Service Unions v Minister for the Civil Service* [1985] AC 374 (*GCHQ* case).
[162] *Miller* (n 1) [53].
[163] The examples given are the exercise of the prerogative to declare war or to extend territorial waters.
[164] *Attorney-General v de Keyser's Royal Hotel* [1920] AC 508.
[165] See the references at *Miller* (n 1) [48] and [51] to *Laker Airways Ltd v Department of Trade* [1977] QB 643; *R v Secretary of State for the Home Department, ex parte Fire Brigades Union* [1995] 2 AC 513. cf *Miller* (n 1) [168] (Lord Reed) and [250] (Lord Carnwath).
[166] *Watkins v Secretary of State for the Home Office* (n 47) [26], [58]–[64].
[167] P Sales, 'Crown Powers, the Royal Prerogative and Fundamental Rights' in H Wilberg and M Elliott (eds), *The Scope and Intensity of Judicial Review: Traversing Taggart's Rainbow* (Oxford, Hart Publishing, 2017) 383–84.

attempting to rely on rights of this kind outside the context of statutory interpretation would be to give them excessive force.[168] The consequence or corollary of that, however, may well be that the exercise of such powers will not generally affect domestic legal rights.

One area in which the exercise of the prerogative may affect domestic legal rights concerns withdrawal at the international level from the ECHR. If the rights domesticated in the HRA 1998 and set out in schedule 1 to the Act would be rendered illusory by this, the reasoning of the majority in *Miller's* case would apply and legislation would be necessary. But the Convention rights have been domesticated by the HRA 1998 in a way very different from the way the ECA 1972 domesticated EU rights. For these reasons, it has been argued that, despite withdrawal at the international level from the Convention, the operation and effect of the HRA 1998's key right-conferring provisions may possibly be preserved. If so, the use of the prerogative to withdraw from the Convention would not be precluded by the decision in *Miller's* case. We agree with those who consider that this would be a difficult argument because of the provisions in the HRA 1998 permitting reservations and derogations from the ECHR in times of war or public emergency, which it is difficult to see could operate if the UK withdrew from the Convention.[169]

iv. *The Role of the Courts in Resolving These Issues*

So far, we have considered issues between the legislature and the executive. But of course the division of opinion in *Miller's* case concerned whether the court had a role in the resolution of such issues. It is apposite at this stage to remind ourselves of the distinction Dicey made between two parts of the constitution. They are: 'understandings, customs and conventions which are not in the true sense laws because they are not enforced by the courts'; and rules that, 'whether embodied in statutes or not, are laws in the strictest sense of the term, and make up the true law of the constitution'.[170] Hickman argues that Dicey was more sensitive to the interface between the legal and the political than his critics recognise.[171] It was the location of this line that divided the judges in *Miller's* case. The dissenters considered that the legal accountability that resulted from the majority's approach unduly underplayed the role of democratic and political accountability, and thus the role of the UK's political constitution. They also pointed to the statutory authorisation for a referendum in the European Union Referendum Act 2015 and the result of the referendum.[172] Lord Carnwath considered that the principle of parliamentary accountability was no less fundamental to the UK's constitution than parliamentary sovereignty.[173] Lord Reed considered that '[i]t is important for courts to understand that the legalisation of political issues is not always constitutionally appropriate, and may be fraught with risk, not least for the judiciary'.[174]

---

[168] See also Elliott, 'The Rule of Law and Access to Justice: Some Home Truths' (n 94) 8: 'There is, and should be, no question of the common law's filling the gap that EU law will leave by morphing into a judicial tool that can be used to override, rather than interpret, legislation.'

[169] G Phillipson and A Young, 'Would Use of the Prerogative to Denounce the ECHR "Frustrate" the Human Rights Act? Lessons from *Miller*' [2017] PL 150, 169, 173–75.

[170] AV Dicey, *Introduction to the Study of the Law of the Constitution*, 10th edn, (London, Macmillan, 1959) 469–70.

[171] Hickman, 'In Defence of the Legal Constitution' (n 99) 988.

[172] *Miller* (n 1) [171], [195], [266]–[268], [272], [275]. The majority dealt with this at [116]–[125].

[173] ibid [249]. See also ibid [254].

[174] ibid [240]. See also ibid [161].

We have referred to the force of the points made by the dissenters and the critics of the decision. We do not, however, consider that the majority underplayed the importance of democratic and political accountability. Their treatment of the devolution arguments showed they were fully aware of the limits of legal accountability. As they stated, withdrawal from the EU 'involves unilateral action by the relevant constitutional bodies [in the UK] which affects a fundamental change in the constitutional arrangements of the [UK]'.[175] The effect of the decision (albeit by asserting a role for the court) was to ensure a role for the sovereign legislature. The decision was, as Rob Murray, Ms Miller's solicitor, stated, about process not politics.[176]

Additionally, those who advocate the use of the prerogative power in the conduct of foreign affairs because, in Blackstone's words, it 'is wisely placed in a single hand by the British constitution, for the sake of unanimity, strength, and despatch',[177] may have underplayed the effect on unanimity, strength and despatch where there is tension or disagreement between the executive and the legislature. Resolving such tensions or disagreement politically may be a difficult and lengthy process without a constitutional 'adjudicator' or a 'mediator'. The advocates of a 'political constitution' focus on the Harlow and Rawlings 'green light' approach of enabling the legislature and the executive to act separately or together and on non-juridical forms of accountability. The fact that over most of our recent history the executive has dominated and controlled the legislature has meant situations of tension and disagreement between the executive and the legislature rarely arise, and thus they may have been overlooked when identifying the paradigm. It is not without significance that the seventeenth century, a time of tension and disagreement between the Crown and Parliament, was a century in which the courts were active.[178] It is true that *Miller's* case was not prompted by what can be described as 'active disagreement' between the legislature and the executive. However, given the sharp difference of views about leaving the EU and how to give effect to the referendum result, the context of the litigation can fairly be described as one of tension and disagreement, and the issue was resolved by the courts with despatch – within seven months of the referendum. Moreover, it would be wrong to characterise the approach of the majority as judicial usurpation of political power. The issue was whether it was the executive or the legislature that had the power to initiate the process for leaving the EU.[179]

The decision that the court may have a role in such circumstances also chimes with the fact that in traditional judicial review of a central/local dispute, the courts may have to decide who Parliament has made the primary decision-maker and give close scrutiny to a decision by the body with secondary responsibility which appears to 'interfere' with the role and responsibilities of the primary decision-maker.[180] In constitutional cases, taking on

---

[175] ibid [78]. See also *Miller* (n 105) [92]–[94].
[176] R Murray, 'The Article 50 Challenge: Clarifying the UK's Constitutional Requirements to Start Brexit' in Galligan (ed), *Constitution in Crisis* (n 98) 102.
[177] See Lord Reed at [160], citing *Blackstone's Commentaries, Book I* (Oxford, Clarendon Press, 1765) 242–43. cf Craig, '*Miller*, Structural Constitutional Review' (n 117) 56–58 for the argument that, in the circumstances before the court, the purpose and rationale of granting prerogative powers in relation to foreign affairs to Ministers was not undermined.
[178] See, eg, *Case of Proclamations* (1611) 12 Co Rep 74.
[179] See P Craig, 'Judicial Power, the Judicial Power Project and the UK' (2017) 36 *University of Queensland Law Journal* 355, 359.
[180] See *Secretary of State for Education v Tameside MBC* [1977] AC 1014; but cf *Nottinghamshire CC v Secretary of State for the Environment* [1986] AC 240, where the council's challenge failed because the Secretary of State's decision had primacy.

such a role makes it important for the courts to articulate a coherent approach to the determination of which part of the state has primary responsibility. It cannot simply be assumed that it is the executive, or in the case of a devolution matter the UK institutions, which has that responsibility. Of course, given the principle of parliamentary sovereignty, it is always open to provide that the executive or the relevant UK institution has primary responsibility on a given issue by enacting legislation. That was not done in the European Union Referendum Act 2015, but it was in the Withdrawal Act 2018. By section 13 of the Withdrawal Act, the House of Commons is to approve by resolution the negotiated withdrawal agreement and the framework for the future relationship with the EU, and the withdrawal agreement may only be ratified if an Act of Parliament is passed providing for its implementation. On 15 January 2019, however, the House of Commons, by a majority of 230, rejected the agreement negotiated by the UK Government.[181] At the time the text of this chapter was finalised, two weeks after the statutorily designated 'exit day',[182] there had been no parliamentary agreement to this or another withdrawal agreement.[183]

Where no provision is made as to whether the executive or the legislature has primary responsibility, it is important for the courts to articulate as coherent an approach to justiciability and the institutional appropriateness of a role for the courts as is possible. In the context of an issue as to the relative competences of the courts and Parliament on the sensitive question of relaxing the statutory prohibition of assisted suicide, the different approaches in the judgments of the Supreme Court in *R (Nicklinson) v Ministry of Justice*[184] to whether the courts have a role or whether the matter is for Parliament alone illustrate the difficulties and left a measure of uncertainty. The consequence of that uncertainty has led to further litigation but not to any resolution of the differences as to whether the matter is for Parliament alone.[185]

Any development of the common law to provide stronger rights protections could be seen as an erosion of parliamentary sovereignty. As we considered in section II, if the courts do not have available the range of EU law and ECHR human rights protections, judges may instead develop the common law and thus enhance the role of the courts. Some will see such a move as a further undesirable tilting of the balance of the constitution away from the political constitution.[186] The way to address this may be to show that such development

---

[181] The controversy centres around what has been termed the Northern Irish backstop, an arrangement to maintain the current open border between Northern Ireland and the Republic of Ireland, which would either involve the UK's remaining within a customs union or introduce regulatory differences between Northern Ireland and the rest of the UK for an unlimited period. 'Brexiteers' objected to the first because it would remove the UK's ability to have an independent trade policy; the Democratic Unionist Party objected to the second, which they see as a threat to the union between Northern Ireland and the rest of the UK.

[182] The European Union (Withdrawal) Act 2018, s 20(1) defines this as 11 pm on 29 March 2019.

[183] If this remains the position, unless 'exit day' is deferred, which requires both an agreement with the EU and UK legislation, the UK will leave the EU with no withdrawal agreement, something which many consider would be detrimental and possibly lead to serious disruption.

[184] *R (Nicklinson) v Ministry of Justice* [2015] AC 657.

[185] *R (Conway) v Secretary of State for Justice* [2018] EWCA Civ 1431, affirming [2017] EWHC 2447 (Admin). Permission to appeal to the Supreme Court was refused on 27 November 2018. For earlier proceedings see [2017] EWCA Civ 275 and [2017] EWHC 640 (Admin).

[186] See, eg, G Gee and AL Young, 'Regaining Sovereignty' in G Gee, L Rubini and M Trybus (eds), *Leaving the EU? The Legal Impact of 'Brexit' on the United Kingdom* (Birmingham, Institute of European Law, 2016) 53, available at https://www.birmingham.ac.uk/Documents/college-artslaw/law/iel/leaving-EU-legal-impact-brexit-gee-rubini-trybus.pdf.

can only occur where it is possible without producing disharmony between parliamentary sovereignty and the rule of law.[187] Sensitivity to this is likely to involve avoiding too robust an approach, save where there is a consensus in the political and legal communities over the right or principle under consideration. In that way, the role of the courts could be less of a threat. In our view, an increased role for the courts in determining the scope of common law rights would be a legitimate consequence of any reduction in rights protection under the Charter, or even in future under the HRA 1998. There is nothing novel in the courts' constitutional role as a guarantor of individual rights. Without EU law's direct influence on the development of rights, the courts are best placed to continue to protect rights, which will necessarily evolve and develop over time.

v. The Devolution Issues

Finally, we turn to the impact of what was said in *Miller's* case about the devolution issues before the Court and the impact of developments since then. The Court referred to two matters. The first was whether primary legislation was required by the Northern Ireland Act 1998, which gave citizens the right to challenge decisions of the Northern Ireland Executive and Assembly on the ground they breached EU law (and by implication required by similar provisions in the Scottish and Welsh devolution legislation). In view of the majority's decision that legislation was required as a result of the ECA 1972, it was not necessary for them to decide this, but they were inclined to say that legislation was required, inter alia because it would be incongruous to remove a statutory constraint on the competence of the devolved administrations by the exercise of the prerogative.[188] This approach has been criticised as side-lining critically important questions of Northern Ireland constitutional law.[189]

The Court also unanimously held that for two reasons there was no legal requirement to consult the devolved legislatures before serving notice under Article 50(2). First, those bodies do not have competence over foreign affairs.[190] Secondly, the 'Sewel convention', that the UK Parliament 'will not normally legislate with regard to devolved matters without the consent of' the devolved legislature, is a political convention the courts do not enforce.[191] Courts can recognise the operation of a political convention when deciding a legal question, but they cannot give legal rulings on their operation or scope 'because those matters are determined in the political world' and policing of the scope and operation of conventions is not 'within the constitutional remit of the judiciary, which is to protect the rule of law'.[192] The fact that the convention is now enshrined in the Scottish and Welsh devolution

---

[187] For suggestions as to how this might be done, see TRS Allan, *Sovereignty of Law: Freedom, Constitution and Common Law* (Oxford, Oxford University Press, 2013) ch 5; and Sales, 'Rights and Fundamental Rights in English Law' (n 150) 99–100.
[188] *Miller* (n 1) [132].
[189] C McCrudden and D Halberstam, '*Miller* and Northern Ireland: A Critical Constitutional Response' in Clarry (ed), *The UK Supreme Court Yearbook* (n 95) 343.
[190] *Miller* (n 1) [129]–[130], [178], [242]–[243].
[191] ibid [140]–[141], [178], [242]–[243]. See also *The UK Withdrawal from the European Union (Legal Continuity) (Scotland) Bill – A Reference by the Attorney General and the Advocate General for Scotland (Scotland)* [2019] 2 WLR 1, [19].
[192] *Miller* (n 1) [146], [151].

legislation[193] did not affect the matter. The language and its context showed that the purpose was not to convert it into a legal rule justiciable by the courts but only to declare 'that it is a permanent feature of the relevant devolution settlement' and thus 'to entrench it as a convention'.[194]

The second reason is of more general significance because of the scope for differences about the roles of the UK and devolved Governments and Parliaments in relation to matters that, under the devolution legislation, are within the competence of the devolved institutions. The most notable difference, and the main development since *Miller*, is that between the UK Government and the devolved institutions about the repatriation of matters which are at present within the competence of the EU. This has led to UK and Scottish and Welsh legislation reflecting the different views.[195] The UK Government challenged the legality of the Bills passed by the devolved Parliaments and referred them to the Supreme Court under its devolution jurisdiction.[196] As explained below, in the event only the challenge to the Scottish Bill came before the Supreme Court, which, in December 2018, upheld the challenge in part.[197]

The position of the devolved institutions that led to the Welsh and Scottish Bills was that after the UK leaves the EU, the powers should be repatriated in accordance with the division of competencies in the devolution legislation and that their agreement pursuant to the Sewel convention is required for any UK legislation. This would, as the Court in *Miller's* case recognised,[198] enhance their competence by removing the present constraint precluding devolved institutions from acting where the EU has competence. The UK Government considers that the EU element of some, although not all, of the competencies devolved under the devolution legislation should be 'repatriated' to the UK institutions and then released, save where a common UK framework is needed 'to protect the essential interests of businesses and consumers in every part of the [UK]'[199] – that is, the operation of the UK's own internal market.

---

[193] Scotland Act 1998, s 28(8), inserted by Scotland Act 2016; Government of Wales Act 2006, s 107(6), inserted by Wales Act 2017. The Wales Bill was before the UK Parliament at the time *Miller's* case was heard by the Supreme Court, and the Court referred to it at *Miller* (n 1) [147]. Royal Assent was granted a week after the judgments in *Miller's* case were handed down.

[194] *Miller* (n 1) [148]–[149], relying on the contrast between s 28(8) and s 63A of the Scotland Act declaring that the Scottish Parliament and Government are not to be abolished except on the basis of a referendum. The word 'entrench' in [149], however, appears too strong. Note also that the Advocate-General had submitted (see [106]–[107]) that the use of the term 'normally' showed that the matter was 'quintessentially a matter of political judgment and that any attempt to enforce the Sewel convention would impinge on the sovereignty of the UK (Westminster) Parliament'.

[195] European Union (Legal Continuity) (Scotland) Bill 2018, the Law Derived from the European Union (Wales) Bill 2018 and the UK European Union (Withdrawal) Act 2018. As devolved government in Northern Ireland has been suspended since January 2017, there is no Northern Irish legislation.

[196] See Scotland Act 1998, ss 32–33 and Government of Wales Act 2006, s 112. See also Northern Ireland Act 1998, s 11. Section 40(4)(b) of the Constitutional Reform Act 2005 transferred the jurisdiction from the Judicial Committee of the Privy Council to the Supreme Court. For a summary of the jurisdiction and analysis of leading decisions on 'devolution issues', see JS Caird, *The Supreme Court on Devolution*, House of Commons, Briefing Paper No 07670 (27 July 2016).

[197] *The UK Withdrawal from the European Union (Legal Continuity) (Scotland) Bill – A Reference by the Attorney General and the Advocate General for Scotland (Scotland)* (n 191).

[198] *Miller* (n 1) [130].

[199] D Lidington MP, 'United at home, stronger abroad', Speech delivered in Broughton (26 February 2018), available at https://www.gov.uk/government/speeches/united-at-home-stronger-abroad.

In April 2018, the Welsh Government agreed to drop its objections to the UK Bill.[200] It did so after an agreement which the responsible UK Minister described as respecting the devolution settlements and also upholding the Sewel Convention.[201] The agreement provided that 'areas already devolved remain devolved', and the UK Government would consult the devolved legislatures and seek their consent about which areas of EU law will be 'frozen' at a UK level while frameworks are agreed.[202] The Scottish institutions maintained their position because, although the devolved legislatures would be consulted about which areas of EU law would be temporarily 'frozen' at a UK level, their consent was not required in respect of those areas. They also considered that the Scottish Parliament has competence to legislate on the consequences of withdrawal in areas in which the Scotland Act gives competence to the Scottish Parliament. On 15 May 2018, the Scottish Parliament voted against the UK Government's proposal.

On 26 June, the UK Withdrawal Act 2018 received Royal Assent. It empowers UK Ministers to make regulations specifying areas of retained EU law in which the devolved legislatures have no competence.[203] The Explanatory Notes state that it thus seeks to empower regulations freezing the position so that, taking into account what are now EU competencies, 'in those areas the current parameters of devolved competence are maintained'.[204] The UK Government's powers in these policy areas are subject to their seeking consent from the devolved authorities, giving reasons for proceeding without consent, and, importantly, to 'sunset' clauses, whereby the powers expire two years after 'exit day'[205] and any regulations made under them expire five years after coming into effect.[206] Significantly, paragraph 21(2)(b) of schedule 3 to the Withdrawal Act amends schedule 4 to the Scotland Act by adding the Withdrawal Act 2018 to the list of provisions that cannot be modified by an Act of the Scottish Parliament.

The hearing of the UK Government's challenge to the Scottish Bill started on 24 July 2018, the 451st anniversary of the deposition of Mary Queen of Scots. The challenge required the UK Supreme Court to consider whether the Scottish legislation is contrary to the constitutional framework underpinning the devolution settlement and is incompetent, inter alia because, contrary to the Scotland Act 1998,[207] it modifies the power of the UK Government to make laws for Scotland and is contrary to section 2(1) of the ECA 1972.[208] It also required it to consider the effect of the provision adding the Withdrawal Act 2018 to the list of provisions that cannot be modified by an Act of the Scottish Parliament.

---

[200] J Gallagher, 'Clause 11: the Schleswig-Holstein question of the EU Withdrawal Bill' The Constitution Unit (2 May 2018), available at https://constitution-unit.com/2018/05/02/clause-11-the-schleswig-holstein-question-of-the-eu-withdrawal-bill/#more-6698, states that if the Welsh Bill survives the Supreme Court it will be repealed.
[201] D Lidington MP, 'Chancellor of the Duchy of Lancaster Speech to CBI Scotland', Speech delivered in Edinburgh (11 May 2018), available at https://www.gov.uk/government/speeches/chancellor-of-the-duchy-of-lancaster-speech-to-cbi-scotland.
[202] Welsh Government, 'Welsh Government agrees deal on Brexit Bill that respects devolution' (24 April 2018), available at https://gov.wales/newsroom/finance1/2018/item/?lang=en.
[203] European Union (Withdrawal) Act 2018, s 12, inserting s 30A to the Scotland Act 1998, s 109A to the Government of Wales Act 2006 and s 6A to the Northern Ireland Act 1998.
[204] European Union (Withdrawal) Act 2018, Explanatory Notes, para 36.
[205] The European Union (Withdrawal) Act 2018, s 20(1) defines this as 11 pm on 29 March 2019.
[206] The European Union (Withdrawal) Act 2018, s 12(9).
[207] Scotland Act 1998, s 28(7).
[208] See the restriction in Scotland Act 1998, para 1(2)(c) of sch 4, which falls under s 29(2)(c).

The Supreme Court rejected the challenges based on incompatibility with EU law and section 2(1) of the ECA 1972. It declined to assume an expansive constitutional role in relation to competencies that formerly belonged to the EU. It stated that it was not for it to express a view as to whether the devolved or UK institutions would acquire these competences. That involved 'questions of policy, which are the responsibility of our elected representatives and in which the wider civil society has an interest'.[209] The Court stated that its role is to determine as a matter of law whether, and to what extent, the Scottish Bill would be within the legislative competence of the Scottish Parliament. This role is, however, also to some extent, constitutional. The Court had regard to the aim of the Scotland Act to achieve a constitutional settlement, and recognised the importance of giving that Act a consistent and predictable interpretation so as to provide a coherent, stable and workable system for the Scottish Parliament. It did so by affirming the supremacy of the Westminster Parliament. Its holding that section 17 of the Scottish Bill would be outside the legislative competence of the Scottish Parliament because it would modify the Scotland Act is an uncontroversial vindication of the existing constitutional settlement. Its holding that a number of other sections of the Bill[210] would be outside the Parliament's competence because they would modify provisions of the UK Withdrawal Act 2018 is more striking. This is because it could be said that the Court thus accepted the power of the UK Parliament to alter the constitutional settlement, or at least the way it works in practice, by provisions such as paragraph 21(2)(b) of schedule 3 to the Withdrawal Act.

That other courts may also have an important role is illustrated by *Wightman v Secretary of State for Exiting the EU*. The issue was whether a notification of intent to withdraw from the EU under Article 50 can unilaterally be revoked. The Inner House of the Court of Session referred the question to the CJEU, which held that the Member State that gave the notification can unilaterally revoke it.[211]

The decision by the Supreme Court in *Miller's* case to leave the determination of the scope of the Sewel convention entirely to political mechanisms, reaffirmed in the decision on the UK Government's challenge to the Scottish Bill, has been criticised as giving insufficient attention to the legal constitution.[212] Leaving aside the tension between such criticism and the criticism that in relation to the use of the prerogative the majority gave insufficient weight to the political constitution, to which we have referred, the position taken is in our view constitutionally entirely orthodox. The challenge to the Scottish Bill demonstrates the importance of the courts' orthodox role: they are required to interpret the requirements of the devolution legislation. Where the issues turn on non-statutory constitutional principles,

---

[209] *The UK Withdrawal from the European Union (Legal Continuity) (Scotland) Bill – A Reference by the Attorney General and the Advocate General for Scotland (Scotland)* (n 191) [11].

[210] Ss 2(2), 5, 7(2)(b), 7(3), 8(2), 9A, 9B, 10(2), 10(3)(a), 10(4)(a), 11, 13B, 14, 14A, 15, 16, 19(1), 22, 26A(6), 33, and paras 11(a) and 16 of sch 1.

[211] *Wightman v Secretary of State for Exiting the EU* 2019 SC 111; *Case C621/18 Wightman & Others (Notification by a Member State of its intention to withdraw from the European Union)* [2019] QB 199.

[212] Elliott, 'The Supreme Court's Judgment in *Miller*' (n 97) 273–80; P Daly, '*Miller*: Legal and Political Fault Lines' [2017] *PL* 73, 80, 90; J Wolffe, 'Devolution Settlement' in Clarry (ed), *The UK Supreme Court Yearbook* (n 95) 356 ff. cf JF Larkin, '*Miller* and Northern Ireland: The Northern Ireland Constitution before the UK Supreme Court' in Clarry (ed), ibid 289 ff. Phillipson and Young, 'Would Use of the Prerogative to Denounce the ECHR "Frustrate" the Human Rights Act?' (n 169) 151, fn 8, state that because the devolved bodies are disabled from legislating contrary to 'the Convention rights', as defined in the HRA 1998, repeal of the HRA 1998 would trigger the Sewel convention since it would modify the distribution of powers between Westminster and the devolved nations.

in the absence of the development of a principle similar to the *Simms* principle of legality,[213] the orthodox approach may be unsatisfactory. This is because, where Sewel consent remains unforthcoming, the Withdrawal Act 2018, and in particular paragraph 21(2)(b) of schedule 3, shows that the consequences may be what Richard Rawlings has described as 'muscular usage of formal law through the medium of Parliamentary Sovereignty'.[214] That may well lead to further litigation on devolution issues and further strain on the Union and the constitutional structure of the UK.

IV. Conclusion

In our view, there is scope for focused doctrinal development of the common law to protect rights of a 'constitutional' or 'fundamental' nature, in particular through further development of the principle of proportionality. The impact and broader constitutional implications of *Miller's* case are less clear. It is possible that Brexit has raised unique constitutional questions, such that possible ramifications will be limited in other contexts. Much will depend on the courts' approach to defining statutory provisions that qualify as 'constitutional' and governing the relationship between the legislature and the executive. We consider that the courts play an important and legitimate role in addressing these difficult constitutional questions.

---

[213] *R v Secretary of State for the Home Department, ex parte Simms* (n 133) 131.
[214] R Rawlings, 'Brexit: Law, Constitution and Market', Miegunyah Lecture delivered at the University of Melbourne (20 March 2018).

PART 2

Public Law and Indigenous Peoples

6
Indigenous Rights, Judges and Judicial Review in New Zealand

MATTHEW SR PALMER[*]

E ngā mana, e ngā waka, e ngā reo, tēnā koutou, tēnā koutou, tēnā koutou katoa. My respects to the Wurundjeri peoples of the Kulin nations, the traditional owners of the land where I originally presented a draft of this chapter.

I. Introduction

In most colonised nations now, indigenous peoples are a minority of the population. They claim rights not on the basis of being a minority but on the basis of being indigenous. This is reflected in the Declaration on the Rights of Indigenous Peoples adopted by the United Nations General Assembly in 2007. The Declaration asserts civil, political, economic, social and cultural rights, of indigenous peoples collectively and of indigenous individuals. Indigeneity adds an additional layer to indigenous claims in terms of morals, politics and law. The deterioration of an indigenous people, or their culture, reduces the cultural diversity of the world.

There are many ways in which indigenous rights can be protected as a matter of constitutional design and law. But at a simplistic macro-constitutional level, a choice appears necessary between protection enforced through political representation and protection enforced by judges. In this chapter I ask: how do law and the judicial branch of government contribute to protection of indigenous rights in New Zealand, a constitutional system that relies primarily on political protection of indigenous rights? I examine the answer in two ways.

First, even under a constitution where indigenous rights are ultimately protected by politics rather than by law, the process of constitutional dialogue over time provides a role for the judiciary, along with other branches of government, in shaping constitutional protection. This only requires the judiciary to fulfil its conventional constitutional role

---

[*] This is a revised version of a paper presented to the Public Law Conference, 'Frontiers of Public Law', 11–13 July 2018, Melbourne Law School, Melbourne, Australia. I thank Sir David Baragwanath, Claire Charters, Dean Knight, Sir Geoffrey Palmer, Jessica Storey, Jason Varuhas, Ruth Wilkie and conference attendees for comments, and Jessica Storey for her research assistance. The views expressed in this paper are personal to the author.

of using reason to apply the law to specific factual contexts. But the iterative dynamic of interactions between the judicial and political branches of government reveals a distinctive judicial contribution to constitutional change over time. In New Zealand, the judiciary contributed significantly to constitutional dialogue regarding the meaning and the legal status of the Treaty of Waitangi, particularly from the 1970s to the 1990s.

Second, the law of judicial review is a primary case study of the judiciary developing law and engaging in constitutional dialogue in relation to claims of indigenous rights. The chapter examines patterns in the contemporary cases of judicial review in New Zealand that have invoked the Treaty of Waitangi. These cases have been a significant vehicle for protection of indigenous rights in some areas of law. They exhibit a more general blurring of grounds of judicial review. And they suggest the substantive principles of the Treaty have been developed to mirror the substantive law of judicial review.

II. Indigenous Rights in New Zealand

A. The Treaty of Waitangi

First, I explain something of the Treaty of Waitangi and New Zealand's constitutional framework and law. The Treaty of Waitangi was signed by the Crown and Māori on a variety of occasions and in a variety of places throughout the country during the course of 1840. This was preceded by a complex evolving context of contrasting private settler and missionary political pressure in London, increasing law and order problems for Māori from Europeans, purported land sales in Aotearoa New Zealand, and Colonial Office wavering about what to do.[1] Eventually, Britain dispatched Captain Hobson to treat with Māori. The Treaty was first signed on 6 February 1840 at Waitangi and then hawked around the country by agents of the Crown. By September 1840, some 530 signatures of Māori rangatira had been obtained. Midway through that process, in response to indications of separate settler negotiations with Māori in May 1840, Captain Hobson proclaimed sovereignty anyway. The Treaty was prepared in two languages: English and te reo Māori. All but 39 of the Māori signatures were to the Māori language version.

The three simple articles of the Treaty, and its preamble, contain serious linguistic and interpretive ambiguities:

- The preamble recited Queen Victoria's interest in protecting Māori rights and property (in the English version) or preserving their rangatiratanga and land (in the Māori version), and her appointment of Captain Hobson to treat with Māori for recognition of her sovereign authority (in English) or establishment of kāwanatanga (in Māori).

- In the first article the rangatira gave to the Queen all the rights and powers of sovereignty (in English) or complete kāwanatanga of their land (in Māori).

---

[1] C Orange, *The Treaty of Waitangi* (Wellington, Allen & Unwin, 1987); The Waitangi Tribunal, *He Whakaputanga me te Tiriti: The Declaration and the Treaty*, Wai 1040 (2014); MSR Palmer, 'Indigenous Rights: The Changing Place of the Treaty of Waitangi in the Constitutional Context of New Zealand' in DS Law (ed), *Constitutionalism in Context* (Cambridge, Cambridge University Press, forthcoming 2019).

- In the second article the Queen guaranteed to rangatira the full, exclusive and undisturbed possession of their lands, estates, forests, fisheries and other properties (in English) or their unqualified exercise of rangatiratanga over their whenua, kainga and taonga (lands, villages and treasures). Rangatira also gave to the Queen the exclusive right of pre-emption (in English) or sale (in Māori) of such lands as they were willing to sell.
- In the third article the Queen guaranteed Māori her protection and imparted to them the rights and privileges (in English) or tikanga (customs, in Māori) of British subjects.

In essence, the Crown acquired sovereignty, or kāwanatanga, a transliteration of governorship. It guaranteed Māori tino rangatiratanga, or full chieftainship. To put it mildly, there was room for disagreement as to what the Treaty meant even in 1840, let alone once British settler demand for Māori land exploded in the 1850s and 1860s.

B. New Zealand's Political Constitution

In the long term the rights of any group in a society are, of course, protected by and exposed to social, political and constitutional norms that evolve over time. Rights enforcement, even under written constitutions, is only as strong as the relationships between the groups of people who tolerate and influence the power arrangements constituting their polity. In the shorter term, individual decisions by those with power over the enforcement of rights have to take wider constitutional structures and processes as a given. In most western democracies, the key constitutional fault-line is that separating political and judicial powers. Which is stronger is a matter of constitutional design and evolution.

In most jurisdictions around the world, indigenous claims to distinctive existence have bubbled up through the relevant legal system. The legal sources, natures and scopes of these manifestations have been shaped by the constitutional culture of each jurisdiction and the pressure points accessible to indigenous peoples. In post-colonial common law jurisdictions, treaties have provided leverage where they exist, such as in Canada, New Zealand and the United States. The common law of aboriginal title, shaped by judicial perceptions of the interests of justice in the individual case, has been an alternative source of leverage in Canada, the United States and Australia. Access to political power has provided leverage in New Zealand.

The comparison between New Zealand and Canada is particularly instructive. They share marked similarities in their systems of Westminster government and their approach to relationships between the state and indigenous peoples. Yet, since the 1980s, they have diverged just as markedly in their respective reliance on political or judicial means of protecting indigenous rights.[2] I do not suggest either is necessarily better or more effective. Rather, each means of protection reflects and responds to the context and circumstances of the jurisdiction in which they have developed.

In 1982 Canada adopted the Charter of Rights and Freedoms, against which the judiciary is empowered to strike down inconsistent legislation. Section 35(1), unqualified by

---

[2] MSR Palmer, 'Constitutional Realism about Constitutional Protection: Indigenous Rights under a Judicialized and a Politicized Constitution' (2006) 29 *Dalhousie Law Journal* 1.

section 1's balancing provision or the section 33 legislative override, provides '[t]he existing aboriginal and treaty rights of the aboriginal peoples of Canada are hereby recognized and affirmed'. Judicial power to protect indigenous rights, against even legislation, has been entrenched ever since. The Court can hold legislation invalid on the basis of inconsistency with aboriginal and treaty rights under section 35. That is not to say the issues are easy. For example, in *Mikisew Cree First Nation v Canada (Governor General in Council)* in 2018, nine judges of the Canadian Supreme Court split four ways over whether indigenous peoples have a constitutional right to be consulted on government legislative proposals that would adversely affect them and, if so, whether legislation enacted in breach of that could be invalid.[3]

In 1985, three years after Canada's judicialisation of indigenous rights, a New Zealand Government proposed something similar: a bill of rights, including the Treaty of Waitangi, against which the judiciary would be empowered to strike down inconsistent legislation. In 1988, after 438 submissions, the Justice and Law Reform Committee of the House of Representatives reported its conclusion that New Zealanders just did not like the idea of such a supreme law.[4] As Professor Paul Rishworth stated, '[s]everal distinct strains of objection emerged, but foremost among them was that a constitutional bill of rights would elevate judicial power over parliamentary power, and be anti-democratic'.[5] Indeed, there was a significant view among Māori that putting the Treaty of Waitangi into law passed by Parliament would *diminish* its status. The Treaty would be transformed from a powerful normative symbol with enduring moral legitimacy into a mere legal instrument, capable of amendment.

The New Zealand Bill of Rights Act 1990 ('the Bill of Rights'), which was passed instead, explicitly disavows the ability of a court to hold any provision of any enactment to be impliedly repealed or revoked or in any way invalid or ineffective, or to decline to apply any provision of the enactment, by reason of its inconsistency with the Bill of Rights.[6] New Zealand courts long flirted with the idea they had jurisdiction to declare legislation inconsistent with the Bill of Rights with no other legal effect. The first declaration only issued in 2015. A majority of the Supreme Court confirmed the jurisdiction in 2018.[7] The Crown has announced its intention to introduce legislation providing explicitly for such jurisdiction, along with a process by which Parliament would respond to declarations of inconsistency. This would be constitutional dialogue indeed, but none of it would directly touch the legal validity of legislation.

So there is currently no supreme law in New Zealand. The judiciary has no legislatively acknowledged power to strike down legislation. Once the New Zealand Parliament attained the ability to amend its own constitution, and the Governor and the United Kingdom stopped refusing assent to legislation, there were no real checks on Parliament's power to

---

[3] *Mikisew Cree First Nation v Canada (Governor General in Council)* 2018 SCC 40.
[4] Justice and Law Reform Select Committee, 'Final Report on a White Paper on a Bill of Rights for New Zealand' [1987–1990] XVII *Appendices to the Journal of the House of Representatives* I8C.
[5] P Rishworth, 'The New Zealand Bill of Rights' in P Rishworth et al, *The New Zealand Bill of Rights* (Melbourne, Oxford University Press, 2003) 7.
[6] New Zealand Bill of Rights Act 1990, s 4.
[7] *Taylor v Attorney-General* [2015] 3 NZLR 791 (HC); *Attorney-General v Taylor* [2017] 3 NZLR 24 (CA); *Attorney-General v Taylor* [2018] NZSC 104, [2019] 1 NZLR 213.

legislate away indigenous rights, including inconsistently with the Treaty. Furthermore, there is only one, relatively small, house of Parliament, of 120 members. With tight party discipline since the 1930s and the abolition of the upper house, the Legislative Council, in 1950, the executive branch acquired 'unbridled power' in New Zealand.[8]

Having considered Canada's model of judicial checks on executive government, New Zealand pursued political checks on the power of executive government. In 1985 the concerns that led to the Bill of Rights White Paper also led to the establishment of a Royal Commission on the Electoral System, which issued a comprehensive report in December 1986.[9] It recommended New Zealand reform its plurality or 'first past the post' electoral system by adopting a system of mixed member proportional (MMP) representation along the lines of West Germany. By the early 1990s there was a public mood to restructure the political system that had itself restructured much of the rest of the government and economy. Referenda in 1992 and 1993 saw the Royal Commission's proposal for electoral reform enacted.[10]

As political science predicts, MMP destroyed the two-party duopoly on public power. This has had fundamental constitutional effects in New Zealand. No one party has won an overall majority of members in the House since. As a result, there must now be bargaining between parliamentary parties to form a government, to formulate policy and to pass legislation. The system of government has slowed down, the executive has less power, and Parliament has been revitalised. The effects of this have changed the basic dynamics of power in New Zealand government. Under MMP, every policy and legislative initiative is the subject of negotiation between parties in the search for a majority position in the House of Representatives. Government decision-making is now transactional. It is less efficient. Change tends to be less thoroughgoing. There are more pressure points at which various groups in society can influence the exercise of government power. A greater range of political opinion is represented in Parliament, is heard in public political debate and can influence New Zealand government decisions. Power has been at least somewhat bridled, through political rather than legal mechanisms.[11]

C. Political Protection of Indigenous Rights

Given the constitutional arrangements, indigenous rights in New Zealand ultimately rely on politics for protection. But compared with First Nations' share of 4 per cent of the population of Canada, Māori are 15 per cent of New Zealand's population. Māori therefore represent a sizable portion of the electorate, and their party votes have a direct influence on which of the two major parties is able to form and lead a government. Furthermore, since 1867, a number of seats in the House of Representatives have been reserved for Māori,

---

[8] G Palmer, *Unbridled Power? An Interpretation of New Zealand's Constitution and Government* (Wellington, Oxford University Press, 1979).
[9] *Report of the Royal Commission on the Electoral System: Towards a Better Democracy*, House of Representatives, H3 (December 1986).
[10] Electoral Act 1993.
[11] G Palmer and M Palmer, *Bridled Power: New Zealand's Constitution and Government*, 4th edn (Auckland, Oxford University Press, 2004).

originally as 'a useful way of rewarding Maori loyalists and placating Maori rebels, while also assuring critics in Britain that the colonists would look after Maori interests'.[12]

Since 1994, the number of Māori seats has varied with the number of Māori choosing to enrol on the parallel Māori electoral roll rather than on the general roll. Māori votes in the House have been crucial to the formation of successive governments since then. Since the 2017 election there have been more Māori members in Parliament, and in government, than ever before. At least 27 of the 120 Members of Parliament (MPs) (22 per cent) are Māori.[13] At least 19 of 63 (30 per cent) of the members of parliamentary caucuses supporting the Government are Māori. Eight of 26 (30 per cent) Ministers are Māori. The Deputy Prime Minister and Leader of the Opposition are Māori. At least six of the nine leaders and deputy leaders of parties in Parliament are Māori.

So New Zealand's constitution, and its constitutional protection of indigenous rights, is fundamentally political. That is so not only in the ultimate sense in which generational shifts in constitutional norms are extra-legal, but in the sense that conflicts between Māori and the Crown are primarily resolved through political means: legislation and negotiations.

Legally, the Treaty of Waitangi is generally incorporated into New Zealand law, in the Treaty of Waitangi Act 1975. But that Act allocates the role of interpreting the two language versions of the Treaty to a specially constituted Waitangi Tribunal, not the courts. In relation to some former Crown land and forestry assets the Tribunal's determinations have binding force. Otherwise they do not. The Treaty can also be said to be reasonably fully incorporated into New Zealand law in relation to Māori language, Māori land and Māori fisheries by the relevant legislation governing those important dimensions of te ao Māori.[14]

Otherwise, the Treaty is part in and part out of New Zealand law.[15] In 2018, the 'principles of the Treaty of Waitangi' were referred to in 25 Acts of the New Zealand Parliament other than those implementing Treaty settlements. Under those Acts, decision-makers are variously required to 'give effect to' the principles, 'not act in a manner inconsistent' with the principles, 'ensure full and balanced account is taken' of the principles, 'give particular recognition', 'take into account', 'have regard to' and 'acknowledge' the principles of the Treaty of Waitangi.[16] The Acts particularly concern natural resources and the environment, but also social services and local government. Such bare unelaborated references are more than lip service. Such a savings clause in section 9 of the State-Owned Enterprises Act 1986 (SOEs Act) was interpreted and applied with significant effect by the Court of Appeal in *New Zealand Māori Council v Attorney-General*, commonly known as the *SOEs case*, as discussed in section III.B.[17] After 2000, there was a trend for more expansive legislative provisions about what the Treaty means in relation to a particular area of law.[18]

---

[12] MPK Sorrenson, 'A History of Māori Representation in Parliament', Appendix B to the *Report of the Royal Commission on the Electoral System: Towards a Better Democracy* (n 9) B-20.

[13] Some additional MPs have Maori heritage but do not appear to self-identify as Māori.

[14] Te Ture Whenua Maori Act 1993; Maori Fisheries Act 2004; Te Ture mō Te Reo Māori 2016.

[15] On the legal status and force of the Treaty in New Zealand law, see MSR Palmer, *The Treaty of Waitangi in New Zealand's Law and Constitution* (Wellington, Victoria University Press, 2008) ch 4.

[16] See Palmer, *The Treaty of Waitangi* (n 15) 182–83.

[17] *New Zealand Māori Council v Attorney-General [SOEs case]* [1987] 1 NZLR 641 (CA).

[18] New Zealand Public Health and Disability Act 2000; Local Government Act 2002; Land Transport Management Act 2003; Public Records Act 2005. See Palmer, *The Treaty of Waitangi* (n 15) 100–01.

As I argued in a book in 2008, the overall effect of the Treaty in New Zealand law is incoherent.[19] The Treaty is part of New Zealand law for some purposes and not others. What it means in law, and what effect it has in practice, depends on how the judiciary interprets particular laws, in the particular factual context in which a case is brought. Hence the overall question addressed by this chapter: how does the judiciary contribute to protection of indigenous rights in an ultimately political constitution?

III. The Treaty of Waitangi and Constitutional Dialogue

A. Dialogue Theory

In 1997, constitutional scholars in Canada, including a New Zealander, Peter Hogg, offered a notion of constitutional dialogue in an article entitled 'The *Charter* Dialogue between Courts and Legislatures (Or Perhaps the *Charter of Rights* Isn't Such a Bad Thing After All)'.[20] Peter Hogg and Allison Bushell conducted empirical analysis, updated 10 years later with additional help from Wade Wright.[21] They identified 89 instances of the Canadian Supreme Court finding acts invalid between 1982 and 2007. In response to 67 of those 89 instances, the Canadian Parliament enacted new legislation to address its objective in a different way.

Elsewhere, I have offered proposals for enriching the dialogue metaphor as a descriptive, not normative, means of understanding constitutional and legal dynamics.[22] I suggest the ordinary exercise by the political and judicial branches of government of their conventional institutional functions, over time, constitutes dialogue not only about constitutional issues but also over more ordinary legal issues. The point is clear in New Zealand, which lacks a written constitution and where the constitutional slides into the legal. But I consider the point is a generic one. When a judge interprets the meaning of a law passed by a legislature, and the legislature reacts by changing it, that is a form of institutional dialogue about what the law is and should be: legal dialogue. When the point at issue is one of constitutional significance, legal dialogue becomes constitutional dialogue.

Legal and constitutional dialogue occur quintessentially between a jurisdiction's highest court and the legislature. But there is no reason why other institutional actors cannot also be conceived of as adding their voices to the mix. In New Zealand, in relation to the Treaty of Waitangi, the Waitangi Tribunal has been an important constitutional interlocutor. Its first four substantive reports, finding and developing a contemporary relational meaning on the Treaty, were influential on the Court of Appeal in the seminal *SOEs case*.

I have also proposed we can extend the metaphor by hearing those engaged in dialogue as speaking more or less loudly or strongly to each other. This provides a way of characterising,

---

[19] Palmer, *The Treaty of Waitangi* (n 15).
[20] PW Hogg and AA Bushell, 'The *Charter* Dialogue Between Courts and Legislatures (Or Perhaps the *Charter of Rights* Isn't Such a Bad Thing After All)' (1997) 35 *Osgoode Hall Law Journal* 75.
[21] PW Hogg, AA Bushell Thornton and WK Wright, '*Charter* Dialogue Revisited – or "Much Ado about Metaphors"' (2007) 45 *Osgoode Hall Law Journal* 1.
[22] For example, MSR Palmer, 'Constitutional Dialogue and the Rule of Law' (2017) 47 *Hong Kong Law Journal* 505.

descriptively, the strength of voice of one branch of government relative to the others, or relative to its own strength in the past. In New Zealand, the judiciary's voice is relatively muted.[23] The lack of a written constitution, supreme law or any other generally accepted power in the judiciary to invalidate an Act of Parliament affects the judicial voice. Proposals to create such a role have been rejected to date, though they are still offered.[24] The evolution of declarations of inconsistency may change that somewhat. The *SOEs case* was an occasion on which the New Zealand appellate courts raised their voice clearly. They did so repeatedly in the series of cases that followed. But, otherwise, as a general rule, New Zealand judges have become used to their relatively quiet role, occasionally talked over by Parliament. Parliament speaks loudly in New Zealand, from its one House. Its messages are more mixed than they used to be, with the executive's influential voice being moderated by negotiations between political parties necessitated by MMP. But there is no doubt Parliament speaks more loudly than the judiciary in New Zealand.

Extending the dialogue metaphor in another direction provides a way of characterising the different perspectives adopted by different institutions as different languages.[25] I have suggested the language of the judiciary is the methodology of the common law, distinctively characterised by the use of reason in applying the law in specific factual contexts. This is an inductive form of reasoning, by analogy and distinction, from the particulars of individual cases towards the general rule. There must be logical links of reasoning that chain the law applied, and the facts to which it is applied, to the result. Those links of reasoning must bear the weight of public scrutiny, according to the principle of open justice.[26] And the requirement to provide reasons for our decisions is a crucial check and balance on the power of the judiciary. It is society's version of requiring judicial decision-making to think slowly, deliberatively and logically, using the body politic's prefrontal cortex.[27]

A court's perspective of a law is very different from that of Parliament or the public service. Decision-making about law by the political branches of government – the executive and legislature – results in legislation. Legislation is usually drafted generally: a general rule, generally stated, with general application. But in applying the law in individual cases, the judiciary confronts the more precise meaning of legislation in a messy factual context of humanity. The judiciary is required to be alive to the effects of applying the general words of an Act's text in a particular circumstance to particular people. That context informs judicial analysis of Parliament's general purpose in passing the Act. As the New Zealand Supreme Court has stated, apparent textual meaning should always be cross-checked against purpose, and in determining purpose the court 'must obviously have regard to both the immediate and the general legislative context'.[28]

---

[23] ibid 516.
[24] G Palmer, 'A Bill of Rights for New Zealand: A White Paper' [1984–1985] I *Appendices to the Journal of the House of Representatives* A6, 29; G Palmer and A Butler, *Towards Democratic Renewal: Ideas for Constitutional Change in New Zealand* (Wellington, Victoria University Press, 2018).
[25] Palmer, 'Constitutional Dialogue' (n 22) 517.
[26] *Lewis v Wilson & Horton Ltd* [2000] 3 NZLR 546 (CA), [76]–[79]; and see *R v Taito* [2003] 3 NZLR 577 (PC), [17].
[27] D Kahneman, *Thinking Fast and Slow* (London, Allen Lane, 2011).
[28] *Commerce Commission v Fonterra Co-operative Group Ltd* [2007] 3 NZLR 767 (SC) [22].

By contrast, the paradigm of public policy analysis, spoken by the public service in proposing policy and legislative reform, is quite different. Policy analysts typically start with the Government's general objectives. They identify the problem to be resolved. They identify not just arguments for and against a binary set of outcomes, but all possible options for addressing the problem. They analyse the options in terms of which will best achieve the general objectives, assessing financial, legal and all other sets of implications. This is deductive reasoning – from the general to the particular. It is more abstract. It is less interested in factual circumstances. Its evidence derives from general social science analysis rather than anecdotes from a particular fact scenario. It looks to the future, not the past. In some ways policy analysis is the direct inverse of legal analysis.

And I have previously suggested politicians tend to speak the language of politics: compromise, negotiation, log-rolling, persuasion;[29] the dark arts of the deal, now taken to an extreme in the United States. While politicians have policy objectives, to greater or lesser extents they have difficulty accomplishing them out of office. The need for electoral popularity lends a primacy to public responsiveness that judges and public servants do not experience so directly.

So I suggest, as a descriptive matter, not only do the institutions of government engage in constitutional dialogue through the routine exercise of their functions in affecting the generic exercise of public power, speaking more or less loudly, but they do so in different languages. As a normative matter, I have suggested the constitutional health of any government is improved by having the different branches of government that exercise public power thinking and speaking in different languages.[30] We want an institution thinking abstractly and generically about the formulation of general policy and legal principles. Separately, as a cross-check, we want an institution thinking contextually about how those general principles apply to the reality of specific facts of particular cases. Each perspective checks the other, consistent with the separation of powers and the rule of law. Not only is the context and use of reason in judicial decision-making of value in itself, but it is distinctive from the perspectives of the other branches of government. Normatively, this reinforces the importance of judges sticking to their conventional role of considering context and using reason in their decision-making.

The value of the insight available from dialogue theory is that it breaks through the tired old binary question of which branch of government is supreme. Hogg and Bushell's analysis immediately demonstrated the staleness of a static view of parliamentary sovereignty or judicial supremacy. Together with the bells and whistles I suggest, the notion of constitutional dialogue offers a dynamic alternative to understanding the location not of supremacy, but of the changing dynamics of relative power between the political and judicial branches of government, exercised over time in a process of constitutional dialogue.

---

[29] MSR Palmer, 'Open the Doors and Where are the People? Constitutional Dialogue in the Shadow of the People' in C Charters and DR Knight (eds), *We, The People(s): Participation in Governance* (Wellington, Victoria University Press, 2011) 50.
[30] Palmer, 'Constitutional Dialogue' (n 22) 523.

B. Constitutional Dialogue Over the Treaty of Waitangi

The dialogue metaphor is useful as a means of exploring the development of one of the most significant constitutional developments in New Zealand in the last 50 years: the reinterpretation of the meaning and status of the Treaty of Waitangi.[31]

As might be expected, after its signing there was continuing political and legal contest over the meaning and status of the Treaty of Waitangi.[32] There was, eventually, expression of a domestic legal status of the Treaty by the courts. Most definitively, in 1941, the Judicial Committee of the Privy Council appears to have affirmed the Treaty is not part of New Zealand law unless Parliament specifically so provides, as with other international treaties.[33]

Then, from 1973 to 1993, the institutions of New Zealand government reinterpreted the meaning and legal and constitutional status of the Treaty of Waitangi through a process of constitutional dialogue.[34] In the late 1960s and early 1970s there was a renaissance of Māori cultural and political assertiveness. In 1971, the National Cabinet asked for a paper about whether the Treaty should have the force of law.[35] The recommendation that it should not, referring to the English language version, was accepted. From 1973 to 1975 a committee of the Labour Government's parliamentary caucus made a proposal to Cabinet for investigation of Māori claims, referring to both language versions. The first proposal was to set up a select committee to inquire into allegations of breaches of the Treaty. Instead, Cabinet decided to propose legislation. The resulting Treaty of Waitangi Act 1975 created the Waitangi Tribunal to interpret and make non-binding recommendations to government about contemporary breaches of the Treaty.

After a delayed start, the Waitangi Tribunal issued four reports, from 1983 to 1986, which interpreted the meaning of the Treaty in a contemporary context. The Treaty represented a relational compromise, 'the gift of the right to make laws in return for the promise to do so, so as to acknowledge and protect the interests of the indigenous inhabitants'.[36]

In 1985, Parliament extended the Tribunal's jurisdiction, retrospectively, to alleged historical breaches of the Treaty by the Crown since 1840. Most alleged breaches involved the taking of land. Yet in the State-Owned Enterprises (SOEs) Bill in 1986, the Crown proposed to transfer, out of Crown ownership, land Māori claimed had been taken from them in breach of the Treaty. Following an urgent recommendation by the Waitangi Tribunal while the SOEs Bill was going through the House of Representatives, a savings clause was included, providing '[n]othing in this Act shall permit the Crown to act in a manner that is inconsistent with the principles of the Treaty of Waitangi'.

---

[31] Palmer, *The Treaty of Waitangi* (n 15) ch 3.

[32] See, eg, H Robinson, 'Simple Nullity or Birth of Law and Order? The Treaty of Waitangi in Legal and Historiographical Discourse from 1877 to 1970' (2010) 24 *New Zealand Universities Law Review* 259; M Hickford, 'John Salmond and Native Title in New Zealand: Developing a Crown Theory on the Treaty of Waitangi, 1910–1920' (2008) 38 *Victoria University of Wellington Law Review* 853.

[33] *Te Heuheu Tukino v Aotea District Māori Land Board* [1941] NZLR 590 (PC). For a contextual view, see A Frame, 'Hoani Te Heuheu's Case in London 1940–1941: An Explosive Story' (2006) 22 *New Zealand Universities Law Review* 148.

[34] Palmer, *The Treaty of Waitangi* (n 15) ch 5.

[35] ibid 131–33, 179; Palmer, 'Indigenous Rights' (n 1).

[36] The Waitangi Tribunal, *Report of the Waitangi Tribunal on the Motunui-Waitara Claim*, 2nd edn, Wai 6 (1989) [11.3].

Section 9 became 'a prompt for litigation'.[37] Based on those apparently innocuous words, the New Zealand Māori Council successfully enjoined the Crown from transferring almost four million hectares of land, worth billions of dollars, to SOEs. The *SOEs case* in 1987 was simply the most constitutionally significant judgment in New Zealand's history. In five separate judgments, using reason and context, the Court of Appeal followed the Tribunal's lead on the meaning of the Treaty, using an analogy with partnership to describe the relationship between the Crown and Māori. The Court required the Crown and the New Zealand Māori Council to negotiate a regime to protect Māori claims to the Waitangi Tribunal before transferring land to SOEs.

The *SOEs case* was decided in the context of specific Māori claims. The Court directed the plaintiffs to nominate three test cases of the loss of Māori land to illustrate their contentions.[38] They nominated:

- a claim by Ngāi Tahu for breach by the Crown of undertakings in taking 600,000 acres of land in Otakou;
- a claim by the then-landless Ngāti Tama for breach by the Crown in unjustly confiscating 462,000 acres of land in 1863; and
- a claim not yet made by Ngāti Whātua over the taking of some 10,000 acres of land, including urupa (burial grounds), for sand-dune reclamation that was no longer required.

Affidavit evidence was adduced. Leading counsel for the plaintiffs, Sir David Baragwanath as he became, considered the evidence of Dame Whina Cooper 'pivotal' in enabling the Court to understand the whole picture and reach the conclusion it did.[39] Cooke P's judgment characterised the affidavit as including 'eloquent and moving passages'.[40] Richardson J's judgment traversed the three illustrative cases, and he was 'satisfied that each raises an arguable case for consideration by the Waitangi Tribunal'.[41]

The outcome of these negotiations was legislated for by Parliament in the Treaty of Waitangi (State Enterprises) Act 1988. Under it, the Waitangi Tribunal acquired power to require that land be resumed, compulsorily and at market value, by the Crown from whomever then owned it and be returned to a Māori claimant in respect of a breach of the Treaty. Further litigation followed over preservation of the Crown's ability to provide other sorts of redress, such as coal and forestry assets. The courts gave the same sorts of answers. Further judicial reinforcement of the Court of Appeal's and Waitangi Tribunal's approaches to the meaning of the Treaty came in 1993 from the Privy Council, then New Zealand's highest court, in relation to broadcasting assets.[42]

---

[37] For an account of the passage of s 9, see M Hickford, 'Quasi-constitutionality and the Treaty of Waitangi: Historicity and the Political' in R Albert and J Colón-Ríos (eds), *Quasi-Constitutionality and Constitutional Statutes: Forms, Functions, Applications* (London, Routledge, 2019).
[38] *SOEs case* (n 17) 654.
[39] D Baragwanath, 'Arguing the Case for the Appellants' in J Ruru (ed), *'In Good Faith': Symposium Proceedings Marking the 20th Anniversary of the Lands Case* (Dunedin, New Zealand Law Foundation and Faculty of Law, University of Otago, 2008) 28.
[40] *SOEs case* (n 17) 662.
[41] ibid 674.
[42] *New Zealand Maori Council v Attorney-General [Broadcasting Assets case]* [1994] 1 NZLR 513; [1994] 1 AC 466 (PC).

The context has changed since then as a series of settlements of historical breaches of the Treaty were negotiated between the Crown and Māori from 1994. Whether that meant a change in the application of law was tested in 2013 when the Crown pursued partial privatisation of SOEs without a special regime to protect Māori claims to water and in the context of a different legislative framework. The Supreme Court confirmed the same legal principles still endure.[43] It accepted 'privatisation may limit the scope to provide some forms of redress which are currently at least theoretically possible'.[44] But this was a policy on which an election campaign had just been fought by a re-elected Government. In its judgment, the Court traversed '[t]he changes in the social and legislative context since the *SOE case* was decided'.[45] It stated 'the trend since the *SOE case* should provide reassurance that Māori claims are not being ignored' and '[i]t appears from the policy initiatives and from the assurances given in the litigation that the message that there is need for action on these claims has been accepted'.[46] The Court was not persuaded material impairment arose from the proposed sale of shares, having regard to:

(a) the assurances given by the Crown, (b) the extent to which such options are substantially in prospect, (c) the capacity of the Crown to provide equivalent and meaningful redress, and (d) the proven willingness and ability of the Crown to provide such redress.[47]

Elsewhere I have characterised this as judicial statecraft (and judicial jujitsu).[48]

As even this potted summary makes clear, the reinterpretation of the legal meaning and status of the Treaty of Waitangi from 1973 to 1993, subtly confirmed in 2013, exemplifies a process of constitutional dialogue. Political pressure led the executive to propose and Parliament to create the Waitangi Tribunal, which subsequently recommended direct legislative reference to the Treaty. That prompted litigation that gave a contemporary relational meaning to the Treaty and, through negotiation with Māori and more legislation, greater legal power to the Tribunal. It has resulted in a reconciliation of authoritative views of the meaning of the Treaty in the context of contemporary New Zealand social, economic, political and cultural conditions. And court decisions have, in turn, guided further decision-making by the Waitangi Tribunal and the executive. Judicial participation in such constitutional dialogue, through courts simply performing their conventional roles, can contribute to protecting the rights of indigenous peoples in a political constitution.

IV. The Treaty of Waitangi and Judicial Review

When the judiciary performs its conventional role of applying the law in specific cases, it also develops the law. This is the other dimension of the courts' role in protecting indigenous rights I examine. Many of the seminal indigenous rights cases in New Zealand, including

---

[43] *New Zealand Māori Council v Attorney-General* [*Water case*] [2013] 3 NZLR 31 (SC).
[44] ibid [149].
[45] ibid [147].
[46] ibid [148].
[47] ibid.
[48] M Palmer, 'Judicial Review' in M-R Russell and M Barber (eds), *The Supreme Court of New Zealand 2004–2013* (Wellington, Thomson Reuters, 2015).

the *SOEs case*, arose out of judicial review of state action claimed to be in conflict with the Treaty. So, in particular, I examine how the New Zealand judiciary has applied the law of judicial review in the Treaty context.

I acknowledge, of course, that cases seeking to uphold customary title and aboriginal rights of Māori also seek to uphold indigenous rights.[49] So do cases concerning Māori land or other Māori property rights or fiduciary duties, some of which have been significant in New Zealand.[50] Of course Māori can also use other law to seek to advance Treaty-related interests, including contract law or trust law.[51] And some cases traditionally viewed as Treaty cases are brought in reliance on statutory provisions that exist because of the background of the Treaty, rather than directly in reliance on the Treaty or its principles.[52] But my focus here is on the use of the law of judicial review to invoke the Treaty of Waitangi. Judicial review is the primary means by which the judiciary supervises the legality of decision-making by those wielding the coercive powers of the state. Examining these judicial review cases reveals patterns in the law of judicial review as well as a close relationship between the substance of judicial review law and the substance of the principles of the Treaty of Waitangi, as interpreted by the judiciary.

I identify 53 cases that invoke the Treaty of Waitangi directly in judicial review proceedings. This list should include almost all such judgments of the senior courts since the *SOEs case*. There are, of course, overlaps with other causes of action such as breach of contract[53] and breach of fiduciary duty.[54] In addition, appeals on the basis of error of law can be viewed as effectively the same as judicial review in substance, as illustrated by these six appeals:

- *Barton-Prescott v Director-General of Social Welfare*: a 1997 appeal of a Family Court decision not to award a grandmother custody of a Māori child being adopted out of the whanau.[55] A full court of the High Court found all Acts dealing with the status, future and control of children are to be interpreted as coloured by the principles of the Treaty of Waitangi, and found family organisation is 'among those things which the Treaty was intended to preserve and protect'.[56] However, the Court concluded the baby's needs would not be best met by awarding custody to the appellant.[57]

- *Watercare Services Ltd v Minhinnick*: a 1997 appeal of an Environment Court decision under the Resource Management Act (RMA) 1991 to cease construction of a sewerage

---

[49] For example, see *Attorney-General v Ngati Apa* [2003] 3 NZLR 643 (CA) and *Takamore v Clarke* [2013] 2 NZLR 733 (SC).
[50] *New Zealand Māori Council v Attorney-General [Te Arawa Cross Claim]* [2008] 1 NZLR 318 (CA); *Paki v Attorney-General (No 2)* [2015] 1 NZLR 67 (SC); *Proprietors of Wakatu v Attorney-General* [2017] 1 NZLR 423 (SC).
[51] *Proprietors of Taharoa C v Māori Trustee* (1993) 7 PRNZ 236 (HC); *New Zealand Māori Council v Foulkes* [2015] NZAR 1441 (HC).
[52] For example, the Maori Fisheries Act 1989.
[53] *Chetham v Mighty River Power* [2014] NZHC 3202; *Te Tai Tokerau Mapo Trust v Chief Executive of Ministry of Health* HC Whangarei CIV-2010-488-307, 5 August 2011.
[54] See, eg, *Te Runanga o Wharekauri Rekohu Inc v Attorney General [Sealords case]* [1993] 2 NZLR 301 (CA); *Kai Tohu Tohu o Puketapu Hapu Inc v Attorney-General* HC Wellington CP344/97, 5 February 1999; *New Zealand Māori Council v Attorney-General* CA134/00, 13 July 2000 [*Radio Spectrum case*]; *Te Runanga o Ngai Tahu v Attorney-General* HC Auckland CIV-1113-03, 6 November 2003; *Manukau Urban Māori Authority Inc v Treaty of Waitangi Fisheries Commission* HC Auckland CP122/95, 28 November 2003.
[55] *Barton-Prescott v Director-General of Social Welfare* [1997] 3 NZLR 179 (Full HC).
[56] ibid 184.
[57] ibid 190.

pipe under a designation, because the ground was wāhi tapu (sacred, often burial, places).[58] The Court of Appeal found the construction was within the designation and the Act's reference to the Treaty did not confer a right of veto.

- *Bleakley v Environmental Risk Management Authority*: a 2001 appeal of an Environmental Risk Management Authority decision to approve testing of a genetically modified organism on Ngati Wairere land.[59] A majority of a full court of the High Court found that, while the Treaty imposed a duty of active protection on the Crown, it did not require action beyond what was reasonable in the prevailing circumstances.[60]
- *Friends and Community of Ngawha Inc v Minister of Corrections*: a 2002 appeal of an Environment Court decision to allow building of a prison on a site said to be occupied by a taniwha.[61] The High Court declined the appeal, finding section 8 of the RMA 1991 did not require consideration of alternative sites to fulfil the Treaty principle of active protection.[62]
- *Takamore Trustees v Kapiti Coast District Council*: a 2003 appeal of an Environment Court decision to confirm designation of a road over land said to be wāhi tāpu.[63] The High Court agreed the Environment Court had failed to take into account Treaty principles as required by the RMA 1991.
- *Taranaki-Whanganui Conservation Board v Environmental Protection Authority*: a 2018 appeal of an Environment Protection Authority decision to grant consents to extract, process and discharge seabed material.[64] The High Court found the Authority was not required to administer and interpret the relevant Act consistently with the principles of the Treaty, but nonetheless still considered the interests of iwi (tribes) under the Treaty.[65]

These were appeals of decisions on the basis of error of law. Errors of law tend either to involve inconsistency with substantive legislation, which also constitutes illegality under judicial review, or inadequacy in the decision-making processes as under judicial review of the process of decision-making. Ironically, given the traditional emphasis on distinguishing appeal and review, it is effectively the same law being applied.

A. The Nature of the Decisions Judicially Reviewed

The 53 cases of judicial review that rely on the Treaty of Waitangi include cases of great significance to government and to Māori. The seminal 1987 *SOEs case* deferred the transfer of billions of dollars' worth of Crown land and assets in pursuance of the Government's

---

[58] *Watercare Services Ltd v Minhinnick* [1998] 1 NZLR 294 (CA).
[59] *Bleakley v Environmental Risk Management Authority* [2001] 3 NZLR 213 (Full HC).
[60] ibid [82]–[83], citing *Broadcasting Assets case* (n 42).
[61] *Friends and Community of Ngawha Inc v Minister of Corrections* [2002] NZRMA 401 (HC). (A taniwha is a supernatural creature in Māori tradition.)
[62] ibid [55].
[63] *Takamore Trustees v Kapiti Coast District Council* [2003] 3 NZLR 496 (HC).
[64] *Taranaki-Whanganui Conservation Board v Environmental Protection Authority* [2018] NZHC 2217.
[65] ibid [238]–[243].

programme of corporatisation, in an election year. The 2013 *Water case* could have done the same with the partial privatisation of hydro-electricity generation companies, which had been a central plank of the Government's re-election campaign in 2011.

There are also patterns in the nature of the decisions under challenge in these cases. I suggest judicial review proceedings based on the Treaty of Waitangi have fallen, so far, into five broad categories of challenge:

- Crown divestment of land and assets that might prejudice Treaty settlements;
- Treaty settlement processes;
- resource management and conservation decisions;
- commercial regulatory decisions; and
- social services and other decisions.

i. Challenges to Crown Divestment of Land and Assets

The earliest but ongoing group of judicial reviews, 14 in number, comprised challenges to divestment of land and assets that could otherwise be used to satisfy Māori Treaty claims. The first four challenges, by the pan-Māori New Zealand Māori Council, were successful:

- the 1987 *SOEs case*;[66]
- the 1989 *Coal case*;[67]
- the 1989 *Forestry case*;[68] and
- the 1990 *Radio frequencies case*.[69]

Five subsequent challenges, mainly involving assets less directly connected to land and culture, were unsuccessful:

- the 1992 *Ngati Whatua o Orakei* case about negotiations over Māori land;[70]
- the 1993 *Broadcasting assets case*;[71]
- the 1993 *Hydro-electric dams case* (against local authorities);[72]
- the 1996 *Commercial radio assets case*;[73] and
- the 2000 *Radio Spectrum case*.[74]

In the 2013 *Water case*, the Supreme Court allowed partial privatisation of electricity-generating former SOEs, as Mixed Ownership Model (MOM) companies, to proceed.[75]

---

[66] *SOEs case* (n 17).
[67] *Tainui Māori Trust Board v Attorney-General* [*Coal case*] [1989] 2 NZLR 513 (CA).
[68] *New Zealand Māori Council v Attorney-General* [*Forestry case*] [1989] 2 NZLR 142 (CA).
[69] *Attorney-General v New Zealand Māori Council* [*Radio Frequencies case*] [1991] 2 NZLR 129 (CA).
[70] *Ngati Whatua O Orakei Māori Trust Board v Attorney-General* HC Auckland M1501/92, 18 November 1992.
[71] *Broadcasting Assets case* (n 42).
[72] *Te Runanganui o Te Ika Whenua Inc Society v Attorney-General* [*Hydro-electric dams case*] [1994] 2 NZLR 20 (CA).
[73] *New Zealand Māori Council v Attorney-General* [*Commercial Radio Assets case*] [1996] 3 NZLR 140 (CA).
[74] *Radio Spectrum case* (n 54).
[75] *Water case* (n 43).

The context mattered. The Court held the Crown to its undertakings to settle claims alleging bodies of water, such as rivers and lakes, were used inconsistently with the Treaty. The difference between success and failure of these claims also appears related to whether the Court considered a system of protection over the assets was necessary for the Crown to fulfil its Treaty obligations in the context of each case. Three other challenges by claimants, to proposed decisions regarding specific properties, failed; perhaps due to the same distinction:

- in 1998, in *Ngati Koata No Rangitoto ki te Tonga Trust v Minister of Transport*, interim relief was refused on a challenge to a Crown decision that would have changed the value of land that could potentially be the subject of a later Treaty settlement;[76]
- a 1999 Tuwharetoa challenge to a transfer of land from an SOE to the Taupo District Council, on the basis of inadequacy of the 1988 compulsory resumption regime;[77] and
- a 2014 challenge to sale, by an MOM company, of land that was not subject to compulsory resumption.[78]

The most recent such case, in 2016, *Ririnui v Landcorp Farming Ltd*, is more opaque and more interesting.[79] A majority of the Supreme Court held a decision by Landcorp, an SOE, to sell land was judicially reviewable given one of its legitimate activities was to assist the Crown to meet its Treaty obligations. It held Ministers were legally entitled to ask Landcorp to halt a tender process to give Ngāti Mākino an opportunity to purchase the land, and Landcorp did not act improperly in acceding to that request. However, the Ministers' decision not to intervene similarly on behalf of Ngāti Whakahemo was held to be based on an error: they wrongly believed Whakahemo's Treaty claim had been settled.[80]

ii. Challenges to Treaty Settlement Processes

Eleven cases involve challenges to decisions regarding the process of settling iwi or hapū (sub-tribe) Treaty claims. By contrast with their willingness to intervene to avoid prejudice to potential Treaty settlements involving redress directly related to Māori land or culture, the courts have been more reluctant to intervene in Treaty settlements that have almost always been effected by legislation. In four challenges to Crown decisions in such 'political' processes, until 2012, the courts declined to get involved, including in relation to cross-claims by one iwi about decisions in relation to another:

- In 1993, the *Sealords case* was an unsuccessful challenge to a settlement by the Crown and Māori of fisheries claims, which was to be effected by legislation.[81] The Court of Appeal held there was no doubt the principle of non-interference by the courts in parliamentary proceedings applied so as to require the courts to refrain from prohibiting a Minister from introducing a Bill into Parliament.[82]

---

[76] *Ngati Koata No Rangitoto ki te Tonga Trust v Minister of Transport* CA296/98, 18 December 1998.
[77] *Te Heu Heu v Attorney-General* [1999] 1 NZLR 98 (HC).
[78] *Chetham v Mighty River Power* (n 53).
[79] *Ririnui v Landcorp Farming Ltd* [2016] 1 NZLR 1056 (SC).
[80] ibid [94]–[96], [147], [186].
[81] *Sealords case* (n 54).
[82] ibid 307–08.

- In 1999, in *Kai Tohu Tohu o Puketapu Hapu Inc v Attorney-General*, the Puketapu hapū challenged the Crown's decision to negotiate with Te Atiawa Iwi Authority on the hapū's behalf.[83] The High Court held the principles of the Treaty were not justiciable because they were not statutorily incorporated, negotiation was a political process and the Minister had not acted outside his powers.
- In 2002, in *Pouwhare v Attorney-General*, a Treaty claimant unsuccessfully challenged the decision of the Minister in charge of Treaty of Waitangi Negotiations about a settlement with Ngāti Awa on grounds it would prejudice any potential settlement with its own iwi.[84] The Court concluded it was fatal to the claim that the decisions challenged 'essentially involve policy and are subject to a ratification process and the political process', which, if passed into legislation, 'will be inviolate and totally beyond the reach of the Courts [sic] supervision'.[85]
- In 2005, a claim similar to *Pouwhare*, challenging the advice to the Crown leading to a settlement deed with another iwi said to prejudice pending Tribunal claims, was also dismissed in *Milroy v Attorney-General*.[86] The Court of Appeal said examining the advice of officials would take the courts 'into the very heart of the policy formation process of government'[87] and that the case was indistinguishable from the principle in *Sealords*.[88]

However, in 2012, in *Port Nicholson Block Settlement Trust v Attorney-General*, Taranaki Whānui challenged the Crown's failure to consult them over settling with Ngāti Toa.[89] The High Court held the issue was justiciable, and there was a legitimate expectation of consultation which was satisfied. Extending this, in 2018, in *Ngāti Whātua Ōrākei Trust v Attorney-General*, a majority of the Supreme Court sounded

> a note of caution about the extent to which the principle of non-interference in parliamentary proceedings has been held to apply to decisions somewhat distant from, for example, the decision of a Minister to introduce a Bill to the House or from debate in the House.[90]

It overturned the striking-out of challenges involving live issues as to the nature and scope of rights claimed by Ngāti Whātua Ōrākei, which it considered would not interfere with parliamentary proceedings.

The identity of the decision-maker also may make a difference. Away from the political and parliamentary context of settlements, courts appear somewhat more comfortable reviewing decisions of the Waitangi Tribunal or Māori Appellate Court, even if they relate to settlement negotiations:

- In 1995, in *Hauraki Maori Trust Board v Waitangi Tribunal*, the applicant sought review of the Tribunal's decision to enquire into the processes adopted by the Treaty of

---

[83] *Kai Tohu Tohu o Puketapu Hapu Inc v Attorney-General* (n 54).
[84] *Pouwhare v Attorney-General* HC Wellington CP78/02, 30 August 2002.
[85] ibid [45].
[86] *Milroy v Attorney-General* [2005] NZAR 562 (CA).
[87] ibid [11].
[88] ibid [14].
[89] *Port Nicholson Block Settlement Trust v Attorney-General* [2012] NZHC 3181.
[90] *Ngāti Whātua Ōrākei Trust v Attorney-General* [2018] NZSC 84, [46].

Waitangi Fisheries Commission.[91] The Court held the Tribunal's inquiry was premature as the Commission had not yet proposed a policy.
- In 2000, in *Ngati Apa ki Te Waipounamu Trust v R*, the applicant challenged a Māori Appellate Court decision in favour of Ngāi Tahu in order to pre-empt impediments to their own settlement.[92] The Court of Appeal ruled they were not prevented from alleging the Māori Appellate Court decision and subsequent legislation breached the Treaty.
- In 2004, in *Ngati Apa ki Te Waipounamu Trust v R*, Ngāti Apa claimants unsuccessfully challenged a decision of the Māori Appellate Court determining tribal boundaries with other South Island iwi on grounds of natural justice.[93] The Court of Appeal held additional duties said to arise from the principles of the Treaty were 'encompassed within the principles of natural justice and fairness'.[94]
- In 2009, in *Attorney-General v Mair*, a Treaty claimant unsuccessfully challenged the Waitangi Tribunal's refusal to give urgency to hearing two claims because of possible prejudice by other settlements.[95]
- In 2018, in *Baker v Waitangi Tribunal*, claimants challenged the Waitangi Tribunal's finding that the Crown should not have recognised the claimants' mandate to negotiate.[96] The Court found the challenge was arguable but declined interim relief.

iii. Challenges to Resource Management and Conservation Decisions

In a grouping of 13 cases, challenges to resource management and conservation decisions have often achieved some success. That has usually been on the basis of a right of Māori under the Treaty to be consulted or for their interests to be considered, but occasionally has rested on protection of substantive rights:

- In 1987, in *Huakina Development Trust v Waikato Valley Authority*, the Huakina Development Trust challenged a planning tribunal decision to grant a right to discharge treated dairy shed water into a stream where the criteria were unspecified in statute.[97] The High Court upheld the challenge, holding the Treaty was 'essential to the foundation of New Zealand' and 'part of the fabric of New Zealand society'.[98]
- In 1990, in the *Fisheries case*, the iwi of Muriwhenua challenged the use of fisheries quota. They were successful in obtaining interim relief, resulting in settlement instead of a substantive hearing.[99] Cooke P, for the Court, observed the Treaty may be an assurance for the protection of customary title.[100]

---

[91] *Hauraki Māori Trust Board v Waitangi Tribunal* HC Wellington CP171/95, 31 July 1995.
[92] *Ngati Apa Ki Te Waipounamu Trust v R* [2000] 2 NZLR 659 (CA).
[93] *Ngati Apa Ki Te Waipounamu Trust v Attorney-General* [2004] 1 NZLR 462 (CA)
[94] ibid [33].
[95] *Attorney-General v Mair* [2009] NZCA 625.
[96] *Baker v Waitangi Tribunal* [2018] NZHC 2348.
[97] *Huakina Development Trust v Waikato Valley Authority* [1987] 2 NZLR 188 (HC).
[98] ibid 210.
[99] *Te Runanga o Muriwhenua Inc v Attorney-General [Fisheries case]* [1990] 2 NZLR 641 (CA).
[100] ibid 655.

- In 1995, in *Ngai Tahu Māori Trust Board v Director-General of Conservation (Whalewatching Case)*, Ngāi Tahu successfully challenged the Director-General of Conservation's decision to issue a competing whale-watching permit.[101] The Court of Appeal held Ngāi Tahu was entitled to a reasonable degree of preference in applying for permits.[102]
- In 1998, in *Ngatiwai Trust Board v Minister of Conservation*, Ngātiwai successfully challenged the Minister's decision to ban all fishing, including customary fishing, in a marine reserve, without considering its position.[103]
- In 1999, in *Ngati Apa ki te Waipounamu Trust v Attorney-General*, iwi challenged the District Council's revocation of a moratorium on coastal permits for marine farms in the Marlborough Sounds in an area over which the iwi had ongoing Treaty claims.[104] The High Court held there was adequate consultation where the Minister had earlier consulted and knew the iwi's position, and there was no Treaty obligation to go through separate consultation as a matter of form.
- In 2002, in *Glenharrow Holdings Ltd v Attorney-General*, a mining company with a licence to mine land containing pounamu (greenstone) successfully challenged a decision of the Crown refusing an extension of its licence.[105] The Minister had consulted with Ngāi Tahu, in which the pounamu was to be vested under a Treaty settlement. The High Court held it was open to the Ministers to consult, but there was no right to consultation and the principle of active protection of taonga could not prevail if inconsistent with the Mining Act.
- In 2004, in *Ngati Maru v Thames-Coromandel District Council*, Ngāti Maru successfully challenged a Council decision to grant consent to earthworks on a historic pā site (a village, often fortified) near a sacred stream without notifying and consulting them (but no relief was granted because of the advanced state of the development).[106]
- In 2007, in *Reihana v Director-General of Conservation*, Mr Reihana unsuccessfully challenged the process of consultation over regulations governing the customary taking of titi ('muttonbirds').[107]
- In 2009, in *Environs Holdings Ltd v the Environment Court at Auckland*, the plaintiff, controlled by Te Uri o Hau Settlement Trust, challenged a decision of the Environment Court not to adjourn hearing an appeal of resource consents relating to restricted coastal activities, pending resolution of a separate customary rights application over the same land.[108] The High Court held the Environment Court had taken Treaty principles into account in refusing to adjourn and was correct that concerns about the consistency

---

[101] *Ngai Tahu Māori Trust Board v Director-General of Conservation [Whalewatching case]* [1995] 3 NZLR 553 (CA).
[102] ibid 561–62.
[103] *Ngatiwai Trust Board v Minister of Conservation* HC CP39/98, 22 December 1998.
[104] *Ngati Apa ki te Waipounamu Trust v Attorney-General* [2000] NZRMA 460 (HC).
[105] *Glenharrow Holdings Ltd v Attorney-General* [2003] 1 NZLR 236 (HC).
[106] *Ngati Maru v Thames-Coromandel District Council* HC Hamilton CIV-2004-485-330, 27 August 2004.
[107] *Reihana v Director-General of Conservation* CA46/05, 29 March 2006; *Reihana v Director-General of Conservation* HC Invercargill CIV-2005-425-75, 19 December 2007.
[108] *Environs Holdings Ltd v The Environment Court at Auckland* [2009] NZRMA 340 (HC).

of the resource consent with Treaty principles could be dealt with at the substantive hearing of the appeal.

- In 2010, in *Waikato Tainui Te Kauhanganui Inc v Hamilton City Council*, Waikato-Tainui successfully challenged the Council's failure to consult them in their capacity as tangata whenua (the people of the land) in addition to their capacity as affected commercial landowners.[109]

- In 2012, in *Greenpeace of New Zealand Inc v Minister of Energy and Resources*, Te Runanga o te Whanau-a-Apanui challenged a Crown decision to allow offshore oil exploration on the basis of failure to consult, to actively protect a taonga or to take into account its fishing rights.[110] The High Court held there were opportunities for the applicant to raise its issues but it did not, the fishing rights were not a relevant consideration and the Crown did not breach its obligations.

- In 2018, in *Ngāti Tama Ki Te Waipounamu Trust v Tasman District Council*, the Council's consent to taking water in Golden Bay without consultation was challenged.[111] The High Court held the consented activities could compromise the objective of involving iwi in water management but struck out the claim because the consent had lapsed.

- In 2018, in *Ngāi Tai ki Tāmaki Tribal Trust v Minister of Conservation*, Ngāi Tai interests claimed tourism permits should not have been granted to non-Māori interests over the islands of Rangitoto and Motutapu.[112] A majority of the Supreme Court held there was an error of law in the official advice to the Minister advising there was no basis for preferential entitlement to concessions, and that economic benefit to iwi cannot be taken into account, under the principle of active protection.[113] It further found the errors diverted the decision-maker from proper consideration of the application of the relevant legislation.[114]

iv. Challenges to Commercial Regulatory Decisions

In six other cases, the courts declined challenges where industry competitors or potential competitors challenged commercial regulatory decisions:

- In 1994, in *Quarantine Waste (NZ) Ltd v Waste Resources Ltd*, an applicant with no particular connection to tangata whenua alleged consultation with Māori over a resource consent to incinerate waste was inadequate.[115] The High Court found it was not.

- In 1994, in *Auckland Casino Ltd v Casino Control Authority*, an applicant with a substantial Māori shareholding challenged the process for granting a casino licence as

---

[109] *Waikato Tainui Te Kauhanganui Inc v Hamilton City Council* [2010] NZRMA 285 (HC).
[110] *Greenpeace of New Zealand Inc v Minister of Energy and Resources* [2012] NZHC 1422.
[111] *Ngāti Tama Ki Te Waipounamu Trust v Tasman District Council* [2018] NZHC 2166.
[112] *Ngāi Tai ki Tāmaki Tribal Trust v Minister of Conservation* [2018] NZSC 122.
[113] ibid [69].
[114] ibid [94].
[115] *Quarantine Waste (NZ) Ltd v Waste Resources Ltd* [1994] NZRMA 529 (HC).

inconsistent with Māori consultation processes and culture.[116] The High Court found there was no such obligation in this context and no disadvantage.

- In 1997, in *New Zealand Fishing Industry Association (Inc) v Minister of Fisheries*, a range of Māori fishing interests challenged the decision of the Minister of Fisheries to reduce the commercial catch and increase the recreational catch.[117] The Court of Appeal declined the challenge, holding Māori were entitled to the same consideration as other quota owners.

- In 1999, in *Te Runanga o Ngati Awa v Attorney-General*, an iwi challenged the Crown's review of forestry licence fees, without Ngāti Awa participation, over land Ngāti Awa was negotiating to acquire from the Crown under a Treaty settlement.[118] The High Court held Ngāti Awa's position was absolutely protected and it was not entitled to participate.

- In 2003, in *Te Runanga o Ngai Tahu v Attorney General*, Ngāi Tahu challenged the Minister of Fisheries' approval of a recommended fishing quota scheme without sending it back to the Treaty of Waitangi Fisheries Commission.[119] The High Court held the Minister was entitled to deal with matters he considered in conflict with the Treaty without sending the report back.

- In 2004, in *Reid v Tararua District Council*, an individual challenged a Council decision to sell land that he wanted to buy to someone else on a variety of grounds, including inconsistency with the Treaty.[120] The High Court held there was no evidence of breach of any Treaty obligation.

v. Social Services and Other Decisions

Finally, nine cases have challenged a range of decisions that could be characterised as relating to social services, including education and health, and to immigration and electoral law. Few succeeded:

- In 1994, in *Taiaroa v Minister of Justice*, there was a challenge to the Chief Electoral Officer's process of providing Māori with the option of choosing whether to enrol on the Māori Electoral Roll or the General Electoral Roll, which occurs every five years.[121] The Court of Appeal dismissed the challenge, finding the Government's decision to reject recommendations by the Waitangi Tribunal to allocate more funding to the option was not perfect but 'passed the test of reasonableness'.[122]

- In 1999, in *Singh v Minister of Immigration*, a decision not to cancel a removal order from New Zealand was challenged for being inconsistent with Mr Singh's Māori family's

---

[116] *Auckland Casino Ltd v Casino Control Authority* HC Auckland M81/94, 13 July 1994.
[117] *New Zealand Fishing Industry Association (Inc) v Minister of Fisheries* CA82/97, 22 July 1997.
[118] *Te Runanga o Ngati Awa v Attorney-General* HC Wellington CP73/99, 21 April 1999.
[119] *Te Runanga o Ngai Tahu* (n 54).
[120] *Reid v Tararua District Council* HC Wellington CIV-2003-454-615, 8 November 2004.
[121] *Taiaroa v Minister of Justice* [1995] 1 NZLR 411 (CA).
[122] ibid 418.

rights under article 2 of the Treaty.[123] The Court found the family members' rights were not implicated as it was their choice whether to stay.

- In 1999, in *Osborne v Attorney-General for Minister of Education*, closure of a school, with eight students, on land gifted to educate future generations of Māori was challenged.[124] The High Court held the Treaty did not extend to a right to education in a particular place based on historical and whakapapa (genealogy) links.

- In 1999, in *Orme v New Zealand Law Society Disciplinary Tribunal*, the striking off of a lawyer for over-charging and breach of the intervention rule was challenged.[125] The High Court held the disciplinary rules were unlikely to be inconsistent with tikanga and, if they were, the rules would prevail.

- In 1999, in *The Association of University Staff of New Zealand Inc v The University of Waikato*, the Association challenged the restructuring of schools and faculties as inconsistent with the Treaty.[126] The High Court did not have to decide this issue but questioned whether it could be consistent to assimilate the Māori Studies unit into a general academic entity.[127]

- In 2003, in *Manukau Urban Māori Authority Inc v Treaty of Waitangi Fisheries Commission*, the report of the Treaty of Waitangi Fisheries Commission was challenged as inconsistent with the Treaty in its proposal on channelling benefits of fisheries assets to the benefit of urban Māori.[128] The High Court held the Commission did have a duty to distribute fairly to and for the benefit of all Māori, but there was a discretion as to how to discharge that and the decisions here did not breach the duty.

- In 2008, *Singh v Minister of Immigration*, a decision to remove the plaintiff from New Zealand was challenged on the basis his spouse was Māori.[129] The High Court held there was nothing indicating the Immigration Officer had not taken into account the principles of the Treaty.

- In 2011, in *Te Tai Tokerau Mapo Trust v Chief Executive of Ministry of Health*, the plaintiffs challenged a decision to terminate an agreement for the provision of health services for failure to take into account Treaty considerations.[130] The High Court held the decision was commercial and could not be challenged, and the Ministry did have sufficient regard to Treaty principles.

- In 2012, in *Te Whanau o Waipareira Trust v Attorney-General*, the Trust challenged a Crown decision to terminate an agreement for provision of Family Start services.[131] The Court held the decision was contractual and could not be challenged, and the principles of the Treaty did not require the Ministry to treat Te Whanau o Waipareira differently from other providers.

---

[123] *Singh v Minister of Immigration* HC Auckland M428/99, 28 April 1999.
[124] *Osborne v Attorney-General for Minister of Education* HC Hamilton M198/99, 4 October 1999.
[125] *Orme v New Zealand Law Society Disciplinary Tribunal* HC Auckland M1305/99, 22 October 1999.
[126] *The Association of University Staff of New Zealand Inc v The University of Waikato* [2002] NZAR 817 (HC).
[127] ibid [89]–[91].
[128] *Manukau Urban Māori Authority Inc* (n 54).
[129] *Singh v Minister of Immigration* HC Auckland CIV-2008-404-7545, 17 December 2008.
[130] *Te Tai Tokerau Mapo Trust v Chief Executive of Ministry of Health* (n 53).
[131] *Te Whanau o Waipareira Trust v Attorney-General* [2012] NZHC 3107.

B. Grounds of Judicial Review

In the first judicial review proceeding I heard as a judge, I asked counsel for the applicant which pleaded ground of judicial review he considered strongest. The adventurous counsel submitted to me the Mexican food analogy to the grounds of judicial review.[132] Tex-Mex dishes are folded and wrapped in different shapes and arrangements and called different names: enchiladas, tacos, burritos, quesadillas. But they often contain the same ingredients: flour and water, tomato, cheese, avocado, chili; or a mix of aspects of substantive law, good process and unreasonableness.

I was not adventurous enough to use this analogy explicitly in my judgment.[133] But the problem with dressing up the same ingredients under different labels is rather more serious in law than in the kitchen. Categorisation is fundamental to a full understanding of the law.[134] As Dean Knight's recent book has authoritatively canvassed, 'grounds' of judicial review is one available schemata by which the law of judicial review is conceptualised.[135] It is the dominant conventional schemata in New Zealand. It is therefore important for both potential challengers and potential defenders to be able to be clear about what are potential grounds of challenge. This is what decision-makers must ensure they do not breach when making decisions. It is what challengers assess in order to decide whether to mount a legal challenge or not. A clear understanding of the grounds of challenge of decisions involving the Treaty of Waitangi, like any other official decisions, is required for the certainty and non-arbitrariness of the rule of law to be maintained.

Unfortunately, it is a lot harder to identify the grounds on which decisions have successfully and unsuccessfully been judicially reviewed in relation to the Treaty of Waitangi than it is to identify the nature of the decisions reviewed. As with most judicial reviews, challengers tend to take a 'kitchen sink' approach to pleadings – pleading all the grounds they can think of. The grounds pleaded do not always make it into the judgment. And judges are not always clear about which grounds they find persuasive. Too often, it is difficult to tell where one ground begins and another ends. It is this feature of judicial review that I consider lends undesirable credence to Philip Joseph's characterisation of judicial review in New Zealand as 'instinctual'.[136]

I have categorised the grounds of judicial review for the 53 Treaty cases, whether successful or unsuccessful, as treated in the judgments, according to five grounds of judicial review, as best as (and if) I can determine. Some fall into more than one category. The relevant propositions from the cases are listed in the annex, appended at the end of the chapter, under each of the five grounds:

- illegality;
- failure to consider mandatory or relevant considerations;

---

[132] Mr Isaac Hikaka.
[133] *Royal Forest and Bird Protection Society of New Zealand Inc v Minister of Conservation* (2016) 19 ELRNZ 370 (HC); *Hawke's Bay Regional Investment Company Ltd v Royal Forest and Bird Protection Society of New Zealand Inc* [2017] 1 NZLR 1041 (SC); *Royal Forest and Bird Protection Society of New Zealand Inc v Minister of Conservation* [2016] 3 NZLR 828 (CA).
[134] JNE Varuhas, 'Taxonomy and Public Law' in M Elliott, JNE Varuhas and S Wilson Stark (eds), *The Unity of Public Law? Doctrinal, Theoretical and Comparative Perspectives* (Oxford, Hart Publishing, 2018) 39.
[135] DR Knight, *Vigilance and Restraint in the Common Law of Judicial Review* (Cambridge, Cambridge University Press, 2018).
[136] PA Joseph, 'Exploratory Questions in Administrative Law' (2012) 25 *New Zealand Universities Law Review* 73.

- breach of legitimate expectations;
- natural justice; and
- unreasonableness.

The first point to notice is that the first ground of illegality, or unlawfulness, is the most often invoked ground of judicial review. Seven of 25 challenges for illegality have succeeded. This is judicial review on the basis of inconsistency with the principles of the Treaty, which is usually illegal on the basis of inconsistency with legislation that explicitly invokes the Treaty. As Cooke P said in the *SOEs case*, '[i]f the judiciary has been able to play a role to some extent creative, that is because the legislature has given the opportunity'.[137] Indeed, much judicial review is simply statutory interpretation. Judges have more or less latitude for interpretation depending on the prescriptiveness of the legislation. The same is true of the appeal decisions referred to earlier, as exercises in statutory interpretation, since illegality is not only a ground of judicial review but also a ground of appeal. It may be comforting for advocates of parliamentary sovereignty in a political constitution that the most important measure against which the judiciary reviews government action is legislation passed by Parliament.

But legislation may prohibit actions inconsistent with the Treaty even if it does not explicitly mention the Treaty. In 1987, in *Huakina*, Chilwell J held the Treaty 'is part of the context in which legislation which impinges upon its principles is to be interpreted when it is proper, in accordance with the principles of statutory interpretation, to have resort to extrinsic material'.[138] He held Māori cultural and spiritual values were a relevant consideration to be taken into account in granting a water right under an Act that did not specify what considerations were relevant.[139]

Where a statute invokes the principles of the Treaty, the judiciary's role on judicial review is to interpret the meaning of the principles of the Treaty, apply that meaning and determine whether a decision is inconsistent with the principles. There has been a lot of work for the judiciary to do in interpreting the meaning of the principles of the Treaty in particular cases, particularly where Parliament has made bare, unelaborated references to the Treaty. But that jurisprudence is now well-established and understood as a relatively sophisticated and nuanced body of principled jurisprudence.[140] It has essentially been accepted by the other branches of government in their own subsequent decisions. The annex appended at the end of this chapter gives some sense of how the principles of the Treaty bear on government decisions.

The greatest proportion of successful challenges were on the ground of failure to consider relevant considerations: seven of 18. But the substantive nature of the challenges appears similar across that ground and the ground of illegality. This might illustrate the porous boundary between these two grounds of judicial review. After all, what is relevant and irrelevant is closely related to the application of the principles of the Treaty in the particular statutory context and, therefore, to statutory interpretation. The successful judicial reviews based on relevant considerations in Treaty cases are frequently that the

---

[137] *SOEs case* (n 17) 668.
[138] *Huakina Development Trust* (n 97) 210.
[139] ibid 223.
[140] Palmer, *The Treaty of Waitangi* (n 15) ch 3.

decision-maker should have considered Treaty interests but did not. That is effectively the same as the ground of illegality. None of the relevant considerations that were said to have grounded successful challenges were purely procedural. They tended to be substantive, in the nature of illegality.

And the relevant considerations ground also shades into the breach of legitimate expectations ground – both often involve challenges to the absence or adequacy of consultation with Māori. The challenges that succeeded on the ground of legitimate expectation – three of 13 – are based on consultation requirements. That might be expected, given New Zealand courts have yet to uphold a case of substantive legitimate expectation. But it appears that the successful challenges under both grounds could potentially be framed in terms of either ground. This emphasises the blurriness of grounds of review. It might also be thought to raise a question as to whether failure to consider a relevant consideration could be cured by consultation. But the Supreme Court's recent decision in *Ngāi Tai Ki Tamaki Tribal Trust* suggests not.[141]

The relative lack of Treaty cases invoking the principles of natural justice is also interesting. One of two succeeded. That may be explicable by the decision in *Ngati Apa*, holding that the Treaty does not impose greater procedural obligations than do the principles of natural justice.[142] So perhaps the Treaty need not be invoked explicitly. But procedural fairness plays a central role in the substance of the principles of the Treaty, according to the language of the appellate courts in their key decisions. That suggests fair process issues might attract scrutiny from courts in Treaty cases that manifests in their application of substantive law and, therefore, be treated as matters of legality or relevant considerations.

Only one of the six challenges obviously based on the ground of reasonableness attained success, and even then success was only potential. But the concept of unreasonableness has a bigger role in Treaty judicial reviews than might be expected. In the law of judicial review generally, the ground of unreasonableness is a poor and somewhat despised cousin. Hammond J, who delivered the judgment in the potentially successful reasonableness challenge, characterised the ground as the destination of the doomed elsewhere.[143] Yet the statements about reasonableness in the cases where it was argued as an explicit ground allow for the possibility of its playing a role in the right circumstances.

And the language of reasonableness and unreasonableness pops up throughout judicial review judgments regarding the Treaty of Waitangi irrespective of the formal 'grounds' of judicial review. Both the illegality cases and the relevant consideration cases tend to be coloured by the language and concept of reasonableness. Where Treaty principles were not considered, the language of reasonableness can be used. Where the decision challenged was judged reasonable, the challenge tends to fail. I suggest this is because reasonableness on the part of the Treaty partners has been found to be part of the substantive requirements of the Treaty of Waitangi and, therefore, part of substantive law where the Treaty is reflected in legislation.

In the *SOEs case* itself, Cooke P said:

> If the Crown acting reasonably and in good faith satisfies itself that known or foreseeable Māori claims do not require retention of certain land, no principle of the Treaty will prevent a transfer.

---

[141] *Ngāi Tai ki Tamaki Tribal Trust v Minister of Conservation* (n 112).
[142] *Ngati Apa Ki Te Waipounamu Trust v Attorney-General* (n 93).
[143] *Lumber Specialties Ltd v Hodgson* [2000] 2 NZLR 347 (HC) [144].

> I use 'reasonably' here in the ordinary sense of in accordance with or within the limits of reason. The distinction is between on the one hand what a reasonable person could do or decide, and on the other what would be irrational or capricious or misdirected. Lawyers often speak of *Wednesbury* unreasonableness, in allusion to the case reported in [1949] 1 KB 223, but I think that it comes to the same thing.[144]

And:

> A reasonably effective and workable safeguard machinery is what is required. Further than that the Crown should not be obliged to go ... The principles of the Treaty do not authorise unreasonable restrictions on the right of a duly elected Government to follow its chosen policy. Indeed to try to shackle the Government unreasonably would itself be inconsistent with those principles. The test of reasonableness is necessarily a broad one and necessarily has to be applied by the Court in the end in a realistic way. The parties owe each other cooperation ...[145]

The most authoritative encapsulations of general Treaty obligations also emphasise reasonableness. Lord Woolf, for the Judicial Committee of the Privy Council, then New Zealand's highest court, said this in the 1993 *Broadcasting Assets case*:

> This relationship the Treaty envisages should be founded on reasonableness, mutual cooperation and trust. It is therefore accepted by both parties that the Crown in carrying out its obligations is not required in protecting taonga to go beyond taking such action as is reasonable in the prevailing circumstances. While the obligation of the Crown is constant, the protective steps which it is reasonable for the Crown to take change depending on the situation which exists at any particular time. For example in times of recession the Crown may be regarded as acting reasonably in not becoming involved in heavy expenditure in order to fulfil its obligations although this would not be acceptable at a time when the economy was buoyant. Again, if as is the case with the Māori language at the present time, a taonga is in a vulnerable state, this has to be taken into account by the Crown in deciding the action it should take to fulfil its obligations and may well require the Crown to take especially vigorous action for its protection. This may arise, for example, if the vulnerable state can be attributed to past breaches by the Crown of its obligations, and may extend to the situation where those breaches are due to legislative action. Indeed any previous default of the Crown could, far from reducing, increase the Crown's responsibility.[146]

In 2013, in the *Water case*, the Supreme Court relied on the *Broadcasting Assets case* and said:

> In deciding whether proposed Crown action will result in 'material impairment', a court must assess the difference between the ability of the Crown to act in a particular way if the proposed action does not occur and its likely post-action capacity. So impairment of an ability to provide a particular form of redress which is not in reasonable or substantial prospect, objectively evaluated, will not be relevantly material. To decide what is reasonable requires a contextual evaluation which may require consideration of the social and economic climate.[147]

Reasonableness appears central to the nature and limits of the substantive Treaty obligations of the Crown, and presumably also Māori, under the Treaty. As an element of

---

[144] *SOEs case* (n 17) 664.
[145] ibid 665–66.
[146] *Broadcasting Assets case* (n 42) 518.
[147] *Water case* (n 43) [89] (footnotes omitted).

substantive law, as a Treaty principle, it has real potential bite. It is not invoked as a stand-alone ground of judicial review relatively often. But because of the substantive content of Treaty obligations, reasonableness is a potentially central aspect, if not ground, of judicial review proceedings that invoke the Treaty of Waitangi under the heading of 'illegality'.

This suggests an alternative explanation for the substantive nature of judicial review based on the Treaty of Waitangi compared to Philip Joseph's proposition that such review is 'constitutional' as opposed to 'administrative'.[148] Treaty-related judicial review is not qualitatively different from judicial review in other areas of law. But the substance of Treaty law – of the principles of the Treaty of Waitangi – may emphasise the requirement for reasonableness on the part of decision-makers more heavily than does the substance of other substantive law.

Perhaps the most salient feature of reviewing the patterns of the grounds of judicial review is the extent to which they have been effectively incorporated into the substantive requirements of the Treaty of Waitangi through the judiciary's interpretation of the meaning of the Treaty. This is true of the procedural grounds of judicial review as well as unreasonableness. The principles of the Treaty are, themselves, deeply rooted in good process. If the Crown were to fail to take into account a relevant consideration, take into account an irrelevant consideration, dishonour a legitimate expectation or breach natural justice, it would probably also be breaching the principles of the Treaty of Waitangi. This flows from the courts' acceptance of the Waitangi Tribunal's perspective of the Treaty in a relational sense.[149] Procedure looms large in the legal parameters on the relationship between the Treaty partners. The language of partnership and references in the *SOEs case* on the duty of the Treaty partners to act in good faith, fairly and reasonably toward each other resonates deeply with the law of judicial review.

V. Conclusion

Judges in New Zealand contribute to the protection of the rights of indigenous people through performing their conventional role of using reason to apply the law to specific factual contexts. This contributes a distinctive judicial voice to the ongoing constitutional dialogue that has reshaped the content and status of the Treaty of Waitangi in New Zealand's law since the 1970s.

In particular, judges contribute to the protection of the rights of indigenous peoples through the application of the law of judicial review. Judicial review for illegality depends on interpretation of the meaning of the relevant statute. That has involved the judiciary in a lot of work in explicating the principles of the Treaty of Waitangi – in order to give substance to statutory provisions that invoke them. In doing so, they have drawn on the law of judicial review. The most salient feature of the substantive principles of the Treaty is that their substantive procedural and reasonableness requirements mirror the substance of the law of judicial review. Recognition of that would allow counsel to argue more clearly and judges to

---

[148] PA Joseph, 'Constitutional Review Now' [1998] *New Zealand Law Review* 85; PA Joseph, *Constitutional and Administrative Law in New Zealand*, 4th edn (Wellington, Brookers, 2014) [22.12].
[149] Palmer, *The Treaty of Waitangi* (n 15) 125–29.

apply the law of judicial review more clearly when the Treaty of Waitangi is invoked. And clarity in the law of judicial review should enhance the judiciary's ability to contribute to constitutional dialogue and to perform its fundamental functions of applying the law to specific factual circumstances, using reason.

Perhaps there is also a more general lesson here for how to conceive of unreasonableness as a ground of judicial review. It is the relevant statute that matters. Whether an Act or area of law emphasises or plays down the importance of process, or invokes or sets its face against unreasonableness, should tell us what is fair process and what is unreasonable in the circumstances of that Act or area of law.

And it is worth reflecting on why the substance of Treaty law might have come to mirror the substance of judicial review law. Part of the answer may be that the essence of the relational view of the Treaty that was originated by the Waitangi Tribunal and endorsed by the courts lies in process and in reason. That is, after all, the essence of good relationships. Or it might be that, in giving legal substance to Treaty relationships, the courts have reached for the tools most familiar to them in mediating the relationships between citizens and the state – the procedural and occasionally reasonableness requirements of the law of judicial review. Perhaps both are true. But, if so, there seems no reason why such a special conceptual linkage between the law of judicial review and the law of the principles of the Treaty of Waitangi should not also inform the laws of other jurisdictions that deploy the law of judicial review to protect the rights of indigenous peoples in their relationships with states. Whether that is so, or should be so, is for others to consider.

Nō reira, tēnā koutou, tēnā koutou, tēnā koutou katoa.

Annex: Decisions Challenged by Ground of Judicial Review

A. Illegality

Successful	Unsuccessful
1) Granting a water right without regard to spiritual, cultural and traditional relationships of Māori to water.[150] 2) Transferring assets to SOEs without establishing any system to avoid prejudicing Māori Treaty claims.[151] 3) Transferring forestry assets without such a system.[152]	1) Transferring land to a local council because a regime protecting claims was sufficient to ensure consistency with Treaty principles.[153] 2) Negotiating and moving to enact the Sealord settlement with all Māori.[154] 3) Not negotiating before selling land, because Treaty principles are not necessarily relevant to a Māori Trust Board.[155]

(continued)

[150] *Huakina Development Trust* (n 97).
[151] *SOEs case* (n 17).
[152] *Forestry case* (n 68).
[153] *Te Heu Heu v Attorney-General* (n 77).
[154] *Sealords case* (n 54).
[155] *Ngāti Whātua O Orakei Trust* (n 70).

(Continued)

Successful	Unsuccessful
4) Transferring coal mining rights without a scheme for protecting Tainui Treaty claims.[156] 5) Allocating individual transferable fisheries quota despite a legislative savings clause protecting 'Māori fishing rights'.[157] 6) The Waitangi Tribunal inquiring into the procedure of the Treaty of Waitangi Fisheries Commission before it had proposed a policy.[158] 7) Granting temporary permit to non-iwi interests to conduct tours over the Rangitoto and Motutapu islands.[159]	4) Transferring dams to new energy companies, allegedly interfering with customary title rights, as Treaty rights did not include electricity generation and so there was no prejudice to potential claims.[160] 5) Selling commercial radio assets owned by the Crown, where there were other ways to discharge Treaty obligations.[161] 6) Negotiating with an iwi authority on behalf of a hapū.[162] 7) Striking off a lawyer for over-charging and breach of the intervention rule is unlikely to be inconsistent with tikanga.[163] 8) Closing a school gifted for the purpose of educating future Māori.[164] 9) Refusing to accept a Waitangi Tribunal recommendation to suspend a radio frequencies auction.[165] 10) Agreeing to a settlement with one iwi, said to prejudice potential settlement with another, as the decision was non-justiciable.[166] 11) Refusing to send a proposed fishing quota scheme back to the Treaty of Waitangi Fisheries Commission.[167] 12) Recommending a trust to channel the benefits from fisheries assets to urban Māori.[168] 13) Selling land to one person rather than another in the absence of any Treaty obligation.[169]

(continued)

---

[156] *Coal case* (n 67).
[157] *Fisheries case* (n 99).
[158] *Hauraki Māori Trust Board* (n 91).
[159] *Ngāi Tai ki Tāmaki Tribal Trust v Minister of Conservation* (n 112).
[160] *Hydro-electric Dams case* (n 72).
[161] *Commercial Radio Assets case* (n 73).
[162] *Kai Tohu Tohu o Puketapu Hapu Inc* (n 54).
[163] *Orme* (n 125).
[164] *Osborne* (n 124).
[165] *Radio Spectrum case* (n 54).
[166] *Pouwhare v Attorney-General* (n 84) and *Milroy v Attorney-General* (n 86).
[167] *Te Runanga o Ngai Tahu* (n 54).
[168] *Manukau Urban Māori Authority* (n 54).
[169] *Reid* (n 120).

(Continued)

Successful	Unsuccessful
	14) Refusing an urgent Waitangi Tribunal hearing without considering the Treaty principles at all stages of the Tribunal inquiry.[170] 15) Terminating a contract for provision of health services, while taking sufficient consideration of Treaty principles.[171] 16) Treating an urban Māori provider of social services in the same way as other providers.[172] 17) Removing a power company from the SOE regime because there was no material impact on the ability to take reasonable actions to remedy Treaty breaches.[173] 18) Selling Crown-owned company land because the company was not subject to Treaty principles, it was private land and the Crown had not assisted in the sale.[174]

B. Failure to Consider Mandatory or Relevant Considerations

Successful	Unsuccessful
1) Failure to consider whether disposition of assets would prejudice Māori Treaty claims.[175] 2) Failure to protect Tainui's claims before transferring coal-mining rights.[176] 3) Failure to consider a pending Waitangi Tribunal report in the planned apportionment of radio frequencies.[177]	1) Failure to consider the plaintiffs' interests when offering land to others with whom the Crown was settling was overriden by the non-justiciability of a claim that would intrude on Parliament's processes.[178] 2) No need to consider the interests of tangata whenua in transferring dams, or of a pending Waitangi Tribunal report or of consultation.[179]

(continued)

---

[170] *Attorney-General v Mair* (n 95).
[171] *Te Tai Tokerau Mapo Trust* (n 53).
[172] *Te Whanau o Waipareira Trust* (n 131).
[173] *Water case* (n 43).
[174] *Chetham v Mighty River Power Ltd* (n 53).
[175] *SOEs case* (n 17).
[176] *Coal case* (n 67).
[177] *Radio Frequencies case* (n 69).
[178] *Ngati Whatua O Orakei Trust* (n 70).
[179] *Hydro-electric dams case* (n 72).

(Continued)

Successful	Unsuccessful
4) Failing to accord Ngāi Tahu interests a reasonable degree of preference in respect of whale-watching permits, subject to overriding conservation considerations.[180] 5) Failing to consult with Waikato-Tainui in their capacity as tangata whenua in addition to their capacity as affected commercial landowners.[181] 6) Failing to consider that Ngāti Whakahemo's claim had not been settled.[182] 7) Failing to consider that consented activities may compromise the objective of involving iwi in water management.[183]	3) No need to establish a system to protect Māori language before transferring broadcasting assets when the transfer would not impair the Crown's ability to take reasonable action to do so.[184] 4) Māori interests were considered in granting a consent to incinerate waste and there was no evidence Māori were unhappy about the consultation or effect.[185] 5) A Māori approach to consultation was not required in regulating gambling where the applicant was functionally commercial and faced no procedural disadvantage as a result.[186] 6) No need to consider Treaty principles in removal proceedings on grounds the removed person's family members are Māori, because those family members can decide whether to stay in New Zealand or not.[187] 7) There was no evidence the principles of the Treaty were not taken into account in deciding to deport the spouse of a Māori.[188] 8) Consulting with non-Māori about regulations governing the taking of tīti (muttonbirds) was not prohibited.[189] 9) An adjournment by the Environment Court of a consent appeal was not required because Treaty principles could be taken into account at the substantive appeal hearing.[190]

(continued)

---

[180] *Whalewatching case* (n 101).
[181] *Waikato Tainui Te Kauhanganui Inc* (n 109).
[182] *Ririnui v Attorney-General* (n 79).
[183] *Ngāti Tama Ki Te Waipounamu Trust* (n 111).
[184] *Broadcasting Assets case* (n 42).
[185] *Quarantine Waste (NZ) Ltd* (n 115).
[186] *Auckland Casino Ltd* (n 116).
[187] *Singh* (n 123).
[188] *Singh* (n 129).
[189] *Reihana v Director-General of Conservation* (n 107).
[190] *Environs Holdings Ltd* (n 108).

(Continued)

Successful	Unsuccessful
	10) Fishing rights were not relevant to a decision to allow offshore oil exploration and there had been opportunities to raise any issues.[191] 11) There was insufficient prejudice to justify interim orders in a claim against the Waitangi Tribunal regarding the claimants' mandate.[192]

C. Breach of Legitimate Expectations

Successful	Unsuccessful
1) Ngāti Wai had a legitimate expectation the Crown would consider its position before banning customary fishing in a marine reserve.[193] 2) Ngāti Maru had a legitimate expectation of being consulted over a proposal for earthworks on a historic pā site near a sacred stream.[194] 3) One Treaty claimant had a legitimate expectation of consultation over settlement with another.[195]	1) There was no legitimate expectation the Crown would establish a system to protect te reo Māori before transferring broadcasting assets; but an undertaking to the Court about implementing Cabinet decisions doing so could give rise to an enforceable legitimate expectation.[196] 2) An expectation that reduction in fishing quota would be applied proportionately to commercial and recreational quota.[197] 3) An expectation of consultation before the Crown terminated a joint venture with local councils altering the status, and possibly the value, of land subject to a Treaty claim.[198] 4) An expectation Ngati Tuwheretoa would be consulted on transfer of land held by an SOE but subject to a Treaty claim, when the original transfer of the land had complied with the provisions of the SOEs Act.[199]

(continued)

---

[191] *Greenpeace of New Zealand Inc* (n 110).
[192] *Baker* (n 96).
[193] *Ngatiwai Trust Board v Minister of Conservation* (n 103).
[194] *Ngati Maru* (n 106).
[195] *Port Nicholson Block Settlement Trust v Attorney-General* (n 89).
[196] *Broadcasting Assets case* (n 42).
[197] *New Zealand Fishing Industry Association (Inc)* (n 117).
[198] *Ngati Koata No Rangitoto ki te Tonga Trust v Minister of Transport* (n 76).
[199] *Te Heu Heu v Attorney-General* (n 77).

(Continued)

Successful	Unsuccessful
	5) An expectation the Crown would accept a Waitangi Tribunal recommendation to suspend a radio frequencies auction.[200]
	6) There was no obligation to go through separate consultation as a matter of form over marine farming permits where the Minister already knew the iwi's position.[201]
	7) An expectation of consultation before extending a mining licence over land in the South Island, where legislation did not provide for such consultation but the pounamu in that land had been granted to Ngai Tahu under a Treaty settlement.[202]
	8) An expectation of participation in Crown review of forestry licences over land subject to a Treaty settlement claim when the claimant's position was absolutely protected.[203]
	9) There was nothing in a contract for provision of health services to found a legitimate expectation wider than those arising from the terms in the contract.[204]
	10) Taranaki Whānui's legitimate expectation of being consulted about the Crown settling with Ngāti Toa was satisfied.[205]

D. Natural Justice

Successful	Unsuccessful
1) A claim of lack of a reasonable opportunity to be heard by the Māori Appellate Court could be pursued for declaratory relief though it would not invalidate the relevant order.[206]	1) The Treaty does not impose greater procedural obligations than do the principles of natural justice.[207]

---

[200] *Radio Spectrum case* (n 54).
[201] *Ngati Apa ki te Waipounamu Trust v Attorney-General* (n 104).
[202] *Glenharrow Holdings Ltd v Attorney-General* (n 105).
[203] *Te Runanga o Ngāti Awa* (n 118).
[204] *Te Tai Tokerau Mapo Trust* (n 53).
[205] *Port Nicholson Block Settlement Trust v Attorney-General* (n 89).
[206] *Ngati Apa Ki Te Waipounamu Trust v R* (n 92).
[207] *Ngati Apa Ki Te Waipounamu Trust v Attorney-General* (n 93).

E. Unreasonableness

Successful	Unsuccessful
1) Potentially, folding Māori Studies into a generalist academic faculty within a University by decision only of the Vice-Chancellor may be contrary to the duty to act reasonably and in good faith.[208]	1) The relationship the Treaty envisages 'should be founded on reasonableness, mutual cooperation and trust' but the Crown does not have to go beyond what is reasonable in the prevailing circumstances.[209] 2) Failure to allow the Waitangi Tribunal time to complete its inquiry before enacting a policy as to apportionment of radio frequencies.[210] 3) The Treaty did not add anything to the obligations on the Crown to take reasonable steps to publicise the Māori Electoral Option.[211] 4) A decrease in commercial fishing quota and an increase in recreational fishing quota was not unreasonable.[212] 5) The sale of shares in a MOM company would not materially impair the Crown's ability to take reasonable action which it is obliged to undertake, which requires a contextual evaluation.[213]

---

[208] *The Association of University Staff of New Zealand Inc* (n 126).
[209] *SOEs case* (n 17) 518.
[210] *Radio Frequencies case* (n 69).
[211] *Taiaroa v Minister of Justice* (n 121).
[212] *New Zealand Fishing Industry Association (Inc)* (n 117).
[213] *Water case* (n 43).

7
Coming to Terms with Communal, Land-related Decision-making by Aboriginal and/or Torres Strait Islander Peoples in a Public Law Context

DEBBIE MORTIMER*

I. Introduction

The idea for this chapter arose out of a case that I heard in 2017, and in which I gave judgment in February 2018: *Ellis v Central Land Council*.[1] An appeal from that decision was dismissed in January 2019.[2] The proceeding invoked the Federal Court of Australia's supervisory jurisdiction under both section 39B of the *Judiciary Act 1903* (Cth) ('Judiciary Act') and section 5 of the *Administrative Decisions (Judicial Review) Act 1977* (Cth). It concerned the nature and operation of a provision of the *Aboriginal Land Rights (Northern Territory) Act 1976* (Cth) ('Land Rights Act'), section 19(5), which requires as a precondition to the grant of Aboriginal land by an Aboriginal Land Trust to a third party, satisfaction of the Land Council of the consent of traditional owners 'as a group'. The proceeding concerned Aboriginal land in a community called Amoonguna, outside Alice Springs, in the Northern Territory. It was brought by some traditional owners who opposed the grant of a number of leases to third parties for community infrastructure and services in Amoonguna, and which had been made by the Amoonguna Aboriginal Land Trust on the direction of the Central Land Council (CLC).

I heard and determined this proceeding after my participation in a decision by three members of the Federal Court, sitting in its original jurisdiction, in *McGlade v Native Title Registrar*.[3] *McGlade* was actually four proceedings, which were heard and determined together by the Court. They were judicial review challenges brought under section 39B of

---

* I gratefully acknowledge the considerable assistance given to me by Daniel Lopez, JD student at Melbourne Law School, in both research and preparing this chapter for publication. My thanks also to my staff in chambers: Alexandra Harrison-Ichlov, Katrina Jobson and Shelby Mclean.
[1] *Ellis v Central Land Council* (2018) 335 ALR 93 (*Ellis*).
[2] *Ellis v Central Land Council* [2019] FCAFC 1.
[3] *McGlade v Native Title Registrar* (2017) 251 FCR 172 (*McGlade*).

the Judiciary Act. Given the importance of the issues in the proceedings, a bench of three judges was constituted by the Chief Justice pursuant to section 20(1A) of the *Federal Court of Australia Act 1976* (Cth), following a remitter to this Court from the High Court by order of Nettle J on 17 February 2016. The proceedings were commenced in the High Court in response to applications by the State of Western Australia to register four agreements as 'Indigenous Land Use Agreements' (ILUAs) on the Register of Indigenous Land Use Agreements under section 24CG of the *Native Title Act 1993* (Cth) ('Native Title Act').

The ILUA registration applications were the culmination of a long and complex negotiation process known as the South West Native Title Settlement, which I describe in more detail later in this chapter.

McGlade raised issues about how a court on judicial review should approach statutory requirements in the Native Title Act about decision-making on behalf of a group of Indigenous people. In this case, the issues were less about the mode of proof, or how a decision-maker (and the Court on review) might be satisfied about consent 'as a group', and more about what the scheme of the Native Title Act required of individuals who had been chosen as representatives of a group of Indigenous people claiming to hold native title over particular areas of land.

Sitting underneath these two examples are questions about how courts are asked to deal with contests about decision-making by or on behalf of a group or groups of Indigenous peoples, where that decision-making has legal consequences. Of course, there are questions about appropriate policy choices in legislative schemes that are framed to recognise and give effect to decision-making by groups of Indigenous peoples. Some of the matters I touch on in this chapter are connected to those policy choices, although the policy choices themselves are not the subject of the chapter.

The public law context of these issues is that proceedings in the nature of judicial review are often the only avenue for members of Indigenous communities or groups who are dissatisfied with the method or outcome of a decision-making process about their land. At some point, as we shall see in both examples I have given, exercises of public power are often involved: whether by way of implementation of a communal decision and its translation into an enforceable statutory outcome, or because the communal decision-making model involves an entity or organisation created by statute, with statutory powers.

These two cases illustrate some of the complexities in public law challenges to such decision-making and provide an opportunity to reflect on forensic and judicial approaches under Australian law[4] to the review or assessment of decision-making by Indigenous peoples.

My suggestion is that courts need to recognise they are applying public law principles in a very different context in such cases, and come to terms with those differences better than we currently do. There will be questions about whether, in applying public law

---

[4] There is no opportunity in this chapter to explore the comparative position in New Zealand and in Canada in any detail, save to say that from what I have seen, Canada seems to have gone down a road, through legislative prescription, of imposing majority decision-making on Indigenous people in relation to consent processes for dealing in or disposition of their traditional lands: see, eg, Indian Act RSC 1985, c I-5, s 39(1)(b). In New Zealand the situation is more nuanced, especially because of the existence of a dedicated Māori Land Court – a judicial structure we do not have in Australia: see Te Ture Whenua Maori Act 1993 (Maori Land Act 1993) (NZ). Australia's preoccupation with anthropologists as the arbiters of consent and articulation of Indigenous decision-making processes does not seem to be replicated in either jurisdiction.

principles and in engaging in statutory interpretation, a disproportionately non-Indigenous framework is imposed on processes that were intended to be, or to recognise, Indigenous processes. There may be ways courts (and indeed decision-makers themselves) can better empower Indigenous people to speak for themselves through evidence, rather than through non-Indigenous methods, such as expert evidence.

In interpreting legislation, recalling the constraints on the judicial function in performing that role, it seems to me to be critical to bear in mind the very different nature of Indigenous communal rights, to recognise the challenges that decision-making in the context of those rights presents and to question whether what seems to be the 'default' position of majority decision-making is one that should become the default position in this space too. Majority decision-making models may be comfortable and familiar to non-Indigenous people, but it is a different issue whether they should be imposed or endorsed (either by judicial decision or legislative requirement) as the default system on Indigenous peoples making decisions about their land.

Now is not the occasion to trace the slow and difficult progression towards recognition of the rights of Indigenous peoples to their lands in Australia.[5] The two key provisions on which I wish to focus in this chapter come from very different statutory regimes, enacted in different eras in the development and recognition of Indigenous rights to land in Australia. Nevertheless, each deals with the conferral of rights and interests in land on Aboriginal peoples (in the case of the Land Rights Act), and Aboriginal and Torres Strait Islander peoples (in the case of the Native Title Act).

II. Consent 'as a Group': The *Aboriginal Land Rights (Northern Territory) Act 1976* (Cth)

The Land Rights Act covers land in the Northern Territory of Australia only, and was enacted pursuant to the Commonwealth's territories power in section 122 of the Constitution. A large proportion of land in the Northern Territory has remained continuously occupied by Aboriginal peoples. At later stages, legislative schemes with some similarities to the Land Rights Act were established elsewhere in Australia;[6] however, the Northern Territory legislation has been the subject of a large number of judicial decisions, covering a range of aspects of its scheme.

The genesis of the Land Rights Act is traced by Brennan J in his reasons for judgment in *R v Toohey; Ex parte Meneling Station Pty Ltd*,[7] including the critical turning point of Blackburn J's judgment in *Milirrpum v Nabalco Pty Ltd* (the Gove land rights case), where the Court found it could not recognise rights held by Indigenous people in land as

---

[5] For an excellent general history and review, see the lecture by former Justice John Mansfield, an expert in this area: J Mansfield, 'Indigenous Land Rights: Australia's Response Following Mabo – the Present and the Future' (University of South Australia, 17 August 2017), available at http://www.fedcourt.gov.au/__data/assets/pdf_file/0020/46127/Mansfield-J-20170817.pdf.

[6] See, eg, *Anangu Pitjantjatjara Yankunytjatjara Land Rights Act 1981* (SA), s 7, and the quite different model in the *Aboriginal Land Rights Act 1983* (NSW), s 42G(1), (5).

[7] *R v Toohey; Ex parte Meneling Station Pty Ltd* (1982) 158 CLR 327, 354–55 (*Meneling Station*).

proprietary rights under Australian law.[8] That conclusion was reached despite some findings sympathetic to the Yonglu People in that judgment. In *Meneling Station*, Brennan J describes the effect of the Land Rights Act scheme as restoring areas of land within the Northern Territory to 'Aboriginal control'.[9] His Honour also describes the effect of section 19(5) in the following way:

> The usufructuary rights of Aboriginals in respect of Aboriginal land, once acquired, might be overridden by the granting of a lease or licence by a Land Trust (s 19(3)), or by a surrender of that land to the Crown (s 19(4)), but any of those events requires the approval of the traditional Aboriginal owners, and of any Aboriginal community or group that might be affected thereby (s 19(5)(a) and (b)). The Aboriginal people connected with a tract of country were thus made competent to use their country in a non-traditional way if and *when an Aboriginal consensus* to do so should be established.[10]

Brennan J did not need to examine in *Meneling Station* what was meant by an 'Aboriginal consensus', but this is a significant evidentiary challenge, as well as a conceptual one.

The Land Rights Act establishes a process through which Aboriginal people in the Northern Territory can secure rights of a proprietary kind in the land over which they have 'affiliations' in accordance with traditional law and custom, thus overcoming the decision in *Milirrpum*. Speaking very broadly (and therefore inviting some inaccuracies), the process of making grants of Aboriginal land under the Land Rights Act is concerned with the identification of who are the 'traditional Aboriginal owners' (as defined in section 3(1)) of the land, through an inquiry by an Aboriginal Land Commissioner and a recommendation to the responsible federal Minister.[11] It is the federal Minister who decides whether or not to make a grant of land, which then becomes known as Aboriginal land.

The legislative scheme does not, however, confer the right to hold proprietary interests directly on Aboriginal people. Instead, a statutory vehicle is created to hold the proprietary right: a Land Trust.[12] The Minister establishes Land Trusts, again speaking broadly, for each group of traditional owners who have been identified as entitled by Aboriginal tradition to the use or occupation of the land concerned. A Land Trust is to exercise its powers – which include the power to deal in the land, and therefore create proprietary interests in third parties by way of leases, for example – for the benefit of the Aboriginal people on whose behalf it holds the land.[13]

The Land Rights Act also establishes Land Councils under section 21. These are regionally based bodies corporate and their functions are wide-ranging. However, all of their functions relate in some way to the acquisition by Aboriginal people of rights and interests in land under the Land Rights Act and then the management of Aboriginal land – including, for example, protection of sacred sites, but also wider functions relating to the use of Aboriginal land, whether for traditional or non-traditional purposes.[14]

---

[8] *Milirrpum v Nabalco Pty Ltd* (1971) 17 FLR 141, 273–74 (*Milirrpum*).
[9] *Meneling Station* (n 7) 355.
[10] ibid 359 (emphasis added).
[11] *Aboriginal Land Rights (Northern Territory) Act 1976* (Cth), ss 5, 10–12.
[12] ibid s 4.
[13] ibid s 5.
[14] ibid ss 22–23.

Thus, the legislative scheme in the Land Rights Act is built on the recognition of communal title in people who are described as 'traditional Aboriginal owners'.

Dealing in or disposing of Aboriginal land by a Land Trust is controlled directly by a Land Council, and indirectly by the traditional owners themselves. By section 19(1) there is a prohibition on a Land Trust's dealing in or disposing of Aboriginal land vested in it, except by a method set out in section 19.

A number of methods are set out in section 19. The one that arose in *Ellis*, and one of the common methods, is in section 19(4):

> With the consent, in writing, of the Minister and at the direction, in writing, of the relevant Land Council, a Land Trust may:
>
> ...
>
> (b) transfer to another Land Trust, or surrender to the Crown, the whole of its estate or interest in the whole, or any part of, the land vested in it.

The power of the Land Council to give such a direction is controlled by section 19(5):

> A Land Council shall not give a direction under this section for the grant, transfer or surrender of an estate or interest in land unless the Land Council is satisfied that:
>
> (a) the traditional Aboriginal owners (if any) of that land understand the nature and purpose of the proposed grant, transfer or surrender and, as a group, consent to it;
> (b) any Aboriginal community or group that may be affected by the proposed grant, transfer or surrender has been consulted and has had adequate opportunity to express its view to the Land Council; and
> (c) in the case of a grant of an estate or interest – the terms and conditions on which the grant is to be made are reasonable.

There is a form of ouster (or privative) clause in section 19(6), the construction and operation of which was in issue in *Ellis*. The CLC relied on section 19(6) in its defence against the applicants' claims. Ultimately, it was not necessary at first instance in *Ellis* to determine the precise construction and operation of section 19(6), and the extent to which it protected the decision of the CLC.

What could constitute consent 'as a group' by traditional owners of Aboriginal land was considered by Muirhead J in the Northern Territory Supreme Court decision of *Alderson v Northern Land Council*.[15] In this case, some traditional owners opposed the grant of leases of Aboriginal land, which had in accordance with the Land Rights Act been vested in a Land Trust. The leases in issue were mining leases. The majority of traditional owners agreed to the leases. An injunction had been sought to restrain the grant of the mining leases on the basis that section 19(5) was not complied with. His Honour's reasons were therefore given in a situation of some urgency, but he referred to the 'delicate and complicated task' of identifying who *are* the traditional owners of Aboriginal land for the purposes of the consent and consultation functions given to Land Councils, finding that ultimately it is a task reposed in the Land Council.[16] Justice Muirhead rejected the contentions of the

---

[15] *Alderson v Northern Land Council* (1983) 20 NTR 1.
[16] ibid 8.

plaintiffs before him that unanimity amongst traditional owners was required for there to be consent 'as a group'.[17]

Section 77A was added to the Land Rights Act in 1987. It appears to confirm the view held by Muirhead J that unanimity is not necessarily required. It provides:

77A Consents of traditional Aboriginal owners

Where, for the purposes of this Act, the traditional Aboriginal owners of an area of land are required to have consented, as a group, to a particular act or thing, the consent shall be taken to have been given if:

(a) in a case where there is a particular process of decision making that, under the Aboriginal tradition of those traditional Aboriginal owners or of the group to which they belong, must be complied with in relation to decisions of that kind – the decision was made in accordance with that process; or

(b) in a case where there is no such process of decision making – the decision was made in accordance with a process of decision making agreed to and adopted by those traditional Aboriginal owners in relation to the decision or in relation to decisions of that kind.

The concepts in section 77A would be reflected, eventually, in the terms of sections 251A and 251B of the Native Title Act, which I discuss in the next section.

In the *Ellis* proceeding at trial, no party really relied on the terms of section 77A. There was no evidence that any specific method of decision-making had been adopted as section 77A contemplated. Thus it fell to be established as a forensic exercise whether it was open to the CLC to be satisfied (satisfaction being the threshold in section 19(5)) that the Amoonguna traditional owners had, as a group, understood and consented to their Land Trust's entering into the leases over land in their community.[18]

The applicants in the *Ellis* proceeding were traditional owners who were also the proponents of the competing lease proposal, which was not the proposal implemented when the CLC granted leases to other third parties (including the Northern Territory Government and National Aboriginal Congress).

Since this was a judicial review, under Australian law, and speaking in broad terms, the question for the Court was whether the material before the CLC when it made its decision under section 19(5) was adequate for it to form a state of satisfaction about consent of traditional owners 'as a group', and whether the CLC properly understood the nature of the satisfaction it had to form.[19] Complicating the issue was the fact that the 'satisfaction' was to be formed by an entity (the Land Council), and on the facts in this case that requirement was (lawfully) delegated to a sub-committee of the CLC. Both the CLC and

---

[17] ibid 10.
[18] The Full Court rejected a ground of appeal based on s 77A: see especially *Ellis v Central Land Council* (n 2) [141]–[146].
[19] For some appreciation of the approach of Australian law to the judicial review of the exercise of powers conditioned by the formation of a state of satisfaction, see: *Shrestha v Minister for Immigration and Border Protection* (2018) 92 ALJR 798, [2] (Kiefel CJ, Gageler and Keane JJ); *Plaintiff M64/2015 v Minister for Immigration and Border Protection* (2015) 258 CLR 173, [63]–[66] (Gageler J); *Minister for Immigration and Citizenship v SZMDS* (2010) 240 CLR 611, [130]–[136] (Crennan and Bell JJ); *He v Minister for Immigration and Border Protection* (2017) 255 FCR 41, [47]–[52] (Siopsis, Kerr and Rangiah JJ); *MZYPZ v Minister for Immigration and Citizenship* [2012] FCA 478, [18]–[20] (Bromberg J) and the authorities cited by his Honour therein.

its sub-committee were composed of Aboriginal people drawn from the various regions covered by the CLC's work, and appointed by the responsible federal Minister.

The principal evidence relied upon by the CLC, defending the decision under section 19(5), was anthropological evidence. The CLC had instructed one of its employee anthropologists to attend a meeting of traditional owners and other members of the Amoonguna community, held to consider the lease proposals. In the lead-up to that meeting the CLC had conducted an information campaign amongst traditional owners about the competing lease proposals.

The CLC anthropologist reported back to the CLC on her observations of the meeting – who was present, who spoke, and what their role in the traditional owner group was. The CLC officers then prepared a briefing report for the sub-committee charged with deciding whether to give a direction to the CLC to grant the leases.

The applicants contended a number of key traditional owners were not present and/ or did not agree to the proposals. They objected to the amount of information provided to traditional owners, and to the way it was provided. They contended these factors meant there was an insufficient basis for the CLC to be satisfied that 'as a group' the traditional owners had consented, particularly when some of the traditional owners, including the applicants, were vociferously opposed to the leasing proposal and some of the 'right' people were not at the meeting. The opposition by the applicants, and those who supported them, was based on their view that leases for community infrastructure and services should not be granted to 'outsiders' but to organisations formed by the Amoonguna community itself, so that members of the Amoonguna community were responsible for how their own community operated. However, the evidence revealed divisions within the Amoonguna traditional owners about the applicants' plans and intentions, and about which was the best model for service delivery in the community.

So here, the decision-maker itself had established a preference for indirect proof of consent, through anthropologists and then through an internal report about the anthropologist's opinion concerning the outcome of a meeting of traditional owners. The other material it had was a report from an employee lawyer about what had occurred at the meeting.

On judicial review in the Federal Court, the anthropologist was called, and her views about the group's consent were tested. A senior CLC anthropologist was also called, to give evidence about the way in which the assessment of traditional owner consent is carried out by CLC anthropologists. There was also evidence from some traditional owners, both for the applicants and for the CLC, seemingly directed at showing there was no reasonable basis for the formation of the state of satisfaction by the CLC about the consent of Amoonguna traditional owners 'as a group'.[20]

Relevantly to this chapter, I found that the phrase 'consent as a group' should not be construed as meaning there must be unanimity amongst the group of traditional owners, nor even unanimity amongst the senior traditional owners with decision-making responsibilities under traditional law and custom. As the senior CLC anthropologist noted in his evidence, 'consent as a group' may also involve some with opposing views effectively electing not to press them. The dynamics are likely to be many and various.[21]

---

[20] See *Ellis* (n 1) [242]–[261].
[21] ibid [278].

Although the grounds of review in *Ellis* led to a different focus, the circumstances of that case illustrate at least two matters. First, there is much room for development, in terms of statutory construction, of a phrase such as 'consent as a group', when it appears in a context such as the Land Rights Act. For example, when will the disagreement of key elders be significant enough to take a situation outside the concept of 'consent as a group'? What if key elders agree, but the majority of the group does not? How are proven (or implied) power differentials within a group to be accommodated in this concept? While at the decision-making level these matters might be expected to be resolved pragmatically through further consultation, if a matter reaches judicial review, there is an opportunity for statutory interpretation to play a role in respecting and recognising the differences between Indigenous decision-making and non-Indigenous decision-making that are raised by the concept of 'consent as a group'. How much of applicable traditional Aboriginal law and custom of the traditional owners can be imported into the interpretation of this phrase? While section 77A may well have a determinative role to play if it is used to specify a method of decision-making, even in the operation of section 77A there are likely to be some real issues about (for example) which members of the group are able to *establish* the decision-making process. That is, who – according to traditional law and custom – can agree to agree in a particular way. It is not difficult to understand how, at an evidentiary level, the details of the decision-making process could give rise to difficulties in applying what might at first glance have looked like a specified and agreed method of decision-making.

There were a number of other grounds of judicial review in *Ellis* that are not relevant to the topic of this chapter. On the issue of section 19(5), the conclusion I reached (in summary) was that the applicants had not proved that the CLC committee had failed to form the requisite state of satisfaction about whether the Amoonguna traditional owners, 'as a group', had consented to the grant of the leases. I found there was enough material before the CLC committee on which its satisfaction about the consent of Amoonguna traditional owners 'as a group' could have been based, and the applicants had not proven any failure to properly consider that material, including the material that highlighted diverging views within the traditional owner group.[22] As I have noted, the grounds of review in *Ellis* did not call for any particular focus on the construction of the phrase 'consent as a group' by reference to traditional law and custom.

The question of how consent 'as a group' could, or rather *should*, be proved, is another aspect of these kinds of provisions that would benefit from further judicial consideration. The resort to the perceptions of non-Indigenous observers about what occurred gives rise to a number of issues. In *Ellis*, I said:

> In this proceeding, there was no issue raised about the process adopted by the CLC: that is, the process of using (largely non-Aboriginal) anthropologists as the persons who express a concluded view, and recommendation, to other CLC officers (such as Mr Gosford) about whether a group of traditional owners have given consent. No challenge was made to the unstated premise of this approach that a group of traditional owners cannot have autonomy over their decision-making so that they simply convey what their views are, without the additional layer of an anthropologist interpreting what they say and do, and measuring it for consistency against prior interpretations of previous expressions of the group's views. I am not aware of any other group of people in Australia whose decision-making processes are subjected to this kind of overlay. Whether it

[22] ibid [373].

be union members, workplace meetings, unincorporated associations, democratic bodies such as local councils, or any other form of collective decision-making, there is no requirement that a person or persons who are culturally separate, and not part of that group, somehow supervise, interpret and give an imprimatur to a collective decision-making process. The Land Rights Act does not require it. The Land Rights Act simply requires consent from traditional owners as a group. As I say, this was not an issue raised in this proceeding however, the evidence in this proceeding makes it clear that the primary source of authoritative information about what the traditional owners say is not considered to be what the traditional owners say, but rather what an anthropologist concludes from what they say, after having measured it against what has been said in the past.[23]

That process of measuring for 'consistency' is, it seems to me, a layer of external validation that is not applied to any other form of collective decision-making by people in Australia. It is also not the evaluative process contemplated by the Land Rights Act. That evaluative process is given by the statute to a Land Council, all of whose members are themselves Aboriginal people drawn from the region over which the Land Council operates. It is not given to anthropologists or Land Council employees.[24] While the Land Rights Act contemplates that a Land Council may receive, and use, expert advice in some circumstances (see section 27(1)(b)), the subject matter of section 19(5) is a matter for the Land Council itself, looking at what a group of traditional owners have or have not agreed to. It is a significant responsibility, because a consequence is the creation and alteration of interests in Aboriginal land.

What the statutory framework requires, and also what it may allow, in terms of proof of the assessment whether there has been 'consent as a group' by traditional owners is, like the concept itself, a matter ripe for further consideration in a public law context.

III. Representative and Majority Decision-making: The *Native Title Act 1993* (Cth)

The circumstances of *McGlade* illustrate a second, and quite different, context in which Australian courts have been called upon, in public law adjudication, to examine communal decision-making of Indigenous peoples, this time under a more prescriptive legislative scheme. The issues that arose in *McGlade* concerned the required level of adherence to the careful and specific scheme in the Native Title Act for the making of an agreement, contractual in nature, on behalf of a native title rights-holding group, or a native title claim group, where the agreement affected the group's native title rights and interests. Again, there were constructional choices to be made about what purposes Parliament sought to advance or achieve with the prescriptive scheme that had been created. The context for the decision, and the issues examined, was once again a level of division and disagreement within the native title claimant group about what the appropriate outcome was, in terms of dealing with the group's rights and interests in land.

---

[23] ibid [262].
[24] Although there are powers to form sub-committees who can make decisions: see s 29A of the Land Rights Act. This occurred in *Ellis*. There is also a delegation power: see s 29. Both these powers have limits relating to certain dealings in Aboriginal land.

A. Background

The Native Title Act was the Commonwealth's legislative reaction to the ground-breaking decision of the High Court in 1992 in *Mabo v Queensland (No 2)*.[25] It is, as might be expected, a piece of legislation reflecting many compromises. However, its purposes, as seen through its Preamble and Objects provision, are broad, and generally intended to be restorative towards Aboriginal and Torres Strait Islander peoples, affording their traditional laws and customs an express place in Australian law. The Preamble sets out the considerations taken into account by the Parliament of Australia in enacting the Native Title Act, including:

(a) That Aboriginal peoples and Torres Strait Islanders 'have been progressively dispossessed of their lands. This dispossession occurred largely without compensation, and successive governments have failed to reach a lasting and equitable agreement with Aboriginal peoples and Torres Strait Islanders concerning the use of their lands'.
(b) That '[a]s a consequence, Aboriginal peoples and Torres Strait Islanders have become, as a group, the most disadvantaged in Australian society'.
(c) Noting Australia's commitment to a range of human rights instruments, the rejection by the High Court of the doctrine that Australia was *terra nullius* (land belonging to no one) at the time of European settlement, and the Court's recognition of 'a form of native title that reflects the entitlement of the indigenous inhabitants of Australia, in accordance with their laws and customs, to their traditional lands', the Preamble also recognises the capacity for native title to be extinguished, but nevertheless identifies that the people of Australia intend 'to rectify the consequences of past injustices by the special measures contained in this Act' and to 'ensure that Aboriginal peoples and Torres Strait Islanders receive the full recognition and status within the Australian nation to which history, their prior rights and interests, and their rich and diverse culture, fully entitle them to aspire'.

The Act provides for a process whereby groups of Aboriginal or Torres Strait Islander peoples, who claim that they are united by traditional law and custom in the possession and enjoyment of rights and interests in particular land and/or waters, can have that 'native title' recognised, on proof of certain matters. The nature of the rights recognised may vary, and may be exclusive or non-exclusive. Rights and interests in land or waters, even if established, may be found to have been validly extinguished by acts of the Crown after sovereignty. In this lies the federal political and legislative compromise between Indigenous and non-Indigenous proprietary rights and interests in land. Extinguishment of native title may lead to compensation being payable. The High Court has recently considered this issue for the first time.[26]

The process of proving native title occurs within the jurisdiction of the Federal Court of Australia, and a 'determination' of native title may occur either after a litigated process, or by consent of all parties with proprietary rights and interests in the land or waters which are claimed. Along the way to such an outcome, the Native Title Act seeks to protect the rights of Aboriginal and Torres Strait Islander Peoples to their native title by the creation

---

[25] *Mabo v Queensland (No 2)* (1992) 175 CLR 1.
[26] *Northern Territory v Griffiths* [2019] HCA 7.

of a complicated 'future act' regime, whereby those claiming native title are intended to have a role in whether the grant of new proprietary interests in land over which claims are made should occur, and what the impact on their native title might be. The adequacy and effectiveness of this legislative 'protection' is a matter of debate.

Although the use of the term 'communal rights' to describe native title has been the subject of judicial comment,[27] the view I expressed in *McGlade* was that whether or not the characterisation of communal title as 'fundamental' is appropriate, a claim for native title made under the Native Title Act is generally made as a communal claim, on behalf of a group of people who assert rights and interests in a particular area or areas of land.[28] The *particular* native title rights and interests that are then contended to arise in accordance with the traditional law and custom acknowledged and observed by that claim group in respect of particular parcels of land may be identified as communal, group or individual, in accordance with the terms of section 223(1) of the Native Title Act.

However, the basis for the claim has a communal aspect. That is because, as the High Court pointed out in *Members of the Yorta Yorta Aboriginal Community v Victoria*,[29] a claim of rights and interests in land under the Native Title Act (and at common law, in accordance with *Mabo v Queensland (No 2)*) must arise from traditional laws and customs that are 'socially derivative and non-autonomous', and normative in that they are the laws of a society or group.[30] They are, the Court said, 'the creatures of the laws and customs of a particular society that exist as a group'.[31]

The premise of section 61 of the Native Title Act – the provision that regulates how a claim for native title, and for any compensation, is to be made – is that there is a 'native title claim group'. Since 1998, claims made under the Native Title Act must be made by an individual who is, or individuals who are, *authorised* by the members of the native title claim group to bring the application. Those individuals constitute 'the applicant': a peculiar kind of statutory concept in the Native Title Act, not a legal entity, but a collective that is required to act 'jointly'.[32]

Thus, agreement and decision-making by the native title claim group, through this peculiar statutory entity called an 'applicant', can be seen as central and integral to how the Native Title Act regulates native title interests, or claimed native title interests.

In *Daniel v Western Australia*,[33] French J (as his Honour then was) examined why the 1998 amendments introducing this concept of an 'applicant' were required, why they are of such importance and how the scheme operates:

> It is of central importance to the conduct of native title determination applications and the exercise of the rights that flow from their registration, that those who purport to bring such applications and to exercise such rights on behalf of a group of asserted native title holders have the authority of that group to do so. Prior to the 1998 amendments there was no requirement under the Native Title Act that an applicant have such authority. The absence of that requirement led, in some cases,

---

[27] For a summary, see *McGlade* (n 3) [357]–[358].
[28] ibid [360].
[29] *Members of the Yorta Yorta Aboriginal Community v Victoria* (2002) 214 CLR 422.
[30] ibid [49] (Gleeson CJ, Gummow and Hayne JJ).
[31] ibid [50] (Gleeson CJ, Gummow and Hayne JJ).
[32] *Native Title Act 1993* (Cth), s 61(2)(c).
[33] *Daniel v Western Australia* [2002] FCA 1147 (*Daniel*).

to conflicting and overlapping claims all carrying with them the statutory right to negotiate in respect of the grant of mineral tenements and the compulsory acquisition by Commonwealth or State Governments of native title rights and interests. Although many aspects of the 1998 amendments were the subject of controversy in the public and parliamentary debates that preceded their enactment, the need for communal authorisation of claims was largely a matter of common ground.[34]

After referring to some earlier authorities[35] that emphasised the importance of those representing a native title claim group being appropriately authorised to do so, French J concluded by describing how the mechanism in the Native Title Act for changing the individuals who are authorised to represent the claim group (section 66B) reinforces the communal control of the group over their claim:

> Section 66B recognises that a claim group which can confer authority on applicants to deal with matters arising in relation to a native title determination application, can also withdraw that authority. Additionally, it provides a remedy where that authority is exceeded. The authority required and recognised by the Native Title Act can be conferred by 'a process of decision-making that, under the traditional laws and custom of the persons in the native title claim group must be complied with in relation to authorising things of that kind'. Absent such a process it may be conferred 'in accordance with a process of decision-making agreed to and adopted by the persons in the native title claim group in relation to authorising the making of the application and dealing with matters or in relation to doing things of that kind'.[36]

With that background, it is necessary to explain the other part of the Native Title Act that gave rise to the issues in *McGlade*; namely, that part dealing with Indigenous Land Use Agreements, or ILUAs.

The Native Title Act provides, in a closely regulated way, for both those claiming native title and those to whom a grant of native title has been made, to negotiate and contract about uses or activities on land subject either to a claim of native title or to a grant of native title. The complicated 'future act' regime in the Native Title Act is designed to set out the circumstances in which acts (generally of third parties) affecting native title rights and interests will be valid, and when they will not. This is part of pursuing one of the objectives of the Act, which is to protect native title from any further extinguishment unless that extinguishment is an intended consequence of the statutory regime. The Native Title Act creates ILUAs, as statutory contracts, for this purpose. The necessary or appropriate parties to an ILUA is a matter of some complexity within the legislative scheme and I return to one relevant aspect of this below. It is possible (but not obligatory), as part of an ILUA, for a native title-holding group, or a native title claim group, to surrender its native title, in return for a range of negotiated benefits, including land access and protection regimes, and compensation.

To be enforceable (leaving the question of validity aside) ILUAs must be registered.[37] What can be registered must, therefore, accord with the statutory concept of an ILUA.

---

[34] ibid [11].
[35] *Western Australia v Strickland* (2000) 99 FCR 33, 52; and *Moran v Minister of Land and Water Conservation for NSW* [1999] FCA 1637.
[36] *Daniel* (n 33) [13]. See also [15]–[16].
[37] See *Native Title Act 1993*, pt 2, div 3, sub-divs A–E.

There are three different kinds of ILUAs established under the Native Title Act. *McGlade* concerned 'area' ILUAs.[38] As their name suggests, they are agreements covering specially identified areas. They may encompass the land of more than one claim group, and this fact had some real significance in *McGlade*.

McGlade concerned the 'Southwest Settlement': a negotiated outcome principally between representatives of the Noongar People and the State of Western Australia, relating to approximately 30,000 Noongar People and covering approximately 200,000 square kilometres of land.[39]

The Noongar People have made claims over the south-west of Western Australia and over metropolitan Perth for more than two decades. The process began with an application in November 1994, with further applications and interlocutory proceedings, until in 2003 what was described as the 'Single Noongar application' was made,[40] with 80 named applicants, 'on behalf of all Noongar people'. For those unfamiliar with native title proceedings, that is a lot of representative applicants, but the number reflected the size of a single Noongar claim group (many thousands) and the complexity of the intra-Indigenous interests represented by that claim. The number of individuals constituting the applicant had reduced considerably by the time of the settlement in 2014/15. The complex history of the claims is traced by Wilcox J in *Bennell v Western Australia*,[41] a decision on a separate question in one iteration of 'the Single Noongar application'. Although five overlapping claims in relation to native title brought by Mr Christopher Robert (Corrie) Bodney were dismissed by Wilcox J,[42] on the Single Noongar application his Honour found (in summary) that but for any question of extinguishment of native title by inconsistent legislative or executive acts, native title existed in relation to the whole of the land and waters in the claim area, and the persons who held the common or group rights and interests comprising the native title were the Noongar People.[43]

Rather than continue to litigate about their native title, the Noongar, through their native title representative body, South West Aboriginal Land and Sea Country Aboriginal Corporation (SWALSC), negotiated with the Western Australian Government to resolve the Noongar native title claims. Agreement in principle was reached in 2014. This provided, amongst other things, for the surrender of Noongar native title in exchange for what was described as 'a comprehensive package of benefits', including some legislative recognition of Noongars as the traditional owners for south-west Western Australia, an economic package of around $1 billion, and a variety of access, joint management, heritage and governance arrangements in relation to Noongar land.

---

[38] ibid pt 2, div 3, sub-div C.
[39] For a summary, see Government of Western Australia, 'South West Native Title Settlement' (11 February 2019), available at https://www.dpc.wa.gov.au/swnts/South-West-Native-Title-Settlement/Pages/default.aspx.
[40] Federal Court case WAD 6006 of 2003.
[41] *Bennell v Western Australia* (2006) 153 FCR 120.
[42] ibid [877]–[878].
[43] As identified in sch A to the application for determination filed on 10 September 2003 in Federal Court case WAD 6006 of 2003. Justice Wilcox's decision was overturned on appeal, on grounds that are not presently relevant. However, the Full Court was prepared to assume, without deciding, that his Honour's finding about the existence of the pre-1829 single Noongar community was correct: *Bodney v Bennell* (2008) 167 FCR 84, [43]. Some seven years later, the six ILUAs the State sought to register arose out of the claims in those proceedings, as well as certain other claims for native title in relation to parts of the land covered by the Single Noongar application.

These agreements were contained in six ILUAs covering land and waters in Noongar country. At meetings in early 2015, SWALSC sought authorisation for the making of these ILUAs under section 251A of the Native Title Act from the Noongar claim group members.

Like section 77A of the Land Rights Act, sections 251A and 251B of the Native Title Act contemplate that the claim group will decide what kind of decision-making process it wishes to use to make decisions.[44] In the case of the Native Title Act, they may be dispositive decisions (such as approving an ILUA), or decisions defining the scope of authority for those individuals who are the group's representatives for the conduct of a claim for native title or for compensation, namely the individuals who constitute the 'applicant' for native title under section 61 of the Native Title Act.

B. The *McGlade* Case

In *McGlade*, five of the 32 individuals who constituted the 'applicant' for the various claim groups did not sign the relevant ILUAs, one person died before the authorisation of the relevant ILUA and one died afterwards, and one person signed the relevant ILUA after it was lodged for registration. The remainder of the 32 individuals did sign the ILUAs.

---

[44] Those sections of the *Native Title Act 1993* provide:

251A Authorising the making of indigenous land use agreements

(1) For the purposes of this Act, persons holding native title in relation to land or waters in the area covered by an indigenous land use agreement authorise the making of the agreement if:

   (a) where there is a process of decision-making that, under the traditional laws and customs of the persons who hold or may hold the common or group rights comprising the native title, must be complied with in relation to authorising things of that kind – the persons authorise the making of the agreement in accordance with that process; or

   (b) where there is no such process – the persons authorise the making of the agreement in accordance with a process of decision-making agreed to and adopted, by the persons who hold or may hold the common or group rights comprising the native title, in relation to authorising the making of the agreement or of things of that kind.

(2) Without limiting subsection (1), when authorising the making of the agreement, a native title claim group may do either or both of the following:

   (a) nominate one or more of the persons who comprise the registered native title claimant for the group to be a party or parties to the agreement;

   (b) specify a process for determining which of the persons who comprise the registered native title claimant for the group is to be a party, or are to be parties, to the agreement.

251B Authorising the making of applications

For the purposes of this Act, all the persons in a native title claim group or compensation claim group authorise a person or persons to make a native title determination application or a compensation application, and to deal with matters arising in relation to it, if:

   (a) where there is a process of decision-making that, under the traditional laws and customs of the persons in the native title claim group or compensation claim group, must be complied with in relation to authorising things of that kind – the persons in the native title claim group or compensation claim group authorise the person or persons to make the application and to deal with the matters in accordance with that process; or

   (b) where there is no such process – the persons in the native title claim group or compensation claim group authorise the other person or persons to make the application and to deal with the matters in accordance with a process of decision-making agreed to and adopted, by the persons in the native title claim group or compensation claim group, in relation to authorising the making of the application and dealing with the matters, or in relation to doing things of that kind.

Four members of the relevant native title claim groups, including some of the individuals who had been nominated to constitute 'the applicant' for their claim group but who had not signed the ILUAs (such as Ms McGlade), challenged the proposed registration of the four ILUAs by the Native Title Registrar, by way of a judicial review proceeding. They sought orders in the nature of prohibition, seeking to prevent the Registrar from placing the ILUAs on the ILUA Register and thus making them enforceable and fully effective.

Relevantly for this chapter, those individuals contended the agreements were not ILUAs as that term was defined in the Native Title Act, because not all individuals who had been identified through the processes under the Native Title Act as applicants had signed them. It was apparent that at least some of the individuals who had not signed were opposed to the settlement reached.

All three members of the Court upheld the applicants' contentions, and found the agreements were not effective under the Native Title Act because not all of those who needed to sign them had done so. The Court focused on the available procedure under section 66B, to which I have referred earlier, and held that process could have been, but was not, used. The Court interpreted the detailed requirements of the Native Title Act as intending that all those who had been chosen by the claim group to comprise 'the applicant' needed to sign an ILUA. A theme of the Court's reasoning was the representative nature of those who had been chosen to constitute the 'applicant'.[45]

In a matter of weeks after the Full Court handed down *McGlade*, the Commonwealth had drafted, introduced and passed amending legalisation to avoid any ongoing effect of the decision, although the invalidation by the Court of the Noongar ILUAs remained effective.[46] The amendments did two things:

(a) they enabled the claim group to select particular individuals to be the contracting parties (whether or not those people are members of the 'applicant'); and
(b) if no such selection process was undertaken then a majority of those individuals who constitute the 'applicant' can sign the ILUA contract.

As before the amendments, the scheme of the Native Title Act is that every member of a claim group is bound by the ILUA contract. After the amendments, however, claim group members may be bound by an ILUA made by only one, or a small number, of claim group members, whether or not they were members of the 'applicant'.[47]

So, to be clear, if an ILUA involves the surrender of all native title rights and interests (as the Noongar ILUAs did) then all those individuals who have previously been chosen as representatives for their claim group need not agree, and need not indicate their agreement by signing an ILUA contract. If there are 20 individuals, and if 11 sign, the amendments appear to intend the ILUA will be valid. In *McGlade*, I expressed some views about the

---

[45] For the reasoning in *McGlade* (n 3) on aspects relevant to the issues in this paper, see: [240]–[246], [252]–[255], [264]–[265], [267]–[268] (North and Barker JJ), [363]–[371], [379]–[380], [435]–[439], [504]–[506] (Mortimer J).
[46] The *McGlade* judgment was handed down on 2 February 2017 and the Native Title Amendment (Indigenous Land Use Agreements) Bill 2017 (Cth) was introduced into the Federal Parliament on 15 February 2017. The Bill was referred for inquiry to the Senate Legal and Constitutional Affairs Legislation Committee on 17 March 2017, and following a consultation process, the Bill passed the Parliament on 14 June 2017 and came into effect on 22 June 2017.
[47] The ILUA must still be authorised under the Native Title Act, s 251A, but as some of the extracts cited in this chapter demonstrate, there are real debates about how authorisation is obtained in some circumstances.

collective nature of an 'applicant' in the scheme of the Native Title Act.[48] The effect of these amendments on the nature and purpose of an 'applicant' as a collective body in the Native Title Act remains to be seen.

Other judges have previously expressed the view that a claim group cannot authorise majority decision-making by those who constitute the applicant.[49] In *Gomeroi People v Attorney-General of New South Wales*, Bromberg J (dissenting in the result) said:

> The short answer to the applicant's reliance upon s 251B, is that the applicant has mischaracterised that provision. Section 251B does not deal with the decision-making process of an applicant. It deals only with the process of decision-making to be utilised when a claim group decides to authorise a person or persons to be an applicant.[50]

In *Tigan v Western Australia*, Gilmour J described the contention that individuals constituting an applicant could act by majority as 'inimical to the object of ss 61 and 62 in the context of the Act as a whole',[51] finding that members of the applicant cannot act by majority but must act in concert.[52] His Honour added:

> If dissension arises, as it seems has occurred here, between the named persons who are the applicant, then there are procedures under the Act for the native title claimant group to effect a change in the membership of the applicant. Indeed that has been foreshadowed in this case.[53]

I noted in *McGlade*, by reference to French J's decision in *Daniel*, that the representative role played by individuals constituting an applicant may mean that it is wrong to see an individual member of the applicant who objects to an ILUA as having a 'dissenting', 'unreasonable' or 'obstructionist' voice.[54] None of those descriptions may be accurate. The individual in *Daniel* could have been described as 'obstructing' the agreement. However, there is no sense in the judgment of French J that this individual was doing anything other than acting conscientiously according to what he saw as being in the best interests of the people he considered he had been authorised to represent, and indeed had been authorised to represent.

The extract from French J's reasons in *Daniel*[55] refers to the provision in the Native Title Act, section 66B, which establishes a process for changing the people who have been authorised to constitute the applicant. A key issue in *McGlade* was whether this was the only way to break a deadlock about an ILUA, or to resolve an issue of incapacity or death: that is, to change the composition of the representative individuals. That process is not only court-supervised, but the Court is also empowered to decide whether the change requested should be made. It can assess, at an evidentiary level, a complaint about whether a claim group does or does not continue to support a particular individual as its representative. In this way, power struggles within a group may be exposed in court.

As Kelsi Forrest points out, there is 'no requirement in entering into an ILUA that the claim group have a particular quorum present in order to ensure the "majority view" present

---

[48] *McGlade* (n 3) [380]–[386].
[49] See *Tigan v Western Australia* (2010) 188 FCR 533, [28] (Gilmour J) (*Tigan*); *Gomeroi People v A-G (NSW)* (2016) 241 FCR 301, [176]–[177] (Bromberg J) (*Gomeroi*).
[50] *Gomeroi* (n 49) [177].
[51] *Tigan* (n 49) [18].
[52] ibid [28].
[53] ibid.
[54] *McGlade* (n 3) [465]–[466].
[55] See n 36.

at an authorisation meeting is in fact the majority view of the wider claim group'.[56] If the majority decision-making method is chosen, it matters not whether senior elders are present – or only some of them. It could be that no one with principal authority to speak for country is present. Whoever is at the meeting may well be able to determine whether an ILUA should be adopted. That places heavy responsibility on those who organise authorisation meetings to ensure the right people are there, even if a traditional decision-making process is not to be adopted. The Federal Court is frequently called upon to determine challenges to authorisation processes, although, as many of my colleagues have emphasised, aside from the broad terms of section 251A (and section 251B in other contexts where authorisation is needed), the Native Title Act itself does not prescribe any detailed requirements for the notification and conduct of such meetings.

The National Congress of Australia's First Peoples, the current peak representative body for Aboriginal and Torres Strait Islander peoples in Australia, made the following submissions to the Senate committee inquiring into the *McGlade* amendments:

> Our membership reports that, in most instances, the people whose names appear on the Native Title Register are *already* a representative of the clan group who has a claim to land. Creating another level of governance within the claim group is not only culturally inappropriate, it opens the door for inadequate representation. If the RNTC [Registered Native Title Claimant] is already a representative of their clan or bloodline, then choosing amongst those representatives to be the party or parties to the ILUA may leave entire clans or bloodlines with legitimate claims to land unrepresented in the ILUA process.
>
> This is particularly concerning given the vital economic resources and employment opportunities made available to our peoples through ILUAs. Overwhelmingly, our members have reported bodies corporate strategically 'paying off' RNTCs to sign ILUAs. We have heard reports of members being given items such as cars, overseas holidays and even houses. *'Suddenly one or two families are driving around in Land Rovers, right after the ILUA has been signed,'* one member reported, *'but other bloodlines who've got claims don't get anything, because they got shut out of the deal.'* Given this reportedly widespread practice, there is a strong risk that nominated persons will be approached by companies with an economic attempting to get them to sign an ILUA which does not cater to all people with claims. This creates an inappropriate distortion of governance based on inducements provided by commercial interests with deep pockets to peoples with limited income, education and business experience.[57]

The Congress also submitted:

> We strongly oppose ... the simple majority requirement in the proposed amendment to s 24CD(2)(a). No Aboriginal or Torres Strait Islander person should have their native title rights violated by an ILUA they do not agree to. Allowing in ILUAs where a potentially large proportion of the native title claim group disagrees is unjust and compromises our native title rights.[58]

---

[56] K Forrest, 'A Wajuk Barladong Mineng Nyungar Perspective on *McGlade v Native Title Registrar* and the Resulting Native Title Amendment (Indigenous Land Use Agreements) Bill 2017' (2017) 8(28) *Indigenous Law Bulletin* 29, 30.

[57] National Congress of Australia's First Peoples, 'Submission No 57' to Senate Legal and Constitutional Affairs Legislation Committee, *Inquiry into the Native Title Amendment (Indigenous Land Use Agreements) Bill 2017*, March 2017, 4–5.

[58] ibid 12.

Hannah McGlade, the daughter of Noongar elder Mingli Wanjurri McGlade, the lead applicant in the *McGlade* litigation, has written:

> The Noongar Settlement ILUA provides substantial benefits that may not have resulted if people had pursed native title under common law, considering the high level of extinguishment that has taken place in Australia through inconsistent tenures and by way of interpretation of Aboriginal culture by the Anglo-Australian courts.
>
> Notwithstanding this, it is still important that we hear and respect the views of many Noongar people who did not support the agreement and who wanted to see Noongar sovereignty recognised. They disagreed with 'selling' Noongar lands and the extinguishment of Noongar native title that is at the heart of the ILUA. Many of these feel they had little or no say in the negotiation for the Noongar agreement and are aggrieved and unhappy by the decision to negotiate extinguishment. They are understandably fearful and concerned that ancestral and sovereign rights to land, which were never conceded through a Treaty, may be lost forever due to the ILUA.[59]

The Cape York Land Council, the Balkanu Cape York Development Corporation and the Cape York Institute for Policy and Leadership made the following submission:

> The Committee should understand that ILUAs are at the centre of this process, and traditional owners are torn apart by the ruthless politicking, dividing and ruling, misinformation, peeling off individuals and subgroups from the native title society: families that lived peacefully and respectfully for all of their lives are torn apart forever, when environmentalists and developers fail to respect proper processes and seek to manipulate traditional owners and cause division. ILUAs are the ground zero of this heartbreaking calamity.
>
> There will be, like any community of interest-holders, people with a range of perspectives on social impact, environmental impact and cultural impact of either development or conservation initiatives on native title land. The native title community should be left to work out their own resolutions to these questions, without being vulnerable to the manipulation and divisiveness caused by third parties with agendas. The Committee should consider law reform that protect[s] ILUA processes from this form of unconscionable dealing either by governments, developers or environmentalists.[60]

The Law Council of Australia submitted:

> The requirement for the people who comprise the registered native title claimant to act as a single entity may be regarded by those groups as a safety net to ensure decisions are made by consensus, rather than a blunt majority, particularly if there is a concern that one large faction may dominate. If a claim group has been operating on that basis, it would be understandable why a particular subgroup may be aggrieved, if that process is suddenly departed from in the authorisation of an Area Agreement.[61]

All these submissions illustrate some of the complexities involved in ensuring that agreement secured on behalf of a claim group is appropriately representative of all the views of

---

[59] H McGlade, 'The McGlade Case: A Noongar History of Social Justice and Activism' (2017) 43 *Australian Feminist Law Journal* 185, 209.

[60] Cape York Land Council, Balkanu Cape York Development Corporation and the Cape York Institute for Policy and Leadership, 'Submission No 14' to Senate Legal and Constitutional Affairs Legislation Committee, *Inquiry into the Native Title Amendment (Indigenous Land Use Agreements) Bill 2017*, 3 March 2017, [32]–[33].

[61] Law Council of Australia, 'Submission No 19' to Senate Legal and Constitutional Affairs Legislation Committee, *Inquiry into the Native Title Amendment (Indigenous Land Use Agreements) Bill 2017*, 6 March 2017, 3.

any of the claim group, and respectful of the role of senior claim group members under traditional law and custom. They also illustrate the potential difficulties in reconciling a majority decision-making method with claim group decision-making, where the whole basis for a claim of native title is the continued observance of traditional law and custom.

Where, as in *McGlade*, these issues are presented to a court in a public law context, once again interpretation of the statutory framework will be a core task of the court. There is, it seems to me, room within that task for greater recognition and support to be afforded to decision-making methods that are consistent with traditional law and custom. There may also be room for greater emphasis on the realities of the composition of claim groups, which generally comprise clan, estate or family groups within a larger society, in circumstances where different clan, estate or family groups 'speak for' different parts of country within a single claim area. There is frequently significant time and effort expended by native title claim groups in selecting the individuals who will constitute an 'applicant': many factors may be weighed in the balance in those choices, and they are generally viewed by claim group members as significant decisions, conferring significant responsibilities on those chosen. In construing the scheme of the Native Title Act, recalling its purposes and objects, there may be justifications for closer consideration of the kinds of decision-making processes that fit most comfortably with those purposes and objects. After the *McGlade* amendments, the Federal Parliament has permitted majority decision-making in some contexts. No doubt Australian courts, and the Federal Court in particular, will be called upon to interpret and apply those amendments in due course.

As a footnote, the controversy over the Noongar settlement continues. In October 2018, the Native Title Registrar registered all six ILUAs, this being the step prevented by the Court's decision in *McGlade*. There are fresh judicial review challenges in the Federal Court to the Registrar's decision. These are likely to be dealt with by the Court in 2019.

IV. Reflections on the Two Cases

Adversarial practice, and judicial method, has some way to travel to accommodate and understand the very different dynamics at work where the Court is faced with challenges to decision-making stemming from communal or group circumstances, and involving traditional laws and customs of Indigenous peoples.

There are possibilities for statutory construction that I do not consider have yet been explored, where statutes incorporate or recognise decision-making in accordance with traditional law and custom. There is room for reflection and perhaps reconsideration of how group decision-making should be proved, and what evidence is the best evidence.

There are challenges, too. Majority decision-making is generally quicker, and may be clearer.[62] It is also capable of resolving what might otherwise appear to be an impasse. However, as I have sought to illustrate in this chapter, majority decision-making may conflict not only with traditional decision-making processes, but also with the whole concept of

---

[62] Both s 77A of the Land Rights Act and ss 251A and 251B of the Native Title Act are capable of being used to give effect to such processes, but the courts' role in construing those provisions, and in reviewing decisions made pursuant to them, is an important one.

communal decision-making. It may encourage practices that are not necessarily conducive to the empowerment of Indigenous peoples, which the Federal Parliament has sought to advance with legislative schemes such as the two discussed in this chapter.

It is worth reflecting on whether it is appropriate to require Indigenous peoples to change their decision-making processes, or to impose majority decision-making processes as a default, if those processes are ill-suited to sustaining and empowering all those within Indigenous communities who share the rights and interests at stake.

In time, it might be hoped that there will need to be less reliance on anthropologists to offer opinions about whether or not a group 'consents', or what might be taken from the conduct and outcome of a meeting of Indigenous people. One might hope that Indigenous voices in evidence will become stronger and more confident of their place in proving the decisions of their communities. It is appropriate that judges are assisted to have the background, skills and knowledge they need to understand and assess the evidence of Indigenous people themselves, directly, about how their traditional law and custom require decisions to be made, or alternatively in narrating how – outside traditional law and custom – their community reached a decision, and why it should be found to reflect the decision of the group as a whole.

Those anthropologists working closely with Indigenous peoples in Australia, often through Land Councils, or native title representative bodies, are to be admired and respected for their dedication to the advancement of the interests of Indigenous peoples. I do not wish to suggest otherwise. However, courts need to show leadership, in my respectful opinion, in encouraging reliance on the evidence of Indigenous people themselves about their decision-making processes, and whether or not consent or agreement has been given, or consultation undertaken. This is a core part of empowering Indigenous peoples to be in charge of their own decision-making processes, and to explain and defend them where necessary. It is also a core part of encouraging and strengthening decision-making in accordance with traditional law and custom, if that is what Indigenous people feel is the right way in their respective communities.

It would be a step along the way to reconciliation for those involved in litigation, including judges, to accept that we should come to terms with the fundamental importance of communal decision-making to Indigenous peoples, and engage actively in approaching our tasks in a public law context with a true sense of respect for the importance of these processes, and the importance of them functioning well so that all Aboriginal and Torres Strait Islander peoples can deal constructively with interests in their own country, in the ways they choose.

8
Representing Jurisdiction: Decolonising Administrative Law in a Multijural State

MARY LISTON*

26. We call upon the federal, provincial, and territorial governments to review and amend their respective statutes of limitations to ensure that they conform to the principle that governments and other entities cannot rely on limitation defences to defend legal actions of historical abuse brought by Aboriginal people.

27. We call upon the Federation of Law Societies of Canada to ensure that lawyers receive appropriate cultural competency training, which includes the history and legacy of residential schools, the United Nations Declaration on the Rights of Indigenous Peoples, Treaties and Aboriginal rights, Indigenous law, and Aboriginal-Crown relations. This will require skills-based training in intercultural competency, conflict resolution, human rights, and anti-racism.

28. We call upon law schools in Canada to require all law students to take a course in Aboriginal people and the law, which includes the history and legacy of residential schools, the United Nations Declaration on the Rights of Indigenous Peoples, Treaties and Aboriginal rights, Indigenous law, and Aboriginal-Crown relations. This will require skills-based training in intercultural competency, conflict resolution, human rights, and antiracism.

…

42. We call upon the federal, provincial, and territorial governments to commit to the recognition and implementation of Aboriginal justice systems in a manner consistent with the Treaty and Aboriginal rights of Aboriginal peoples, the Constitution Act, 1982, and the United Nations Declaration on the Rights of Indigenous Peoples …[1]

I. Introduction: Public Law for a Postcolonial Age?

How should twenty-first-century Canadians understand the complex relationship among Indigenous authorities, Indigenous customary laws and Canadian public law – in particular, the relationships embedded in judicial review of Indigenous decision-makers?

---

*This is a revised version of a paper presented at the Public Law Conference 'Frontiers of Public Law', 11–13 July 2018, Melbourne Law School, Melbourne, Australia. I would like to thank fellow panellists and conference attendees, Shona Wilson Stark, my colleague Darlene Johnston and the editors for constructive feedback.
[1] Truth and Reconciliation Commission of Canada, *Calls to Action* (Winnipeg, 2015) available at http://www.trc.ca/.

178 Mary Liston

This question animates my analysis of a rapidly evolving set of jurisprudential relations between Indigenous peoples[2] and the Canadian state, a state that is now clearly recognised as a 'multijural' entity comprised of an overarching common law system, a hybrid civil law–common law system in Quebec, and numerous Indigenous legal orders across the country.[3] This challenge has been made more urgent following the completion of Canada's Truth and Reconciliation Commission (TRC) mandate and demands to implement its 94 Calls to Action.[4] The extract reproduced at the start of this chapter sets out the four Calls to Action that specifically concern the recognition, integration, teaching and competent understanding of Indigenous legal orders.

This chapter examines judicial review of Indigenous laws and governance systems from two places that are usually not a part of the Canadian public law conversation – a conversation that normally is constitutional in substance – administrative law and

---

[2] Following current practice in Canada, I shall use the term 'Indigenous' as the appropriate general referent for the original peoples of North America and their systems of law. Both 'Aboriginal' and especially 'Indian' are now considered outdated terms and are only used in reference to legal categories and texts. For example, s 35(2) of the Constitution Act 1982 (being sch B to the Canada Act 1982 (UK)) uses 'aboriginal' as the umbrella term under which three constitutional categories of Indigenous peoples are recognised: Indian, Inuit and Métis peoples. 'Indian', in s 35(2), originally solely referred to one of these three constitutional peoples, but 'First Nations' has replaced this term and is commonly used in legislation, policy and regarding Indigenous communities with reserve lands under the Indian Act RSC 1985, c I-5 ('Indian Act 1985'; more will be said about this statute in section II). To summarise this complicated set of terms: (i) 'Indigenous' is the preferred 'pan' term; (ii) 'Aboriginal' and 'Indian' are terms that refer to specific legal categories in historical time; and (iii) 'First Nations' replaces the term 'Indian', distinguishes one constitutional category of Indigenous peoples from the Inuit and Métis peoples, and indicates a set of Indigenous communities recognised as an administrative unit federally for the purpose of implementing the Indian Act 1985. See J Promislow and N Metallic, 'Realizing Aboriginal Administrative Law' in CM Flood and L Sossin (eds), *Administrative Law in Context*, 3rd edn (Toronto, Emond Montgomery, 2018) 88.

[3] For discussions of the multijural or pluralistic nature of the Canadian legal order, see J Borrows, *Canada's Indigenous Constitution* (Toronto, University of Toronto Press, 2010); and P Macklem, 'Indigenous Peoples and the Ethos of Legal Pluralism in Canada' in P Macklem and D Sanderson (eds), *From Recognition to Reconciliation: Essays on the Constitutional Entrenchment of Aboriginal and Treaty Rights* (Toronto, University of Toronto Press, 2016).

[4] From the 19th century to the late 20th century, over 150,000 Indigenous (First Nations, Inuit and Métis) children were (often forcibly) removed and separated from their families and communities to attend what were known as 'residential schools'. Residential schools, originally run by the various Christian churches nationwide, sought to 'take the Indian out of the child' – in the words of then Prime Minister John A Macdonald – through a coercive and assimilationist education system. Many children were subject to physical, sexual and psychological abuse. Most of the 139 Indian Residential Schools had closed by the mid-1970s, but the last federally-run school did not close until the late 1990s. The legacy of the residential school system has had a profound impact on Indigenous individuals, their families and their communities. Redress was sought both politically and legally. In May 2006, the Indian Residential School Settlement Agreement was approved (see Indigenous and Northern Affairs Canada, 'Indian Residential Schools', available at https://www.aadnc-aandc.gc.ca/eng/1100100015576/110010001 5577). This was the largest class-action settlement in Canadian history. Its implementation began in September 2007, with the aim of bringing a fair and lasting resolution to the legacy of the residential schools. One of the elements of the agreement was the establishment of the TRC by the federal Government to facilitate reconciliation among former students, their families their communities and all Canadians. On 11 June 2008, then Prime Minister Stephen Harper, on behalf of the Government of Canada, formally apologised in Parliament for the damage done by the residential school system: see Indigenous and Northern Affairs Canada, 'Statement of Apology to Former Students of Indian Residential Schools' (11 June 2008), available at https://www.aadnc-aandc.gc.ca/eng/110010001 5644/1100100015649. The TRC, also established in 2008, documented the history of the Indian residential school system and its legacy on Indigenous students, their families and their communities. Residential school survivors had an opportunity to share their experiences during public and private meetings held across the country. The TRC released an Executive Summary of its findings in 2015 along with its Calls to Action regarding reconciliation between Canadians and Indigenous peoples: Truth and Reconciliation Commission of Canada, *Calls to Action* (n 1). It published a multi-volume report in December 2015 that concluded the residential school system amounted to cultural genocide. The National Centre for Truth and Reconciliation, which opened in November 2015, is home to much of the research, documents and testimony that the TRC collected. Other parts of the TRC's

Indigenous local 'governance law'.[5] This is a topic that necessarily involves the determination of jurisdictions – the jurisdiction of the Canadian state, the jurisdiction of a reviewing court and the jurisdiction of the Indigenous authority under review. In Canada, this is an under-explored area that contains a fascinating set of legal questions at the intersection of public law (both administrative and constitutional), the law of democracy and the laws of Indigenous self-governance.[6] Such self-governance laws are often contained in, and communicated through, a variety of First Nations Customary Codes concerning procedures for elections, by-law enactment and membership in the community.[7]

Other ways of framing the central question in this chapter are: How do laws *in relation to* Indigenous peoples recognise and reinforce Indigenous law? Does administrative law *in relation to* Indigenous decision-makers and norms build helpful bridges or construct unhelpful barriers? And does judicial review facilitate or obstruct recognition and reconciliation? Seen from this angle, the chapter argues that Canadian law cannot ignore jurisprudential fences and walls that may need to be brought down if they obstruct proper recognition of Indigenous decision-makers or, conversely, be maintained where they justifiably protect Indigenous legal orders. The Calls to Action therefore implicitly require the re-examination and renovation of Canadian administrative law, so that it will appropriately recognise the distinctiveness of Indigenous decision-makers and norms at judicial review.

This chapter sets out the legal status of Indigenous peoples prior to and at the moment of Confederation in 1867. It then analyses how administrative law traditionally understands these Indigenous decision-makers and reviews their powers. The chapter turns to examine the emergence of a distinct field of public law – one now labelled Aboriginal administrative law[8] – in section IV. Lastly, section V begins the task of considering what it means to begin decolonising Canadian public law, and sets out how administrative law may assist in what appears to be Canada's postcolonial project of deep legal pluralism.

II. Indigenous Peoples *Before* the Indian Act

The elective system had two goals. The first was to acculturate the Indian people in the political mores of the prevalent society, through the operation of local self-government; the second, to eliminate the vestiges of the indigenous Indian political system. It would, as William Spragge, the

---

archives are housed at the Indian Residential School History and Dialogue Centre, which opened in April 2018 at the University of British Columbia.

[5] Note that in this chapter I am not considering treaty relationships, the duty to consult and accommodate, or the United Nations Declaration on the Rights of Indigenous Peoples, UN GA Res 61/295, 61st Sess, Supp No 53 (2007) (UNDRIP), which Canada endorsed on 12 November 2010.

[6] For more comprehensive overviews, see S Imai, 'Indigenous Self-Determination and the State' in BJ Richardson, S Imai and K McNeil (eds), *Indigenous Peoples and the Law: Comparative and Critical Perspectives* (Oxford, Hart Publishing, 2009); and WB Shipley, 'Governance Disputes Involving First Nations in Canada: Culture, Custom, and Dispute Resolution Outside of the Indian Act' in JAR Nafziger (ed), *Comparative Law and Anthropology* (Cheltenham, Edward Elgar, 2017). For an excellent discussion of Canadian colonialism see D Johnston, 'Aboriginal Traditions of Tolerance and Reparation: Introducing Canadian Colonialism' in M Labelle, R Antoinius and G Leroux (eds), *Le devoir de mémoire et les politiques du pardon* (Sainte-Foy, Presses de l'Université du Québec, 2005).

[7] See the Centre for First Nations Governance's 'Custom leadership selection codes for First Nations' for a detailed overview of the current issues around, and models and elements of, custom electoral codes, available at http://fngovernance.org/resources_docs/CustomElectionCod_BackgroundTemplate.pdf.

[8] See n 2.

Deputy Superintendent General of Indian Affairs, had asserted in 1870, 'establish a responsible for an irresponsible system'.[9]

Before examining the judicial treatment of Indigenous decision-makers in the administrative law electoral context, this chapter first explains what the immediate precolonial world of Indigenous governance looked like, what the Indian Act's changes signified and where it is possible to see how some of the tensions contained in the Indian Act point towards a potentially more fruitful future jurisprudence. I have divided this section into three parts unified by the concept of 'before' the Indian Act.[10] I am using 'before' in three senses in this section: at an earlier time (section II.A); in front of or confronting (section II.B); and under the jurisdiction of (section II.C). The overall objective is twofold: (i) to ensure that Canadian and non-Canadian readers have a sense of both the colonial and the legislative history; and (ii) to provide baselines for further comparative analysis of the legal treatment of Indigenous decision-makers in administrative law in the future. The extract above establishes this basic colonial baseline.

A. Before the Indian Act: Precolonial Promises

Before and at first contact, Indigenous communities were legally and politically sovereign in Canada. Their legal form varied across North America, but centred around family units now called tribes, clans, houses and so on. Some Indigenous communities have retained these forms (such as the Gitksan House system in northwestern British Columbia) and many communities continue to maintain hereditary chiefs and consult their Elders on governance matters. Their political nature also varied, from explicit aristocracies (especially in British Columbia) to democracies (such as was found in the Iroquois Confederacy in the East), but many Indigenous communities shared the traditional practice of consensus-based decision-making.[11] Regardless of their legal form and political nature, their sovereign status was recognised and confirmed in the Royal Proclamation of 1763:

> And whereas it is just and reasonable, and essential to our Interest, and the Security of our Colonies, that the *several Nations or Tribes of Indians with whom We are connected, and who live under our Protection*, should not be molested or disturbed in the Possession of such Parts of Our Dominions and Territories as, not having been ceded to or purchased by Us, are reserved to them, or any of them, as their Hunting Grounds.[12]

---

[9] W Daugherty and D Madill, *Indian Government under Indian Act Legislation 1868–1951* (Ottawa, Indian and Northern Affairs, 1980) 77.

[10] Not unlike Franz Kafka's invocation of the term in his parable 'Before the Law': F Kafka, *The Penal Colony: Stories and Short Pieces*, trs Willa and Edwin Muir (New York, Schocken Books, 1961) 148–50.

[11] Indigenous democracies, in turn, influenced European thought: see JD Stubben, 'The Indigenous Influence Theory of American Democracy' (2000) 81 *Social Science Quarterly* 716. See also K Horn-Miller, 'What Does Indigenous Participatory Democracy Look Like? Kahnawà:ke's Community Decision Making Process' (2013) 18 *Review of Constitutional Studies* 111. For more detailed information on historical and contemporary Indigenous societies, see Canadian Geographic's four-volume *Indigenous Peoples of Atlas Canada* (Ottawa, Royal Canadian Geographical Society, 2018), created in partnership with the Assembly of First Nations, Inuit Tapiriit Kantami, the Métis Nation, the National Centre for Truth and Reconciliation and Indspire.

[12] Royal Proclamation (1763) RSC 1985, App II, No 1 ('Royal Proclamation of 1763') (emphasis added). The Royal Proclamation also set out the boundaries of several new settler colonies in North America.

The Royal Proclamation is the first codification of the *sui generis*[13] Crown–Indigenous relationship for Canadian public law that, originally, began as sovereign to sovereigns. Its significance is threefold – legal, moral and political.[14] This document is therefore often called the 'Magna Carta of Indian rights', and all treaties negotiated after 1763 share a source in the legal principles, which are fundamental, contained in the Royal Proclamation.

The document promised to protect Indigenous peoples' interests in their unceded lands, and also provided a framework for making treaties where land and rights could be exchanged for the ceding of land to the Crown:

> And whereas great Frauds and Abuses have been committed in purchasing Lands of the Indians, to the great Prejudice of our Interests and to the great Dissatisfaction of the said Indians: In order, therefore, to prevent such Irregularities for the future, and to the end that the Indians may be convinced of our Justice and determined Resolution to remove all reasonable Cause of Discontent, We do with the Advice of our Privy Council strictly enjoin and require that no private Person do presume to make any purchase from the said Indians of any Lands reserved to the said Indians, within those parts of our Colonies where, We have thought proper to allow Settlement: but that if at any Time any of the Said Indians should be inclined to dispose of the said Lands, the same shall be Purchased only for Us, in our Name, *at some public Meeting or Assembly of the said Indians*, to be held for that Purpose by the Governor or Commander in Chief of our Colony respectively within which they shall lie: and in case they shall lie within the limits of any Proprietary Government they shall be purchased only for the Use and in the name of such Proprietaries, conformable to such Directions and Instructions as We or they shall think proper to give for that Purpose.[15]

The text has been interpreted to underscore the Crown's undertaking to assume primary responsibility to protect and manage Indigenous interests in their lands in order to prevent exploitation by settlers. It also signifies that the Royal Proclamation recognises a separate legal source for Indigenous interests in their lands, because Indigenous peoples had pre-existing legal rights prior to colonisation.[16] As a result of the Royal Proclamation, the Crown continues to have the monopoly on both the alienation of Indian land and accompanying responsibilities.[17] Lastly, as the words in italics emphasise, it imperfectly recognises Indigenous governance.

Crown responsibility forms the bedrock of the Crown–Indigenous public law relationship, and the Royal Proclamation stands as the key source for the constitutional, fiduciary principle of the honour of the Crown.[18] Importantly, this principle has been interpreted

---

[13] The term *sui generis* first described the distinctive interest that Indigenous peoples have in the land, which distinguishes them from settlers: see *Guerin v The Queen* [1984] 2 SCR 335, [387]. The term has since broadened to include multiple facets of the legal relationship Indigenous peoples have with the state. In this chapter, for example, I describe Indigenous decision-makers as *sui generis* because of pre-existing governance rights, which entails that they be treated differently when reviewed in administrative law. See also the majority decision in *R v Van der Peet* [1996] 2 SCR 507, [42] which affirmed, citing Professor Brian Slattery, a conception of the law of aboriginal rights as 'neither English nor aboriginal in origin: it is a form of intersocietal law that evolved from long-standing practices linking the various communities'.

[14] RA Reiter, 'Aboriginal and Treaty Rights: A Survey of Case Law and Future Directions in Law and Policies' (2000) 48 *Canadian Tax Journal* 1199.

[15] Royal Proclamation of 1763 (n 12) (emphasis added).

[16] See n 13 and text therein.

[17] Alienated Indian land, however, vests in the province. Only the federal Government can accept a surrender of aboriginal rights, but provinces can infringe (but not extinguish) with justification.

[18] The principle regulates Crown conduct. The honour of the Crown must always be upheld, which places significant duties on federal and provincial Crowns: the administration of surrendered lands; honouring aboriginal and

to acknowledge that the 'process of reconciliation flows from the Crown's duty of honourable dealing toward Aboriginal peoples, which arises in turn from the Crown's *assertion* of sovereignty over an Aboriginal people and *de facto* control of land and resources that were formerly in the control of that people'.[19]

Prior to 1982, the Royal Proclamation was held to have the force similar to that of a statute on the Crown[20] – but it now has at least quasi-constitutional, if not full constitutional status (but note that its force is becoming stronger, though still not full). The Crown's obligation to protect and manage Indigenous interests in their lands became codified in section 18 of the Indian Act,[21] while the rights and freedoms of Indigenous peoples that were recognised by the Royal Proclamation are now affirmed in section 25 of the Constitution Act 1982,[22] which guarantees that they will not be diminished.

For this subsection, the main takeaway is this: that while extending the laws of England and the power of the sovereign to the colonies, the Royal Proclamation did not displace or extinguish Indigenous legal orders (absent treaties) and it affirmed an ongoing relationship grounded in shared legal principles. The chapter argues that while the Crown asserted sovereignty over Indigenous modes of governance, it only ever had *de facto* control over some Indigenous communities, and had *de jure* over none as a result of the unilateral imposition of Western structures. This will be discussed next.

B. Before the Indian Act: Confronting 1876

At Confederation in 1867, the federal level assumed jurisdiction and responsibility for Indians under section 91(24) ('Indians, and Lands reserved for the Indians'[23]) of the British North America Act, with the chief government officer being the Superintendent General of Indian Affairs. Along with the power to make laws and regulations, significant discretionary power inhered in the Superintendent General and, later, other key federal actors. The breadth of this power is communicated in section 2 of the Indian Act 1876:

Superintendent General.

2. The Minister of the Interior shall be Superintendent-General of Indian Affairs, and shall be governed in the supervision of the said affairs, and in the control and management of the reserves, lands, moneys and property of Indians in Canada by the provisions of this Act.[24]

With this legislation, Indigenous communities had the legal form 'band' imposed on them:

Band.

1. The term 'band' means any tribe, band or body of Indians who own or are interested in a reserve or in Indian lands in common, of which the legal title is vested in the Crown, or who share alike

---

treaty rights; and, engaging in adequate consultation and accommodation when proved or unproved rights are potentially affected by Crown action. If Crown conduct infringes an Aboriginal right, it must be justified (*R v Sparrow* [1990] 1 SCR 1075).

[19] *Haida Nation v British Columbia (Minister of Forests)* [2004] 3 SCR 511, [32] ('*Haida Nation*').
[20] *The King v Lady McMaster* [1926] Ex CR 68, [72].
[21] Indian Act 1985 (n 2).
[22] See n 2.
[23] British North America Act 1867 (UK), now The Constitution Act 1867 (UK).
[24] An Act to amend and consolidate the laws respecting Indians, SC 1876 ('Indian Act 1876'). The Indian Act does not govern Métis and Inuit communities.

in the distribution of any annuities or interest moneys for which the Government of Canada is responsible; the term 'the band' means the band to which the context relates; and the term 'band,' when action is being taken by the band as such, means the band in council.[25]

This is also the moment where elective and customary band councils were firmly distinguished, and this distinction has carried forward in time to present-day legislation.

Prior to the enactment of the first Indian Act in 1876, the federal Government had already passed legislation affecting the governance powers of Indigenous peoples and tied this to their ability to participate politically. The Gradual Civilization Act 1857 awarded any First Nation male (who met the conditions of literacy, good moral character and freedom from debt) full ownership of 50 acres of reserve land. He would then be enfranchised and compelled to cut ties with the band and cease to be an Indian.[26] This, of course, was an early assimilation policy.[27] Shortly thereafter, the Gradual Enfranchisement Act 1869 consolidated the federal Government's control of the on-reserve political system by enabling the Superintendent General to determine when and how elections would take place.[28] The federal Government introduced a Western-style voting system for choosing leadership, with the aim of replacing traditional modes. Every three years a community would select a band council and a band chief using a Western-style plurality system through a secret ballot.[29] Under this legislation, band councils were meant to be 'local mouthpieces for the federal government for the primary purpose of realizing control over the Aboriginal population'.[30]

The Indian Act 1876 was enacted outside of the treaty process and without the participation of any First Nation. Its main purpose was to facilitate the colonisation and assimilation specifically of First Nations, but this purpose ultimately later encompassed all Indigenous communities in Canada. This legislation was, in effect, the 'capstone' to the earlier legislation just discussed. It confirmed that all First Nations would be treated the same by the federal authority, as each community would be organised along patrilineal lines (though many were traditionally matriarchal)[31] and all would use the Western-style method of choosing their leadership discussed immediately above.

In 1880, the Department of Indian Affairs was created to administer the Indian Act.[32] So-called 'Indian agents' were delegated powers to make decisions over Indigenous

---

[25] ibid s 3(1).
[26] An Act to Encourage the Gradual Civilization of Indian Tribes in this Province, and to Amend the Laws Relating to Indians, 3rd Session, 5th Parliament, 1857.
[27] Similar legislation existed in Australia during this period: see, eg, Aboriginal Protection Act 1869 (Vic).
[28] An Act for the gradual enfranchisement of Indians, the better management of Indian affairs, and to extend the provisions of the Act, 31 Victoria, Chapter 42, SC 1869.
[29] For example, the current Indian Act 1985, s 2(3) describes the exercise of powers conferred on band or council as follows: 'Unless the context otherwise requires or this Act otherwise provides, (a) a power conferred on a band shall be deemed not to be exercised unless it is exercised pursuant to the *consent of a majority* of the electors of the band; and (b) a power conferred on the council of a band shall be deemed not to be exercised unless it is exercised pursuant to the *consent of a majority* of the councillors of the band present at a meeting of the council duly convened' (emphasis added).
[30] A Gatensby, 'The Legal Obligations of Band Councils: The Exclusion of Off-Reserve Members from Per-Capita Distributions' (2014) 12 *Indigenous Law Journal* 1, 13.
[31] See, eg, the voting requirements for electing chiefs in 1876: 'At the election of a chief or chiefs, or the granting of any ordinary consent required of a band of Indians under this Act, *those entitled to vote at the council or meeting thereof shall be the male members of the band* of the full age of twenty-one years; and the vote of a majority of such members at a council or meeting of the band summoned according to their rules, and held in the presence of the Superintendent-General, or an agent acting under his instructions, shall be sufficient to determine such election, or grant such consent': Indian Act 1876, s 61 (emphasis added).
[32] Indian Act, 43 Victoria, Chapter 28, SC 1880.

individuals and their communities, to regulate intrusively in Indigenous lives and to enforce the Indian Act. The Indian Act's scope ranged from constitutive matters such as defining who qualifies to be a status Indian (a power which had a disproportionate effect on Indigenous women who lost their Indian status if they married non-Indigenous men, as did their children), putting into place the 'pass system' where Indian agents could control which Indigenous individuals could come and go on the reserve (and, if found off the reserve without a valid pass, could be arrested), to legal matters concerning wills, land and resource use, and so on.[33] Further colonial legislation banned spiritual ceremonies and dances, introduced the assimilatory residential schools and compulsory attendance at them, and prohibited Indigenous persons from hiring lawyers. During this period, First Nations had to obtain the approval of the Superintendent General – later the Minister of Indian Affairs – for 'almost every aspect of life from land allocation to dog control by-laws'.[34]

Bands were governed by elected chiefs and councils who had jurisdiction over the reserve territory. A band would be recognised through the treaty process or unilaterally by the federal Government (recognition, therefore, was a discretionary power subject to abuse). Bands could retain their precolonial form and so might coincide with pre-existing family groups or clans, sub-units of nations or groups of a number of nations.[35] But recall that both of the terms 'Indian' and 'band'[36] are colonial impositions, which have now been replaced by 'First Nations' and 'government' or 'authority'.

During this phase, communities could use the Western-style electoral system to elect more than one chief in a community or even life chiefs[37] – but always subject to the discretion of the federal Government and the Superintendent General.[38] The band chiefs and councils would also be responsible for implementing aspects of the Indian Act, thereby painfully participating in a governance model that was both assimilationist and paternalistic.

At this historical juncture, the colonial project clearly aimed to end what was then continuing self-government, to lay to rest any future inherent right to self-government, and to provide only bare recognition of Indigenous laws and customary norms. Nevertheless, a bare modicum of recognition existed for some aspects of the constitutive life of Indigenous communities such as their traditional form and the continuance of some types of leadership such as life chiefs.[39] More will be said about this bare modicum in section II.C.

---

[33] For a brief overview, see JF Leslie, 'The *Indian Act*: An Historical Perspective' (2002) 25(2) *Canadian Parliamentary Review* 23.
[34] S Imai, *Aboriginal Law Handbook* (Toronto, Carswell, 1999) 131.
[35] ibid 132.
[36] See quote accompanying n 25. The current Indian Act defines 'band' as follows: 'band means a body of Indians: (a) for whose use and benefit in common, lands, the legal title to which is vested in Her Majesty, have been set apart before, on or after September 4, 1951; (b) for whose use and benefit in common, moneys are held by Her Majesty, or (c) declared by the Governor in Council to be a band for the purposes of this Act: Indian Act 1985, s 2(1).
[37] See Indian Act 1876, s 62.
[38] Chiefs would remain in office 'unless deposed by the Governor [in Council] for dishonesty, intemperance, immorality, or incompetency': ibid.
[39] Compare with Australia, where Aboriginal customary laws have never been recognised by general public law. See Australian Law Reform Commission, *Recognition of Aboriginal Customary Laws* (ALRC Report 31) (12 June 1986). Note that the customary laws focused on in this report related to criminal law (punishment, sentencing) and rehabilitation.

C. Before the Indian Act: Imperfect Jurisdictions

Not surprisingly, the imposition of a foreign governance model, combined with the high paternalism of the Superintendent General and his Indian agents, met with both active and passive resistance. This reality, along with other aggravating factors, led to the inconsistent application of the Indian Act's provisions – the electoral provisions being of significance here.[40]

In 1884, the federal Government enacted the Indian Advancement Act, legislation that offered more 'advanced' bands the opportunity to govern themselves like a municipality using a ward system.[41] The assimilative purpose of this Act is best expressed by then Superintendent General Sir John A Macdonald,[42] who, in a response to a question during parliamentary debate about possible resistance from band chiefs, stated:

> In some of the tribes there are hereditary and elective chiefs combined. There are great varieties of organizations in the different bands. It is not proposed in any way to affect the status or the rank of the chiefs; but, as in the Act of 1880, *where an elective system of chiefs has been adopted, the hereditary chiefs retain their rank, but lose their power.* I will say to my hon. friend that I have received a good many suggestions from different bands of Indians – from educated men, who are quite capable of judging the effect of this law. On the whole, the Bill has been favourably received by more advanced bands. There is to be no force exercised on the Indians; this measure is also intended to give them the opportunity of adapting themselves to the white system as much as possible.[43]

Of significance here is the explicit goal of emptying the traditional power of hereditary or lifelong chiefs, while maintaining the shell of their formal rank under the proposed municipal elective system.[44] Macdonald's words also evince the alternative 'cooperative' governmental approach (as opposed to the mode of unilateral imposition) to secure the 'advancement' and assimilation of Indigenous peoples. Whether unilateral or cooperative, however, the end goal remained the same. At this time, the Canadian Government's oscillation reflected its continued paternalistic adherence to Indian protection (inherited from the Royal Proclamation) *and* its continued hope that Indian people and their cultures would disappear through intermarriage and the imposition of foreign processes in relation to their governments, lands and customs. While clearly misguided, it was not until the early decades of the twentieth century that the turn to a predominantly destructive bent became very clear

---

[40] The historical backdrop is complicated, but two of the key dynamics that aggravated matters at this time were the drive to construct a national railway and the project of settling the West. To achieve these purposes, treaties had to be negotiated with Indigenous peoples across the West, but many Indigenous communities were also forcibly relocated in order to build the railway and ensure that settlers could access arable land. Also at this time, Canada faced continued pressure due to the American embrace of the expansionist manifest destiny ideology.

[41] An Act for conferring certain privileges on the more advanced Bands of the Indians of Canada, with the view of training them for the exercise of municipal power, 47 Victoria, Chapter 28, SC 1884. This legislation mainly focused on bands located in Eastern Canada and those communities who, in the opinion of the Government, exhibited the capacity and competence to engage in municipal-style government and democratic processes. The determination of which community was 'advanced' was at the discretion of the Superintendent General. Again, this is an example of an assimilationist policy where 'advanced' affirmed the superiority of Western civilisation. See also Leslie, 'The *Indian Act*: An Historical Perspective' (n 33).

[42] Note that at this time, Macdonald held the positions of Superintendent General, Secretary of the Interior, Minister of Railways and Canals and, of course, Prime Minister.

[43] Daugherty and Madill, *Indian Government under Indian Act Legislation 1868-1951* (n 9) 14 (emphasis added).

[44] See also ME Walls, *No Need of a Chief for this Band* (Vancouver, University of British Columbia Press, 2010) 63.

when Deputy Superintendent-General Duncan Campbell Scott said the following about new legislative measures for the compulsory enfranchisement of Indians:

> I want to get rid of the Indian problem. I do not think as a matter of fact, that this country ought to continuously protect a class of people who are able to stand alone. Our objective is to continue until there is not a single Indian in Canada that has not been absorbed into the body politic and there is no Indian question, and no Indian Department, that is the object of this Bill.[45]

According to Wayne Daugherty and Dennis Madill, 1899 saw a federal attempt at blanket application of the Indian Act across the country, a move that was successful in the eastern part of Canada (ie, the Maritimes, Quebec, Ontario) where the three-year elective system was in fact imposed without Indigenous consent by Order in Council.[46] But, some communities, like the Six Nations of Brantford, remained notable exceptions in the East by retaining their hereditary system of government due to federal fears about the strength of their resistance. The years between 1890 and 1906 marked the 'high point' for rolling out the electoral programme. But the new territories located in the Canadian West (ie, from Manitoba to British Columbia and up to the far North) proved very difficult to control.[47]

In 1906 the Indian Act and the Indian Advancement Act were consolidated, with the Indian Advancement Act becoming Part II of the Indian Act. The purpose of the 'advancement' provisions expressly aimed to put into effect a process of assimilation that amounted to cultural genocide.[48] But the classification of some Indigenous communities as less advanced – particularly in the West – inadvertently enabled their customary systems to survive and operate. As Wayne Daugherty and Dennis Madill confirm:

> The most innovative measure implemented by the Department was the matter [sic] in which it dealt with the bands not considered 'advanced'. The Department permitted these bands to form councils through tribal custom.[49]

Still, Indigenous autonomy remained a struggle to achieve. Before 1951, 400 bands selected their leadership through custom, 185 used the three-year system and nine used the Indian Advancement one-year system. By 1971, approximately 384 bands had been placed under the three-year elective system,[50] while 169 retained customary methods.[51] In section III, we shall see how much this trajectory has now changed.

---

[45] EB Titley, *A Narrow Vision: Duncan Campbell Scott and the Administration of Indian Affairs in Canada* (Vancouver, University of British Columbia Press, 1986) 50.

[46] Daugherty and Madill, *Indian Government under Indian Act Legislation 1868–1951* (n 9) 22.

[47] Two historical moments of significant Indigenous resistance occurred in this period: the Red River Rebellion in 1869 and the North-West Rebellion in 1885, both led by Métis politician and political leader Louis Riel. For discussion of the legal significance of these events for the rule of law in Canada, see M Liston, 'The Canadian Rule of Law: Past, Present, Future' in E Mendes (ed), *Canada's Constitutional Democracy: The 150th Anniversary Celebration* (Toronto, Lexis Nexis, 2017).

[48] As a result of the TRC, Canada has come to recognise residential schools as a tool to effect cultural genocide. One of the most important acknowledgements came when then Chief Justice of the Supreme Court of Canada Beverly McLachlin used the term in a 2015 speech at the Global Centre for Pluralism. At that time, she was the highest-ranking Canadian official to use the phrase: see S Fine, 'Chief Justice says Canada attempted "Cultural Genocide" on Aboriginals', *The Globe and Mail* (28 May 2015), available at https://www.theglobeandmail.com/news/national/chief-justice-says-canada-attempted-cultural-genocide-on-aboriginals/article24688854/. The TRC's finding is now starting to find its place in current case law involving Indigenous legal matters.

[49] Daugherty and Madill, *Indian Government under Indian Act Legislation 1868–1951* (n 9) 80.

[50] In 1951, the Indian Advancement part of the Indian Act was rescinded by Order in Council: ibid 6.

[51] ibid 74.

D. Before the Indian Act: Recovering the Future?

This brief history underscores three key points to take to the next section. The first is the precolonial recognition of Indigenous governance in 1763, a principled recognition that carried forward in time despite the assimilative colonial project. The second is that the sovereign jurisdiction of the Canadian state was imperfect. It did not have *de jure* perfect sovereignty and it also did not have full *de facto* control. The Crown could not and did not eradicate customary forms of governance. Indeed, it was compelled to tolerate such modes – a toleration made easier by classifying them as inferior. This backhanded recognition has turned out to be a blessing in disguise, since customary practices continued to survive, particularly in the West, producing distinctive Indigenous decision-makers. Third, the pinnacle of 'advanced' self-government imagined for Indigenous communities during the early years of the Indian Act was that of a municipality or local government. As we shall see, this preferred colonial model continues in the jurisprudence, but nothing in the jurisprudence compels the recognition of only one form of band governance. Lastly, it is worth noting again that the focus on Indigenous decision-makers who are elected using the Indian Act model or traditional modes is deliberate, as the selection of representative leadership is a constitutive act made by self-governing Indigenous individuals and communities, especially in a democratic order.

III. Administrative Decision-makers Elect?

> The band, as an enduring entity with its own government, is a unique type of legal entity under Canadian law. … What distinguishes a band from a club is that a band exists apart from any voluntary act of its members. In this respect a band is more like a nation state than a club. But no comparison is totally apt. In law a band is in a class by itself.[52]

This section sets out the legal status of Indigenous authorities in administrative law, as well as the current parameters of judicial review under the administrative law principles of procedural fairness and substantive review. The connection I wish to make in this section through the use of the word 'elect' is twofold. The first is the obvious political dimension of elections and voting. Secondly, it refers to the *sui generis* nature of band governance, using 'elect' in the sense of a specially selected or an exclusive group of people.

As we have seen, one of the chief effects of the Indian Act was to impose a Western governance framework on Indigenous communities. By the mid- to late-twentieth century, the majority of Indigenous 'bands' employed a plurality-type electoral process to select their representatives and enacted their by-laws by majoritarian means. Traditional customary laws and processes were therefore displaced, but not eradicated. As of 2018, a little less than 40 per cent of the 618 recognised First Nations governments or bands currently hold their elections under the colonial electoral system.[53] Under this Indian Act

---

[52] Imai, *Aboriginal Law Handbook* (n 34) 133, citing Jack Woodward's *Native Law* text.
[53] For data, see Indigenous and Northern Affairs Canada, 'First Nations Electoral System Breakdown, by Province and Territory, in Canada' (4 July 2015), available at http://www.aadnc-aandc.gc.ca/eng/1337794249355/1337794353857.

framework, colonialism continues since the chief and council, though elected by their community, are ultimately accountable to the federal Government rather than the Indigenous community per se. The federal Minister also continues to retain considerable powers to intervene in the affairs of the community. Today's Indian Act, then, is not substantially different from its nineteenth-century predecessor legislation when it comes to governance matters.

But a sea change has recently occurred, and now the majority of First Nations – a little over 55 per cent – use customary election systems.[54] Section III.B discusses this sea change and its implications for Canadian public law. A resurgence is underway and, as the quotation at the beginning of this section adverts, public law has begun to grapple with the true *sui generis* nature of Indigenous peoples as self-determining bodies in a class by themselves.

A. The Traditional Baseline Slightly Tweaked

In 2014, the federal Government under then Prime Minister Stephen Harper enacted the First Nations Elections Act (FNEA).[55] This legislation offers an alternative to the Indian Act election system, with the aim to create greater stability and reduce the number of weaknesses contained the earlier system.[56] One prominent flaw was that a two-year electoral cycle resulted in much turmoil, frustration and, ultimately, litigation over disputed electoral processes and outcomes. First Nations can now choose to opt out of the Indian Act and sign onto the revised FNEA election system, which has a four-year cycle. The FNEA is not, however, a return to traditional governance. One of the key shortcomings of the FNEA is that the capacious discretionary powers of the Minister over elections remains unaffected in both the FNEA and the Indian Act:

> **Elected councils**
>
> 74 (1) *Whenever he deems it advisable for the good government of a band, the Minister may declare* by order that after a day to be named therein the council of the band, consisting of a chief and councillors, shall be selected by elections to be held in accordance with this Act.[57]

Because of this criticism and the fact that the FNEA does not change the Indian Act election system, the FNEA is generally not perceived to represent a true alternative. The instability that FNEA sought to mitigate is a profound problem, originating in the devastating effects of colonial laws and policies. Such instability, however, will continue under customary electoral methods that must grapple with this legacy of constitutive questions around identity, membership and citizenship into the future.

---

[54] ibid. The remaining First Nations have different arrangements through negotiated self-government agreements (the next largest category at 5%) or operate under the FNEA (the smallest category). See also J Quesnel and K Ishkanian, *Custom Election Codes for First Nations: A Double-Edged Sword* (Fraser Institute, 2017), available at https://www.fraserinstitute.org/sites/default/files/custom-election-codes-for-first-nations.pdf.

[55] First Nations Elections Act SC 2014, c 5. This chapter will not consider this legislation any further.

[56] For further discussion of these flaws, see *Report of the Standing Senate Committee on Aboriginal Peoples, First Nations Elections: The Choice is Inherently Theirs* (2010), available at https://sencanada.ca/Content/SEN/Committee/403/abor/rep/rep03may10-e.pdf.

[57] Indian Act 1985 (emphasis added).

B. Getting Outside the Indian Act

How, then, do Indigenous communities get 'outside' of the Indian Act's domination, homogenisation and continued imposition of European-derived electoral practices that section 74 represents? Fortunately, as section II concluded, the Indian Act did not extinguish or completely replace traditional modes of Indigenous governance.[58]

One central way that Indigenous communities can revert to traditional forms is through the treaty process or self-government agreements.[59] Alternatively, the community may develop its own community election code by opting out of the Indian Act. There is no explicit provision in the Indian Act for reverting to custom. One can see that this is implicitly intended in the current definition of a band council:

council of the band means

(a) in the case of a band to which section 74 applies, the council established pursuant to that section,

(b) in the case of a band that is named in the schedule to the First Nations Elections Act, the council elected or in office in accordance with that Act,

(c) in the case of a band whose name has been removed from the schedule to the First Nations Elections Act in accordance with section 42 of that Act, the council elected or in office in accordance with the community election code referred to in that section, or

(d) in the case of any other band, *the council chosen according to the custom of the band, or, if there is no council, the chief of the band chosen according to the custom of the band.*[60]

A First Nation that chooses to govern itself through a customary elections code must ask the Minister of Indigenous and Northern Affairs (now called Crown-Indigenous Relations and Northern Affairs Canada[61]) to issue an order that removes that First Nation from the application of the Indian Act's electoral provisions.[62] Once that order is made, the evolution of the Indigenous community's customary laws proceeds without oversight by, or intervention from, the federal Government. Nevertheless, a custom must meet the following criteria, criteria that assure both continued incursion from the Canadian legal system and judicial review: protection of the rights of individual members; provisions for appeals and for amending the custom; compliance with the principles of natural justice and consistency

---

[58] Other cultural and familial aspects of Indigenous societies were, however, targeted for extinction, such as language, religion and cultural identity through initiatives such as banning speech and religious practices like the potlatch, removal of children into residential schools and denial of basic rights. The potlatch is a ceremony integral to the governing structure, culture and spiritual traditions of First Nations of the Northwest Pacific coast. The ceremony served a number of important communal and legal functions, such as redistributing wealth, conferring status and rank upon individuals, and establishing claims to various names, powers and rights in the territory.

[59] These treaties will also not be the focus of this chapter.

[60] Indian Act 1985, s 2(1) (emphasis added).

[61] In August 2017, Prime Minister Justin Trudeau's Government dissolved Indigenous and Northern Affairs Canada in order to create two new departments: Indigenous Services Canada, and Crown-Indigenous Relations and Northern Affairs Canada.

[62] This is called a 'section 74' order. One of the significant requirements is that the community election system must be consistent with the Canadian Charter of Rights and Freedoms with respect to guaranteeing voting rights to off-reserve members, and also ensuring the opportunity for off-reserve electors to hold positions on the band council. See Indigenous and Northern Affairs Canada, 'Conversion to Community Election System Policy' (1 June 2015), available at https://www.aadnc-aandc.gc.ca/eng/1433166668652/1433166766343.

with the Canadian Charter of Rights and Freedoms; and expression in a clear, written format.[63]

A variety of electoral models therefore currently exist: communities may continue to fall under the authority of the Indian Act or the FNEA; they may keep their Indigenous governance and Indian Act systems apart, but maintain both for different functions; or they can replace the Indian Act governance structure with traditional forms, values or principles through self-government agreements or by opting out of the Indian Act.[64] A little over half of First Nations (55 per cent) have community-designed or custom election codes, while 5 per cent of First Nations select leaders pursuant to constitutions contained in their self-government agreements. Significantly, then, since the early 2000s – and in a very short space of time – Indian Act governance structures have become a minority – albeit a significant minority – across the country.

C. Creatures of Administrative Law

While many First Nations still hold elections under the Indian Act, section III.B underscored the salient fact that more than half of First Nations have chosen to organise political affairs in their communities in accordance with their own customs, and not under the Indian Act.[65]

But while an Indigenous process for selecting a governing body may be outside of the colonial Indian Act, the community is not outside of administrative law. Following public law scholar Lorne Sossin, I define administrative law as 'any law, rule, principle, or practice that governs decision making by government or an entity governed by a statute'.[66] Those communities under the Indian Act or the First Nations Elections Act are clearly public actors whose powers are delegated under that enabling legislation: they are therefore statutory delegates, just like any other statutory authority, for the purposes of judicial review. They are conventionally described as follows: 'As *municipal councils* are the "creatures" of the legislatures of the provinces so *Indian band councils* are the "creatures" of the Parliament of Canada.'[67]

---

[63] J Giokas, *The Indian Act: Evolution, Overview and Options for Amendment and Transition* (Ottawa, Royal Commission on Aboriginal Peoples, 1995) 211. See Canadian Charter of Rights and Freedoms, Part I of the Constitution Act 1982, being Schedule B to the Canada Act 1982 (UK) ('the Charter').

[64] For further discussion, see JJ Borrows and LI Rotman, *Aboriginal Legal Issues: Cases, Materials & Commentary*, 5th edn (Toronto, Lexis-Nexis Canada, 2018) ch 1.

[65] Why different Indigenous communities select customary elections, opt for the FNEA model or continue to use the Indian Act election system is a topic that is beyond the scope of this chapter. That said, part of the reason is that securing consensus to change to another electoral model is always difficult to achieve. Another reason is that some communities are split into factions, with part of the community preferring the traditional form of governance and the other part of the community preferring the Indian Act model – this situation often leads to very divisive politics. For a current example of this kind of conflict in the Wet'suwet'en First Nation, see M Abedi, 'Band Councils, Hereditary Chiefs – Here's what to know about Indigenous governance' *Global News* (10 January 2019), available at https://globalnews.ca/news/4833830/band-councils-hereditary-chiefs-indigenous-governance/.

[66] L Sossin, 'Indigenous Self-Government and the Future of Administrative Law' (2012) 45 *UBC Law Review* 595, 603. In this piece he sets out a narrower definition of administration law as 'the substantive and procedural standards by which those who exercise public authority will be held legally accountable'.

[67] *Re Whitebear Band Council v Carpenters Provincial Council of Saskatchewan et al* (1982) 135 DLR (3d) 128, [13].

But, as it turns out, while the current legal framework incentivises Indigenous communities to remove themselves from those sections of the Indian Act that concern leadership selection, membership, administration of governance codes and other matters, it does not preclude judicial review of their procedures and decisions. They remain, subject to conventional administrative law review as: (i) local governments; or (ii) agents of the Minister; or (iii) statutory delegates; or (iv) intermediaries between the members of the band and other governments. The question for the future – which will be examined in section IV – is whether judicial review will treat Indigenous decision-makers differently if they exercise powers under their own customary laws, rather than under non-Indigenous legislation.

If a band chooses to govern with customary election laws, it can no longer be affected by either the relevant provisions of the Indian Act or by the Minister in this governance area. Customary election laws may be protected from other non-Indigenous laws as well but, as was noted earlier, the Charter still applies.[68] 'Customary' can mean a reversion to traditional forms and processes of choosing representatives and leaders, or First Nations can create new customs. A community, for example, can have a mix, such as a two-tiered governance system with an elected Village Council (elected either by custom or under the Indian Act) and a hereditary Clan Council.[69] Regardless of whether the custom is old or new, customs are fundamentally understood to be dynamic, not static or rooted in originalism.[70] Those applicants relying on 'custom' are obliged to specify what the custom is – for example, identify and describe it in the relevant Electoral Code – and indicate its source.[71]

The next two subsections set out in brief how Indigenous electoral processes and authorities are currently reviewed in administrative law, turning to review for procedural fairness first and then substantive review.

D. The Scope of Governance under Common Law Judicial Review: Procedural Fairness Review

Electoral processes and decisions made in relation to these processes will be reviewed under the two principles of fairness in relation to procedure: the duty to hear the other side; and the right to an unbiased, impartial and independent decision-maker.[72] As in all procedural fairness cases, the principles will be contextually applied (discussed further in the next section), with fairness reviewed on a correctness standard (or, alternatively, a standard akin to correctness).[73] But, as will be discussed in section IV, the principles of fairness have long

---

[68] See *Kahkewistahaw First Nation v Taypotat* [2015] 2 SCR 548 ('*KFN v Taypotat*'), which involved a Charter challenge to the Grade 12 educational requirement in the community Election Code.
[69] *Clifton v Hartley Bay Village Council* 2005 FC 1594.
[70] *McLeod Lake Indian Band v Chingee* (1998) 165 DLR (4th) 358, [40].
[71] *Francis v Mohawk Council of Kanesatake* [2003] 4 FC 1133, citing *McArthur v Canada (Department of Indian Affairs and Northern Development)* (1992) 91 DLR (4th), 666. For a behaviour to become custom, a practice must be firmly established, generalised and followed consistently by a majority of the community. If evidence of broad consensus exists, the views of an insignificant number of members who have persistently objected to the practice or behaviour can be disregarded.
[72] *Baker v Canada (Minister of Citizenship and Immigration)* [1999] 2 SCR 817 ('*Baker*').
[73] *Mission Institution v Khela* [2014] 1 SCR 502, [89].

been considered 'universal' in Canada, a view best expressed by Lamer CJ of the Supreme Court:

> In my view, principles of natural justice apply to the bands' tribunals *as they would apply to any tribunal performing similar functions*. The fact that the tribunals have been constituted within the context of a federal policy promoting Aboriginal self-government does not, in itself, dilute natural justice.[74]

Reviewing courts have the inherent authority to supplement or expand statutory guarantees, but if a statute ousts procedural fairness necessarily or by implication, it is reviewed through constitutional law. A margin of appreciation may be shown to the choice of procedures and deference may be shown to the expertise of the decision-maker. These common law principles are not ousted by a self-government context, as the quotation above confirms.

Electoral disputes often centre on the issues of adequacy of notice to appear before a decision-making body, lack of an opportunity to make representations and allegedly biased tribunals. Indigenous customary election codes are recognised. If, for example, a customary code sets out an eligibility requirement grounded in Indigenous values, this will be recognised and applied by a reviewing court. Due to the flaws contained in the Indian Act and through the process of running customary elections, this is a very active area of administrative law. Many of the cases turn on the facts – especially for bias findings – rather than on Indigenous customary law or values *per se*.

E. The Scope of Governance under Common Law Judicial Review: Substantive Review

In addition to the judicial review of procedures and decisions for fairness, Canadian administrative law reviews the content of these decisions to ensure that they are either correct or reasonable in terms of their substantive content and outcome.[75] Contemporary administrative law accords broad 'deference as respect' to administrative decision-makers, and even more so to municipal authorities in judicial review on substantive grounds.[76] In *Catalyst Paper*, McLachlin CJ, for a unanimous Supreme Court, developed a highly deferential standard to review the content of by-laws made by municipal authorities:

> The case law suggests that review of municipal bylaws must reflect the broad discretion provincial legislators have traditionally accorded to municipalities engaged in delegated legislation. Municipal councillors passing bylaws fulfill a task that affects their community as a whole and is legislative rather than adjudicative in nature. Bylaws are not quasi-judicial decisions. Rather, they involve an array of social, economic, political and other non-legal considerations. 'Municipal governments are democratic institutions', per LeBel J for the majority in *Pacific National*

---

[74] *Canadian Pacific Ltd v Matsqui Indian Band* [1995] 1 SCR 3, [74] ('*CP v Matsqui IB*') (emphasis added).

[75] Because Indigenous authorities are subject to the Charter, even when governing through customary election codes, a large jurisprudence exists about discriminatory voting requirements that appear to disadvantage off-reserve voters. Both Indian Act and customary governance practices have often been held to offend the Charter's s 15 equality guarantee, and election rules that exclude off-reserve members can be found unconstitutional. See, eg, *Corbiere v Canada (Minister of Indian and Northern Affairs)* [1999] 2 SCR 203, which concerns Indian Act elections, and *KFN v Taypotat* (n 68), which concerns customary elections. I am not considering this line of jurisprudence in this chapter.

[76] *Baker* (n 72) [65].

Investments Ltd v Victoria (City) ... [2000] 2 SCR 919, at para 33. In this context, reasonableness means courts must respect the responsibility of elected representatives to serve the people who elected them and to whom they are ultimately accountable.[77]

This case stands for the proposition that only truly egregious examples of by-law making and content will not survive judicial scrutiny.[78]

As will be discussed further in the next section, currently the delegated authority given to municipalities and the authority possessed by Indigenous bands under the Indian Act or customary codes share some similarities. The important difference is that municipalities are treated as a level of democratic government that should be given heightened respectful treatment when by-laws are reviewed. The jurisprudence reveals that Indigenous authorities are not shown the same level of deference, even when they are enacting their own by-laws.[79]

Older jurisprudence follows a pattern encapsulated in *Jackson v Piikani Nation Election Appeals Board*.[80] In this garden variety customary elections case, the Federal Court considered the nomination process for a disputed band customary election where a traditional band principle of behaviour was factored into the consideration of the applicants' eligibility to run for office, and resulted in the disqualification of their candidacies. The principle of behaviour – part of the traditional values called *piikanissini* – demanded that members of the community should not engage in behaviour that dishonours, brings shame, and/or negatively affects the dignity and integrity of the First Nation. This principle captured a wide variety of behaviour, not just criminal, such as corrupt practices (the scope of which were determined by the principle) and abuse of office. The band's Chief Electoral Officer (CEO) applied the principle and determined that the applicants were ineligible to run as councillors, because she was in receipt of a letter from the Piikani Elders that these individuals had engaged in corrupt practices. The Code specifically indicated that the principles of *piikanissini* applied to the eligibility to hold office, but not explicitly to running for the office of Chief or councillor. The applicants appealed to the Piikani Nation Election Appeals Board, which upheld the CEO's decision. At judicial review, the court asked: Did the CEO misinterpret the Code and lose jurisdiction because she did not have the authority to refuse to list a person as eligible to run for office? And, moreover, did the appeals board lose jurisdiction for the same mistake too?

In coming to its conclusion, the reviewing court considered several of the standard of review factors to determine the intensity of judicial review.[81] Phelan J held that neither the CEO nor the Board 'possess any particular expertise that the Court does not possess. The issues before the Court deal with jurisdiction and statutory interpretation: the core of a court's work'.[82] He therefore chose the least deferential standard: correctness. Using a strict approach to interpret the Election Code, Phelan J employed the common law canon *expressio unius est exclusio alterius* to confirm that it would be against intent and inconsistent to apply the principles of *piikanissini* where they were evidently omitted in other parts of

---

[77] *Catalyst Paper Corp v North Cowichan (District)* [2012] 1 SCR 5, [19].
[78] ibid [20]–[21]. A *Wednesbury*-like standard is employed.
[79] For a fuller discussion of Indigenous by-law making, see N Metallic, 'Indian Act By-Laws: A Viable Means for First Nations to (Re)Assert Control over Local Matters Now and not Later' (2016) 67 *University of New Brunswick Law Journal* 211.
[80] *Jackson v Piikani Nation Election Appeals Board* 2008 FC 130 ('*Jackson v Piikani Nation*').
[81] *Dunsmuir v New Brunswick* [2008] 1 SCR 190.
[82] *Jackson v Piikani Nation* (n 80) [17].

the Code.[83] He buttressed this conclusion by pointing to the fact that the Election Code is a 'modern' document, enacted in 2002.

He called the principles 'noble principles'[84] mandating a conduct of loyalty and honesty toward the community. He also recognised the role of the Elders, who act as 'a senate and have a governing voice in the community. Their wisdom and direction are to be respected and followed'.[85] But not, apparently, by the reviewing court. In his analysis of the intent behind the Election Code, Phelan J surmised:

> It may well be, and the evidence suggests it, that the people believed that the Elders could invoke PIIKANISSINI and declare a person ineligible to stand for election. The Elders who wrote to the CEO thought so and the CEO thought so. But this conclusion is at odds with the Election Code.[86]

Phelan J declared that the CEO's decision was made without proper authority. Sufficient evidence had also not been provided about the role of the Elders, the nature of *their* authority, and the evidence that they provided. He ordered the Piikani Nation to amend their by-law to make the Code consistent by revising the eligibility requirements to run in the election to match the grounds for removal from office. They had six months to do so or else pay the applicants' costs.

This relatively recent decision stands at odds with contemporary administrative law review for substance. In the latest cases, the principle of deference (as respect) is held to be a requirement of the law of judicial review and a principle of modern statutory interpretation.[87] Reasonableness has become the presumptive standard at judicial review when: the enabling legislation contains a privative clause; and/or the case concerns a legal matter where the authority is operating in its 'home' statute (ie, enabling legislation) or a closely related statute; and/or the authority possesses expertise that reviewing courts do not have. The reasonableness standard is contextually applied in conjunction with the modern approach to statutory interpretation. Jurisdiction – narrowly construed – is reviewed on a correctness standard.[88] Correctness concerns only particular questions of law, but not matters of statutory interpretation generally. Expertise of the decision-maker is relative to the courts and interpretive pluralism is recognised: public authorities share the task of interpreting legislation with courts.[89] Reasons play a justificatory role and can work to support the reasonableness of the decision and the outcome, but need not be perfect.[90] The usual remedy for procedural and substantive review is to quash and send the decision back to the original authority, sometimes with directions. *Jackson v Piikani Nation* overtly contradicts several of these requirements of the law of judicial review.

Older jurisprudence involving Indigenous authorities therefore sets out administrative law baselines and attitudes that require change. The next section revisits the precedents that

---

[83] ibid [25].
[84] ibid [22].
[85] ibid.
[86] ibid [23].
[87] *McLean v British Columbia (Securities Commission)* [2013] 3 SCR 895, [40].
[88] *Alberta (Information and Privacy Commissioner) v Alberta Teachers' Association* [2011] 3 SCR 654, [34].
[89] For greater analysis of these jurisprudential baselines, see M Liston, 'Six Impossible Things' in C Hunt, L Neudorf and M Rankin (eds), *Legislating Statutory Interpretation: Perspectives from the Common Law World* (Toronto, Carswell, 2018).
[90] *Newfoundland and Labrador Nurses' Union v Newfoundland and Labrador (Treasury Board)* [2011] 3 SCR 708, [18].

inform current jurisprudence. Current case law has moved away from some of the negative attitudes, but as *Jackson v Piikani Nation* illustrates, Indigenous authorities are not always the beneficiaries of the changes in contemporary administrative law. Because of this, the administrative law framework requires further work to move review of Indigenous authorities out of the colonial past and into the twenty-first century.

IV. Extending or Reclaiming Jurisdiction?

> I do not think that the power of the Band to choose its council in a customary manner is a 'power conferred on the Band' as is contemplated [under] the Indian Act. Rather it is an inherent power of the Band; it is a power the Band has always had, which the Indian Act only interferes with in limited circumstances, as provided for under section 74 of the Act.[91]

Despite Canada's colonial history and cases like *Jackson v Piikani Nation*, contemporary case law has come to affirm that the power of a Band to choose its council in a customary manner is an inherent power and one that a Band has always had. It is therefore not conferred or delegated, even if it may be reviewed as such. The legal proposition quoted above has now become a true new baseline in the jurisprudence.

This section turns to the chapter's secondary objective, which is to re-examine the current 'leading' administrative law cases in order to assess what elements might be jurisprudentially beneficial for Indigenous communities and identify where the case law must evolve to, for example, recognise Indigenous laws and distinct governance values. Particular attention is paid to changing judicial perceptions of their supervisory role vis-à-vis Indigenous communities, and whether or not judges have tried to reconstruct Canadian public law to reflect the changing boundaries of their own and these other actors' powers. This section therefore seeks to understand where and how courts have recognised the inherent authority of Indigenous communities to choose their own leaders and modes of governance.

It is important to note two facts here: (i) the leading cases are from the 1990s and are therefore seriously out of date; and (ii) few cases go beyond Federal Courts, with the 1995 Supreme Court case *CP v Matsqui IB*[92] (discussed next) representing a significant exception. The two cases examined in this section ostensibly concern procedural fairness but, as will be no surprise to many public law scholars, they also delve into substantive issues.

A. More Fences Than Bridges: *CP v Matsqui IB*

The first case is *CP v Matsqui IB*. This case concerns judicial review of an on-reserve taxation appellate body, the Assessment Review Committee, which was tasked with assessing the Canadian Pacific (CP) railway company whose rail lines ran through the reserve. The Matsqui band had passed their own by-laws to levy taxes on real property on reserve lands

---

[91] *Bone v Sioux Valley Indian Band No 290 Council et al* (1996) 107 FTR 133, [32]. No doubt the emergence of this baseline was buttressed by the foundational work of the Royal Commission on Aboriginal Peoples and its five-volume final report that was released in 1996.
[92] *CP v Matsqui IB* (n 74).

(as had several other bands at the time). The by-laws provided that members of the appeal tribunal could be paid, but did not mandate that they must be paid, and gave no tenure of office so that members might not be appointed to sit on future assessment appeals. Members of the bands could be appointed to the tribunal. The jurisdiction to create the by-laws, including an appeals mechanism to Federal Court, Trial Division,[93] was not disputed and the Minister of Indian Affairs and Northern Development had allowed the by-laws;[94] the by-laws were therefore *intra vires*.

The Indigenous appellate body, however, only existed on paper in the enabling legislation, and this case was in fact a preliminary move by CP to delegitimise the appeal body – in effect, euthanising it before it even got off the ground. One administrative law issue was CP's attempt to prevent the Matsqui band from taxing the land CP used for its rail line, using the argument that this land was not 'in the reserve' and so outside the band's jurisdiction. The other issue was CP's use of the second principle of procedural fairness to argue that the structure of the appeal body led to violation of the right to an unbiased, impartial and independent decision-maker. The company argued that the Indigenous appellate body could be considered neither an adequate institution in itself nor an adequate alternative remedial route to the Federal Courts. Band members appointed to the appeal body would act in a self-interested way when it came to assessing the fairness of the taxes that the Council imposed on companies like CP.

The case presents the first older baseline concerning the politics of Indigenous governance in the Canadian legal system. The decision is a complex judgment that mainly focuses on the discretion of the first-level Federal Court judge, rather than on the Indigenous decision-maker as such.

We begin with the analogy (discussed in section III.E) between municipal levels of government and Indigenous governments: 'Although the scheme resembles the kind of tax assessment regime we see at the municipal level of government in Canada, it is more ambitious in what it sets out to achieve.'[95] Both are statutory delegates. Matsqui band became one via the Indian Act. This is a conventional administrative law baseline, and it is not a bad one, since municipalities benefit from a great deal of deference at judicial review due to their democratic pedigree (see section III.E). In his judgment, Lamer CJ appears to be slotting the tax assessment body into this political typology and gestures towards its role in developing self-government. Yet even he seems to recognise that this is a highly imperfect analogy because of the different aspiration between enabling municipal governance and enabling Indigenous governance. As the chapter emphasised earlier, Indigenous governance bodies are *sui generis* by virtue of their pre-existing or continuing sovereignty, a status or pedigree that makes them very unlike municipalities.

---

[93] The Matsqui band's assessment by-law enabled the appointment of Courts of Revision to hear appeals from the assessments, the appointment of an Assessment Review Committee to hear appeals from the decisions of the Courts of Revision and, finally, an appeal on questions of law to the Federal Court, Trial Division from the decisions of the Assessment Review Committee. The other bands provided for a single hearing before a Board of Review, with an appeal directly to the Federal Court, Trial Division.

[94] Under the Indian Act at that time, the Minister did not approve by-laws but, rather, 'allowed' them. This is because the Minister had a disallowance power delegated in s 82(2) of the Act to disallow rather than power to approve band by-laws. In 2014, the Indian Act Amendment and Replacement Act SC 2014, c 38 removed the Minister's ability to disallow band council by-laws.

[95] *CP v Matsqui IB* (n 74) [43].

But Lamer CJ does not move to assert this fuller *sui generis* status. Instead he considers another analogy. This analogy compares Indigenous governing authorities to universities: 'the university thus being given the chance to correct its own errors, consonantly with the traditional autonomy of universities as well as with expeditiousness and low cost for the public and the members of the university'.[96] Again, it seems to be a promising direction because universities benefit from a great deal of jurisdictional autonomy, including their arm's-length relationship to government that partly shields them from Charter application.[97] Does this mean that Indigenous bodies, like universities, should benefit from the shield that protects them from intensive judicial review (whether administrative law review or Charter review) because of history, democratic pedigree or protective provisions in their enabling documents? At this point it looks as if Lamer CJ will agree with Mr Justice Joyal in the original Federal Court Trial Division decision that the issue should be resolved 'over there' in that *other* jurisdiction. It also seems to be the case that he recognises that the tax assessment body is linked to, and essential for, the realisation of greater self-government. But this view is what I shall ultimately call *negatively evolutionary*.

According to Lamer CJ, Indigenous decision-makers and their governing institutions will be held to the *same* or perhaps higher standards of procedural fairness as non-Indigenous authorities in administrative law. According to him, *all* appellate tribunal bodies should have similar guarantees of independence, impartiality and lack of bias as a universal common law guarantee of fairness, no matter where they are located in the state. Moreover, we find ourselves between a rock and a hard place, for the remedy that Lamer CJ imagines is for the appeal board members to be appointed by the federal Government, not the Band, and that these appointees need not be members of the community. This of course guts self-government, and we have more than a fence; we have a serious wall constructed in the Majority's approach to self-government.[98]

This, then, is what I meant by negatively evolutionary. Lamer CJ does not think that Indigenous communities – despite governing themselves for thousands of years – had or currently have the capacity for self-government. They are in an infant state as pre-modern noble savages, and self-government must be paternalistically facilitated by the Canadian state. The Majority's decision therefore does not move us very far forward, but it is still considered good law.

It would be a sad story to end there, but the dissent written by Sopinka J builds a precedential bridge going forward. In his judgment, Sopinka J invokes something like the modern

---

[96] ibid [45].
[97] Universities, like hospitals, do not fully 'fit' within the concept of 'legislature and government' under s 32(1) of the Charter. See *McKinney v University of Guelph* [1990] 3 SCR 229 and *Eldridge v British Columbia* [1997] 3 SCR 624, where the Supreme Court concludes that universities and hospitals are not government entities for the purpose of Charter review, but the Charter may apply in limited circumstances where the activity in question implements a government policy or programme. Private entities may also be subject to the Charter if they perform inherently governmental functions.
[98] This majority decision violates the simple condition of equality that Harry Hobbs discusses in ch 10 in this volume, because it cannot recognise the Indigenous institutional body and does not want it to look radically different from existing non-Indigenous institutions. The dissenting opinion, as well as the judgment discussed next, both exhibit the creative, flexible accommodation of difference that is required in this context.

approach to statutory interpretation (not yet adopted until *Rizzo Shoes*[99] in 1998) and blends it with the dynamic, liberal approach to the interpretation of Aboriginal rights:[100]

> The self-government policy context is relevant to the entire exercise of judicial discretion. ... Accordingly, before concluding that the by-laws in question do not establish band taxation tribunals with sufficient institutional independence, they should be interpreted in the context of the fullest knowledge of how they are applied in practice.[101]

Even more, we can see how he fits with the current approach to reasonableness review – reasonableness contextually understood. It therefore provides a bridge to a more contemporary approach to reviewing Indigenous decision-makers, where Indigenous self-government (in terms of bodies, decisions, procedures) is conceived of as a factor central to understanding context and should receive great weight at judicial review. To my mind, this passage emphasises the duty that now lies on the judiciary and the legal profession – so important post-TRC – to familiarise oneself with the history of Canada and the different decision-making context in Indigenous communities.

B. Building Bridges and Future Paths:
Sparvier v Cowessess Indian Band

We now turn to the second leading case from the 1990s, but this time from a more typical lower court: *Sparvier v Cowessess Indian Band*.[102] This case concerns judicial review of an election run using customary law. In this election for Band Chief, a dispute emerged regarding the residency of several of the candidates (but not that of the applicant, Ken Sparvier). Sparvier, an unsuccessful electoral candidate, initiated the appeal. The Election Appeal Tribunal made overt procedural errors, which are not the real focus of the case. The case concerned the subsequent ability of the Cowessess Election Appeal Tribunal to overturn the election and call for a new one. The tribunal was constituted under the Cowessess Indian Reserve Elections Act. But the real salience of the choice of opting out of the Indian Act and organising the political affairs of the community in accordance with one's own customs had not yet been recognised.

This case is of particular interest for two other reasons: (i) the reviewing judge, Mr Justice Marshall Rothstein, rendered this decision before he was elevated to the Supreme Court; and (ii) he is an expert in statutory interpretation and general interpretation in public law contexts. We begin with jurisdiction:

> If *Gabriel v Canatonquin* is correct and a council of a band, elected pursuant to customary Indian law, is a federal board in the same manner as would be the case had it been elected pursuant to a federal statute such as the Indian Act, then an appeal tribunal, elected pursuant to customary Indian law would, by similar logic, be a federal board. ... This Court thus has jurisdiction to decide this application. ... Applying *Gabriel v Canatonquin*, the Appeal Tribunal is a federal board.[103]

---

[99] *Rizzo & Rizzo Shoes Ltd (Re)* [1998] 1 SCR 27.
[100] *Nowegijick v The Queen* [1983] 1 SCR 2; and *Mitchell v Peguis Indian Band* [1990] 2 SCR 85.
[101] *CP v Matsqui IB* (n 74) [114]–[115].
[102] *Sparvier v Cowessess Indian Band* [1993] 3 FC 142 ('*Sparvier v Cowessess IB*').
[103] ibid, 151.

I want to begin with the administrative law jurisdictional baseline: a council of a Band elected under customary law (or an internal appeal tribunal created under the by-law making powers of the Indian Act as in *CP v Matsqui IB*) is considered a federal decision-maker for the purposes of judicial review. It is worth noting that this administrative law jurisdictional baseline appears to exhibit some internal tensions. What, exactly, is the jurisdiction of federal courts at judicial review over an Indigenous community that has elected to govern itself using customary law? The case is used to affirm the principle that a band council elected under customary law is a federal decision-maker for the purposes of administrative law judicial review, just like the appeal body in *CP v Matsqui IB* or any other statutorily created federal tribunal. One can see, however, that Rothstein J mulls over the jurisdiction question using the key word '*if*. This case raises an interesting proposition. If a band chooses to govern itself through customary law, does this choice function as a kind of privative clause protecting jurisdiction for the purposes of judicial review? No authority exists to say no. No authority exists to say yes either. In 1993, when this case was decided, there was little to no authority on these foundational matters.

Concerning the application of the principles of procedural fairness, Rothstein J considers the issue and resolves it in favour of conventional administrative law – but he does not take us to the same place as Lamer CJ in *CP v Matsqui IB*: 'While I accept the importance of an autonomous process for electing band governments, in my opinion, minimum standards of natural justice or procedural fairness must be met.'[104] It is the minimum, not the maximum, standards of procedural fairness that should be met in order to recognise the different context, the different identity of the decision-maker and the principle of deference, because otherwise it would be imposing non-Indigenous standards of procedure in the place of customary practices. The jurisprudential bridge he extends is the question I am facing today in my administrative law class: to what extent should courts have jurisdiction over Indigenous authorities engaged in the project of self-government?

I do not wish to deny that notions of fairness or due process should inform Indigenous governance contexts. If there is some universal content to justice then the concept of procedural fairness is certainly the most likely candidate. But what is important here is that a federal judge raises the jurisdiction question squarely and faces the reality that there is no authority, other than the assertion of Crown sovereignty and its accompanying legal system, that these customary contexts should be subject to judicial review. Rothstein J seems to suggest that judicial review is not precluded, but that the context modifies the intensity of judicial review. We might read in that this is the continuing effect of prior sovereignty, which acts as a kind of implicit common law privative clause in this context.

In *Sparvier v Cowessess IB*, Rothstein J appears to recognise the fact of pluralism inherent within administrative law: a multiplicity of types of administrative decision-makers exists and they are not to be treated the same way at judicial review. These decision-makers also possess expertise, though not necessarily 'legal' in the strict or formal sense:

> Even though Appeal Tribunal members may not be legally trained, it appears that they are to decide, based on facts and their application of the Act or other Band customs, traditions or perhaps other laws, whether or not to uphold an election or order a new election. Members are

[104] ibid, 160.

not popularly elected. Although the Act uses the term 'elected', members are selected by the Band Council.[105]

Nevertheless, where empowered they are competent to decide questions of law, especially if it is their *own* law. The jurisdiction to interpret and apply the law is therefore shared generally throughout administrative law. Matters of governance are also contextual and will not always take a purely democratic form, as Rothstein J notes about the specific manner of 'election' – and that is fine, because Canada is not a pure democracy; rather, it is a liberal-democratic constitutional monarchy.

These insights lead Rothstein J to a jurisprudential baseline different from that of Lamer CJ in *CP v Matsqui IB*. He recognises the essential need for common law calibration and builds a true bridge forward:

> If a rigorous test for reasonable apprehension of bias were applied, the membership of decision-making bodies such as the Appeal Tribunal, in bands of small populations, would constantly be challenged on grounds of bias stemming from a connection that a member of the decision-making body had with one or another of the potential candidates. Such a rigorous application of principles relating to the apprehension of bias could potentially lead to situations where the election process would be frustrated under the weight of these assertions. Such procedural frustration could, as stated by counsel for the respondents, be a danger to the process of autonomous elections of band governments.[106]

Though it is a lower court decision, I believe *Sparvier v Cowessess IB* to be the more fruitful and generative case than *CP v Matsqui IB*. As Rothstein J intuits, the solution for procedural flaws in customary elections should be found in that alternative institutional context and process 'over there'.[107] This is the real remedy for self-governance and also access to justice for Indigenous communities.

The next section will take these insights and use them to set out a framework that could apply to Indigenous decision-makers in contemporary administrative law.

V. Decolonising Administrative Law in a Multijural State: A Beginning

> Band councils are created under the Indian Act and derive their authority to operate qua band councils exclusively from that Act. ... They have no other source of power.[108]

The above quotation lays down a bottom line that must now be viewed as completely antiquated. Since the 1990s, Canada has been working with a new jurisprudential framework for thinking about Aboriginal law and Indigenous governance, first set out in the *Haida*

---

[105] ibid, 164. Note that the Code in question is not a comprehensive enactment covering chiefs, councillors and other governance matters.

[106] ibid, 168.

[107] Rothstein J's intuition comports with the views expressed by Justice Debbie Mortimer in her chapter in this volume, where she emphasises the pressing need for judges (and others involved in litigation) to respect and understand Indigenous decision-making involving their traditional laws and customs. See ch 7 of this volume.

[108] Per Belzil JA in *Paul Band (Indian Reserve No 133) v R* [1984] 1 CNLR 87, [94] (Alta CA).

Nation case.[109] In this case and in subsequent developments, the following propositions have become clear. First, the Canadian legal system is in the process of coming to recognise the full panoply of Indigenous powers (ie, rights, title, governance). This process aspires to convert what were primarily moral and political governmental duties towards Indigenous peoples into effective legal obligations.[110] Indigenous persons should be able to call upon courts to affirm this historically continuing legal obligation, sourced back to the Royal Proclamation of 1763, and demand that rights be recognised and duties be fulfilled. The special role of administrative law is to check the power of the Crown and constrain both the structured and unstructured discretionary powers the Crown exercises in public law.

As this chapter has argued in previous sections, we need to move farther away from the older baselines to a new administrative law framework for Indigenous authorities. The first step is the affirmation of Indigenous authorities as *sui generis*, even when exercising delegated powers. They need to be treated very differently in public law than conventional statutory delegates. This *sui generis* nature grounds a multijural perspective where courts share jurisdiction with Indigenous institutions and acknowledge the reality of plural interpreters of law.

In terms of jurisdiction, these principles militate in favour of interpreting the principle of deference as respect in a way that is fully informed by the Indigenous governance context. This will affect how reviewing courts interpret the context such as institutional independence, shared authority over questions of law, expertise regarding facts, policy and customs, and a very narrow construction of jurisdiction that avoids judicial intrusiveness. The modern principle of statutory interpretation needs to be further 'indigenised', with Indigenous authorities recognised as experts clearly over customary law, but also over other governance issues.

For procedural fairness, these principles argue for fuller contextual application of principles of fairness and a greater margin of appreciation for the role of Indigenous norms and procedures. They take up where Rothstein J left off in *Sparvier v Cowessess IB* to demand a deeply contextualised bias test. This chapter does not argue for the more radical proposition that procedural fairness is a colonial imposition that First Nations can reject by creating a 'legal firewall' around their communities. Instead, it suggests that Indigenous governments have the power to – like other legislative bodies – explicitly oust the content of common law procedural fairness in their own jurisprudence.

The contemporary approach to the review of substance – summarised in section III.E – needs to be consistently extended to Indigenous authorities. Reasonableness should be the presumptive standard and Indigenous expertise over Indigenous norms confirmed.[111] Indeed, expertise should explicitly mean legal knowledge of Indigenous norms and contexts so as to counsel humility in judicial (and lawyers') attitudes and ensure that considerable deference is shown to Bands who choose to govern themselves through customary law.

---

[109] *Haida Nation* (n 19).
[110] ibid [8]–[10].
[111] See the similar analysis in chapter 6 of this volume by Justice Matthew Palmer concerning the grounds of judicial review in relation to the Treaty of Waitangi in New Zealand. He discusses how reviewing courts have found that Māori cultural and spiritual values are always relevant considerations when assessing the legality of government action and/or the reasonableness of the decision where Treaty principles inform the context.

Customary norms ought to be treated with great weight as a significant factor in the deference calculus.[112] More radically, new principles, including those recognising rights to governance or jurisdiction, may act similarly to privative clauses like a kind of 'Indigenous supremacy' parallel to Parliamentary supremacy; or, alternatively, ensure that deferential respect accords with that provided to a municipality. As Grammond J notes in a recent Federal Court case, we would do well to consider by-laws and elections regulations as 'Indigenous legislation' and not just 'custom'.[113] The content of administrative law will be further developed in tandem with Aboriginal law principles such as the honour of the Crown and reconciliation, as well as with principles derived from Indigenous legal orders.[114] Obligations will be enforced through improvements to frameworks such as the duty to consult and accommodate.[115] The scope of correctness review for Indigenous authorities, however, still requires fleshing out.

With respect to remedies, Indigenous norms will act as a 'jurisgenerative'[116] source for new remedies. The spirit of Sopinka J's dissent in *CP v Matsqui IB*, as well as the careful contextual and interpretative analysis undertaken by Rothstein J in *Sparvier v Cowessess IB*, should be embraced regarding a broader understanding of Indigenous institutions not only as adequate forums for alternative remedies, but also as institutional remedies in and of themselves for the project of self-government. This view is buttressed by the constitutional principle of access to justice. In my view, the constitutional principle of access to justice demands the most effective resolution in the most appropriate forum available.[117] As a recent case confirmed, it may be appropriate for reviewing courts to recognise 'the alternative Indigenous process of seeking resolution through agreement as contrasted with the process of litigation and adjudication'.[118] This understanding of remedies, combined with a narrow conception of jurisdiction, ensures that judicial review remains the last resort.

VI. Conclusion

It is clear that the Indian Act must be repealed. As Indigenous leaders Ovide Mercredi and Mary Ellen Turpel-Lafond have long argued, 'It must be remembered that there is an

---

[112] *Clifton v Benton* [2005] FC 1030, [42].

[113] *Pastion v Dene Tha' First Nation* [2018] FC 648, [13].

[114] See chapter 11 in this volume by Andrew Geddis and Jacinta Ruru for a fascinating discussion of New Zealand's adoption of the concept of 'person' to apply to natural things (the Whanganui River and Te Urewera National Park) – a creative, flexible legal development that both recognises the ways in which Māori conceive of and relate to places in their cosmology as well as changing the way that the majority non-Indigenous Pākehā will interact with these places in the future. Recognising personhood, they suggest, creates the basis for a new future relationship.

[115] The Australian Uluru Statement from the Heart also recommends a model of consultation so that Indigenous peoples can be heard in law-making that directly affects their interests. See ch 9 of this volume by Kirsty Gover.

[116] See Seyla Benhabib, following Robert Cover, on the concept of jurisgenerative: 'the law's capacity to create a normative universe of meaning which can often escape the "provenance of formal lawmaking"': S Benhabib, *Exile, Statelessness, and Migration: Playing Chess with History from Hannah Arendt to Isaiah Berlin* (Princeton, NJ, Princeton University Press, 2018) 28.

[117] Canadian jurisprudence affirms that, as an unwritten constitutional principle, access to justice no longer means only access to the public court system and that all forums should be effective and efficient. See, eg, *Seidel v TELUS Communications Inc* [2011] 1 SCR 531; *Hryniak v Mauldin* [2014] 1 SCR 87; and *Trial Lawyers Association of British Columbia v British Columbia (Attorney General)* [2014] 3 SCR 3.

[118] *Henry v Roseau River Anishinabe First Nation Government* [2017] FC 1038, [4].

important distinction between self-determination and self-administration. One means we design our own institutions and rely on our own values, the other that we apply someone else's programs.'[119] The Canadian Government, currently led by Prime Minister Justin Trudeau, has been working on a new post-TRC Indigenous rights framework that would form the basis for new relations between the federal Government and Indigenous communities across the country. But in 2018 this project was put on hold, as disagreement exists about whether this new framework properly recognises Indigenous rights or whether it still continues to assert that the authority of a First Nation to govern itself is not inherent but, rather, solely found in federal authority.[120] Until this changes, other legal efforts must continue.

As a JD student 20 years ago, I studied both administrative law and Aboriginal law. In these courses back then, the two areas of law did not intersect and I therefore learned little of the content this chapter hopes to convey. It is my hope that this chapter's discussion will be of interest to other similarly-situated settler states, as well as to those interested in the conversation about the many intersections of Indigenous and non-Indigenous laws and values. I have been teaching administrative law for almost a decade now, and have only recently taken a hard look at the two leading cases analysed in section IV. I began this chapter with the four Calls to Action that concern legal education and the justice system. I did this to remind myself of the learning that I still need to undertake in order to become a more competent teacher of administrative and public law in Canada. It is therefore also my hope that administrative law can better assist in achieving truth, reconciliation and the recognition of a multijural Canada.

---

[119] O Mercredi and ME Turpel, *In the Rapids: Navigating the Future of First Nations* (Toronto, Viking, 1993) 93. When this book was published, her name was Mary Ellen Turpel, but it is now Turpel-Lafond and she is more widely known by this name in Canada.

[120] Most agree that repealing or reforming the Indian Act in one fell swoop would be too disruptive, given that it has shaped and continues to shape First Nations' communities. But consensus does not exist on what a post-Indian Act world should look like. Another point of disagreement concerns what the role of UNDRIP should be (n 5). For further discussion, see J Barrera, 'Trudeau's Words don't match early indicators on Indigenous rights framework: Letter', *CBC News* (11 September 2018), available at https://www.cbc.ca/news/indigenous/indigenous-rights-framework-letter-trudeau-1.4818000.

9

From the Heart: The Indigenous Challenge to Australian Public Law

KIRSTY GOVER*

The 2017 Uluru Statement from the Heart is an expression of Indigenous sovereignty. As the Statement explains, the ancient sovereignty of Aboriginal and Torres Strait Islanders 'is a spiritual notion' that has persisted for some 60,000 years as an 'ancestral tie' between the land and its peoples.[1] Australian courts have closed their doors to this sovereignty and to any assertion of Indigenous law or jurisdiction that might invoke it. Likewise, the Constitution contains no recognition of Indigenous peoples' status or rights, nor of their relationship with Australian governments. Indigenous peoples are conceived of in constitutional terms only so far as they are 'a people of [a] race', with respect to whom Australian governments may 'make special laws' when deemed necessary (a power that has only ever been deployed in support of laws targeting Indigenous peoples).[2] In contrast to our common law peers, Canada and New Zealand, in Australia there are no Indigenous–state treaties.

These absences are the constitutive flaws at 'the heart' of Australian public law, to which the Uluru Statement attends. The Statement confirms the continuity of Indigenous sovereignty, acknowledges that it 'co-exists with the sovereignty of the Crown', and sets out three proposed reforms to correct the deficiencies of Australian public law and shore up the legitimacy of the Australian state. The authors of the Statement 'seek constitutional reforms to empower our people and take *a rightful place* in our own country', calling for 'a First Nations Voice enshrined in the Constitution' and a 'Makarrata Commission to supervise a process of agreement-making between governments and First Nations and truth-telling about our history'.[3] These three proposals have come to be known by the short-form 'Voice, Treaty, Truth'.[4]

---

* Many thanks to participants at the 2018 Public Law Conference, *The Frontiers of Public Law*, held at Melbourne Law School, 11–13 July 2018.
[1] Referendum Council, 'Uluru Statement from the Heart', *Final Report of the Referendum Council* (2017) i.
[2] Australian Constitution, s 51(xxvi) (the race power).
[3] Emphasis in original. Makarrata is a Yolngu concept, sometimes equated with the idea of a treaty or treaties, that 'captures the idea of two parties coming together after a struggle, healing the divisions of the past': N Pearson, 'Uluru Statement Practical on Indigenous Recognition' *The Australian* (27 May 2017). See also Referendum Council, 'Uluru Statement from the Heart' (n 1) 21.
[4] See, eg, the theme adopted for NAIDOC week 2019: National Aborigines and Islanders Day Observance Committee, 'Voice. Treaty. Truth.' (2019), available at https://www.naidoc.org.au/get-involved/2019-theme.

This chapter explores the potential for the Uluru proposals to transform Australia's public law and augment its democratic processes. It argues that the Statement provides an opportunity for Australia's peoples to address the incompleteness of the Australian Commonwealth Constitution, in ways comparable to advances made in the public law of Canada and New Zealand. The chapter's major claim is that, seen in comparative context, the proposals are modest and reasonable, and given the Australian context, they are vitally necessary. In particular, it argues that the Uluru proposals go some way towards remedying a striking deficit in Australian public law: the absence of any duty obliging governments to consult Indigenous peoples before making decisions that impact directly on their interests. Such a duty has evolved in Canada and New Zealand as a corollary of the constitutional recognition afforded to Indigenous peoples by section 35 of the Canadian Constitution and by the 1840 Treaty of Waitangi. Both mechanisms effect and express a distinctive constitutional relationship between settler and Indigenous peoples, and between their respective representatives and governments. Australian public law is impoverished to the extent it lacks anything comparable.

As a case in point, because of the directions followed in Australian public law, Indigenous Australians are now more vulnerable to discriminatory legal measures than any other community in Australia, precisely because they are already disadvantaged in the enjoyment of human rights, and because they are identified in law primarily as members of a race. This peculiar vulnerability is confirmed by the High Court's reasoning in the 2013 case of *Maloney v The Queen* (*Maloney*).[5] The case establishes a precedent that enables Australian governments to impose uniquely burdensome measures on Indigenous communities, and to do so in the absence of any obligation to consult them.

Section I reviews the recent history of the constitutional recognition debates that precede and post-date the 2017 Uluru Statement from the Heart. Section II explains that the tension evident in these debates turns on competing conceptions of the Australian public, one which conceives of the ideal to be a single Australian people as a politically undifferentiated group, and the other that takes as its starting point the popular sovereignty of Indigenous peoples in a multi-people state. Section III offers a comparative perspective on Australian public law, discussing counter-majoritarian innovations in Canadian and New Zealand public law that facilitate a distinctive and constitutional Indigenous–state relationship, with a particular focus on the consultative obligations understood to flow from the proper conduct of such a relationship. Section IV examines the judicial reasoning deployed in *Maloney*, with a view to demonstrating the type of unilateralism that is enabled by the absence of a constitutionally salient Indigenous–state relationship. Section V concludes.

I. The Statement and the Constitutional Recognition Debate

The Uluru Statement from the Heart was endorsed by Indigenous leaders on 27 May 2017, at an Indigenous Constitutional Convention held at Uluru (Ayers Rock) on Anangu land in the Western Desert. The Statement is just one page in length, and the language used

---

[5] *Maloney v The Queen* (2013) 252 CLR 168.

in it is forthright, reflective and decidedly non-legal. The deliberative process leading to the Uluru convention is unprecedented in Australia, as is the degree of consensus reached there. The Statement is the culmination of 13 Regional Dialogues, in which 1,200 Indigenous delegates participated.[6] At Uluru, of the 250 delegates in attendance, 243 endorsed the Statement.[7] This demonstration of political solidarity is all the more remarkable given the diversity of the participant peoples, who represent hundreds of different language and kinship groups from all parts of the Australian landmass, who have widely varied political views and aspirations, and who live in the full range of urban and rural settings in accordance with distinct local traditions and law.

The Uluru Statement finds its place within a convoluted recent institutional history. For brevity, this history is addressed here only in outline, with the aim of recording the hurdles that have been overcome to date, and identifying the challenges yet to be faced.

The possibility of constitutional recognition for Indigenous peoples was first officially raised in 2010 by the then Labor Government Prime Minister, Julia Gillard.[8] The Expert Panel on Constitutional Recognition of Indigenous Australians was established that year, and reported in 2012,[9] followed by the 2012 Joint Select Committee on Constitutional Recognition of Aboriginal and Torres Strait Islander Peoples, which reported in mid-2015.[10] Later in 2015, a 16-member Referendum Council was established, with a hard-won mandate to consult separately with Indigenous peoples in a series of Regional Dialogues on constitutional recognition of Indigenous Australians. These culminated in the Indigenous Constitutional Convention at Uluru on 26–27 May 2017, followed a month later by the report of Referendum Council, showcasing the Uluru Statement as the cornerstone of its recommendations.[11]

In its Final Report the Referendum Council endorsed the Uluru Statement, recommending that a 'referendum be held to provide in the Australian Constitution for a representative body that gives Aboriginal and Torres Strait Islander First Nations a Voice to the Commonwealth Parliament'.[12] The Referendum Council envisaged that the functions of the representative body would be specified in legislation, and that these functions would include oversight of the exercise of the two constitutional powers that most directly and frequently enable legislation directed to Indigenous communities: the 'race power' (section 51 (xxvi)), noted at the start of this chapter, and the 'territories power' (section 122). The territories power enables the Commonwealth (but not the States) to

---

[6] 'Meetings were capped at 100 participants: 60% of places were reserved for first nations/traditional owner groups, 20% for community organisations and 20% for key individuals. The Council worked in partnership with a host organisation at each location, to ensure the local community was appropriately represented in the process.' Referendum Council, 'Dialogues', available at https://www.referendumcouncil.org.au/dialogues.html.

[7] C Wahlquist, 'Uluru Talks: Delegates Walk Out Due to Sovereignty and Treaty Fears' *The Guardian* (25 May 2017), available at https://www.theguardian.com/australia-news/2017/may/25/uluru-talks-delegates-walk-out-due-to-sovereignty-and-treaty-fears.

[8] K Lazzaro, 'Julia Gillard wants Indigenous People Recognised in Constitution' *ABC Radio National* (8 November 2010).

[9] Expert Panel on Constitutional Recognition of Indigenous Australians, 'Recognising Aboriginal and Torres Strait Islander Peoples in the Constitution: Final Report of the Expert Panel' (15 January 2012).

[10] Joint Select Committee on Constitutional Recognition of Aboriginal and Torres Strait Islander Peoples, *Final Report* (Canberra, Commonwealth of Australia, 2015).

[11] Referendum Council, 'Uluru Statement from the Heart' (n 1).

[12] ibid 2.

make laws for the territories, specifically the Northern Territory, in which 26 per cent of residents are Indigenous[13] and where more than 70 per cent of land is subject to Indigenous property rights.[14] The Referendum Council's recommendations mark a shift away from approach taken by the 2010 Expert Panel, which proposed replacing the race power with a head of power enabling laws to be made for Aboriginal and Torres Strait Islanders and adding a provision prohibiting racial discrimination.[15]

The Commonwealth Government responded to the Referendum Council's Report by rejecting the proposed Voice to Parliament (for reasons discussed in section II). It then established a second Joint Select Committee (the Joint Select Committee on Constitutional Recognition relating to Aboriginal and Torres Strait Islander Peoples) to consider the recommendations of the previously appointed bodies, along with the Uluru Statement from the Heart, and make recommendations on constitutional change. That body reported in November 2018, taking up the Uluru Statement's proposal for an entrenched Voice to Parliament, and noting that other proposals for constitutional amendment had been 'taken off the table' by the support shown for the Statement.[16] The Committee further recommended 'that the Australian Government initiate a process of co-design with Aboriginal and Torres Strait Islander peoples' and 'support the process of truth-telling'.[17] At the time of writing the incumbent Liberal–National Coalition Government had not provided a formal response to the Joint Select Committee's Report, although the Minister for Indigenous Australians had announced his intention to begin 'a process of co-design' in response to the Voice proposal (albeit without committing to support for constitutional amendment).

As this circuitous history shows, neither the Labor party nor the Liberal-National Coalition party has decisively taken up the recommendations of the bodies appointed to advise them. This does not augur well for the type of determined bipartisanship that would ensure the proposals have the best chance of succeeding in a referendum on constitutional amendment.[18] Notwithstanding the lack of a formal commitment, in the lead up to the May 2019 federal election, the Liberal–National Coalition Government allocated 7.3 million dollars in its 2019 budget for the 'co-design of an Indigenous Voice to Parliament', an initiative that seems in line with the Joint Select Committee's recommendations. The party secured a third term as government in the federal election

---

[13] Australian Bureau of Statistics, '2016 Census Quickstats: Northern Territory', available at https://quickstats.censusdata.abs.gov.au/census_services/getproduct/census/2016/quickstat/7?opendocument.

[14] In the Northern Territory, 22.6% of land is subject to native title rights and 48% is held as Aboriginal freehold under the *Aboriginal Land Rights Act 1976*: National Native Title Tribunal, personal communication, 20 May 2019; Northern Territory Government, 'Northern Territory Aboriginal Land and Sea Action Plan' (2019) 5. The 'Territories power' and the 'race power' together provided the justification for the Commonwealth's 2007 Northern Territory Emergency Response legislative package, imposing sweeping restrictions on the lives of residents in 'prescribed communities' on Aboriginal land in the Northern Territory.

[15] Expert Panel on Constitutional Recognition of Indigenous Australians, 'Final Report of the Expert Panel' (n 9) xviii.

[16] Referendum Council, 'Uluru Statement from the Heart' (n 1) viii.

[17] Joint Select Committee on Constitutional Recognition relating to Aboriginal and Torres Strait Islander Peoples, *Final Report* (Canberra, Parliament of the Commonwealth of Australia, 2018) ('Joint Select Committee Report').

[18] Only 8 of 44 referenda proposals have succeeded in meeting the constitutional criteria specified in s 128 of the Australian Constitution, a fact that weighed heavily on the second Joint Parliamentary Select Committee, which noted that all successful referenda have proceeded with 'strong bipartisan support': Joint Select Committee Report (n 17) ix.

but has not committed to advancing constitutional reform.[19] Recent polls suggest that the support of the Australian electorate has outpaced the ambivalence of their leaders, reporting that some 64 per cent of Australians are in favour of the proposition that 'Australia should amend its constitution to establish a representative Indigenous body to advise Parliament on laws and policies affecting Indigenous people'.[20]

Even in light of this impressive level of majority support, the hurdles yet to be faced are significant. Amendments to Australia's Constitution require a majority of voters in each State and a majority of voters nationwide to vote affirmatively in a referendum.[21] To take their 'rightful place' in Australia's constitutional order as the Uluru Statement proposes, Indigenous peoples must convince a 'double majority' of Australian voters that this is what justice requires. In this democratic exercise as in all others, Australian Indigenous peoples will be outnumbered 35 to 1 by their settler counterparts.[22]

II. Official Responses to Proposals for Indigenous Representation

This section outlines some of the substantial, conceptual and constitutional challenges faced by Indigenous Australians in their efforts to secure constitutional recognition. Chief among these is the insistence of Australian political leaders (and some judges) that Australian democracy is best served by representative mechanisms that do not distinguish between Indigenous and settler citizens.

Five months after the Uluru Convention, then Prime Minister Malcolm Turnbull, along with the Attorney-General and Minister for Indigenous Affairs, issued a statement on behalf of the Government, rejecting the proposed Voice to Parliament, citing its incompatibility with Australian democratic principles:

> Our democracy is built on the foundation of all Australian citizens having equal civic rights ... A constitutionally enshrined additional representative assembly for which only Indigenous Australians could vote for or serve in is inconsistent with this fundamental principle.[23]

Later he confirmed his view that the proposed Voice to Parliament 'is contrary to the principles of equality of citizenship in Australia [and] would inevitably be seen as a third chamber ... of Parliament'.[24] Notwithstanding that the form of the Indigenous

---

[19] D McCulloch, 'Minister Optimistic about Indigenous Voice' *Canberra Times* (21 May 2019); D Weber and E Parke, 'Indigenous MPs split on what Federal Election 2019 Result means for Aboriginal Affairs' ABC News (20 May 2019), available at https://www.abc.net.au/news/2019-05-20/indigenous-mps-at-odds-over-federal-election-aboriginal-affairs/11128600).

[20] I Higgins and S Collards, 'Federal Election 2019: Vote Compass Finds Australians are Ready to Back Indigenous "Voice To Parliament"' ABC News (3 May 2019), available at https://www.abc.net.au/news/2019-05-03/vote-compass-federal-election-voice-to-parliament/11071384.

[21] Australian Constitution, s 128.

[22] Australian Bureau of Statistics, 'Aboriginal and Torres Strait Islander Population: 2016 Census Data Summary' (2017) shows that Aboriginal and Torres Strait Islander peoples represented 2.8% of the national population.

[23] Department of Prime Minister and Cabinet, 'Response to Referendum Council's Report on Constitutional Recognition' (26 October 2017).

[24] M Turnbull, Press Conference with The Right Honourable Jacinda Ardern, Prime Minister of New Zealand (5 November 2017).

representative body has not been settled, Turnbull's successor Prime Minister Scott Morrison has reinforced his Government's view that a representative advisory body for Indigenous peoples is incompatible with Australian democracy, stating in October 2018 that he did not support the Voice proposal, because it was a 'third chamber of parliament', adding '[i]t really is. People can dress it up any way they like – but I think two chambers is enough.'[25]

This is not the first time that an Australian Prime Minister has expressed scepticism about Indigenous representative bodies. In 2005, for example, when former Prime Minister John Howard's Government abolished the Aboriginal and Torres Strait Island Commission (ATSIC), the country's primary national Indigenous representative body, he explained that 'We believe very strongly that the experiment in separate representation, elected representation, for indigenous people has been a failure.'[26] In 2000, he rejected the possibility of a treaty with Indigenous Australians, saying 'a nation, an undivided united nation does not make a treaty with itself. I mean to talk about one part of Australia making a treaty with another part is to accept that we are in effect two nations.'[27] A similar view is reflected in former Prime Minister Tony Abbott's view of reconciliation as a process that should erase differentiation between Indigenous and settler Australians: 'I am a supporter of constitutional recognition because I want our country to transcend the "them and us" mindset to embrace "all of us" in [a] spirit of generous inclusion', adding, with a chilling choice of words, 'Not "them" and "us" anymore – just us.'[28]

These comments reflect a long-standing preoccupation in Australian law and politics with an idealised, politically undifferentiated Australian body politic, within which Indigenous peoples are represented, if they are at all, as racial minorities with no other constitutional or political status. It is a vision sustained by an unusually formal and symmetrical view of equality and non-discrimination norms in Australian public law, as is discussed further in section IV.

The difficulty of designing legitimate and effective democratic institutions in settler states has been the subject of scholarship in political theory calling into question the assumptions underpinning official views of Australian democracy. Paul Patton, for example, points out that many theories of democratic legitimacy rest on the idea that all participants should enjoy equal influence over governmental decisions, so that 'if a decision of government is not in accordance with your wishes, you must be able to think that it was just unfortunate that the decision went that way.'[29] In countries established by colonisation, Patton observes, the nature and history of the relationship between settler majorities and Indigenous minorities often ensures that 'not all individuals and groups

---

[25] P Karp, 'Scott Morrison claims Indigenous Voice to Parliament would be a Third Chamber' *The Guardian* (26 September 2018).
[26] J Howard, Joint Press Conference with Senator Amanda Vanstone (15 April 2004). On this history of ATSIC, see H Hobbs, 'Public Law, Legitimacy and Indigenous Aspirations', ch 10 in this volume.
[27] J Howard, Interview With John Laws, *2UE Radio* (29 May 2000).
[28] T Abbott, Address to the RECOGNISE Inaugural Gala Dinner (11 December 2014).
[29] P Patton, 'The Limits of Decolonization and the Problem of Legitimacy' in D Boucher and A Omar (eds), *Decolonisation: Evolution and Revolution* (Johannesburg, Wits University Press, 2019) 4 (discussing Philip Pettit's account in P Pettit, *On The People's Terms: A Republican Theory and Model of Democracy* (Cambridge, Cambridge University Press, 2012)).

have the same *ex ante* chance of being in the majority on certain issues'.[30] Instead, he notes, in some settler societies:

> From the perspective of [Indigenous] minorities, the idea that they participate equally in the effective control of government appears at best a hollow ideal. It is not just a matter of tough luck that a majority of their fellow citizens harbour active or passive racist beliefs that lead them to consistently oppose the full and equal enjoyment of basic rights by Indigenous people. It is a matter of colonial aspects of individual and collective identity that are not readily subject to change. It is not the case that members of such minorities could just as easily have been on the winning side. On the contrary, they are consistently and systematically on the losing side in majority decision-making processes.[31]

He goes on to note that in accounts valuing equal influence as a precondition of democratic legitimacy (in this case Philip Pettit's), it is accepted that '[w]here there are entrenched differences of the kind that we see in countries established by colonization, equal individual votes are not sufficient to ensure equally accessible influence over government policy'.[32] Likewise Duncan Ivison has argued that a political theory for liberal democratic *settler* states should

> conceptualise [those] states very differently. They should be seen as being composed of constellations of normative orders that overlap and intersect in complex ways both above and below the state, as opposed to a singular people or sovereign. And it should take seriously the historical and political legacies of the way those normative orders came into being and the interactions between them over time.[33]

Additionally, as Noel Pearson has argued, even if historic dispossession and denigration had not operated to exclude Indigenous peoples from effective democratic participation, the demographic challenge alone would be formidable. He says:

> I want to focus on our extreme minority because I believe it is a defining feature of our condition. It is a crucial explanation of our predicament. If we were not so small a minority, we could participate in the Australian democracy and influence its institutions towards our aspirations. It would help combat the baggage of race and represent our indigeneity. … Australian parliaments and executive governments simply do not work for Aboriginal and Torres Strait Islander peoples. Routinely and invariably. While Australians complain about politicians, governments and bureaucracies, our democratic institutions, systems and processes generally work for the majority. The electoral system ultimately drives responsive government. Not so for extreme minorities whose presence in that electoral system is negligible.[34]

The fact remains, as Pearson concludes, that 'The scale and moral urgency of the indigenous predicament far exceeds the power of indigenous participation in the country's democratic process'.[35] His concerns are echoed in the Uluru Statement from the Heart, which aims in part to more accurately reflect the character of Australia as a multi-people state, and

---

[30] Patton, 'The Limits of Decolonization' (n 29) 4.
[31] ibid 5.
[32] ibid.
[33] D Ivison, 'Justification, not Recognition' (2016) 8(24) *Indigenous Law Bulletin* 1.
[34] N Pearson, 'A Rightful Place: Race, Recognition and a More Complete Commonwealth' (2014) 55 *Quarterly Essay* 1, 38–39.
[35] ibid 40.

so address the 'torment of powerlessness' endured by Indigenous peoples in Australia's democracy. As Djawa Yunupingu commented in 2018:

> [T]he Truth is that we are not United in this country – we are not Comfortable – and we remain uncertain and troubled by this Truth. Because we live side by side – Two People – Two Laws – One Country … 'One Country' because that is what we want and it must happen in the Constitution.[36]

As the foregoing illustrates, debates about the constitutional recognition of Australian Indigenous peoples reveal competing visions of the composition of the 'public' that is to be served by public law. In the model promoted by settler leaders and officials, the Australian public comprises a single 'people' from whom the legitimacy of the state derives and to whom public institutions are ultimately accountable. In such a model undifferentiated political rights serve the interests of all citizens equally. Australia is a multi-people state, however, and this changes the preconditions for the legitimate exercise of governmental power. For Indigenous peoples, then, who did not participate in the political bargain that formed the Australian federation, the Constitution and the public institutions it mandates do not derive from Indigenous popular sovereignty or the exercise of Indigenous constituent power. The Uluru proposals seek to modify the Constitution to mitigate the effects of this constitutive flaw, by enabling Indigenous peoples to more effectively influence political decision-making, and ensuring they participate *as peoples* in law-making that directly affects them.[37]

These foundational questions about the identity and composition of 'the people' underpin debates about distributive justice and political equality in settler societies. Historic Indigenous rights are not premised on claims to an equitable share of primary goods on terms equal to those of other individuals, but instead are claims to *particular* property and powers, those that were held by the predecessors of Indigenous communities and have been or should have been inherited by their descendants. These rights are not necessarily, or as a matter of principle, 'capped' by concepts of distributive justice, equality and non-discrimination. As Duncan Ivison has pointed out, Indigenous claims challenge the base-line from which distributive exercises are to be evaluated:

> [H]istoric injustices continue to shape not only the distribution of 'primary goods', but also the meaning and equal value of those very goods (as well as the boundaries of the political community within which they are to be distributed).[38]

Indigenous rights, then, refer for their justification to Indigenous arrangements of power, property and law that preceded the establishment of the settler state, and propose a counterfactual modelling of what a just society might have looked like had those arrangements been inviolable, so that only changes consented to would be legitimate. This is a model of justice and legitimacy that takes into account the distinctive circumstances and histories of settler states.

In order to accommodate at least some of these distinctive features of democracy in liberal democratic settler states, the public law of Canada and New Zealand has evolved to

---

[36] D Yunupingu, Speech at the Garma Festival (4 August 2018).

[37] For an extended discussion of these and related ideas, see L Beckman, K Gover and U Morkenstam, 'Popular Sovereignty in Multi-people States: The Indigenous Challenge to Conceptions of Popular Sovereignty as Democratic Participation' (unpublished manuscript, on file with author).

[38] Ivison, 'Justification, not Recognition' (n 33) 13.

include 'counter-majoritarian' mechanisms that ensure Indigenous peoples have a better chance of influencing settler law and policy, and which better reflect the special constitutive status of Indigenous peoples. In the section that follows I outline some of these measures and their justifications. All accept that the relationship between settler and Indigenous peoples is qualitatively different from the relationship governments have with other citizens, and is one that cannot be properly conducted or assessed using unaugmented general public and administrative law mechanisms. In Australian public law this foundational conceptual understanding has far less purchase, and it is this deficit that the Uluru Statement seeks to address.

III. The Public Law of Indigenous–State Relationships

Canadian and New Zealand public law adaptations for Indigenous–state relationships have their constitutional basis in section 35 of Canada's Constitution and in New Zealand's 1840 Treaty of Waitangi respectively, and are elaborated in judge-made law ascribing obligations to settler governments in their dealings with Indigenous interests and in the conduct of treaty relationships. This section focuses on the purposes of these adaptations and their justifications, rather than on their detail. As the discussion below indicates, relative to its peers in the Commonwealth settler state fraternity, Australian public law is marked by:

- the absence of Indigenous–state treaties;
- the absence of a federal legislative or constitutional bill of rights that could house protections for Indigenous rights, or for the rights of ethnic or cultural minorities;
- the lack of common law qualifications on the exercise of state power, such as the constitutional principle of the Honour of the Crown and doctrines enforcing a state–Indigenous fiduciary relationship;
- the absence (relative to New Zealand) of secured seats for Indigenous Members of Parliament (MPs).

All four of the above features require, when present, that Indigenous peoples be regarded for at least some purposes as polities or political groupings. Their absence in Australia is evidenced in two further features of Australian public law: the persistent classification of Indigenous peoples as members of a 'particular race', rather than as, for example, members of political communities, nations, ethnic minorities or holders of historic property rights; and the absence of obligations on the part of Australian governments to consult with Indigenous peoples about measures that impact on their interests.

A. New Zealand

The distinctive political and constitutional status of Māori in New Zealand is secured by and expressed in the 1840 Treaty of Waitangi, signed by representatives of the British Crown and the rangatira or leaders of more than 500 tribal groupings. 'The Treaty', as it is known in New Zealand, is described in the *Cabinet Manual* as a 'major source of the constitution'[39] that 'may indicate limits in our polity on majority decision-making'.[40] It is not, however, an independent source of rights and duties in New Zealand law, and is typically considered by courts only where its principles are referred to in legislation, or, less frequently, when it is drawn on as an extrinsic aid to statutory interpretation of legislation that does not refer to it.[41] Courts interpreting legislative references to the Treaty principles have emphasised that the Treaty effects a partnership between peoples that 'require[s] the Pākehā and Māori Treaty partners to act towards each other reasonably and with the utmost good faith'.[42] In *Te Runanga o Wharekauri Rekohu Inc v Attorney-General*, President Cooke of the Court of Appeal explained:

> The Treaty created an enduring relationship of a fiduciary nature akin to partnership, each party accepting a positive duty to act in good faith, fairly, reasonably and honourably towards each other.[43]

The exchange evident in the Treaty supports the legitimacy of New Zealand's settler government, because it records an agreement in which 'the Crown sought legitimacy from the indigenous people for its acquisition of sovereignty'.[44] In this way, the Treaty embodies 'the obligations which the Crown undertook of protecting and preserving Māori property ... in return for being recognised as the legitimate government of the whole nation by Māori'.[45] It is clear that the Crown's Treaty obligations to Māori are not 'absolute and unqualified', and that the Crown has 'other responsibilities as the government of New Zealand'.[46] The Crown's Treaty obligations are thus sensitive to changes in the fortunes and aspirations of the Treaty partners, and 'will evolve from generation to generation as conditions change'.[47]

Courts have also explained that the Crown's obligation to act 'fairly and reasonably' towards its Māori Treaty partner[48] requires it 'to make 'informed decisions', that is, 'decision[s] where it is sufficiently informed as to the relevant facts and law to be able to say it had proper regard to the impact of the principles of the Treaty'.[49] The Treaty principles do not, however, extend to 'an absolute duty to consult' Māori,[50] nor do they entail an 'open-ended and formless duty to consult' that would be 'incapable of practical fulfilment':[51]

> In some [cases] extensive consultation and cooperation will be necessary. In others the partner may have sufficient information in its possession for it to act consistently with the principles of the Treaty without any specific consultation.[52]

---

[39] New Zealand Cabinet Office, *Cabinet Manual 2017* (Wellington, Department of the Prime Minister and Cabinet, 2017) 1.
[40] ibid 2. For a more detailed explanation of the Treaty, including the two language texts, see M Palmer, 'Indigenous Rights, Judges and Judicial Review in New Zealand', ch 6 in this volume.
[41] For examples of the latter, see *Huakina Development Trust v Waikato Valley Authority* [1987] 2 NZLR 188 (HC); *Barton-Prescott v Director-General of Social Welfare* [1997] 3 NZLR 179 (HC), 184.
[42] *New Zealand Māori Council v Attorney-General* [1987] 1 NZLR 641, 667 (Cooke P).
[43] *Te Runanga o Wharekauri Rekohu Inc v Attorney-General* [1993] 2 NZLR 301, 304 (Cooke P).
[44] *New Zealand Māori Council v Attorney-General* (n 42) 674 (Richardson J).
[45] *New Zealand Māori Council v Attorney-General (Broadcasting Assets)* [1994] 1 NZLR 513, 517.
[46] ibid.
[47] *Muriwhenua Inc v Attorney-General* [1990] 2 NZLR 641, 656.
[48] *New Zealand Māori Council v Attorney-General* (n 42) 673.
[49] ibid 683 (Richardson J).
[50] ibid.
[51] ibid.
[52] ibid.

Nonetheless, the Court of Appeal has determined that the principle of good faith 'must extend to consultation on truly major issues', noting that this 'is really clearly beyond argument'.[53]

Also in New Zealand, Ministers submitting bills to Parliament must draw attention to any implications of the proposed law for the principles of the Treaty of Waitangi.[54] Such a requirement ensures that proposed laws affecting Māori are debated by Māori Members of Parliament in both the general and the reserved Māori seats. Four 'Māori seats' were first introduced in 1867. Since 1993 the number of seats has been adjusted every five years, during the 'Māori Electoral Option', to be proportionate to the number of voters who register on the Māori electoral roll. Typically just over half of Māori choose to be on the Māori roll.[55] The current cohort of Māori MPs includes seven elected to reserved Māori seats, and a further 22 Māori elected to general seats across the major political parties (a figure that corresponds to 24 per cent of the 120 MPs in the New Zealand Parliament, well above parity for the Māori population as a whole, which is at 15 per cent of the national population).[56]

Taken together, the Treaty relationship, the consultation requirement, and the reserved Māori seats amount to something broadly similar to the national participation (the Voice) and local negotiation (Makarrata Commission) proposals expressed in the Uluru Statement.

B. Canada

Section 35 of the Canadian Constitution provides that '[t]he existing aboriginal and treaty rights of the aboriginal people in Canada are hereby recognized and affirmed'.[57] The section sits outside of the Constitution's Charter of Human Rights and Freedoms, and is thus shielded from the application of competing Charter protections. It is not subject to section 1 of the Charter, which permits reasonable limits on rights, while section 25 of the Constitution specifies that '[t]he guarantee in this Charter of certain rights and freedoms shall not be construed as to abrogate or derogate from any aboriginal, treaty or other rights or freedoms that pertain to the aboriginal peoples of Canada'.[58] The Canadian Constitution thus recognises that the rights of Indigenous peoples (including but not limited to those protected by section 35) are distinct from, and vulnerable to, rights held by

---

[53] ibid 152 (Cooke P). Lower courts have accepted that the duty to consult arises where a Treaty interest is at stake, and not as a more general duty. See *Te Waero v Minister of Conservation* HC Auckland, M360-SW01, 19 February 2002, [61] (Harrison J): '[C]onsultation is not of itself a discrete, substantive Treaty principle. It does not exist in a vacuum without an underlying purpose. In this statutory context consultation is the medium for Maori to advise the Minister of a distinct Treaty interest.' See also *Te Tai Tokerau Mapo Trust v Chief Executive of Ministry of Health* HC Whangarei, 5 August 2011, [151] (Woodhouse J).
[54] New Zealand Cabinet Office, *Cabinet Manual 2017* (n 39) [7.65].
[55] Electoral Commission, 'Māori Electoral Option 2018 Results and Statistics' (13 August 2018), available at https://www.elections.org.nz/events/maori-electoral-option-2018/results-statistics.
[56] T Koti, 'Who are our Māori Members of Parliament now?' *Te Ao Māori News* (24 September 2017), available at https://www.Maoritelevision.com/news/politics/who-are-our-Māori-members-parliament-now. Most, but not all, MPs with Māori ancestry identify as Māori in their political and public roles.
[57] Canadian Constitution, s 35.
[58] ibid s 25.

other Canadians and so should be protected in the event that these rights conflict. As was explained by the then Chief Justice of the Supreme Court in *R v Van der Peet*, speaking for the majority:

> In the liberal enlightenment view, reflected in the American Bill of Rights and, more indirectly, in the Charter, rights are held by all people in society because each person is entitled to dignity and respect. Rights are general and universal; they are the way in which the 'inherent dignity' of each individual in society is respected: ... Aboriginal rights cannot, however, be defined on the basis of the philosophical precepts of the liberal enlightenment. Although equal in importance and significance to the rights enshrined in the Charter, aboriginal rights must be viewed differently from Charter rights because they are rights held only by aboriginal members of Canadian society. They arise from the fact that aboriginal people are aboriginal.[59]

Section 35 also provides a basis for the common law constitutional principle of the 'Honour of the Crown', which expresses distinctive obligations owed by the Canadian Crown to Indigenous peoples, including the duty to consult Indigenous communities about measures that may impact on their claimed or proven interests.[60] The 'Honour of the Crown' is a 'constitutional principle'[61] and a 'constitutional imperative',[62] which applies to the Crown 'in all of its dealings with indigenous peoples, from the assertion of sovereignty to the resolution of claims and the implementation of treaties'.[63] The principle derives from the political and moral import of the act of sovereign acquisition, 'aris[ing] from the Crown's assertion of sovereignty over an Aboriginal people and *de facto* control of land and resources that were formerly in the control of that people'.[64] The duty to consult is thus 'an essential corollary to the honourable process of reconciliation that s 35 demands'.[65]

The Honour of the Crown encompasses and builds upon common law principles identifying the Crown's fiduciary duties to Indigenous peoples. Duties arising from the state–Indigenous fiduciary relationship, including in some cases an obligation to consult the Indigenous beneficiary, pre-date and inform the jurisprudence on consultation that has since developed in elaboration of section 35.[66] The constitutional law expression of the consultative duty was first addressed in jurisprudence assessing the validity of legislative infringements of section 35, and more recently has evolved into a 'free-standing duty',[67] arising whenever claimed or established section 35 rights are affected by legislative or executive action.[68]

In its first constitutional instantiation, the conduct of consultation is a relevant consideration in judicial assessments of the validity of legislation affecting section 35 rights. These rights may only be validly infringed by federal legislation that satisfies the judicial test

---

[59] *R v Van der Peet* [1996] 2 SCR 507, 534.
[60] *Haida Nation v British Columbia (Minister of Forests)* [2004] 3 SCR 511.
[61] *Beckman v Little Salmon/Carmacks First Nation* [2010] 3 SCR 103, [42].
[62] *Mikisew Cree First Nation v Canada* [2018] SCC 40, 55 (Abella and Martin JJ).
[63] *Haida Nation v British Columbia* (n 60) [17].
[64] ibid [32].
[65] ibid [38].
[66] See, eg, *Guerin v The Queen* [1984] 2 SCR 335, 362 (Wilson J), 389 (Dickson J); *R v Sparrow* [1990] 1 SCR 1075, 1108.
[67] *Mikisew Cree First Nation v Canada* (n 62) [67] (Abella and Martin JJ).
[68] But the duty is not owed by executive officials when acting in a legislative capacity during the law-making process: ibid.

laid out in *R v Sparrow*[69] and later cases, requiring a 'valid legislative objective', the attainment of which 'must uphold the honour of the Crown and must be in keeping with the unique contemporary relationship, grounded in history and policy, between the Crown and Canada's aboriginal peoples'.[70] The test requires attention to 'whether the aboriginal group in question has been consulted with respect to the measures being implemented'.[71]

As a free-standing duty, the duty to consult arises as a corollary to action that may impact on Indigenous interests, even where the interests at stake are 'unproven'.[72] The duty is triggered wherever 'the Crown has knowledge, real or constructive, of the potential existence of the Aboriginal right or title and contemplates conduct that might adversely affect it',[73] and is calibrated to match 'the strength of the case supporting the existence of the right or title, and ... the seriousness of the potentially adverse effect upon the right or title claimed'.[74] As the Supreme Court put it in *Delgamuukw v British Columbia*:

> There is always a duty of consultation. ... The nature and scope of the duty of consultation will vary with the circumstances. In occasional cases, when the breach is less serious or relatively minor, it will be no more than a duty to discuss important decisions that will be taken ... [E]ven in these rare cases when the minimum acceptable standard is consultation, this consultation must be in good faith, and with the intention of substantially addressing the concerns of the aboriginal peoples whose lands are at issue. In most cases, it will be significantly deeper than mere consultation. Some cases may even require the full consent of an aboriginal nation.[75]

Thus where Aboriginal (native) title has been asserted but not established, section 35 requires the Crown 'to consult with the group asserting title and, if appropriate, accommodate its interests'; and once title is established, incursions are permitted 'only with the consent of the Aboriginal group or if they are justified by a compelling and substantial public purpose and are not inconsistent with the Crown's fiduciary duty to [that] group'.[76] In this way, the Honour of the Crown and the duty to consult that derives from it are important qualifications on state power, as is expressed by the Supreme Court in *R v Sparrow*:

> There is no explicit language in [section 35 of the Canadian Constitution] that authorizes this Court or any court to assess the legitimacy of any government legislation that restricts aboriginal rights. Yet, we find that the words 'recognition and affirmation' incorporate the fiduciary relationship referred to earlier and so import some restraint on the exercise of sovereign power.[77]

C. Australia

As indicated previously, there is currently no recognition in the Australian Constitution of Indigenous peoples or their rights. There is no constitutional or federal legislative bill

---

[69] *R v Sparrow* (n 66).
[70] ibid 1119.
[71] ibid 1120. See also *Haida Nation v British Columbia* (n 60) [21].
[72] *Haida Nation v British Columbia* (n 60) [32].
[73] ibid [35].
[74] ibid [34].
[75] *Delgamuukw v British Columbia* [1997] 3 SCR 1010, 1113. See also *Tsilhqot'in Nation v British Columbia* [2014] 2 SCR 256, 294.
[76] *Tsilhqot'in Nation v British Columbia* (n 75) 269.
[77] *R v Sparrow* (n 66) 1109.

of rights that could support distinctive rights for Indigenous Australians, either in a stand-alone provision or by reference to the rights of cultural or ethnic minorities.[78] There are no reserved seats in Parliament for Indigenous representatives, and no treaties concluded between Australian governments and Indigenous peoples. Nor is there a common law duty requiring governments to consult Indigenous peoples or to make informed decisions where their interests are at stake.

A general state–Indigenous trust or fiduciary duty, one that could have provided a seedbed for the emergence of a consultative duty, possibly as part of a general set of obligations akin to the 'Honour of the Crown', might have emerged in Australia alongside the common law recognition of native title rights in the 1992 *Mabo (No 2)* decision.[79] This possibility did not, however, form part of the High Court's reasoning in that case.[80] It was given substantive consideration by one judge, Justice Toohey, who found that the Crown had the obligations of a constructive trustee with respect to the Meriam people, emerging from the 'circumstances of the relationship' and the inalienability of native title rights.[81] The *Mabo (No 2)* decision was, however, swiftly followed by the federal *Native Title Act 1993* (of which there is no equivalent in Canada or New Zealand), which has rather comprehensively regulated the field of native title, reducing the scope for judges to elaborate on the concomitant obligations of Australian governments, including consultative obligations, outside of those expressly provided for in the legislation.

There appears as yet no formal reason, that is, nothing exclusionary in the *Native Title Act*, and no majority in the High Court on this point, to suggest that some future exploration of trust principles in connection to proven native title rights might not yield a set of fiduciary obligations supportive of consultative obligations. As Justice Kirby noted more than 20 years ago in *Thorpe v The Commonwealth*, the ambivalence of judicial determinations on an Australian state–Indigenous fiduciary relationship means the possibility is unrealised, and the question unresolved:

> [W]hether a fiduciary duty is owed by the Crown to the [I]ndigenous peoples of Australia remains an open question. This Court has simply not determined it. Certainly, it has not determined it adversely to the proposition. On the other hand, there is no holding endorsing such a fiduciary duty.[82]

As the above indicates, Australian public law diverges from that of its Commonwealth settler state peers in its failure to protect the distinctive rights of Indigenous peoples (beyond the protections provided for native title rights and interests), or to establish and monitor a constitutional relationship between Indigenous peoples and settler governments. As a result, the capacity of Indigenous peoples to influence decision-making that affects their interests is, in Australia, severely curtailed. As the examples drawn from Canada and New Zealand show, despite periodic missteps and with much work left to be done, sound

---

[78] See, eg, s 20 of the New Zealand Bill of Rights Act, protecting the rights of members of ethnic, religious or linguistic minorities in New Zealand to enjoy their culture, to profess and practise their religion, or to use their language, in community with others. See also the Victorian *Charter of Human Rights and Responsibilities 2010*, s 19 (protecting cultural rights, with specific reference in s 19(2) to the cultural rights of Aboriginal peoples).

[79] *Mabo v Queensland (No 2)* (1992) 175 CLR 1.

[80] For a more in-depth analysis of this possibility, see K Gover, 'The Honour of the Crowns: State–Indigenous Fiduciary Relationships and Australian Exceptionalism' (2016) 38 *Sydney Law Review* 339.

[81] *Mabo v Queensland (No 2)* (n 79) 202.

[82] *Thorpe v Commonwealth (No 3)* (1997) 144 ALR 677 [37].

procedural requirements ensuring political participation and consultation enable the parties to commit to the process of working out how to respond to concrete issues when they arise. These processes are guided by the judicial expectation that the parties will act in good faith, and that Indigenous views will be sought and taken into account where their interests are at stake. This much provides the constitutional conditions for justice, even if it does not suffice on its own to ensure just outcomes.

In light of these commitments, in the settler societies 'reconciliation' can manifest in the day to day as good faith dialogue between peoples rather than as a final settlement of Indigenous claims. This model has been suggested by James Tully, who argues that that negotiation between equals is a 'democratic way' to achieve reconciliation 'acceptable to both parties' in a settler society:

> It consists in Indigenous and non-Indigenous peoples negotiating a relationship of reconciliation. On this view reconciliation is neither a form of recognition handed down to Indigenous peoples from the state nor a final settlement of some kind. It is an on-going partnership negotiated by free peoples based on principles they can both endorse and open to modification *en passant*.[83]

Given the lack of a federal or constitutional bill of rights, the lack of treaties, and the lack of consultative obligations on the part of Australian governments, the Uluru Statement is very understandably an appeal to the Australian people themselves, asking them to consider and endorse a relationship of a kind that no branch of government has so far been willing to pursue on their behalf. Most importantly, the Uluru Statement's proposed Voice to Parliament could mitigate against the excesses of governmental unilateralism in Indigenous affairs. It would provide a basis on which meaningful consultation with Indigenous peoples could be conducted, and through which 'rules of engagement' can be agreed to ensure dealings are undertaken in good faith and with honour. In Australia, however, for the time being and in the absence of a constitutional relationship, Indigenous claims are forced into the very narrow and inhospitable avenues provided by anti-discrimination legislation, most significantly, the federal *Racial Discrimination Act 1975* (RDA). Within this framework, the 2013 case of *Maloney* provided an opportunity for the High Court to require that measures burdening Indigenous communities be accompanied by consultation with those communities. It declined to take up this opportunity, and in the course of dismissing Joan Maloney's claim, rendered Australian Indigenous peoples uniquely vulnerable to discriminatory laws. The aim of the following section is to show that for Australian Indigenous peoples the stakes are high, and that the deficits addressed by the Uluru Statement are current and serious.[84]

IV. *Maloney v The Queen*: Some Rights, No Relationship

The Australian Indigenous–state relationship is to a very large extent structured by legal concepts of race and of racial discrimination. Perhaps because of the dominance of the

---

[83] J Tully, *Public Philosophy in a New Key*, vol 1: *Democracy and Civic Freedom* (Cambridge, Cambridge University Press, 2008) 223.
[84] This section draws on analysis in K Gover, 'Indigenous–State Relationships and the Paradoxical Effects of Anti-discrimination Law: Lessons from the Australian High Court in *Maloney v The Queen*' in M Tatum et al (eds), *Indigenous Justice: New Tools, Approaches, and Spaces* (Basingstoke, Palgrave MacMillan, 2018).

RDA, indigeneity and race appear as interchangeable cognates in Australian public law. The RDA and its underpinning concept of racial difference have been used to adjudicate differential treatment between traditional land owners and persons who are not traditional land owners;[85] between holders of native title and holders of other types of property;[86] and between Aboriginal and non-Aboriginal persons.[87] Accordingly, in Australia, non-Aboriginality has been held to be a marker of 'race', and the collective of all persons who are not traditional owners or native title holders (including Indigenous persons) has been deemed to constitute a 'particular race' in the terms of the Act.[88] The effect is to characterise measures giving effect to Indigenous rights as measures that deny those rights to others on the basis of their race. As a result, in Australia, laws that benefit or burden Indigenous persons must run the gauntlet of the RDA, which implements the International Convention on the Elimination of All Forms of Racial Discrimination (ICERD).[89] In the absence of anything else, the RDA has become the default architecture for the evaluation of any law that is specifically directed to an Indigenous community. It is not equipped to do this well.

Crucially, the only allowance made in the RDA for measures that differentiate between groups on the basis of their race is the so-called 'special measures' exception, permitting and requiring governments to take measures 'necessary to ensure the adequate development and protection of certain racial groups or individuals belonging to them, for the purpose of guaranteeing them the full and equal enjoyment of human rights and fundamental freedoms'.[90] The special measures exception has been used by Australian governments to defend State laws for Indigenous communities from challenges brought by non-Indigenous applicants[91] and by Indigenous non-beneficiaries.[92] Most controversially, however, it has served to defend measures rejected by Indigenous 'beneficiaries' themselves, as in Joan Maloney's case.[93] The assumption had been, in the earlier jurisprudence of the High Court and in the recommendations of the Committee on the Elimination of Racial Discrimination (CERD) tasked with oversight of ICERD,[94] that special measures provisions were to be used to defend and justify preferential treatment for disadvantaged racial minorities where these are challenged by members of the majority. The High Court's 2013 decision in *Maloney* has turned this assumption on its head.

In *Maloney*, the High Court found that regulatory measures imposed by the Queensland Crown, criminalising the possession of certain volumes and types of alcohol in 19 identified Indigenous communities, and *only* in those Indigenous communities, were 'special measures', having the sole purpose of securing adequate advancement of a disadvantaged group.

---

[85] *Gerhardy v Brown* (1985) 159 CLR 70, 118 (Brennan J).
[86] *Mabo v Queensland (No 1)* (1988) 166 CLR 186; *Western Australia v Ward* (2002) 213 CLR 1, [117]; *Western Australia v Commonwealth (Native Title Act Case)* (1995) 183 CLR 373, [438].
[87] *Carr v Boree Aboriginal Corporation* [2003] FMCA 408, [9].
[88] *Gerhardy v Brown* (n 85) 84 (Gibbs CJ), 100–01 (Mason J), 118 (Brennan J).
[89] International Convention on the Elimination of All Forms of Racial Discrimination (21 December 1965) 660 UNTS 195.
[90] RDA 1975, s 8 (cross-referencing to ICERD Art 1(4)).
[91] *Bruch v Commonwealth* [2002] FMCA 29.
[92] *Gerhardy v Brown* (n 85).
[93] *Bropho v Western Australia* (2008) 169 FCR 59; *Aurukun Shire Council v Chief Executive Officer, Office of Liquor Gaming and Racing in the Department of Treasury* [2012] 1 Qd R 1; *Maloney* (n 5).
[94] CERD, *General Recommendation No 32: The Meaning and Scope of Special Measures in the International Convention on the Elimination of All Forms Racial Discrimination* CERD/C/GC/32 (24 September 2009) [12].

In other words, these regulations were permitted as measures furthering substantive equality through affirmative action. Before discussing the reasoning that led to this result, it is important to note first that when Joan Maloney was arrested and charged with the unlawful possession of two bottles of alcohol, she was 55 years old and had no criminal record. The fact that she now has a criminal record is because she is an Indigenous person living in an Indigenous community. It is equally important to note that, as might be expected given the complexity of the issues raised by alcohol consumption, Australian Indigenous peoples have diverse views about how the supply and use of alcohol in their communities should be regulated. Many Indigenous communities have chosen to limit the supply of alcohol to curb alcohol-related violence and dysfunction, and especially to mitigate against its disproportionate effects on the safety of women and children. Some have used their local government powers and their own traditional law to regulate alcohol, with the cooperation of State and Territory governments. Whatever the views of Indigenous peoples contemplating the regulation of alcohol use and supply in their communities, *Maloney* establishes that officials need not ask them for those views before imposing their own measures, even when those measures criminalise conduct that is lawful in non-Indigenous communities.

In total the Queensland Government has designated 19 Aboriginal communities, including Palm Island, as 'restricted areas' to be governed by Alcohol Management Plans (AMPs).[95] All 'restricted areas' are Indigenous communities and, as was noted in the Court of Appeal, '[t]he relevant provisions do not apply to dysfunctional non-Indigenous communities with problems of alcohol-related violence'.[96] While the applicable legislation specifies that the responsible Minister may impose an AMP only if he or she has consulted with the community, it also provides that failure to consult 'does not affect the validity' of an AMP.[97] Joan Maloney's community on Bwgcolman or Palm Island was the last of the 19 communities to be subjected to an AMP, in 2006. The Island's particular history is relevant to the way in which the AMP was designed and imposed, and helps to explain the reluctance of Queensland officials to consult with the community's representative bodies. Some of that history is briefly summarised here for context.

Palm Island has a population of approximately 2,000 people, an 'overwhelming majority' of whom (probably in the realm of 97 per cent) are Indigenous.[98] It has a long association with Indigenous civil disobedience. The Island was first established as a reserve in 1914, and by the 1920s it had become the most populous Aboriginal reserve in Queensland, one used as a 'penal settlement' in which to incarcerate Indigenous persons from other reserves who were considered troublesome or 'incorrigible'.[99] The Island is still known amongst Queensland indigenous peoples as 'Punishment Island'. As is the case for many Indigenous communities, rates of domestic and alcohol-related violence are much higher on Palm Island than elsewhere in Queensland.[100] The Island's tragic history and the ongoing struggle of its residents with poverty and dysfunction have long contributed to a difficult relationship between the Bwgcolman community and its resident police.

---

[95] *Indigenous Communities Liquor Licenses Act 2002* (Qld).
[96] *R v Maloney* [2013] 1 Qd R 32, [28].
[97] *Liquor Act 1992* (Qld), s 173I(2).
[98] *Maloney v The Queen* [2012] HCA Trans 342, 11 December 2012, at 10.15am (French CJ).
[99] *Wotton v Queensland (No 5)* [2016] FCA 1457, [44].
[100] *Maloney* (n 5) [125] (Crennan J).

In 2004, longstanding tensions and frustrations erupted in a series of violent encounters between police and Indigenous residents, catalysed by the death in police custody of Mulrunji, previously known as Cameron Doomadgee, on 19 November 2004 (his family prefer that after his death he be called by his traditional name).[101]

Mulrunji's preliminary autopsy report advised that his death was caused by 'a compressive force ... which caused heavy internal bleeding',[102] a finding that appeared to confirm the community's suspicion that Mulrunji had been killed by his arresting officer. Immediately after the autopsy results were announced, violence flared up on the Island. Rocks were thrown at police and a police car was stolen and burnt. Later, the home of the arresting officer, the police station and the Island's courthouse were set alight and destroyed by fire.[103] The Queensland Government immediately issued an emergency declaration, allowing Palm Island police to exercise 'a variety of coercive powers, and powers of entry, search and seizure, which otherwise would not be available to them without warrant'.[104] A 'special emergency response team' was dispatched to the Island, and over the course of three days police officers searched 18 homes, often in the very early morning, and arrested 11 people. Three of those arrested subsequently brought a class action suit that was heard by the Federal Court in 2016, resulting in a finding that the Queensland police had discriminated on the basis of race in their conduct of the raids, and requiring the payment of compensation to the applicants.[105] In 2018, Palm Islanders and the Queensland Government negotiated a 30 million dollar settlement of related claims.[106]

The civil unrest on the Island intensified the Government's insistence on the need to restrict the availability of alcohol in the community. It pushed forward with its proposed AMP in circumstances characterised by great mutual suspicion and animosity. Two days after the riots occurred, the Queensland Government presented a 'Five Point Plan' to the Palm Island community, referencing its intention to finalise an AMP for the Island, and several months later 'the Palm Island Aboriginal Shire Council was informed that an Alcohol Management Plan would be introduced in early 2006'.[107] It was by virtue of this measure that Joan Maloney came to be charged in the Magistrate's Court in 2008.

Maloney appealed against her conviction in the Supreme Court of Queensland, arguing that the AMP and its enabling legislative provisions were inconsistent with the RDA and so invalid, because their effect was to limit her human rights and fundamental freedoms, and to prevent her from enjoying those rights to the same extent as non-Aboriginal persons.[108] Queensland countered that the AMP was a special measure satisfying the terms of section 8 of the RDA, because it was enacted 'for the sole purpose of securing adequate advancement' of its beneficiaries. In response Maloney produced affidavits from 14 Palm Islanders as evidence that the consultation on the AMP was inadequate.[109] She argued that in the

---

[101] *Wotton v Queensland* (n 99) [4].
[102] ibid [318].
[103] ibid [322]–[326].
[104] ibid [329].
[105] ibid.
[106] S Kohlbacher and W Barnsley, 'Palm Islanders reach $30m settlement' *The Courier* (1 May 2018).
[107] Queensland Government, 'Queensland Government Response to the Palm Island Select Committee' (November 2005), 39.
[108] In accordance with RDA 1975, s 10.
[109] *R v Maloney* [2012] QCA 105, [41] (McMurdo P) and [207] (Chesterman J).

absence of appropriate consultation with the Bwgcolman people, the purported special measure must be accompanied by a 'compelling justification' and subjected to a higher degree of judicial scrutiny.[110] In support of this claim she urged a reading of the RDA that is 'consistent with principles of international law', including the recommendations of the CERD Committee. These emphasise the need for consultation with the beneficiaries of special measures, even while the ICERD contains no reference to consultation.[111]

The judges of the High Court confirmed that the measures constituted a prima facie violation of the RDA, but agreed with Queensland that they were exempted as 'special measures' within the terms of the Act. Perhaps most importantly, they unanimously held that special measures need not be accompanied by consultation with the community that is to be the beneficiary of those measures, because no such requirement is found in the text of the RDA.[112] Several judges thought that a lack of consultation might, in some circumstances, be a factor relevant to the question of whether a measure could reasonably be deemed a 'special measure', but did not think this limitation was applicable on the facts in *Maloney*.[113] As the Chief Justice explained:

> The criminalization of the conduct prohibited by [the AMP] does not take the law out of the category of 'special measure' as defined in Art 1(4) of the ICERD and incorporated in s 8 of the RDA. Such a provision is not in terms excluded by the text or by implication from the scope of special measures, which must be capable of application to a wide variety of circumstances. In so saying, it may be accepted that 'special measures' are ordinarily measures of the kind generally covered by the rubric 'affirmative action'.[114]

As noted, while neither the RDA nor the ICERD makes reference to consultation requirements, the CERD Committee, which is tasked with oversight of the ICERD, has advised state parties that consultation is a required element of 'special measures', advising that states 'should ensure that special measures are designed and implemented on the basis of prior consultation with affected communities and the active participation of such communities'.[115] The Committee has also called on states to 'ensure that members of indigenous peoples have equal rights in respect of effective participation in public life and that no decisions directly relating to their rights and interests are taken without their informed consent'.[116]

---

[110] *Maloney* (n 5) [117] (Crennan J).
[111] ibid [233].
[112] ibid [24] (French CJ), [91] (Hayne J), [128] and [131] (Crennan J), [186] (Kiefel J), [240] (Bell J), [357] (Gageler J).
[113] French CJ left open the possibility that 'in the absence of genuine consultation with those to be affected by a special measure, it may be open to a court to conclude that the measure is not reasonably capable of being appropriate and adapted for the sole purpose it purports to serve': ibid [25]. Hayne J noted that '[a]t most, the fact that consultation has taken place may assist, in some cases, in determining whether a particular law meets the statutory criteria for a "special measure"': at [91]. Bell J at [247] allowed that 'The nature and extent of the burden imposed by the law and the adequacy of the consultation with those who are to be affected by it are matters that may be relevant to the determination of whether it is a special measure. This is because a law limiting the enjoyment of the rights of a group enacted without adequate consultation with the group may not be capable of being reasonably considered to be appropriate and adapted to the sole purpose of securing the group's adequate advancement.'
[114] *Maloney* (n 5) [21] (French CJ).
[115] Committee on the Elimination of Racial Discrimination, *General Recommendation No 32* (n 94) [18].
[116] Committee on the Elimination of Racial Discrimination, *General Recommendation No 23: Indigenous Peoples* (18 August 1997) 4(d), extracted in *Report of the Committee on the Elimination of Racial Discrimination*, UN Doc A/52/18 (26 September 1997), Annex V.

All but one of the judges in the High Court declined, for various reasons, to use the recommendations of the CERD Committee as extrinsic material in the interpretation of the RDA.[117] All judges likewise declined to consider the relevance of the United Nations Declaration on the Rights of Indigenous Peoples 2007, including its provisions on 'free, prior and informed consent'.[118] Through *Maloney*, the High Court has confirmed that when Indigenous peoples seek to influence law and policy affecting their interests, even where those interests are uniquely and directly affected, they must take their chances alongside everyone else in the Australian electorate. Justice Bell, for example, discussed the international instruments and materials relevant to the issue of consultation with Indigenous peoples, but deemed them irrelevant to the statutory interpretation exercise at hand, concluding that:

> In any event, and just as importantly, those materials take democratic society as their background, which includes democratic mechanisms by which representative governments resolve contested policy. Those mechanisms include free, informed public debate, a free press and regular elections. Because of those mechanisms, however precautionary or desirable in some sense consultation with constituents may be (and even if a legislature encourages consultation, as here), ordinarily neither consultation with constituents nor their consent to a law is a precondition to the legality of a statute, particularly a protective measure, passed in Australia by an elected Parliament.[119]

By implication, then, communities in need of 'protective measures' have an even weaker claim to be consulted about those measures than the population at large. For members of an 'extreme minority', who are outnumbered 35 to 1 in the best of circumstances and live with the colonial legacy of exclusion and dispossession, a recommendation to pursue one's interests (in this case, one's interest in not being singled out for criminal sanction) through 'informed public debate, a free press and regular elections', must seem like a further act of exclusion.

Significantly for the purposes of this chapter, the High Court failed to accept the observations offered in obiter by one of the judges presiding in the High Court's 1985 decision in *Gerhardy v Brown* (the only other High Court case considering the special measures defence for acts affecting an Indigenous community). In this case, Brennan J (alone on this point) thought that the concept of advancement animating the special measures exception was intrinsically linked to 'the wishes of the beneficiaries' and to their agency and human dignity, which are supported by the opportunity to exercise choice. He observed:

> 'Advancement' is not necessarily what the person who takes the measure regards as a benefit for the beneficiaries. The purpose of securing advancement for a racial group is not established by showing that the branch of government or the person who takes the measure does so for the purpose of conferring what it or he regards as a benefit for the group if the group does not seek or wish to have the benefit. The wishes of the beneficiaries for the measure are of great importance (perhaps essential) in determining whether a measure is taken for the purpose of securing their

---

[117] *Maloney* (n 5) [61] (Hayne J), [175]–[176] (Kiefel J), [236] (Bell J), [134] (Crennan J), see also [326]–[328] (Gageler J).

[118] United Nations Declaration on the Rights of Indigenous Peoples, GA Res 61/295, 61st sess, 107th plenary meeting, Supp No 49, UN Doc A/RES/61295 (13 September 2007), Arts 19, 32.

[119] *Maloney* (n 5) [135].

advancement. The dignity of the beneficiaries is impaired and they are not advanced by having an unwanted material benefit foisted on them.[120]

Finally, to conclude this section, an important aspect of the High Court's decision lies in its findings on the concept of 'advancement' in Australian non-discrimination law. These have an analogue in judicial reasoning on the idea of 'benefit' in cases considering the Constitutional 'race power'. As previously noted, the 'race power' enables Australian governments to make laws for '[t]he people of any race for whom it is deemed necessary to make special laws'. This head of power has been used by the Commonwealth only to enact legislation for Indigenous peoples.[121] It was amended in a successful referendum held in 1967, enabling the Commonwealth to make laws under its auspices 'with regard to the Aboriginal race', a capacity formerly reserved to the States. In cases considering the scope of the race power, the High Court has failed to resolve the question of whether power is confined to laws for the benefit of members of a particular race, or should be so confined when used to enact laws for Indigenous peoples. When the matter was directly argued in the 1998 case of *Kartinyeri v Commonwealth*,[122] of the four judges who considered the scope of the race power, two decided the power was not confined to beneficial laws, and two admitted the possibility that at least *some* discriminatory laws could be ultra vires the race power. On this point it is arguable there is no majority finding. In *Maloney*, the High Court has further affirmed its agnosticism on the question of whether laws may be made for Indigenous peoples, on the basis of their race, that either do not benefit them, or indeed significantly burden them. It has confirmed that in Australian law, 'advancement' entails not just the type of benefits associated with 'affirmative action', but also burdens designed to correct behaviours thought not to be in the community's best interests. These burdens are valid even if the community has itself determined through its own representative institutions that the measures are unnecessary and undesirable. Consequently, anti-discrimination principles in Australia tend to obscure and undermine intergovernmental modes of engagement (including consultation) that could support Indigenous agency and self-governance.

Most worryingly, the decision suggests that it is precisely *because* of their disadvantage and their designation as members of a 'race' that Indigenous peoples are now more vulnerable to targeted race-based law-making than any other community in Australia. Because they are already disadvantaged in the enjoyment of human rights and fundamental freedoms, itself the legacy of colonial policies, and because they are defined in law as members of a racial group, discriminatory actions that would otherwise be impermissible can be defended as special measures. This is precisely the type of top-down coercive approach to law-making that a Voice to Parliament could identify, caution against, and propose alternatives to. The Voice to Parliament could help to ensure that Indigenous peoples are recognised as polities, with differing views on what is in the best interests of their communities, rather than being positioned as undifferentiated members of a racial minority. It could further ensure that

---

[120] *Gerhardy v Brown* (n 85) 135.
[121] eg *Native Title Act 1993*; *Aboriginal and Torres Strait Islander Heritage Protection Act 1984*; *Aboriginal and Torres Strait Islander Commission Act 1989*.
[122] *Kartinyeri v Commonwealth* (1998) 152 ALR 540.

Indigenous polities are recognised as having a distinctive constitutional status that requires they be included, as peoples, in the making of laws that affect their interests.

V. Conclusion

The proposals set out in the Uluru Statement are orientated above all else towards the maintenance of a just ongoing collaborative relationship, and in this sense they are optimistic and forward-looking 'rules of engagement' that do not insist on the outcome of that engagement but instead direct us to act respectfully and honestly in our dealings with one another. Perhaps most fundamentally, implementing the proposals set out in the Uluru Statement from the Heart would go some way to alleviating what is described in the Statement as the 'torment of powerlessness' experienced by Indigenous peoples, who are subject to laws that they had almost no say in making, some of which expressly apply only to them and some of which are overtly coercive and intrusive. Seen in this context, and given everything that has happened, the Uluru Statement is an immensely generous invitation.

10
Public Law, Legitimacy and Indigenous Aspirations

HARRY HOBBS*

I. Introduction

Across the globe, settler-states are debating whether and how their political and legal governance framework can recognise and accommodate the Indigenous nations whose traditional lands they claim. The terms of each discussion vary, as do the languages in which that debate is conducted, but the central issue remains consistent: existing arrangements fail to do justice to Indigenous demands, whether for sovereignty, autonomy, self-government or some level of decision-making authority.[1] Questions of public law and institutional design are a key site for this debate, as a diverse array of mechanisms that empower Indigenous peoples with the capacity to have their voices heard in the processes of settler-state government have been established, and others proposed, in recent years.[2] In status and scope, these mechanisms range from appointed or elected administrative agencies to representative bodies exercising limited policy-making functions, to relatively self-governing autonomous units within federations. Depending on their mandate, powers and authority, these institutional arrangements provide a measure of input into and control over public decision-making, ensuring that government remains responsive to the interests and values of Indigenous peoples. Considered as an element of a burgeoning or emergent notion of shared rule, these bodies signal, even if they do not necessarily demonstrate in practice, the public and political equality of Indigenous peoples within the state.[3]

The emergence of Indigenous decision-making bodies connected to, or embedded within, state processes suggests a growing recognition and institutional acknowledgement

---

*I thank Annabel Johnson, Aishani Gupta, Patrick Macklem and Jason Varuhas for their comments on earlier drafts. I also thank Nicole Roughan, Kirsty Gover and other participants at the Third Public Law Conference, Melbourne, 11–13 July 2018.
[1] *United Nations Declaration on the Rights of Indigenous Peoples*, GA Res 61/295, 61st sess, 107th plen mtg, Supp No 49, UN Doc A/RES/61295 (13 September 2007), Arts 3–5 (hereinafter '*UNDRIP*').
[2] Human Rights Council, *Final Report of the Study on Indigenous Peoples and the Right to Participate in Decision-Making: Report of the Expert Mechanism on the Rights of Indigenous Peoples*, 18th sess, Agenda Item 5, UN Doc A/HRC/18/42 (17 August 2011) 5–11, [16]–[39].
[3] P Macklem, 'Distributing Sovereignty: Indian Nations and Equality of Peoples' (1993) 45 *Stanford Law Review* 1311.

of Indigenous rights. Though differently structured and situated, each mechanism is predicated on an ethos that Indigenous peoples are entitled to have their views considered in decisions that affect them. At the same time, however, this development gives rise to two interrelated concerns regarding public law's relationship with Indigenous law, rights and culture. On one hand sit Indigenous peoples and communities, who quite rightly contend that any decision-making institution must reflect their own ontologies and values,[4] which may differ considerably from the institutional forms of the state. On the other hand, some members of the dominant community (and indeed some Indigenous peoples themselves) question whether such institutions can be accommodated within existing public law frameworks. When these competing conceptions of the state meet, Indigenous claims are often subducted beneath state rationality. This does not defuse tensions, but it can lead to faults and eruptions now and into the future.

The challenge is that even when Indigenous decision-making bodies are validly established, it is not clear that they meet Indigenous demands of and for legitimacy. Public law may be dynamic and flexible, but accommodating Indigenous forms of decision-making within the political and legal architecture of the state will necessarily involve transforming those governance institutions in some manner. For more radical Indigenous scholars and activists, this fact belies the existence of Indigenous self-governance, rendering it 'meaningless'.[5] Even if this is not always the case, however, in practice, the act of translation can do violence to Indigenous normative orders.

In this chapter, I explore the tensions involved in designing Indigenous decision-making institutions connected to or embedded within the public law apparatus of the state. My goal is to identify indicia of institutional design to ensure that public law remains both flexible and substantively accommodative of diverse normative orders, as well as to highlight the inherent challenges in this process. I do so by examining the notion of legitimacy.

This issue has recently achieved prominence in Australia. In May 2017, around 250 Aboriginal and Torres Strait Islander delegates 'from all points of the southern sky' gathered on the red dust of Mutitjulu to call for meaningful substantive reform to Australia's public law framework.[6] The culmination of the most extensive deliberative constitutional process in the country's history, delegates characterised their aspirations as 'voice, treaty, and truth'.[7] In the Uluru Statement from the Heart, they called for the establishment of a Makarrata Commission to supervise a process of agreement-making and truth-telling about Australia's colonial history, as well as constitutional reform to embed a First Nations Voice – a national Indigenous representative body empowered to advise Parliament on laws that affect Aboriginal and Torres Strait Islander people. Although the federal Government rejected the proposal for an Indigenous representative body, the Opposition has committed to holding a referendum to entrench a First Nations

---

[4] *UNDRIP*, Art 18.

[5] T Alfred, *Peace, Power Righteousness: An Indigenous Manifesto*, 2nd edn (New York, Oxford University Press, 2009) 5. As pre-existing self-governing communities, these scholars argue that Indigenous communities and nations must exercise self-government on the same level as existing states.

[6] Referendum Council, 'Uluru Statement from the Heart', *Final Report of the Referendum Council* (2017) i.

[7] P Anderson, 'Our Hope for the Future: Voice. Treaty. Truth', 17th Vincent Lingiari Memorial Lecture, Darwin (16 August 2017).

Voice in the Australian Constitution if it wins the next election.[8] If it is to be established, issues of public law and legitimacy will be critical.

I explore these issues in three parts but start with a brief note on methodology. Torres Strait Islander scholar Martin Nakata has explained that a critique of Western epistemologies is 'not sufficient for the defence of Indigenous systems of thought or the re-building of Indigenous lives and communities'.[9] A central task of academics is therefore to '[re-assert] and [draw] in concepts and meanings from Indigenous knowledge and systems of thought and experience of the colonial'.[10] While, as a non-Indigenous person, I am unable to re-assert Indigenous knowledge, I can attempt, faithfully and with sensitivity, to draw on Indigenous thinking and aspirations and carry these to other non-Indigenous persons. Section II begins this task, by responding to Indigenous scholars and activists who cast doubt on the validity of establishing Indigenous institutions embedded within the state. Whether or not public law is flexible enough to accommodate Indigenous ontologies and institutions of governance in theory, these scholars powerfully argue both that the practice has failed and that the goal is undesirable. In this section I take these challenges seriously, but nonetheless argue that there are strong reasons for Indigenous peoples and communities to work within the state in order to have their interests taken into account by the state.

Recognising that there are challenges in implementation, I argue that culturally appropriate Indigenous decision-making institutions can be accommodated within the state's broader public law framework, though this requires flexibility on both sides. Flexibility is the central focus of section III, where I examine the concept of legitimacy. Drawing on sociological accounts, I tease out three indicia that can guide judgement in assessing whether an Indigenous decision-making institution is likely to be credible in the eyes of its constituents; that is, whether public law has accommodated Indigenous normative orders in and on their own terms.

The indicia provide a language with which to assess Indigenous decision-making bodies acting within state frameworks. I demonstrate this by applying them to the Aboriginal and Torres Strait Islander Commission (ATSIC) in section IV. ATSIC was an Indigenous representative body with executive authority that operated in Australia between 1989 and 2005. Intended to give Aboriginal and Torres Strait Islander peoples 'a real say in the management of their own affairs' and 'a real say in the decision-making process',[11] the Commission was ultimately abolished with bipartisan support. Ideological opposition to the Commission played a role, but public law notions of accountability, governance

---

[8] Department of Prime Minister and Cabinet, 'Response to Referendum Council's Report on Constitutional Recognition' (26 October 2017), available at https://ministers.pmc.gov.au/scullion/2017/responsereferendum-councils-report-constitutional-recognition; C Wahlquist, 'Bill Shorten Says Labor Will Pursue Indigenous Voice to Parliament Without Coalition', *Guardian Australia* (12 February 2018), available at https://www.theguardian.com/australia-news/2018/feb/12/bill-shorten-says-labor-will-pursue-indigenous-voice-to-parliament-without-coalition.

[9] M Nakata et al, 'Decolonial Goals and Pedagogies for Indigenous Students' (2012) 1 *Decolonisation: Indigeneity, Education & Society* 120, 124.

[10] ibid.

[11] Australia Cth, House of Representatives, Aboriginal and Torres Strait Islander Commission Bill 1989, 4 May 1989, vol 166, 1994 (Gerry Hand).

and integrity served as the catalyst for its removal. Today, ATSIC is largely – though not entirely – considered a failure by non-Indigenous politicians. As Indigenous aspirations for constitutional reform coalesce around a national representative body, however, it is important to revisit the Commission.

This study is not aimed at a comprehensive evaluation of ATSIC. Rather, the indicia reveal the opportunities and challenges inherent in accommodating Indigenous institutions within public law frameworks. The goal is therefore not to interrogate Indigenous decision-making institutions or to problematise Indigeneity, a practice Māori professor Linda Tuhiwai Smith condemns as a 'Western obsession',[12] but to challenge public law and prevailing conceptions of governance; to, as Robert Cover implored, 'stop circumscribing the *nomos* ... [and] ... invite new worlds'.[13] Concluding comments on future institutional design are offered in section V.

II. Indigenous Institutions and the State

A significant strain of Indigenous scholarship and activism critiques the idea of Indigenous decision-making bodies operating within existing state frameworks. Kanien'kehá:ka professor Taiaiake Alfred, for instance, forcefully contends that self-governance or self-rule 'within the legal and structural confines of the state' is 'an assimilative goal',[14] and ends with the 'defeat of the idea of an independent Onkwehonwe [original person] existence'.[15] Tanganekald/Meintangk scholar Irene Watson agrees with Alfred, dismissing forms of recognition of Indigenous self-determination by or within state institutions as 'inevitably reinstat[ing] colonial law',[16] and thus leaving Indigenous peoples 'subservient to the rules of the state'.[17] In a persuasive critique of state-sponsored efforts at 'recognition' and 'reconciliation', Yellowknives Dene political theorist Glen Coulthard adopts a similar position. Coulthard argues that conceiving recognition as something that is 'granted' or 'accorded' by the state to subaltern groups, 'prefigures its failure to significantly modify, let alone transcend, the breadth of power at play in colonial relations'.[18] Rather, it is a form of 'domestication'[19] of Indigenous sovereignty, that 'subtly reproduce[s] nonmutual and unfree relations rather than free and mutual ones'.[20] Kahnawake Mohawk anthropologist

---

[12] LT Smith, *Decolonizing Methodologies: Research and Indigenous Peoples* (Dunedin, University of Otago Press, 1999) 91–92.
[13] R Cover, 'The Supreme Court 1982 Term: Foreword: Nomos and Narrative' (1983) 97 *Harvard Law Review* 4, 68.
[14] Alfred, *Peace, Power Righteousness* (n 5) 122.
[15] T Alfred, *Wasáse: Indigenous Pathways of Action and Freedom* (Toronto, University of Toronto Press, 2005) 23; J Mack, 'Thickening Totems and Thinning Imperialism', Thesis submitted to Victoria University in fulfilment of the requirements for the degree of Master of Laws (2007) 10.
[16] I Watson, *Aboriginal Peoples, Colonialism and International Law: Raw Law* (New York, Routledge, 2014) 2.
[17] ibid 91.
[18] G Coulthard, *Red Skins, White Masks: Rejecting the Colonial Politics of Recognition* (Minneapolis, MN, University of Minnesota Press, 2014) 30–31.
[19] ibid 40.
[20] ibid 17.

Audra Simpson concurs, arguing that policies of state recognition are merely a 'gentler form' of continuing the perennial problem of 'managing Indians'.[21]

These scholars posit refusal as a political alternative to recognition. Because enhanced decision-making authority or autonomy within the state cannot provide a place 'with the freedom for the song law to be sung',[22] Indigenous peoples should turn away from the oppressor and resist the act of recognition.[23] As Indigenous sovereignty has never been surrendered or extinguished, what is required is self-rule emanating not from delegated authority but inhering in Indigenous nations themselves.[24] Drawing on ideas of cultural and political resurgence, Alfred argues that meaningful change in Indigenous–Settler relations is only possible after Indigenous communities 'regenerate ourselves and take back our dignity'.[25] Contending that 'continued cooperation with state power structures is morally unacceptable',[26] Alfred urges Indigenous communities to 'recreat[e] our existences, regenerat[e] our cultures',[27] and live as Onkwehonwe 'with integrity'.[28] For Alfred, Indigenous peoples must develop solutions 'within their own cultural frameworks, reuniting themselves as individuals with their collectivity'.[29]

It is tempting to deflect these challenging positions by asserting that they merely reflect historical approaches and colonial attitudes towards Indigenous peoples. Surely the existence of diverse institutional mechanisms empowering Indigenous peoples to exercise decision-making authority and/or channelling Indigenous interests into the processes of settler-state government across the globe must demonstrate a renewed focus, or at least an emergent understanding of the moral and ethical force of Indigenous claims, as well as a commitment to reconcile them with/in redrawn governance frameworks? To some extent this is true, but the present cannot be excised from the past for it remains fundamentally shaped by it. Perhaps unsurprisingly then, scholars and activists have identified a host of problems in existing institutional attempts to broaden public law institutions. In many cases, existing institutions simply paste 'a thin layer' of 'Aboriginal content ... over a colonial foundation',[30] or marginalise Indigenous peoples' distinct nationhood status,[31] rather than meaningfully grapple with the challenge of respecting Indigenous forms of decision-making on their own terms.

---

[21] A Simpson, *Mohawk Interruptus: Political Life Across the Borders of Settler States* (Durham, NC, Duke University Press, 2014) 20.
[22] Watson, *Aboriginal Peoples, Colonialism and International Law* (n 16) 152.
[23] G Coulthard, 'Subjects of Empire: Indigenous Peoples and the "Politics of Recognition" in Canada' (2007) 6 *Contemporary Political Theory* 444, 454–56; Simpson, *Mohawk Interruptus* (n 21) 11.
[24] Watson, *Aboriginal Peoples, Colonialism and International Law* (n 16) 161. See further A Moreton-Robinson, 'Writing off Indigenous Sovereignty: The Discourse of Security and Patriarchal White Sovereignty' in A Moreton-Robinson (ed), *Sovereign Subjects* (St Leonards, Allen & Unwin, 2007) 99.
[25] Alfred, *Wasáse* (n 15) 38. See further T Alfred, 'Colonialism and State Dependency' (2009) 5 *Journal of Aboriginal Health* 42, 48.
[26] Alfred, *Wasáse* (n 15) 36.
[27] ibid 19.
[28] ibid 24.
[29] Alfred, *Peace, Power Righteousness* (n 5) 29.
[30] J Green, 'Self-Determination, Citizenship, and Federalism: Indigenous and Canadian Palimpsest' in M Murphy (ed), *Canada: State of the Federation 2000 – Reconfiguring Aboriginal-State Relations* (Montreal, McGill-Queen's University Press, 2003) 347.
[31] J Corntassel and R Witmer II, *Forced Federalism: Contemporary Challenges to Indigenous Nationhood* (Norman, OK, University of Oklahoma Press, 2008).

These critiques must be taken seriously, but it is not clear whether and how they can displace existing entrenched power imbalances. In this light, Indigenous peoples may choose to adopt a *modus vivendi* that allows them to respond to the world as it is. After all, as Gabrielle Slowey has argued in the context of resource development projects in Canada's north, the issue facing Indigenous peoples is not a question between exclusion or inclusion but 'about how to secure the best of both worlds'.[32] Indigenous participation within state institutions and public law frameworks does not discount or prevent alternative oppositional strategies or the building of culturally resurgent institutions of self-government outside of the state. Rather, participation in culturally appropriate institutions 'can be viewed as simply one additional means of facilitating Aboriginal control over Aboriginal affairs' and of incorporating Indigenous voices in decisions that affect the state as a whole.[33] In any case, it is a brute fact that many significant issues facing Indigenous communities may most effectively be addressed by leveraging the power of the state, including its coercive powers of redistribution. Many Indigenous scholars and activists agree, arguing that meaningful reform requires that Indigenous peoples 'engage the state's legal and political discourses in more effective ways',[34] transforming colonial structures and ways of thinking. As these scholars caution, however, engaging the state and establishing a dialogue across the Settler–Indigenous divide cannot occur when both parties are working within settler frameworks. A true dialogue must 'not assume' Western superiority but 'acknowledge and understand those who are different in their own terms'.[35] This requires meaningful accommodation on the part of the state.

In an ideal governance framework reflective of Indigenous peoples' equal status as a distinct normative community, Indigenous decision-making institutions would be accepted in whatever manifestation they take. This is a simple condition of equality: 'Aboriginal people must be free, like other people, to choose the political structures suitable to their needs'.[36] If those structures look radically different from existing institutional design then so be it – public law institutions and governing frameworks should accommodate that difference. In the absence of an entirely renegotiated framework premised on something akin to a Rawlsian original position, however, this is improbable. Indigenous peoples seeking governance reform to more accurately reflect their priorities are operating within an elaborate public law architecture that, by and large, does a good job of maintaining public order,[37] coordinating behaviour[38] and providing reasons for citizens

---

[32] GA Slowey, 'A Fine Balance? Aboriginal Peoples in the Canadian North and the Dilemma of Development' in AM Timpson (ed), *First Nations, First Thoughts: The Impact of Indigenous Thought in Canada* (Vancouver, University of British Columbia Press, 2009) 236.

[33] M Murphy, 'Relational Self-Determination and Federal Reform' in M Murphy (ed), *Canada: State of the Federation 2000 – Reconfiguring Aboriginal-State Relations* (McGill-Queen's University Press, Montreal, 2003) 16.

[34] D Turner, *This Is Not a Peace Pipe: Towards a Critical Indigenous Philosophy* (University of Toronto Press, Toronto, 2006) 5.

[35] P Dodson and D Cronin, 'An Australian Dialogue: Decolonising the Country' in S Maddison and M Brigg (eds), *Unsettling the Settler State: Creativity and Resistance in Indigenous Settler-State Governance* (Sydney, Federation Press, 2011) 193. See further D Ivison, *Postcolonial Liberalism* (Cambridge, Cambridge University Press, 2002).

[36] M Mansell, *Treaty and Statehood: Aboriginal Self-Determination* (Sydney, Federation Press, 2016) 141.

[37] T Hobbes, *Leviathan* (Indianapolis, IN, Hackett Publishing, 1994 [1651]).

[38] J Waldron, *Law and Disagreement* (New York, Oxford University Press, 1999).

to act that mirror their own.[39] Even where a particular manifestation fails to meet certain criteria of respect and dignity – and for many Indigenous peoples this is certainly true – disassembling the framework may produce other forms of injustice.[40] For this reason, Indigenous peoples designing culturally appropriate institutions of governance and decision-making that are to be effective, will need to find forms that are 'intelligible within the broader legal framework'.[41]

Accommodation is a complex term that masks a broad spectrum of approaches. In a helpful intervention under the guise of recognition, Bruce Buchan distinguishes between 'recognition as familiarity' and 'recognition as acceptance'. Buchan argues that non-Indigenous peoples must recognise Indigenous institutions of decision-making in Indigenous forms, language and voice, rather than transforming them into our (non-Indigenous) image.[42] Buchan's distinction is key. It points to the fact that despite the necessity of some degree of translation, accommodation should not be unidirectional: whatever form is adopted must be identifiable by Indigenous peoples as reflecting their ways of knowing and being, rather than merely replicating state forms of knowledge.[43]

This is a critical point. Indigenous institutions operating within the state should empower Indigenous peoples to, in the words of Anishinaabe scholar Leanne Simpson, 'practice ways of being and living in the world that are profoundly Nishnaabeg'.[44] This project – the integration of Indigenous ontologies within public law – requires a politico-legal structure that strengthens traditional forms of governance, political cultures and intellectual traditions, so as to 're-create the conditions for living as Nishnaabeg peoples following our own inherent processes and expressions of life',[45] within a wider normative community.

Variations from existing governance frameworks will not necessarily be dramatic or radical. Historical decision-making institutions and processes do not need to be recreated, for 'the authenticity of Indigenous law and governance is not measured by how closely they mirror the perceived past, but by how consistent they are with the current ideas of their communities'.[46] Indeed, reflecting the fact that the increasing complexity of personal and legal relations in contemporary society means that Indigenous and non-Indigenous peoples are 'inextricably entwined in a relationship of interdependence',[47] it should not be surprising that culturally appropriate governance institutions may have evolved 'as a result

---

[39] J Raz, *The Morality of Freedom* (New York, Oxford University Press, 1986).

[40] J Waldron, 'Superseding Historic Injustice' (1992) 103 *Ethics* 4; D Sanderson, 'Redressing the Right Wrong: The Argument from Corrective Justice' (2012) 62 *University of Toronto Law Journal* 93.

[41] J Webber, 'Beyond Regret: Mabo's Implications for Australian Constitutionalism' in D Ivison, P Patten and W Sanders (eds), *Political Theory and the Rights of Indigenous Peoples* (Cambridge, Cambridge University Press, 2000) 66.

[42] B Buchan, *Empire of Political Thought: Indigenous Australians and the Language of Colonial Government* (London, Pickering & Chatto, 2008) 143.

[43] K Gilbert, *Because A White Man'll Never Do It* (Sydney, Angus and Robertson, 1973) 173.

[44] L Simpson, *Dancing on Our Turtle's Back: Stories of Nishnaabeg Re-Creation, Resurgence and a New Emergence* (Winnipeg, ARP Books, 2011) 52–53; J Borrows, *Freedom and Indigenous Constitutionalism* (Toronto, University of Toronto Press, 2016) 9–11.

[45] Simpson, *Dancing on Our Turtle's Back* (n 44) 53, 144.

[46] J Borrows, *Canada's Indigenous Constitution* (Toronto, University of Toronto Press, 2010) 60. See also K Gilbert, *Living Black: Blacks Talk to Kevin Gilbert* (Sydney, Penguin, 1977) 3–4.

[47] Turner, *This Is Not a Peace Pipe* (n 34) 54.

of discussion and dialogue, or even agreement, with the State'.[48] In some cases, it may not even require jettisoning Western forms of governance; after all, as Narungga, Kaurna and Ngarrindjeri educationalist Lester-Irabinna Rigney notes, Indigenous communities 'will – and must – use Western institutions and processes as part of a range of strategies to pursue our governance and wider political goals'.[49] What it does mean, of course, is that Indigenous peoples and communities themselves should be empowered to make this decision.

III. Legitimacy

Public law scholarship is often concerned with legitimacy in a narrow sense, focused on examining whether a public authority acted beyond its legal powers. This approach owes much to the predominance of legal positivism, which centres analysis on the legal validity of decision-making. This is not the only approach. Section II intimated that legitimacy is broader than mere legal validity. As the 'quality that leads people … to accept authority – independent of coercion, self-interest, or rational persuasion',[50] legitimacy has both normative and sociological dimensions. An Indigenous organisation may be normatively legitimate because it was established in accordance with legal requirements set out in an Act of Parliament, but if the relevant Indigenous nation or nations does or do not accept or perceive it as capable of representing their interests, accountable to them, or as reflecting their norms and values, it will unlikely be sociologically legitimate. In this sense, sociological legitimacy is relational and external. It is concerned with the attitudes of individuals and focuses on whether a community considers a particular public institution as worthy of support or justifiable beyond its legal validity, mere habit or fear of sanction.[51] Efforts at permeating public law's boundaries to incorporate Indigenous institutions of decision-making strike at the heart of this distinction. Broadening state orders of governance to recognise and accommodate Indigenous forms of authority requires legal and political institutions that meet both criteria. More than embedding Indigenous values in public law, it requires public law institutions to accept difference. Public law scholarship should recognise and grapple with legitimacy's broader domain.

The concerns raised by Taiaiake Alfred and others are valuable in this endeavour. These scholars caution that Indigenous governance institutions connected to or embedded within the state in some respect may not be capable of acting in the interests of Indigenous peoples. At the same time, however, there are strong arguments for Indigenous peoples to challenge existing public law institutional frameworks and force the state to recognise and accommodate Indigenous governance mechanisms that reflect their values. Such an institution may be 'an adaptation to the social and political circumstances of

---

[48] Human Rights Council, *Final Report* (n 2) 5, [16].

[49] L-I Rigney, 'Epilogue: Can the Settler State Settle with Whom It Colonises? Reasons for Hope and Priorities for Action' in S Maddison and M Brigg (eds), *Unsettling the Settler State: Creativity and Resistance in Indigenous Settler-State Governance* (Sydney, Federation Press, 2011) 209.

[50] D Bodansky, 'The Legitimacy of International Governance: A Coming Challenge for International Environmental Law?' (1999) 93 *American Journal of International Law* 596, 600.

[51] R Fallon Jr, 'Legitimacy and the Constitution' (2005) 118(6) *Harvard Law Review* 1789, 1795; C McEwen and R Maiman, 'In Search of Legitimacy: Toward an Empirical Analysis' (1986) 8 *Law and Policy* 257, 258.

the state',[52] but it must nonetheless be a culturally appropriate institution with Indigenous leaders accountable to Indigenous peoples. How can we assess whether a body meets this standard? This section sketches three indicia useful in assessing whether an Indigenous decision-making institution operating within the state may satisfy Indigenous demands for sociological legitimacy.

My starting point is David Beetham's influential account of legitimacy. In *The Legitimation of Power*, Beetham draws on insights from social science and political philosophy to strike a position between positivistic legal accounts that stand and fall on legal validity and the Weberian tradition that limits the concept to a descriptive examination of a participant's belief. Contra Weber, Beetham contends that 'a given power relationship is not legitimate [simply] because people believe in its legitimacy, but because it can be justified in terms of their beliefs'.[53] For Beetham, legitimacy is a multi-dimensional concept. Power can be exercised legitimately if:

  i. it conforms to legal rules
  ii. the rules can be justified by reference to beliefs shared by both dominant and subordinate, and
  iii. there is evidence of consent by the subordinate to the particular power relation.[54]

The first level of Beetham's account of legitimacy is a formal requirement concerning legal validity. It requires that an institution be established in accordance with valid legal norms, and that any action taken by the body be consistent with its legal authority, whether that authority is conceptually understood to be delegated from the state or inherent to the Indigenous nation(s). I agree with Beetham that this is a necessary, though insufficient component; more important for my purposes are his second and third dimensions.

The second element concerns the cultural and social norms of those affected by decisions made. It highlights that although power may be exercised in accordance with legal norms, its exercise may still be seen as illegitimate; actions must also accord with the cultural and social values of the relevant community. Beetham developed his account to explore the legitimacy of shared public institutions. In examining Indigenous-specific bodies, however, the relevant norms that should guide the acquisition and exercise of public power are those of the Indigenous nation(s). Authority must be exercised in a manner recognisable to and justifiable within the norms of those communities,[55] because the institution must be accountable and answerable to them. This element hints at our first challenge. It is unlikely that members of the dominant community will accept an institution exercising public authority operating under rules that differ radically from their own conceptions of the proper exercise of power. This is not to say that Indigenous institutions must operate in the precise manner of other public law institutions, under the same form or mechanisms of public accountability for instance, but that some degree of give and take,

---

[52] C Jones, *New Treaty, New Tradition: Reconciling New Zealand and Māori Law* (Vancouver, University of British Columbia Press, 2016) 86.
[53] D Beetham, *The Legitimation of Power*, 2nd edn (Basingstoke, Palgrave MacMillan, 2013) 11.
[54] ibid 15–16.
[55] *UNDRIP*, Arts 3–5. See further N Roughan, 'From Authority to Authorities: Bridging the Social/Normative Divide' in R Cotterrell and M Del Mar (eds), *Authority in Transnational Legal Theory: Theorising Across Disciplines* (Cheltenham, Edward Elgar, 2016) 280.

of mutual respect and compromise, will be necessary. The question, as always, is where that line lands in practice.

The third dimension focuses on consent. For Beetham, political authority is legitimate to the extent that participants provide a 'demonstrable expression of consent'.[56] This element both binds individuals into a relationship with the persons exercising authority, and publicly conveys declaratory or expressive force. Consent is not hypothetical here but plays a significant constitutive role in the establishment of legitimacy.[57] As Beetham notes, however, what counts for consent is 'a culturally specific matter, determined by the conventions of a given society'.[58] In some Indigenous polities consent may not be recognised by voting but through other mechanisms.

Beetham's analysis is valuable but, as I have noted, it needs to be adapted to provide indicia relevant to assessing the legitimacy of institutions designed to empower Indigenous peoples within the public law framework of the state. As the previous section illustrated, the history of this relationship leads many to presumptively view such institutions with suspicion. Stringent as Beetham's dimensions may be, something more is needed in this context. Three points are relevant. First, the absence of Indigenous peoples in deliberative discussions that led to the adoption of the state's legal and political architecture emphasises the importance of designing institutions that reflect the norms and values of Indigenous communities. Of course, as Beetham reminds us, any durable public institution must be based on values shared by both Indigenous and non-Indigenous communities, but care should be taken to ensure an Indigenous decision-making body is nonetheless genuinely drawn from the values of the Indigenous communities it is intended to serve. While it may not always be possible to derive a uniform set of values from multiple political communities and nations, Indigenous peoples themselves must be allowed to identify and interpret the values that they consider important.

Second, state-sponsored efforts at assimilating Indigenous political communities suggest that any institution to empower Indigenous peoples must obtain more than simply their passive consent. Third, in order both to build and maintain that support, an institution must be effective in protecting and promoting Indigenous interests. This can be understood both in terms of realising substantive outcomes as well as the process for reaching those outcomes. These three points will be developed below. Here, it is worth restating them. *Pace* Beetham, an Indigenous decision-making body operating within the state may (but will not necessarily) be sociologically legitimate if:

(a) its rules, structure and operation reflect Indigenous ontologies and values (*norms*);
(b) there is evidence of active support, rather than mere consent (*actions*); and
(c) it is capable of realising Indigenous aspirations (*outcomes*).

Articulating legitimacy into three dimensions of *norms*, *actions* and *outcomes*, is somewhat artificial. These concepts are fluid and may be satisfied to greater or lesser degrees

---

[56] Beetham, *The Legitimation of Power* (n 53) 18.
[57] On this point, as well as the role consent plays in the theories of Thomas Hobbes and Joseph Raz, see D Dyzenhaus, 'Consent, Legitimacy, and the Foundation of Political Authority' in J Webber and CM Macleod (eds), *Between Consenting Peoples: Political Community and the Meaning of Consent* (Vancouver, University of British Columbia Press, 2010) 163.
[58] Beetham, *The Legitimation of Power* (n 53) 19.

throughout an institution's life. For instance, securing active support relies both on the way that power is exercised and whether the institution is capable of securing transformative results, for a culturally appropriate institution unable to realise positive outcomes will not enjoy support for long. Similarly, an institution's structure, including how it relates to other public institutions and bodies, is directly connected to its ability to undertake its work. An institution with no formal interface with key stakeholders will struggle to realise outcomes and undertake actions in appropriate ways. Nonetheless, notwithstanding some overlap, this tripartite model offers a valuable framework of analysis and provides a necessary structure to examine the legitimacy of institutions designed to empower Indigenous peoples within the state.

A. Norms

The first indicium examines the congruence between the norms and values of an institution and the cultural principles of the constituents it serves. It requires that Indigenous institutions embedded within or acting in concert with the state reflect the ontologies and values of the relevant Indigenous nation(s), rather than unconsciously replicate settler-state forms of governance. In this sense it draws on Apache and Purépecha international lawyer James Anaya's distinction between constitutive and ongoing self-determination. As Anaya explains, constitutive self-determination requires that 'the governing institutional order be substantially the creation of processes guided by the will of [all] people[s]', while ongoing self-determination ignores the process of creation of the state, inquiring only whether it is one 'under which people may live and develop freely on a continuous basis'.[59] In view of the difficulty of renegotiating foundational frameworks, this indicium aims at meeting conditions of ongoing self-determination. An institution that satisfies this standard permits Indigenous peoples to 'continue [their] distinct character and to have this character reflected in the institutions of government under which [they live]'.[60]

Its value is reflected in two recent substantive community consultative forums conducted in Australia in 2016 and 2017. In 2016, the Victorian Aboriginal Treaty Interim Working Group conducted community consultations at 10 locations across Victoria. These consultations were designed to enable Aboriginal peoples to discuss what principles should ground a state-wide body to represent them in Treaty negotiations with the state.[61] Similarly, in 2017, the Referendum Council, a body established with bipartisan support to 'advise … on progress and next steps towards a referendum' on constitutional recognition of Aboriginal and Torres Strait Islander peoples,[62] conducted 12 deliberative dialogues in communities across the country.

---

[59] J Anaya, *Indigenous Peoples in International Law* (New York, Oxford University Press, 2004) 105.
[60] ibid 106.
[61] For more information on this process, see H Hobbs, 'Treaty Making and the United Nations Declaration on the Rights of Indigenous Peoples: Lessons from Emerging Negotiations in Australia' (2019) 23(1-2) *International Journal of Human Rights* 174; H Hobbs and G Williams, 'Treaty-Making in the Australian Federation' (2019) 43 *Melbourne University Law Review* (forthcoming).
[62] M Turnbull and B Shorten, 'Referendum Council' Media Release (7 December 2015), available at https://www.pm.gov.au/media/2015-12-07/referendum-council.

Both community-driven processes revealed the significance of a culturally grounded Indigenous institution. Frequently asserted at consultations in Victoria was the desire that an Indigenous representative body be 'accountable to the Aboriginal Community', 'meaning the Representative Body must answer to the Aboriginal Community'.[63] At all locations, an institution that 'answers to the Aboriginal Community' was understood to be one built on cultural principles, processes and knowledge, but flexible enough to accommodate development of those principles and practices. In Mildura, for instance, participants considered that 'culture must underpin the foundation of the design of the Representative Body',[64] while in Melbourne participants explained that the body must '[respect] and [embed] customs and values'.[65] The significance of grounding the design of any institution or process on cultural principles was also underscored in Shepparton and Ballarat, where participants agreed that culture is necessary 'if it is to hold any integrity in the community',[66] 'because if there is no culture base then it is not for black fellas'.[67] Similar views were expressed across the country as part of the Referendum Council's Regional Dialogues. Repeatedly emphasised was the desire that a First Nations Voice to Parliament 'must not be a hand-picked, advisory government body, but have legitimacy in the eyes of the community',[68] and therefore be 'structured in a way that respects culture'.[69]

Participants also recognised the need to ensure that any Indigenous institution was comprehensible to the state and to non-Indigenous ontologies. At the Swan Hill community consultation in northwest Victoria, it was argued that an Indigenous organisation should be 'able to live in two worlds'.[70] This requires the 'best warriors at the table',[71] those with the requisite 'skills, connections and resources to discharge their responsibilities'.[72] Similarly, in the Uluru Statement from the Heart, Aboriginal and Torres Strait Islander peoples from across the country emphasised that the goal of structural reform is to ensure that 'our children ... walk in two worlds'.[73] As these comments indicate, a sustainable Indigenous

---

[63] Aboriginal Treaty Interim Working Group, *Aboriginal Community Consultations on the Design of a Representative Body* (December 2016) 23 (Bendigo).
[64] ibid 29 (Mildura).
[65] ibid 39 (Melbourne).
[66] ibid 49 (Shepparton).
[67] ibid 44 (Ballarat). See also 53 (Warrnambool), 59 (Horsham), 62 (Bairnsdale).
[68] Referendum Council, 'First Nations Regional Dialogue in Dubbo' Media Release (17–19 February 2017), available at https://www.referendumcouncil.org.au/event/first-nations-regional-dialogue-in-dubbo. See also Referendum Council, 'Broome Regional Dialogue Discusses Constitutional Reform' Media Release (13 February 2017), available at https://www.referendumcouncil.org.au/sites/default/files/2017-03/Referendum_Council_media_release_Broome_Regional_Dialogue_Discusses_Constitutional_Reform_940KB.pdf.
[69] Referendum Council, 'Uluru Statement from the Heart' (n 6) 30. See also Referendum Council, 'Delegates Determine Self-Determination Is a Priority' Media Release (28 March 2017), available at https://www.referendumcouncil.org.au/sites/default/files/2017-03/Referendum%20Council%20media%20release%20-%20Cairns%20Regional%20Dialogue_1.pdf) (Cairns); Referendum Council, 'Constitutional Reform: Speaking the Same Language' Media Release (7 April 2017), available at https://www.referendumcouncil.org.au/sites/default/files/2017-04/Referendum%20Council%20media%20release%20Ross%20River%20Regional%20Dialogue.pdf (Ross River).
[70] Aboriginal Treaty Interim Working Group, *Aboriginal Community Consultations on the Design of a Representative Body* (n 63) 34.
[71] ibid.
[72] ibid 13.
[73] Referendum Council, 'Uluru Statement from the Heart' (n 6).

decision-making institution must be drawn from Indigenous values, but it also needs to connect with the norms of the larger non-Indigenous community.

Congruence of norms and values can be assessed in multiple ways. One approach is to identify the extent to which Indigenous people and communities were involved in choices around the structural design of the body prior to its establishment.[74] Was consultation undertaken and, if so, what did it look like? Was it conducted in a respectful manner? Did Indigenous peoples and communities lead the debate, or were their voices limited to proposing minor amendments to an existing proposal? It may be difficult to precisely identify causality here, as it is not always clear why amendments to a Bill or legislative proposal are adopted. This indicium can therefore also be viewed from the opposite angle; we can ask whether the institution is materially distinct in its structure, powers or legal status from comparable public law bodies. The greater the distinction, the greater the likelihood the state has at least attempted to modify its own understandings of political authority to accommodate Indigenous peoples' values and traditions.

B. Actions

Institutions are not static. The second indicium understands that support for, or belief in, an Indigenous decision-making body may rise and fall depending on whether it becomes grounded within the community, irrespective of whether its design satisfies the first indicium. By acting in congruence with the cultural and social values of their constituents, members of Indigenous decision-making bodies can shape the structure and operation of the institution. As this suggests, this indicium largely concerns internal procedures and approaches to decision-making within an Indigenous body. It understands that while jurisdictional authority is necessary to protect and promote Indigenous interests, the manner in which that authority is exercised is also important because it affects the likelihood of active support from the community, which in turn enhances legitimacy. Power and authority must be exercised in a culturally grounded and appropriate way.

The procedural component can be seen most clearly in two examples from the Canadian Territory of Nunavut. Nunavut is a public rather than ethnic government, but as Inuit comprise around 85 per cent of the population, governance is largely conducted by Inuit people, providing them with an opportunity to shape its operation, albeit within a broader non-Inuit structure. Significantly, although Nunavut largely follows Westminster traditions, no political parties run or are present in the Legislative Assembly. Instead, the Territory operates under a form of consensus government, where all members are elected as independents and cabinet is appointed by the legislature. Empirical studies suggest that this practice both contributes to and reflects Inuit values of respect, teamwork and sharing, while minimising adversarial and confrontational politics more common in partisan systems.[75]

---

[74] *UNDRIP*, Art 19.
[75] G White, 'Traditional Aboriginal Values in a Westminster Parliament: The Legislative Assembly of Nunavut' (2006) 12 *The Journal of Legislative Studies* 8, 29.

Legislative and policy development in Nunavut is guided by the concept of Inuit Qaujimajatuqangit (IQ). Emerging from a conference on traditional knowledge held in 1998 aimed at identifying 'processes designed to ensure that Inuit culture, language, and values are democratically reflected in the policies, programs, and day-to-day operations of the new Nunavut government',[76] IQ is understood as 'the very foundation' of Nunavut.[77] Translated literally as 'that which has long been known by Inuit',[78] the extent to which IQ has infused Nunavut governance and public administration has, for some, become 'the benchmark against which the success'[79] of Nunavut is judged.

In recent years, the Nunavut Court of Justice has explored how IQ can be meaningfully developed and applied. In two cases in 2018, the Court held that courts must 'strive to incorporate the precepts of IQ into our judgments and practices',[80] and affirmed that 'Inuit norms *must* be considered by the judge when crafting a just and fit sentence'.[81] In *R v Itturiligaq*, for instance, Bychok J relied on IQ values of 'forgiveness, reconciliation, reintegration, restitution and understanding', to hold that a federal mandatory minimum penalty imposing a four-year sentence to be served in a federal gaol, thousands of miles from Nunavut, would be grossly disproportionate and thus in violation of the *Charter of Rights and Freedoms*.[82] As Bychok J explained, such a sentence 'would be considered intolerable by fair minded Nunavummiut'.[83]

Challenges certainly exist. It is not always easy to identify diffuse and diverse 'Inuit values', let alone articulate and apply them in a modern state bureaucracy. Nonetheless, the prioritisation of IQ reflects the right of Nunavummiut to have a government they 'can recognise as embodying their values'.[84] The experience in Nunavut also reveals the flexibility of public law. In many cases, politics rather than law is the more significant impediment to meaningful accommodation.

These examples are helpful in articulating how an Indigenous institution may act to ensure congruence with the norms and values of its constituents, but it is still necessary to formulate a way to assess success. For representative bodies, success could be assessed through electoral turnout and nomination for office. Voter turnout is the 'most common and important act of political participation in any democracy'[85] and is often identified as a 'powerful [symbol] of ... democratic legitimacy'.[86] As such, political scientists have

---

[76] Nunavut Social Development Council, *A Discussion Paper: Towards an Inuit Qaujimajatuqangit (IQ) Policy for Nunavut* (1998) 5.

[77] ibid 1. See also F Lévesque, 'Revisiting Inuit Qaujimajatuqangit: Inuit Knowledge, Culture, Language, and Values in Nunavut Institutions since 1999' (2014) 38 *Études/Inuit/Studies* 115, 121.

[78] Pikialasorsuaq Commission, 'Inuit Knowledge' Inuit Circumpolar Council, available at http://pikialasorsuaq.org/en/Inuit-knowledge.

[79] A Henderson, *Nunavut: Rethinking Political Culture* (Vancouver, University of British Columbia Press, 2007) 190.

[80] *R v Anugaa* [2018] NUCJ 2, [42].

[81] *R v Itturiligaq* [2018] NUCJ 31, [108] (emphasis in original).

[82] ibid [106], [113]–[124].

[83] ibid [124]. Nunavummiut is the Inuktitut word for the people of Nunavut.

[84] G Dacks, 'Nunavut: Aboriginal Self-Determination through Public Government', Report prepared for the Royal Commission on Aboriginal Peoples (1993) 36.

[85] J Aldrich, 'Rational Choice and Turnout' (1993) 37 *American Journal of Political Science* 246, 246.

[86] R Topf, 'Electoral Participation' in H-D Klingemann and D Fuchs (eds), *Citizens and the State: Beliefs in Government* (New York, Oxford University Press, 1995) 27.

sought to identify causal relationships between turnout, legitimacy and trust in political institutions. Despite difficulty in accounting for multiple variables and settings, it is generally accepted that at the macro-level, trust in democratic institutions and representatives increases the probability of voting.[87] Consequently, increased voter support and increased candidature nomination over time may indicate a growing acceptance of the institution. Conversely, low turnout and nomination may suggest that the body is not regarded as legitimate, either because its members fail to act in a culturally appropriate manner, or perhaps, as discussed in section IV, in protest against its limited authority or effectiveness. If the latter, the solution will involve imbuing the body with real power and establishing new institutional mechanisms to exert that authority. This indicium needs to be assessed with caution, however. Voting is a 'culturally specific practice',[88] and may not be the most appropriate measure to assess active consent.

C. Outcomes

These considerations lead to the third indicium: outcomes. Indigenous communities often find themselves comprising numerical minorities subsumed within state borders. In liberal democracies, particularly those with few constitutional or statutory rights protections, this can mean that law and policy that affect Indigenous peoples are largely formulated without their consideration or in the absence of their voices. An Indigenous decision-making institution operating within the state must therefore have the power to realise Indigenous interests. As Yawuru scholar Mick Dodson and non-Indigenous academic Diane Smith have explained, this indicium is a central element of legitimacy:

> [W]hile Indigenous governance arrangements need to be informed by local cultural standards if they are to be regarded as legitimate by community members, the governing arrangements also have to work – governing bodies have to be practically capable of responding and taking action in the contemporary environment.[89]

Unsurprisingly, this site is where conflict between Indigenous aspirations and state constraints is most pronounced. Indigenous nations contend that any decision-making institution must empower them to exercise autonomy over internal affairs,[90] to 'steer their own vessel' by articulating their own concerns, identifying their own priorities, and developing law and policy to address those challenges, independent of state action.[91] In contrast, states are often wary of recognising extensive jurisdictional powers, anxious that

---

[87] K Gronlund and M Setala, 'Political Trust, Satisfaction and Voter Turnout' (2007) 5 *Comparative European Politics* 400, 416.

[88] D Lino, 'The Indigenous Franchise and Assimilation' (2017) 48 *Australian Historical Studies* 363, 366.

[89] M Dodson and D Smith, 'Governance for Sustainable Development: Strategic Issues and Principles for Indigenous Australian Communities', Centre for Aboriginal Economic Policy Research Discussion Paper No 250 (2003) 19.

[90] *UNDRIP*, Art 4.

[91] *Gus-Wen-Tah*, or Two-Row Wampum Treaty, signed in 1613 by representatives of the Five Nations of the Haudenosaunee and representatives of the Dutch Government in what is now upstate New York. Cited in Alfred, *Peace, Power Righteousness* (n 5) 76; Turner, *This Is Not a Peace Pipe* (n 34) 54.

doing so may weaken their own claims to authority. Of course, the extent of an institution or mechanism's authority can be gradated, ranging from broad legislative and executive powers at one end, to regulatory functions and to responsibilities of service delivery at the other. Even within more limited domains, however, Indigenous people should have the opportunity to design and manage programs that preserve and develop culture and ways of thinking, if this indicium is to be satisfied.

***

As this brief discussion has revealed, the three dimensions of legitimacy are fluid and interconnected. Enhancing one may have positive or neutral effects on the others, and all may rise and fall across the life of an institution. Nonetheless, although not determinative, these three indicia are useful in guiding judgement as to the legitimacy of an Indigenous institution operating within the public law framework of the state. They speak to a simple proposition. Institutions that are designed and supported by Indigenous peoples, and realise outcomes for Indigenous communities, are likely to be regarded as legitimate by those communities, even if they are formally connected to the state.

IV. The Aboriginal and Torres Strait Islander Commission

The preceding discussion developed a way to speak about sociological legitimacy in relation to Indigenous decision-making institutions operating within the state. In this section, I demonstrate the explanatory power of the indicia by adopting them as a frame to analyse ATSIC's legitimacy. Although a full exploration of the Commission is not possible here, the discussion highlights the inherent tensions involved in seeking to design Indigenous institutions embedded within the public law apparatus of the state.

ATSIC was a national elected representative body for Indigenous peoples in Australia that operated between 1989 and 2005. Formally established as an independent statutory commission, rather than by ministerial directive or privately incorporated, the Commission's moorings exemplified the capacity of public law to accommodate Indigenous representative and decision-making institutions. This legal form also ensured that ATSIC had clearly defined powers and responsibilities, providing Indigenous representatives with a measure of control so as to 'shape the social context in which they live'.[92] Its objectives were set out in section 3 of the *Aboriginal and Torres Strait Islander Commission Act 1989* (Cth) (*ATSIC Act*). The Commission was:

(a) to ensure maximum participation of Aboriginal and Torres Strait Islander people in government policy formulation and implementation;
(b) to promote indigenous self-management and self-sufficiency;
(c) to further indigenous economic, social and cultural development; and
(d) to ensure coordination of Commonwealth, State, Territory and local government policy affecting indigenous people.

---

[92] T Pogge, 'Creating Supra-National Institutions Democratically: Reflections on the European Union's "Democratic Deficit"' (1997) 5 *The Journal of Political Philosophy* 163, 179.

ATSIC was not the first institutional attempt in Australia to hear 'the Aboriginal voice'.[93] Its structure, powers and responsibilities were developed out of lessons learned from previous efforts at building a national Indigenous representative body. Two key innovations stand out. First, concern that predecessor organisations were 'out of touch with Aboriginal communities' led to a decentralised, regional structure, whose authority was based on and derived from local communities.[94] The country was divided into 35 Regional Councils, directly elected every three years. The Councils were then grouped into 16 Zones, each of which elected a full-time Commissioner to the national board. Another Commissioner was elected from the Torres Strait, which comprised its own zone.[95] Second, criticisms that previous bodies offered elected Indigenous representatives' roles that were 'merely consultative'[96] meant that the Commission would be empowered with limited decision-making authority. This decision was significant, as it marked the first time that Aboriginal and Torres Strait Islander peoples had been given executive rather than merely advisory powers over Commonwealth programmes dedicated to their welfare.

The Commission had three key responsibilities. It advised governments at all levels on Indigenous issues; advocated for the recognition of Indigenous rights on behalf of Indigenous peoples regionally, nationally and internationally; and delivered and monitored most of the Commonwealth Government's Indigenous programmes and services. Elected Indigenous representatives therefore exercised substantial authority. They were empowered to identify local funding priorities, formulate and implement regional plans, make decisions over public expenditure, protect cultural material and information, and speak directly to government. Nonetheless, as a creature of the Australian Parliament, the Commission was not entirely autonomous. The Minister for Aboriginal Affairs appointed ATSIC's Chairperson until 1999 and the head of the Commission's administrative arm throughout its existence, complicating layers of accountability. These and other tensions are teased out in what follows.

A. Norms

The Bill that established the Aboriginal and Torres Strait Islander Commission was preceded by the 'most extensive' consultation undertaken on a single piece of legislation in recent Australian history.[97] Over 21,000 copies of the Minister for Aboriginal Affairs policy statement setting out the proposed structure and powers of the Commission had been distributed to around 1,000 Indigenous communities and organisations, and the Minister, Gerry Hand, held over 530 meetings involving 14,500 people to discuss

---

[93] Australia Cth, House of Representatives, Department of Aboriginal Affairs Report, *The Road Ahead*, 24 November 1978, vol 47, 3449 (Ian Viner).

[94] HC Coombs, *The Role of the National Aboriginal Conference* (Canberra, Australian Government Publishing Service, 1984) 11; LR Hiatt, *Australian Committee of Inquiry into the Role of the National Aboriginal Consultative Committee* (Canberra, Australian Government Publishing Service, 1976) 32, 48.

[95] *ATSIC Act*, sch 1.

[96] Hiatt, *Australian Committee of Inquiry into the Role of the National Aboriginal Consultative Committee* (n 94) viii.

[97] Australia Cth, House of Representatives, Aboriginal and Torres Strait Islander Commission Bill 1989 (n 11) (Gerry Hand).

the proposal.[98] Even ATSIC's detractors acknowledged that the consultation process 'was among the most exhaustive and protracted ... ever undertaken'.[99] Nonetheless, its adequacy, and the extent to which Indigenous peoples had a determinative say over questions of institutional design, has been the subject of considerable controversy. Negotiation and compromise may be inherent to legislative enactment, but the process that culminated in the Commission reveals challenges for future institutional design.

Most significantly, consultation with Aboriginal and Torres Strait Islander communities occurred only after the Government had already devised a substantial initial proposal. Although this proposal was informed by the views of some Indigenous peoples, there was no sustained, let alone representative, process of discussion or deliberation. The proposal that was distributed to Indigenous communities was developed in-house, largely by consultants and officials attached to the office of the Minister of Aboriginal Affairs, as well as by some senior staff from the Department of Aboriginal Affairs (DAA),[100] and owed much to the model laid out in a 1984 review of a previous Indigenous representative body. While that report had been informed by consultation with Indigenous peoples and communities, the author, Dr Nugget Coombs, acknowledged that such engagement was severely limited and confined to 'a period of less than three months'.[101] There was thus little sustained scope for Aboriginal and Torres Strait Islander peoples to propose key elements of the putative Commission.

The nationwide consultations were similarly problematic. A 1989 Senate Select Committee examining the development of the ATSIC Bill found that 'the nature of the meetings precluded effective consultation'.[102] Meetings were only three hours long and were not conducted in a manner familiar to Indigenous Australians. The proposal was presented on a 'take it or leave it basis', communities were pressured to reach a quick decision that would bind all participants and senior departmental staff responsible for allocating funding to communities were present.[103] The Government was aware of these criticisms. Meeting reports drafted by DAA staff revealed considerable limitations. For instance, in April 1988, Brian Stacey, the DAA Darwin Regional Manager, noted that consultations with representatives from Maningrida, Oenpelli and Warruwi in West Arnhem Land on 11 April 1988 were not effective: 'most Aboriginal people did not have any understanding of the concept ... [because] the consultation process was too rushed'.[104] Changes to the process were not forthcoming. The Committee concluded that the 'failure to provide adequate time or resources for proper examination of the legislation'

---

[98] Australia Cth, House of Representatives, Aboriginal and Torres Strait Islander Commission Bill 1988, 24 August 1988, vol 162, 252 (Gerry Hand).
[99] R Tickner, *Taking a Stand: Land Rights to Reconciliation* (St Leonards, Allen & Unwin, 2001) 51.
[100] Senate Select Committee on the Administration of Aboriginal Affairs, Parliament of Australia, *Administration of Aboriginal Affairs* (1989) 71–72, [4.2]–[4.3].
[101] Coombs, *The Role of the National Aboriginal Conference* (n 94) 4.
[102] Senate Select Committee on the Administration of Aboriginal Affairs, *Administration of Aboriginal Affairs* (n 100) 77, [4.24].
[103] ibid 77–79, [4.25]–[4.30].
[104] B Stacey, *Report of ATSIC Meetings: Darwin Region* (12 April 1988) 5. Cited in Senate Select Committee on the Administration of Aboriginal Affairs, *Administration of Aboriginal Affairs* (n 100) 83, [4.48].

constituted a 'glaring fault'[105] that was the 'inevitable result of the "whistle-stop" nature of the Minister's tour'.[106]

The development of the Commission illustrates some of the complexities in designing Indigenous institutions within democratic states. The views of Indigenous peoples and communities were considered important and substantial effort was taken to ascertain them – but not to the extent that they might have derailed the Government's preferred process. Acutely conscious of broader political considerations, Hand warned Indigenous communities that 'dragging out the period of consultation could endanger ATSIC'.[107] The Government may well have believed this, but it reveals that while consultation was prized, efficacy was prioritised.

Problems existed with the Government's consultation process, but some issues raised by Indigenous communities were incorporated. Indigenous views were integral in initially expanding the number of Regional Councils from 36 to 60,[108] for instance, more accurately reflecting Indigenous concerns with localism and regionalism. Indigenous successes were rare, however; senior Indigenous executives of the Department of Aboriginal Affairs, including its head, Arrernte and Kalkadoon administrator Charles Perkins, were not permitted to see a copy of the Bill until August 1988 – and none of their proposed changes was accepted.[109]

Indigenous peoples' limited ability to effect change can be contrasted with the relative ease with which non-Indigenous peoples were able to make amendments to the proposal once the Bill had been introduced into Parliament. Concern by non-Government parties that the initial Bill included inadequate accountability mechanisms catalysed five inquiries into the administration of Aboriginal affairs.[110] These inquiries reported between late 1988 and early 1989 and led to 'no less than 91 amendments'.[111] As Prime Minister Bob Hawke explained in Parliament, those amendments were aimed at 'finding the right balance' between self-determination and accountability,[112] but it ultimately meant that the Commission operated under a more stringent accountability framework than any other department or statutory authority. While good public administration requires public monies be properly accounted for, the scope and extent of the amendments to the initial proposal led some Indigenous organisations to question whether it any longer 'resembled the original intention of ATSIC'.[113]

---

[105] Senate Select Committee on the Administration of Aboriginal Affairs, *Administration of Aboriginal Affairs* (n 100) 89, [4.76].

[106] ibid 80, [4.36].

[107] ibid 78, [4.29]. Minister Hand to the Amoonguna community on 29 January 1988.

[108] Subsequent amendments to the *ATSIC Act* revised the number of Regional Councils back down to 36. *Aboriginal and Torres Strait Islander Commission Amendment Act 1993* (Cth), cl 23, replacing sch 1 to the *ATSIC Act*. While this was at ATSIC's request, the result was 'an even more classically western structure': J Hannaford, J Huggins and B Collins, *Review of the Aboriginal and Torres Strait Islander Commission*, Discussion Paper (2003) 13, [2.12].

[109] P Read, *Charles Perkins: A Biography* (Ringwood, Viking, 1990) 289.

[110] W Sanders, 'Reconciling Public Accountability and Aboriginal Self-Determination/Self-Management: Is ATSIC Succeeding?' (1994) 53 *Australian Journal of Public Administration* 475, 476.

[111] ibid 477.

[112] Australia Cth, House of Representatives, Administration of Aboriginal Affairs, 11 April 1989, vol 166, 1325–26.

[113] John Ah Kit, Director Northern Land Council, cited in F Brennan, 'ATSIC: Seeking a National Mouthpiece for Local Voices' (1990) 2(43) *Aboriginal Law Bulletin* 4, 5.

Other design challenges had little to do with the capacity to introduce amendments but reflected the inherent tensions in designing institutions reflective of Indigenous normative orders into the existing public law framework of the state. In particular, difficulties were encountered in setting Regional Council and Zone electoral boundaries, which did not always correspond with or acknowledge traditional community boundaries.[114] The challenge here involved mediating two competing principles: how to ensure that distinct Indigenous communities were adequately represented while maintaining administrative efficacy in a federation that divides responsibilities between State and federal governments.[115] As the 1995 Boundary Review Panel explained, while an effort was made to align electoral and regional boundaries along tribal and group affiliations, this goal often conflicted with 'the pursuit and achievement of community and organisational objectives';[116] delineating electoral boundaries along community cleavages meant issues would need to be negotiated 'with two and sometimes three state/territory governments' and required several ATSIC offices to coordinate the handling of issues. This caused 'extreme difficulties' and was 'unworkable'.[117]

The Commission determined to prioritise administrative ease. This decision is understandable, as electoral boundaries did not prevent or inhibit communities from continuing to observe those connections, but it nonetheless did cause complications. Boundaries alienated communities, detaching Councils, Zones and the national Board from the concerns of their constituents.[118] In some cases this led communities to refuse to take part. Trisha Gray notes that when electoral boundaries 'were altered to bring the Warburton/Ceduna boundary into line with the Western Australia and South Australia border, the new line divided the Warburton community who refused to vote in the 1993 ATSIC election'.[119] Regular boundary reviews reveal both persistent challenges in mediating these competing priorities and continuing efforts to do so.

Concerns were also raised over the Commission's relationship with the public service. Members of ATSIC's administrative arm were employed under the *Public Service Act* and led by a CEO appointed by the Minister. The Royal Commission into Aboriginal Deaths in Custody highlighted this arrangement, noting that legally it meant Commission staff were primarily accountable to government rather than the Indigenous community.[120] Although the Royal Commission recommended the Commonwealth reconsider this relationship as part of a path to self-determination,[121] government demurred. Complicating easy analysis, however, it was rejected 'expressly at the request of the ATSIC Board', who believed

---

[114] P Coe, 'ATSIC: Self-determination or Otherwise' (1994) 4 *Race & Class* 35, 36; Senate Select Committee on the Administration of Aboriginal Affairs, *Administration of Aboriginal Affairs* (n 100) 38, [2.106].

[115] L O'Donoghue, *An Aboriginal and Islander Consultative Organisation* (Department of Aboriginal Affairs, 1986) 29–30.

[116] ATSIC, *Review of Boundaries: The Report of the Panel Convened by the Minister for Aboriginal and Torres Strait Islander Affairs to Review Matters Relating to the Boundaries of ATSIC's Zones, Regions and Wards* (February 1995) 6.

[117] ibid.

[118] J Hannaford, J Huggins and B Collins, *In the Hands of the Regions – A New ATSIC*, Report of the Review of the Aboriginal and Torres Strait Islander Commission (2003) 45.

[119] T Gray, 'Realistic Accommodation: The Influence of Traditional Aboriginal Political Culture on Contemporary Aboriginal Political Institutions', Honours Thesis submitted to Department of Political Science, ANU (1994) 60. Cited in S Bennett, *White Politics and Black Australians* (St Leonards, Allen & Unwin, 1999) 134.

[120] Commonwealth, Royal Commission into Aboriginal Deaths in Custody, *National Report* (1991) vol 4, 8.

[121] ibid (Recommendation 189).

that being situated within the public service would enhance the Commission's capacity to influence public policy and ease employee mobility.[122] ATSIC reversed its position in 1997,[123] but this issue, once again, illustrates the tensions faced by an independent statutory commission operating within and outside government.

Choices made at the development and design stage had a direct impact as to whether Aboriginal and Torres Strait Islander people and communities initially viewed the Commission as legitimate. For many, including Kuku Yalanji magistrate Pat O'Shane, those choices meant that the Commission was a 'creation of non-Aboriginal Australia',[124] as its rules, structure and operation failed to reflect Indigenous norms. Revealing the fluidity of the indicia, many Indigenous Australians who agreed with O'Shane boycotted ATSIC's initial elections. By withdrawing their support in frustration and anger over its design, these boycotts further weakened the Commission's legitimacy.

B. Actions

Electoral boycotts revealed significant concern within Indigenous communities over ATSIC's legitimacy. Legitimacy is fluid, however. It can rise and fall as its constituents come to accept it, or nonetheless view it as acting in an appropriate manner. Did ATSIC come to receive the active support of the Indigenous community?

It is difficult to measure active support for an institution, but the political science literature discussed in section III.B suggests that voter turnout figures may indicate a causal relationship between trust in and support for the Commission. Examining voter turnout for the Regional Council direct elections held every three years reveals a complicated picture. At a national level, the Commission was largely unable to overcome its inauspicious start, but distinctions existed across the country. Nationally, voting rates averaged around 20–25 per cent of estimated eligible voters across ATSIC's existence.[125] Although this figure compares favourably to similar non-compulsory local government elections held in South Australia and Western Australia in the early 1990s,[126] it hardly suggests widespread endorsement from the community. Indeed, even as the number of voters grew between 1990 and 2002, the voting rate improved only slightly,[127] revealing that the Commission struggled to obtain, or demonstrate, active support throughout the Indigenous community.

Focusing on the national figure elides distinctions across the country. The Commission's decentralised, regional structure meant each community played a significant role in the design and delivery of programmes and services tailored to their needs. In regional and remote areas, where ATSIC played a larger proportionate role in Indigenous

---

[122] Tickner, *Taking a Stand* (n 99) 75.
[123] ATSIC, *Strengthening ATSIC: The 1997 Review of the ATSIC Act* (1998) 43 (Recommendation 28).
[124] P O'Shane, 'Aboriginal Political Movements: Some Observations', 13th Frank Archibald Memorial Lecture, University of New England (14 October 1998) 6.
[125] W Sanders, J Taylor and K Ross, 'Participation and Representation in ATSIC Elections: A 10 Year Perspective' (2000) 35 *Australian Journal of Political Science* 493, 502.
[126] W Sanders, 'Participation and Representation in the 2002 ATSIC Elections', Centre for Aboriginal Economic Policy Research Discussion Paper No 252 (2003) 7.
[127] W Sanders, 'ATSIC's Achievements and Strengths: Implications for Institutional Reform', Centre for Aboriginal Economic Policy Research (2004) 1.

communities, turnout was consistently higher.[128] In some places, this distinction was marked: in the 1993 elections, for instance, turnout in Cooktown in regional Queensland reached 79 per cent, evidencing significant support. In contrast, in Sydney turnout lagged at 9 per cent.[129] It appears that this considerable regional distinction persisted throughout ATSIC's life: in 2002, the last election, the top 18 regions with turnout above 30 per cent were all in 'sparsely settled northern and central Australia'.[130]

These figures should be treated carefully. First, no national register of people eligible to vote in ATSIC elections was ever created; rather, all voters had to be registered on the Commonwealth electoral roll. In the absence of an Indigenous-specific roll, turnout was measured against estimates of the eligible Indigenous population as recorded in the census. This is problematic, as the Indigenous population enumerated in the five-yearly national censuses 'increased faster than can be explained by demographic factors alone', perhaps as the propensity of Indigenous people to identify as such increased, or enhanced enumeration methods were adopted.[131] It is not clear whether individuals who newly identified as being of Indigenous origin in the census considered themselves eligible to vote in ATSIC elections.[132] If this is the case then the voting rate is lower than it should be. Indeed, in Tasmania in 2002, where a separate roll was drawn up, a more respectable 55 per cent of those enrolled voted.[133]

Second, many Aboriginal and Torres Strait Islander people did not support voting as the mechanism to choose representatives. The House of Representatives Standing Committee on Aboriginal Affairs acknowledged this in 1990, remarking that the electoral process challenged traditional power structures in many remote Aboriginal communities,[134] where positions of power and cultural authority are not won 'through democratic election, but earned through knowledge, experience and initiation'.[135] This concern reverberated throughout ATSIC's existence: a 2003 review found dissatisfaction with the uniformity of the electoral model, suggesting that different approaches could be adopted in different regions.[136] Although this suggests that voter turnout may not be the best indicator of trust in the Commission, the failure to adopt a more culturally appropriate or contextualised model certainly weakened the Commission's capacity to gain support over its life.

C. Outcomes

ATSIC's decentralised structure empowered it with different responsibilities at local and national levels, and it is important to appreciate these distinctions when assessing

---

[128] L Behrendt, 'Representative Structures – Lessons Learned from the ATSIC Era' (2009) 10 *Journal of Indigenous Policy* 35, 58.
[129] Sanders, 'Reconciling Public Accountability and Aboriginal Self-Determination/Self-Management' (n 110) 486.
[130] Sanders, 'Participation and Representation in the 2002 ATSIC Elections' (n 126) 7.
[131] ibid.
[132] ibid.
[133] ibid 1–2.
[134] House of Representatives Standing Committee on Aboriginal Affairs, Parliament of Australia, *Our Future, Our Selves: Aboriginal and Torres Strait Islander Community Control, Management and Resources* (1990) 20, [2.18]–[2.19].
[135] C Gibson, 'Cartographies of the Colonial/Capitalist State: A Geopolitics of Indigenous Self-Determination in Australia' (1999) 31 *Antipode* 45, 68.
[136] Hannaford, Huggins and Collins, *In the Hands of the Regions* (n 118) (Recommendation 67).

its outcomes. At the local level, Regional Councils were responsible for formulating and implementing plans for improving the economic, social and cultural status of Indigenous peoples living in the region.[137] To ensure that these plans reflected local concerns, they were developed through a process of community consultation. Regional plans were submitted to the national Board, which was required to determine financial priorities and develop an overall budget. Subject to government sign off, the Board allocated funds to the Regional Councils in line with the priorities identified in their regional plans.[138] At the federal level, in contrast, the national Board advocated for Indigenous rights across the country, and advised government on legislation and policy.

The Commission proved relatively effective at the local level in some communities. Regional Councils were an innovative way to allow ATSIC to flexibly and sensitively meet heterogeneous and diverse community needs across the country, while by-passing traditional bureaucratic structures where policy was formulated by largely non-Indigenous public servants in Canberra. This regional structure also established and empowered significant institutional arrangements at the local level, enabling Aboriginal and Torres Strait Islander peoples to articulate their own concerns, identify their own priorities and develop policy (though not law) to address those challenges. While their decisions, and their capacity to effectuate those decisions, were always subject to ministerial and parliamentary review, communities had some latitude in which they could steer their own vessel.

ATSIC was also capable of protecting and promoting the interests of Aboriginal and Torres Strait Islander peoples and communities at national and international levels. Nonetheless, structural and political challenges inhibited its effectiveness. The Commonwealth Parliament enjoys only a concurrent power to legislate with respect to Aboriginal and Torres Strait Islander affairs, and responsibility for many issues of concern for Indigenous peoples, including health, education and housing, lies with the States. Yet ATSIC had no formal structural interface with the States and Territories, weakening its ability to effectively articulate Indigenous interests to relevant decision-makers.

More problematic, however, were the inherent political tensions that arose from the Commission's position as a government-established body when it sought to realise Indigenous interests. ATSIC laboured under persistent criticism of its goals and independence throughout its life. Highlighting these frictions, the Commission weathered this censure most directly when it sought to engage with government. For instance, ATSIC's inaugural Chair, Lois O'Donoghue, was heavily involved in negotiations with the Keating Government over the legislative response to *Mabo v Queensland (No 2)*,[139] which recognised native title. ATSIC's role 'within and without' government, operating inside intergovernmental channels while remaining responsive to its constituents, proved challenging.[140] Although some more radical Indigenous activists acknowledged that ATSIC 'extract[ed] the best deal from the government',[141] others continued to criticise its role.[142]

---

[137] *ATSIC Act*, s 94.
[138] *ATSIC Act*, s 7(1).
[139] *Mabo v Queensland (No 2)* (1992) 175 CLR 1.
[140] T Rowse, *Obliged to be Difficult: Nugget Coombs' Legacy in Indigenous Affairs* (Cambridge, Cambridge University Press, 2000) 204–09.
[141] Statement from the Aboriginal Provisional Government cited in F Brennan, *One Land, One Nation: Mabo – Towards 2001* (Brisbane, University of Queensland Press, 2001) 71.
[142] Coe, 'ATSIC: Self-determination or Otherwise' (n 114) 38–39.

Conscious of the political challenges inherent in its position, ATSIC strived to develop a sense of independence. The Commission engaged in international advocacy, obtaining NGO status at the United Nations, submitting communications and lodging comprehensive reports to international treaty bodies. Domestically, it funded Native Title Representative Bodies to litigate native title claims where the federal Government was a party, and lobbied for a treaty between Indigenous peoples and the state. These activities more clearly demarcated ATSIC from government and more directly articulated Indigenous aspirations. At the same time, however, in actively challenging government policy, this strategy likely weakened government support for the Commission, and consequently its effectiveness as an operative within government.[143] Indeed, a comprehensive 2003 review found 'a significant decline over time in ATSIC's input and access to the Cabinet policy development process',[144] while the Commission's increasingly independent action likely catalysed government attempts to marginalise and abolish it.[145] ATSIC's ultimate fate reveals the inherent tension facing all Indigenous institutions operating within the public law apparatus of the state. If they become too troublesome, government may look for opportunities to silence them. Sociological legitimacy is no guarantee of survival.

D. Assessment

The establishment of ATSIC was lauded as marking 'the turning point' in Indigenous–non-Indigenous relations; a moment 'when Australia moved from a position of, firstly, contempt and ridicule of Aboriginal Australians; secondly, to a position of paternalism; and now to a period in which Aboriginal Australians are entitled to self-management, self-respect and self-determination'.[146] And yet, just 15 years later, the Commission was abolished with bipartisan support. Scholars accounting for this fall suggest that ATSIC's demise owes much to ideological opposition to the Commission, as well as to poor leadership and governance.[147] These factors are critical, but assessing ATSIC against the indicia identified in section III also reveals a more foundational problem: the Commission struggled to be regarded as legitimate by Indigenous communities.

As a non-Indigenous designed body situated within the state's public law architecture, the Commission 'hover[ed] in the uncertain space between autonomy and state bureaucracy',[148] never able to transcend 'existing or imposed structures'.[149] Structural choices certainly hampered ATSIC from the beginning, but over the course of its life the Commission sought to increase its legitimacy in the eyes of Indigenous peoples and communities. It endeavoured to develop an independent streak, agitating for priorities

---

[143] M Dillon, 'Institutional Structures in Indigenous Affairs' in P Sullivan (ed), *Shooting the Banker* (North Australian Research Unit, 1996) 100.

[144] Hannaford, Huggins and Collins, *Review of the Aboriginal and Torres Strait Islander Commission* (n 108) 36, [5.6].

[145] L Behrendt, 'The Abolition of ATSIC – Implications for Democracy' (Democratic Audit of Australia, 2006) 6.

[146] Australia Cth, House of Representatives, Aboriginal and Torres Strait Islander Commission Bill 1989, 2 November 1989, vol 169, 2439 (Duncan Kerr).

[147] Sanders, 'ATSIC's Achievements and Strengths' (n 127).

[148] S Bradfield, 'Separatism or Status-Quo? Indigenous Affairs from the Birth of Land Rights to the Death of ATSIC' (2006) 52 *Australian Journal of Politics and History* 80, 88.

[149] M Dodson and L Strelein, 'Australia's Nation-Building' (2001) 24 *UNSW Law Journal* 826, 834.

meaningful to Indigenous peoples and challenging government policy. In regional and remote communities, areas where ATSIC had the greatest footprint, it was rewarded by generally increased voter turnout at successive elections. And yet, nationally and in urban areas, its turnout figures remained poor, suggesting that the Commission did not achieve active support and was not generally regarded by Aboriginal and Torres Strait Islander peoples as reflecting their ontologies and values. Indigenous Australians worked with and through ATSIC to realise their interests, but it largely struggled to meet demands of and for legitimacy.

V. Future Institutional Design

Law generates expectations and structures behaviour. In Australia, like many other settler-states, the political and legal framework of government was built on the exclusion of Indigenous peoples and their approaches to, and understanding of, legitimate political authority. Shifts in social and legal attitudes towards Indigenous peoples may have moderated some of its extremes, but the public law artifice that it established endures. The institutions that exercise and regulate public power in Australia remain both constructed and enlivened by those 'deep substantive commitments'[150] that ignored and discounted the interests of Aboriginal and Torres Strait Islander peoples. Amending this framework to equitably accommodate Indigenous decision-making bodies is challenging.

ATSIC was a victim of this history. Criticism of the Commission often centred on its apparent anomalous position within Australia's system of governance. During debate on the ATSIC Bill, members of the Opposition attacked the proposed body as a 'black parliament',[151] which 'smacks of separatism of the worst possible kind in a nation'.[152] Similar criticisms have been made towards the proposed First Nations Voice. In rejecting the body, Prime Minister Malcolm Turnbull explained that 'our democracy is built on the foundation of all Australian citizens having equal civic rights', and that a constitutionally enshrined Indigenous representative body with advisory powers would 'undermine the universal principles of unity, equality and "one person one vote"'.[153]

These and other like statements reveal once again the tension inherent to our indicia. A durable Indigenous institution must be drawn from Indigenous ontologies, but it must also accord with the norms of the state. Yet those norms are themselves contestable. As already noted, the Labor Opposition has committed to holding a referendum to entrench a First Nations Voice in the Constitution, and strong political leadership can shift the values of the dominant community. In any case, I suggest that arguments against Indigenous decision-making institutions are premised on excessively narrow understandings

---

[150] E Arcioni and A Stone, 'The Small Brown Bird: Values and Aspirations in the Australian Constitution' (2016) 14 *International Journal of Constitutional Law* 60, 60–61.
[151] Australia Cth, Senate, Aboriginal and Torres Strait Islander Commission Bill 1989, 18 August 1989, vol 135, 395 (Jim Short); Australia Cth, Senate, Aboriginal and Torres Strait Islander Commission Bill 1989, 30 August 1989, vol 135, 641 (Florence Bjelke-Petersen).
[152] Australia Cth, Senate, Aboriginal and Torres Strait Islander Commission Bill 1989, 17 October 1989, vol 136, 2014 (Jim Short).
[153] Department of Prime Minister and Cabinet, 'Response to Referendum Council's Report' (n 8).

of democratic governance.[154] In structuring relationships among the community and between the state, there is nothing inherent in public law that discounts creative and flexible accommodations of difference. Exploration of ATSIC's sociological legitimacy offers several valuable lessons for future institutional design in Australia and elsewhere.

First, this study reveals the inherent tensions involved in designing Indigenous decision-making bodies within the confines of the state. Unfortunately, simply adopting design choices grounded in Indigenous ontologies would not have resolved all the Commission's challenges; translation is a necessary element of this process, but at some point, Indigenous peoples must make difficult choices to ensure that they are effective at operating within state structures. For instance, even with creative institutional design, it is difficult to see how Regional Council boundaries could align with community affiliations that crossed State or Territory borders while maintaining administrative efficacy in a federal system. Although this inhibited the capacity or desire of some Indigenous peoples and communities to engage with the body, weakening its legitimacy among and within those communities, such a decision was necessary to ensure that the Commission could be effective at advocating for Indigenous peoples at all levels of government.

Second, positively and notwithstanding the above, many of the challenges ATSIC faced were problems of institutional choice and can be traced to the fact that Aboriginal and Torres Strait Islander peoples were not permitted to lead debate on the design of the Commission. The requirement that all members of Regional Councils be directly elected, for example, was in tension with some communities whose cultural practices favoured alternative non-electoral means of leadership. Similarly, the overwhelming focus on mechanisms of public accountability ensured that state priorities would place continued pressure on Regional Councillors and members of the national Board to remain answerable to their Indigenous constituents. A design process centred on and driven by Aboriginal and Torres Strait Islander peoples and communities would likely have resulted in an institution more directly connected to the norms and values of Indigenous peoples. This would have strengthened the initial legitimacy of the Commission and may have had positive consequences into the future. Future institutional design should take heart from this lesson.

Empowering Indigenous peoples to drive design is critical but will not necessarily lead to positive results. This challenge is pronounced in an environment where legislation and policy are developed or finally enacted in the absence of Indigenous voices. The fact that no Aboriginal and Torres Strait Islander peoples were present in Parliament during debate over the ATSIC Bill meant that amendments could be made contrary to their wishes. In this sense, attempts to rectify foundational injustices that denied Indigenous peoples a place in the government of their land were exacerbated by that initial injustice.

Creative approaches can resolve some, but not all, of these tensions. In Victoria, for example, the Parliament has recently passed legislation requiring government to recognise an Aboriginal Representative Body, on the recommendation of the Victorian Treaty Advancement Commissioner.[155] This statutory hook ensures that the State will consult in

---

[154] H Hobbs, 'Constitutional Recognition and Reform: Developing an Inclusive Australian Citizenship through Treaty' (2018) 53 *Australian Journal of Political Science* 176; H Hobbs, 'Aboriginal and Torres Strait Islander Peoples and Multinational Federalism in Australia' (2018) 27 *Griffith Law Review* 307.

[155] *Advancing the Treaty Process with Aboriginal Victorians Act 2018* (Vic), ss 8, 10–11.

'partnership and good faith' with the body in the development of a treaty framework,[156] but it leaves questions of structure and design to be determined by Aboriginal Victorians.[157] Without clear legal authority or financial security, however, the body's effectiveness remains reliant on government determination to meaningfully engage.

This points to a fourth conclusion. ATSIC demonstrates that the greatest challenge to establishing Indigenous decision-making bodies within the public law framework of the state is generally *not* public law but politics. Public law *is* sufficiently flexible and dynamic to accommodate diverse institutional processes and mechanisms that empower Indigenous peoples with the capacity to be heard in the processes of government. Statements that the Commission involved a 'truly radical reorientation of governmental institutions relating to Indigenous affairs'[158] may be hyperbolic, but the Commission was an innovative and novel approach to empowering Aboriginal and Torres Strait Islander peoples that could be established with relatively little stress on Australia's existing political and legal governance system.

Relatedly, a final lesson from ATSIC's experience concerns the state. An Indigenous decision-making body formally embedded within the state must be allowed to succeed. State anxiety over an Indigenous institution's jurisdictional authority or capacity to realise outcomes is self-defeating. These bodies are intended to empower Indigenous peoples to be heard in the processes of government. Such a role is impossible to carry out where state interference weakens community trust and confidence in the institution to the extent that it is regarded as illegitimate. This is a problem of all state-supported national Indigenous organisations with pressure-group functions.[159] As Sally Weaver argued many years ago, one solution is to support and enhance the autonomy of such bodies.[160] By fostering the political development of Indigenous peoples – recognising a real domain of authority and permitting representatives the conceptual and political space to develop long-term policy that reflects Indigenous values – Indigenous peoples will have confidence in their institution, and it will become an effective instrument of and in government. This will necessarily require the state to rethink its current approach. Public law can, and must, create institutions that are drawn from and 'have currency within Aboriginal traditions of legality and authority',[161] but whether those institutions are established is a question of politics, not law.

---

[156] *Advancing the Treaty Process with Aboriginal Victorians Act 2018* (Vic), ss 20(2), 22.
[157] *Advancing the Treaty Process with Aboriginal Victorians Act 2018* (Vic), s 11(2).
[158] Dillon, 'Institutional Structures in Indigenous Affairs' (n 143) 92.
[159] This is also a more general problem in Australia, as government criticism of Gillian Triggs during her tenure as President of the Human Rights Commission demonstrates.
[160] S Weaver, 'Australian Aboriginal Policy: Aboriginal Pressure Groups or Government Advisory Bodies? Part II' (1983) 54 *Oceania* 85.
[161] J Webber, *The Constitution of Canada: A Contextual Analysis* (Oxford, Hart Publishing, 2015) 264.

11
Places as Persons: Creating a New Framework for Māori-Crown Relations

ANDREW GEDDIS AND JACINTA RURU*

This chapter describes a novel legal development in Aotearoa New Zealand, co-written by a Māori-Pākehā and Pākehā (NZ European) author team. We recognise at the outset that this story primarily belongs to the peoples of Ngai Tūhoe and Whanganui Iwi. This is our attempt to contribute in a purely legal sense the significance in law of what these Iwi (Māori tribal federations) have achieved for the nation.

I. Introduction

In 2014, an Act of the Aotearoa New Zealand Parliament recognised the 2,127 square kilometre former Te Urewera National Park as being a 'legal entity' possessing 'all the rights, powers, duties, and liabilities of a legal person'.[1] In March of 2017, another enactment acknowledged the country's 300-kilometre-long Whanganui River as 'a legal person [with] all the rights, powers, duties, and liabilities of a legal person'.[2] In late 2017, the Crown and Taranaki Māori signed a record of understanding that Parliament will in the future legislate to grant the 2,518-metre-tall Mount Taranaki/Mount Egmont legal personhood.[3] By virtue of these legislative acts, the various geographic entities gain an independent existence in the eyes of the law. Rather than being mere Crown or public property, they own themselves. They are deemed to be holders of their own rights, which may be asserted in legal proceedings and other fora. In short, they are no longer 'things' over which human beings exercise dominion; they are 'persons' with which humans have a relationship.

---

* Our thanks to Laura MacKay for research assistance. This research contributes to the Ngā Pae o te Māramatanga Ngā Ture o Te Tai Ao Research Project.
[1] Te Urewera Act 2014, s 11(1).
[2] Te Awa Tupua (Whanganui River Claims Settlement) Act 2017, s 14(1).
[3] See D Cheng, 'Mt Taranaki Will Be Granted Special Legal Status Similar to Urewera and the Whanganui River', *NZ Herald* (21 December 2017), available at https://www.nzherald.co.nz/nz/news/article.cfm?c_id=1&objectid=11963982.

Declaring places to be persons in law was without precedent in those parts of the world hewing to the common law tradition.[4] As such, it has attracted substantial media[5] and academic[6] interest. Some of this attention may be due to the apparent incongruity of putting earth, trees and water on the same legal footing as human beings. The very fact that this novel step has been taken excites curiosity and invites explanation. But interest also is driven by claims that the move represents the recognition of so-called 'Rights of Nature'[7] in Aotearoa New Zealand law. That is to say, many have interpreted the granting of legal personality primarily as a mechanism to improve the environmental protection afforded to these places, by better empowering them to defend themselves against forms of human development and degradation.[8] We think that such understandings and explanations of this legal development are at worst mistaken and at least are incomplete, and fail to capture the crucial context in which these developments have occurred. The granting of legal personality rather recognises the way in which Māori, the Indigenous peoples of Aotearoa New Zealand, conceive of and relate to the particular places at issue. As the Iwi along the Whanganui River say, 'Ko au te awa, Ko te awa ko au.'[9] Or, as legal academic Catherine Iorns Magallanes puts it, deeming places such as Te Urewera, the

---

[4] However, prior to 2014, the Constitutions of Bolivia and Ecuador both give constitutional recognition to 'Pachamama' (nature); while India and Colombia also have taken steps to confer legal personality on individual rivers: see E O'Donnell, *Legal Rights for Rivers: Competition, Collaboration and Water Governance* (Abingdon, Routledge, 2018).

[5] See, eg, A Fairbrother, 'New Zealand's Whanganui River Gains a Legal Voice' *Huffington Post* (15 October 2012), available at http://www.huffingtonpost.com/2012/09/18/new-zealand-whanganui-river_n_1894893.html; B Rouseau, 'In New Zealand, Lands and Rivers Can Be People (Legally Speaking)' *New York Times* (13 July 2016), available at http://www.nytimes.com/2016/07/14/world/what-in-the-world/in-new-zealand-lands-and-rivers-can-be-people-legally-speaking.html?_r=0; K Calderwood, 'Why New Zealand is granting a river the same rights as a citizen' *ABC Online* (6 September 2016), available at http://www.abc.net.au/radionational/programs/sundayextra/new-zealand-granting-rivers-and-forests-same-rights-as-citizens/7816456; J Turkewitz, 'Corporations have rights, why shouldn't rivers?' *New York Times* (26 September 2017), available at https://www.nytimes.com/2017/09/26/us/does-the-colorado-river-have-rights-a-lawsuit-seeks-to-declare-it-a-person.html; E Ainge Roy, 'New Zealand Gives Mt Taranaki the same legal rights as a person' *The Guardian* (22 December 2017), available at https://www.theguardian.com/world/2017/dec/22/new-zealand-gives-mount-taranaki-same-legal-rights-as-a-person.

[6] See, eg, A Hutchison, 'Whanganui River as a Legal Person' (2014) 39 *Alternative Law Journal* 179; CJ Iorns Magallanes, 'Nature as an Ancestor: Two Examples of Legal Personality for Nature in New Zealand' (September 2015) 22 *VertigO – La Revue Électronique en Sciences de l'Environnement*, available at https://vertigo.revues.org/16199; D Shelton, 'Nature as a Legal Person' (September 2015) 22 *VertigO – La Revue Électronique en Sciences de l'Environnement*, available at http://vertigo.revues.org/16188; CJ Iorns Magallanes, 'Māori Cultural Rights in Aotearoa New Zealand: Protecting the Cosmology That Protects the Environment'(2015) 21 *Widener Law Review* 271; G Gordon, 'Environmental Personhood' (2018) 43 *Columbia Journal of Environmental Law* 49; L Charpleix, 'The Whanganui River as Te Awa Tupua: Place-based Law in a Legally Pluralistic Society' (2018) 184 *Geographic Journal* 19.

[7] C Stone, 'Should Trees Have Standing? Towards Legal Rights for Material Agents' (1972) 45 *Southern California Law Review* 450; DR Boyd, *The Rights of Nature: A Legal Revolution That Could Save the World* (Toronto, ECW Press, 2017).

[8] See, eg, M Margil, 'Building an International Movement for Rights of Nature' in M Maloney and P Burdon (eds), *Wild Law – In Practice* (Abingdon, Routledge, 2014) 156; CG Gonzalez, 'Bridging the North-South Divide: International Environmental Law in the Anthropocene' (2015) 32 *Pace Environmental Law Review* 407, 425; M Maloney and P Siemen, 'Responding to the Great Work: The Role of Earth Jurisprudence and Wild Law in the 21st Century' (2015) 5 *Environmental and Earth Law Journal* 6, 17–18; EL O'Donnell, 'At the Intersection of the Sacred and the Legal: Rights for Nature in Uttarakhand, India' (2018) 30 *Journal of Environmental Law* 135, 136.

[9] 'I am the river. The river is me.' See Te Awa Tupua (Whanganui River Claims Settlement) Act 2017, s 13(c). Ngai Tūhoe express a similar view towards Te Urewera: 'Te Urewera expresses and gives meaning to Tūhoe culture, language, customs, and identity.' See Te Urewera Act 2014, s 3(6).

Whanganui River and Mt Taranaki to be persons 'truly reflects the indigenous cosmological view of people as part of nature, not separate nor above it'.[10]

The question, then, is *why* did Aotearoa New Zealand's Parliament make the decision to grant legal personality to these natural features in order to reflect the 'cosmological view' of Māori? Our answer in this chapter is fundamentally constitutional in nature.[11] Recognising personhood broke a deadlock between the Crown and some individual Iwi when settling historical pre-1992 injustices within the context of the Treaty of Waitangi.[12] It was thus a form of principled compromise that permitted redress for the extensive Crown breaches of the Treaty, whilst creating the basis for a new future relationship. But beyond permitting a solution to historical injuries, the legal recognition of these places-as-persons also changes the way in which they are conceived of by the majority Pākehā nation and how all citizens will interact with them in the future. In part, this change will come from the different stewardship arrangements that have been established to speak for these now-persons and to safeguard their interests. That change also will reflect the fact that a legal shift in what these entities are seen as being – a move from conceiving of them purely in state law as instrumental things to persons with which an ongoing relationship exists – will alter how human interactions with them take place. That is to say, the inclusion of these places as persons within the web of laws and practices that govern Aotearoa New Zealand inevitably will make a difference to how those laws and practices operate in relation to those places beyond the norm of conservation law.

We explore this issue as follows. In section II, we traverse the background to Te Urewera and the Whanganui River legislation, explaining how the previous legal status of these geographic features formed a blockage in the Crown's efforts to settle historical breaches of the Treaty of Waitangi with particular Iwi. In particular, a deadlock over the question of who 'owned' each place – which in turn reflected disputes over who possesses 'sovereignty' within the nation's constitutional framework – threatened to prevent those settlements from occurring. Reconceiving of the places in law as being their own persons thus resolved the issue in a way that allowed for a mutually satisfactory solution to those long-standing disputes.

Section III outlines the legislation conferring legal personality on Te Urewera and the Whanganui River. We explain how the structure and content of each piece of legislation reflects the differing legal regimes that governed each entity prior to its being declared a legal person. Even so, each enactment has in common that it: defines the entity that is being granted personhood status; gives a particular legal meaning to that status; establishes a governance structure for each entity; and continues to subject the entity to some ongoing constraints by others.

Overall, we argue that Aotearoa New Zealand's reasons for giving Te Urewera and the Whanganui River personhood status is an acknowledgement of their intrinsic value and

---

[10] Magallanes, 'Māori Cultural Rights' (n 6) 325. For an introduction to the Māori worldview, see HM Mead, *Tikanga Māori: Living By Māori Values*, revised edn (Wellington, Huai Publishers, 2016); ET Durie, 'Will the Settlers Settle? Cultural Conciliation and the Law' (1996) 8 *Otago Law Review* 449; M Reilly et al (eds), *Te Kōparapara: An Introduction to the Māori World* (Auckland, Auckland University Press, 2018).

[11] For a similar analysis, see K Saunders, '"Beyond Human Ownership"? Property, Power and Legal Personality for Nature in Aotearoa New Zealand' (2018) 30 *Journal of Environmental Law* 207.

[12] See generally NR Wheen and J Hayward (eds), *Treaty of Waitangi Settlements* (Wellington, Bridget Williams Books, 2012).

moral worth, which does accord with the Rights of Nature account of the development. However, that recognition also encompasses an understanding of these places as being deeply interconnected with Iwi in ways that permit (indeed, envision) future forms of development or utilisation of these places to meet human needs. As such, the entities themselves are not conceived of as separate from or independent of the people who interact with them. Rather, they are only understandable in relation to those human beings who live with, use and care for the places in question; in particular, the Māori tangata whenua ('people of the land') of Aotearoa New Zealand.

II. Recognising Personhood in the Context of Sovereignty

As with many once-colonial jurisdictions, ongoing issues of sovereignty and property lie at the heart of Aotearoa New Zealand's constitutional narrative. In 1840, the British Crown relied on a combination of the signed Treaty of Waitangi ('the Treaty') and the common law doctrine of discovery to assert sovereignty over the new colony.[13] Despite the Māori language version of the Treaty's promising otherwise, the constitutional framework established thereafter denied Māori their ongoing sovereign powers. In Māori, the Treaty recognises that Māori were to retain 'te tino rangatiratanga' (sovereignty/chieftainship), whilst permitting the Crown to exercise 'kawanatanga' (governorship) over incoming Europeans. In contrast, in English, the Treaty records a transfer of sovereignty from Māori to the British, but in return recognises the retention by Māori of 'full exclusive and undisturbed possession of their Lands and Estates Forests Fisheries and other properties which they may collectively or individually possess'. This clash of original intent has continued to mark relations between the Crown and Māori ever since, heightened by a long-continuing series of Crown actions breaching the basic principles of the Treaty, including the ongoing false assumption that Māori voluntarily ceded their sovereignty.[14] In response, Māori consistently fought to retain both their sovereignty and property in the face of both military[15] and judicial[16] hostility.

---

[13] C Orange, *The Treaty of Waitangi*, 2nd edn (Wellington, Bridget Williams Books, 2011); R Miller et al, *Discovering Indigenous Lands: The Doctrine of Discovery in the English Colonies* (Oxford, Oxford University Press, 2010); A Anderson, J Binney and A Harris, *Tangata Whenua: An Illustrated History* (Wellington, Bridget Williams Books, 2014).
[14] See The Waitangi Tribunal, *He Whakaputanga me te Tiriti, The Declaration and the Treaty: The Report on Stage 1 of the Te Paparahi o Te Raki Inquiry*, Wai 1080 (2014) 527.
[15] See J Belich, *The New Zealand Wars and the Victorian Interpretation of Racial Conflict* (Auckland, Auckland University Press, 1988); V O'Malley, *The Great War for New Zealand, Waikato 1800–2000* (Wellington, Bridget Williams Books, 2016). For a broader understanding of Māori history and protest see, eg, A Harris, *Hikoi: Forty Years of Māori Protest* (Auckland, Penguin Books, 2004); and M Bargh (ed), *Resistance: An Indigenous Response to Neoliberalism* (Auckland, Penguin Books, 2007).
[16] *Wi Parata v Bishop of Wellington* [1877] 3 NZ Jur (NS) 72, 78. See also D Williams, '*Te Kooti Tango Whenua*': *The Native Land Court, 1864–1909* (Auckland, Penguin Books, 1999); R Boast, *Buying the Land, Selling the Land: Governments and Māori Land on the North Island 1865–1921* (Wellington, Victoria University Press, 2008); R Boast and R Hill (eds), *Raupatu: The Confiscation of Māori Land*, (Wellington, Victoria University Press, 2009); D Williams, *A Simple Nullity? The Wi Parata Case in New Zealand Law and History* (Auckland, Auckland University Press, 2011); R Boast, *The Native Land Court 1862–1887: A Historical Study, Cases and Commentary* (Wellington, Victoria University Press, 2013); R Boast, *The Native Land Court 1888–1909: A Historical Study, Cases and Commentary* (Wellington, Victoria University Press, 2015).

The creation of the country's conservation estate in the late 1800s sat firmly within this colonial context. British colonisers arriving on the shores of this 'new world' set about putting to use the expansive lands they regarded as wild and empty.[17] Some lands were ring-fenced as Crown land for conservation purposes. Rationalised first as a tourist and recreation tool, it was not until the twentieth century that protected land, such as national parks, became firmly embedded in explicitly conservation goals.

Te Urewera, the Whanganui River and Mt Taranaki all share a history within this conservation estate. The slopes of Mt Taranaki first were protected as a forest reserve in 1881, and then fully encased within the country's second national park: Egmont National Park, formally created in 1900. It was established with no appreciation of the cultural, historical, traditional and spiritual importance of this mountain to the Taranaki Iwi.[18] Likewise, the densely covered forested land of Te Urewera was designated a national park in 1954 without regard for Ngai Tūhoe. The Tūhoe Claims Settlement Act 2014 accepts 'The Crown neither consulted Tūhoe about the establishment of the park nor about its 1957 expansion and did not recognise Tūhoe as having any special interest in the park or its governance.'[19] Later, in 1987, the Whanganui National Park was officially opened, encompassing a vast area of lowland forest and a significant part of the Whanganui River catchment. While it did not include the water in the river or its tributaries, it did include parts of the bed of the river. Whanganui Iwi had reluctantly agreed to the Park on the condition that their ancestral river be excluded from it.[20]

Today, the conservation estate is extensive (nearly one-third of Aotearoa New Zealand's landmass) and is managed by the Department of Conservation in a manner that is committed to preserving and protecting these lands 'for the purpose of maintaining their intrinsic values, providing for their appreciation and recreational enjoyment by the public, and safeguarding the options of future generations'.[21] Since 1987, the law has required those empowered to care for the conservation estate to give effect to the principles of the Treaty.[22] However, from a Māori perspective, the Department has been slow to realise this legal mandate. Present conservation legislation and practices arguably continue to reflect antiquated ideas about the little value of Māori in contributing to biodiversity restoration.[23] This is because most of the conservation legislation was enacted prior to the modern reconciliation Treaty of Waitangi settlement statutes. Many of these conservation

---

[17] W Cronon, 'The Creation of National Parks and Equivalent Resources in Ontario and the Anitpodes: A Comparative History and its Contemporary Expression' in JS March and BW Hodgins (eds), *Changing Parks: The History, Future and Cultural Context of Parks and Heritage Landscapes* (Ottawa, Natural Heritage, 1998). See also PS Kopas, *Taking the Air: Ideas and Change in Canada's National Parks* (Vancouver, UBC Press, 2007).
[18] See The Waitangi Tribunal, *The Taranaki Report: Kaupapa Tuatahi*, Wai 143 (1996).
[19] Tūhoe Claims Settlement Act 2014, s 8(10). J Binney, *Encircled Lands: Te Urewera, 1820–1921* (Wellington, Bridget Williams Books, 2009); The Waitangi Tribunal, *Te Urewera*, Wai 894 (2014).
[20] The Waitangi Tribunal, *He Whiritaunoka: The Whanganui Land Report*, Wai 903 (2015), in particular ch 22.
[21] Conservation Act 1987, s 2 (definition of 'conservation').
[22] Conservation Act 1987, s 4.
[23] J Ruru et al, 'Reversing the Decline in New Zealand's Biodiversity: Empowering Māori Within Reformed Conservation Law' (2017) 13 *Policy Quarterly* 65; POB Lyver et al, 'Building Biocultural Approaches into Aotearoa – New Zealand's Conservation Future' (2018) *Journal of the Royal Society of New Zealand*, available at https://doi.org/10.1080/03036758.2018.1539405; The Waitangi Tribunal, *Ko Aotearoa Tenei: A Report into Claims Concerning New Zealand Law and Policy Affecting Māori Culture and Identity*, Wai 262 (2011); J Ruru, 'Managing Our Treasured Home: The Conservation Estate and the Principles of the Treaty of Waitangi' (2004) 8 *NZ Journal of Environmental Law* 243.

statutes emerged from a period when policymakers and government members were heavily influenced by the monocultural Western conservation ideals of the nineteenth and early twentieth centuries. Consequently, Māori leaders have for some time criticised the conservation protection objective as 'hostile to the customary principle of sustainable use and the spiritual linkage of iwi with indigenous resources is subjected to paternalistic control'.[24] They have criticised national parks more broadly as 'gated areas where we are obstructed from our customary practices, locked out from decision making, and held back from continuing our relationship with sites of deep spiritual or cultural significance'.[25]

For these reasons, Māori entering into Treaty settlement negotiations with the Crown have prioritised the return of their lands, which have been caged in the conservation estate. Settlement redress typically consists of a Crown apology and financial, commercial and cultural redress. They are intended to be full and final settlements. Often included in a settlement package will be the return to Iwi ownership of a small quantity of Crown-owned land that was wrongfully acquired from the Iwi concerned. However, the Crown has laid several parameters around the negotiations, including a general rule that the lands within the conservation estate are not available for return to Iwi ownership. Recognition of legal personality has broken this deadlock between the Crown and some Iwi.

A. Te Urewera Negotiations

Settlement of Ngai Tūhoe Treaty claims through the passage of the Te Urewera Act was the culmination of a process dating back to the early 2000s.[26] From the beginning of its negotiations, the return of the Te Urewera National Park was one of Tūhoe's 'bottom lines'. The mandated negotiating body, Te Kotahi a Tūhoe, was instructed by Tūhoe not to engage with any settlement that did not include Te Urewera.[27] Consequently, the initial Deed of Settlement prepared in 2009 agreed that Tūhoe would gain ownership of Te Urewera National Park and manage it in partnership with the Crown for 10 years, after which the relationship would be reconsidered and either extended or terminated, with Tūhoe fully taking over management of the park.[28] However, on the eve of Tūhoe signing this Deed of Settlement, then Prime Minister Sir John Key intervened and removed Te Urewera from the negotiating table.[29] It appears that the Prime Minister was concerned with the political ramifications of transferring 'ownership' of the park in question to Tūhoe and the possibility of subsequent limits being imposed on general public access to the park.[30]

---

[24] E Ellison, *Deficiencies in Conservation Subsidiary Legislation*, Report to the New Zealand Conservation Authority (25 July 2001) (unpublished; file with authors).
[25] M Solomon, 'Locked Out of National Parks, A Call to Action from Kaiwhakahaere Ta Mark Solomon' Te Karaka (2014), available at http://ngaitahu.iwi.nz/our_stories/locked-national-parks/.
[26] Tūhoe Establishment Trust, *He Waihanga i te Whare Kaha o Tūhoe* (2009) 6. R Higgins, 'Te Wharehou o Tūhoe: The House that "We" Built' [2014] *Māori Law Review* 7, 9.
[27] The other bottom lines were Mana Motuhake (autonomy/self-determination), and the settlement's quantum; see Higgins, 'Te Wharehou o Tūhoe' (n 26) 8.
[28] 'Iwi Wants to Run Te Urewera National Park', *NZ Herald* (22 April 2010), available at https://www.nzherald.co.nz/nz/news/article.cfm?c_id=1&objectid=10639994.
[29] Higgins, 'Te Wharehou o Tūhoe' (n 26) 10.
[30] T Kruger, 'We Are Not Who We Should Be as Tūhoe People', Bruce Jesson Memorial Lecture (31 October 2017), available at https://e-tangata.co.nz/identity/tamati-kruger-we-are-not-who-we-should-be-as-tuhoe-people/; 'Tūhoe Were Never Promised Te Urewera – Key', *NZ Herald* (17 May 2010), available at https://www.nzherald.co.nz/nz/news/article.cfm?c_id=1&objectid=10645529.

For many Tūhoe persons, this was yet another example of the Crown undermining Tūhoe Mana Motuhake (autonomy/self-determination).[31] Despite this setback, Te Kotahi a Tūhoe continued to negotiate with the Crown, and also with Iwi members, and in 2011 a significant turning point was reached.[32] A political compact was signed between Tūhoe and the Crown in Ruatāhuna on 2 July 2011, stating:

> Tatū mai ki tēnei wā, kua herea a Tūhoe me Te Karauna kia rite tētahi puretumu e whakatikaina ai nā tini hē i whakawhiua poka noatia ai a Tūhoe i roto i nā rau tau, otiia, ki tēnā whakatipurana ki tēnā whakatipurana. He wā momoho tēnei mā māua, mā Tūhoe me Te Karauna kia hīkoi, kia mahi tahi hoki kia kaua ai e tāmatemate te āhua ranatira, kia mau pū tonu ai te whakamanawatana o tāua tahi, kia ana whakamua ai anō te ora mō tāua tahi. E tika ana anō hoki, hai whāina pae tata mā tāua, kia whakaae tahi tāua ki ō tāua āheina mana, tēnā ki tō tēnā.
>
> Now, however Tūhoe and the Crown have committed themselves to achieving a just and honourable redress for the manifold wrongs inflicted on Tūhoe over centuries and many generations. It is timely, therefore, that we, Tūhoe and the Crown, resolve to walk and work together for our mutual honour, dignity, advantage and progress. And it is fitting that in furtherance of such resolve the Crown and Tūhoe should acknowledge their respective mana.[33]

This compact was significant because it went some way towards restoring trust between the parties, and to Tūhoe it meant that the Crown was willing to acknowledge their mana (authority) and work towards a settlement.[34] This was especially so given that the signatories of the compact were the Crown and the hapū (sub-tribe federations) of Tūhoe, as opposed to Te Kotahi a Tūhoe. Tūhoe remains a strongly hapū-based iwi,[35] and issues relating to individual hapū are managed by Tūhoe Tribal Executive Committees to ensure the protection and maintenance of Tūhoe Mana Motuhake, particularly over resources and boundaries.[36] A compromise regarding Te Urewera was reached under the auspices of this compact, and in March 2013 a Deed of Settlement was initialled by both Te Kotahi a Tūhoe and a member from each hapū of Tūhoe.[37] Two separate pieces of legislation were then enacted to give force to this Deed: the Tūhoe Claims Settlement Act 2014 and the Te Urewera Act 2014.

While the second Deed of Settlement did not return ownership of Te Urewera to Tūhoe, the granting of legal personality to the park was considered an acceptable compromise.[38] The concept of 'ownership' simply was too big a hurdle to the success of the negotiations. As Tūhoe's Chief Negotiator, Tamati Kruger, has said:

> [D]uring the negotiations, not only did I get some advice from John Key around engineering bridges, but we found ourselves struggling with opposing ideas where John Key was very, very concerned about ownership of things. And he felt that, however the Crown got to own Te Urewera

---

[31] Higgins, 'Te Wharehou o Tūhoe' (n 26) 10.
[32] ibid.
[33] 'Nā Kōrero Ranatira ā Tūhoe me Te Karauna – Ngā Kōrero Rangatira a Tūhoe me Te Karauna: Political compact document signed by the hapū of Tūhoe and the Crown' (2 July 2011).
[34] Higgins, 'Te Wharehou o Tūhoe' (n 26) 11.
[35] While iwi (tribe) were the largest political grouping in pre-European Māori society, the hapū (clan or descent group) was the primary forum for collective decision-making.
[36] Higgins, 'Te Wharehou o Tūhoe' (n 26) 11.
[37] ibid.
[38] S Warren, 'Whanganui River and Te Urewera Treaty Settlements: Innovative Developments for the Practice of Rangatiratanga in Resource Management', Thesis submitted to Victoria University of Wellington in fulfilment of the requirements for the degree of Master of New Zealand Studies (2016) 66, available at http://researcharchive.vuw.ac.nz/handle/10063/6198.

was irrelevant, it was now public land and all New Zealanders owned it, and loved it and admired it. Even more so perhaps than Tūhoe people. The engineering advice to me was we couldn't build a bridge over that – and something else had to happen. So our mission was to delete ownership from the negotiations.[39]

Kruger stated that Tūhoe spent approximately five years researching the overseas co-management models and ideas that the Crown put forward for managing Te Urewera. He sent people worldwide to analyse the effectiveness of the models the Crown was proposing, from the Northern Territories to the Arctic Circle, and the response from Indigenous peoples in these places was that these models did not work. Only then was the Crown prepared to accept a local solution to the issue of ownership, allowing the negotiations to proceed to a successful settlement.[40]

B. Whanganui River Negotiations

The Iwi of the Whanganui River began their claim of ownership by protest and formal objections from 1873 onwards, initially in the form of parliamentary petitions.[41] In 1988, the Whanganui River Māori Trust Board was established by the Whanganui River Trust Board Act 1988 to negotiate for the settlement of all outstanding Whanganui Iwi claims over the Whanganui River.[42] In 1990, the Trust Board lodged a claim with the Waitangi Tribunal – a standing commission of inquiry into alleged Crown breaches of the principles of the Treaty – in regard to the Whanganui River. Nine years later the Tribunal released its Report, finding that the Treaty of Waitangi had guaranteed Whanganui Iwi the rights to ownership, management and control of the river, which Whanganui Iwi had never freely and willingly relinquished.[43]

Following the release of the Waitangi Tribunal Report, negotiations between Whanganui Iwi and the Crown in relation to the status of the Whanganui River took place between 2002 and 2004. However, these were unsuccessful.[44] After a five-year hiatus, negotiations recommenced in 2009.[45] In 2011, the Crown approved a process of exploratory discussions involving a series of intensive workshops with Whanganui Iwi, the Office of Treaty Settlements and other government departments with an interest in the status of the Whanganui River.[46] The purpose of these discussions was to develop a settlement framework for the key elements of a proposed settlement, to be documented in a Record of Understanding, which would set the stage for formal negotiations.[47]

---

[39] Kruger, 'We Are Not Who We Should Be as Tūhoe People' (n 30).
[40] ibid.
[41] The Waitangi Tribunal, *The Whanganui River Report*, Wai 167 (1999) 4. See also *Re the Bed of the Wanganui River* [1962] NZLR 600 (CA).
[42] Whanganui River Trust Board Act 1988, ss 4 and 6.
[43] The Waitangi Tribunal, *The Whanganui River Report*, Wai 167 (1999) xiii.
[44] *Record of Understanding in Relation to Whanganui River Settlement* (13 October 2011) [1.16].
[45] ibid [1.17].
[46] ibid [1.20].
[47] ibid [1.21].

The exploratory discussions resulted in a framework that focused on:
1. Recognising the status of the Whanganui River as Te Awa Tupua.
2. Facilitating an integrated approach to the governance and management of the Whanganui River and its health and wellbeing.
3. Involving Whanganui Iwi, alongside the Crown, local government and the catchment community in the governance and management of the Whanganui River.[48]

By using the framework developed in the *Record of Understanding*, a High-Level Agreement (Tūtohu Whakatupua) was reached in 2012. This proposed to recognise the Whanganui River as Te Awa Tupua – 'a whole and indivisible entity from the mountains to the sea' – which we shall discuss in detail in section III.A.[49] Finally, in 2014, a Deed of Settlement was signed, and the legislation to give effect to this was introduced in May 2016.[50]

Similar to Te Urewera Act, Te Awa Tupua (Whanganui River Claims Settlement) Act 2017 is a solution to the issue of 'ownership' in negotiating a settlement. The Waitangi Tribunal Report of 1999 had explicitly stated that Māori had, and continue to claim, interests in the Whanganui River that equate to ownership; however, this was not something the Crown was eager to recognise.[51] Recognising the river as a legal entity provided a solution to this issue.

C. Legal Personality as a Bridging Concept

As noted, Catherine Iorns Magallanes has placed the granting of personhood to Te Urewera and the Whanganui River in the context of Aotearoa New Zealand's increasing legal recognition of the 'cosmological view' of Māori, in which 'people [are] part of nature, not separate nor above it'.[52] From a Māori perspective, this interconnected kinship is central to Māori identity. A prominent Māori appeal court judge, Joe Williams, positions kinship as the glue that holds Māori society together, expanding to regulate and inform human relationships with both the physical and spiritual worlds. For example, as he writes:

> Thus the story of what happened to Rata when he felled his totara tree without proper procedure confirms that good relations must be maintained with the forest itself as a related descent group in order to maintain the human right to be a user of forest resources.[53]

---

[48] ibid [1.22].
[49] Minister of Treaty Settlements, 'Whanganui River Deed of Settlement initialled' (27 March 2014), available at https://www.beehive.govt.nz/release/whanganui-river-deed-settlement-initialled.
[50] L Te Aho, 'Legislation – Te Awa Tupua (Whanganui River Claims Settlement) Bill – the Endless Quest for Justice' [2016] *Māori Law Review*, available at http://maorilawreview.co.nz/2016/08/legislation-te-awa-tupua-whanganui-river-claims-settlement-bill-the-endless-quest-for-justice/; L Te Aho, 'Ngā Whakatunga Waimāori: Freshwater Settlements' in NR Wheen and J Hayward (eds), *Treaty of Waitangi Settlements* (Wellington, Bridget Williams Books, 2012).
[51] A Geddis, 'Te Awa Tupua – Ding an Sich Selbst', *Pundit* (20 March 2017), available at https://www.pundit.co.nz/content/te-awa-tupua-ding-an-sich-selbst.
[52] Magallanes, 'Māori Cultural Rights' (n 6) 325.
[53] J Williams, 'Lex Aotearoa: An Heroic Attempt to Map the Māori Dimension in Modern New Zealand Law' (2013) 21 *Waikato Law Review* 1, 4.

This view is shared by other First Nations peoples:

> The traditional knowledge of indigenous peoples reflects a distinctive land ethic on many different levels. Many indigenous peoples share the belief that the Earth is a living, conscious being that must be treated with respect and care. The natural forces of wind, water, earth, and fire are understood to be quite powerful and capable of destroying humans who abuse their own tentative relationship with the natural world. Thus, within the traditional world view of many indigenous peoples, the relationship of human beings to the natural world must be premised on an ethic of respect and reciprocity, sometimes linked up to a model of stewardship rather than the Western property-based notion of dominion. In a way of thinking that perceives man and nature as part of an ordered, balanced, and living whole, human beings have social and kinship relationships with other beings. ... In sum, the traditional laws of Native peoples acknowledge a unique relationship between the indigenous peoples and the specific places and landscapes that have facilitated their existence for thousands of years. The very identity of many Native peoples is circumscribed by particular landforms and waterways.[54]

This is true, too, for those Iwi that have successfully negotiated legal personality of their ancestral lands and waters. Legal personality then provides a bridge whereby such Māori understandings of natural features can connect with existing common law concepts in a manner that accommodates both worldviews. Reaching that solution required a leap of both state legal imagination and political faith. For example, the then Minister for Conservation, Hon Dr Nick Smith, stated in the House when Te Urewera Bill was being read for the third time:

> It is surprising for me, as a Minister of Conservation in the 1990s who was involved under the leadership of the Rt Hon Jim Bolger – who is in the House – in the huge debate that occurred around the provisions of the Ngāi Tahu settlement in respect of conservation land, how far this country and this Parliament have come when we now get to this Tūhoe settlement in respect of the treasured Te Urewera National Park. If you had told me 15 years ago that Parliament would almost unanimously be able to agree to this bill, I would have said 'You're dreaming mate.' It has been a real journey for New Zealand, iwi, and Parliament to get used to the idea that Māori are perfectly capable of conserving New Zealand treasures at least as well as Pākehā and departments of State ...[55]

On that same occasion the then Minister for Māori Affairs, Hon Pita Sharples, reiterated the development's importance:

> The settlement is a profound alternative to the human presumption of sovereignty over the natural world. It restores to Tūhoe their role as kaitiaki and it embodies their hopes of self-determination – Tūhoe autonomy for the 21st century, Tūhoe services for Tūhoe, benefit on Tūhoe terms, and Tūhoe living by Tūhoe traditions and Tūhoe aspirations ...[56]

---

[54] R Tsosie, 'The Impacts of Climate Change on Indigenous Peoples' (2013) 26 *Tulane Environmental Law Journal* 239, 244–45 (internal citations omitted). See also MY Teran, 'The Nagoya Protocol and Indigenous Peoples' (2016) 7(2) *The International Indigenous Policy Journal*, available at https://ir.lib.uwo.ca/cgi/viewcontent.cgi?article=1267&context=iipj.
[55] Hon Nick Smith, NZPD vol 700 (23 July 2014) 19463.
[56] ibid. See also J Ruru, 'Reimagining Governance for National Parks' in L Elenius, C Allard and C Sandström (eds), *Indigenous Rights in Modern Landscapes: Nordic Conservation Regimes in Global Context* (Abingdon, Routledge, 2017) 113–25.

Thus, these two settlements, and the third in progress for Mt Taranaki, are principled compromises that demonstrate the possibilities for innovatively reframing Iwi–Crown relationships. We turn now to explain the way in which the legislative frameworks do so in each case.

III. The Legislative Framework for Recognising Personhood

The enactments conferring legal personality on Te Urewera and the Whanganui River are somewhat lengthy and complex, meaning a complete account of every provision is beyond the scope of this chapter. Consequently, this section will summarise the essential common features of both pieces of legislation, while noting where they diverge in approach.

In doing so, the different legal background to each enactment becomes important. As noted, Te Urewera previously was a National Park, fully controlled by the Crown and managed under the National Parks Act 1980 by the Department of Conservation. That legislation required the land comprising the Park to 'be preserved as far as possible in [its] natural state',[57] with the general purpose of 'preserving in perpetuity … [its] intrinsic worth … for the benefit, use, and enjoyment of the public'.[58] In contrast, the Whanganui River was a navigable waterway used for a range of purposes (commercial and otherwise), with competing demands for its use primarily managed by a range of local authorities in accordance with the Resource Management Act 1991, and also a place bounded both by private landholdings and the Whanganui National Park. Consequently, while those parts of the river bed previously owned by the Crown and managed as part of the conservation estate have now been vested in Te Awa Tupua (the entity associated with the Whanganui River), that land's previous conservation status continues to apply.[59] Equally, some portions were (and still are) owned by private interests, while ownership of the river's water was and is a deeply contested issue.

This differing pre-existing legal status and regulatory framework for each place is important for two reasons. First, the granting of legal personality does not represent a dramatic change in the previous purpose or form of legal regulation applied to each entity. Whilst Te Urewera no longer has National Park status, Te Urewera Act requires that it continue to be, so far as possible, 'preserved in its natural state';[60] that 'the value of Te Urewera for soil, water, and forest conservation [be] maintained';[61] and that the entity be managed 'as a place for public use and enjoyment'.[62] In other words, Parliament has mandated that Te Urewera retain a particular teleology – one that continues to reflect the notion of a forest protected from private spoliation, which all New Zealanders may access and enjoy. Equally, despite the Whanganui River's new status as a person, the activities permitted in relation to it still are decided by the various local authorities through which it runs. While Te Awa Tupua

---

[57] National Parks Act 1980, s 4(2)(a).
[58] National Parks Act 1980, s 4(1).
[59] See Te Awa Tupua (Whanganui River Claims Settlement) Act 2017, ss 41–42.
[60] Te Urewera Act 2014, s 5(a).
[61] Te Urewera Act 2014, s 5(f).
[62] Te Urewera Act 2014, s 4(c).

may now be heard before such decisions are made (as discussed in section III.B), and while Te Awa Tupua Act contains processes for establishing new frameworks to guide such local authority decision-making, the ultimate say on what occurs on and is done to the river remains governed by general resource management and conservation law. Te Awa Tupua is thus not an autonomous being that may choose what does and does not happen to it; rather, such decisions over it remain vested in local governmental bodies.

Second, the previous legal and regulatory regime applied to these entities is reflected in differing guardianship and decision-making structures contained in each piece of legislation. Te Urewera's former National Park status meant the Department of Conservation could consult with other societal groups (including Ngai Tūhoe) when deciding how to manage the land. It was thus relatively straightforward administratively to place the guardianship of Te Urewera with a body in which the Crown and Ngai Tūhoe work together, while empowering that body to continue to liaise with others when making decisions, and in some instances formally requiring cooperation, for example with the Fish and Game Council.[63] Doing so limits the exclusion of any person or group that previously enjoyed a right of input into the management of the land. In contrast, the Whanganui River had multiple users with potentially conflicting interests that were balanced through the exercise of discretionary powers by elected local representatives. Enabling these various interests to continue to have input into Te Awa Tupua's future has resulted in a far more complex guardianship structure, with one body established to speak on behalf of the entity and another, separate one to create a strategy for promoting its health and wellbeing.

However, taking these differing starting points into account, each piece of legislation has four common features:

(a) defining the entity in question and conferring personhood status on it;
(b) outlining the effect of that personhood status, in terms of the legal standing and rights, powers and duties that it confers upon the entity; and
(c) establishing a guardianship regime for the new entity; and
(d) setting out the ongoing constraints on the decisions that may be made on the entity's behalf.

We discuss each of these features in turn.

A. Defining the Entity and its Status

Both enactments first have to identify the entity in question. Te Urewera Act 2014 does so by initially defining the concept or ethos of Te Urewera:

Te Urewera

(1) Te Urewera is ancient and enduring, a fortress of nature, alive with history; its scenery is abundant with mystery, adventure, and remote beauty.
(2) Te Urewera is a place of spiritual value, with its own mana and mauri.
(3) Te Urewera has an identity in and of itself, inspiring people to commit to its care.

---

[63] Te Urewera Act 2014, s 61 requires the Board and the Fish and Game Council to commence discussion to enter a memorandum of understanding for working together.

Te Urewera and Tūhoe

(4) For Tūhoe, Te Urewera is Te Manawa o te Ika a Māui; it is the heart of the great fish of Maui, its name being derived from Murakareke, the son of the ancestor Tūhoe.
(5) For Tūhoe, Te Urewera is their ewe whenua, their place of origin and return, their homeland.
(6) Te Urewera expresses and gives meaning to Tūhoe culture, language, customs, and identity. There Tūhoe hold mana by ahikāroa; they are tangata whenua and kaitiaki of Te Urewera.

Te Urewera and all New Zealanders

(7) Te Urewera is prized by other iwi and hapū who have acknowledged special associations with, and customary interests in, parts of Te Urewera.
(8) Te Urewera is also prized by all New Zealanders as a place of outstanding national value and intrinsic worth; it is treasured by all for the distinctive natural values of its vast and rugged primeval forest, and for the integrity of those values; for its indigenous ecological systems and biodiversity, its historical and cultural heritage, its scientific importance, and as a place for outdoor recreation and spiritual reflection.[64]

The legislation then establishes a geographic boundary by defining 'Te Urewera lands', upon which Te Urewera resides.[65] These boundaries initially encompass the former National Park, although there is scope for expanding them if the relevant land meets certain qualifying characteristics.[66] Consequently, Te Urewera may generally be understood as being the special place that is within the land boundaries specified in the enactment.

Te Awa Tupua Act contains a more complex definition, with the entity being described as 'an indivisible and living whole, comprising the Whanganui River from the mountains to the sea, incorporating all its physical and metaphysical elements'.[67] In comparison with Te Urewera, the physical boundaries of this entity are not precisely defined. Therefore, Te Awa Tupua cannot just be understood as comprising 'the Whanganui River', nor even 'the Whanganui River and its various tributaries'. Rather, it encompasses both the physical river (its waters, its banks, its bed), the ecosystems which exist within it and the meaning the river has for all those who interact with it.

This conceptual (as opposed to geographic) definition is required because fused with the entity are 'Tupua te Kawa',[68] comprising:

> the intrinsic values that represent the essence of Te Awa Tupua, namely—
>
> *Ko Te Kawa Tuatahi*
>
> (a) *Ko te Awa te mātāpuna o te ora*: the River is the source of spiritual and physical sustenance:
>
> Te Awa Tupua is a spiritual and physical entity that supports and sustains both the life and natural resources within the Whanganui River and the health and well-being of the iwi, hapū, and other communities of the River.
>
> *Ko Te Kawa Tuarua*
>
> (b) *E rere kau mai i te Awa nui mai i te Kahui Maunga ki Tangaroa*: the great River flows from the mountains to the sea:
>
> Te Awa Tupua is an indivisible and living whole from the mountains to the sea, incorporating the Whanganui River and all of its physical and metaphysical elements.

---

[64] Te Urewera Act 2014, s 3.
[65] Te Urewera Act 2014, s 12, sch 1.
[66] Te Urewera Act 2014, ss 100–101.
[67] Te Awa Tupua (Whanganui River Claims Settlement) Act 2017, s 12.
[68] Te Awa Tupua (Whanganui River Claims Settlement) Act 2017, s 13.

Ko Te Kawa Tuatoru

(c) *Ko au te Awa, ko te Awa ko au*: I am the River and the River is me:

The iwi and hapū of the Whanganui River have an inalienable connection with, and responsibility to, Te Awa Tupua and its health and well-being.

Ko Te Kawa Tuawhā

(d) *Ngā manga iti, ngā manga nui e honohono kau ana, ka tupu hei Awa Tupua*: the small and large streams that flow into one another form one River:

Te Awa Tupua is a singular entity comprised of many elements and communities, working collaboratively for the common purpose of the health and well-being of Te Awa Tupua.

Despite their differing definitional approaches, both enactments proceed to confer legal personhood on each of these entities, as well as 'all the rights, powers, duties, and liabilities of a legal person'.[69] Exactly what that means, however, is coloured by the statutory context.

B. Effect of 'Personhood' Status

In the case of Te Urewera, the rights, powers and duties accompanying its personhood status must be exercised and performed 'in the manner provided for in this Act'.[70] Consequently, the overall purpose for and specific provisions of Te Urewera Act 2014 constrain the scope of the personhood designation accorded to the place. Te Urewera is not able to, for instance, establish a farm animal petting zoo or Radiata Pine plantation within its borders, as that would be contrary to the requirement that 'introduced plants and animals are exterminated'.[71] Equally, Te Urewera cannot charge non-commercial users for access, as the legislation 'provide[s] for Te Urewera as a place for public use and enjoyment, for recreation, learning, and spiritual reflection, and as an inspiration for all';[72] whilst requiring that in achieving this purpose, 'the public has freedom of entry and access to Te Urewera'.[73] Section 56 of the enactment then specifies that no prior authorisation is necessary for any 'cultural, recreational, or educational activity' carried out without 'specific gain or reward for that activity'.[74] As noted in section III.A, Parliament has mandated that Te Urewera retain a particular teleology, which then defines the sort of 'person' it is and the actions it may undertake (or permit to be undertaken in respect of it).

There are no equivalent legislative constraints on how Te Awa Tupua's rights, powers and duties may be exercised and performed. However, the Te Awa Tupua (Whanganui River Claims Settlement) Act 2017 does specify what those rights amount to in relation to certain identified pieces of legislation that confer regulatory decision-making powers over

---

[69] Te Urewera Act 2014, s 11(1); Te Awa Tupua (Whanganui River Claims Settlement) Act 2017, s 14(1).
[70] Te Urewera Act 2014, s11(2)(a)(ii).
[71] Te Urewera Act 2014, s 5(1)(b).
[72] Te Urewera Act 2014, s 4(c).
[73] Te Urewera Act 2014, s 5(2).
[74] However, commercial activities in Te Urewera require the granting of a concession, for which a charge may be levied: Te Urewera Act 2014, s 62.

the Whanganui River and its catchment. Decision-makers operating under 25 specified statutes must affirmatively 'recognise and provide' for Te Awa Tupua's personhood status when taking action.[75] This includes the decision-makers' preparing and changing regional policy statements and regional and district plans pursuant to the Resource Management Act 1991, as well as the Taranaki/Whanganui Conservation Board's operating under the National Parks Act 1980. In relation to another three specified statutes, the decision-makers only 'must have particular regard to' that personhood status.[76] This relates to decision-makers working under the Heritage New Zealand Pouhere Taonga Act 2014, Public Works Act 1981 and a large component of the Resource Management Act 1991, including importantly the specific resource consent process for using the river.

These requirements do not, then, have the effect of removing any discretion the decision-makers may have under the relevant enactments, but they do permit the decision-makers to 'consider the Te Awa Tupua status and Tupua te Kawa as determining factors' when they exercise it.[77] Some entities, then, have new, specifically enhanced mandates. For example, the Taranaki/Whanagnui Conservation Board must 'have regard to the spiritual, historical, and cultural significance of the Whanganui River to the Whanganui iwi' and 'seek and have regard to the advice of the trustees of Ngā Tāngata Tiaki o Whanganui … on any matter that involves the spiritual, historical, and cultural significance of the park to the Whanganui iwi'.[78]

As such, the Te Awa Tupua (Whanganui River Claims Settlement) Act 2017 does not expressly constrain how the entity may go about exercising its various legal rights, powers and duties. As discussed in section III.C, those rights, powers and duties are then expressed through a governance arrangement that reflects Māori understandings of the physical river, the human values that relate to it and how these phenomena interact. However, the fact that Te Awa Tupua as an entity remains subject to discretionary decision-making control by a range of regulatory bodies, most particularly the elected representatives of local authorities, means that it has only limited autonomy. It can be, and is, subject to a range of uses by others, over which it has no veto rights. At most, its interests are, in consequence of its new status, accorded some stronger role in the decision-making process, in a manner described in the following section.

C. Establishing a Guardianship Regime for Each Entity

As noted in the introduction to this section, the pre-existing legal status of and form of regulation for each entity has resulted in quite different guardianship structures being created.[79]

---

[75] Te Awa Tupua (Whanganui River Claims Settlement) Act 2017, s 15(2). Other statutes listed include, eg, the Biosecurity Act 1993, Fisheries Act 1996, Local Government Act 2002 and the Wildlife Act 1953. The effect of such requirements is discussed in section III.C.
[76] Te Awa Tupua (Whanganui River Claims Settlement) Act 2017, s 15(3).
[77] Te Awa Tupua (Whanganui River Claims Settlement) Act 2017, s 15(5).
[78] National Parks Act 1980, s 30(2). See also Conservation Act 1987, s 6P(7).
[79] As Trevor Daya-Winterbottom notes, the creation of 'guardians' to provide a representative voice for geographical features in New Zealand dates back to 1973: see T Daya-Winterbottom, 'Personality and Representation in Environmental Law' [2018] *New Zealand Law Journal* 130, 131.

Te Urewera has a reasonably simple model applied to it. The legislation creates a Board[80] that acts for and provides governance to Te Urewera.[81] It does so primarily by preparing and approving a management plan for Te Urewera,[82] which then is implemented by the Chief Executive of Tūhoe Te Uru Taumatua and the Director-General of the Department of Conservation.[83] The Board also may make by-laws to regulate conduct within Te Urewera,[84] as well as issue authorisations and concessions to permit certain otherwise prohibited activities within the entity's boundaries.[85] This Board consists of nine members, six of whom are now appointed by Tūhoe and three of whom are appointed by the Crown. When making decisions:

(a) It must begin by seeking full unanimity.
(b) If this is not possible, then a decision by consensus must be sought.
(c) If this is not initially possible then the chair of the Board may initiate mediation to try and reach consensus.
(d) Finally, if necessary, a vote must be taken on the issue, which requires the support of at least 80 per cent of all Board members and at least two out of three Crown appointees to pass.[86]

Consequently, the guardianship structure of Te Urewera places extensive decision-making and regulatory powers in the hands of representatives of Tūhoe, albeit subject to the requirement that they are used in a way that at least a majority of the Crown's representatives will accept. While those powers are constrained by both the legislative purpose and specific requirements of Te Urewera Act, they still allow for the substantial incorporation of Māori law. The Te Urewera management plan, launched in 2017, is highly innovative and distinctly different from existing conservation management plans in Aotearoa New Zealand and worldwide. It is centred on creating and applying rules to manage the people rather than the land.[87] Its opening words include 'Deliberatively, we are resetting our human relationship and behaviour towards nature. Our disconnection from Te Urewera has changed our humanness. We wish for its return.'[88]

In contrast, Te Awa Tupua has a more complex set of governance arrangements. The primary representative body is the office of Te Pou Tupua, which is 'to be the human face of Te Awa Tupua and act in the name of Te Awa Tupua'.[89] Consisting of two individuals appointed jointly by the Crown and those iwi with interests in the Whanganui River, Te Pou Tupua has a number of specific functions in terms of publicly representing Te Awa Tupua's interests.[90] However, Te Pou Tupua possesses no decision-making power over Te Awa Tupua; its function is to speak for the entity when others are making decisions. The legislation confers upon Te Pou Tupua 'full capacity and all the powers reasonably necessary

---

[80] Te Urewera Act 2014, s 16.
[81] Te Urewera Act 2014, s 17.
[82] Te Urewera Act 2014, ss 18(1)(a), 44–47.
[83] Te Urewera Act 2014, s 50.
[84] Te Urewera Act 2014, ss 18(1)(d), 70.
[85] Te Urewera Act 2014, s 18(1)(e), 57.
[86] Te Urewera Act 2014, ss 33–36.
[87] See 'Te Kawa o Te Urewera' (2017), available at www.ngaituhoe.iwi.nz/te-kawa-o-te-urewera.
[88] ibid 8.
[89] Te Awa Tupua (Whanganui River Claims Settlement) Act 2017, s 18(2).
[90] Te Awa Tupua (Whanganui River Claims Settlement) Act 2017, s 19.

to achieve its purpose and perform and exercise its functions, powers, and duties in accordance with this Act'.[91] It is in turn advised and supported in its activities by Te Karewao,[92] consisting of three representatives from: the trustees of Ngā Tāngata Tiaki o Whanganui;[93] those iwi with interests in the Whanganui river; and the local authorities with resource management obligations to Te Awa Tupua.

An additional body, Te Kōpuka, operates as 'a strategy group for Te Awa Tupua'.[94] Consisting of up to 17 members widely drawn from across commercial, recreational and iwi stakeholders in the river's use, Te Kōpuka's sole role is to create and maintain Te Heke Ngahuru ki Te Awa Tupua – a collaborative document that recognises issues relevant to the health and wellbeing of Te Awa Tupua, identifies a strategy to address these issues and recommends specific actions to deal with them. In so doing, Te Kōpuka is obliged to have particular regard to Te Awa Tupua's status and to Tupua te Kawa.[95] Once Te Heke Ngahuru has been formulated, statutory decision-makers exercising powers over Te Awa Tupua must pay particular regard to it and the recommendations contained therein.

The actual decision over what may and may not be done in relation to Te Awa Tupua then remains with these statutory decision-makers. In particular, local authorities continue to permit or prohibit various activities that affect Te Awa Tupua under the auspices of the Resource Management Act 1991. The difference now is that Whanganui Iwi have legislative certainty that Te Awa Tupua – the interests of this entity, as conceived of in a way that is consistent with Māori understandings of nature and its relationship with human beings – will be recognised and provided for in resource management policy and planning concerning the river. In comparison, before the enactment of Te Awa Tupua Act, Whanganui Iwi only had a legislative expectation that the local authority in this process would 'take into account' any of their relevant iwi planning documents that they had lodged with that authority.[96] In the resource consent process, Whanganui Iwi now have a stronger legislative expectation that the decision-makers will have particular regard to the personhood of the river, in addition to the more general statutory obligation to 'take into account the principles of the Treaty of Waitangi (Te Tiriti o Waitangi)'.[97] That expectation may then be supported by judicial challenge to decisions which fail to meet it, with Te Pou Tupua able to mount such cases on behalf of the entity itself.

Consequently, authority over Te Awa Tupua is subject to an intricate web of processes and procedures. Ultimate decision-making power over the entity continues to rest with, for example, elected local authorities exercising general resource management and other statutory powers. When doing so, however, those local authorities must have particular regard to Te Heke Ngahuru – a strategy for addressing the entity's future health and wellbeing developed by the entity's stakeholders. And any general or specific decisions can only be taken after hearing from Te Pou Tupua, speaking on behalf of Te Awa Tupua itself.

---

[91] Te Awa Tupua (Whanganui River Claims Settlement) Act 2017, s 18(3).
[92] Te Awa Tupua (Whanganui River Claims Settlement) Act 2017, s 27.
[93] This is the entity that manages the settlement assets given to Whanganui Iwi as part of their 2014 Treaty Settlement with the Crown.
[94] Te Awa Tupua (Whanganui River Claims Settlement) Act 2017, s 29.
[95] Te Awa Tupua (Whanganui River Claims Settlement) Act 2017, s 30(3).
[96] See Resource Management Act 1991, ss 66(2A)(a), 74(2A).
[97] Resource Management Act 1991, s 8.

Such an approach requires those decision-makers to consider the Whanganui River in a new way that directly reflects Māori understandings and values, and they must accord these a greater weight than under general law. However, it is not then a given that those expressed interests will be adopted in a final decision. While they must be 'recognised and provided' for or given 'particular regard', depending upon the statutory decision-making context in question, they do not remove the decision-maker's discretion as to what may be done to, on or in Te Awa Tupua.

D. Ongoing Constraints

The legislation defining both entities imposes a range of constraints on their capacity to act. One common constraint is a virtual prohibition on alienating any land that comprises the entity.[98] Consequently, neither Te Urewera Board nor Te Pou Tupua can determine that a part of the entity is no longer required for its purposes (although new pieces of land may be added to it). This 'lockbox' model for the two entities reflects their intrinsic nature; 'an indivisible and living whole', in the language of Te Awa Tupua (Whanganui River Claims Settlement) Act 2017.[99] Another common constraint is that each entity is subject to 'the liabilities and obligations placed on a person' by income tax legislation.[100] So, while each place may not face a natural person's inevitable death, it cannot escape the requirement to contribute taxes to the state.

Further external constraints are then imposed upon each entity. Section 41 of Te Urewera Act 2014 continues to apply the general laws of Aotearoa New Zealand to and within the new entity:

Except as expressly provided in this Act, this Act and the deed of settlement do not limit—

(a) any enactment or rule of law; or
(b) the statutory functions and powers exercised by a body within Te Urewera, including the statutory powers and functions of—
   (i) a local authority; or
   (ii) the New Zealand Fish and Game Council; or
   (iii) a Fish and Game Council with jurisdiction in the locality of Te Urewera.

In particular, any mining activities authorised under the Crown Minerals Act 1991 still may take place without requiring any further authorisation under Te Urewera Act 2014.[101] However, the designation of Te Urewera as being the equivalent of Crown-owned land under schedule 4 to the Crown Minerals Act 1991 radically limits the sorts of mining activity that presently may take place within its boundaries.[102] In practice, only minor, non-invasive forms of prospecting are permitted, with further extraction of mineral resources effectively prohibited under current law. Also retaining powers over Te Urewera is the Fish and Game Council, which has a statutory mandate to enforce hunting and fishing

---

[98] Te Urewera Act 2014, s 13; Te Awa Tupua (Whanganui River Claims Settlement) Act 2017, s 43(1).
[99] Te Awa Tupua (Whanganui River Claims Settlement) Act 2017, s 12.
[100] Te Urewera Act 2014, s 40(2); Te Awa Tupua (Whanganui River Claims Settlement) Act 2017, s 25(1).
[101] Te Urewera Act 2014, s 56(b).
[102] Te Urewera Act 2014, s 64(1); Crown Minerals Act 1991, s 61(1A).

regulations under the Conservation Act 1987, part 5A. While this Council and Te Urewera's Board are required to 'work together in a coordinated and cooperative way',[103] fish and game rangers still may exercise their extensive powers under section 40 of the Conservation Act 1987, to stop and search persons and seize property within Te Urewera's borders.

A range of existing legal interests and entitlements also continue to apply in respect of Te Awa Tupua. In particular, section 46(2) mandates that:

> The following matters are preserved and not affected by the vesting of the Crown-owned parts of the Whanganui River ...:
> (a) existing public use of, and access to and across, the Whanganui River, including navigation rights; and
> (b) existing private property rights, including customary rights and title; and
> (c) the existing rights of State-owned enterprises and mixed ownership model companies; and
> (d) existing resource consents and other existing statutory authorisations; and
> (e) fishing rights recognised under—
>   (i) the Conservation Act 1987;
>   (ii) the Fisheries Act 1996;
>   (iii) the Treaty of Waitangi (Fisheries Claims) Settlement Act 1992; and
> (f) the existing ownership of, and consents for, lawful structures in or on any part of the Whanganui River, and any existing lawful rights to use, access, occupy, maintain, remove, repair, or demolish those structures; and
> (g) the statutory functions, powers, and duties of the relevant local authorities, except as otherwise provided in this Act; and
> (h) the application of any other enactment, unless expressly provided otherwise by this Act.

Consequently, although Te Awa Tupua is described as being 'an indivisible whole', in reality parts of the entity remain in the ownership of private individuals, while existing legal rights to make use of the entity continue to apply.

IV. Conclusions

In this chapter, we suggest that the legal recognition of places-as-persons represents a principled compromise that permits redress for the Crown wrongs of the past, whilst creating the basis for a new future relationship. We also argue that this recognition changes the way in which these places are conceived of by the nation and how public decision-makers will interact with them in the future. In a similar vein, Katherine Saunders has argued convincingly that the development should be considered constitutional in nature, as 'it highlights the role law may play in contests over fundamental values, and brings attention to the contribution that this legislation makes to ongoing debate about land, authority and colonisation'.[104] She draws attention to the way in which the governing structures created for each entity permit ongoing deliberation over contesting purposes and principles. They do so by reframing that contest, 'reflect[ing] the understanding that settlement is

---

[103] Te Urewera Act 2014, s 61.
[104] Saunders, '"Beyond Human Ownership?"' (n 11) 231.

contingent upon the maintenance of relationships between peoples, and, perhaps between peoples and land'.[105] In other words, the recognition of places-as-persons is not merely the conclusion of a settlement process between Māori and the Crown. It also marks the beginning of a new and ongoing process of joint stewardship for the entity in question, which commences from a prioritised Māori worldview of place.

If, then, it is the case that the recent recognition of places-as-people constitutes a constitutional development in Aotearoa New Zealand, a number of questions arise for the future. Exactly how and where do these new legal persons sit in our constitutional structures? For as well as being persons in the eyes of the law, they also are a novel form of public authority over a geographic area that is able to exercise decision-making power over how others may use it. This dualistic nature – both person subject to law and also regulator of others – raises interesting issues about the entities' place within the nation's wider legal framework. To take but one example, section 29 of the New Zealand Bill of Rights Act 1990 states 'the provisions of this Bill of Rights apply, so far as practicable, for the benefit of all legal persons as well as for the benefit of all natural persons'. How, then, might the rights guaranteed by that legislation apply to these entities as against other public actors? And as exercisers of public powers and functions in terms of section 3(b) of that legislation, how do the duties in that Bill of Rights apply to these entities themselves?

Another set of questions involves whether the governance processes for the entities in question really are significantly different from other environmental decision-making processes being negotiated between the Crown and Iwi. For example, forms of 'co-management' or 'co-governance' of natural resources between the Crown and iwi have become relatively commonplace in recent years.[106] Does the recognition of the entities in question as persons then add anything meaningful to such arrangements? Our suspicion is that it does, and that focusing governing arrangements on Māori principles and values said to be inherent in the entity itself will result in different decisions being reached. For example, the management plan formed for Te Urewera is markedly different in both rhetoric and content from those in place for the country's National Parks.[107] But exactly how (and even how much) this difference will manifest is a matter that requires further attention.

Beyond these questions, however, we believe that the recognition of these places-as-persons tells a story about legal potential that is worth noting. It demonstrates the possibilities of law's acting as a bridge between worlds. By adapting a concept from one legal tradition to incorporate the understandings of another, granting legal personality to Te Urewera and the Whanganui River has permitted the Crown and Iwi to reconcile over past Crown breaches of the Treaty and move their relationship forward. This action, however, represents more than a purely pragmatic form of problem solving. It represents a respectful way of acknowledging the meaning of these places for Māori that can operate within the existing legal order. That the Crown and iwi were able to find a way to use legal mechanisms to achieve this social outcome seems, to us, a hopeful and encouraging story to tell about the law.

---

[105] ibid 233.
[106] Auditor General, *Principles for Effectively Governing Natural Resources* (February 2016), available at https://www.oag.govt.nz/2016/co-governance/docs/co-governance-amended.pdf. As an example, see Waikato-Tainui Raupatu Claims (Waikato River) Settlement Act 2010.
[107] See text from n 57 of this chapter onwards.

PART 3

Public Law, Criminal Law and Private Law

12
Changing Boundaries: Crime, Punishment and Public Law

DAVID FELDMAN*

I. Due Process Values and Criminal Justice before the 1970s

In the 1970s, administrative law first penetrated parts of the criminal justice system operating outside courtrooms. Whilst judges in criminal trials had long tended to give defendants (many unrepresented) fair hearings according to law, the law did far less to safeguard fairness in relation to criminal investigations, charging decisions and the implementation of punishments. The 'Judges' Rules' gave administrative guidance to police officers when questioning suspects,[1] but otherwise investigative practice depended on police discretion, to which the law gave wide scope.[2] In relation to control of prosecutions and the operation of penal institutions, too, official discretion reigned.

By the mid-1980s, by contrast, police powers were more carefully regulated, decisions to prosecute (or not) were made independently of the police and were increasingly subject to judicial review, important aspects of prison life (especially discipline) had been opened to judicial scrutiny, and post-sentence discretion had started to be challengeable before courts. The 1970s were a turning point in subjecting several fields of criminal justice to public law principles. This was achieved by a combination of statutory and institutional reform, and in some areas by extension of judicial review. Factors influencing developments often originated well before the 1970s, and much of the real change was realised significantly later, but it was in the 1970s that aspirations began to turn into principled reforms.

Section II identifies some social, professional and political changes that reduced complacency about the police, prisons and Ministers. Subsequent sections examine their

---

* I am grateful to Phillippa Kaufmann QC, Justice Maxwell, President of the Court of Appeal of Victoria, Shona Wilson Stark, Findlay Stark and participants at the Third Biennial Public Law Conference for valuable insights, comments and suggestions. Remaining errors are my own.

[1] *Police Enquiries: Memorandum by HM Judges of the King's Bench Division* (1912). These administrative guidelines were promulgated by the King's Bench judges at the request of the Home Secretary, Reginald McKenna, in 1912, in an attempt to make police practice consistent and reduce the risk that trial judges would exclude statements which they regarded as improperly obtained. See *R v Voisin* [1918] 1 KB 531, 539, fn 29. The Rules, revised from time to time, were circulated to forces as a Home Office Circular. The 1964 version was published in the Law Reports: *Note* [1964] 1 WLR 152. They were superseded when the Police and Criminal Evidence Act 1984 and its associated Codes of Practice came into force on 1 January 1986.

[2] See, eg, *Kuruma v R* [1955] AC 197.

effects in the contexts of policing (section III), charging decisions (section IV) and prison discipline (section V).[3] Section VI then draws together the threads. Some reference is made to other aspects of criminal justice in which important developments have taken place, including the parole system, but they are not at the heart of the chapter; and other important matters, like the use of Convention rights under the European Convention on Human Rights (ECHR) and the Human Rights Act 1998 to require authorities to conduct effective inquiries into deaths and some mistreatment of people in custody, lie outside the scope of the chapter.

II. Social and Legal Attitudes in the 1960s and 1970s

Deference to age and all kinds of authority had begun to wane in the 1960s, especially among young people.[4] This spawned a rash of satirical magazines and television and radio programmes.[5] *Private Eye* was launched in 1961. On television, the BBC, usually a pillar of the establishment, broadcast *That Was The Week That Was* in 1962 and 1963, with young satirists who had a sharp eye for political hypocrisy and pomposity. This was followed by *The Frost Report* in 1966 and 1967 on BBC television, *Week Ending* on Friday evenings on BBC Radio 4 from 1970 to 1998, and *Not the Nine O'Clock News* on BBC2 television between 1979 and 1982. The independent broadcaster ITV followed suit with a Central Independent Television satirical puppet show, *Spitting Image*, from 1984 until 1996, which took advantage of changing times to be even more scurrilous than the BBC's shows.

The risk of oppression when authority was insufficiently limited and scrutinised, especially in closed institutions, was shown in popular dramas such as *The Winslow Boy*,[6] *The Caine Mutiny*[7] and *Mutiny on the Bounty*.[8] Concern of this sort chimed with the more general reduction of deference to authority. The police came under special scrutiny. Constables, in theory merely citizens in uniform, enjoyed considerable social authority, reinforcing social order through more or less informal social interactions. Their power was legitimated and incorporated into popular culture through books, films and television programmes like *Dixon of Dock Green*, which ran on BBC TV from 1955 to 1976.[9]

---

[3] Other fields, including the sentencing process, regimes and conditions of imprisonment, and early release on licence of prisoners serving a sentence, are relevant but space prevents their examination here.

[4] B Levin, *The Pendulum Years: Britain in the Sixties* (London, Jonathan Cape, 1970) gives an excellent flavour of that decade.

[5] SH Bailey, 'The Big Four' in TT Arvind et al (eds), *Executive Decision-Making and the Courts: Revisiting the Origins of Judicial Review* (Oxford, Hart Publishing, forthcoming).

[6] *The Winslow Boy*, a 1946 play by Terence Rattigan based on the real-life case of a cadet at a naval academy who was dismissed after being wrongly accused of theft, was made into a popular film in 1948.

[7] This was a 1951 novel by Herman Wouk, which was made into a play in 1953 and a successful film in 1954, about a naval officer who started to suffer from mental illness, made his crew's lives a misery and was removed from his command by junior officers who then faced court martial for mutiny.

[8] This was the real-life story of a harsh Royal Navy captain who, in 1789, was overwhelmed and set loose in an open boat by mutineers including Fletcher Christian. It was made into successful films in 1935 and 1962.

[9] Jack Warner played George Dixon, a beat constable and later (when he became too infirm to patrol) station sergeant, whose combination of humanity, fairness and firmness in administering the law bolstered the belief in the police service as benevolent and worthy of respect and support. (In Warner's first appearance as Dixon in a film, *The Blue Lamp*, produced by Ealing Studios in 1950, his character was shot dead, but this did not prevent his reincarnation on television.) See R Reiner, *The Politics of the Police*, 1st edn (Brighton, Wheatsheaf, 1985) ch 5; see now 4th edn (Oxford, Oxford University Press, 2010) ch 6, on the media's role in promoting an idealised view of the police.

But television also noted changes in police strategies and methods: the BBC's *Z Cars*, set in the north of England and rather grittier than *Dixon*, was broadcast from 1962 to 1978; and ITV's *The Sweeney*, based on the Metropolitan Police Flying Squad and screened from 1975 to 1978, portrayed a rough edge to policing in London.

Public institutions came under examination by official inquiries and non-governmental organisations (NGOs). Trades Unions and the Labour Party had long been suspicious of the police, whom they regarded as agents of employers and the establishment against workers and left-wing movements.[10] Labour Governments of 1964–70 and 1974–79 were particularly willing to cast light on police practices, but it had become common for Conservative as well as Labour Governments to use Royal Commissions and other official inquiries for investigation and policy-making in an attempt to depoliticise them. For example, the Criminal Law Revision Committee, established in 1959 by then Conservative Home Secretary RA Butler, influenced reform of criminal law and evidence. In the 1970s an independent inquiry into a botched investigation into the murder of Maxwell Confait exposed serious flaws in the ways in which the police had treated young and mentally handicapped suspects,[11] and helped to persuade the Labour Home Secretary, Merlyn Rees, to establish the Royal Commission on Criminal Procedure in 1978.[12] This laid the ground for major innovations in police powers and the conduct of prosecutions.

Other influential inquiries and reports came from NGOs operating in the field of criminal justice, either conducting inquiries and campaigning (like JUSTICE, founded in 1957) or supporting or conducting litigation allied to campaigns (like the National Council for Civil Liberties (NCCL), founded in 1934, which later became Liberty). They helped to dispel complacency and generated a head of steam behind efforts for reform. Official inquiries also cast light on heavy-handed and discriminatory policing practices in relation to minority ethnic and cultural groups, and the social conditions that made those practices potentially explosive. A classic example was Lord Justice Scarman's public inquiry into anti-police disorders in London in 1974.[13]

Emerging academic disciplines also contributed to changing social perceptions. From the 1960s to the 1980s, socio-legal studies, criminology and penology took off. Empirical researchers gained access to courts and police forces, and studied their day-to-day dynamics and their interactions with each other and the public. They then provided theoretical models that helped to explain what appeared to be aberrant or counter-productive official behaviour, at least when judged by classical rule-of-law criteria. A generation of penologists conducted rigorous, empirical research on prisons, based on extended periods of observation and interviews with prisoners, prison officers and governors, and revealed in a scholarly way the power structures and informal management systems that operated alongside, and tended to subvert the fairness of, formal systems.[14]

---

[10] For some background, see KD Ewing and CA Gearty, *The Struggle for Civil Liberties: Political Freedom and the Rule of Law in Britain, 1914–1945* (Oxford, Oxford University Press, 2000).

[11] *The Confait Case: Report by the Hon Sir Henry Fisher*, HC Paper 90 of 1977–78 (London, HMSO, 1977).

[12] Royal Commission on Criminal Procedure, *Report*, Cmnd 8092 (London, HMSO, 1981).

[13] L Scarman, *Report of the Inquiry on the Red Lion Square Disorders of 15 June 1974*, Cmnd 5919 (London, HMSO, 1975).

[14] The USA led the way, but scholarship in the UK was growing: see, eg, T Morris and P Morris, *Pentonville: A Sociological Study of an English Prison* (London, Routledge & Kegan Paul, 1963); T Morris, 'Research on the Prison Community' in *Collected Studies in Criminology*, vol 1 (Strasbourg, Council of Europe, 1967). See the

They painted a realistic picture of the dynamics operating within police forces, prosecuting agencies and prisons, puncturing the complacency which earlier representations of the police and courts had induced.[15] This was not popular with the authorities, and it took some time for the research and researchers to establish their trustworthiness and usefulness with policy-makers.[16]

Two linked developments that made judicial scrutiny of the policing and prisons possible were the advent of publicly funded legal aid and the appearance of solicitors and barristers who could make litigation by suspects and prisoners legally and financially viable. After the Legal Aid and Assistance Act 1949 and later the Legal Aid Act 1974, courts became accessible, and people charged with criminal offences could reliably secure competent representation. BM Birnberg & Co (now Birnberg Peirce), established in the 1960s 'to provide what was then hardly recognised as a focus of legal practice, the establishment and upholding of the "civil rights and liberties" of individuals under threat of unjust or oppressive treatment by police or state agencies or authorities',[17] and Bindman & Partners (now Bindmans LLP), formed in 1974, were pioneers. They instructed barristers who came to share their concerns, and formed a closely knit group of specialists in police and prison law, including Louis Blom-Cooper, Anthony Lester and Stephen Sedley. The next generation took up the cudgels, including Edward Fitzgerald and Phillippa Kaufmann. Gradually, strategic litigation regarding prisoners was made possible by the concentration of cases in the hands of a small number of solicitors and barristers, sometimes supported and coordinated by NGOs.[18] In law schools, some socially committed future practitioners encountered academics who taught and wrote on civil liberties, stimulating a new generation to practise in the field.[19]

Judges too were becoming more alert to the dangers of authoritarianism. By the 1960s and 1970s most were post-Victorian, and a growing number had fought in World War II, usually with responsibility for service personnel from all social classes. When put on the High Court bench they exercised authority with confidence, and were not afraid to stand up to Ministers and officials. Conscious of the importance of order, they were nonetheless alive to the risks that accompanied unchecked power over others in a closed, hierarchical

---

overviews in N Walker, *Crime and Punishment in Britain: An Analysis of the Penal System in Theory, Law and Practice* (Edinburgh, Edinburgh University Press, 1965; 2nd edn, 1967); JD McClean and JC Wood, *Criminal Justice and the Treatment of Offenders* (London, Sweet & Maxwell, 1969) 91–124; and R Hood and R Sparks, *Key Issues in Criminology* (London, Weidenfeld & Nicolson, 1970) ch 8.

[15] John Baldwin, David Brown, David Dixon, John Lambert, Ken Lidstone, Mike McConville, Rod Morgan, Robert Reiner, Andrew Sanders, David J Smith and Richard Young are among the most prominent of a large number of researchers.

[16] See J Baldwin, 'Flies on the Legal Carcass: The Disreputable Study of Judicial Administration' (1993–94) 16 *Holdsworth Law Review* 22 (Professor Baldwin's inaugural lecture as Professor of Judicial Administration at the University of Birmingham); and J Baldwin, 'Four Decades of the Institute of Judicial Administration: 1968–2012', University of Birmingham (April 2012), available at https://www.birmingham.ac.uk/research/activity/ija/history/index.aspx.

[17] This is the description by Birnberg Peirce: see their website at http://www.birnbergpeirce.co.uk/who-we-are/.

[18] This paragraph has gained from insights generously offered by Phillippa Kaufmann QC in private conversation on 29 November 2018.

[19] See, eg, H Street, *Freedom, The Individual and The Law*, 1st edn (Harmondsworth, Penguin, 1963; 4th edn, 1977); LH Leigh, *Police Powers in England and Wales*, 1st edn (London, Butterworths, 1975; 2nd edn, 1986).

institution. Sir Tasker Watkins VC was the most famous of them[20] but was not alone. Lord Denning MR was perhaps the least favourably disposed towards suspects and prisoners; he had been too young to serve in World War I (born 1899) and too old for World War II, whilst Roskill LJ (born 1911) had contracted tuberculosis, so was unfit for military service,[21] and Shaw LJ limped as a result of polio. But the judges who extended judicial review over prisons included war heroes. Ackner LJ had served in the Royal Artillery before contracting polio in 1942 and being transferred to the Admiralty Naval Law Branch.[22] Cumming-Bruce LJ and Widgery LJ had been Lt-Colonels in the Royal Artillery. Widgery had won the French Croix de Guerre, been appointed to the Order of Leopold (the highest order of knighthood in Belgium) and appointed OBE, going on after the war to the rank of Brigadier in the Territorial Army, while Megaw LJ, also in the Royal Artillery, had reached the rank of Colonel. Ormrod LJ, a physician and lecturer in forensic medicine by background, had served as a Major in the Royal Army Medical Corps in Normandy and North-Western Europe from 1942 to 1945.[23] Geoffrey Lane LJ and Waller LJ had served with distinction in the RAF, the former starting as a bomber pilot flying missions over Germany and occupied France, then on other dangerous and important missions, being awarded the Air Force Cross,[24] and the latter as a Wing Commander mentioned in despatches and awarded the OBE. Such experiences generate a mixture of authority and sympathy with those under authority.

Shaw LJ had been a member from 1970–74, and Vice-Chairman 1973–74, of the Parole Board, while Lord Widgery CJ had been Vice-Chairman of the Home Office Advisory Council on the Penal System (1966–70). Such judges were markedly less likely to defer on matters of penal policy to the Home Office or to prison governors than previous or, indeed, post-war generations of senior judges. In short, the social environment in which police and courts operated was better informed, more open to reform, less complacent, and more

---

[20] See the description of an exchange in *R v Secretary of State for Education and Science, ex parte Hardy* (DC, 27 July 1988) by S Sedley, *Lions Under the Throne: Essays on the History of English Public Law* (Cambridge, Cambridge University Press, 2015) 14–15; Sedley's comment in fn 43, 'Tasker Watkins, who had won a VC in the war, usually got his way', can hardly be bettered. For Sir Tasker's history, see M Pill, 'Watkins, Sir Tasker, Judge' in *Oxford Dictionary of National Biography*, online edn (Oxford, Oxford University Press, 2013), available at http://www.oxforddnb.com.ezp.lib.cam.ac.uk/view/10.1093/ref:odnb/9780198614128.001.0001/odnb-9780198614128-e-99120?rskey=YPzbNI&result=2; Anon, 'Sir Tasker Watkins, VC', Obituary in *Daily Telegraph* (10 September 2007), available at https://www.telegraph.co.uk/news/obituaries/1562637/Sir-Tasker-Watkins-VC.html; and see also 'Sir Tasker Watkins VC, GBE', The Comprehensive Guide to the Victoria & George Cross, available at www.vconline.org.uk/sir-tasker-watkins-vc/4588487548.
[21] Lord Templeman, 'Roskill, Eustace Wentworth, Baron Roskill (1911-1996), Judge' in *Oxford Dictionary of National Biography*, online edn (Oxford, Oxford University Press, 2004), available at http://www.oxforddnb.com.ezp.lib.cam.ac.uk/view/10.1093/ref:odnb/9780198614128.001.0001/odnb-9780198614128-e-63307?rskey=FGMgHA&result=1.
[22] M Beloff, 'Ackner, Desmond James Conrad, Baron Ackner (1920-2006), Judge' in *Oxford Dictionary of National Biography*, online edn (Oxford, Oxford University Press, 2010), available at http://www.oxforddnb.com.ezp.lib.cam.ac.uk/search?q=Ackner&searchBtn=Search&isQuickSearch=true.
[23] R Dunn, 'Ormrod, Sir Roger Fray Greenwood (1911–1992), Judge' in *Oxford Dictionary of National Biography*, online edn (Oxford, Oxford University Press, 2004), available at http://www.oxforddnb.com.ezp.lib.cam.ac.uk/search?q=Roger+Ormrod&searchBtn=Search&isQuickSearch=true.
[24] I Judge and C Colston, 'Lane, Geoffrey Dawson, Baron Lane (1918–2005), Judge' in *Oxford Dictionary of National Biography*, online edition (Oxford, Oxford University Press, 2009), available at http://www.oxforddnb.com.ezp.lib.cam.ac.uk/view/10.1093/ref:odnb/9780198614128.001.0001/odnb-9780198614128-e-95983?rskey=nRhyky&result=1.

confident and better supported in challenging abuse of power in state institutions than had previously been the case.

A final factor facilitating legal intervention in criminal justice was the developing content and scope, particularly in the 1960s and 1970s, of judicial review of administrative action more generally. The Tribunals and Inquiries Acts of 1958 and 1971 repealed many 'ouster' clauses in earlier statutes. Landmark judicial decisions helped to systematise the law limited by the technical restrictions on remedies. Grounds of review such as excess of jurisdiction and natural justice or fairness were being strengthened and made generally applicable, while new grounds, such as breach of legitimate expectation, were starting to emerge.[25] Academic work helped to make the field more principled.[26] Following a report by the Law Commission for England and Wales, a reformed Order 53 of the Rules of the Supreme Court provided a unified system for applying for prerogative orders[27] and so facilitated public law challenges. The 'application for judicial review' procedure required litigants to bring proceedings in the High Court, but until 1982 it remained possible to seek declarations and injunctions in public law matters more cheaply in the county court.[28]

To sum up, by the later 1970s social and legal conditions and attitudes had moved to a point where it became far easier than previously to advocate legal control of official discretion within the criminal justice system, both in Parliament and in the courts. How did this affect policing, prosecution and prisons?

III. Policing and Public Law

Despite revelations in the 1960s, such as the way Sheffield police officers used offensive weapons, including a rhino whip, to beat suspects into confessing,[29] public support for the police remained fairly consistent. Whilst people were increasingly aware of the risk of police malpractice, courts did not consider it their job to oversee police behaviour as long as officers did not induce confessions or instigate criminal offences. Legal powers of the police were seen as haphazard and inadequate, so both judges and senior officers might condone excess of power where they thought it justified by investigative exigency. As Lord Denning MR pointed out in *Ghani v Jones*:

> No magistrate – no judge even – has any power to issue a search warrant for murder. He can issue a search warrant for stolen goods and for some statutory offences, such as coinage. But not for

---

[25] See, eg, *Ridge v Baldwin* [1964] AC 40; *Re HK (an infant)* [1967] 2 QB 617; *Anisminic v Foreign Commonwealth Commission* [1969] 2 AC 147; *R v Liverpool Corporation, ex parte Liverpool Taxi Fleet Operators Association* [1972] 2 QB 299.

[26] See, eg, SA de Smith, *Judicial Review of Administrative Action*, 1st edn (London, Sweet & Maxwell, 1959) and subsequent editions; HWR Wade, *Administrative Law*, 1st edn (Oxford, Clarendon Press, 1961) and subsequent editions; JAG Griffith and H Street, *Principles of Administrative Law*, 1st edn (London, Pitmans, 1952) and subsequent editions.

[27] Law Commission, *Remedies in Administrative Law*, Report No 73, Cmnd 6407 (London, HMSO, 1976). 'Orders' replaced 'writs' in the nomenclature of certiorari, prohibition and mandamus.

[28] This route was effectively cut off by *O'Reilly v Mackman* [1983] 2 AC 237.

[29] Much credit went to a campaign in 1963 by *The Sheffield Telegraph* newspaper and its editor David Hopkinson (obituary, *The Times*, 17 October 2018), which led Conservative Home Secretary Henry Brooke to establish an inquiry.

murder. Not to dig for the body. Nor to look for the axe, the gun or the poison dregs. The police have to get the consent of the householder to enter if they can: or, if not, do it by stealth or by force. Somehow they seem to manage. No decent person refuses them permission. If he does, he is probably implicated in some way or other. So the police risk an action for trespass. It is not much risk.[30]

Denning considered it to be his role to facilitate rather than control police action. When the 'Birmingham Six', who had been convicted of bombing pubs in Birmingham in 1974, sought to bring a civil action against the Chief Constable of the West Midlands alleging that police officers had beaten confessions out of them, he said:

> If the six men fail, it will mean that much time and money and worry will have been expended by many people for no good purpose. If the six men win, it will mean that the police were guilty of perjury, and they were guilty of violence and threats, that the confessions were involuntary and were improperly admitted in evidence, and that the convictions were erroneous. That would mean that the Home Secretary would have either to recommend they be pardoned or he would have to remit the case to the Court of Appeal under section 17 of the Criminal Appeal Act 1968. This is such an appalling vista that every sensible person in the land would say: 'It cannot be right that these actions should go any further'.[31]

It took a further 11 years before the Court of Appeal overturned the men's convictions on the ground that they were unsafe and unsatisfactory, and a decade after that before the vindicated defendants received huge sums in compensation for their wrongful conviction and imprisonment.

Turning a blind eye to police malpractice, however, facilitated excess and abuse of authority and corruption. Scandals in the Metropolitan Police (including cases of bribery of officers and mistreatment of suspects) led, in 1972, to the appointment as Metropolitan Police Commissioner of Sir Robert Mark, who set about driving out corrupt officers and cleaning up the force. In 1979, Sir David McNee, the Metropolitan Police Commissioner, accepted that officers' frustration with inadequate, unclear legal powers of arrest and search meant that many officers, 'early in their careers, learned to use methods bordering on trickery or stealth in their investigations', including 'so-called pious perjury', which might 'led to even more serious perjury on other matters later in their careers'.[32] Some judges consciously sought to modernise the law by creating powers at common law that did not exist under statute. For example, in a 1968 judgment concerning the execution of search warrants, Diplock LJ sought to rebalance police powers and property rights, where the matter was, in his view, untrammelled by authority.[33] This made it look as if judges were trespassing on the province of Parliament, and made legislative intervention desirable if not inevitable.[34]

Nevertheless, there was social concern about the extent to which the use of police powers was effectively in the unfettered control of constables on the beat, and influenced

---

[30] *Ghani v Jones* [1970] 1 QB 693, 705.
[31] *Hunter v Chief Constable of the West Midland Police Force* [1980] 2 QB 283, 323–24. An appeal to the House of Lords was dismissed without reference to this passage: [1982] AC 529.
[32] JUSTICE, *Pre-Trial Criminal Procedure: Police Powers and the Prosecution Process* (London, Sweet & Maxwell, 1979) 4.
[33] In *Chic Fashions (West Wales) Ltd v Jones* [1968] 2 QB 299, 315, 318.
[34] D Feldman, *The Law Relating to Entry, Search and Seizure* (London, Butterworths, 1986) 14–15.

by the culture of a particular police station, shift or squad rather than by consistent rules or principles.[35] Complaints of racial discrimination in policing grew. Riots in protest at the use of stop-and-search powers on the street encouraged empirical research that showed how far such practices reflected racial profiling without evidence that it was related to a greater likelihood of offending by members of the targeted community.[36] When added to a number of scandals about police corruption and ineffectiveness, it produced a public and political view of police forces as out of control.

High-profile miscarriages of justice and campaigning by JUSTICE and others[37] led to the establishment of the Royal Commission on Criminal Procedure in 1978. The Commission bolstered its work with a body of specially commissioned empirical research. Reporting in 1981 to a Conservative Government, its main recommendations were unpopular with many rank-and-file police officers on whom the Government was soon to depend during the miners' strike of 1984–85, when many came to see the police as waging a class war on behalf of the Conservative Party. But the political head of steam behind reform was such that the Government made legislative time available to push through the legislation over several parliamentary sessions. The Police and Criminal Evidence Act 1984 and its associated Codes of Practice, provided for the first time a more or less comprehensive statutory code of powers of stop and search, arrest, detention and questioning of suspects, and taking fingerprints and samples. Additional powers for the police were balanced by procedural safeguards for suspects' rights, such as access to legal advice in the police station, and to a significant extent overseen by courts as well as senior officers and inspectors of constabulary.

Litigation could not have achieved that, nor could it secure comprehensive accountability for senior police officers' decisions on deployment of resources as between different kinds of crimes and threats to public order. Nevertheless, it provided publicity that could generate political pressure and legislative reform. For example, Raymond Blackburn, a former MP, used litigation to direct public attention to the failure of the Metropolitan Police to control illegal gambling and pornography. The courts would not tell the Commissioner how to deploy his forces against gambling, although the campaign led to legislation establishing the Gaming Board for Great Britain to regulate the gaming industry.[38] But courts were otherwise unable to exercise much control; for example, no remedy was available against a police force that had called off pursuit of suspected thieves on encountering armed youths blocking the pavement,[39] and it remains the case that courts will not lightly review a decision

---

[35] DJ Smith and J Gray, *Police and People in London: The PSI Report* (Aldershot, Gower, 1985) ch 16.
[36] See, eg, P Stevens and CF Willis, *Race, Crime and Arrests*, Home Office Research Study No 58 (London, Home Office Research and Policy Unit, 1979); Lord Scarman, *The Brixton Disorders*, Cmnd 8427 (London, HMSO, 1981) 64–65; M McConville, 'Search of Persons and Premises: New Data From London' [1983] *Crim LR* 605, 605–14; Smith and Gray, *Police and People in London* (n 35) ch 15.
[37] See, eg, *The Confait Case: Report by the Hon Sir Henry Fisher* (n 11); JUSTICE, *Pre-Trial Criminal Procedure: Police Powers and the Prosecution Process* (n 32).
[38] Betting and Gaming Act 1968, after *R v Commissioner of Police of the Metropolis, ex parte Blackburn* [1968] 2 QB 118. For less productive litigation regarding pornography in Soho, see *R v Commissioner of Police of the Metropolis, ex parte Blackburn (No 3)* [1973] QB 241; *R v Commissioner of Police of the Metropolis, ex parte Blackburn* The Times, 6 March 1980 (CA).
[39] *R v Oxford, ex parte Levey* The Times, 1 November 1986 (CA).

to end an investigation prematurely on the ground that continuing it would be contrary to the public interest.[40]

Nonetheless, efforts were being made to create a principled framework for judicial scrutiny of police action. A major practitioners' textbook was soon to be published on civil actions against the police.[41] The police resented it (and its authors), not least because the book encouraged and facilitated the work of other lawyers in commencing similar litigation. Other texts for practitioners helped to create a principled framework within which to litigate,[42] and students' texts contributed to developing a generation of young lawyers who saw the control of public power as important and had the equipment to use law to advance it.[43] In relation to public order policing, the 1980s saw legislative systematisation and modernisation of parts of the law of public order, affected by the Scarman Report on the Brixton riots but also by a Home Office review of powers to control demonstrations and meetings and a Law Commission report on criminal offences.[44] Considering that the Public Order Bill that became the Act of 1986 was introduced to Parliament in the wake of the massive disturbances provoked by unions' and police officers' tactics during the miners' strike of 1984–85, the legislation was remarkably balanced in its treatment of the competing interests in freedom of association and expression and in the maintenance of order.

However, the Public Order Act 1986 left untouched police discretion in relation to preventing breaches of the peace, and even in statutory contexts judicial review of police discretion relating to prevention of public disorder had little success. Whilst constables (like all citizens) have a duty at common law to take reasonable steps to stop breaches of the peace, their discretion is wide, and judges respect the judgement of officers having to make immediate decisions in difficult circumstances, so they could never be successfully challenged on the ground of *Wednesbury* unreasonableness.[45] The rare successes followed the enactment of the Human Rights Act 1998, and usually involved police behaviour that goes beyond a mere excess of discretion and violates a Convention right, as in *R (Laporte) v Chief Constable of Gloucestershire*.[46] Even in this context, the English courts and the

---

[40] *R (Corner House Research) v Director of the Serious Fraud Office* [2009] 1 AC 756, where the House of Lords held that the discretion of the Director to discontinue an investigation into supply of military equipment to Saudi Arabia was wide enough to take account of wider, public-interest considerations, including the Saudi Arabian Government's threatened refusal to offer further cooperation in security and intelligence matters; this was not an irrelevant consideration.

[41] R Clayton and H Tomlinson, *Civil Actions against the Police* (London, Sweet & Maxwell, 1987; 3rd edn, 2005).

[42] See, eg, Feldman, *The Law Relating to Entry, Search and Seizure* (n 34); R Stone, *The Law of Entry, Search and Seizure* (London, Sweet & Maxwell, 1985; 5th edn, Oxford, Oxford University Press, 2013).

[43] See, eg, SH Bailey, DJ Harris and BL Jones, *Civil Liberties Cases and Materials* (London, Butterworths, 1980) and subsequent editions; and the growing number of student texts to include substantial coverage of both freedoms and judicial review, eg SA de Smith, *Constitutional and Administrative Law*, 1st edn (Harmondsworth, Penguin, 1971) and subsequent editions; M Zander, *Cases and Materials on the English Legal System* (London, Weidenfeld & Nicolson, 1973; 2nd edn, 1975) ch 3.

[44] Home Office, *Review of the Public Order Act 1936 and Related Legislation*, Cmnd 7891 (London, HMSO, 1980); and The Law Commission, *Criminal Law: Offences Relating to Public Order*, Report No 123 (London, HMSO, 1983).

[45] *Moss v McLachlan* [1984] IRLR 76; *G v Chief Superintendent of Police, Stroud* (1988) 86 Cr App R 92; *Lewis v Chief Constable of Greater Manchester* Independent, 23 October 1991 (CA). Similar leeway is allowed under statutory powers: see, eg, *Kent v Metropolitan Police Commissioner* The Times, 13 May 1981 (CA). See D Galligan, 'Preserving Public Protest: The Legal Approach' in L Gostin (ed), *Civil Liberties in Conflict* (London, Routledge, 1988) 39–64.

[46] *R (Laporte) v Chief Constable of Gloucestershire* [2007] 2 AC 105.

European Court of Human Rights have shown themselves keener to give the police room to preserve the peace than to insist on a rigorous, consistent interpretation of the right not to be deprived of liberty.[47] Nevertheless, litigation has allowed courts to establish guidelines for the police regarding considerations that should be taken into account when deciding how to conduct public order policing, and there have more recently been signs of a more demanding standard of scrutiny creeping in, at any rate in extreme circumstances. In *ZH v Commissioner of Police of the Metropolis*, for example, a particularly egregious case, Lord Dyson MR said:

> I accept that operational discretion is important to the police … But operational discretion is not sacrosanct. It cannot be invoked by the police in order to give them immunity from liability for everything that they do … One is bound to have some sympathy for the police in this case. They were intent on securing the best interests of everyone, not least ZH. But as the judge said, they behaved as if they were faced with an emergency when there was no emergency.[48]

But on the whole, little judicial control was or is exercised over decisions about policing, except where statute has provided strict rules for police to follow or human rights are engaged. Even in the latter context, it remains rare for judges to hold that public order policing measures are disproportionate to a legitimate aim so as to violate rights and be unlawful. The main effect of agitation in the 1970s was to produce more legislation and greater managerial rather than judicial control of the police.

IV. Prosecution Decisions and Control of Discretion

Concerns about policing in the 1970s were aggravated by the absence of an independent prosecution service. Nearly all criminal prosecutions were brought by police officers, and in magistrates' courts officers would usually also present the cases, although by 1970 it was gradually becoming more common for solicitors to prosecute, either from a prosecuting solicitors' department of the local authority – in 1970 just over two-thirds of police forces had a prosecuting solicitor – or from local private practice.[49] 'The solicitor acts upon the instructions of the police; the solicitor may advise, but the chief constable is not bound by that advice.'[50] Police officers who had investigated a case could lack the objectivity needed to assess the strength of evidence fairly when deciding whether a court was likely to convict, and appreciate the need to consider the strength of any public interest in prosecuting when deciding whether to do so. There was a risk of abuse where the prosecutor was part of the investigation and had direct dealings with the suspect. Police officers were not trained advocates or lawyers, increasing the risk that convictions would be successfully appealed on procedural grounds. There was evidence that the police sometimes failed to disclose evidence that could help the defence. At the level of summary proceedings in

---

[47] See, eg, *Re E (A Child)* [2009] 1 AC 536; *Austin v Commissioner of Police of the Metropolis* [2009] 1 AC 564; *Austin v United Kingdom* (2012) 55 EHRR 14.
[48] *ZH v Commissioner of Police of the Metropolis* [2013] 1 WLR 3021, [90]. I am grateful to Dr Shona Wilson Stark for this point.
[49] JUSTICE, *The Prosecution Process in England and Wales* (London, JUSTICE, 1970) 3–5, 19–20.
[50] Royal Commission on Criminal Procedure, *Report* (n 12) 127.

magistrates' courts there was a great deal of variation between the principles applied and the way procedures were followed in different police areas.[51]

Historically, courts had left the institution of prosecutions to the prosecutors. A declaration of guilt or innocence in civil proceedings could not bind criminal courts, which were masters of their own procedures and empowered to prevent abuse of process by staying proceedings.[52] It was perhaps possible to seek certiorari to bring up and quash general policies as to prosecution. If, for example, 'a chief constable were to issue a directive to his men that no person should be prosecuted for stealing any goods less than £100 in value[,] I should have thought that the court could countermand it. He would be failing in his duty to enforce the law',[53] but in practice it was never done. The prerogative writ of prohibition was available when an inferior court was contemplating hearing a case that was outside its jurisdiction, but could not be used to challenge prosecutorial discretion or outflank criminal courts. Second, criminal law was concerned with the public good, while civil law protected individual goods. People should not be liable to have their liberties restricted by civil injunction unless the proceedings were brought by a recognised guardian of the public interest, particularly the Attorney-General as *parens patriae* or a local authority using its statutory power under the Local Government Acts.[54] Administrative controls were available; the Attorney-General could exercise the prerogative power to enter a *nolle prosequi* to stop proceedings, and the Director of Public Prosecutions (DPP) had statutory power to take over a prosecution and offer no evidence.

Nevertheless, concern about inconsistency of practice and lack of accountability had stimulated proposals for reform, especially from the 1960s. A series of reports recommended that there should be a review of police officers acting as prosecutors,[55] and that England and Wales should move to something like the Scottish system, where the Lord Advocate (in effect the Scottish equivalent of the Attorney-General) was responsible for prosecuting all but the most minor offences, assisted by the Solicitor-General for Scotland, a number of Advocates-Depute and local Procurators Fiscal.[56] The Royal Commission on Criminal Procedure in 1981 recognised the unfairness of local variations in methods of disposal of suspects, but recommended establishing a locally- rather than nationally-based Crown prosecutor responsible to local police authorities, but working on national guidelines issued by the DPP.[57] After much debate, the Prosecution of Offences Act 1985 instead instituted a national Crown Prosecution Service (CPS), headed by the DPP, who was operationally independent of, though accountable to, the Attorney-General.

This did much to make prosecutorial decision-making consistent across England and Wales. By putting the service on a statutory basis, it also made it more amenable to administrative law. The DPP's duty to draw up and publish a Code for Crown Prosecutors

---

[51] JUSTICE, *The Prosecution Process in England and Wales* (n 49) 5–8.
[52] *Imperial Tobacco Ltd v Attorney-General* [1981] AC 718; D Feldman, 'Declarations and The Control of Prosecutions' [1981] *Crim LR* 25.
[53] *R v Commissioner of Metropolitan Police, ex parte Blackburn* [1968] (n 38) 336 (Lord Denning MR).
[54] *Gouriet v Union of Post Office Workers and others* [1978] AC 435; D Feldman, 'Injunctions and the Criminal Law' (1979) 42 *MLR* 369.
[55] Royal Commission on the Police, *Report*, Cmnd 1782 (London, HMSO, 1962) [381].
[56] JUSTICE, *The Prosecution Process in England and Wales* (n 49) 9–13.
[57] Royal Commission on Criminal Procedure, *Report* (n 12) [6.40]–[6.41], [6.57]–[6.59], [7.25].

to guide decision-making[58] provided ammunition for judicial review, as it might be regarded as unreasonable not to follow published guidance. Judicial review extended to individual charging decisions as well as policies. The CPS was a public decision-maker exercising statutory functions, and reviewable accordingly. By 1994, courts were reviewing, at the instance of alleged victims of crime, decisions not to prosecute if made '(1) because of some unlawful policy ...; or (2) because the Director of Public Prosecutions failed to act in accordance with her own settled policy as set out in the Code; or (3) because the decision was perverse' in the sense of being one 'at which no reasonable prosecutor could have arrived'.[59] In 2013, the CPS formalised an internal review of a decision not to charge or to discontinue a prosecution if an alleged victim requests it, through the Victims' Right to Review (VRR) Scheme, introduced to give effect to EU Directive 2012/29 on the minimum rights of victims of crime.[60] The CPS retains a discretion not to follow the guidance and to limit its application, as long as that can be justified on judicial review principles.[61] Courts will not usually entertain an application for judicial review until the CPS has had an opportunity to conduct an internal review. Where the CPS has, at the request of a victim, already carefully reconsidered a decision not to prosecute, the decision will only rarely be judicially reviewed.[62]

The DPP and CPS now issue guidance on particular kinds of offence, such as prosecution of journalists for offences committed while undertaking journalistic activities.[63] And judges have required the DPP to issue special guidance relating to people who assist others to die, in order to help the law to meet the rule-of-law standard of reasonable predictability needed to make it justifiable to interfere with respect for people's private lives under Article 8 ECHR. In *R (Purdy) v DPP*,[64] the House of Lords decided that the crime of assisting suicide engaged the right to respect for private life in Article 8 of the ECHR. In order to make that law compatible with Article 8, the House of Lords held that the DPP had an obligation to issue guidance to prosecutors as to the factors that should be taken into account when deciding whether to bring prosecutions for assisting suicide. This gave legal significance to the guidance, and placed a significant burden on the DPP as, effectively, a legislator.[65]

To sum up, between 1977 and 1985, continued concern about police controlling prosecutions, expressed by scholars, NGOs and the Royal Commission on Criminal Procedure, became concentrated on Government and politicians to a point at which prosecution

---

[58] Prosecution of Offences Act 1985, s 10.
[59] *R v DPP, ex parte Chaudhary* [1995] 1 Cr App R 136, 141 (Kennedy LJ).
[60] CPS, 'Victims' Right to Review Scheme' (2016 revised version), available at https://www.cps.gov.uk/legal-guidance/victims-right-review-scheme.
[61] *R (Hayes) v CPS* [2018] 1 WLR 4106.
[62] *R (L) v DPP* [2013] EWHC 1752 (Admin). See further *R (C) v DPP* [2019] 1 WLR 917 as noted by P Hungerford-Welch, 'Right to Review Decision, Not to Prosecute: *R (on the application of C) v Director of Public Prosecutions*' [2019] *Crim LR* 55.
[63] CPS, 'Media: Prosecuting Cases where Public Servants Have Disclosed Confidential Information to Journalists', available at https://www.cps.gov.uk/legal-guidance/media-prosecuting-cases-where-public-servants-have-disclosed-confidential. All such cases must be referred to Special Crime Division.
[64] *R (Purdy) v DPP* [2010] 1 AC 345.
[65] DPP, 'Suicide: Policy for Prosecutors in respect of Cases of Encouraging or Assisting Suicide' (originally issued in 2010 and updated in 2014), available at https://www.cps.gov.uk/legal-guidance/suicide-policy-prosecutors-respect-cases-encouraging-or-assisting-suicide.

decisions were taken away from the police, and decisions by the CPS then became progressively opened to scrutiny by reference to guidance drawn up and published by the DPP. This blurred the barrier between criminal and civil jurisdictions, allowing public law to intrude increasingly into criminal justice.

V. Invisible Places: Penal Institutions

Prisons were closed institutions in the early 1970s. Most people rarely, if ever, experienced them; those who did tended to be people who were suspected or convicted of crimes. Prison gates were locked, and this kept ordinary people out as well as prisoners in. Prisoners had no political leverage. It was regarded as inevitable and necessary that prisons should be authoritarian, hierarchical places in which ideas of openness and fairness had little traction. The legal framework for prisons, contained in the Prison Act 1952 and the Prison Rules (then in the 1964 edition),[66] imposed certain duties on the Home Secretary and prison governors; but the Court of Appeal held in 1972 that those were regulatory, not mandatory, and did not give a right of action to a prisoner in respect of a failure to comply with the obligations.[67] Disciplinary decisions were seen as entirely separate from criminal charges, even if they arose out of the same facts. The power of prison governors over prisoners was as great as that of a ship's master over crew and passengers. Prisons were akin to the armed services in this respect. The idea of subjecting conditions or the system of discipline to outside oversight seemed absurd, and 'prisoners' rights' an oxymoron. A prisoner might be released 'on parole' before the end of his or her sentence, but that would be a matter for the Home Secretary, exercising the royal prerogative of mercy on behalf of the Crown, on advice from the prison governor. It was entirely discretionary. A Parole Board was established in 1968 under the Criminal Justice Act 1967, which for the first time put early release on a statutory footing. The Board advised the Home Secretary, but the final decision remained within the Home Secretary's discretion.

Legal protection was limited. A dictum of Atkin LJ was usually thought to have restricted the prerogative writs of certiorari and prohibition to cases brought against judicial or quasi-judicial decision-makers making final decisions about rights.[68] In reality, both writs were historically flexible and capable of being shaped according to need, but this was not established authoritatively until much later. Prisoners were not usually regarded as having rights, and Governors and Boards of Visitors were not obliged to act judicially or quasi-judicially. In *Ex parte Fry*, Lord Goddard CJ opined that the prerogative writs, including certiorari, did not extend to the domestic authorities of prisons (except for habeas corpus in cases of unauthorised detention), and the Court of Appeal affirmed the decision, though on the ground that the court should, even if it had jurisdiction, exercise its discretion to refuse relief in such cases.[69] In a setting where many prisoners were controlled by a small number

---

[66] SI 1964/388.
[67] *Becker v Home Office* [1972] 2 QB 407.
[68] *R v Electricity Commissioners, ex parte London Electricity Joint Committee (1920) Ltd* [1924] 1 KB 171, 204–05 (Atkin LJ).
[69] *Ex parte Fry* [1954] 1 WLR 730, 733.

of staff, coercive, hierarchical structures were seen as essential, and external review of governors' decisions would have threatened to undermine the coercive authority of the staff and increase the risk of disorder or mutiny.

Lord Denning MR summarised the prevailing view on prisoners trenchantly in *Fraser v Mudge*,[70] in which a prisoner sought a declaration that a Board of Visitors would act unlawfully if it commenced inquiring into charges against him without giving him the opportunity to have legal representation. The prisoner was represented by Stephen Sedley, briefed by Bindman & Partners, soon to be a familiar pairing in prison cases. Both section 47(2) of the Prison Act 1952 and the Prison Rules made pursuant to the Act provided that a person charged was to have a fair opportunity of presenting his case, before both the Governor and a Board of Visitors. In a case concerning an accusation of doping a greyhound, being inquired into by the Greyhound Racing Association, Lord Denning had thought that it might be proper to allow legal representation.[71] But in *Fraser v Mudge* Lord Denning was clear that this did not extend to breaches of prison discipline. In the armed forces, it was 'of the first importance that the cases should be decided quickly. If legal representation were allowed, it would mean considerable delay. So also with breaches of prison discipline.'[72]

The court accepted that fairness was required: 'Those who hear the cases must, of course, act fairly. They must let the man know the charge and give him a proper opportunity of presenting his case. But that can be done and is done without the matter being held up for legal representation.'[73] There was, however, this difference: in the armed forces, courts martial provided a system of formal justice for serious cases. Prisons lacked such a system, and the need for it was not obvious to policy-makers: prisoners, unlike sailors, soldiers and airmen, were there because they had committed criminal offences, and were seen as having forfeited normal civil rights for the duration of their sentences. Provision for petitioning the Secretary of State sufficed, and impliedly excluded certiorari.

It is, therefore, surprising that it was in relation to prisons that administrative law had its first and most extensive impact on criminal justice. The first, big doctrinal step came in a series of challenges to the disciplinary powers of prison governors and Boards of Visitors. Governors had very wide powers to sentence prisoners for breaches of prison discipline. Proceedings were usually summary, although for more serious offences the governor could refer the matter to a Board of Visitors, whose varied responsibilities as external monitors of prison life included adjudicating on serious disciplinary charges against prisoners. Members often included a number of lay magistrates. In practice, both governors and Boards of Visitors tended to support the word of prison officers against prisoners, and accused prisoners facing sanctions including loss of privileges, solitary confinement and loss of parole had few fair-hearing rights. Prisoners could petition the Home Secretary (in England and Wales) seeking remission of disciplinary sanctions, but there was no judicial redress.

The decisive turn came in *R v Board of Visitors of Hull Prison, ex parte St Germain and others*,[74] where prisoners who had allegedly been involved in prison riots at Hull Prison

---

[70] *Fraser v Mudge* [1975] 1 WLR 1132.
[71] *Pett v Greyhound Racing Association* [1969] 1 QB 125.
[72] *Fraser v Mudge* (n 70) 1133.
[73] ibid 1133–34; see also 1134 (Roskill LJ).
[74] *R v Board of Visitors of Hull Prison, ex parte St Germain and others* [1978] QB 678. Bindman & Partners representing Saxton, one of the prisoners, briefed Michael Beloff, who also represented other applicants. Andrew Collins, later a High Court judge, appeared for Hague. Harry Woolf represented the Visitors, led in the Court of Appeal by Philip Otton QC.

sought certiorari to quash disciplinary awards, including loss of 150 days' remission, made against them, arguing that the Board of Visitors had failed to accord them natural justice. They argued that the duty to act fairly was, since *Ridge v Baldwin* and subsequent cases, of general application; Boards of Visitors were not exempt. The Visitors argued that certiorari was not available in respect of internal disciplinary processes, relying on cases relating to prisons and the police.[75] The issue was one of the court's jurisdiction to grant the remedy, which could not be affected by developments in the law of natural justice and fairness. Next, they argued that their disciplinary decisions did not affect the prisoners' legal rights, since early release was a privilege, not a right. Andrew Collins, for one of the prisoners, argued that certiorari could run to Boards of Visitors, although the court had a discretion as to whether to issue it, and would not do so where the disciplinary body was an individual person with administrative authority rather than a separate body exercising disciplinary functions.[76]

The Divisional Court broadly accepted the Visitors' jurisdictional argument. Whilst the boundaries to the scope of certiorari were not, and should never be, firmly settled, the Governor acting alone would certainly not be subject to certiorari,[77] and there was no basis for distinguishing between the Governor's disciplinary function and that of the Visitors, especially in view of the right to petition the Secretary of State.

The Court of Appeal, however, reversed the decision. Megaw, Shaw and Waller LJJ all agreed that Boards of Visitors were required to act judicially and comply with natural justice when exercising disciplinary functions.[78] Disciplinary decisions generally were no longer exempt from judicial control,[79] and the Court did not regard the prison context as preventing certiorari from running, as Boards of Visitors exercising disciplinary functions were independent of ordinary prison administration. The reviewability of prison governors remained unclear. Megaw LJ did not consider that certiorari would lie against an officer in a hierarchy.[80] Waller LJ reserved his opinion on the point.[81] Shaw LJ found it difficult to find a principled basis for distinguishing between governors and Boards of Visitors in this respect, and, unlike the Divisional Court, thought that both (rather than neither) were amenable to certiorari.[82]

When the prisoners in *Ex parte St Germain* returned to the Divisional Court, having established that Boards of Visitors were required to act fairly and were amenable to certiorari, the court held that several of them had been treated unfairly and unlawfully, because the Board had taken into account evidence from the Governor based on written statements from prison officers who were not named and did not give evidence at the hearing. The prisoners did not know the names of the officers or the contents of the statements on which the Governor's evidence was based. Some prisoners were not allowed to call witnesses to support their defences, including alibis.[83] The court said:

---

[75] *Ex parte Fry* (n 69); *R v Commissioner of Police of the Metropolis, ex parte Parker* [1953] 1 WLR 1150.
[76] Collins relied on *R v Secretary of State for War, ex parte Martyn* [1949] 1 All ER 242, and *ex parte Parker* (n 75).
[77] *R v Board of Visitors of Hull Prison, ex parte St Germain* (n 74) 691 (Lord Widgery CJ).
[78] *R v Board of Visitors of Hull Prison, ex parte St Germain* [1979] QB 425.
[79] *R v Gaming Board for Great Britain, ex parte Benaim and Khaida* [1970] 2 QB 417, 425, 428, and *Buckoke v Greater London Council* [1971] Ch 655, 669 (Lord Denning MR).
[80] *R v Board of Visitors of Hull Prison, ex parte St Germain* (n 78) 447.
[81] ibid 458.
[82] ibid 456.
[83] *R v Board of Visitors of Hull Prison, ex parte St Germain (No 2)* [1979] 1 WLR 1401 (Lord Widgery CJ, Geoffrey Lane and Ackner LJJ).

The rules of natural justice are a compendious reference to those rules of procedure which the common law requires persons who exercise quasi-judicial functions to observe (*R v Deputy Industrial Injuries Commissioner, ex parte Moore*[84]). Natural justice requires that the procedure before any tribunal which is acting judicially shall be fair in all the circumstances. For a long time the courts have without objection from Parliament supplemented procedure laid down in legislation where they have found that to be necessary for this purpose (see *Wiseman v Borneman*[85] per Lord Reid).[86]

Thus while the strict rules of evidence were not applicable and Boards of Visitors retained some discretion as to their procedure, they could not adopt a procedure that deprived prisoners of a fair hearing. Considerations of administrative convenience would not deprive the prisoners of the right to know the case against them, or of the right to call evidence and cross-examine witnesses if that was essential to the fairness of the hearing. Requirements vary with context, and Boards must take account of the nature of the charge, the nature of the defence, and what in the circumstances is needed for the person charged to have a fair chance to put his or her case and counter the evidence supporting the charge.

This encouraged prisoners to initiate a steady flow of cases, which gave the courts opportunities to rethink their approach to the status of prisoners and prisons. Determined litigators such as Mark Leech had notable successes.[87] Before long, judges held that where disciplinary charges raise difficult issues of law or fact, and the consequences for the prisoner of an adverse finding might be serious, fairness may require a prisoner to be allowed legal representation. Boards of Visitors had no duty to allow legal representation, but they had a discretion to do so, and the discretion had to be exercised fairly in the light of the seriousness of the charge, the capacity of the prisoner and the legal complexity of the case, among other considerations.[88]

What of the position of prison governors, left open in *Ex parte Hague*? By the early 1980s, key members of the legal profession came to share Shaw LJ's view that it was impossible to find a principled distinction between disciplinary functions exercised by governors and those exercised by Boards of Visitors; both should be required to act fairly and be subject to judicial review. The view of 'Treasury Devils', or Junior Treasury Counsel, who represent the executive in most of its litigation, was particularly important. A key moment came in *Leech v Deputy Governor of Parkhurst Prison*:[89] John Laws, 'Treasury Devil' representing the Deputy Governor,

> declined to invite the House of Lords to reverse the High Court's landmark decision in *St Germain* that the procedures of prison boards of visitors were justiciable – a reversal that would have won

---

[84] *R v Deputy Industrial Injuries Commissioner, ex parte Moore* [1965] 1 QB 456, 487.
[85] *Wiseman v Borneman* [1971] AC 297, 308.
[86] *Ex parte St Germain (No 2)* (n 83) 1408 in the single judgment of the court, read by Geoffrey Lane LJ.
[87] See, eg, *R v Board of Visitors of Hull Prison, ex parte St Germain* (n 78); *R v Board of Visitors of Hull Prison, ex parte St Germain (No 2)* (n 83); *R v Secretary of State for the Home Department, ex parte Leech (No 1)* [1991] COD 491; *Leech v Secretary of State for Scotland* 1992 SC 89; *R v Secretary of State for the Home Department, ex parte Leech (No 2)* [1994] QB 198; *Leech v United Kingdom* (1994) 18 EHRR CD 116; *R v Deputy Governor of Parkhurst Prison, ex parte Hague* [1992] 1 AC 58.
[88] *R v Secretary of State for the Home Department, ex parte Tarrant* [1985] QB 251. The prisoners were represented by Stephen Sedley QC, Edward Fitzgerald, Andrew Collins and Nigel Seed, briefed by BM Birnberg & Co and other solicitors.
[89] *Leech v Deputy Governor of Parkhurst Prison* [1988] AC 533, 554, 556–57.

him the case – and instead undertook the sisyphean task of attempting to carve out an exception for adjudications by prison governors.[90]

Thereafter certiorari could be deployed against prison governors and deputy governors in respect of disciplinary hearings, at least where the nature of the governor's alleged error was such as to deprive him or her of jurisdiction to hear the charge.[91]

These developments did not transform prisons or even ensure consistent accountability. Much remained – and still remains – to be done.[92] When the Human Rights Act 1998 made Article 6 ECHR part of national law, and our courts followed the Strasbourg Court in treating a disciplinary charge as capable of being a 'criminal charge' for the purpose of bringing protections of Article 6 into play, serious disciplinary charges that put a prisoner at risk of being sentenced to extra days of imprisonment had become equivalent in many respects to a trial before a criminal court. Judgments of the European Court of Human Rights and domestic courts were to lead to a transfer of decision-making from the Home Secretary to sentencing judges and the Parole Board, and in due course an extension of judicial review to the Parole Board. Such things take time, but the process started in the 1970s.

One effect has been to make us reconsider the relationship between prison disciplinary decisions and criminal law. While disciplinary decisions regarding prisons were seen as entirely separate from criminal charges against prisoners that arose out of the same facts, and prison Boards of Visitors were not regarded as 'courts of competent jurisdiction', the rule against double jeopardy did not prevent a person from being charged sequentially with a criminal offence and a breach of prison discipline.[93] In *R v Robinson (Anthony)*,[94] however, the Divisional Court held that it was unlawful for an Independent Adjudicator to determine a disciplinary charge of escape contrary to the Prison Rules, and to impose a sentence of 14 days' imprisonment, when a charge of escape from lawful custody, at common law, was pending before the Crown Court, for which the defendant was later convicted and sentenced to two months' imprisonment.[95] Developments in English and European human rights law led to the inexorable conclusion that '[w]here a prison adjudication proceeding involves punishment by loss of liberty such proceedings amount to "criminal proceedings" by a body of competent jurisdiction and the rule against double jeopardy applies'.[96] The borderline between disciplinary proceedings and criminal proceedings has become permeable as public law principles have flowed into the field of prison discipline.

---

[90] S Sedley, 'The Lion Beneath the Throne: Law as History', The 16th Annual Sir David Williams Lecture, Faculty of Law, University of Cambridge (5 March 2016) 5, available at https://www.cpl.law.cam.ac.uk/sites/www.law.cam. ac.uk/files/images/www.cpl.law.cam.ac.uk/legacy/File/stephen_sedley_2016_david_williams_lecture.pdf. Stephen Sedley was counsel for Leech.
[91] See, eg, *R v Governor of Pentonville Prison, ex parte Watkins* [1992] COD 329; *R v Governor of Crumlin Road Prison, ex parte Jordan* [1992] NI 148.
[92] See, eg, R Morgan, 'Prisons Accountability Revisited' [1993] *PL* 314; G Richardson, *Law, Process and Custody: Prisoners and Patients* (London, Weidenfeld & Nicolson, 1993) chs 5–8.
[93] *R v Hogan* [1960] 2 QB 513.
[94] *R v Robinson (Anthony)* [2018] QB 941.
[95] The defendant contended that the later, criminal sentence was voidable on account of double jeopardy. The Court held that the earlier, disciplinary sentence was void, because it was so erroneous in law to expose the defendant to a risk of double jeopardy, when, for reasons of policy, it was wrong to allow 'prisoner adjudications … to prevent or disable the Crown Court from proceedings to exercise its proper jurisdiction in relation to criminal law': *Robinson* (n 94) [19].
[96] ibid [25], disapproving *R v Hogan* (n 93).

A series of social influences continued to change expectations of prison regimes. The work of organisations such as JUSTICE, the National Council for Civil Liberties (now Liberty), the National Association for the Care and Resettlement of Officers (NACRO) and the Howard League for Penal Reform in publicising problems and conditions encouraged reform through government and Parliament as well as the courts.[97] Public figures with a long-standing concern about prison conditions and treatment of prisoners, most famously Lord Longford, and some formerly celebrated politicians who served prison sentences and publicised their experiences,[98] kept issues in the public eye. Pressure grew to take seriously the injunction (now in Rule 3 of the Prison Rules 1999 (SI 1999/728)), 'The purpose of the training and treatment of convicted prisoners shall be to encourage and assist them to lead a good and useful life.' Prisoners themselves became advocates for change. Since his release, Mark Leech has published excellent books for prisoners, staff and others on prisons and prison law.[99]

This kept the state of prisons fitfully in the consciousness of politicians, and stimulated some significant developments. First, following a review of the Prison Service by Mr Justice May,[100] the Conservative Government created the office of Chief Inspector of Prisons in 1982.[101] The Office became a potent force for prison reform from 1987, when former Circuit Judge, His Honour Sir Stephen Tumim, was appointed to the office and, instead of merely reporting to the Home Secretary through official channels, publicised his findings and concerns widely, becoming something of a media personality. He was followed by retired army General Sir David Ramsbotham, a dedicated reformer, and a former Director of JUSTICE, Dame Anne Owers. The Office has become a safeguard and advocate on prison conditions and the treatment of offenders.

In 1991, Lord Justice (later Lord) Woolf reported on a riot by prisoners at Strangeways Prison, where prisoners had been complaining, without effect, about conditions and other matters. The Woolf Inquiry was unusual in that Sir Harry Woolf was joined by another judge (Judge Tumim, Chief Inspector of Prisons) and assisted by a sociology professor specialising in prisons and policing, Professor Rod Morgan. They adopted a procedure that included seminars in prisons and interviews with prisoners. The Report[102] recommended major changes in the way in which prisons were run. This further stimulated a growing literature. Stephen Livingstone, an academic, and Tim Owen QC produced a practitioners' text, *Prison Law* (first published by Oxford University Press in 1993), which itself encouraged further interest and inventiveness among practitioners and NGOs.[103]

---

[97] See, eg, JUSTICE, *Punishment in Prison* (London, Justice, 1983); V Stern, *Bricks of Shame: Britain's Prisons* (Harmondsworth, Penguin, 1987).

[98] See, eg, J Archer, *A Prison Diary*, vols 1–3 (London, Pan, 2003); J Aitken, *Porridge and Passion* (London, Continuum, 2005).

[99] M Leech, *The Prisoners' Handbook* (Oxford, Oxford University Press, 1995); M Leech, *The Prisons Handbook 2018* (High Peak, prisons.org.uk, 2018) with Foreword by D Gauke MP, Secretary of State for Justice; M Leech, *The Cell Companion 2018/19* (Bury, Lancs: prisons.org.uk, 2018). Leech's website, available at http://markleech.com/, provides a wealth of information about prisons.

[100] JD May (Chairman), *Committee of Inquiry into the United Kingdom Prison Services: Report*, vols 1–2, Cmnd 7673 (London, HMSO, 1979).

[101] Criminal Justice Act 1982, s 57(1), inserting s 5A into the Prison Act 1952.

[102] Lord Justice Woolf and His Honour Judge Stephen Tumim, *Prison Disturbances 1990*, Cm 1456 (London, HMSO, 1991).

[103] The current edition is T Owen and A Macdonald (eds), *Livingstone, Owen and Macdonald on Prison Law*, 5th edn (Oxford, Oxford University Press, 2015).

Among the changes that followed was the replacement of the disciplinary powers of prison Boards of Visitors, who were no longer seen as sufficiently independent of the prison administration to satisfy the independence requirement in Article 6(1) ECHR after the Human Rights Act 1998 took effect, as it became clear that adjudicating on disciplinary charges where there was a risk of a sentence of additional loss of liberty involved what the European Court of Human Rights regarded as a 'criminal charge' for the purposes of the procedural protections provided for in Article 6 ECHR.[104] Whilst disciplinary charges that are not serious enough to lead to a sentence of additional days of imprisonment are still heard by the Governor, more serious charges, or a charge which for some other reason it is expedient to refer to an Independent Adjudicator (who is a District Judge (Magistrates' Courts), formerly known as stipendiary magistrate),[105] must be so referred.

VI. Conclusion

Since the 1970s, in the context of what one may loosely call the 'criminal justice' domain, the gradual adoption of public law has occurred by way of a gradual accumulation of public inquiries, socially sensitive politicians, and litigation before increasingly informed and critical judges. Achieving this depended on there being pressure from outside the legal system for greater accountability of coercive institutions, triggered by increasing public and political understanding of previously hidden practices and conditions. This additional knowledge came from empirical sociologists and from pressure groups, aided by specialist solicitors and barristers, litigants supported by legal aid, and an active group of NGOs. Courts were more likely and able to respond to such developments in some fields than in others; where courts were unable or unwilling to move in, legislation was needed. Where courts decided to extend their supervision to an area of criminal justice, it was usually as a result of the application to that field of doctrinal or procedural changes first made in other contexts and applied by analogy to particular contexts of criminal justice. But while judges could help to change procedures, it required Parliament to create and reform institutions. Constitutionalising criminal justice required both techniques. They were not isolated from each other or from the social trends that fuelled reform. Six particular elements seem particularly important to the story.

First, there developed a perception that (i) there were particular problems in the administration of different aspects of criminal justice, (ii) there were inadequate, or insufficiently reliable and accessible, means of resolving those problems within the institutions of criminal justice themselves, and (iii) it mattered. The personnel of public law and politics needed to be aware of the problems and care about them, before they could use public law principles, procedures and remedies to try to offer assistance in them. To alert the personnel of public law and inform public opinion so as to make change acceptable, activists, NGOs, scholars and people who had been on the receiving end of the system needed to do research, share their knowledge and experiences with people who might be able to help and with society more broadly, build networks for action, and make use

---

[104] See *Ezeh and Connors v United Kingdom* (2004) 39 EHRR 1.
[105] Prison Rules 1999 (SI 1999/728), rr 53–53A.

of journalists and broadcasters (today social media would be included), lobby political representatives for administrative action and, if necessary, legislative change, and, in the last resort, litigate.

Second, social and cultural conditions were needed in which a questioning attitude was adopted to claims to traditional or unaccountable authority. Political leaders had to be reformers by inclination, or at least open-minded enough to take seriously informed criticisms of the system, to initiate inquiries and to be ready to legislate in the light of their recommendations. For the common law to play a part in reform, judges had to share this attitude; they needed to be alive to the dangers of unconstrained power exercised by unaccountable people in closed settings, and had to have respect for the idea of law as a system in which relevantly similar situations should be governed by similar rules and principles. Alongside a commitment to principled consistency, they (or at least the more senior of them) needed to be prepared to reassess previously accepted decisions or assumptions about which situations are relevantly similar, and what remedies could be used in different contexts and for different purposes.

Third, litigants with potentially viable cases needed access to legal professionals who had imbibed, or were open to, the latest knowledge about the criminal justice system and were concerned about it, and who also felt that it was constitutionally and professionally proper to address problems through law. These professionals had to understand the practice and law of policing or prisons. It helped that they were in touch with the networks mentioned above. But they also needed to have their fingers on the pulse of the living body of public law as a whole. They were then able to draw forensically on developing principles that seemed inconsistent with current practices in the particular field of criminal justice.

Fourth, litigants and legal professionals needed either a source of funding for legal activity, in the form of the legal aid system, or lawyers willing to cross-subsidise this work from their other earnings, or both. State generosity inspired by respect for the rule of law was bolstered by individuals' willingness sometimes to act pro bono.

Fifth, arguments could not respectably be addressed to courts, or could not be advanced with reasonable hope of success, until a sound, doctrinal basis for them had developed in public law generally. In this respect, the 1970s were a fertile time. The prospect for judicially extending principles of fairness to prison disciplinary matters would have been weak had a general duty of fairness not been articulated in a case about dismissing a Chief Constable. If there is a hint in another context that a boundary-fence is weakening, imaginative lawyers can generalise it. This is how the common law develops.[106]

Sixth, the judges needed to be confident that they would get their way, and that Ministers and administrators would accept judgments and be prepared to change institutions and procedures to give effect to them.

In the 1970s and early 1980s, the UK generally, and England and Wales in particular, benefited from each of these elements being present together to a significant degree. It is hard to maintain this confluence. Several of the factors are now under pressure, or have passed away, at least temporarily. To the extent to which they can be maintained, both the rule of law and constitutional government may be upheld and strengthened.

---

[106] For an assessment, see A Lester, 'English Judges as Law Makers' [1993] *PL* 269.

13

Discretionary Power and Consistency: Is the Sentencing Discretion Different?

CHRIS MAXWELL*

Ultimately every sentence imposed represents the sentencing judge's instinctive synthesis of all the various aspects involved in the punitive process.[1]

There must be a synthesising of the relevant factors. In that process, greater and lesser weight will be allocated to some factors depending on their relevance to the person convicted and his or her crime. Ultimately, community and legal values are translated into a number of years, months and days. That process must involve an instinctive judgment.[2]

'Instinctive synthesis' is a concept unique to Australian sentencing jurisprudence. The term was first coined in 1975, by the Full Court of the Supreme Court of Victoria, as a way of capturing what was evidently seen as the special character of the sentencing decision.[3] Its place at the centre of sentencing orthodoxy was confirmed by the High Court of Australia in 2005.[4]

The administration of the criminal law involves 'individualised justice', the High Court has held, 'the attainment of which is acknowledged to involve the exercise of a wide sentencing discretion'.[5] In order to do justice in the particular case, the judge must be allowed 'as much flexibility in sentencing as is consonant with consistency of approach and as accords with the statutory regime that applies'.[6]

These characteristics of the sentencing discretion have been held – as a matter of principle – to preclude recourse to mechanisms, such as sentencing guidelines, designed to produce reasonable consistency of outcome. Practical attempts to guide the exercise

---

* The author has been President of the Court of Appeal of Victoria since 2005. Amongst the decisions of the High Court of Australia discussed in this chapter, there are three in which the High Court reversed a decision of the Victorian Court of Appeal to which the author was a party: *R v Pham* (2015) 256 CLR 550; *DPP v Dalgliesh* (2017) 262 CLR 428; *Barbaro v The Queen* (2014) 253 CLR 58.
[1] *R v Williscroft* [1975] VR 292, 300 (*Williscroft*).
[2] *Markarian v The Queen* (2005) 228 CLR 357, [73] (*Markarian*).
[3] *Williscroft* (n 1) 300.
[4] *Markarian* (n 2). For recent examples of the concept's being invoked to describe the sentencing judge's decision-making process, see *McKeon-Muller v The Queen* [2018] VSCA 199, [14] and *DPP v Macarthur* [2019] VSCA 71, [57].
[5] *Elias v The Queen* (2013) 248 CLR 483, [27].
[6] *Markarian* (n 2) [27].

of the discretion have been repeatedly characterised by the High Court as 'inappropriate intrusions' into the discretion.[7]

In this chapter, I seek to challenge the prevailing exceptionalism of Australian sentencing law. I argue that the power to impose punishment for criminal offences should be seen as a species of public power, of pre-eminent importance, to which accepted public law principles of equal treatment should be applied with full rigour. Aids to consistency of sentencing should therefore be seen as indispensable.

I begin with the proposition that criminal law is public law.

I. Criminal Law as Public Law

There are several significant intersections between administrative law and criminal law. The first is that decisions made in the course of criminal proceedings in inferior courts are amenable to judicial review or appeal on a question of law.[8] The second is that the basic requirements of a fair trial are grounded in the principles of natural justice – the right of the accused to know the case against him or her and to have a reasonable opportunity to answer it, and the right to be tried by an impartial tribunal.[9]

The third intersection lies in the field of criminal appeals. Familiar public law notions are routinely deployed in appellate review of both conviction and sentence. Thus, in sentence appeals, in deciding whether a sentence was 'manifestly excessive', the Court must consider whether the sentence imposed was outside the range reasonably open to the judge in the circumstances of the case.[10] I have argued elsewhere that this amounts in substance to the application of *Wednesbury* unreasonableness to sentence appeals.[11]

In the same way, disparity in sentencing between co-offenders raises the question whether it was reasonably open to the judge to differentiate between them;[12] and a complaint of factual error will only succeed if it is shown that there was no evidence to support the finding, or that it was not reasonably open to the sentencing judge to arrive at the finding in question.[13]

On appeal against conviction, the jury's verdict may be challenged on the ground that it was 'unreasonable or cannot be supported having regard to the evidence'.[14] In addressing

---

[7] S Krasnostein, '*Boulton v The Queen*: Guideline Judgments in Australia' (2015) 27 *Current Issues in Criminal Justice* 42.
[8] See D Feldman, 'Changing Boundaries: Crime, Punishment and Public Law', in ch 12 of this volume. It is notable that, in contrast to the position in the United Kingdom, Australian law treats prosecutorial decisions as immune from judicial review: see *Likiardopoulos v The Queen* (2012) 247 CLR 265, [37]; *Magaming v The Queen* (2013) 252 CLR 381, [20].
[9] See, eg, *Ward (a pseudonym) v The Queen* (2017) 54 VR 68, [12], [119]–[123]; *Jarratt (a pseudonym) v The Queen* [2018] VSCA 150, [64].
[10] See, eg, *Clarkson v The Queen* (2011) 32 VR 361, [89].
[11] C Maxwell, 'The Statutory Implication of Reasonableness and the Scope of *Wednesbury* Unreasonableness' (2017) 28 *Public Law Review* 3.
[12] *Teng v The Queen* (2009) 22 VR 706, [17].
[13] See, eg, *AB v The Queen* [2014] NSWCCA 339, [38]–[40].
[14] In Victoria: *Criminal Procedure Act 2009*, s 276(1)(a). In England, the equivalent ground of appeal is that 'under all the circumstances of the case [the verdict] is unsafe or unsatisfactory': Criminal Appeal Act 1968, s 2(1)(a). In Canada, the ground of appeal is expressed in language identical to that of the Victorian provision: Criminal Code 1985, s 686(1)(a)(i).

that ground, the appeal court will ask whether it was reasonably open to the jury, on the evidence before it, to be satisfied beyond reasonable doubt of the accused's guilt.[15]

My present concern is not, however, with the relationship *between* administrative law and criminal law. Rather, I start from the proposition that criminal law is itself a species of public law. Whether criminal law is viewed structurally or functionally, this classification seems entirely appropriate.

Criminal law has long since been transformed 'from a system of private remedy to one of public administration'.[16] As Vincent Chiao has argued, the criminal law

> is a means to an end, and that end is: to help secure the role of stable and just public institutions. The basic principle of public institutions, in turn, is to extend the equal protection of the law to all – that is, to promote the common good on terms befitting social and political equals. In this sense, criminal law rests on the same principle of universal entitlement that animates public law more broadly.[17]

More concretely, the operation of the criminal justice system is concerned with 'the justified exercise of coercive power by the state'.[18] Indeed, as Chief Justice Allsop of the Federal Court has said, criminal law can properly be viewed as 'the epitome of public power, underpinned as it is by the potential for raw, State-sanctioned force'.[19]

Relevantly for present purposes, 'State-sanctioned force' is exerted through the exercise of the judicial discretion to impose punishment upon proof of a breach of the criminal law.[20]

On this view, the invocation of public law remedies, and the utilisation of public law concepts, in connection with criminal proceedings reflects the true character of the branch of law to which criminal law belongs. The corollary, I shall argue, is that the exercise of discretionary power in criminal law can properly be examined by reference to public law principles.

My focus will be on the sentencing discretion vested in judges and magistrates, and on the supervisory jurisdiction of courts of appeal with respect to the exercise of that discretion. My contention is that the exercise of that discretion should be governed by the same requirements of consistency – equal treatment – as apply to discretionary decision-making in other areas of public law.

There is, in my view, no principled basis for treating the exercise of the sentencing discretion differently from any other exercise of public power, whether administrative or judicial. The judge making the sentencing decision should have available 'tools for consistency' of the kind routinely deployed in other fields.[21]

---

[15] *R v Klamo* (2008) 18 VR 644, [38]–[40].
[16] V Chiao, *Criminal Law in The Age of the Administrative State* (New York, Oxford University Press, 2018) 11.
[17] ibid 5.
[18] M Thorburn, 'Criminal Law as Public Law' in A Duff and S Green (eds), *Philosophical Foundations of Criminal Law* (Oxford, Oxford University Press, 2011).
[19] J Allsop, 'Values in Public Law' in N Williams (ed), *Key Issues in Public Law* (Annandale, Federation Press, 2017).
[20] As the High Court of Australia has affirmed, 'adjudging and punishing criminal guilt is an exclusively judicial function': *Magaming v The Queen* (n 8) [47].
[21] S Krasnostein and A Freiberg, 'Pursuing Consistency in an Individualistic Sentencing Framework: If You Know Where You're Going, How Do You Know When You've Got There?' (2013) *Law and Contemporary Problems* 265, 267.

As in other fields of public law, tools of this kind promote reasonable consistency of treatment, while preserving sufficient discretion to ensure justice in the individual case.[22] In addition, enabling judges to achieve their goal of treating like cases alike promotes other rule-of-law values, such as certainty, predictability and finality.[23]

II. Guidelines and Consistency: Administrative Discretion

In administrative law, decision-makers – and courts undertaking judicial review – have long recognised the importance of consistency in decision-making, and the utility of guidelines and policies in achieving that end. In *Re Drake and Minister for Immigration and Ethnic Affairs [No 2]*, the first President of the Administrative Appeals Tribunal, Brennan J, said:

> Decision-making is facilitated by the guidance given by an adopted policy, and the integrity of decision-making in particular cases is the better assured if decisions can be tested against such a policy. By diminishing the importance of individual predilection, an adopted policy can diminish the inconsistencies which might otherwise appear in a series of decisions, and enhance the sense of satisfaction with the fairness and continuity of the administrative process.[24]

In the same year, in *Drake v Minister for Immigration and Ethnic Affairs*, the Full Federal Court (Bowen CJ and Deane J) said 'the consistent exercise of discretionary administrative power in the absence of legislative guidelines will, in itself, almost inevitably lead to the formulation of some general policy or rules relating to the exercise of the relevant power'.[25]

The weight to be given to the policy, the Court said, was for the decision-maker to determine

> in the context of the particular case and in the light of the need for compromise, in the interests of good government, between, on the one hand, the desirability of consistency and the treatment of citizens under the law and, on the other hand, the ideal of justice in the individual case.[26]

Subsequently, in *Nevistic v Minister for Immigration and Ethnic Affairs*, Deane J affirmed the significance of consistency as emblematic of the rule of law:

> There are many reasons for the desirability of consistency in the making of decisions affecting rights, opportunities and obligations under the law. Paramount among them is the fact that inconsistency in the treatment of those amenable to the law involves an element of injustice. Particularly where there is competition or correlativity between rights, advantages, obligations and disadvantages, equality of treatment under the law is an ingredient of modern concepts of justice and the rule of law.[27]

---

[22] *Kalala v The Queen* [2017] VSCA 223, [40]–[41].
[23] *R v MacNeil-Brown* (2008) 20 VR 677, [4].
[24] *Re Drake and Minister for Immigration and Ethnic Affairs [No 2]* (1979) 2 ALD 634, 640 (*Drake [No 2]*).
[25] *Drake v Minister for Immigration and Ethnic Affairs* (1979) 24 ALR 577, 590.
[26] ibid 590–91.
[27] *Nevistic v Minister for Immigration and Ethnic Affairs* (1981) 34 ALR 639, 646–47.

More recently, in *Plaintiff M64/2015 v Minister for Immigration and Border Protection*, the plurality (French CJ, Bell, Keane and Gordon JJ) rejected a complaint about a decision-maker's application of departmental policy, saying:

> Policy guidelines ... promote values of consistency and rationality in decision-making, and *the principle that administrative decision-makers should treat like cases alike*. In particular, policies or guidelines may help to promote consistency in 'high-volume decision-making'.[28]

In the same case, Gageler J relied on the passage from Deane J in *Nevistic* (above) in stating:

> It is open to the Minister in the exercise of non-statutory executive power to lay down a policy for the guidance of his or her delegates in making those determinations. Indeed it is inconceivable that the Minister would not do so.[29]

Consistency of treatment is both an end in itself and a necessary condition of maintaining public confidence in the decision-making process. As Brennan J said in *Drake [No 2]*, '[i]nconsistency is not merely inelegant: it brings the process of deciding into disrepute, suggesting an antithesis which is incompatible with commonly accepted notions of justice'.[30]

In *Federal Commissioner of Taxation v Swift*, French J cited this passage from *Drake [No 2]* and said 'the need to maintain the perception and reality of equal treatment is an important factor in the administration of all laws'.[31]

For well over a decade, Mark Elliott has been making a persuasive case for the recognition of consistency as a 'free-standing' principle of administrative law, to be accorded the same status as the principles of rationality and (in England) legitimate expectations. Consistency of treatment, he argues, is 'a norm worthy of protection in its own right', having its normative roots in the dignity and equality of individuals.[32]

For the present, however, consistency of treatment remains 'a particular application of the ordinary requirement of rationality imposed on public authorities'.[33] This means that unjustified differentiation in the treatment of like cases may attract judicial review on the unreasonableness ground.[34] The reviewing court will apply the 'cardinal principle of public administration that all persons in a similar position should be treated similarly'.[35]

The application of policies or guidelines in particular cases is limited, of course, by the 'non-fettering' principle. Axiomatically, the decision-maker must give consideration to the merits of the case at hand and may not treat the outcome as 'dictated' by the policy or guideline.[36]

---

[28] *Plaintiff M64/2015 v Minister for Immigration and Border Protection* (2015) 258 CLR 173, [54] (emphasis added).
[29] ibid [68]. See also *R (Lumba) v Secretary of State for the Home Department* [2012] 1 AC 245 [190], [315].
[30] *Drake [No 2]* (n 24) 639.
[31] *Federal Commissioner of Taxation v Swift* (1989) 18 ALD 679, 692.
[32] M Elliott, 'Legitimate Expectation, Consistency and Abuse of Power' [2005] *Judicial Review* 281, 286; M Elliott, 'A "Principle" of Consistency? The Doctrinal Configuration of the Law of Judicial Review' [2018] *CLJ* 444.
[33] *R (Gallaher Group Ltd) v Competition and Markets Authority* [2019] AC 96, [50] (*Gallaher*).
[34] *Fares Rural Meat and Livestock Co Pty Ltd v Australian Meat and Livestock Corporation* (1990) 96 ALR 153, 167–68; *Bellinz Pty Ltd v Commissioner of Taxation (Cth)* (1998) 84 FCR 154, 167; *Matadeen v Pointu* [1999] 1 AC 98, [9].
[35] *Gallaher* (n 33) [28].
[36] *SSHD v R* [2007] EWCA Civ 546, [50].

III. Guidelines and Consistency: Judicial Discretion

Importantly for present purposes, the High Court of Australia has affirmed the importance of consistency in the exercise of *judicial* discretions, and the appropriateness of guidelines as an aid to consistency. In *Norbis v Norbis*,[37] the Court was concerned with the judicial discretion conferred the *Family Law Act 1974* (Cth) to make a 'just and equitable' division of the assets between the parties to the marriage. The Full Court of the Family Court had developed guidelines to assist judges in the exercise of this discretion.

The majority of the High Court (Mason, Deane and Brennan JJ) affirmed the appropriateness of the Full Court's having done so:

> The point of preserving the width of the discretion which Parliament has created is that it maximises the possibility of doing justice in every case. But the need for consistency in judicial adjudication, which is the antithesis of arbitrary and capricious decision-making, provides an important countervailing consideration supporting the giving of guidance by appellate courts, whether in the form of principles or guidelines.[38]

Reference should also be made to the judicial discretion under Lord Cairns' Act to award damages in lieu of an injunction. Since the decision of the English Court of Appeal in *Shelfer v City of London Electric Lighting Co*,[39] courts have had no hesitation in applying the 'good working rule' laid down by AL Smith LJ in that case. It has never been suggested that the enunciation, or application, of that rule was wrong in principle or impermissibly constrained the judge's discretion.[40]

There is an instructive parallel with judgments about proportionality in constitutional law. The High Court has pointed out the benefits of a structured 'analytical framework for evaluating legislation which effects a restriction on a right or freedom'.[41] Such a structure

> has the advantage of transparency. Its structured nature assists members of the legislature, those advising the legislature, and those drafting legislative materials, to understand how the sufficiency of the justification for a legislative restriction on a freedom will be tested.
>
> …
>
> Accepting that value judgments cannot be avoided altogether, their subjectivity is lessened and a more objective analysis encouraged by this process.[42]

Judicial opinion has, however, been far from unanimous. The decision to uphold the guidelines in *Norbis v Norbis* was by a narrow majority of three to two, and the minority disagreed strongly about the appropriateness of guidelines. Wilson and Dawson JJ said:

> [W]e believe that the sound development of the law, in this area as in others, is served best by following the tradition of the common law. The genius of the common law is to be found in its case-by-case approach. The decision and reasoning of one case contributes its wisdom to the accumulated wisdom of past cases. The authoritative guidance available to aid in the resolution

---

[37] *Norbis v Norbis* (1986) 161 CLR 513.
[38] ibid 519–20.
[39] *Shelfer v City of London Electric Lighting Co* (1874) 9 LR Ch App 221.
[40] For a recent example of its application, see *Janney v Steller Works Pty Ltd* (2017) 53 VR 677, 687–88.
[41] *McCloy v New South Wales* (2015) 257 CLR 178, [74].
[42] ibid [74], [76].

of the next case lies in that accumulated wisdom. It does not lie in the abstract formulation of principles or guidelines designed to constrain judicial discretion within a predetermined framework.[43]

This view echoes what the High Court had said two decades earlier regarding the discretion to award general damages. In *Planet Fisheries Pty Ltd v La Rosa*, the High Court 'emphatically' rejected a submission that, in deciding whether an award of general damages was excessive, the appeal court should seek 'a norm or standard' in other decisions on that question.[44] The Court (Barwick CJ, Kitto and Menzies JJ) said:

> It is the relationship of the award to the injury and its consequences as established in the evidence in the case in question which is to be proportionate. It is only if, there being no other error, the award is grossly disproportionate to those injuries and consequences that it can be set aside. Whether it is so or not is a matter of judgment in the sound exercise of a sense of proportion. It is not a matter to be resolved by reference to some norm or standard supposedly to be derived from a consideration of amounts awarded in a number of other specific cases.[45]

Eventually, Australian legislatures intervened to rectify the position. Section 28HA of the *Wrongs Act 1958* now authorises a court, in determining damages for non-economic loss, to refer to 'earlier decisions of that or other courts for the purpose of establishing the appropriate award in the proceedings'.[46]

There is a similar divergence of opinion with respect to the judicial discretion to impose sentence. For example, in *R v Jurisic*, Spigelman CJ explained how sentencing guidelines promote consistency:

> The preservation of a broad sentencing discretion is central to the ability of the criminal courts to ensure justice is done in all the extraordinary variety of circumstances of individual offences and individual offenders. However, public confidence in the administration of criminal justice requires consistency in sentencing decisions. As I have said, inconsistency is a form of injustice. ... Guideline judgments are a mechanism for structuring discretion, rather than restricting discretion.[47]

By contrast, in *R v Ngui and Tiong*, Winneke P of the Victorian Court of Appeal said:

> I have reservations about the use which can or should be made in the sentencing process of judicially expressed guidelines, based on existing 'sentencing patterns' which are themselves the product of the accumulated wisdom of sentencing judges exercising individual discretion in respect of individual cases over a number of years. It must, of course, be acknowledged that consistency in sentences imposed for like offences upon like offenders is an objective to which the system of criminal justice aspires. ... To the extent that judicially expressed guidelines can assist the production of such consistency, then they may be of use. *However, the search for sentencing consistency should not be permitted to usurp the discretion of the sentencing judge.* ... Experience in other areas of the law has shown that judicially expressed guidelines can have a tendency, with the passage of time, to fetter judicial discretion by assuming the status of rules of universal application which they were never intended to have.[48]

---

[43] *Norbis v Norbis* (n 37) 533–34.
[44] *Planet Fisheries Pty Ltd v La Rosa* (1968) 119 CLR 118, 124.
[45] ibid 124–25.
[46] See also *Rogers v Nationwide News Pty Ltd* (2003) 216 CLR 237, [69]–[70].
[47] *R v Jurisic* (1998) 45 NSWLR 209, 221 (*Jurisic*).
[48] *R v Ngui and Tiong* [2000] 1 VR 579, [12] (emphasis added).

IV. Why Does Sentencing Consistency Matter?

Self-evidently, the power to impose sentence is a power of the utmost significance for the community. This is most obviously so when the sentence imposed is one of imprisonment. The deprivation of liberty has profound consequences for the offender and for those affected by his or her incarceration.

It is not surprising, therefore, that the largest single area of work in the Victorian Court of Appeal concerns appeals against sentence. In 2016–17 and again in 2017–18, sentence appeals accounted for almost 50 per cent of the work of the Victorian Court. The only other discretionary power whose exercise has comparable life-changing implications for individuals is the Ministerial power to refuse a person entry to a country or to deport a person from a country. The appellate work of the Federal Court is likewise dominated by challenges to migration decisions.

The exercise of the power to punish therefore merits the closest scrutiny. The community is entitled to be satisfied that this most potent of discretions is being fairly exercised. In particular, the community needs to be assured that sentencing courts adhere to the principle of equality before the law and the principle of equal treatment. As Lord Devlin said 40 years ago, 'a sense of injustice is more easily aroused by the apprehension of unequal treatment than by anything else'.[49]

The principle of equal justice has been repeatedly affirmed in the sentencing decisions of the High Court of Australia. In *Wong v The Queen*, Gaudron, Gummow and Hayne JJ said 'Equal justice requires identity of outcome in cases that are *relevantly* identical. It requires *different* outcomes in cases that are different in some relevant respect'.[50] Quoting that passage, French CJ, Crennan and Kiefel JJ said, in *Green v The Queen*:

> 'Equal justice' embodies the norm expressed in the term 'equality before the law'. It is an aspect of the rule of law. It was characterised by Kelsen as 'the principle of legality, of lawfulness, which is immanent in every legal order'. It has been called 'the starting point of all other liberties'. It applies to the interpretation of statutes and thereby to the exercise of statutory powers. It requires, so far as the law permits, that like cases be treated alike. Equal justice according to law also requires, where the law permits, differential treatment of persons according to differences between them relevant to the scope, purpose and subject matter of the law.[51]

Earlier, in *Lowe v The Queen*, Mason J had highlighted the link between consistency in punishment and public confidence in the criminal justice system:

> Just as consistency in punishment – a reflection of the notion of equal justice – is a fundamental element in any rational and fair system of criminal justice, so inconsistency in punishment, because it is regarded as a badge of unfairness and unequal treatment under the law, is calculated to lead to an erosion of public confidence in the integrity of the administration of justice. It is for this reason that the avoidance and elimination of unjustifiable discrepancy in sentencing is a matter of abiding importance to the administration of justice and to the community.[52]

---

[49] P Devlin, *The Judge* (Oxford, Oxford University Press, 1979) 85.
[50] *Wong v The Queen* (2001) 207 CLR 584, [65].
[51] *Green v The Queen* (2011) 244 CLR 462, [28].
[52] *Lowe v The Queen* (1984) 154 CLR 606, 610–11.

Spigelman CJ made similar points in *Jurisic*:

> Inconsistency in sentencing offends the principle of equality before the law. It is itself a manifestation of injustice. It can lead to a sense of grievance amongst individuals on whom uncharacteristically severe sentences are imposed and amongst the broader community, or victims and their families, in the case of uncharacteristically light sentences.[53]

But what does 'consistency' mean in this context? While acknowledging that 'reasonable consistency in sentencing should be maintained as an aspect of the rule of law', the High Court has repeatedly stated that this requirement is satisfied by 'reasonable consistency in the application of the relevant legal principles'.[54]

In practice, of course, the focus of sentencing hearings – and of appeals against sentence – is on (in)consistency of *outcome*. As Gleeson CJ said, '[d]ay by day, sentencing judges and appellate courts are referred to sentences imposed in what are said to be comparable cases'.[55]

At first instance, comparable cases are relied on because counsel – and the judge – seek to ensure that like cases are treated alike. On appeal, the reference to such cases is designed to show that the appellant has received a heavier sentence than other persons sentenced for comparable offending in comparable circumstances, without there being reasonable justification for the difference of treatment.

This is, in short, a complaint of unequal treatment. Since the difference in outcome is typically measured in months or years of incarceration, the complaint deserves careful attention. It is not an adequate answer, in my view, to say that there was 'reasonable consistency in the application of the relevant legal principles'. Given the well-established framework of sentencing principle, consistency of that kind is unremarkable. Sentencing reasons invariably recite the governing principles set out in section 5(1) of the *Sentencing Act 1991* (Vic): just punishment, denunciation, specific deterrence, general deterrence, community protection and rehabilitation.

Crucially, consistency of principle is no safeguard against unjustifiably disparate outcomes in comparable cases. This reflects the inherent difficulty of deciding what *quantitative* outcome is required by the application of *qualitative* principles to the offender, and the offence, before the Court.

That difficulty was eloquently described by McHugh J in *AB v The Queen*, as follows:

> Many, probably the large bulk of, sentences reflect compromises between conflicting objectives of sentencing. One objective is to impose a sentence that reflects adequate punishment for the culpability of the convicted person, having regard to the community's view concerning the need for retribution, denunciation, deterrence, community protection and sometimes vindication. Another objective is to impose a sentence, with or without conditions, that will further the public interest by encouraging and not discouraging the convicted person to renounce criminal activity and to re-establish himself or herself as a law-abiding citizen. Still another objective is that the sentence should reflect an allowance for those circumstances, personal to the convicted person, which call for mitigation.[56]

---

[53] *Jurisic* (n 47) 216.
[54] *Hili v The Queen* (2010) 242 CLR 520, [49]; *DPP v Dalgliesh* (2017) 262 CLR 428, [49]–[50].
[55] *Wong v The Queen* (n 50) [7].
[56] *AB v The Queen* (1999) 198 CLR 111, [14].

V. Guideline Judgments

In June 1999, the Chief Justice of New South Wales declared that the Court of Criminal Appeal (NSWCCA) had established 'a formal system of guideline judgments'.[57] Spigelman CJ described this as 'a significant development in this State with respect to the exercise of discretion by sentencing judges, a context which is, perhaps, the most controversial single area of judicial decision-making'.[58]

Later that year, in *R v Wong*,[59] the NSWCCA delivered a guideline judgment with respect to sentencing for drug importation offences. In affirming the jurisdiction of the Court to give such a judgment, Spigelman CJ said:

> The nature and purpose of [a court of criminal appeal] encompasses the identification of sentencing principles and formulation of guidelines about the exercise of the sentencing discretion by trial judges.
>
> ...
>
> Courts of criminal appeal have frequently stated principles of general application with respect to appropriate sentences for particular offences. The step of promulgating a guideline in quantitative terms is a logical development of what such courts have long done.[60]

The guideline in question was structured by reference to the quantity of drugs imported, with a sentencing range specified for each quantity level. As Spigelman CJ noted, the English Court of Appeal had developed similar guidelines for drug importation in the 1980s.[61] That Court's jurisdiction to promulgate sentencing guidelines – and the utility of doing so – has never been doubted.[62]

The High Court of Australia took a different view, however, and struck down the *Wong* guideline. The NSWCCA's selection of the weight of narcotic imported as the chief factor to be taken into account in fixing a sentence was characterised as 'a departure from fundamental principle'.[63] In the view of the majority, to have a 'starting point' for sentence based on the weight of narcotic

> departs from principle because it does not take account of the fact that there are many conflicting and contradictory elements which bear upon sentencing an offender. Attributing a particular weight to some factors, while leaving the significance of all other factors substantially unaltered, may be quite wrong. We say 'may be' quite wrong because the task of the sentencer is to take account of *all* of the relevant factors and to arrive at a single result which takes due account of them all. That is what is meant by saying that the task is to arrive at an 'instinctive synthesis'. This expression is used, not as might be supposed, to cloak the task of the sentencer in some mystery, but to make plain that the sentencer is called on to reach a single sentence which, in the case of an offence like the one now under discussion, balances many different and conflicting features.[64]

---

[57] JJ Spigelman, 'Sentencing Guideline Judgments' (1999) 73 *Australian Law Journal* 876, 876.
[58] ibid.
[59] *R v Wong* (1999) 48 NSWLR 340.
[60] ibid [15]–[16].
[61] ibid [135].
[62] See also *Avis v R* [1997] EWCA Crim 3423.
[63] *Wong v The Queen* (n 50) [70].
[64] ibid [75].

Their Honours continued:

> The core of the difficulty lies in the complexity of the sentencing task. A sentencing judge must take into account a wide variety of matters which concern the seriousness of the offence for which the offender stands to be sentenced and the personal history and circumstances of the offender. Very often there are competing and contradictory considerations. What may mitigate the seriousness of one offence may aggravate the seriousness of another. Yet from these the sentencing judge must distil an answer which reflects human behaviour in the time or monetary units of punishment.
>
> Numerical guidelines either take account of only some of the relevant considerations or would have to be so complicated as to make their application difficult, if not impossible. Most importantly of all, numerical guidelines cannot address considerations of proportionality. Their application cannot avoid outcomes which fail to reflect the circumstances of the offence *and* the offender (with absurd and unforeseen results) if they do not articulate and reflect the principles which will lead to the just sentencing of offenders whose offending behaviour is every bit as diverse as is their personal history and circumstances.[65]

Gleeson CJ dissented, saying

> there is a growing need for the Court of Criminal Appeal to give practical guidance to primary judges. The form that such guidance might properly take is an important issue in the administration of criminal justice. If there is insufficient guidance, and resulting inconsistency, public confidence in the value of discretionary sentencing will suffer.[66]

And further:

> One of the legitimate objectives of such guidance is to reduce the incidence of unnecessary and inappropriate inconsistency. All discretionary decision-making carries with it the probability of some degree of inconsistency. But there are limits beyond which such inconsistency itself constitutes a form of injustice. The outcome of discretionary decision-making can never be uniform, but it ought to depend as little as possible upon the identity of the judge who happens to hear the case. Like cases should be treated in like manner. The administration of criminal justice works as a system; not merely as a multiplicity of unconnected single instances. It should be systematically fair, and that involves, amongst other things, reasonable consistency.[67]

In 2004, the Victorian Parliament expressly authorised the Court of Appeal – either on its own initiative or on application by a party to an appeal – to give a guideline judgment. Such a judgment would 'contain guidelines to be taken into account by courts in sentencing offenders'.[68]

A guideline judgment might set out:

(a) criteria to be applied in selecting among various sentencing alternatives;
(b) the weight to be given to the various purposes specified in section 5(1) for which a sentence may be imposed;
(c) the criteria by which a sentencing court is to determine the gravity of an offence.[69]

---

[65] ibid [77]–[78].
[66] ibid [10].
[67] ibid [6].
[68] *Sentencing Act 1991* (Vic), s 6AA.
[69] ibid s 6AC.

These provisions remained unused for a decade, in part because of ambivalence amongst judges and criminal lawyers about the appropriateness of sentencing guidelines. Finally, in 2014, the Victorian Director of Public Prosecutions applied for a guideline judgment in respect of a relatively new type of sanction, the community correction order (CCO).

In *Boulton v R*,[70] a unanimous five-member bench of the Court granted the Director's application and published a detailed guideline judgment highlighting the scope for the CCO to be used to achieve rehabilitation and punishment simultaneously. In the view of the Court, the giving of such a judgment should promote consistency in sentencing and public confidence in the criminal justice system. The Court emphasised that the guidelines would assist sentencing judges without fettering their discretion:

> By enacting the provisions of pt 2AA, Parliament affirmed the importance of this Court providing guidance to sentencing courts. The giving of a guideline judgment is not a substitute for the case-by-case development of the law. The one complements the other. The great advantage of the case-by-case process is that it ensures that the development of legal principles is informed by the practical realities of individual cases. The great advantage of a guideline judgment is that it enables this Court to deal systematically and comprehensively with a particular topic or topics relevant to sentencing, rather than being confined to the questions raised by particular appeals.
>
> Just as importantly, the giving of a guideline judgment does not fetter the discretion of the sentencing court in any way. The only constraints on the exercise of the sentencing discretion are those imposed by the common law and by the substantive provisions of the Act. The function of a guideline judgment is to provide assistance to sentencing courts in the application of the law.[71]

VI. Preserving Flexibility

Markarian v The Queen[72] concerned sentencing for supply of a commercial quantity of a prohibited drug. In upholding a Crown appeal against sentence, the NSWCCA had taken as its starting point the quantity of heroin the subject of the offence. The High Court of Australia concluded that this was an error of principle. The plurality (Gleeson CJ, Gummow, Hayne and Callinan JJ) said:

> Express legislative provisions apart, neither principle, nor any of the grounds of appellate review, dictates the particular path that a sentencer, passing sentence in a case where the penalty is not fixed by statute, must follow in reasoning to the conclusion that the sentence to be imposed should be fixed as it is. The judgment is a discretionary judgment and, as the bases for appellate review reveal, what is required is that the sentencer must take into account all relevant considerations (and only relevant considerations) in forming the conclusion reached. As has now been pointed out more than once, there is no single correct sentence. *And judges at first instance are to be allowed as much flexibility in sentencing as is consonant with consistency of approach and as accords with the statutory regime that applies.*[73]

---

[70] *Boulton v R* (2014) 46 VR 308.
[71] ibid [26]–[27].
[72] *Markarian* (n 2).
[73] ibid [27] (emphasis added).

In *Hili v The Queen*,[74] the High Court rejected as wrong in principle the adoption of a 'norm' of between 60 and 66 per cent for the minimum term of imprisonment under the applicable legislation. The Court (French CJ, Gummow, Hayne, Crennan, Kiefel and Bell JJ) noted that the arguments in favour of the 'mathematical approach' had been based on the need for consistency in sentencing. The Court said:

> Consistency is not demonstrated by, and does not require, numerical equivalence. Presentation of the sentences that have been passed on federal offenders in numerical tables, bar charts or graphs is not useful to a sentencing judge. It is not useful because referring only to the lengths of sentences passed says nothing about why sentences were fixed as they were. Presentation in any of these forms suggests, wrongly, that the task of a sentencing judge is to interpolate the result of the instant case on a graph that depicts the available outcomes. ...
>
> *The consistency that is sought is consistency in the application of the relevant legal principles.* ... When it is said that the search is for *'reasonable consistency'*, what is sought is the treatment of like cases alike, and different cases differently. Consistency of that kind is not capable of mathematical expression. It is not capable of expression in tabular form.[75]

Similar views were expressed more recently in *R v Pham*.[76] In that case, the offender had been sentenced for drug importation. In allowing an appeal against sentence on the ground of manifest excess, the Victorian Court of Appeal tabulated for the purposes of comparison the sentences imposed in 32 other cases decided by intermediate courts of appeal. The cases were said to be relevantly comparable because each involved an offender who had performed the role of courier, had pleaded guilty and had no relevant prior convictions. As a result, it was said, 'a large number of sentencing decisions can be assembled – for the purposes of comparison – in which the only variable factor affecting offence seriousness is the quantity imported'.[77]

The High Court plurality (French CJ, Keane and Nettle JJ) described this approach as involving 'two departures from fundamental principle'. The first was that to characterise an offender as a 'courier' or a 'principal' was likely to 'obscure the assessment of what the offender did'. The second was in attributing chief importance to the weight of the drug in distinguishing between offenders for the purposes of sentence.[78]

In *Elias v The Queen*, a unanimous High Court (French CJ, Hayne, Kiefel, Bell and Keane JJ) said:

> As this Court has explained on more than one occasion, the factors bearing on the determination of sentence will frequently pull in different directions. It is the duty of the judge to balance often incommensurable factors and to arrive at a sentence that is just in all of the circumstances. The administration of the criminal law involves individualised justice, the attainment of which is acknowledged to involve the exercise of a wide sentencing discretion.[79]

The primacy of 'individualised justice' was reaffirmed recently in *DPP v Dalgliesh*.[80] In that case, the plurality (Kiefel CJ, Bell and Keane JJ) said '[t]he imposition of a just sentence on

---

[74] *Hili v The Queen* (n 54).
[75] ibid [48]–[49] (emphasis added).
[76] *R v Pham* (2015) 256 CLR 550.
[77] *Pham v The Queen* (2014) 244 A Crim R 252, [3].
[78] *R v Pham* (n 76) [37].
[79] *Elias v The Queen* (n 5) [27].
[80] *DPP v Dalgliesh* (n 54).

an offender in a particular case is an exercise of judicial discretion concerned to do justice in that case'.[81]

Their Honours endorsed the statement that the administration of criminal justice 'should be systematically fair, and that involves … reasonable consistency'. They reiterated, however, the consistency sought was 'consistency in the application of the relevant legal principles'.[82]

The minority judges in *R v Pham* (Bell and Gageler JJ) expressed a different view:

> The 'reasonable consistency' to which the joint reasons in *Hili* refer is with respect to sentencing outcomes. The qualifier 'reasonable' in this context is an acknowledgement both that sentencing is a discretionary judgment and that the mix of factors that must be weighed in determining the appropriate sentence will never be precisely the same as in a past case or cases.[83]

VII. Why is the Sentencing Discretion Seen as Special?

The effect of the High Court's jurisprudence has been summed up by Chief Justice Allsop of the Federal Court as follows:

> The emphasis of the High Court … upon the necessity to have complete regard to the individual circumstances of the human evaluation of proper punishment has seen a rejection of any form of structured approach, or any rule, whether judicial or statutory, that may affect or impede the evaluation of the individual human context of the offender, in a manner reflecting justice and equality.[84]

Writing after the Victorian Court of Appeal's first guideline judgment, Sarah Krasnostein drew a contrast with the decisions of the High Court which, in her view,

> strongly assert the inherent value of a broadly unfettered sentencing discretion and the notion that it should be as wide as possible within the parameters of the maximum penalty, the limiting principle of proportionality, and any statutory constraints … This 'individualist' approach measures fairness largely in relation to what it sees as each case's unique circumstances and therefore rigorously protects unregulated discretion to tailor punishment to individual case facts.[85]

Why does the sentencing discretion require 'rigorous protection'? It is scarcely unique in requiring that the individual case be justly dealt with, that is, after proper consideration of the circumstances of the individual in question. Those requirements apply with equal force to the exercise of a multiplicity of administrative discretions. The oft-repeated statement that 'no two cases are the same' is as true of applications for medical benefits based on post-traumatic stress disorder (for example) as it is of criminal offenders and offences.

As suggested earlier, the concept of 'instinctive synthesis' carries with it the implication that – precisely because of the uniqueness of the case and the myriad of often conflicting

---

[81] ibid [49].
[82] ibid.
[83] *R v Pham* (n 76) [46].
[84] Allsop, 'Values in Public Law' (n 19) 19–20.
[85] Krasnostein, '*Boulton v The Queen*' (n 7) 43.

considerations to be brought to bear – the decision arrived at is a product of the judge's 'instinct' or intuition and is therefore, in some relevant sense, unexaminable.

The foundational decision was that of the Full Court of the Victorian Supreme Court in *R v Williscroft*.[86] In that case, Adam and Crockett JJ said:

> [U]ltimately every sentence imposed represents the sentencing judge's instinctive synthesis of all various aspects involved in the punitive process. Moreover, in our view, it is profitless … to attempt to allot to the various considerations their proper part in the assessment of the particular punishments presently under examination.[87]

Likewise, an appellate court's conclusion that the sentencing discretion has miscarried 'rests upon what is essentially a subjective judgment largely intuitively reached by an appellate judge as to what punishment is appropriate'.[88]

But a reading of the full judgment casts a different light on the references to instinct and intuition. In particular, Adam and Crockett JJ went on to emphasise the need for the appellate court to have information about comparable cases:

> [A] judgment as to what is appropriate by way of sentence must depend upon knowledge of sentences for the same or similar offences which is derived from personal experience or any other source. To this end, the Court asked for and was supplied with some statistical data relating to sentences imposed in this State during the past 18 months for armed robbery of banks, TAB agencies and service stations.[89]

More strikingly still, their Honours then set out in their judgment the terms of a memorandum, prepared by English judges in 1901, which said:

> The judges of the King's Bench Division are agreed that it would be convenient and of public advantage in regard to certain classes of crime to come to an agreement, or, at least to an approximate agreement, as to what may be called a 'normal' standard of punishment: a standard of punishment, that is to say, which should be proved to be properly applicable, unless the particular case under consideration presented some special features of aggravation or extenuation.[90]

In the same vein, Lord Devlin said that 'above all [the judge] should know the tariff'. Explaining why, his Lordship said:

> The tariff figure is a conventional one. It is no more possible to relate wicked or unsocial behaviour to a number of days in prison than it is to measure pain and suffering in pounds sterling. *In neither of these spheres can a judge do his own arithmetic; the fruits of diversity would be general injustice.* A judge can take into account that a prison regime will affect some more painfully than others, but the application of that depends mainly on his appreciation of the individual he is sentencing. *He must start from the tariff figure.*[91]

As has been seen, the concept of 'instinctive synthesis' has been central to the sentencing jurisprudence of the High Court of Australia. What appears to have been overlooked,

---

[86] *R v Williscroft* (n 1).
[87] ibid 300.
[88] ibid.
[89] ibid 301.
[90] ibid.
[91] Devlin (n 49) 40–42 (emphasis added).

however, is the recognition by the Full Court in *Williscroft* of the indispensability of information about sentences imposed for like offending and of the appropriateness of a 'tariff', or starting point, for sentencing. Paradoxically, the notion of 'instinctive synthesis' has been said to preclude any notion of 'tariff' or 'two-stage sentencing'.[92]

The question remains as to why the exercise of the sentencing discretion is seen to have its own special character. Further insight may be gained from examining the sharp divergence of opinion over the appropriateness of a prosecutor's providing a submission to a sentencing judge on the sentencing range reasonably open to the judge in the circumstances of the case.

In *R v MacNeil-Brown*, a majority of the Victorian Court of Appeal held that it was part of the prosecutor's duty to the court to make such a submission, either when requested to do so or when it was necessary to avoid a risk of the judge's falling into error.[93] Such submissions would, it was said, promote consistency of sentencing and reduce the likelihood of appealable error.[94]

Buchanan and Kellam JJA dissented. Buchanan JA concluded that 'the expression of counsel's opinion as to the outer limits of an acceptable range of sentences' was of no utility to a sentencing judge. This turned, his Honour said, on the nature of the sentencing judge's discretion:

> The task of a sentencing judge is complex. The discretion which he exercises is unlike other judicial discretions, due to the number of factors which inform the discretion, the relevant factors or their combination differing from one case to another and being, for the most part, incommensurable.
>
> ...
>
> The myriad facts identified, found and classified by the sentencing judge are to be intuitively synthesised, that is, considered, in the light of general sentencing considerations, for the purpose of assessing their contribution to the determination of an appropriate sentence. This synthesis is generally not to be done mechanically by arriving at a starting point and adding or subtracting a period of time attached to each relevant sentencing factor.[95]

In his Honour's view,

> to require counsel to nominate what counsel considers to be the limits of a range is to seek to enlist counsel as a surrogate judge. The opinions of counsel are simply irrelevant. ... The synthesis of the raw material is the task of the sentencing judge, not counsel.[96]

Kellam JA expressed similar views:

> It is the judge who exercises the sentencing discretion, and not counsel. ... The ultimate sentence to be imposed involves the exercise of a judicial discretion, which is the result of an 'intuitive synthesis' of all the relevant facts, circumstances and sentencing principles. The exercise of that discretion is the function of the judge and the judge alone. It is not the function of counsel. Neither counsel for the prosecution nor counsel for the defence will have examined all of the relevant

---

[92] See *AB v The Queen* (n 56) [16]; *Wong v The Queen* (n 50) [74]–[75]; *DPP v OJA* (2007) 172 A Crim R 181, [29].
[93] *R v MacNeil-Brown* (n 23).
[94] ibid [2]–[4].
[95] ibid [124]–[126].
[96] ibid [128].

factors with the same scrutiny and impartiality prior to the plea hearing. Nor should they be expected to do so, for it is not their function. It is difficult to see how counsel on either side by quoting a range of head sentences and a range of non-parole periods could provide a considered and impartial view which would be of any assistance at all to a judge whose duty it is to synthesise all of the relevant factors intuitively.[97]

The High Court refused special leave to appeal from the decision in R v MacNeil-Brown. Several years later, however, the Court permitted the Victorian Director of Public Prosecutions to intervene in a Commonwealth sentence appeal and submit that the practice of prosecutors making submissions on range was wrong in principle and should cease.[98] The majority of the Court (French CJ, Hayne, Kiefel and Bell JJ) upheld that submission, endorsing the view of Buchanan JA that the practice depended upon the prosecution's acting – inappropriately – in the role of 'a surrogate judge'.[99] The making of a prosecution submission on the limits of the available range might 'lead to erroneous views about its importance in the process of sentencing with consequential blurring of what should be a sharp distinction between the role of the judge and the role of the prosecution in that process'.[100]

VIII. Conclusion

The sentencing discretion is 'of vital importance in the administration of our system of criminal justice'.[101] Both the judge's and the community's sense of justice demand that the sentencing decision be – and be seen to be – responsive to the circumstances of the case at hand. Mandatory sentencing is objectionable precisely because it requires unlike cases to be treated alike.

But the need for 'individualised' justice is not confined to the exercise of the sentencing discretion. Nor is the process of reasoning any more 'intuitive' or 'instinctive' than any other process of judicial reasoning to a conclusion. In sentencing, as in any other field of adjudication, the judge is required to arrive at a considered judgment, applying legal principles to the facts of the case at hand. It is a rational, analytical process, which must be capable of explanation in the form of clear, logical reasons.

The foundational requirement of equal treatment means that this process of reasoning must, of necessity, involve comparative analysis. The reliance on comparable cases recognises the obvious truth that – at a level of detail – every case is unique,[102] but it maintains that relevant sentencing trends and patterns can – and must – be discerned by identifying the common features between one case and the next.[103]

---

[97] ibid [140].
[98] *Barbaro v The Queen* (2014) 253 CLR 58, [23].
[99] ibid [29].
[100] ibid [33]. For a comparison with the position in New Zealand, see A Britton, 'Pressing for Sentence? An Examination of the New Zealand Crown Prosecutor's Role in Sentencing' (2018) 29 *Criminal Law Forum* 377.
[101] *Lowndes v The Queen* (1999) 195 CLR 665, [16].
[102] See *Kane v The Queen* [2010] VSCA 213 [25]; *Russell v The Queen* [2011] VSCA 147, [57].
[103] Cf *Hudson v The Queen* (2010) 30 VR 610, [33]–[34].

As Lon Fuller said in 1968, 'In its most rudimentary expression, justice demands the like decision of like cases. Since no two cases are ever exactly alike, one cannot act justly unless one is able to define what constitutes an essential likeness'.[104]

Sentencing guidelines can assist by defining 'what constitutes an essential likeness' and identifying the relevant criteria for comparison. Tables of cases, and sentencing submissions from prosecutors, can assist by identifying cases which are 'materially the same or ... instructively different'.[105] These are simply efficient ways of distilling the 'accumulated wisdom' of past decisions and making it accessible to the judge deciding the case at hand.

A structured discretion is not a fettered discretion.[106] Most sentencing judges – concerned to do justice in the individual case – regard equal treatment as a matter of fundamental obligation. So far from regarding such 'tools for consistency' as an impermissible incursion into their discretion, they welcome assistance of this kind as indispensable to its lawful exercise.

---

[104] LL Fuller, *Anatomy of the Law* (New York, FA Praeger, 1968) 94.
[105] *DPP (Cth) v Thomas* (2016) 53 VR 546, 609, [182].
[106] *R v Zakaria* (1984) 12 A Crim R 386, 388, 390.

14

Public and Private Law: A Redundant Divide

CAROL HARLOW*

Over the years of my working life, the frontiers of public law have changed considerably. At the start of my career, the public/private divide was seen by English administrative lawyers as highly significant, as they sought to re-establish their subject in the face of executive powers that had expanded exponentially after a prolonged period of wartime emergency powers and the growth of a highly centralised administrative state, skewing, in their view, the balance of power. The debate at that point centred on the distinctiveness of public law and the need for a 'separate' jurisdiction with 'separate' administrative law rules and principles. This was the background to '"Public" and "Private" Law: Definition without Distinction',[1] an article that I published in 1980, in which I argued against any sharp public/private distinction and against a set of public law principles separate from the common law. My preference as a common lawyer was – and remains – for a functional approach, in which the law applicable to institutions, bodies, acts, decisions and activities is tailored to the part they play in public life, where all are in principle subject, in the Diceyan phrase, to the 'ordinary' law of the land. Moreover, I believe that it is to the legislature rather than the courts that we should look primarily for the allocation of functions and demarcation of boundaries.

Two decades later, on the cusp of a new millennium, that distinguished common lawyer, Michael Taggart, spoke of the absence of any clear boundary between public and private law as a 'peculiarity of the English', though one that was 'still worthy of discussion'.[2] Perhaps surprisingly then, in his own contribution to *The Province of Administrative Law*, the book of essays that he edited, Taggart sought common law sources for many of the principles of public law, suggesting that they were a common resource.[3] Other contributors to the collection made it clear that the preoccupations of public lawyers had changed. The priority was

---

* I should like to thank Professors Richard Rawlings, Mark Aronson and Javier Barnes for insightful comments on earlier drafts of this paper.
[1] C Harlow, '"Public" and "Private" Law: Definition without Distinction' (1980) 43 *MLR* 241.
[2] M Taggart, '"The Peculiarities of the English": Resisting the Public/Private Law Distinction' in P Craig and R Rawlings (eds), *Law and Administration in Europe: Essays in Honour of Carol Harlow* (Oxford, Oxford University Press, 2003).
[3] M Taggart, 'The Province of Administrative Law Determined' in M Taggart (ed), *The Province of Administrative Law* (Oxford, Hart Publishing, 1997) (hereinafter *The Province*).

no longer a separate jurisdiction but concern lest the values and principles of their subject be overthrown by a move to privatisation.

Taking my 1980 article as the starting-point, I shall try in this chapter to chart the shifting course of the public/private debate and to assess its relevance to contemporary debates. The chapter is grounded at the domestic level in the United Kingdom (UK), but I have tried to draw on the common experience of, and exchanges between, common lawyers in several jurisdictions and to profit too from debates amongst European public lawyers.

I. 'Definition without Distinction'?

The modest article that I published in 1980 made four straightforward points:

1. There is no case for a separate administrative jurisdiction in the English legal system. It creates as many problems as it resolves. A remedial distinction, whereby the 'public law remedies' are obtainable via judicial review in the High Court, is more in line with the remedy-oriented common law.
2. There is no case either for separate principles of administrative law in the sense used by Professor Georges Vedel of 'a body of wholly autonomous rules entirely separate from the common law (*le droit commun*)'.[4]
3. The common law is strong enough to find answers to most problems – though the judges often fail to do so.
4. In deciding cases or decision-making, the characteristics of the act and functions of the actor under consideration should be decisive in arriving at a solution. I added, citing a handful of cases that I thought wrongly decided,[5] that a binary public/private classification was too often used by the judiciary as a formalist shield for an authoritarian jurisprudence.

This last proposition was widely misunderstood.[6] I was not saying that there is *never* any distinction to be made between public and private spheres and law, but that the distinction should be based on functional and substantive reasoning and not drawn on purely formal lines. Later, the opposing case was strongly argued by comparatist Geoffrey Samuel, who saw the public/private distinction as 'fundamental to Western legal thought', rooted in our common Roman law heritage and, like the distinctions between property and obligations or contract and tort, a useful classificatory device. Bad decisions were attributable not to the public/private distinction itself but to the way the judges had utilised it.[7]

The background against which these arguments were advanced was, as indicated earlier, that of a transitional period in which the UK had emerged from an authoritarian wartime

---

[4] G Vedel, *Droit Administratif*, 5th edn (Paris, Presses Universitaire de France, 1973) 57–58.

[5] Notably *Town Investments v Department of the Environment* [1978] AC 359, which I had noted in C Harlow, 'The Crown: Wrong Once Again?' (1977) 40 *MLR* 728, and *Hoffman-La Roche v Trade Secretary* [1975] AC 295.

[6] Taggart, '"The Peculiarities of the English"' (n 2) asserts that 'for Carol Harlow *any* distinction between public and private law is irrelevant, devoid of intrinsic merit, dysfunctional, outmoded, too rigid, ill timed bridge-building within Europe, and productive of executive-minded decisions' (emphasis added). This was not the case.

[7] G Samuel, 'Public and Private Law: A Private Lawyer's Response' (1983) 46 *MLR* 558.

regime followed by a period of socialist reconstruction, and was, largely unknowingly, coming to the end of an era of 'big government'. It was a time of discontent with the performance of English public law, which, it was felt by many, had failed to come to terms with the development of 'the administrative state' (terminology not then in general use) and to respond adequately to its manifestations.[8] It was being said that the common law was unable to provide remedies for abuse of power; it had come to the end of its creative life. Lord Scarman thought a new constitutional settlement necessary; party politics had undercut Parliament's autonomous position and 'a legal system at the mercy of a legislature, which is itself, save in a minority situation, at the mercy of the executive, is no sure guarantee of human rights'.[9] Theorists blamed the failure of the common law to elaborate 'a developed concept of the state' or to grapple systematically with the monarchical structure of British government – a thesis challenged cogently by Janet McLean.[10] More directly political arguments were directed at the inadequacy of 'traditional versions of English public law' to shake off the influence of laissez-faire economic theory and take on board the power of the state in 'post liberal-capitalist society' and its essential role in economic management.[11] Specifically invoking the public/private divide, Loughlin attributed deficiencies in public law theory to the English tendency to analogise from private law to the public sphere, a propensity that he saw as the core constituent of the (Diceyan) 'private law model of public law'[12] and to which he attributed the absence of both a 'developed concept of state responsibility' and, more generally, a 'sufficiently distinct' body of public law.[13]

Doctrinally, amongst a small elite, there was a love affair with France.[14] French administrative law boasted a sophisticated law of administrative contract in contrast to the English private law of contract, which had many weaknesses where administrative contracts were concerned.[15] The right of the Crown to contract as a private person concealed the inherent imbalance between the parties and allowed central government to benefit from the use of private law instruments for public purposes, in this way evading the controls of public law.[16]

---

[8] See for a general discussion of legal thinking in the period, M Loughlin, *Public Law and Political Theory* (Oxford, Clarendon Press, 1992).

[9] L Scarman, *English Law – The New Dimension* (London, Stevens Publishing, 1975) 69. Contrast FH Lawson, *The Rational Strength of English Law* (London, Stevens & Sons Ltd, 1951). And see P Devlin, 'The Common Law, Public Policy and the Executive' [1954] *Current Legal Problems* 1, 14; Lord Hailsham, *The Dilemma of Democracy: Diagnosis and Prescription* (London, Collins, 1978).

[10] McLean argued that the absence of a doctrine of the state in English law is not a failure but simply a different way of looking at questions posed by the state and sovereignty: see J McLean, *Searching for the State in British Legal Thought* (Cambridge, Cambridge University Press, 2012).

[11] T Prosser, 'Towards a Critical Public Law' (1982) 9 *Journal of Law and Society* 1. And see E Kamenka and AE-S Tay, 'Beyond Bourgeois Individualism: The Contemporary Crisis in Law and Legal Ideology' in E Kamenka and RS Neale (eds), *Feudalism, Capitalism and Beyond* (Canberra, Australian National University Press, 1975).

[12] For Loughlin's argument that public law is 'special' in character and represents the legal language of politics, see Loughlin, *Public Law and Political Theory* (n 8).

[13] M Loughlin, 'The State, the Crown and the Law' in M Sunkin and S Payne (eds), *The Nature of the Crown: A Legal and Political Analysis* (Oxford, Oxford University Press, 1999).

[14] CJ Hamson, *Executive Discretion and Judicial Control: An Aspect of the French Conseil d'Etat* (London, Stevens & Sons Ltd, 1954); LN Brown and JF Garner, *French Administrative Law*, 2nd edn (Oxford, Butterworth-Heinemann, 1973); JDB Mitchell, 'The Causes and Effects of the Absence of a System of Public Law in the United Kingdom' [1965] *PL* 95; JDB Mitchell, 'The State of Public Law in the United Kingdom' (1966) 15 *ICLQ* 133.

[15] JDB Mitchell, *The Contracts of Public Authorities* (London, Bell, 1954). But see C Turpin, *Government Procurement and Contracts* (Harlow, Longman, 1989).

[16] T Daintith, 'Regulation by Contract: The New Prerogative' [1979] *Current Legal Problems* 41.

Government had recently benefited from this type of reasoning in the widely-criticised *Town Investments* case, where the argument was accepted that a government department was 'carrying on the business of government' and so able to benefit from a reduced rent for a 'business tenancy' in terms of the Counter-Inflation Business Rents Order 1972.[17] Again, French administrative law had developed a sophisticated system of administrative tort liability, developed by an administrative court, 'which knows how to, and does, adapt an appropriate liability to the constantly changing demands of society';[18] the best that the English courts could manage was the *Dorset Yacht* case.[19] Mitchell saw these defects as endemic; they could be cured only by the installation of a powerful public law court closely modelled on that of France.[20]

Against this background, my argument was controversial, if in retrospect surprisingly formalist. There is no comparison of Anglo-French administrative law traditions.[21] There is no discussion of pluralism or defence of diversity, and although beliefs concerning the place of cultural tradition in legitimating legal orders that I would express later are perhaps latent in my argument, they are never clearly articulated.[22] There is no consideration of social context or reference to socio-legal materials and no prevision of the emergent feminist debate, which would later prove transformative.[23] The focus was strictly legal and atheoretical.

A. A Lost Cause: The Separate Jurisdiction

Within the judiciary, the case for a public law court had notable support around this time from Lord Diplock, who engineered and actively espoused the 'exclusive jurisdiction' principle, according to which a litigant seeking to establish 'rights to which he was entitled to protection under public law' could proceed only by way of judicial review.[24] At least initially, the principle was strongly defended by Lord Woolf on the ground that public law proceedings

> serve a different purpose to private law proceedings. In the case of private law proceedings it is the parties alone who are directly concerned with the outcome of the litigation. The public at large are not usually interested in the outcome of private law proceedings. The public as a whole are concerned that private law proceedings should provide a fair and efficient manner of resolving disputes between individuals and of enforcing the rights of one individual over another. However, public law proceedings much more frequently directly affect many members of the public or even the public at large as well as the parties to the proceedings.[25]

---

[17] SI 1972/1848. And see *Town Investments v Department of the Environment* (n 5); Harlow, 'The Crown: Wrong Once Again?' (n 5).
[18] CJ Hamson, 'Escaping Borstal Boys and the Immunity of Office' (1969) 27 *CLJ* 273, 283 in a note on *Home Office v Dorset Yacht Co Ltd* [1970] AC 1004. See similarly JF Garner, 'Public Law and Private Law' [1978] *PL* 230.
[19] *Dorset Yacht* (n 18).
[20] Mitchell, 'The Causes and Effects of the Absence of the System of Public Law in the United Kingdom' (n 14).
[21] As was done later by JWF Allison, *A Continental Distinction in the Common Law: A Historical and Comparative Perspective on English Public Law*, revised edn (Oxford, Oxford University Press, 2000).
[22] C Harlow, 'Voices of Difference in a Plural Community' [2002] 1(3) *American Journal of Comparative Law* 339.
[23] See, eg, M Thornton (ed), *Public and Private: Feminist Legal Debates* (Oxford, Oxford University Press, 1995).
[24] *O'Reilly v Mackman* [1983] 2 AC 237; *Cocks v Thanet District Council* [1983] 2 AC 286.
[25] H Woolf, *Protection of the Public: A New Challenge* (London, Stevens & Sons Ltd, 1990) 12.

Most private lawyers would find this proposition surprising.

Fortunately, given the powerful position of the proponents, the 'exclusive jurisdiction' principle was vigorously attacked by Sir William Wade, who called it a 'seismic disturbance' that 'created a host of new problems for litigants that had by no means yet been resolved'.[26] Similarly, the influential JUSTICE/All Souls Committee thought *O'Reilly v Mackman*, in which the principle was embedded, 'an unfortunate decision', the effects of which were 'quite imprecise' since no clear test for deciding what is a 'public-law case' had been provided.[27] A few wasteful cases were fought on procedural grounds[28] before the tide turned. *Boddington v British Transport Police*[29] affirmed the practice of 'collateral challenge', whereby someone charged with a criminal offence created in regulations or a bye-law can stand on the invalidity of the bye-law as a defence in civil or criminal proceedings.

Aronson suggests, however, that procedural exclusivity was not without consequences. The idea of a 'separate jurisdiction' helped to embolden and empower the British judiciary; it should thus be credited with re-shaping the modern practice of judicial review, moving it from a primarily rule-bound, rights model to a process 'subject to huge swathes of judicial discretion based upon shifting judicial assessments of where the greater public interest might be'.[30] This is debatable. Arguably, it was the passage of the Human Rights Act 1998 that emboldened the British judiciary in the sense referred to by Aronson.[31] And similar developments have taken place in other common law jurisdictions, notably Canada in the late 1960s and early 1970s and again after the entry into force of the Canadian Charter of Rights and Freedoms.[32]

Reforms of judicial review procedure in England and Wales have usually taken place within the parameters of the Supreme Court Act 1981 and Order 53 procedure.[33] By and large, matters have been left to the judges and changes have been minimal (though recently government has been more intrusive).[34] Thus, a Crown Office List with

---

[26] HWR Wade, *Administrative Law*, 6th edn (Oxford, Oxford University Press, 1988) viii.

[27] Committee of the JUSTICE-All Souls Review of Administrative Law in the United Kingdom, *Administrative Justice: Some Necessary Reforms* (Oxford, Clarendon Press,1988) [6.18] and generally [6.15]–[6.22]. And see *Davy v Spelthorne BC* [1984] 1 AC 262 (Lord Wilberforce).

[28] *Wandsworth LBC v Winder* [1985] AC 461; *Roy v Kensington and Chelsea LBC* [1992] 1 AC 624.

[29] *Boddington v British Transport Police* [1999] 2 AC 143. And see M Aronson, M Groves and G Weeks, *Judicial Review of Administrative Action and Government Liability*, 6th edn (Sydney, Thompson Reuters, 2017) 'Collateral Challenge' at [10.6].

[30] M Aronson, 'Public Law Values in the Common Law' in M Elliott and D Feldman (eds), *The Cambridge Companion to Public Law* (Cambridge, Cambridge University Press, 2015) 140. And compare JNE Varuhas, 'The Public Interest Conception of Public Law: Its Procedural Origins and Substantive Implications' in J Bell, M Elliott, JNE Varuhas and P Murray (eds), *Public Law Adjudication in Common Law Systems* (Oxford, Hart Publishing, 2016).

[31] M Groves, 'The Surrogacy Principle and Motherhood Statements in Administrative Law' in L Pearson, C Harlow and M Taggart (eds), *Administrative Law in a Changing State: Essays in Honour of Mark Aronson* (Portland, OR, Hart Publishing, 2008).

[32] D Mullan, 'The Canadian Charter of Rights and Freedom: A "Direct Driver" of Judicial Review of Administrative Action in Canada?' in L Pearson, C Harlow and M Taggart (eds), *Law in a Changing State: Essays in Honour of Mark Aronson* (Oxford, Hart Publishing, 2008); B McLachlin, 'Academe and the Courts: Professor Mullan's Contribution' in G Huscroft and M Taggart (eds), *Inside and Outside Canadian Administrative Law: Essays in Honour of David Mullan* (Toronto, University of Toronto Press, 2006) 15–18. Contrast M Taggart, '"Australian Exceptionalism" in Judicial Review' (2008) 36 *Federal Law Review* 1.

[33] Now s 31 of the Senior Courts Act 1981 and pt 54 of the Civil Procedure Rules (CPR) (SI 1998/3132).

[34] See notably s 15 of the Immigration Act 2014 and ss 84–90 of the Criminal Justice and Courts Act 2015.

dedicated judges was followed by the creation of a nominal Administrative Court within the High Court.[35] Significantly, the Leggatt Committee, on whose report[36] the Tribunals, Courts and Enforcement Act 2007 (TCEA 2007) is based, looked to Australia, where appeals go to a generalist tribunal whose members are (largely) judges, rather than to the dualist French model. The TCEA 2007 can be said to have concluded the process of public/private alignment by firmly integrating tribunals into the courts system as a single, unified courts and tribunals service,[37] and by providing for transfer of cases and interchange of personnel with the appellate Upper Tribunal, which now handles the bulk of judicial review applications.

With appropriate variations, flexible, jurisdictional models of judicial review prevail in all common law jurisdictions. Courts and tribunals in the common law world generally adhere rather strictly to the bipolar adversarial pattern, and although to a limited extent senior courts have accepted third-party interventions,[38] no substantial procedural changes of the type suggested in the 1970s by American academic Richard Stewart to ensure interest-representation for stakeholders, and by Abram Chayes to accommodate policy-centred, group litigation, have ever come about.[39] It is noticeable too that transnational courts – notably the European Court of Justice, though patterned on a French model – have disregarded the model of a dual jurisdiction. Calls for a separate administrative jurisdiction have died away to be replaced by demands for specialist tribunals and courts. Indeed, leafing through the dusty reports and literature, it is hard to see why so much ink was spilled and time spent on a matter that, even in France, where the public/private distinction is deeply embedded in the national culture and hence serves an essential and fundamental purpose,[40] has been questioned in recent years.[41]

B. The Distinctiveness of the State

Much of the argument in favour of 'special' public law rules was grounded in ideas about the state. Public law is concerned with power and authority, with both of which the state has been identified in the modern era. For Dunleavy and O'Leary, the state is 'so differentiated from the rest of its society as to create identifiable public and private spheres'; it is 'the ultimate authority for all law', while public law is 'made by state officials and

---

[35] On the recommendation of J Bowman, *Review of the Crown Office List* (London, Lord Chancellor's Department, 2000).

[36] A Leggatt, *Tribunals for Users: One System, One Service: Report of the Review of Tribunals* (London, The Stationery Office, 2001).

[37] Joint Statement by the Lord Chancellor, the Lord Chief Justice and the Senior President of Tribunals: *Transforming Our Justice System* (Department of Justice, 2016).

[38] H Samuels, 'Public Interest Litigation and the Civil Society Factor' (2018) 38(4) *Legal Studies* 515; M Kirby, 'Deconstructing the Law's Hostility to Public Interest Litigation' (2011) 127 *LQR* 537; G Williams, 'The Amicus Curiae and Intervention in the High Court of Australia' (2000) 28(3) *Federal Law Review* 365; S Shah, T Poole and M Blackwell, 'Rights, Interveners and the Law Lords' (2014) 34(2) *Oxford Journal of Legal Studies* 295.

[39] R Stewart, 'The Reformation of American Administrative Law' (1975) 88 *Harvard Law Review* 1667; A Chayes, 'The Role of the Judge in Public Law Litigation' (1976) 89 *Harvard Law Review* 1281.

[40] See J-B Auby, 'Le Rôle de la Distinction du Droit Public et du Droit Privé dans le Droit Français' and O Beaud, 'La Distinction entre Droit Public et Droit Privé: un dualisme qui résiste aux critiques' in M Freedland and J-B Auby (eds), *The Public Law/Private Law Divide, Une entente assez cordiale?* (Portland, OR, Hart Publishing, 2006).

[41] B Stirn, 'Quelques Réfléxions sur le Dualisme Juridictionnel' (January–June 1996) 3 *Justices* 41, 43–45.

backed by a formal monopoly of force'.[42] How far this statement is true today, we shall leave for section III. The notion that the British lacked 'a developed concept of the state' and had instead to fall back on the Crown as a 'poor substitute' or 'distraction' was, however, an influential element in the argument for a special public law. The archaic symbol of the Crown was said to inhibit lawyers from recognising both 'a modern state apparatus and an associated and distinct public law',[43] allowing the functions of government to be shielded behind it.

Modern case law suggests otherwise. In the key *GCHQ case*, the House of Lords were dismissive of arguments based on the royal prerogative and thought that there was no reason why, 'simply because a decision-making power is derived from a common law and not a statutory source, it should *for that reason only* be immune from judicial review'.[44] Significantly, Lord Roskill added 'In either case the act in question is the act of the executive. To talk of that act as the act of the sovereign savours of the archaism of past centuries.'[45] While in the *GCHQ* case the Lords made an exception for 'the most important prerogative power concerned with the control of the armed forces and with foreign policy', later case law makes it clear that even these areas are not sacrosanct and are subject to a form of judicial review, even if highly deferential.[46] The case of the Chagos Islanders is admittedly a dishonourable exception.[47] But for the time being the saga culminates in the UK with the celebrated Brexit challenge, where the Supreme Court brushed the prerogative powers to one side in ruling that an Act of Parliament was required to authorise Ministers to give notice to the European Union of the UK's decision to withdraw.[48]

C. Uneasy Partners: Tort Law and Government Liability

Perhaps the strongest case for special public law rules of liability lay (and may still lie) in the private law realm of tort. In France, the separate jurisdiction enabled the building of a system of administrative liability with distinctive rules, which provide for compensation to persons injured through the fault of a public service (*faute de service*) and – admittedly on rare occasions – where 'abnormal damage' has been suffered through a legal administrative act (*égalité devant les charges publiques*). Today, these principles form the basis for Council of Europe recommendations to member states on public liability.[49]

---

[42] P Dunleavy and B O'Leary, *Theories of the State: The Politics of Liberal Democracy* (London, Macmillan, 1987) 2. For O'Leary's formalist and positivist view of law, see B O'Leary, 'What Should Public Lawyers Do?' (1992) 12 *OJLS* 404.
[43] Loughlin, 'The State, the Crown and the Law' (n 13).
[44] *Council for Civil Service Unions v Minister for the Civil Service* [1985] AC 374, 410 (Lord Diplock) (hereinafter '*GCHQ* case').
[45] ibid 417 (Lord Roskill).
[46] Aronson, Groves and Weeks, *Judicial Review* (n 29) [3.60]; D Mullan, 'Judicial Review of the Executive: Principled Exasperation' (2010) 8(1) *New Zealand Journal of Public and International Law* 145; T Poole, 'Judicial Review at the Margins: Law, Power and Prerogative' (2010) 60 *University of Toronto Law Journal* 81. And see similarly in the tort context, *Smith v Ministry of Defence* [2013] UKSC 41.
[47] *R (Bancoult) v Secretary of State for Foreign and Commonwealth Affairs (No 2)* [2009] 1 AC 453; *R (Bancoult (No 2)) v Secretary of State for Foreign and Commonwealth Affairs* [2016] UKSC 35.
[48] *R (Miller and Dos Santos) v Secretary of State for Exiting the European Union* [2017] UKSC 5.
[49] Council of Europe, Recommendation No R (84) 15 of the Committee of Ministers to Member States Relating to Public Liability (1984).

The private law model of public law can offer nothing similar. Dicey's ideal-type of the personal responsibility of public officials before the 'ordinary' courts may 'reflect a popular sentiment about officialdom'[50] and help 'to put government on a level playing field with the rest of us';[51] in most respects, however, the idea 'seems quaintly old-fashioned'.[52] The playing field has tilted. Officials are endowed with a multiplicity of statutory powers and duties that often entail considerable discretion but, like all employees, they are largely sheltered from the financial consequences of liability by radical changes to the principles of vicarious liability designed to ensure a solvent respondent.[53] The state is now expected to deliver significant public services and deliver them well. It is also expected to ensure and oversee the delivery of such services – more problematic in terms of proximity and causation.[54] It is a significant and often intrusive regulator, causing loss and damage.[55] Public liability gives rise to difficult questions – whether the police service should owe a general duty of care to protect individuals against criminal activity,[56] whether economic loss caused by a financial regulator should give rise to liability,[57] what the status is of torts actionable *per se*[58] for example. Not surprisingly, judges throughout the common law world where the private law model prevails have vacillated, producing a complex and confused case law in dealing with these questions.

But similarly complex problems arise in the private sector. It is not the case (as Lord Woolf asserted) that in private law proceedings the parties alone are directly concerned. Group tort claims may involve many hundreds of potential claimants, not to say employers dragged into the legal net by extensions to the law of vicarious liability mentioned above. Injury caused by the 'miracle mineral', asbestos, had by 2001 triggered a flood of litigation throughout the world from 600,000 individuals on which more than $54 billion had been spent. Eighty-five firms. including more than 10 of the largest asbestos manufacturers, and several insurers had failed.[59] In the UK alone, government has set aside a £380 million package to compensate victims who cannot trace a liable employer or insurer.[60] It is not necessarily in the public interest that private corporations are bankrupted, and it should not be assumed that losses in public liability cases always fall on the taxpayer; public authorities are often insured. It was indeed the failure of just such an

---

[50] P Hogg, *The Liability of the Crown*, 2nd edn (Scarborough, Carswell Press, 1989) 1–2.
[51] M Aronson, 'Government Liability in Negligence' (2008) 32 *Melbourne University Law Review* 44.
[52] Aronson, Groves and Weeks, *Judicial Review* (n 29) [19.60].
[53] *Various Claimants v Catholic Child Welfare Society* [2013] 2 AC 1; *Armes v Nottinghamshire County Council* [2017] UKSC 60. And see P Giliker, *Vicarious Liability in Tort: A Comparative Perspective* (New York, Cambridge University Press, 2010).
[54] *Graham Barclay Oysters Pty Ltd v Ryan* (2002) 211 CLR 540.
[55] *Trent Strategic Health Authority v Jain and Another* [2009] 2 WLR 248.
[56] *Michael and others v Chief Constable of South Wales Police and Another* [2015] 2 WLR 343.
[57] *Three Rivers District Council v Governor and Company of the Bank of England (No 3)* [2003] 2 AC 1.
[58] *Wainwright v Home Office* [2004] 2 AC 406; *R v Governor of Brockhill Prison, ex parte Evans (No 2)* [2001] 2 AC 19; *R (Lumba) v Secretary of State for the Home Department* [2012] 1 AC 245.
[59] MJ White, 'Asbestos and the Future of Mass Torts' (2004) 18(2) *Journal of Economic Perspectives* 183. See also DR Hensler et al, *Asbestos in the Courts: The Challenge of Mass Toxic Torts* (The Rand Corporation, 1985). Updates on asbestosis litigation are published regularly on the Rand website at https://www.rand.org/.
[60] Department for Work and Pensions, 'Asbestos victims to get £123,000 in compensation' GOV.UK (6 March 2014), available at https://www.gov.uk/government/news/asbestos-victims-to-get-123000-in-compensation.

insurer that led to the Australian *Review of the Law of Negligence* with a view to a *general* limitation of liability,[61] though the outcome in some states was a conveniently restrictive defence for public authorities.[62] Private liability is, in short, not always wholly private and public liability is not wholly public.

A well-argued case for a special law of administrative tort liability to deal with such questions has recently been propounded.[63] But could a 'special law' really have done better? In his detailed comparison of the French and English systems, Fairgrieve noted striking parallels: the judges' desire to avoid defensive administrative practices; to limit excessive liability for repercussive claims; to admit a 'margin of manoeuvre' to public authorities involved in sensitive activities; to avoid second-guessing discretionary administrative choices; to avoid extending liability for certain types of loss – all the familiar arguments are to be found in the jurisprudence of the French administrative courts.[64] The truth is that these are difficult policy questions, multi-layered and polycentric and often unsuited for judicial decision.[65] They require legislative solutions, which too often are not forthcoming,[66] or involve compensation schemes that are inadequate or unsatisfactory.[67] Governments tend in an era of retrenchment to avoid general debates on public liability, as we saw when the English and Welsh Law Commission took the initiative to rationalise the law.[68] The response from the British Government was immediate and negative, pushing the question back to courts to resolve.

II. Public Law at Risk?

A. The 'Hands Off' State

By the end of the twentieth century, the landscape was very different. An era of privatisation and economic liberalism had been ushered in by the election of Conservative governments in the United States (US) and UK, which was seen by many public lawyers to threaten their discipline. The frontiers of public law were retracting and 'public law values' were thought to be at risk. Deficiencies of the private law of contract became a key concern, with privatisation, outsourcing, competitive tendering and franchising all areas for disquiet.[69] Contract law, born into a world of relationships between individuals, seemed ill-adapted

---

[61] Commonwealth of Australia, *Review of the Law of Negligence: Final Report* (2002).
[62] Aronson, Groves and Weeks, *Judicial Review* (n 29) [19.280].
[63] T Cornford, *Towards a Public Law of Tort* (Aldershot, Ashgate Publishing, 2008). My counter-arguments were expressed in C Harlow, *State Liability, Tort Law and Beyond* (Oxford, Oxford University Press, 2004).
[64] D Fairgrieve, *State Liability in Tort: A Comparative Law Study* (Oxford, Oxford University Press, 2003) 263.
[65] See famously L Fuller, 'The Forms and Limits of Adjudication' (1978) 92 *Harvard Law Review* 353.
[66] P Hogg, 'Compensation for Damage Caused by Government' (1995) 6(1) *National Journal of Constitutional Law* 7, 12–13.
[67] C Harlow, 'Rationalising Administrative Compensation' [2010] *PL* 321.
[68] Law Commission, *Administrative Redress: Public Bodies and the Citizen, A Consultation Paper*, CP No 187 (2008).
[69] M Freedland, 'Government by Contract and Public Law' [1994] *PL* 86.

to the modern world of million-pound public/private initiatives,[70] while the interests of public service users, who had no direct contractual relationship with the service, were poorly protected.[71] Prosser questioned the morality of selling 'public goods' into private hands and, drawing the near-obligatory French comparison, pointed to the absence of any British constitutional provision on which to base protection.[72] The 'private law model' was censured for its failure to take account of the collective public interest,[73] and private law was characterised as a shield for selfish, profit-oriented individualism. The debate revealed a clear ideological dimension; it was very much an attack on political values couched in legal terminology.

In an astringent contribution to *The Province*, however, Aronson queried the view that 'only a public law response is appropriate for an issue involving public power'.[74] He saw an 'inter-penetration of state and private sector power' emerging and (echoing the point I had made in 1980) thought the best way to deal with problems might be 'the adaptation of private law doctrines, such as contract or tort law'.[75] In the US too, Jody Freeman called in a seminal set of papers for a more positive attitude. Public lawyers should view privatisation as a means of publicisation, through which 'private actors increasingly commit themselves to traditionally public goals as the price of access to lucrative opportunities to deliver goods and services that might otherwise be provided directly by the state'.[76] Administrative law concepts and doctrines were hierarchical and bureaucratic, and 'badly out of synch' with a reality in which many public services and functions were produced by 'a highly interdependent network of public/private partnerships' woven together by history and practice.[77] Rather than compromising democratic norms of accountability, due process, equality and rationality, privatisation might extend them to private actors. Anticipating the contemporary trend, US legislation, designed to increase the transparency, integrity and accountability of public companies – in the sense, be it noted, of a company whose shares can be bought by the general public – called for corporate codes of behaviour based on professional ethical standards, enforceable through report-back mechanisms.[78] Looking back from a time after the collapse of Carillion, much of the debate seems naive.[79]

---

[70] See R Rawlings, 'Poetic Justice: Public Contracting and the Case of the London Tube' in Pearson, Harlow and Taggart (eds), *Administrative Law in a Changing State* (n 31).

[71] I Harden, *The Contracting State* (Buckingham, PA, Open University Press, 1992). But see ACL Davies, *Accountability: A Public Law Analysis of Government by Contract* (New York, Oxford University Press, 2001); P Vincent-Jones, *The New Public Contracting: Regulation, responsiveness relationality* (Oxford, Oxford University Press, 2006). And see N Seddon, *Government Contracts Federal, State and Local*, 6th edn (Leichhardt, The Federation Press, 2018).

[72] T Prosser, 'Bringing Constitutional Principles Back In' in R Bellamy, V Bufacchi and D Castiglione (eds), *Democratic and Constitutional Culture in the Union of Europe* (London, Lothian Foundation Press, 1995). And see M Hunt, 'The Constitutionalisation and the Contractualisation of Governance' in *The Province* (n 3).

[73] P McAuslan, 'Administrative Law, Collective Consumption and Judicial Policy' (1983) 46 *MLR* 1.

[74] M Aronson, 'A Public Lawyer's Responses to Privatisation and Outsourcing' in *The Province* (n 3).

[75] ibid 51, 70.

[76] J Freeman, 'Extending Public Law Norms through Privatization' (2002–03) 116 *Harvard Law Review* 1258.

[77] ibid 1288, citing her seminal article 'The Private Role in Public Governance' (2000) 75 *NYU Law Review* 543, 547–48.

[78] Note: 'The Good, The Bad, and Their Corporate Codes of Ethics: Enron, Sarbanes-Oxley, and the Problems with Legislating Good Behaviour' (2002) 116 *Harvard Law Review* 2123.

[79] House of Commons Public Administration and Constitutional Affairs Committee, *After Carillion: Public Sector Outsourcing and Contracting* and *Government Response*, HC 748 and 1685 (2017–19).

B. A Regulatory Reshape

The intention had been for privatised industry to be regulated by the market; regulation, 'if needed at all, would only be needed for a transitional phase'.[80] But as the deficiencies of the market model were recognised, supervisory bodies were set in place to protect the public interest. By the turn of the century, the state had once more been transformed; out of the crucible of privatisation had come a 'new regulatory state'. Graham and Prosser thought the difference between *direct* control of nationalised industry and *indirect* control of commercial enterprise through regulation 'largely nominal'. Just as nationalisation had begun with an arm's-length relationship with government that had soon become much closer, so privatisation was heading in the same direction.[81]

Public tasks were delegated to bodies that were nominally self-regulatory, closing the public/private gap. The new entities did not sit comfortably within a conventional public/private framework; they operated across and on both sides of the divide. Professional associations and their disciplinary bodies carried out public functions and trade associations were entrusted with quasi-legislative, standard-setting functions. Such bodies might work to private rather than publicly-set standards, but their autonomy was offset by increased regulatory oversight, and they were subject to varying requirements of transparency and degrees of accountability.[82] Non-state regulation grew very fast 'within and between other social actors … all without the government's involvement or indeed formal approval'.[83] The term 'decentring' came into use, conveying that regulation was not a state monopoly. Noting the rapid rise of 'hybrid' organisations and 'networks', composed of differing combinations of governmental and non-governmental actors, Black pronounced 'the collapse of the public/private distinction in socio-political terms', and called for a 'rethinking of the role of formal authority in governance and regulation'.[84] A conceptual blending of public and private followed, as the term 'regulatory capitalism' was substituted for 'regulatory state'.[85] Yet behind the curtain of 'decentred regulation' the outlines of a regulatory state are always clearly visible; at the end of the day, it is always open to government to intervene.[86]

---

[80] M Moran, 'The Rise of the Regulatory State in Britain' (2001) 54 *Parliamentary Affairs* 15, 26.

[81] C Graham and T Prosser, 'The Privatisation of State Enterprises' in C Graham and T Prosser (eds), *Waiving the Rules: The Constitution under Thatcherism* (Milton Keynes, Open University Press, 1988) 76–78.

[82] See C Scott, 'Private Regulation of the Public Sector: A Neglected Facet of Contemporary Governance' (2002) 29(1) *Journal of Law and Society* 56.

[83] J Black, 'Decentering Regulation: The Role of Regulation and Self-Regulation in a "Post-Regulatory" World' (2001) 54 *Current Legal Problems* 103.

[84] ibid 110. And see I Bartle and P Vass, 'Self-Regulation within the Regulatory State: Towards a New Regulatory Paradigm?' (2007) 85 *Public Administration* 885.

[85] J Jordana and D Levi-Faur (eds), *The Politics of Regulation: Institutions and Regulatory Reforms for the Age of Governance* (Cheltenham, Edward Elgar, 2004); J Braithwaite, *Regulatory Capitalism: How it Works, Ideas for Making it Work Better* (Cheltenham, Edward Elgar, 2008).

[86] In the UK, only the press has to date been strong enough to resist a call for public regulation. Lord Justice Leveson, *An Inquiry into the Culture, Practices and Ethics of the Press*, HC 780 (2012/13), recommended statutory regulation of the press with a statutory body to handle complaints. Agreement could not be reached and the present regulatory body, IPSO, is set up and funded by the press and membership is voluntary. Contrast broadcast media regulated by Ofcom in terms of the Communications Act 2003.

By the turn of the century, regulation was no longer merely a device to correct market failure; it had spread widely across the social and into the private domain. Moran observed:

> Vast new areas of social life have been colonised by regulatory agencies. The food we eat, the physical conditions we work under, the machines and equipment we use in our home, office and on the road – all are increasingly subject to legal controls, usually administered by a specialised agency.[87]

Almost unremarked, the frontiers of public law expanded. Government appropriated contract as a tool of public law. A 'workfare' or 'work to welfare' ethos, based on the idea of welfare benefits as one side of a contract between community and citizen of which the obligation to work was the other,[88] pinned benefits to an undertaking to work or undergo training in which consent was nominal.[89] Contractual ideology, introduced as a justification for harsher conditions on welfare programmes, proliferated through the social services:[90] 'Acceptable behaviour contracts' were used systematically in behaviour modification schemes, governing parental conduct, for example, in cases of truancy or anti-social behaviour.

Associated with self-regulation but common to public and private sectors is the practice of issuing 'soft law' or 'non-legal rules'.[91] The non-justiciable 'Citizens' Charter', which formed a keynote of John Major's public administration programme,[92] exemplifies the soft-law technique. The Charter called for individual service charters, designed to form 'a *kind of* contract' between service users and providers. Providers would publish clear targets for levels of service, which would encourage them to improve their services, but although it suggested compensation where appropriate, the Charter significantly steered clear of creating legal rights.

As the regulatory state moved stealthily into previously unregulated areas of family and social life, it became accepted that family relationships should cease to be 'a sacrosanct private sphere' virtually immune from public scrutiny, to become the legitimate concern of government and target of political interventions.[93] Incursions into private life are popular with politicians as a way to be seen to be doing something while avoiding excessive regulation or prohibitions affecting personal choice. 'Nudge theory' is the art of steering people in a particular direction while apparently preserving their right to make their own decisions. Derived from private sector techniques such as the use by supermarkets of loyalty cards and the more insidious streaming of advertising at online consumers,[94] nudge

---

[87] Moran, 'The Rise of the Regulatory State' (n 80) 20.

[88] S White, 'Social Rights and the Social Contract: Political Theory and the New Welfare Politics' (2000) 30 *British Journal of Political Science* 507; D King, *In the Name of Liberalism: Illiberal Social Policy in the United States and Britain* (Oxford, Oxford University Press, 1999).

[89] M Freedland and D King, 'Contractual Governance and Illiberal Contracts: Some Problems of Contractualism as an Instrument of Behaviour Management by Agencies of Government' (2003) 27 *Cambridge Journal of Economics* 465.

[90] On the spread of the contractual ideology throughout social services, see A Paz-Fuchs, *Welfare to Work: Conditional Rights in Social Policy* (New York, Oxford University Press, 2008).

[91] See R Rawlings, 'Soft Law Never Dies' in M Elliott and D Feldman (eds), *The Cambridge Companion to Public Law* (Cambridge, Cambridge University Press, 2015).

[92] Introduced in the UK by *The Citizen's Charter: Raising the Standard*, Cm 1599 (1991).

[93] M Thornton, 'Introduction' in *Public and Private: Feminist Legal Debates* (n 23) 9.

[94] C Sunstein, 'Nudging: A Very Short Guide' (2014) 37 *Journal of Consumer Policy* 583; RH Thaler and CR Sunstein, *Nudge: Improving Decisions about Health, Wealth, and Happiness* (New Haven, CT, Yale University Press, 2008).

theory has many public law parallels. Public health policies are routinely promoted not only by 'command-and-control' public law techniques – the outright prohibition, say, of tobacco advertising – or through a self-policing, soft-law method such as a code of industry practice, but also by pressure on manufacturers, say, to cut the level of salt and sugar in processed food. The classic public law tools of differential taxation, grants and subsidies are pressed into service to 'nudge' citizens into green choices; as diesel is taxed, green policies are promoted by subsidies for the manufacture of solar panels or wind-farm development, quotas regulate fishery catches, and schemes cap and allocate noxious emissions and allow for trading in emissions. These techniques imply a significant shift in conceptualisation away from a traditional view of private rights to property and self-interested commercial enterprise (such as trading in emissions) towards a concept of public resources, access to and use of which may be apportioned, rationed or, indeed, traded.[95] At every level, but perhaps especially at the supranational level of environmental law and climate change, these 'soft' or 'sub-legal' regulatory techniques are in use to encourage cooperative action and avoid political discord.

C. Values and Tenets

Because public law bodies act for 'the public at large', Lord Woolf had argued, they were subject to 'higher ethical standards'.[96] But what were the standards, and what should they be? Do we really tolerate lower ethical standards in someone who works in the private sector than in a public employee? Aronson is orthodox, selecting values that, as he pointed out, all relate closely to judicial review – legality, good faith, the rule of law, fairness, impartiality, consistency, rationality, accessibility of grievance procedures – though adding accountability and transparency to the mix.[97] Taggart thought that, 'at a reasonably high level of abstraction', public and private law shared several underlying values, yet he classified openness, fairness, participation, impartiality, accountability, honesty and rationality as public law values.[98] But are these really public law values, and are they applicable only to public law bodies? The rule of law references law in general and is not a specifically legal doctrine, although lawyers lay claim to it. It can be traced back to the Greek philosophers. The widely-recognised value of rationality was an Enlightenment ideal, distributed in the nineteenth century through the worlds of science, sociology and political economy. (Perhaps ironically, the common law spoke until very recently in terms of reasonableness.[99])

Transparency and accountability are pre-eminently market values, which travelled across the private/public border in the toolkit of managerial governance. Latecomers to

---

[95] G Winter, 'Rationing the Use of Common Resources: Problems of Design and Constitutionality' in D Oliver, T Prosser and R Rawlings (eds), *Regulatory State: Constitutional Implications* (New York, Oxford University Press, 2010) 129. For a much earlier instance of a similar problem, see M Taggart, *Private Property and Abuse of Rights in Victorian England: The Story of Edward Pickles and the Bradford Water Supply* (New York, Oxford University Press, 2002).
[96] H Woolf, 'Public and Private Law – Why the Divide? [1986] *PL* 273.
[97] Aronson, 'Public Law Values' (n 30) 144–45.
[98] *The Province* (n 3) 3.
[99] The introduction of rationality as a ground of review is generally attributed to Lord Diplock in the *GCHQ* case (n 44).

public law,[100] the terminology is now used 'almost to saturation point' in the jargon of both public and corporate business management.[101] Accountability, transparency, participation and the rule of law are core 'good governance values', propagated at national and transnational levels by institutions such as the UN, OECD and European Commission, together with fringe values, such as fairness, equality, responsiveness, and economy and efficiency. Much like the seven values of selflessness, integrity, objectivity, accountability, openness, honesty and leadership chosen by the Nolan Committee as standards for conduct in public life, these values are generally recognised as basic standards of conduct in corporate administration.[102] They are not specifically legal in content or character and, bridging the public/private barrier, they apply generally across 'public space'. Oliver sees them as 'paramount values of democracy' common to public and private law;[103] Auby (whose choices are compendious) calls them 'public values'[104] – an implicit reference perhaps to the classical division between the 'public' world, which embraced government and commerce, and the 'private' life of the home. They are best described as 'societal values', a common currency that forms part of the 'background theory' against which our institutions and behaviour, public and private, are to be evaluated.[105]

Human rights, which flooded into legal systems in the second half of the twentieth century providing a new and potent source of values, are clearly public law principles in that they can be asserted, like bills of rights embedded in national constitutions, only against the state. But this sharp public/private divide has shown itself to be problematic. In the regrettable English case of *YL v Birmingham City Council*,[106] the House of Lords faced the question whether the Human Rights Act 1998 covered a care home run by a private company but subject to statutory regulation and largely financed through local authority placements made in the exercise of its statutory care obligations. The minority thought that it did: the state had assumed responsibility for seeing that care was provided; there was a strong public interest in the welfare system and a close connection between the care service and 'the core values underlying the Convention rights'.[107] The majority thought otherwise. The home was 'a company carrying on a socially useful business for profit' and neither a charity nor a philanthropist. It operated in a commercial market with commercial competitors, and was consequently entitled to enter into private law contracts with the residents in its care homes and with local authorities. Its activities therefore did not fall within the statutory definition of a body 'carrying on functions of a public nature'.[108] It is hard to support this reasoning;

---

[100] But see P Daly, 'Administrative Law: A Values-based Approach' in J Bell, M Elliott, J Varuhas and P Murray (eds), *Public Law Adjudication in Common Law Systems: Process and Substance* (Oxford, Hart Publishing, 2016).

[101] C Hood, 'Transparency in Historical Perspective' in C Hood and D Heald (eds), *Transparency: The Key to Better Governance?* (New York, Oxford University Press, 2006).

[102] *First Report of the Committee on Standards in Public Life*, Cm 2850 (1995). And see Committee on Standards in Public Life, *Ethical Standards for Public Service Providers* (2014).

[103] D Oliver, 'The Underlying Values of Public and Private Law' in *The Province* (n 3) 217. She lists dignity, autonomy, respect, status and security, citizenship and participation.

[104] J-B Auby, 'Contracting Out and "Public Values": A Theoretical and Comparative Approach' in S Rose-Ackerman, PL Lindseth and B Emerson (eds), *Comparative Administrative Law*, 2nd edn (Cheltenham, Edward Elgar, 2017) 553.

[105] C Harlow, 'Changing the Mindset: The Place of Theory in English Administrative Law' (1994) 14 *OJLS* 419.

[106] *YL v Birmingham City Council* [2008] 1 AC 95.

[107] ibid [66]-[71] (Lady Hale dissenting).

[108] ibid [26], [33] (Lord Scott).

as Cane has remarked, 'functions are public or private only because we make them so for particular and varied purposes'.[109] Our concern should surely be not whether a commercial company is subject to judicial review proceedings or covered by the Human Rights Act but what standards we expect of any company operating care homes, a question scarcely touched on by a House of Lords mired in procedure?

Similarly, in the seminal Canadian case of *Dolphin Delivery*,[110] the Canadian Supreme Court had to decide whether the Charter freedoms of expression and association could be relied on in a case involving secondary picketing between a trade union and commercial company, where there was no reliance on any form of government action. The Court ruled that in limited circumstances they could, but Hutchinson and Petter homed in on the Court's reliance on a binary public/private distinction as a basis for its ruling:

> [T]he labelling of market activity as 'private' and regulatory activity as 'public' can be exposed as wholly arbitrary ... the state is implicated in the market in the same way as it is implicated in any other choice made within its territorial jurisdiction.[111]

It is unwise in human rights discourse, the authors argued, to look on the state as the main enemy of freedom. The state can of course act arbitrarily 'as an enemy of freedom', but to overstate the dichotomy 'makes liberals blind to the threat of unchecked private power and the role of government as a promoter of liberty, particularly for the disadvantaged and oppressed'.[112] I shall pick this point up in section III.

Three years into the new millennium, Peter Cane, in a thoughtful survey of the public/private debate as it stood at the turn of the century, noted two divergent aspects: the distinction was 'deeply embedded in the law', recognised, accepted and sometimes put to use by the courts; it was, on the other hand, largely rejected by academics 'as a way of understanding social life'.[113] Functional analysis was coming into use, with acceptance of the principle that private bodies delivering services for government or carrying out functions normally (or at least frequently) executed by government might find themselves subject to a public law jurisdiction and consequently to public law principles and rules. And the public/private border was becoming more porous, as legal principles crossed from side to side and standards such as transparency, accountability and 'good governance' had gained normative status and recognition as 'societal values', widely expected of public and private bodies alike. Nor was the state in decline domestically; indeed, as argued in the previous section, the 'hidden paw' of the regulatory state was intensifying its grip.[114]

---

[109] P Cane, 'Church, State and Human Rights; Are Parish Councils Public Authorities?' (2004) 120 *LQR* 41, 45, a comment on *Parochial Church Council of the Parish of Aston Cantlow and Wilmcote with Billesley, Warwickshire v Wallbank* [2004] 1 AC 546.

[110] *Retail, Wholesale and Department Store Union v Dolphin Delivery Ltd* [1986] 2 SCR 578.

[111] A Hutchinson and A Petter, 'Private Rights/Public Wrongs: The Liberal Lie of the Charter' (1988) 38 *University of Toronto Law Journal* 278, 285.

[112] ibid 283–84. See for the liberal answer, D Dyzenhaus, 'The New Positivism' (1989) 39 *University of Toronto Law Journal* 361.

[113] P Cane, 'Accountability and the Public/Private Distinction' in N Bamforth and P Leyland (eds), *Public Law in a Multi-Layered Constitution* (Portland, OR, Hart Publishing, 2003) 275.

[114] See C Harlow, 'The "Hidden Paw" of the State and the Publicisation of Private Law' in D Dyzenhuas, M Hunt, and G Huscroft (eds), *A Simple Common Lawyer: Essays in Honour of Michael Taggart* (Oxford, Hart Publishing, 2009).

III. The Decentred State

At the heart of the public/private debates described in the previous sections lay arguments over the state. Public law was territorial; 'a state-centred product', focused on the state's internal ordering. The focus of administrative law was public administration, a function seen as vested primarily in an executive theoretically subordinate to the legislature. Against this background, Cane defended the public/private distinction on the ground that it 'embodies a particular theory about the way power ought to be distributed in societies and about the forms that accountability for the exercise of power should take'.[115] In his prescient contribution to *The Province*, Aman, however, suggested that the public/private distinction was collapsing. If administrative law were to survive in 'the global era of administrative law', it would need to undergo a 'basic shift in focus' towards 'legitimating new mixes of public and private power, new uses of private power and increased reliance on market approaches to further public interest goals'.[116] Changes, such as downsizing, decentralised regulatory responsibilities and moves to greater efficiency, were common to both public and private sectors. The mix was compounded by a market-oriented approach throughout the public sector, and interconnectedness was intensified by the growth of automation and information technologies.

By the end of the twentieth century, when Aman wrote, technology was sufficiently advanced for the term 'e-government' to be in use to cover the use of information technology internally and for interaction with other branches of governments, citizens and the private sector. Computerised form-filling was in use by public services and courts, and tribunals had begun to introduce video links and other forms of technological assistance. Since those early days, technology has leapt ahead. Online tribunals are being developed[117] – a possible forecast of judgeless adjudication? Algorithms in automated service delivery, risk assessment programs and the processing of 'big data' are programmed to learn, adapt and self-improve.[118] They raise very traditional administrative law questions over bias,[119] due process and values,[120] and new and original questions over the status of 'code' as rules,[121] its need to be compatible with human rights[122] and so on. The Australian Government was in the lead, with a comprehensive *Better Practice Guide* published for

---

[115] Cane, 'Accountability and the Public/Private Distinction' (n 113).

[116] AC Aman Jr, 'Administrative Law for a New Century' in *The Province* (n 3). Aman had argued the case more fully in *Administrative Law for a Global Era* (Ithaca, NY, Cornell University Press, 1992) 90–92.

[117] J Tomlinson and R Thomas, 'Remodelling Social Security Appeals (Again): The Advent of Online Tribunals' (2018) 25(2) *Journal of Social Security Law* 84.

[118] A Vedder and L Naudts, 'Accountability for the Use of Algorithms in a Big Data Environment' [2017] *International Review of Law, Computers & Technology* 206. A solution is suggested in J Kroll et al, 'Accountable Algorithms' (2017) 165 *University of Pennsylvania Law Review* 633.

[119] See notably Waitangi Tribunal, *The Offender Assessment Policies Report*, Wai 1024 (2005); *Ewert v Canada* [2018] 2 SCR 165.

[120] See R Brownsword, *Rights, Regulation and the Technological Revolution* (New York, Oxford University Press, 2008); D Morgan, 'Technology in the Age of Anxiety – the Moral Economy of Regulation' (2009) 29 *Legal Studies* 492.

[121] M Goldoni, 'The Politics of Code as Law: Toward Input Reasons' in A-S Lind, J Reichel and I Österdahl (eds), *Information and Law in Transition – Freedom of Speech, the Internet, Privacy and Democracy in the 21st Century* (Stockholm, Liber AB, 2015).

[122] R Brownsword, 'What the World Needs Now: Techno-Regulation, Human Rights and Human Dignity' in R Brownsword (ed), *Human Rights* (Oxford, Hart Publishing, 2004).

those in charge of installing automated systems.[123] It insists that care must be taken that every automated decision is duly authorised and that members of the design team 'share an understanding of the primacy of the law [which] must be reinforced at all stages and levels of the project'.[124] A recent House of Lords inquiry demanded greater oversight of the private sector, which carries out the majority of public digital programs.[125] The Committee thought that unless technology companies and organisations improved the transparency and intelligibility of their AI systems, regulation might be needed to 'prohibit the use of opaque technology in significant and sensitive areas of life and society and prevent discrimination and bias'.[126] Government should also 'incentivise the development of new approaches to the auditing of datasets used in AI and encourage greater diversity in the training and recruitment of AI specialists'[127] (nudging). Perhaps more pertinent would be insistence on a set of statutory principles to govern the subject, corresponding to the 10 guiding principles set in place by the Younger Committee[128] for computers that process personal data, which form the basis of subsequent data protection legislation and are largely replicated in the six data protection principles in Article 5 of the EU General Data Protection Regulation (GDPR)[129] and UK Data Protection Act 2018.

Solutions that blur the public/private divide are beginning to take shape in the field of digitisation. The 'right to know' was born in the public sector and freedom of information legislation was (in general) applicable only to public authorities.[130] There is a clear case in the digitised era for extending the reach of legislation to commercial enterprises such as banks, noted for their culture of secrecy. Privacy, in contrast, was in essence a private law right,[131] though it is today beginning to find its way into human rights texts and, indeed, has gained official recognition in the common law via human rights texts.[132] Data protection legislation leaps the divide, extending to private parties and corporations and enforceable in the UK by a regulator with a dual jurisdiction.[133] Security does not; intelligence gathering by government for purposes of security or criminal investigation is governed by 'special' rules and privileges and secretive adjudicative procedures, with which this chapter cannot deal. But speaking in the debate on the new UK Data Protection Bill, Lord McNally noted the threat to civil liberties and personal freedoms, 'not only

---

[123] Australian Government, *Automated Assistance in Administrative Decision-Making: Better Practice Guide* (2007).
[124] ibid 34.
[125] House of Lords Select Committee on Artificial Intelligence, *AI in the UK: Ready, Willing and Able*, HL 100 (2017–19).
[126] ibid, Summary at 5.
[127] ibid.
[128] *Report of the Committee on Privacy*, Cmnd 5012 (1972).
[129] Regulation (EU) 2016/679 of the European Parliament and of the Council of 27 April 2016 on the protection of natural persons with regard to the processing of personal data and on the free movement of such data, and repealing Directive 95/46/EC (General Data Protection Regulation) [2016] OJ L119/1.
[130] M Siraj, 'Exclusion of Private Sector from Freedom of Information Laws: Implications from a Human Rights Perspective' (2010) 2(1) *Journal of Alternative Perspectives in the Social Sciences* 211, 221–23.
[131] See the famous article by S Warren and L Brandeis, 'The Right to Privacy' (1890) 4 *Harvard Law Review* 193; and P Winfield, 'The Right to Privacy' (1931) 47 *LQR* 23.
[132] See ECHR, Art 8 and EU Charter of Fundamental Rights, Art 7.
[133] See GDPR (n 129). The UK Data Protection Act 2018 follows the GDPR in covering public and private sectors, and for the first time includes some provisions covering intelligence and police. The Information Commissioner regulates access to information held by public authorities and data protection with respect to public bodies, private individuals and commercial concerns.

from agencies of the state but from corporate power as well'.[134] He posed the wider question whether, just as some financial institutions were too big to fail, we were approaching a situation where 'global tech giants' were too big to regulate?[135]

A plethora of tech giants and multi-national enterprises, global international institutions, agencies and bodies, regulatory systems, policy-making networks and private regulatory bodies now operate in global space and carry out 'transnational governance functions of … public significance'.[136] This lends to the actions of multi-national enterprises many of the characteristics of the exercise of public power, and renders the line between public and private increasingly variable and unclear. Public law was previously territorial – 'a state-centred product' concerned with the state's internal ordering – and the focus of administrative law was public administration. An increasingly globalised economy has undercut these central public law tenets together with the territorial autonomy on which they were based.[137] In this new framework, Aman called for a re-drawing of boundaries between the domestic and the global as the basis for a 'new administrative law'. Two decades into the new millennium, his predictions have proved insightful. The state's external borders no longer coincide with the limits of political authority over economy and society, the essence of globalisation being that processes are occurring in which direct agency of the state is not necessary. Indeed, Cassese regards 'the centrality of the state to the notion of public powers as an optical illusion'.[138]

As a global space is opening up without effective public institutions, there are two main ways forward for administrative law: national and pluralistic, which implies centrality of the state, recognition of the subsidiarity principle and acknowledgement of pluralism,[139] or global and universal. Global administrative law aims modestly for a measure of convergence, transmitting its essentially western values through international institutions.[140] As Krisch observes, bodies such as the World Bank and IMF 'are largely regulated by their home states, and they incidentally spread concepts, values and norms from their original context to the rest of the world'[141] – one reason why it is plausible for Stewart to argue the case for American administrative law as a model for a global administrative law.[142]

Powerful states and funding bodies may impose human rights law on the agencies and voluntary organisations that perform central functions in global governance and

---

[134] HL Deb 10 October 2018, vol 785, col 134 (Lord McNally).
[135] ibid.
[136] B Kingsbury, N Krisch and R Stewart, 'The Emergence of Global Administrative Law' (2005) 68 *Law and Contemporary Problems* 15, 22–23.
[137] S Strange, *The Retreat of the State: The Diffusion of Power in the World Economy* (Cambridge, Cambridge University Press, 1996).
[138] S Cassese, 'Administrative Law without the State? The Challenge of Global Regulation' [2005] 37 *NYU Journal of International Law and Politics* 663, 673, 679.
[139] See for discussion, N Krisch, *Beyond Constitutionalism, The Pluralist Structure of Postnational Law* (Oxford, Oxford University Press, 2010).
[140] S Cassese, 'Introduction' in S Cassese (ed), *Research Handbook on Global Administrative Law* (Cheltenham, Edward Elgar, 2017); V van Doeveren, 'Rethinking Good Governance: Identifying Common Principles' (2011) 13(4) *Public Integrity* 301.
[141] N Krisch, 'Imperial International Law', NYU Global Law Working Paper 01/04 (2004) 57, available at https://nicokrisch.files.wordpress.com/2014/05/krisch-n-imperial-international-law-global-law-wp-2004.pdf.
[142] R Stewart, 'US Administrative Law: A Model for Global Administrative Law?' (2005) 68 *Law & Contemporary Problems* 7.

rule-making, not least in development programmes and situations of humanitarian crisis.[143] In respect of accountability, the United Nations (UN) goes further, arguing that not only governmental institutions but also the private sector and civil society organisations must be accountable to the public and to their institutional stakeholders – a point that carries particular weight in view of the tendency of supranational institutions (including the EU) to treat non-governmental or civil society organisations as proxies for global civil society.[144] In recent years too, human rights standards have been imposed on the donor institutions, as in the case of targeted sanctions imposed by the UN Security Council[145] or the criticisms levelled by the European Ombudsman at Frontex, the EU borders agency, for its failure to respect the fundamental rights of migrants forced to return to their countries of origin.[146] In global space, where, as already noted, the actions of giant commercial enterprises may differ very little in outcome from those of a public authority, there is a strong case for the horizontal application of human rights law. A strict application of the public/private distinction might create the expectation that commercial activities at international level would be infused by an ethos of market liberalism and that a 'thin', procedural understanding of the slippery rule of law principle as requiring access to an independent legal system for the enforcement of contracts would apply.[147] Muchlinski suggests, however, that 'an ethical floor of responsibilities that [multi-national enterprises] should observe is coming into being'.[148] This he attributes to a process of 'international rule making' by 'the international community', comprised of states and NGOs – a bottom-up, participatory, public law style infused into an essentially private law situation.

The purpose of this chapter has been to examine the uses to which the public/private distinction has been put in the post-war years. I have argued for a reconceptualisation, which involves decoupling the word 'public' from the state and public authorities. The word has other and more inclusive meanings that are more consonant with contemporary life and mores. The terms 'general public' or 'public at large' equate with civil society. To participate in public affairs or take part in public life is to play a part or involve oneself in activities open to the general public or that take place in the public arena. In this sense, the media exercise important public functions, though they may well be privately owned, and the special privileges that they have been granted depend upon the functions they perform. Public goods are those that, like education or healthcare, are purchased or contributed to by

---

[143] B Simma, J Aschenbrenner and C Schulte, 'Human Rights Considerations in the Development Co-operation of the EU' and E Riedel and M Will, 'Human Rights Clauses in External Agreements of the EC', both in P Alston (ed), *The EU and Human Rights* (Oxford, Oxford University Press, 1999).
[144] UN, 'Governance for Sustainable Human Development', UNDP Policy Document (1997); UNESCAP, 'What is Good Governance?' (10 July 2009), available at https://www.unescap.org/resources/what-good-governance.
[145] G della Cananea, *Due Process of Law Beyond the State: Requirements of Administrative Procedure* (New York, Oxford University Press, 2016); D Hovell, *The Power of Process: The Value of Due Process in Security Council Sanctions Decision-Making* (New York, Oxford University Press, 2016).
[146] European Ombudsman, Case: OI/9/2014/MHZ; European Ombudsman, Press Release No 7/2015 (6 May 2015), available at https://www.ombudsman.europa.eu/en/press-release/en/59744; L Gianetto, 'Frontex and Fundamental Rights: A Love Story?' (2014) 23 *Statewatch Journal* 16.
[147] See for discussion, P Muchlinski, 'Human Rights, Social Responsibility and the Regulation of International Business: The Development of International Standards by Intergovernmental Organisations' (2003) 3 *Non-state Actors and International Law* 123.
[148] P Muchlinski, 'International Business Regulation: An Ethical Discourse in the Making?' in T Campbell and S Miller (eds), *Human Rights and the Moral Responsibilities of Corporate and Public Sector Organisations* (Dordrecht, Kluwer Academic Publishers, 2004) 125.

citizens collectively, while the 'public interest' means (or should mean) the collective interest of society rather than the interests of government or individuals. We have opted for a mixed society and not one in which the private sector is swallowed up, submerged in regulation and juridified. I believe, however, that similar ethical standards should apply to private law transactions, and that on both sides of the notional public/private border a similar set of legal norms should apply.

It has not been my purpose in this chapter to suggest answers for the complex problems posed by the globalised and digitised era in which public law must function now and in the future. Nor do I believe that public law has no further role. Rather the reverse. Public law needs to extend its frontiers so that its traditional control functions can be exercised in a global space where the parameters of the public and private are fluid and constantly changing. In the current global era, states will need, in Aman's words, to 'forge new alliances with the private sector to carry out public interest goals'.[149] Where the boundary should lie in specific cases will always be contestable. All that I have argued in this chapter is that the boundary should fluctuate and not be fixed.

---

[149] Aman, 'Administrative Law for a New Century' (n 116) 115.

15

The 'Contracting State' and the Public/Private Divide

ACL DAVIES*

I. Introduction

Governments have always used private contractors to supply the goods and services they need to perform their functions. However, over the latter part of the twentieth century, there was a marked quantitative and qualitative increase in this activity in many countries, including the United Kingdom (UK).[1] Quantitatively, the amount of public money spent with private contractors (rather than used to pay for direct service provision by government and its agencies) increased considerably. Qualitatively, the Government broadened the range of activities that were considered acceptable for private provision, to include areas often thought of as uniquely public, such as prisons; used private contractors to deliver services directly to the public, rather than just to provide supplies and 'back office' functions to the Government; and engaged in long-term, complex contractual relationships through policies such as the 'private finance initiative' (PFI) or 'public/private partnerships' (PPPs).

This phenomenon has been analysed by mainstream public lawyers principally through the lens of the 'public/private divide'. From this perspective, the central question was whether private contractors performing public services were subject to (in English law at least) judicial review and, later, Human Rights Act 1998 (HRA 1998) review.[2] This was not an inappropriate starting-point: the case law had already begun to tackle the question whether formally non-governmental bodies, such as sports associations, might be subject to judicial review when they performed regulatory functions,[3] and there were reasonably clear indications that the use of the expression 'functions of a public nature' in section 6 of

---

*This chapter considers developments up to 11 February 2019. I am grateful to Jason Varuhas for comments on an earlier draft. Responsibility for errors and opinions remains my own.
[1] This chapter focuses on the UK experience and on English law for reasons of space.
[2] For example, P Craig, 'Contracting Out, the Human Rights Act and the Scope of Judicial Review' (2002) 118 LQR 551; CM Donnelly, *Delegation of Governmental Power to Private Parties: A Comparative Perspective* (Oxford, Oxford University Press, 2007) chs 6–7; D Oliver, 'Functions of a Public Nature Under the Human Rights Act' [2004] PL 329.
[3] See, eg, *R v Disciplinary Committee of the Jockey Club, ex parte Aga Khan* [1993] 1 WLR 909 (CA); *R (Mullins) v Jockey Club Appeal Board* [2005] EWHC 2197 (Admin).

the HRA 1998 was intended to bring contractors within its scope.[4] In theory at least, judicial review and review under the Act would have offered important safeguards to citizens and service users.

In turn, discussion about the scope of judicial review triggered, or at least contributed to, a deeper enquiry about the extent and nature of any differences between public and private law, because obviously the significance of the boundary question is much reduced if the two bodies of law promote similar 'values' in practice. This view was advanced by writers such as Oliver, who argued that it was possible to identify a common core of values underpinning public and private law.[5] In the specific context of government contracts, attempts were made to identify ways in which contractors might be held to account and citizens' and service users' rights protected through contractual techniques.[6] The more recent trend towards arguing that public law can be reconceptualised as a form of fiduciary law is, arguably, in the same tradition, though it seems somewhat less clear how contractors might be factored in to that particular analysis.[7]

It is, of course, important to determine whether or not contractors are subject to judicial review or review under the HRA 1998. But my aim in this chapter is to argue that this is only one component of a comprehensive legal regime for outsourced public services. At least two other important elements are required. One is to establish the extent to which the Government itself is subject to judicial review or review under the Act in respect of its activities as a contracting party, and how this relates to the contractor's subjection to public law and to the contractual relationship between the parties. In English law, the position on this is unclear, largely because of some older decisions relating to the Government's susceptibility to judicial review in respect of its functions as an employer, even though – as I shall argue – the principles involved are not difficult to grasp.[8] The other is to determine whether the doctrines of judicial review themselves are fit for purpose in order to ensure that the Government and its contractors are accountable for the proper use of public funds and the effective delivery of public services. They may require further development, adaptation and even supplementation to fit the contracting environment. For example, some of the core assumptions of public law – that the Government is the stronger party in the relationship, or that government activity is best conceptualised as a series of particular decisions – may be unhelpful in this context.

I recognise that this chapter is perhaps rather unfashionable. Public law, at least in the UK, has been experiencing something of a 'golden age', with excitement generated by the HRA 1998, and then by the judges' rediscovery and promotion of 'common law rights',[9] and now by the profound constitutional questions generated by the UK's exit from the European Union (EU).[10] But the collapse of the UK's second-largest construction

---

[4] See *Hansard*, HC Deb vol 306, col 773 (16 February 1998) (Rt Hon Jack Straw MP).
[5] D Oliver, *Common Values and the Public-Private Divide* (London, Butterworths, 1999).
[6] For critical analysis, see CM Donnelly, '*Leonard Cheshire* Again and Beyond: Private Contractors, Contract and s 6(3)(b) of the Human Rights Act' [2005] *PL* 785.
[7] See, generally, E Fox-Decent et al (eds), *Fiduciary Government* (New York, Cambridge University Press, 2019).
[8] See, eg, *R v Lord Chancellor's Department, ex parte Nangle* [1991] ICR 743 (QB).
[9] See, eg, *R (Unison) v Lord Chancellor* [2017] 3 WLR 409 (SC).
[10] *R (Miller) v Secretary of State for Exiting the European Union* [2018] AC 61 (SC).

company, Carillion, in January 2018, is a timely reminder that while we may have got used to outsourced public services, none of the problems associated with them have either gone away or been addressed.[11] Carillion had some 450 public sector contracts.[12] It was responsible for, among other things, maintaining housing for military families, providing facilities management in prisons, schools and hospitals, and maintaining road and rail infrastructure. It is estimated that, in 2016, Carillion earned £2 billion from the UK public sector, representing some 38 per cent of its total revenue.[13] While a lot of Carillion's business has been picked up by other contractors, the situation has caused considerable uncertainty and disruption for its workers, suppliers and public sector clients alike. Of course, it would be wrong to suggest that Carillion's collapse is somehow a failure of public law: it was a complex situation and involved a variety of different problems within the firm itself, as well as in its relationships with the public sector. What it highlights for me is the considerable financial and social importance of outsourcing in public services, and therefore the strangeness of the fact that, after a small flurry of interest in the early years, it has been relegated to the margins of public lawyers' concerns.

II. Context

This section will provide some background for the rest of the chapter, by examining the place of outsourcing in UK public services. I begin by defining the concept, and then consider some of the statistical data on its usage. I shall also consider the argument sometimes encountered that there is no place for private firms in the delivery of public services.

My focus in this chapter will be on situations in which the Government, broadly defined to include central and local government, and agencies and public bodies, enters into a contractual relationship with an entity that is not itself formally a part of the Government, such as a private firm or a charity, which I shall label the 'contractor', in the discharge of its functions.[14] That contract might either be for the provision of goods or services to the Government, to enable it to provide services to the public, or it might be for the direct provision of goods or services to the public by the contractor. These two types of contract are not formally distinguished in English law, but the difference between them may be important in some circumstances. The contract itself may be more or less complex. A contract for the provision of goods may be for a standard product that is readily available from a number of suppliers in the market, or it may involve the design and manufacture of a bespoke product for the Government. A contract for the provision of services may be for something

---

[11] The two main parliamentary reports are House of Commons Business, Energy and Industrial Strategy and Work and Pensions Committees, *Carillion*, HC 769 (HMSO, 2018); House of Commons Public Administration and Constitutional Affairs Committee, *After Carillion: Public Sector Outsourcing and Contracting*, HC 748 (HMSO, 2018). See also NAO, *Investigation into the Government's Handling of the Collapse of Carillion*, HC 1002 (HMSO, 2018).
[12] House of Commons Library, *The Collapse of Carillion*, Briefing Paper No 8206 (HMSO, 2018) 28.
[13] ibid.
[14] For a more detailed treatment, see ACL Davies, *The Public Law of Government Contracts* (Oxford, Oxford University Press, 2008).

relatively standard, such as office cleaning, or for something highly specialised, such as the rehabilitation of offenders paid for on a 'results' basis. Some of the Government's most ambitious contracts involve up-front investment by the contractor and a long-term relationship, such as concessions, in which the private contractor provides (for example) a new road in return for a share of tolls paid by motorists, or public/private partnerships, in which the private contractor provides, maintains and manages (for example) a new hospital over many decades, in exchange for regular payments by the Government.[15] 'Outsourcing' is a useful, if ugly and non-technical, umbrella term to cover the variety of arrangements.

In the October 2018 Budget, the Chancellor of the Exchequer announced that PFI would be abolished.[16] This striking announcement deflected some of the criticism arising out of the collapse of Carillion, which was a party to some high-profile PFI deals. However, this change of direction is not quite as radical as it sounds. Existing PFI contracts are unaffected: despite the high cost of servicing them, the cost (both financial and reputational) of early termination is likely to be higher. And there were few, if any, new PFI contracts in the pipeline, as public sector decision-makers became nervous about using the scheme.[17] It seems likely that, in the future, the Government will still need to enter into partnerships with the private sector for some infrastructure projects, given that it is unlikely to be able to find the capital to finance them all itself. However, it is to be hoped that these will avoid some of the failings associated with PFI, and in particular the expense of bundling together high- and low-risk activities into the same, poorly negotiated deal. Importantly for present purposes, outsourcing outside the field of capital projects continues unaffected by this development.

A helpful report by the UK National Audit Office (NAO) in 2016 gives some statistics on the use of outsourcing in the UK.[18] Of a total public expenditure figure of £734 billion, £192 billion is spent with contractors, plus £50 billion on capital costs and £3 billion on financing PFI schemes. The NAO estimates that about half the £192 billion is on services and half on goods. Within that figure, around £55 billion is spent by central government and the devolved administrations in Scotland, Wales and Northern Ireland, £61 billion by the National Health Service and £69 billion by local government. The total spend on contractors is roughly equivalent to the total spend on the Government's other two big areas of expenditure: welfare benefits and direct staffing costs.

It is sometimes argued that contractors have no place in government at all: that the Government should provide all public services itself, and should use contractors only to supply it with the means to do so. But this is no more likely to be plausible than the alternative extreme: that the Government should function solely as a 'purchaser', buying all goods and services from contractors and providing nothing itself. The point is that buying

---

[15] In the UK, the Private Finance Initiative (PFI) and its successor PF2 were particular incarnations of the policy of public/private partnerships.

[16] *Hansard*, HC Deb vol 648, cols 659–60 (29 October 2018) and see HM Treasury, *Budget 2018: Private Finance Initiative (PFI) and Private Finance 2 (PF2)* (October 2018).

[17] For statistics, see HM Treasury, *Private Finance Initiative and Private Finance 2 Projects: 2017 Summary Data* (March 2018).

[18] NAO, *Government Commercial and Contracting: An Overview of the NAO's Work* (May 2016).

goods and services in the market and providing them in-house have different advantages and disadvantages. The competitive forces at play in a market should bring costs down, but there are many circumstances in which this will not obtain, for example where the product being purchased is highly specialised and must be made to order, or where the services to be provided are complex and their quality difficult to specify in advance or observe during delivery. In these latter cases, in-house provision may be preferable. But even these relatively basic economic assumptions are questioned in the context of public services. For example, it is often suggested that firms' need to deliver profits to their shareholders may make contracted-out services more, rather than less, expensive, or that making government contracts work is simply a question of better design, using 'payment by results' contracts that overcome problems of contractual specification. Ultimately, then, there are complex economic and political judgements to be made, but these are not the focus of the present chapter.

What can be said with some certainty is that it would be a mammoth task to bring £96 billion-worth of public spending back in-house, and while government contracts are in use, it is worth devoting attention to whether, and if so how, public law might make a greater contribution to improving the fairness, efficiency and effectiveness of this aspect of government. That is my objective here. Of course, this is not my first foray into this topic, and it is a large one, so to narrow things down I shall devote particular attention to issues that have become more apparent (to me at least) in the last 10 years or so, as experience with outsourcing, particularly in its more elaborate forms, has grown.[19]

III. The Public/Private Divide

That the Government's increased use of outsourcing has been seen as raising questions of the public/private divide is, at first sight, a mystery because, at least in formal terms, the legal status of the contracting parties is quite clear: as defined in section II, the Government is buying goods or services from a contractor that is not a part of the Government. But the public/private divide questions that arise are regulatory: should the Government be regulated by public law when it is placing and managing contracts, and should the contractor be regulated by public law when it is carrying out tasks on behalf of the Government under the contract? Although the institutional and regulatory questions are thus separable, they have a tendency to collapse back into each other in practice, particularly if the approach taken is to ask whether what is being performed is a 'public function'. The greatest attention has been focused on how contractors should be regulated. In this section, I offer a brief, critical overview of English law on this point. The courts have considered the meaning of 'public function' in relation to section 6 of the HRA 1998, which subjects private firms to human rights where they are performing public functions, and in judicial review cases.[20]

---

[19] Davies, *The Public Law of Government Contracts* (n 14).
[20] For a detailed analysis, see the literature cited in n 2. It may be worth pointing out that while most cases involve an argument that a contractor should be 'subject to judicial review' in both a procedural and a substantive sense, making this a useful shorthand, it is also possible for public law norms to be applied outside the judicial review procedure: *O'Reilly v Mackman* [1983] 2 AC 237 (HL).

The courts' approach in judicial review cases generally is summarised in the following passage approved by the Court of Appeal in the recent case of *Holmcroft*:[21]

> [T]he law has now been developed to the point where, unless the source of power clearly provides the answer, the question whether the decision of a body is amenable to judicial review requires a careful consideration of the nature of the power and function that has been exercised to see whether the decision has a sufficient public element, flavour or character to bring it within the purview of public law.[22]

In relation to government contractors, the mere presence of a contract with a public body has not been found to be sufficient in itself to generate the required 'public law flavour'.[23] The extra element is often captured in the expression 'statutory underpinning'. The facts of the two leading cases, *Servite*[24] and *Partnerships in Care*,[25] help to illuminate this concept.

In *Servite*, Wandsworth LBC placed a contract with Servite, a housing association, to run a residential home for the elderly.[26] The claimants were residents of the home who believed that they had been promised a home for life, and sought to bring judicial review against Servite for breach of their legitimate expectation when it decided to close the home.[27] The court held that section 26 of the National Assistance Act 1948 only governed the local authority's activities. It did not provide Servite with any special statutory powers or duties. There was no 'statutory penetration' sufficient to make Servite amenable to judicial review.[28]

In *Partnerships in Care*, by contrast, the firm was the provider of a hospital.[29] The claimant was compulsorily detained under the Mental Health Act 1983 in the hospital while she received treatment for a personality disorder. Managers proposed changes to the way care would be delivered that would have left the claimant without appropriate care. It was held:

> Whether facilities can and should be provided, and adequate staff made available, to enable the treatment which the psychiatrists say should take place ... is the subject of specific statutory underpinning directed at the hospital: the statutory duty imposed by regulation 12(1) of the [Nursing Homes and Mental Nursing Homes Regulations 1984 (SI 1984/1578)] on the hospital to provide adequate professional staff and adequate treatment facilities was cast directly on the hospital as the registered person under the Registered Homes Act 1984.[30]

In this case, the hospital was under a direct statutory duty to provide adequate care. Breaches of this duty could be challenged by the claimant through judicial review.

---

[21] *R (Holmcroft Properties Ltd) v KPMG LLP* [2018] EWCA Civ 2093.
[22] *R (Beer (t/a Hammer Trout Farm)) v Hampshire Farmers Markets Ltd* [2004] 1 WLR 233 (CA), [16] (Dyson LJ), approved, *Holmcroft* (n 21) [47] (Arden LJ).
[23] *R (Holmcroft Properties Ltd) v KPMG LLP* [2016] EWHC 323 (Admin), [44], approved by the Court of Appeal, *Holmcroft* (n 21).
[24] *R v Servite Houses, ex parte Goldsmith* (2001) 33 HLR 35 (QB).
[25] *R (A) v Partnerships in Care Ltd* [2002] 1 WLR 2610 (QB).
[26] *Goldsmith* (n 24).
[27] *R v North and East Devon HA, ex parte Coughlan* [2001] QB 213 (CA).
[28] *Goldsmith* (n 24) [76] (Moses J).
[29] *Partnerships in Care Ltd* (n 25).
[30] ibid [24] (Keith J).

These two cases do, of course, form part of a long-running line of litigation about the availability of judicial review. The 'statutory underpinning' test has developed from older cases not concerned with contractors. In the well-known *Datafin* case, the City Takeover Panel was a body that lacked 'visible means of legal support'.[31] Thus, the question facing the court was whether a body not created by statute could be subject to judicial review. Although the phrase 'statutory underpinning' does not feature in the judgments, the concept was clearly influential. The Court of Appeal noted that the Panel fitted into a scheme of statutory regulation even though it had not itself been set up by statute. In subsequent cases concerning regulatory bodies for sport, notably the Jockey Club, the 'statutory underpinning' test or some version of it formed part of the courts' reasons for excluding such bodies from the scope of judicial review.[32] The Jockey Club was not a statutory body, nor did it fit into any kind of statutory scheme. It was a private organisation based on a series of contractual relationships with its members.

The statutory underpinning test thus performs two roles. On the one hand, it allows bodies not created by statute to be subject to judicial review, moving from a source-based approach to one more focused on the functions being performed. On the other hand, it controls contractors' susceptibility to judicial review by requiring claimants to show that any particular contractor has public powers or duties, giving its activities a 'public flavour', and is not just in a contractual relationship with a public body.

Similar issues arise under the HRA 1998. While section 3 of the Act has horizontal effect, applying in wholly private cases, section 6 draws a distinction between what have been termed (somewhat unhelpfully) 'pure' public authorities and 'hybrid' public authorities.[33] The former are caught by the HRA 1998 in respect of all their activities. The latter group is made up of non-public bodies that perform some public functions, and they are subject to the 1998 Act in respect of their public functions only. In this respect, the HRA 1998 test is clearly and explicitly about the functions being performed rather than the source of the body's power. Contractors have the potential to fall within the hybrid group.[34] But the courts have taken the view that not all government contractors are hybrid public authorities and that some additional public element must be shown.[35]

In *Poplar Housing*, the claimant sought to challenge her eviction from social housing provided by Poplar, a housing association, under contract to a local authority.[36] The court held that there was a sufficient public element to bring the housing association within the scope of the HRA 1998. This was because the housing association had played a major role in assessing the claimant's housing needs and, at a later date, in evicting her from the property.[37] The housing association would not have been able to do this without exercising the local authority's public powers. A similar result was reached in *Weaver*.[38]

---

[31] *R v Panel on Takeovers and Mergers, ex parte Datafin* [1987] QB 815 (CA), 824 (Sir John Donaldson MR).
[32] *Aga Khan* (n 3); *Mullins* (n 3).
[33] *Aston Cantlow and Wilmcote with Billesley Parochial Church Council v Wallbank* [2004] 1 AC 546 (HL), [5]–[12] (Lord Nicholls).
[34] The material cited in n 16 indicates that this was the Government's intention.
[35] *R (Heather) v Leonard Cheshire Foundation* [2002] 2 All ER 936 (CA), [15] (Lord Woolf CJ).
[36] *Poplar Housing & Regeneration Community Association Ltd v Donoghue* [2002] QB 48 (CA).
[37] ibid 70 (Lord Woolf CJ).
[38] *R (Weaver) v London & Quadrant Housing Trust* [2010] 1 WLR 363 (CA).

However, where there is no element of coercion or determination of entitlements in the contractor's activities, the courts have found that there is no case for subjecting the contractor to the HRA 1998. The leading case is the decision of the House of Lords in *YL*.[39] The claimant had been placed in a privately-run care home by Birmingham City Council. She was threatened with eviction because the owner of the home took exception to her family's behaviour during visits. She sought to assert Article 8 rights against the private provider of the home. A majority in the House of Lords held that the provider was not subject to the HRA 1998. Their Lordships emphasised the fact that the care home had no special statutory powers, and argued that the functions would not be regarded as 'governmental' in nature.[40] They argued that the care was not 'publicly funded' because, although it was paid for by the council, it was obtained by contract (arguably, importing an inappropriate focus on the source of the contractor's power rather than on its functions).[41] They considered the argument that this created a gap in protection, in that those who benefited from 'in-house' services were better protected than those who benefited from contracted-out services. But they rejected this, largely on the ground that to hold the care home liable under the HRA 1998 would create another kind of unfairness as between those whose care was paid for by the local council and those who could afford to pay for their own care.[42] In powerful dissenting judgments, Lord Bingham and Baroness Hale argued that the parliamentary intention underlying section 6 was to include contracted-out services, and that the function of providing care to individuals in need was public because it was in fulfilment of the council's duty under section 21 of the National Assistance Act 1948 and was provided at public expense. The fact that this might create differences between publicly- and privately-funded care home residents was seen as a more readily justifiable difference than that between residents in contracted-out and in-house services. The decision in *YL* has since been reversed by statute in the social care context.[43]

There are obvious similarities between the HRA 1998 approach and the judicial review cases, although judges have differed as to the precedential value of the judicial review case law in deciding cases under the 1998 Act given the need to apply the statutory wording.[44] A close examination of the statutory framework governing the activity in question is required to determine whether the contractor itself is exercising public powers or performing public duties. A contract with a public body is not enough on its own to bring the contractor within the scope of the HRA 1998. Indeed, *YL* indicates that contractor liability under the Act is likely to be the exception rather than the rule.

The problem with both these lines of case law is that, in deciding whether a contractor should be subject to judicial review or the HRA 1998, the courts are making a policy choice about how contracted-out public services should be regulated, but disguising that

---

[39] *YL v Birmingham City Council* [2007] 3 WLR 112 (HL).
[40] ibid [115] (Lord Mance).
[41] ibid [142] (Lord Neuberger).
[42] ibid [119] (Lord Mance).
[43] Initially by the Health and Social Care Act 2008, s 145, in relation to care homes; now by the Care Act 2014, s 73, which covers care homes and the provision of domiciliary care.
[44] For example, *Aston Cantlow and Wilmcote with Billesley Parochial Church Council v Wallbank* (n 33) [52] (Lord Hope).

choice as the application of a legal test. This has the unfortunate effect of obscuring the reasons underlying the policy choice, though it is possible to infer what these might be from dicta in the cases. Concerns about 'burdening' contractors with unfamiliar public law obligations appear to play a substantial role, even though such arguments are unconvincing. Contractors undertaking to provide public services are on notice that different rules may apply, and could factor this into their behaviour and pricing or indemnity arrangements with the public authority. Moreover, there is a strong argument in the other direction, that the Government should not be able to reduce the scope of application of the HRA 1998 and other public law norms simply by engaging contractors to provide public services. As I have argued elsewhere, there are more helpful ways of thinking about this set of issues.[45]

IV. The Missing Links

The question whether contractors can be subject to judicial review or to the HRA 1998 is undoubtedly important, but it tends to obscure the other two sides of what we might think of as the government contracting 'triangle': the citizen's relationship with the Government, and the Government's relationship with the contractor. A comprehensive legal regime for government contracts would address these aspects too. Indeed, I would go so far as to argue that such a regime should prioritise them, with the consequence that the subjection of government contractors to judicial review (which is now quite unlikely anyway, given the courts' approach) would become much less significant in practice.

A. Citizens and Government

The relationship between citizens, service users or lobby groups in respect of contracted-out public services has two dimensions: the possibility of challenging various aspects of the contracting process itself, such as the decision to contract a particular service out, the development of the invitation to tender and the conduct of the contracting process; and the possibility of seeking judicial review of the Government in respect of the delivery of the contracted-out service. In practice, the courts have placed a variety of different obstacles in the way of concerned citizens and others seeking to bring claims, and this, in turn, has served to ensure that claims have not multiplied, despite the prevalence of the policy of outsourcing. This means that there has been little opportunity for the courts to adapt the doctrines of judicial review to the contracting context, which of course acts as a deterrent in itself to further litigation. Of course, it is important to be alert to the fact that an applicant for judicial review may be using the process for political ends, to disrupt a government activity with which they disagree on the merits. However, the courts have ample power and opportunity to strike out unmeritorious claims, and my concern is that applicants with well-founded claims may be deterred too. Constraints of space preclude a comprehensive analysis of the case law, so I shall confine myself to a few pertinent examples.

---

[45] Davies, *The Public Law of Government Contracts* (n 14) ch 8.

One 'threshold' issue is that the courts can be reluctant to find that a citizen or an interest group has the necessary standing to bring an application for judicial review. This is striking, because it has become relatively unusual for applications to fail on this ground outside the contracting context. Sometimes, the courts will deny standing to a party when there are other, more suitable, applicants before the court, as was the case for the Mayor of London in *R (DSD) v Parole Board*, a challenge to a Parole Board ruling that was thought to be more appropriately brought by the Secretary of State and the victims of the offender who was the subject of the decision, all of whom were already before the court.[46] But it is perfectly possible for someone with no particular interest in the matter to be able to bring a 'public interest' claim:

> In some contexts, it is appropriate to require an applicant for judicial review to demonstrate that he has a particular interest in the matter complained of: the type of interest which is relevant, and therefore required in order to have standing, will depend upon the particular context. In other situations, such as where the excess or abuse of power affects the public generally, insistence upon a particular interest could prevent the matter being brought before the court, and that in turn might disable the court from performing its function to protect the rule of law ...[47]

This point was recognised in principle in the *Chandler* case.[48] In that case, the applicant brought a challenge to the Minister's choice of partner to run an academy school, arguing that the process was not compliant with the EU public procurement regime (under both the Regulations and the Treaty provisions).[49] She was a parent of children in the relevant London borough but otherwise had no particular interest in the choice. The Court of Appeal held that it was too extreme to state, as the judge at first instance had done, that the only recourse in the event of a breach of the Regulations was a complaint by an economic operator under what was then regulation 47.[50] It was possible in principle for an interested person to seek judicial review if the public authority had acted unlawfully, particularly where that had led to a different outcome and he or she was affected by the outcome. It was also stated that the Court could 'envisage cases where the gravity of a departure from public law obligations may justify the grant of a public law remedy in any event'.[51] However, the applicant herself did not have standing because she was regarded simply as an opponent of the policy of academy schools, and had not succeeded on the substance.

In the more recent *Wylde* case, there was no clear acknowledgement of the broader public interest point, despite a detailed discussion of *Chandler*.[52] Instead, the judge

---

[46] *R (DSD) v Parole Board* [2018] 3 WLR 829 (QB).

[47] *AXA General Insurance Ltd v HM Advocate* [2012] 1 AC 868 (SC), [170] (Lord Reed JSC).

[48] *R (Chandler) v Secretary of State for Children, Schools and Families* [2010] 1 CMLR 19 (CA). See also *R (Law Society) v Legal Services Commission* [2007] EWHC 1848 (Admin), [108]–[114] (this aspect of the Divisional Court's decision was not challenged on appeal: *R (Law Society) v Legal Services Commission* [2007] EWCA Civ 1264); *R (UNISON) v NHS Wiltshire Primary Care Trust* [2012] EWHC 624 (Admin); *R (Gottlieb) v Winchester City Council* [2015] EWHC 231 (Admin).

[49] At the relevant time the applicable Regulations were the Public Contracts Regulations 2006 (SI 2006/5).

[50] An 'economic operator' is the term used in procurement law to refer to any legal or natural person providing the relevant goods, services or works on the market, and thus (in essence) to other firms that might have been interested in or capable of bidding for the contract. See now Public Contracts Regulations 2015 (SI 2015/102), reg 2.

[51] *Chandler* (n 48) [77] (Arden LJ).

[52] *R (Wylde) v Waverley Borough Council* [2017] EWHC 466 (Admin). See also *R (Kathro) v Rhondda Cynon Taff County BC* [2002] Env LR 15 (QB).

identified the purpose of the procurement rules as being to protect economic operators, and determined that the only people who would be likely to be able to demonstrate sufficient interest would be those who could show some sort of connection with an economic operator (for example, as a supplier) and thus that they would have been affected had the outcome of the procurement process been different.[53]

Of course, it is important to approach the small group of cases in this context with caution. None of them has been particularly persuasive on the facts, and it is often clear that an application for judicial review is another weapon in an armoury of tactics designed to disrupt a policy with which the applicant disagrees. However, there is a real reluctance on the part of some judges to accept the point that the procurement rules have wider public benefits and that a failure to follow them is not just a 'private' matter for disappointed bidders.

Another problem facing applicants for judicial review is deciding when exactly to make a claim. This reflects the fact that judicial review is, as Freedland has explained, a 'decision-based' process, with short time limits for bringing claims, whereas outsourcing usually involves a series of interlocking decisions.[54] The *Barnet* case is a neat illustration.[55] In that case, the London Borough of Barnet decided to adopt a radical outsourcing policy that would involve placing two substantial contracts with private sector partners, one dealing with various customer service aspects of the council's work, and the other dealing with various elements of its regulatory functions. Both contracts were advertised in the *Official Journal*, and by the time the application for judicial review was made, one had been awarded and the other was about to be awarded. The applicants argued that the contract award decisions should be quashed because the council had failed to consult as required by the Local Government Act 1999, section 3(2). This imposes a duty on councils to consult on how they intend to fulfil a broadly-framed duty under section 3(1) to secure 'continuous improvement' in the performance of their functions. Because of the strict three-month time limit for bringing an application for judicial review, it was crucial to determine precisely when the 'failure to consult' had occurred. The council successfully argued that the applicants' real objection was to the policy of outsourcing as a whole, and that therefore their application was out of time.

I do not want to suggest that the *Barnet* case is wrongly decided. It contains some unfortunate obiter remarks about the reviewability by citizens of the contracting process, but leaving those aside, the ratio is sound.[56] The applicants did want to challenge Barnet's decision to engage in a large-scale programme of outsourcing without any specific consultation, and (leaving aside the court's remedial discretion) there was potential for considerable disruption in allowing a challenge to proceed once the council had completed the procurement process and was ready to award the contracts. However, what is harder to pin down is when exactly the challenge should have been brought. The judgment refers to a review's being initiated in 2008, two discussions in the Cabinet in July and October 2009, and the approval of a report entitled 'One Barnet Programme Framework' in November 2010.

---

[53] *Wylde* (n 52) [44].
[54] MR Freedland, 'Government by Contract and Public Law' [1994] *PL* 86, 97–99.
[55] *R (Nash) v Barnet London Borough Council* [2013] EWCA Civ 1004.
[56] ibid [34], [55] (Davis LJ).

The first of the invitations to tender was published in March 2011 and the second in June 2011. It is clear from the judgment that these are simply the significant moments picked out by the judge in a long-running process of debate and discussion within the council. Leaving aside the need for individuals or campaigners to be paying close attention to council meetings and minutes, the challenge lies in determining which of these decisions finally brought the outsourcing policy into being. Although the problem faced by the applicants in *Barnet* was that they were too late, courts are equally alert to cases in which a claim is brought too early. For example, an application for judicial review at the time of the 2008 review might have been regarded as premature because, at that stage, the council had not taken a decision about the outsourcing policy and was simply considering its options.[57]

Perhaps in part because of these procedural difficulties, and the lack of precedent more generally, it remains the case that there are virtually no challenges to public authorities' decision-making once a service has been contracted out.[58] It is clear as a matter of legal principle that a public authority remains responsible even where it has delegated the day-to-day operation of the service to a contractor.[59] Indeed, the basis for much of the practical conduct of modern government is that decisions may be made and actions taken by officials in the department or agency (or contractor) in the name of the Minister, provided that certain conditions are met – most importantly, that the Minister takes responsibility for those decisions and actions.[60] Greater recognition of this point would reduce the need to find that contractors were subject to review, and would create much stronger incentives for government departments to engage in regular and careful monitoring of contractors' activities.

B. Government and Contractors

The relationship between the Government and its contractors might well be seen, in English law at least, as outside the realm of public law altogether. English law knows no concept of 'public contract', and the ordinary law of contract is what facilitates and regulates government contracts just like any other contract. However, I want to make two points here. One is a structural or constitutional point, that the structure of government and the structure of the market can mean that the Government is in a weak bargaining position and exposed to a great deal of risk, contrary to the usual public law assumption that the Government is the powerful party in need of restraint. The other is to note that it has proved easier for contractors than for citizens to make use of judicial review to challenge government decisions in the contracting context. This is not to suggest that contractors

---

[57] See, generally, *R (Burkett) v Hammersmith and Fulham LBC (No 1)* [2002] 1 WLR 1593 (HL).
[58] One (limited) exception is *R (Chatting) v Viridian Housing* [2012] EWHC 3595 (Admin).
[59] Davies, *The Public Law of Government Contracts* (n 14) ch 8. For a helpful analysis in the context of the public sector equality duty, see *R (Brown) v Secretary of State for Work and Pensions* [2008] EWHC 3158 (Admin), [94] (Aikens LJ).
[60] The well-known principle in *Carltona Ltd v Commissioners of Works* [1943] 2 All ER 560 (CA). For a modern example, see *Castle v Crown Prosecution Service* [2014] 1 WLR 4279 (QB).

should be denied access to judicial review, particularly when they have no other option, but the judicial approach to these cases stands in some contrast with the position for citizens.

It goes without saying that much of public law reflects what Harlow and Rawlings famously described as a 'red light' approach to the regulation of government: the starting assumptions that it is powerful, prone to overreaching and in need of restraint.[61] This attitude translates across relatively easily into the contracting context, in which it might be suggested that the relationship between the Government and a contractor is one of inequality of bargaining power, with the Government in the position of power due to its size, its wealth and its ability to set or at least influence the rules of the game.

However, there are two features of the government contracting landscape, in the UK at least, that should lead us to question this simple view. First, despite the convenience of using 'government' as a shorthand, the Government has never been a single monolithic entity, and nowadays it is often broken up into ever-smaller units, ever more distant from the centre. There have always been reasonably clear distinctions between central and local government and, within central government, between different units and actors with the capacity to contract in their own name. For example, Secretaries of State appear to be able to contract in their own name and not just in the name of the Crown.[62] But nowadays it is common to find numerous smaller public bodies under each of these broad headings. For example, the 1980s policy of 'agencification' led to the creation of agencies within government departments, so that what was once a single department might now consist of a department and multiple agencies.[63] Even more strikingly, attempts to introduce market disciplines into public services led to the break-up of hierarchical structures within public bodies (for example, health authorities or local education authorities responsible for the bulk of healthcare providers or schools within a particular geographical area) into a series of 'autonomous' bodies such as NHS Foundation Trusts or academy schools.[64]

Second, the structure of the market, by contrast, has become (or perhaps just turned out to be) much more monolithic than anyone envisaged. One of the selling points for contracting out in the early years was that the Government would be able to engage expert contractors that were specialists in a particular area of service delivery. They would use their expertise to achieve efficiency savings for the Government and better outcomes for service users. Of course, an obvious flaw in this argument was that, particularly where a service had not previously been contracted out, there might be no relevant expertise in the private sector. It is arguable that some of the early problems with private prisons and prisoner transport services reflected the fact that these were areas in which all the expertise was in the public sector. Leaving that aside, what has emerged in practice is a different sort of specialisation: in bidding for and running government contracts. As noted in section I,

---

[61] C Harlow and R Rawlings, *Law and Administration*, 3rd edn (Cambridge, Cambridge University Press, 2009) ch 1.
[62] Davies, *The Public Law of Government Contracts* (n 14) ch 4.
[63] See, generally, P Greer, *Transforming Central Government: The Next Steps Initiative* (Buckingham, Open University Press 1994).
[64] For an overview see R Klein, *The New Politics of the NHS: From Creation to Reinvention*, 7th edn (Oxford, CRC Press, 2013); A West and E Bailey, 'The Development of the Academies Programme: "Privatising" School-Based Education in England 1986–2013' (2013) 61 *British Journal of Educational Studies* 137.

Carillion was an example of this. It began as a construction company but developed into a business providing a variety of public sector services. There are a number of similar examples. 'Being a government contractor' has become a specialisation in itself.

These two structural features give rise to two significant problems for the Government. First, although in theory the Government should be able to use its very considerable bargaining power to minimise transaction costs and to negotiate good deals, it has organised itself in such a way as to lose these advantages by devolving the job of procurement to the lowest level: hospitals, schools, agencies within government departments and so on. There are some efforts to overcome this, for example through the support offered by the Crown Commercial Service, which has negotiated framework deals in a variety of common areas such as vehicles, stationery, office equipment and marketing services for any public body to use.[65] Nevertheless, it is still the case that smaller units in the public sector may be paying wildly different prices for the same things. Second, the Government (in a collective sense) may expose itself to unexpectedly high levels of risk because different public bodies have all placed contracts with a particular contractor. In the case of Carillion, the Government had appointed a senior civil servant (known as the 'Crown representative') to have oversight of the firm, a practice that is now used where a particular firm holds a substantial portfolio of contracts, but a key issue in any enquiry into the firm's collapse will no doubt be whether that official could or should have done more to protect the Government's interests as the firm got into difficulties.[66]

Of course, none of this is to say that the contracting process should drive the way in which the Government chooses to structure itself, or that the Government is entirely responsible for the shape of the market, but it does show that different aspects of the overall policy of 'marketisation' of public services have not necessarily worked together particularly well. More specifically, it shows that the development of contracting policies or judicial review doctrines derived from an ambition to restrain the Government – or the failure to develop policies or doctrines to support the Government – may be misguided.

One possible example of this is the problem of contractor failure. One of the major issues with government contracts in the UK over the past 30 or 40 years, illustrated by Carillion and many other examples (including rail franchising[67] and London Underground[68]), is that contractors have entered into a contract with the Government to provide a service and then have either abandoned the performance of the contract or gone out of business altogether because it did not prove possible to deliver the contract profitably or at all at the quoted price. Although the Government often describes itself as 'transferring risk' to the private sector when it enters into a contract, these situations make clear that

---

[65] Crown Commercial Service, available at https://www.gov.uk/government/organisations/crown-commercial-service.
[66] See generally Cabinet Office, *Strategic Supplier Risk Management Policy* (November 2012). *Carillion* (n 11) para 169 is critical of the Crown representative's role in relation to the firm, and at the time of writing there is an ongoing Public Accounts Committee enquiry with a greater focus on this issue among others.
[67] See, eg, NAO, *The South Eastern Passenger Rail Franchise*, HC 457 (December 2005).
[68] See, eg, NAO, *The Failure of Metronet*, HC 512 (June 2009); and for critique, R Rawlings, 'Poetic Justice: Public Contracting and the Case of the London Tube' in L Pearson et al (eds), *Administrative Law in a Changing State* (Oxford, Hart Publishing, 2008).

there is one ultimate risk that the Government must always bear: the need to ensure that the service is provided.[69] In cases of contractor failure, the Government usually has to intervene, to bail out the contractor, to bring the service back in-house or to provide an interim solution until another provider can be found. The cost to the taxpayer of the collapse of Carillion is estimated at £148 million.[70]

The causes of contractor failure are complex, but one potentially relevant factor is the procurement process itself. This is a highly regulated area for the Government, in marked contrast to the largely unfettered freedom of contract enjoyed by private actors. The procurement regime is derived from EU law, which is concerned to ensure that, in the context of the internal market, bidders from all Member States are able to compete for government contracts by making it difficult for governments to favour national firms. Moreover, from the perspective of governments, while there may be some political disadvantage in not being able to give business to national firms (and thus to promote employment opportunities, for example), there is the prospect of securing a good deal after a competitive bidding process. While I do not seek to question the wisdom of any of this, it is worth noting that competitive bidding has a disadvantage: that firms may place especially low bids in order to win the contract, only to find that they are then unable to provide the service at the quoted price. EU law does allow governments to reject 'abnormally low' bids,[71] and to accept the 'best value' bid, which need not be the lowest.[72] But it may still be difficult to discern at the bidding stage that a bid is implausible rather than just optimistic. More generally, the process creates an environment in which the bid is a matter for the contractor and the Government must be kept at arm's length, within a strict legal framework, when it might be quite important for the Government to understand the contractor's business in depth in order to evaluate its soundness and reliability.[73]

Another interesting dimension to the relationship between the Government and its contractors is the emergence of judicial review as a possible action for contractors in some circumstances. This may also reflect a 'red light' perception of the situation – that the Government may be abusing its power in relation to contractors and is therefore in need of restraint – and is in some contrast to the position regarding citizens, discussed in section IV.A. It is important to be clear that there are, quite rightly, special remedies for disappointed bidders under the procurement regime, and that the courts have tended not to allow contractors to 'dress up' straightforward contract claims as raising public law issues.[74] However, there is a grey area in which judicial review does appear to be permitted. One curious example is the decision in *R (Trafford) v Blackpool BC*.[75] The applicant in that case was a solicitor who rented her offices from the local council. A significant part of her

---

[69] For critique, see M Freedland, 'Public Law and Private Finance – Placing the Private Finance Initiative in a Public Frame' [1998] *PL* 288.
[70] See NAO, *Investigation into the Government's Handling of the Collapse of Carillion* (n 11) para 5.9.
[71] Directive 2014/24/EU on Public Procurement [2014] OJ L94/65, Art 69.
[72] ibid Art 67.
[73] Though see now 'Government Announces Major Changes to Rebuild Trust After Carillion' (25 June 2018), available at https://www.gov.uk/government/news/government-announces-major-changes-to-rebuild-trust-after-carillion-25-june-2018.
[74] See, eg, *R (Supportways Community Services Ltd) v Hampshire CC* [2006] EWCA Civ 1035.
[75] *R (Trafford) v Blackpool BC* [2014] 2 All ER 947 (QB).

practice involved bringing personal injury claims against the same council by clients who had tripped or otherwise had accidents on the highways. The council decided not to renew her lease on the basis that her business was injurious to its interests. The judge held that the decision was amenable to judicial review because, even though there was a limited public element to the decision, given the nature of the contract and the powers under which the authority was acting, it would still be possible to bring a claim where the ground of review was that the authority had infringed one of a limited group of grounds of review, including acting for improper purposes.[76] The judge then found that this claim was made out on the facts. The case is an interesting one because it highlights the tension around the oft-repeated notion that the Government can (and perhaps also should) have a 'private life' when it is engaged in commercial activities. While a private landlord could probably decide not to renew a business lease for its own capricious reasons,[77] there is a real reluctance to say that a public body should enjoy the same freedom, even though the solicitor could have found other premises and had no right to a renewal of the lease.

Another challenging and topical line of case law has addressed the question of whether local authorities are amenable to judicial review when they set the weekly rate per patient for the provision of residential care. This issue was first raised directly in *R (Bevan & Clarke LLP) v Neath Port Talbot CBC*.[78] In effect, these decisions involve setting the price the authority is willing to pay under contracts with providers of care in the local area. Beatson J (as he then was) found that the council's decision was amenable to judicial review because 'the statutory and regulatory framework shows that [it] does not have the freedom that a private individual would have to use its bargaining power to drive down the price as far as possible'.[79] This included guidance requiring local authorities to consult with local providers and to set the price in a way that would secure their long-term sustainability. Again, the contractual analysis of the situation would probably be rather different. If A sets an upper limit on the price it is willing to pay for a service offered by B, it is up to B to determine whether or not there is a profit to be made at that price. The difference in the care home context, of course, is that it is more difficult for a provider simply to exit the market, because it owes duties to the residents who would need to be rehoused. Although in general terms one would expect the courts to exercise a relatively light-touch scrutiny of these decisions, given their economic complexities, it is important to note that applications for judicial review in this area do sometimes succeed.[80]

It is important to be clear that I am not suggesting that contractors should be unable to seek judicial review of government decisions, or that there is a direct connection between the availability of judicial review and any of the all-too-familiar problems with government contracts. I want to make two points. First, it is not always appropriate to equate the Government's bargaining power in a contractual setting with its power in an administrative

---

[76] ibid [55] (HHJ Stephen Davies).
[77] Subject, of course, to the courts' occasional application of reasonableness and similar requirements in private contractual settings: see, eg, *Braganza v BP Shipping Ltd* [2015] 1 WLR 1661 (SC).
[78] *R (Bevan & Clarke LLP) v Neath Port Talbot CBC* [2012] EWHC 236 (Admin).
[79] ibid [48].
[80] See, eg, *R (Redcar and Cleveland Independent Providers Association) v Redcar and Cleveland Borough Council* [2013] EWHC 4 (Admin).

setting. This means that, particularly if there was any appetite for law reform in this area, it would be appropriate to consider facilitative as well as restrictive policies and doctrines. Second, it seems to be easier for contractors or prospective contractors to hold public bodies to account via judicial review than it is for citizens to do so, perhaps because of an overspill of contractual notions of privity into the public law context. This is unfortunate, because it disregards the now well-established principle that a claimant with an arguable challenge should not be turned away on grounds of insufficient standing, which in turn creates a greater range of opportunities to vindicate the rule of law.[81]

V. Conclusion

It is very striking that, despite the growth – both quantitative and qualitative – of the Government's contracting activity over time, public law has not developed very much at all to accommodate this change of approach. Of course, in the UK constitutional context, it is highly unlikely that the Government would seek to regulate itself in this area by introducing legislation (other than when required to do so by the EU, while the UK remains a Member State) and it is difficult for legislation proposed by backbench or opposition MPs to succeed without government support. But the common law has not kept pace either. It is true that the courts have had limited opportunities to intervene, perhaps because it is just too daunting for pressure groups or citizens to bring cases in the face of procedural hurdles and doctrinal uncertainty; but even when the courts have had cases to decide, there have been few bold decisions.

Perhaps this does not matter very much, because there is some evidence that contracting is falling out of favour with governments. Problems such as the collapse of Carillion and the return of some rail franchises to public ownership have made the Government more cautious and, as we have seen, PFI schemes as traditionally understood will not be used in future. But it seems unlikely that 'ordinary' outsourcing could be abandoned altogether. If we think that public law makes a contribution to legality, rationality, procedural fairness and human rights compliance when government acts alone, there is no reason why it should not also do so when government engages and supervises a contractor. This is an area in which there is a real need for creative thinking, strategic litigation and thoughtful lobbying to improve our outsourced public services.

---

[81] *R v Secretary of State for Foreign and Commonwealth Affairs, ex parte World Development Movement Ltd* [1995] 1 WLR 386 (QB).

16

Public and Private Boundaries of Administrative Law

MARGARET ALLARS

I. Introduction

To assume that the boundary of administrative law is marked solely by the justiciability of administrative action would be simple, but mistaken. Whether administrative action is amenable to judicial review can be a complex question. It is not for that reason that it is wrong to see justiciability as the single boundary. Judicial review is at the centre of the richly developed domain that is administrative law because it enjoys some constitutional protection from incursions by the executive and legislative branches of government, and offers binding final determinations as to the reach of the power exercised by those branches. However, the domain of administrative law includes external review by independent tribunals, investigative and grievance-handling bodies, and proactive regulation by privacy legislation, freedom of information legislation, duties to give reasons and consultation requirements. These mechanisms claim their own boundaries. Some, such as privacy legislation, unashamedly seize space partially within the domain conventionally held by private law.

Justiciability remains an important boundary, because of what it delivers, application of the standards of administrative law. When attention shifts to those standards, further boundaries are identified. These are reflected in the principles relating to standing to seek judicial review, the grounds of review, admissibility of evidence, the availability of remedies and the discretion to decline relief. Justiciability is the entry point for the standards of administrative law, in judicial review. However, administrative law standards may also operate beyond the boundary of judicial review, and within the private sphere. The entry point is different. The final focus of this chapter is contract law and implied contractual terms requiring conformity with administrative law standards. This extended operation of administrative law standards, within the domain of private law and unconstrained by a justiciability gateway, is so well established that it can be described as obvious. It is also under active development. Here administrative law spills over into private law.

To demonstrate that this further terrain of administrative law lies beyond the boundary of judicial review, the limits of justiciability should be identified. Those limits have been fought on several fronts. The first, developed in section III, considers whether it is settled that an exercise of statutory power is justiciable, and the extent to which non-statutory power is justiciable. Reference is made to the idea of a public law element, so familiar in the English search for the key to justiciability that opens the door to administrative law, but arising sporadically in Australia as a vehicle for expansion and contraction of the justiciability boundary. A second area of contention, examined in section IV, concerns the justiciability of an exercise of a capacity of the executive branch, such as the power to enter a contract. Bearing some affinity to this is the third question, considered in section V, as to whether an exercise of power by a non-statutory decision-maker, possibly with a regulatory function under contractual arrangements, is justiciable. Attention then turns from justiciability to administrative law standards. Section VI explores the basis on which these standards apply to domestic bodies, via contract law. The scope for implication of terms requiring conformity to administrative law standards in other contracts is then considered in section VII.

II. Entrenched Minimum Provision of Judicial Review

Judicial review is vulnerable to incursions by the legislative branch, although that is limited by constitutional protections. The original jurisdiction of the High Court under section 75(v) of the Commonwealth Constitution, to issue mandamus, prohibition and injunctions against an officer of the Commonwealth for jurisdictional error, is an entrenched constitutional jurisdiction, which may not be ousted by a privative clause.[1] The Constitution contemplates that State Supreme Courts should not be deprived of their supervisory jurisdiction, to enforce the limits on State executive and judicial power on the ground of jurisdictional error, as this was a defining characteristic of the Supreme Courts at federation.[2] A similar entrenched minimum provision for judicial review has thus been secured for State and Territory Supreme Courts. There is no constitutional bar to a State statutory provision ousting jurisdiction of the Supreme Court to supervise an inferior court, tribunal or other administrator for non-jurisdictional error of law on the face of the record.[3] A distinction between jurisdictional and non-jurisdictional error thus marks the constitutional boundary of legislative power to exclude judicial review.

By denying the executive branch 'islands of power' unreviewable by a court for jurisdictional error,[4] the High Court secured for the judicial branch an island of power that is judicial, exercised by courts in judicial review. That non-negotiable boundary of the island of judicial power is demarcated not only by federal constitutional principle entrenching the minimum provision of judicial review, but also by common law constitutional principle, which concurrently defines the province and duty of a court in judicial review as the ultimate guardian of the limits of legislative and executive power. This common law boundary is 'the declaration and enforcing of the law which determines the limits and governs the exercise of the repository's power',[5] without trespassing upon the merits. Since access to this island of judicial power is via justiciability, an obsession with the test of justiciability is understandable.

---

[1] *Plaintiff S157/2002 v Commonwealth of Australia* (2003) 211 CLR 476.
[2] *Kirk v Industrial Court (NSW)* (2010) 239 CLR 531, 580–81, [97]–[99].
[3] ibid 581, [100].
[4] ibid 580–81, [98]–[99].
[5] *Attorney-General v Quin* (1990) 170 CLR 1, 35–36 (Brennan J), referring to *Marbury v Madison* 5 US 137 (1803) 177; *Graham v Minister for Immigration and Border Protection* (2017) 347 ALR 350, [39].

According to a minority opinion, expressed by Edelman J, the entrenched minimum provision for judicial review under section 75(v) may consist in no more than the jurisdiction to issue relief, rather than some larger conception of the *content* of judicial review.[6] Justice Edelman regarded that broader conception as dependent upon establishing that the rule of law underlying the Constitution,[7] whatever that means,[8] supports the entrenched protection of the content of judicial review.

While there can be no doubt that entrenchment of a minimum provision of judicial review is an aspect of the rule of law, there may be no need to justify the content of judicial review, including administrative law standards, independently by reference to the rule of law. The constitutional writs and injunctions, and remedies issued under the pendent jurisdiction, have content, in that their availability and the appropriateness of the exercise of the discretion to issue them are governed by principle. The content of judicial review, including justiciability and jurisdictional error, is inextricable from the historical and contemporary content of the principles governing remedies. Nor could content, for the purposes of the entrenched minimum provision of judicial review, be frozen at the time of federation. That would mean that constitutional law would turn its face against the administrative law principles that are the foundation for the entrenched minimum provision of judicial review. Jurisdictional error and the constitutional writs that enforce the limits of executive power are concepts that, consistently with having an evolving content, inform and lie at the heart of the constitutional limits of the legislature's power to erode judicial review, whether by privative clauses or provisions denying judicial access to relevant evidence.[9] It would be odd if the administrative law principles applied as the content of the entrenched minimum provision of judicial review are not those that define its boundaries.

III. Power Sourced in Statute and Justiciability

A. Statutory and Non-statutory Power and the General Law Test

Justiciability opens the door to judicial review, unleashing the application of administrative law standards. Subject to the possible ouster by a privative clause of judicial review for non-jurisdictional error of law on the face of the record, it has long been settled that an exercise of statutory power, whether by an inferior court, statutory authority, tribunal or Minister, is justiciable at general law.[10] The hidden premise is that power conferred by the legislative branch is public power, and that it is the province and duty of the judicial branch to identify the extent of that power and prevent its excess.[11] Justiciability has not turned upon any

---

[6] *Graham v Minister for Immigration and Border Protection* (n 5) 376–78, [103]–[107]; cf the majority opinion in *Graham* at [47]–[48], [65].
[7] *Australian Communist Party v The Commonwealth* (1951) 83 CLR 1, 193 (Dixon J).
[8] *Graham v Minister for Immigration and Border Protection* (n 5) 377–78, [105]–[106] (Edelman J).
[9] *Kirk v Industrial Court (NSW)* (n 2) 569–71, [60]–[65]; *Graham v Minister for Immigration and Border Protection* (n 5) 359–62, [38]–[49] (Kiefel CJ, Bell, Gageler, Keane, Nettle and Gordon JJ).
[10] *State of South Australia v O'Shea* (1987) 163 CLR 378; *Minister for Arts, Heritage and Environment v Peko-Wallsend Ltd* (1987) 15 FCR 274; *Victoria v Master Builders' Association (Vic)* [1995] 2 VR 121; *Chase Oyster Bar Pty Ltd v Home Industries Pty Ltd* (2010) 78 NSWLR 393 (Spigelman CJ) (Basten JA agreeing).
[11] *Attorney-General v Quin* (n 5) 35–36 (Brennan J) referring to *Marbury v Madison* (n 5) 177.

definition of the executive branch or the state in order to identify the decision-makers whose excesses the court may bring to book. That the power whose exercise is challenged was conferred by statute has largely sufficed to establish justiciability, without attempts to justify that position by characterising statutory power as public power. In contrast to the United Kingdom, the concept of public power in Australia has surfaced in an erratic fashion, when justiciability is stretched beyond power that is sourced in statute or to a decision-maker not obviously belonging to the executive branch.

The justiciability of an exercise of statutory power was reinforced when significant exceptions based upon the status of the repository of power fell away. By the early 1980s, the Queen's representative's exercise of statutory power to make delegated legislation had been held justiciable.[12] This harmonised the general law test of justiciability with the weakening of old ideas about Crown immunity, and with the reality of the convention that the Queen's representative acts on the advice of ministers, whose status is not a reason for denying justiciability.[13] Whether cabinet decisions were justiciable remained uncertain.[14] Whether a decision of a private sector corporation could be justiciable had not been tested, mostly likely because that was thought to be impossible.

At the same time another limit of justiciability, the source of the power, started to weaken. Justiciability was extended to some prerogative powers, while others by reason of their subject matter continued to be non-justiciable.[15] A similar conclusion was reached in the United Kingdom in *Council of Civil Service Unions v Minister for the Civil Service* ('*GCHQ*').[16]

Two different tests of justiciability at general law emerged from the judgments of the Full Federal Court in *Minister for Arts, Heritage and Environment v Peko-Wallsend Ltd*.[17] Implementing Australia's obligations under an international convention, cabinet made a decision to nominate a site for inclusion on the World Heritage List, with the consequence that under a federal statute the site would be subject to a management plan, with adverse consequences for a company with mining interests. According to the political questions test, the whole subject matter of the decision, in conjunction with its relationship with the convention and the fact that the decision-maker was cabinet, indicated that it was not justiciable.[18]

The second test largely adopted Lord Diplock's test in *GCHQ*, identifying as justiciable those decisions that alter rights or obligations, or deprive a person of a benefit or advantage the person holds or legitimately can expect to continue, adding that the presence of national security or international relations considerations are also relevant factors.[19] Later attempts

---

[12] *R v Toohey (Aboriginal Land Commissioner), ex parte Northern Land Council* (1981) 151 CLR 170; *FAI Insurances Ltd v Winneke* (1982) 151 CLR 342.

[13] *R v Toohey (Aboriginal Land Commissioner), ex parte Northern Land Council* (n 12) 220 (Mason J).

[14] See *Minister for Arts, Heritage and Environment v Peko-Wallsend Ltd* (n 10) 278–90 (Bowen CJ) (cabinet decision not reviewable where it decides a 'political question', but could be if it were ever vested with statutory power), 280–81 (Sheppard J) (expressly not answering the question but suggesting this could occur only if cabinet were vested with statutory power), 305 (Wilcox J) (a rare case but not to be excluded). See also *State of South Australia v O'Shea* (n 10) 387–89 (Mason CJ).

[15] *R v Toohey (Aboriginal Land Commissioner), ex parte Northern Land Council* (n 12) 219–20 (Mason J), 283 (Wilson J).

[16] *Council of Civil Service Unions v Minister for the Civil Service* [1985] AC 374.

[17] *Minister for Arts, Heritage and Environment v Peko-Wallsend Ltd* (n 10).

[18] ibid 278–79 (Bowen CJ).

[19] ibid 303 (Wilcox J).

to tighten the second test by invocation of the act of state doctrine were unsuccessful[20] but suggested that an absence of 'judicial or manageable standards' of judgment would render a matter unsuitable for resolution by the judicial branch.[21]

While aspects of the second test now bring it close to the first, both tests remain available. In any event, the justiciability question often disintegrates into a contest as to whether a prerogative power has been abrogated by statute and thus placed entirely on a statutory footing, or whether the decision-maker's source of power is nothing more than the general executive power conferred by section 61 of the Commonwealth Constitution. In *Ruddock v Vardalis* ('*Tampa case*'),[22] the Full Federal Court by majority held not justiciable action taken by the Australian Navy to remove asylum seekers from a Norwegian vessel that had rescued them from a sinking fishing boat in Australian territorial waters, and to transport them to Nauru. The Navy's actions were an exercise of executive power derived from section 61 of the Commonwealth Constitution, which includes power to prevent the entry of non-citizens. Detailed powers to detain non-citizens were conferred by the *Migration Act 1958* (Cth), but they did not expressly or by necessary implication abrogate the prerogative power.[23] Had abrogation of prerogative power been established, those rescued may have been entitled to the issue of habeas corpus, given the absence of any statutory provision authorising their detention.

The outcome of such contests can be unpredictable. More recently, in similar circumstances to those in the *Tampa case*, the detention and transfer of asylum seekers to a border protection boat, and their transportation from Australia's contiguous zone to India, was justiciable. The majority opinion was that this was a valid exercise of power under a statute conferring maritime powers.[24] The dissenting justices held that the action was ultra vires the statutory power, and not supported by the non-statutory executive power of the Commonwealth derived from section 61 of the Commonwealth Constitution.[25] These dicta in *CPCF* reflect an increasing judicial boldness in identifying the nature of non-statutory power, or that it does not exist.[26] Once the source of power is identified to be statutory rather than non-statutory, justiciability may be readily established, and the gateway opened for the application of administrative law standards.

B. Embracing the Penumbra of Statutory Power

The battleground of contested sources of power, in statute or the prerogative, lost some significance when the justiciability of an exercise of statutory power extended its reach to a

---

[20] According to this common law doctrine, courts are not to examine the validity of acts of foreign states, as this would imperil amicable relations between governments and hence the peace of nations. See *Re Ditfort, ex parte Deputy Commissioner of Taxation* (1988) 19 FCR 347; *Petrotimor v Commonwealth of Australia* (2003) 126 FCR 354; *Hicks v Ruddock* (2007) 156 FCR 574; *Habib v Commonwealth* (2010) 183 FCR 62.
[21] *Hicks v Ruddock* (n 20); *Habib v Commonwealth* (n 20) [119] (finding that in this case there were clear and identifiable standards by which the conduct could be judged).
[22] *Ruddock v Vardalis* (2001) 110 FCR 491 (Beaumont and French JJ) (Black CJ dissenting).
[23] ibid 543, [193]; 544, [197] (French J) (Beaumont J agreeing).
[24] *CPCF v Minister for Immigration and Border Protection* (2015) 255 CLR 514 (Hayne and Bell JJ dissenting). See the *Maritime Powers Act 2013* (Cth), s 72(4).
[25] *Chu Kheng Lim v Minister for Immigration, Local Government and Ethnic Affairs* (1992) 176 CLR 1, 567–68, [149]–[150] (Hayne and Bell JJ).
[26] See also *Williams v Commonwealth of Australia* (2012) 248 CLR 156; *Williams v Commonwealth of Australia (No 2)* (2014) 252 CLR 416.

penumbral area, with little regard for the status of the decision-maker. *Plaintiff M61/2010E v Commonwealth* ('*Offshore Processing case*')[27] was concerned with 'offshore entrants', two Sri Lankan asylum seekers who sought to arrive in Australia by boat without a visa. An offshore entrant was not entitled to make a valid application for a protection visa, or to utilise the processes of internal departmental review and external tribunal review available to an onshore entrant. If an offshore entrant applied for a visa, the *Migration Act* expressly provided that the Minister did not need to consider exercising the power to grant a visa. The Minister had a personal, non-compellable power to grant a protection visa, dubbed a 'dispensing power'.[28] Departmental officers made an initial assessment, either making no submission to the Minister, or recommending that the Minister lift the bar upon consideration of the application. An offshore entrant could seek external review of the departmental decision in an Independent Merits Review (IMR), designed for offshore applicants.

In the *Offshore Processing case*, the Minister had decided to consider whether to exercise the power, and therefore the bar on making a valid application had been lifted.[29] The general law test of justiciability applied, but it was also necessary to establish the jurisdictional requirement under section 75(v) that the respondent was an 'officer of the Commonwealth'. What received little attention in the judgment is that the IMR decisions were made by a private sector company, Wizard People Pty Ltd, under contract to the Department. The company was not an 'officer of the Commonwealth' and could not be the Minister's delegate, as the Minister was expressly precluded from delegating the dispensing power. The Court left for another day the question whether a contractor to the Commonwealth could qualify as an 'officer of the Commonwealth',[30] side-stepping the issue of jurisdiction under section 75(v) by relying upon its other original jurisdiction.[31]

The Court held that even if the IMR exercised non-statutory power, its decisions had sufficient 'statutory foundations'[32] to be justiciable, and were infected by jurisdictional error. The IMR's decisions were, given the Minister's decision to consider exercising the power, 'directed to', or 'the taking of the first step towards' and 'for the purpose of' the Minister's possible exercise of the power.[33] The Court declared that the person within Wizard People Pty Ltd who made the IMR assessments made an error of law and denied procedural fairness.[34]

---

[27] *Plaintiff M61/2010E v Commonwealth* (2010) 243 CLR 319.

[28] Section 46A of the *Migration Act 1958* (Cth) provided that an application for a visa by an offshore entry person who was in Australia and was an unlawful non-citizen was not a valid application The Minister 'may but need not consider' whether to grant a visa to such an applicant (s 46A(7)), had to exercise the power personally (s 46A(3)), but had power to determine this provision did not apply to an application (s 46A(2)).

[29] The Minister had made an announcement that offshore entrants, such as the plaintiffs, would be dealt with in accordance with procedures set out in a manual, which included a description of the IMR. The High Court treated this statement as evidence that the Minister had decided to consider their applications: *Plaintiff M61/2010E v Commonwealth* (n 27) 350–51, [69]–[70].

[30] ibid 345, [51].

[31] This was s 75(iii) of the Constitution, which gives the Court jurisdiction in matters in which the Commonwealth or a person being sued on behalf of the Commonwealth is a party and, perhaps, s 75(i), which gives jurisdiction in a matter arising under a treaty, in this case the Refugees Convention and the Refugees Protocol: *Plaintiff M61/2010E v Commonwealth* (n 27) 345, [51].

[32] ibid 351, [73].

[33] ibid 348, [62]; 351, [71]; 353, [77].

[34] The IMR denied procedural fairness by failing to address a claimed basis for the visa and by failing to disclose country information for comment, and made an error of law in that the manual incorrectly stated that the IMR need not apply Australian legislation or case law on the Refugees Convention.

Put bluntly, the *Offshore Processing case* extended justiciability at general law to a decision made by a private sector corporation carrying out a function under contract to government, on the basis that the decision was directed towards a possible exercise by a Minister of a personal, non-delegable discretionary statutory power. The boundary of justiciability now extended to the penumbra of statutory power. It was of no moment that a decision of a private sector corporation was the subject of review.

C. Erosion of the Test of Statutory Power

Unexpectedly, the extension of justiciability to some non-statutory powers was countered by an erosion of the justiciability of decisions made in exercise of statutory power, where the power holder was not created by statute. The High Court has held that features of a statutory scheme, including its vesting of adjudicative power in a decision-maker not created by the statute, may impliedly indicate a legislative intention to oust judicial review, to which the Court should give effect, subject to constitutional limitations ousting review for jurisdictional error. The hidden driver for this development appears to be the private nature of the adjudicator. This seems to set at nought the Court's preparedness in the *Offshore Processing case* in a judicial review action to grant a declaration that a private sector corporation failed to meet administrative law standards.

This erosion occurred in connection with determinations made by 'adjudicators', appointed to resolve disputes under the *Building and Construction Industry Security of Payment Act 1999* (SOP Act), that progress payments were payable. An adjudicator was appointed by an 'authorised nominating authority', which itself was appointed by the Minister exercising power under the SOP Act. If a progress payment was not made in accordance with an adjudicator's determination that the payment was due, the nominating authority could issue a certificate. The certificate could be filed in the District Court so as to give the determination effect as a judgment debt. In *Probuild Constructions (Aust) Pty Ltd v Shade Systems Pty Ltd*,[35] the High Court held that the SOP Act impliedly excluded the New South Wales (NSW) Supreme Court's supervisory jurisdiction to issue certiorari or prohibition against an adjudicator for non-jurisdictional error of law on the face of the record.[36]

The legislative intention to exclude review for non-jurisdictional error of law on the face of the record was discerned in a statutory object of providing a method of dispute resolution that is informal, speedy and interim and not intended to be subjected to close scrutiny, because the parties can always later pursue separate civil proceedings for breach of contract.[37] There is no doubt that an express, comprehensively formulated, privative clause may oust a State Supreme Court's jurisdiction to review for non-jurisdictional error of law

---

[35] *Probuild Constructions (Aust) Pty Ltd v Shade Systems Pty Ltd* (2018) 351 ALR 225. See also *Maxcon Constructions Pty Ltd v Vadasz (t/as Australasian Piling Company)* (2018) 351 ALR 369.
[36] *Maxcon Constructions Pty Ltd v Vadasz (t/as Australasian Piling Company)* (n 35) 234, [35]; 236, [45]; 237, [47] (Kiefel CJ, Bell, Keane, Nettle, and Gordon JJ) (Gageler and Edelman JJ agreeing in the result in separate judgments with slightly different reasoning).
[37] This is the thrust of the plurality's reason for discerning the legislative intention: ibid 234–36, [35]–[44].

on the face of the record,[38] but the *SOP Act* contained no express privative clause.[39] In introducing the novel idea of what is for practical purposes an implied privative clause,[40] the Court gave little weight to the principle of legality, which requires express and unambiguous words in order to abrogate the fundamental common law right of access to the courts.[41]

Probuild casts a menacing shadow over the settled principle that an exercise of statutory power is justiciable at general law. The judgment upholds a line of cases resting on a view that an adjudicator's determination under the *SOP Act* is expert, interim, divorced from the statutory scheme that gives it force and inherently unsuited to the application of administrative law standards.[42] It removed from judicial review errors characterised as non-jurisdictional errors, most likely to be errors in the construction of the building contract.

The attrition of justiciability was executed only in part. Judicial review of adjudicators' determinations for jurisdictional error remained available. Before the High Court decided *Probuild*, in *Chase Oyster Bar Pty Ltd v Hamo Industries Pty Ltd*[43] the NSW Court of Appeal had confirmed that certiorari may be issued for jurisdictional error by an adjudicator, say where the adjudicator fails to comply with certain procedures in the *SOP Act*.[44] In *Chase Oyster*, Spigelman CJ re-affirmed the fundamental principle that at general law the supervisory jurisdiction of the courts should be available in relation to any exercise of statutory power, regardless of whether the decision-maker is a statutory officer.[45] In *Probuild*, the High Court accepted that the entrenched minimum provision of judicial review of State Supreme Courts does not countenance that a privative clause, express or implied, removes review for jurisdictional error.[46] Here administrative law standards such as denial of procedural fairness, which constitutes a jurisdictional error, must be applied.

---

[38] *Plaintiff S157/2002 v Commonwealth of Australia* (n 1); *Kirk v Industrial Court (NSW)* (n 2) 581, [100].

[39] A respondent to an adjudication determination in respect of which a certificate had been issued and filed, was entitled to bring a proceeding in the District Court to set aside the judgment debt thereby created: *SOP Act*, s 25. In these set-aside proceedings a party was precluded from 'challeng[ing] the adjudicator's determination', or bringing a cross-claim against the claimant, or raising a defence in relation to matters arising under the building contract: *SOP Act*, s 25(4). This was a limitation on the jurisdiction of the District Court in the proceedings to set aside a determination. The provision did not seek to limit judicial review by the Supreme Court, and indeed probably ought not to be described as a privative clause. The Court referred to the set-aside proceedings, including s 25(4), as part of one of five points as to the construction of the *SOP Act* leading to its conclusion, but did not expressly state that preclusion of such arguments in set-aside proceedings impliedly ousted judicial review of an adjudicator's determination: *Probuild Constructions (Aust) Pty Ltd v Shade Systems Pty Ltd* (n 35) 230, [17]; 236, [43]; 246, [78].

[40] ibid 237, [50] (Kiefel CJ, Bell, Keane, Nettle and Gordon JJ); 246, [78] (Gageler J); 255, [104]–[105] (Edelman J). Dicta cited at 253, [98], fn 176, as recognising the implied ouster of judicial review jurisdiction do not in terms support the proposition.

[41] *Plaintiff S157/2002 v Commonwealth of Australia* (n 1).

[42] *Brodyn Pty Ltd (t/as Time Cost and Quality) v Davenport* (2004) 61 NSWLR 421, [51] (Hodgson JA) (Mason P and agreeing).

[43] *Chase Oyster Bar Pty Ltd v Hamo Industries Pty Ltd* (n 10) 398, [3].

[44] ibid (Spigelman CJ, Basten JA and McDougall J). The *Building and Construction Industry Security of Payment Amendment Act 2018* (NSW) inserted into the *SOP Act*, s 32A, which confirms that the Supreme Court may set aside an adjudicator's determination in whole or in part, on the ground of jurisdictional error.

[45] *Chase Oyster Bar Pty Ltd v Hamo Industries Pty Ltd* (n 10) 398–403, [2]–[32] (without disapproving the line of Supreme Court cases holding that review for non-jurisdictional error of law on the face of the record was not available, but questioning whether non-compliance with an essential condition can constitute a non-jurisdictional error).

[46] *Probuild Constructions (Aust) Pty Ltd v Shade Systems Pty Ltd* (n 35) 232, [29]; 237, [50]; 238, [52] (approval of *Brodyn Pty Ltd t/a Time Cost and Quality v Davenport* (n 42) where (at 437, [44]) a line of cases accepted that review for jurisdictional error was available but not review for non-jurisdictional error of law on the face of the record). For the entrenched minimum provision of judicial review, see text accompanying nn 1–9 above.

The line of cases in NSW, approved in *Probuild*, had its origins in assumptions about the status of an adjudicator who resembled a private sector arbitrator. Doubt was sown by a single judge of the Supreme Court of NSW, as to whether an adjudicator was an 'administrative tribunal' to which the principles of jurisdictional error apply, since an adjudicator is more akin to 'an expert by whose determination the parties have agreed to be bound'.[47] Reliance upon the concept of an administrative tribunal was misconceived. This expression has been used in jurisdictional error cases, not as a term of art defining the scope of jurisdictional error, but rather as a loose way of identifying administrative decision-makers that are not inferior courts. It is not part of the test of justiciability. The doubt persisted,[48] including with regard to similar statutory schemes in other States.[49]

The flavour of private arbitration conveyed by the word 'adjudicator' in the *SOP Act* may account to some extent for the surprising outcome in *Probuild*. Arbitration may be described as 'private' because it is founded on the agreement of the parties to submit the dispute to the arbitrator, rather than upon coercion.[50] The prerogative remedies do not issue to arbitrators for error of law, because the source of their jurisdiction to resolve the dispute is contractual.[51] The adjudicators appointed under the *SOP Act* may resemble arbitrators because they do not have statutory terms of appointment and the protections typically enjoyed by tribunal members. However, the adjudicators were vested with power to determine disputes not by agreement of the parties, but pursuant to a compulsory process established by the *SOP Act* which the parties could not avoid by contract.[52] While *Probuild* says otherwise, an adjudicator established or appointed by statute to determine disputes should be amenable to judicial review on the same basis as a tribunal established by statute. In a statutory context, 'adjudicator' and 'tribunal' are labels, no doubt attractive at the time of drafting but otherwise arbitrarily selected, for a decision-maker whose source of power is the statute, regardless of whether the statute created the decision-maker.

By time the issue reached the High Court in *Probuild*, the justification for the implied ouster of review for non-jurisdictional error of law on the face of the record was based in cumulative aspects of the statutory scheme rather than purely the flavour of private adjudication. While the status of the decision-maker had been contentious with regard to justiciability of cabinet or a private sector corporation, *Probuild* stealthily made status an issue in relation to an exercise of statutory power by another kind of decision-maker.

---

[47] *Musico v Davenport* [2003] NSWSC 977, [51] (McDougall J).
[48] *Brodyn Pty Ltd t/a Time Cost and Quality v Davenport* (n 42) 438, [46]; 443, [58] (Hodgson JA); *Chase Oyster Bar Pty Ltd v Hamo Industries Pty Ltd* (n 10) 443 [245] (McDougall J), querying whether an adjudicator exercises 'governmental power'.
[49] *Northbuild Construction Pty Ltd v Central Interior Linings Pty Ltd* [2012] 1 Qd R 525; *McNab Developments (Qld) Pty Ltd v MAK Construction Services Pty Ltd* [2015] 1 Qd R 350; *Grocon Constructors Pty Ltd v Planit Cocciardi Joint Venture (No 2)* (2009) 26 VR 172.
[50] *TCL Air Conditioner (Zhongshan) Co Ltd v Judges of the Federal Court of Australia* (2013) 251 CLR 533, 554, [29].
[51] *R v National Joint Council for the Craft of Dental Technicians (Disputes Committee), ex parte Neate* [1953] 1 QB 704, 709–10; *Bremer Vulcan Schiffbau and Maschinenfabrik v South India Shipping Corporation Ltd* [1981] AC 909, 978–79; *TCL Air Conditioner (Zhongshan) Co Ltd v Judges of the Federal Court of Australia* (n 50) 556, [37]; 568, [82]. However, a relevant commercial arbitration statute ordinarily may provide for a court to refuse to enforce an award, or to intervene on grounds such as fraud or denial of procedural fairness in connection with the making of the award: see discussion in *TCL Air Conditioner (Zhongshan) Co Ltd v Judges of the Federal Court of Australia* (n 50) 561, [53].
[52] *SOP Act*, s 34.

D. *ADJR Act* Test

The status of the decision-maker has also proved to be a limitation upon justiciability under the *Administrative Decisions (Judicial Review) Act 1977* (Cth) (*ADJR Act*), a remedial and procedural statute enacted to avoid the technicalities of prerogative remedies in the judicial review jurisdiction of the Federal Court. From the outset justiciability was firmly rooted in a requirement under the *ADJR Act* that the decision or conduct challenged be made 'under an enactment'.[53] This reflected an assumption apparently made as to the ambit of the general law test of justiciability when the *ADJR Act* was drafted. The assumption was quickly overtaken in the early 1980s by the expansion of the general law test to cover some exercises of non-statutory power. The Federal Court caught up in 1983 and 1997, when additional judicial review jurisdiction under section 39B(1) and (1A)(c) of the *Judiciary Act 1903* (Cth) was vested in the Court, enabling reliance upon the general law test of justiciability.[54]

Occasionally a statutory scheme gives significance to a private sector decision, without that decision's having been made 'under an enactment'. A private sector corporation that issues a certificate assessing the occupational skills of an applicant for a visa does not make a decision under an enactment if the enactment does not authorise or give force to the issue of the certificate.[55] The existence of the certificate is no more than a criterion to be met in order for the Minister to be satisfied that that the visa should be granted.

This kind of reasoning could not explain the displacement of the core role of statute in the *ADJR Act* test of justiciability in *NEAT Domestic Trading Pty Ltd v AWB Ltd*.[56] A private sector company (AWBI) was impliedly vested with statutory power to grant or refuse approval for a wheat export.[57] This approval was a statutory precondition to the power of a statutory authority, the Wheat Export Authority (WEA), to grant consent to the export. According to the minority view in the High Court, AWBI's decision to refuse approval was made under an enactment and therefore justiciable under the *ADJR Act*.[58] The majority baulked at the imposition of administrative law standards upon a private sector company. Effectively side-stepping the *ADJR Act* test, the majority held that administrative law remedies did not lie, because of the structure of the statute; the 'private' character of the company; and because it was not possible to impose administrative law obligations on the company whilst also accommodating its pursuit of its private interests.[59]

NEAT is perplexing. The driving concern was that a decision-maker obliged to meet private law standards of decision-making could not also be subject to administrative law standards. Once the power exercised by AWBI had been characterised as private, the *ADJR*

---

[53] *ADJR Act*, s 3(1).
[54] From 1983, s 39B(1) of the *Judiciary Act 1903* (Cth) conferred jurisdiction parallel to that of the High Court under s 75(v) of the Constitution, with exclusions relating to criminal prosecutorial matters. From 1997, s 39B(1A)(c) of the *Judiciary Act 1903* (Cth) conferred jurisdiction with respect to any matter arising under a law made by the Parliament.
[55] *Silveira v Institute of Management* (2001) 113 FCR 218, 226, [33]–[34].
[56] *NEAT Domestic Trading Pty Ltd v AWB Ltd* (2004) 216 CLR 277.
[57] In addition, from 1990 a restrictive interpretation of the concept of 'decision' in the justiciability test under the *ADJR Act* had also significantly restricted review to decisions that were final, or ultimate or operative decisions: *Australian Broadcasting Tribunal v Bond* (1990) 170 CLR 321.
[58] *NEAT Domestic Trading Pty Ltd v AWB Ltd* (n 56) (Gleeson CJ and Kirby J).
[59] ibid [51].

Act test failed. This means that under the *ADJR Act* the decision challenged must not be made in exercise of private power. However, the exercise of private power, or its apparent antithesis, public power, is not the test of justiciability under the *ADJR Act*, nor indeed under the test that has developed at general law.

The applicant in *NEAT* had not invoked the Federal Court's jurisdiction under section 39B of the *Judiciary Act*, where the general law test of justiciability, still in a fluid state, applied. Six years later, in the *Offshore Processing case*, in the context of the general law test, the High Court would hold justiciable an exercise of private power by a company because it was directed towards a possible exercise of statutory power by the Minister. If that approach had been adopted in *NEAT*, at general law AWBI's refusal to approve the export would most likely be justiciable. If not an exercise of the implied statutory power to refuse approval, the refusal was at least directed to it, and was in turn directed to WEA's express statutory power to consent to the wheat export.

The outcome in *NEAT* may be the product of the unusual statutory circumstances. It is not often that a statute vests power in a private sector company. However, on reflection these were the circumstances in *Chase Oyster* and *Probuild*, where the statute vested power to determine a dispute in a private sector adjudicator. In *Chase Oyster*, such a determination was justiciable at general law for jurisdictional error. In *Probuild*, such a determination was not justiciable for non-jurisdictional error of law on the face of the record. Here jurisdictional error was not argued, and the Court cast no doubt upon *Chase Oyster*, which it referred to in passing. In *Hinkley v Star City Pty Ltd*,[60] considered in section IV.A, the statute vested power in a company that operated a casino, but its exercise of that power was characterised as a non-justiciable exercise of a common law capacity.

A statutory scheme may establish institutional arrangements apparently privatising regulation or the adjudication of disputes. It does not follow that the statute does not confer power on private sector decision-makers, or that an exercise of that power cannot satisfy the applicable, unmodified test of justiciability.

IV. Executive Capacities and Justiciability

A. General Law

Another category of non-statutory power, which may be prerogative or non-prerogative, consists in the capacities of the executive branch.[61] The capacities of the executive branch include capacities similar but not necessarily identical to the powers of a natural person, such as the powers to enter contracts and manage property, and extend to other capacities, such as, for example, in the case of the Commonwealth executive, the power to expend public funds.[62] A capacity of the executive branch may also be sourced in statute or regulated by statute. A statutory authority's exercise of statutory power to enter a contract, including

---

[60] *Hinkley v Star City Pty Ltd* (2011) 284 ALR 154.
[61] *Plaintiff M68-2015 v Minister for Immigration and Border Protection* [2016] 257 CLR 42, [132]–[143], drawing upon the judgment of Brennan J in *Davis v The Commonwealth* (1988) 166 CLR 79, 108.
[62] *Williams v Commonwealth of Australia* (n 26) [38], [154]–[155], [204], [518]–[524], [595].

by making a tendering decision, appears to be justiciable at general law.[63] However, where the capacity is non-statutory it may not be justiciable.[64] Judicial wariness of extending the boundaries of administrative law no doubt accounts for a tendency to characterise a decision as a non-justiciable exercise of a common law capacity when it appears to be authorised by statute. Even where the decision is clearly authorised by statute and justiciable, caution is evident in applying administrative law standards, including resistance to implying the principles of procedural fairness in a tendering process.[65]

Three examples illustrate the point. In *Khuu & Lee Pty Ltd v Corporation of the City of Adelaide*,[66] a local council's decision not to renew a stallholder's licence was held not justiciable. The refusal was characterised as part of a 'conventional commercial relationship' and not as an exercise of the council's statutory powers.[67] In *L v State of South Australia*,[68] the Full Court of the South Australian Supreme Court observed without qualification that an exercise by the executive branch of its common law capacity to enter a contract is an exercise of a private law power, which should not be subject to judicial review, because it would be surprising and burdensome for an administrative law standard such as procedural fairness to apply in the executive's commercial relationships with third parties.[69]

The third example, *Hinkley v Star City Pty Ltd*,[70] deserves close consideration. A casino patron, Mr Hinkley, sought judicial review of a decision to exclude him from a casino operated by Star City Casino Pty Ltd ('Star City'), on the ground of denial of procedural fairness.[71] The NSW Court of Appeal held that Hinkley entered and remained in the casino only by the common law licence granted to him by Star City. A corporation's exercise of its common law contractual capacity to revoke a licence was not justiciable.[72]

It is true that the statute provided that patrons entered only by licence granted by Star City.[73] However, Star City excluded Hinkley by handing him a document described as an exclusion notice, apparently purporting to exercise its express statutory power to issue such a notice.[74] That power was coupled with a duty to issue a notice where appropriate circumstances existed. Star City may have been exercising both its common law capacity as licensor and its statutory power to issue an exclusion notice.[75] This was an extraordinary statutory

---

[63] *Cubic Transportation Systems Inc v State of New South Wales* [2002] NSWSC 656, referring to *White Industries Ltd v The Electricity Commission of NSW* (unreported, NSWSC, Yeldham J, 20 May 1987) and *Cord Holdings Ltd v Burke* (unreported, Supreme Court of Western Australia, Smith J, 22 January 1985).
[64] *KC Park Safe (Brisbane) Pty Ltd v Cairns City Council* (1997) 1 Qd R 497, 501.
[65] *White Industries Ltd v The Electricity Commission of NSW* (n 63); *KC Park Safe (Brisbane) Pty Ltd v Cairns City Council* (n 64) 503–05. cf *Cubic Transportation Systems Inc v State of New South Wales* (n 63), where Adams J implied procedural fairness but held that the bias rule was confined to actual bias rather than apprehended bias. See also *Hinkley v Star City Pty Ltd* (n 60) 156–57, [5]–[15]; 194–95, [184]–[191], where without having accepted that a decision was a justiciable exercise of a statutory power to issue an exclusion notice, the Court addressed the question whether procedural fairness was implied in the exercise of such power, with Giles JA (Young JA agreeing) concluding it was not, and Tobias AJA (Young JA agreeing) not deciding.
[66] *Khuu & Lee Pty Ltd v Corporation of the City of Adelaide* (2011) 110 SASR 235.
[67] ibid 240 [19].
[68] *L v State of South Australia* (2017) 129 SASR 180.
[69] ibid 221–22, [153].
[70] *Hinkley v Star City Pty Ltd* (n 60).
[71] The action faced a likely insurmountable hurdle in that s 141(4) of the *Casino Control Act 1992* (NSW) expressly excluded procedural fairness. The Court of Appeal nonetheless determined the justiciability issue.
[72] *Hinkley v Star City Pty Ltd* (n 60) (Giles, Young, JJA, Tobias AJA).
[73] *Casino Control Act 1992* (NSW), s 77.
[74] ibid, s 79.
[75] As Giles JA appeared to accept: *Hinkley v Star City Pty Ltd* (n 60) 159, [23]–[24].

scheme, as was the scheme in *NEAT*, where a statutory power, coupled with a duty, was vested in a private sector corporation. An exercise by Star City of statutory power should have met the general law test of justiciability applying in the Supreme Court of NSW.

B. ADJR Act

From the outset, the boundary of review under the *ADJR Act*, being drawn in part by the 'under an enactment' requirement, stopped where non-statutory power started.[76] Replicating the reluctance at general law, where courts are liable to characterise a decision as an exercise of a general common law capacity rather than one made pursuant to a statutory grant of power to enter contracts, the former characterisation could prevail.[77] Thus, when Telstra Corporation Ltd ('Telstra'), a corporatised government business enterprise, made a tendering decision, it exercised its capacity as a corporation to enter contracts, rather than the power to enter contracts vested in it by statute in the course of its statutory corporatisation.[78] If an empowering statute does no more than confer capacity to enter contracts, the statute does not give force and effect to the decision to enter the contract.[79] As a consequence, the decision is not made 'under an enactment' and is not justiciable under the *ADJR Act*.[80]

C. Public Power

In the late 1970s, two High Court Justices made a surprising proposal in obiter: that procedural fairness should be implied where a landowner exercises public power to exclude a person from a public venue. Having invited the public to attend a public race meeting or other event, the landowner should not defeat the legitimate expectations of an individual who wishes to accept the invitation, by arbitrary exclusion.[81] These dicta in *Forbes v NSW Trotting Club Ltd*[82] implied that decisions of private sector landowners to exclude persons from public venues should be justiciable, at least on the ground of denial of procedural

---

[76] See, eg, *Hawker Pacific Pty Ltd v Freeland* (1983) 52 ALR 185.
[77] It may not be possible to characterise the decision as made under an enactment. See, eg, *JJ Richards & Sons Pty Ltd v Bowen Shire Council* (2008) 2 Qd R 342, where it was accepted that a decision not to accept a tender was made under an enactment but not a decision to terminate a tender process or to institute a new tender process, which was not authorised by any particular statutory power.
[78] *General Newspapers Pty Ltd v Telstra* (1993) 45 FCR 164; *Giorgas v Federal Airports Corporation* (1995) 37 ALD 623.
[79] See also *Griffith University v Tang* (2005) 221 CLR 99, 128, [80], where an additional restriction derived from 'under an enactment' was developed, of requiring that legal rights or obligations owe in an immediate sense their existence to the decision, or depend upon the presence of the decision for their enforcement.
[80] The Queensland procedure statute including an *ADJR Act* procedure differs from the federal *ADJR Act*, in that it extends justiciability to decisions made under non-statutory funding schemes: *Judicial Review Act 1991* (Qld), s 4(b) (definition of 'decision to which this Act applies').
[81] *Forbes v NSW Trotting Club Ltd* (1979) 143 CLR 242, 264 (Gibbs J), 274–76 (Murphy J). Stephen and Aickin JJ expressly rejected the proposition. Since *Forbes* was decided, the High Court has disapproved the concept of legitimate expectation: *Re Minister for Immigration and Multicultural Affairs, ex parte Lam* (2003) 214 CLR 1; *Plaintiff S10-2011 v Minister for Immigration and Citizenship* (2012) 246 CLR 636; *Minister for Immigration and Border Protection v WZARH* (2015) 256 CLR 326.
[82] *Forbes v NSW Trotting Club Ltd* (n 81).

fairness. If this path were taken, some corporatised government business enterprises that had slipped out of the domain of justiciability would be returned, at least in respect of their activities engaging with the public, exercising 'public power'. Captured with them would be some private sector entities that had not previously faced the prospect of being subject to administrative law standards.

The idea that a private sector corporation could exercise public power and therefore be subject to procedural fairness in doing so, had festered, continuing to fascinate commentators eager to extend the boundaries of administrative law. That path was all but closed, when 30 years later the dicta in *Forbes* were emphatically rejected by the NSW Court of Appeal in *Hinkley*.[83]

The idea of public power as a test of justiciability was mooted in a very particular context in *Forbes*. The NSW Trotting Club Ltd ('Club') was not only the racecourse owner but also the operator of the Trotting Rules in NSW, which included the rule under which a racegoer, Mr Forbes, was warned off. In issuing a warning-off notice the Club acted in its capacity as a domestic body, as the club responsible for operating the rules on behalf of the Australian Trotting Council, an overarching domestic body regulating the trotting industry. This was not a judicial review case but an action seeking equitable relief against a domestic body for breach of contract. The High Court made a declaration that the Club had denied Forbes procedural fairness, in breach of an implied contractual term. If the dicta were obiter and arguably unnecessary in *Forbes* in order to secure the application of administrative law standards, the fascination that the dicta held for commentators, until *Hinkley* was decided, may have been excessive.

V. Non-statutory Regulators

A. *Datafin* in Australia

Like the dicta in *Forbes*, the decision of the English Court of Appeal in *R v Panel on Take-overs and Mergers, ex parte Datafin Plc*[84] held out the promise of extension of the boundaries of administrative law, but wilted for decades in Australia until it attracted unflattering attention in obiter. In *Datafin*, a decision made by the Panel on Take-overs and Mergers, an unincorporated association lacking any statutory power and established by agreement for the purpose of industry self-regulation, was justiciable, being an exercise of public power.

Australian courts hesitated, indeed faltered, in responding to the invitation *Datafin* presented. Intermediate appellate courts deferred, waiting for a High Court decision on the question, with Kirby J having observed in obiter in *NEAT* that making a decision as to whether to accept *Datafin* was a question on which the High Court should not take a wrong turning.[85] As the forms of delivery of government services change, the justiciability of outsourced exercises of public power could scarcely be more important for the future of

---

[83] *Hinkley v Star City Pty Ltd* (n 60) 158, [16], [19] (Giles JA); 160, [29] (Young JA); 187, [150] (Tobias AJA).
[84] *R v Panel on Take-overs and Mergers, ex parte Datafin Plc* [1987] QB 815.
[85] *NEAT Domestic Trading Pty Ltd v AWB Ltd* (n 56) 300, [68].

administrative law.[86] The High Court has still not yet decided the question. However, the significance of any response to *Datafin* has been over-emphasised by many commentators and by some courts.

First, the assumption that to answer the *Datafin* question is to answer the entire question of extending justiciability is misconceived. Justiciability of federal administrative decisions is affected by jurisdictional limits. The entrenched minimum provision of judicial review carries its own inherent limitations. Relief under section 75(v) of the Constitution or section 39B(1) of the *Judiciary Act* must be sought against an 'officer of the Commonwealth', and a constitutional writ of prohibition or mandamus, or an injunction, must be available, or a remedy in the pendent jurisdiction which is not colourably invoked. In the absence of its further development by the High Court, the 'officer of the Commonwealth' element may be a stumbling block for a non-statutory body plaintiff relying on *Datafin*. In review under section 39B(1A)(c) it is pointless to invite the Federal Court to rely on *Datafin* when there is no 'matter arising under any law made by the Parliament'.[87] As the *Offshore Processing case* demonstrates, where the High Court is disposed to intervene it may do so by declaration or injunction, relying on jurisdiction under section 75(iii) or 75(i) of the Constitution. Nonetheless, arguments about *Datafin* have greater practical potential to extend justiciability when made at general law, where such jurisdictional limitations do not apply.

Second, *Datafin* offered a marginal extension of justiciability. *Datafin* did not effect a general reversal of the settled principle, discussed in section VI.A, that domestic bodies are not amenable to certiorari and prohibition.[88] While the presence of a public element was a central requirement in establishing the justiciability of the Panel's decision, *Datafin* does not stand for the justiciability of any exercise of power capable of characterisation as public power, or involving a public element. Nor did *Datafin* put in place a broad principle as to justiciability of decisions made by a private sector body that exercises outsourced functions of government, whether statutory or non-statutory. *Datafin* caught a private sector body performing a regulatory function that could have been undertaken by government, in circumstances involving a public element.[89] *Datafin* identified, as it was put in *R v Disciplinary Committee of the Jockey Club, ex parte Aga Khan*,[90] a body 'whose birth and constitution owed nothing to any exercise of governmental power but which had been woven into the fabric of public regulation' in a particular field.[91] In *Aga Khan*, a jockey

---

[86] ibid 300, [67]–[68]. See also *Mickovski v Financial Ombudsman Service Ltd* (2012) 36 VR 456, 466, [32].
[87] See, eg, *Australasian College of Cosmetic Surgery Ltd v Australian Medical Council Ltd* (2015) 232 FCR 225.
[88] *Law v National Greyhound Racing Club Ltd* [1983] 3 All ER 300; *R v Disciplinary Committee of the Jockey Club, ex parte Aga Kahn* [1993] 2 All ER 853, 870.
[89] *R v Disciplinary Committee of the Jockey Club, ex parte Aga Kahn* (n 88) 870.
[90] ibid.
[91] ibid 864 (Lord Bingham MR). The Jockey Club did not meet that test because its powers were in no sense governmental (at 867 (Lord Bingham MR), 875 (Hoffmann LJ)) and/or there was no public element (at 872 (Farquharson LJ)) and/or because there was no public source for its powers (at 873 (Hoffmann LJ)). In the United Kingdom there has been mixed success in meeting *R v Panel on Take-overs and Mergers, ex parte Datafin Plc* (n 84). Falling within *Datafin* are industry self-regulatory bodies (*R v Advertising Standards Authority Ltd, ex parte Insurance Service Plc* (1989) 2 Admin LR 77). Falling outside *Datafin* are some private bodies operating services on behalf of, and standing in the shoes of, local government (*Poplar Housing and Regeneration Community Association Ltd v Donoghue* [2002] QB 48). A body operating a market held on land dedicated to public use and standing in the shoes of a local authority exercised public functions bringing it within *Datafin* (*R (Beer) v Hampshire Farmers' Market Ltd (CA)* [2004] 1 WLR 233). Falling outside *Datafin* are some private bodies operating services on behalf of, but not standing in the shoes of, local or national government (*R (Heather) v Leonard Cheshire Foundation and*

club did not fall within *Datafin* because its power to discipline a racehorse owner was not governmental and there was no public element.[92]

Third, it was accepted in *Victoria v Master Builders' Association (Vic)*[93] that a decision made by a non-statutory body acting as the alter ego of the State was justiciable at general law. A Building Industry Taskforce requested builders seeking to contract with the Victorian Government to make declarations that they had not been involved in unlawful tendering practices. The Taskforce was non-statutory, established 'under the auspices of' the Victorian Government Solicitor to inquire into collusive tendering and other corrupt practices in the building industry. It compiled a blacklist of builders as part of a scheme designed to induce former contractors and tenderers to atone for their presumed past misconduct. The Full Court of the Victorian Supreme Court held that the Taskforce's actions were justiciable. The Taskforce 'directly represent[ed]' and was the 'alter ego' of the State of Victoria, could be assumed to have been established to 'carry out government policy' and to have been 'instructed to act in the public interest and not contrary to it', and exercised 'a power in the performance of a public duty … [with] … far-reaching public significance, obviously extending well beyond the government's own interests'.[94] The Taskforce's exercise of power involved public rights or duties, or a public law element, or had public law consequences.[95]

In *Master Builders*, *Datafin* was acknowledged, but not relied upon, as the basis for justiciability.[96] *Master Builders* was a stronger case than *Datafin*, as it was patent that the State of Victoria was acting through the Taskforce, which was applying the coercive force of the State.[97] Nonetheless *Master Builders* and *Datafin* are both points on a spectrum that covers a body acting as the alter ego of government and one acting under an 'implied devolution' of power, apparently under the authority of government.[98]

Fourth, the question mark that has hung over *Datafin* in Australia is replete with misconceptions, contributing to *Datafin's* eroding the boundaries of administrative law rather than resting as an unaccepted invitation to expand them. When a decision-making body is found not to fall within the narrow compass of *Datafin*, the possibility of establishing justiciability on another basis may be overlooked. Unnecessary reference may be made to *Datafin*, in cases of review of statutory power where there should be no doubt as to the justiciability of its exercise.[99] The non-acceptance of *Datafin* in Australia has encouraged characterisation of a decision as an exercise of a common law capacity, propelling a conclusion that it is

---

HM Attorney-General (2002) 2 All ER 936; *R (A) v Partnerships in Care Ltd* [2002] EWHC 529 (Admin)). Other private bodies, such as the Medical Defence Union Ltd and the British Council, have not fallen within *Datafin* (*R (on the application of Moreton) v Medical Defence Union Ltd* [2006] All ER (D) 370; *R (on the application of Oxford Study Centre Ltd) v British Council* [2001] All ER (D) 213 (Mar)).

[92] *R v Disciplinary Committee of the Jockey Club, ex parte Aga Kahn* (n 88) 867, 872.
[93] *Victoria v Master Builders' Association (Vic)* (n 10).
[94] ibid 137, 138 (Tadgell JA).
[95] ibid 162–63 (Eames J).
[96] ibid 137 (Tadgell JA), 152, 154 (Eames JA).
[97] ibid 164 (Eames J).
[98] *R v Panel on Take-overs and Mergers, ex parte Datafin Plc* (n 84) 849 (Lloyd LJ).
[99] eg *Chase Oyster Bar Pty Ltd v Home Industries Pty Ltd* (n 10) 410–13, [74]–[81] (Basten JA).

not justiciable, when the decision involves an exercise of statutory power.[100] *Hinkley*, where *Datafin* was unsuccessfully invoked, is an example.[101]

Distraction by *Datafin* from the nature of the power actually exercised is also illustrated by *L v State of South Australia*,[102] where reports by departmental officers relating to the conduct of foster carers were held non-justiciable exercises of non-statutory power.[103] The Court distinguished, and apparently also declined to follow, *Datafin* and *Master Builders*.[104] However, the circumstances did not involve a non-statutory regulatory body, or raise any potential application of *Datafin* or *Master Builders*.

Attempts to establish the justiciability of decisions made by the Financial Ombudsman Service Ltd (FOS) in a complaint-handling scheme, superficially of a non-statutory and consensual nature but with a slender statutory link, have largely foundered when relying on *Datafin*, as discussed in section V.B. Yet without reliance on *Datafin*, the *Offshore Processing* case extended justiciability to Wizard People Pty Ltd, administering an external complaints scheme at the cusp of the penumbra of statutory power.

A fascination with *Datafin* has also distracted attention from the long common law tradition by which declaratory and injunctive relief are granted in respect of breaches by domestic bodies of the contract between them and their members. Since these are not judicial review actions, the test of justiciability is inapplicable. It does not operate as a boundary for the application of administrative law standards as implied contractual terms, as discussed in section VI.B.

B. Testing the Application of *Datafin*

The creation of new institutional functions for domestic bodies, arguably of a regulatory nature, intensified the urgency of resolving uncertainty regarding the application of *Datafin*. Yet it proved difficult in any event in Australia to fit a case within *Datafin*. In *CECA Institute Pty Ltd v Australian Council of Private Education and Training* ('*CECA*'),[105] the Australian Council of Private Education and Training (ACPET), a national industry association, refused a registered training organisation membership of its overseas student assurance scheme. Membership of such an assurance scheme, approved by the Minister, was a statutory condition for obtaining registration to operate overseas student educational programmes. A single judge of the Supreme Court of Victoria held that *Datafin* is a natural development in

---

[100] See, eg, *Khuu & Lee Pty Ltd v Corporation of the City of Adelaide* (n 66) 242–43, [26], [30]–[31]; *L v State of South Australia* (n 68) 216–19, [138]–[142], [147].
[101] *Hinkley v Star City Pty Ltd* (n 60) 158, [19]; 193, [181]–[183]. See also *Colonial Range Pty Ltd v Victoria Building Authority* [2014] VSC 272, [109]–[121], where it was not necessary for Vickery J to decide upon the justiciability under the *Administrative Law Act 1978* (Vic), with reference to *R v Panel on Take-overs and Mergers, ex parte Datafin Plc* (n 84), of an exercise of power by a property owner under s 78 of the *Building Act 1993* (Vic) to appoint a private building surveyor. The Victorian Building Authority, established under the Act, was empowered under the Act to give consent to a termination of a surveyor or to give a direction to facilitate transfer of functions to a new surveyor, or to direct a surveyor regarding carrying out of functions. There was no doubt that the Authority's statutory powers were justiciable.
[102] *L v State of South Australia* (n 68).
[103] ibid 184, [6]; 185, [13]; 205, [99]; 216–22, [137]–[154] (Kourakis CJ) (Park and Doyle JJ agreeing).
[104] ibid 221–22, [152]–[154].
[105] *CECA Institute Pty Ltd v Australian Council of Private Education and Training* (2010) 245 FLR 86.

the evolution of principle, and necessary to ensure adaptation of judicial review to modern government practices, including contracting out of governmental functions.[106] In the absence of High Court authority to the contrary, *Master Builders* provided some support for the application of *Datafin* in Victoria.[107] Because the plaintiff organisation was not a member of the scheme and other pathways existed by which it could attain registration or an exemption, the decision was not justiciable on the basis of *Datafin*.[108]

The applicability of *Datafin* has been tested in numerous challenges to decisions made by a complaint-handling body called FOS, whose predecessor was the Financial Industry Complaints Service Ltd (FICS). Both were registered corporations funded by industry members, whose function was to handle complaints about operators in the financial services industry. Neither was created by statute. The single statutory link was section 912A(1)(g) and (2) of the *Corporations Act 1901* (Cth), which required Australian Financial Services Licensees, as a condition of their financial services licences, to become members of an external dispute resolution scheme whose terms were approved by the Australian Securities and Investment Commission (ASIC).[109] Having been created by a merger of FICS with two private sector ombudsmen (the Banking and Financial Service Ombudsman Ltd and the Insurance Ombudsman Service Ltd), FOS appeared to owe its existence to the regulatory requirements of ASIC, imposed by indirect mechanisms, rather than private sector contractual preferences.[110]

In an early judicial review challenge to FICS, a single judge of the NSW Supreme Court did not hesitate in concluding that FICS's decision was justiciable on the basis of *Datafin*, and that several legal errors were established.[111] However, caution prevailed in *Mickovski v Financial Ombudsman Service Ltd*.[112] The Victorian Court of Appeal adverted to the statutory licence condition, and to the fact that FOS's rules had been approved by ASIC, accepting that this gave some force to the argument that FOS had governmental underpinning.[113] The Court also observed that the *Datafin* principle is appealing, offering 'a logical if still to be perfected'[114] approach to a need for the availability of judicial review in relation to a wide range of public functions, in the face of increasing privatisation of governmental functions.[115] However, a decision on *Datafin* should be made by the High Court.[116] Even if *Datafin* were taken to be accepted in Australia, the Court doubted whether it applied

---

[106] ibid 109, [99] (Kyrou J).
[107] ibid 109, [100].
[108] ibid 110-11, [107]-[113].
[109] *Corporations Act 2001* (Cth), ss 912A(1)(g), 912A(2). The first reference by ASIC to external dispute resolution in the financial services industry was contained in a 1991 ASIC policy. This was replaced in 2007 by a Regulatory Guide setting out the requirements for an external dispute resolution scheme, which were progressively amended: *Policy Statement 139* (8 July 1991), rebadged *Regulatory Guide 139* on 5 July 2007, re-issued in 2009, 2010 and 2011, and 2018.
[110] The history is set out in Australian Securities and Investments Commission, *Consultation Paper No 102*.
[111] *Masu Financial Management Pty Ltd v Financial Industry Complaints Service Ltd (No 2)* (2004) 186 FLR 289 (Shaw J).
[112] *Mickovski v Financial Ombudsman Service Ltd* (n 86). In *Wealthcare Planning Pty Ltd v Financial Industry Complaints Service Ltd* [2009] VSC 7 the plaintiff both invoked judicial review proceedings and sought declaratory relief for breach of contract. It was not necessary to determine justiciability because there was no breach of the rules of FOS. See also *AXA Australia v Financial Industry Complaints Service Ltd* [2006] VSC 121.
[113] *Mickovski v Financial Ombudsman Service Ltd* (n 86) 465-66, [30]-[31] (Buchanan and Nettle JJA and Beach AJA).
[114] ibid 466, [31].
[115] ibid.
[116] ibid 466, [32].

'in relation to contractually based decisions'.[117] Moreover, any 'public interest in having a mechanism for private dispute resolution of insurers' claims',[118] reflected by section 912A, did not amount to a public duty or a public function involving a public element. This was a 'private dispute resolution' mechanism, because FOS's jurisdiction was consensually invoked by the parties to the complaint.[119]

The presence of a consensual element was taken to preclude satisfaction of the *Datafin* requirement of a public element. The rules of FOS provided that they formed a tripartite contract between FOS, the financial services provider that was a member and a complainant, who became a party to the contract upon making a complaint. Under the rules, a recommendation by FOS for the resolution of the dispute, if the complainant elected to accept it, became a determination by FOS that was binding on the member.

While formally a consensual arrangement, the provider was required to be a member of FOS in order to hold its licence. The scheme was designed to ensure that the provider was subject to a particular complaint-handling body. Arguably, membership of FOS was not truly consensual but was an element of a regulatory scheme. A provider was free to forgo holding a licence, but as a consequence would not be entitled to operate its financial services business. It is true that by making a complaint to FOS the complainant voluntarily agreed to be bound by FOS's rules. That one party to the contract has chosen to use a complaint-handling body when others are available with overlapping jurisdiction does not without more justify characterisation of the review mechanism as 'consensual'.

Whether or not the label 'consensual' is warranted, it is not clear why the presence of a consensual element negatives the idea of regulation, or a public element. The Panel in *Datafin* was an unincorporated association, whose members represented industry associations and agreed to be members.[120] Moreover, if statute can supply a public element, in contrast to the Panel in *Datafin*, FOS did not entirely lack any visible means of statutory support. The link in the *Corporations Act*, slender as it was, should have been sufficient to establish that FOS was woven into the fabric of public regulation. Outwardly FOS was a complaint-handling body, but providers were required to submit to FOS's rules, and the requirement of consent was imposed for the regulatory purpose of enforcing standards of conduct in the financial services industry.

If the presence of a consensual element takes a body outside the class of regulatory agencies contemplated by *Datafin*, it was to be expected that in general domestic bodies of the conventional kind, explained further in section VI.A, were doomed to fail the *Datafin* profile. An example is the Agricultural Societies Council of NSW (ASC), a company limited by guarantee and not-for-profit organisation, whose members were show societies. The ASC made disciplinary rules for use by its member show societies, and provided drug testing of horses and disciplinary inquiries at shows on their behalf. The ASC's disciplinary committee

---

[117] ibid.
[118] ibid.
[119] ibid.
[120] It is true that the members of the Panel were not those who were the subject of its determinations applying the City Code on Take-overs and Mergers, so that the consensual element was not of the same order as that occurring in the case of FOS. However, the Panel was a domestic body and therefore consensual in the sense used by the Court in *Mickovski v Financial Ombudsman Service Ltd* (n 86). For further discussion, see n 176 below.

found that a horse trainer breached the rules and suspended him from competition for 12 months. In *Agricultural Societies Council of NSW v Christie*,[121] the Court of Appeal held that the status of *Datafin* was highly uncertain in Australia and did not provide a basis for justiciability.[122] In any event, the ASC was a private body that did not exercise a regulatory role and was not an integral part of government.[123]

Private sector corporations that are not domestic bodies have failed the *Datafin* test. In *Hinkley*, while the Casino Liquor and Gaming Authority was the regulator, Star City's statutory power to issue exclusion notices was an integral part of the statutory scheme for securing the order and integrity of gaming at the casino. On the basis of a constrained view of what is regulatory, the Court concluded that *Datafin* would not in any event have supported justiciability of Star City's exercise of that power.[124]

The idea of a regulatory agency for the purposes of *Datafin* would have to be very narrow, lest any disciplinary decision made by a private sector decision-maker be subjected to administrative law standards, via the *Datafin* vortex.[125] That topic is now addressed, at the outset by focusing on domestic bodies, to identify the justiciability of their decisions and then the scope for a basis other than judicial review by which administrative law standards may apply to them. That basis is contract.

VI. Domestic Bodies

A. Justiciability

The debate about *Datafin* has touched upon entities called domestic bodies, sometimes described as voluntary or consensual bodies, which include trade unions, political organisations and sporting associations. Since a domestic body may effectively regulate the practice of an occupation, activity or endeavour, membership may not be truly voluntary, in that it is necessary in order to carry on a trade, occupation or activity. Domestic bodies may be incorporated or unincorporated associations, whose constitutions consist of rules intended to create legally binding rights and obligations between the members, often including rules dealing with the discipline of members. Domestic bodies may also be established as companies limited by guarantee, where the company's constitution has effect as a contract between the company and each member, and between the members, with each agreeing to observe and perform the constitution.[126]

---

[121] *Agricultural Societies Council of NSW v Christie* (2016) 340 ALR 560.
[122] ibid 577, [89] (Leeming JA).
[123] ibid 570, [48] (Meagher JA) (Ward and Leeming JJA agreeing).
[124] *Hinkley v Star City Pty Ltd* (n 60) 158, [19]; 193, [181]–[182].
[125] In *Agricultural Societies Council of NSW v Christie* (n 121), Leeming JA considered that if accepting *R v Panel on Take-overs and Mergers, ex parte Datafin Plc* (n 84) meant that the ASC's decision were justiciable, it would follow that a decision by a private school to suspend or expel a student would also be justiciable: at 587, [93]. See also *Bird v Ford* [2014] NSWCA 242, [18]–[23], where the NSW Court of Appeal accepted that it would be problematic to establish justiciability of a private school's decision to expel a student, but accepted, referring to United Kingdom and Canadian authority, that a private school's denial of procedural fairness in making a disciplinary decision could be a breach of an implied term of the student's contract with the school.
[126] *Corporations Act 2011* (Cth), s 140.

It is well established that certiorari and prohibition are not available against a domestic body, largely on account of the body's power being sourced in consensus rather than statute.[127] Decisions of a domestic body are thus not justiciable at general law, subject to the *Datafin* debate.[128] By contrast, a statutory authority, even if vested with functions similar to those of a domestic body, is, like other statutory power holders, generally amenable to judicial review, and required to meet administrative law standards such as procedural fairness.[129]

The complexity of modern institutional design for achieving governmental objectives has weakened the utility of simply identifying an entity as a domestic body or a corporation, as a lazy way of answering the question of justiciability. Four examples will suffice. First, a domestic body may be vested with specific statutory power but remain constituted as an incorporated or unincorporated association or a company limited by guarantee. It may have been established for the very purpose of administering a regulatory or grievance-handling scheme, contemplated by the statute but only fully articulated in the rules of the domestic body, to which its members agree. An example is the Australian Financial Services Authority (AFCA), which in late 2018 replaced FOS and the Superannuation Complaints Tribunal and the Credit and Investments Ombudsman. AFCA is a domestic body, but it is referred to in the *Corporations Act*, which also requires ministerial approval of AFCA's scheme rules for external dispute resolution. As was the case with FOS, it is a statutory condition of an Australian Financial Services Licence to become a member of AFCA.[130] On account of its detailed statutory footing as part of a regulatory scheme, AFCA should readily meet the *Datafin* test if that were an accepted extension of the general law test of justiciability. In any event, AFCA's decisions are most likely justiciable without resort to *Datafin*, under section 39B(1A)(c) of the *Judiciary Act*, as matters arising under a law made by the Federal Parliament.

Second, a corporation may be established under the *Corporations Act* but not as a company limited by guarantee and with no claim to be a domestic body, with shareholders that are participants in an industry, having been created wholly or partly for the purpose of enabling it to play a part in a regulatory scheme. The company may be vested with statutory power, perhaps impliedly, as illustrated by *NEAT*.

Third, a statutory authority with the function of providing a publicly consumed commodity such as a telecommunications service, may, by a series of legislative amendments, be converted into a corporatised government business enterprise. While having been vested with a general statutory power to enter contracts, the company is established under the *Corporations Act*, with the majority of its shares initially owned by government Ministers. One example is Telstra, considered in section IV.B.

---

[127] *R v Criminal Injuries Compensation Board, ex parte Lain* [1967] 2 QB 864; *Law v National Greyhound Racing Club Ltd* (n 88); *Whitehead v Griffith University* [2003] 1 Qd R 220; *D'Souza v Royal Australian & New Zealand College of Psychiatrists* (2005) 12 VR 42; *McClelland v Burning Palms Surf Life Saving Club* (2002) 191 ALR 759; *Agricultural Societies Council of NSW v Christie* (n 121).

[128] While the plaintiffs in *R v Panel on Take-overs and Mergers, ex parte Datafin Plc* (n 84) sought certiorari, mandamus and injunction, all that the case itself decided was that they had leave to seek judicial review.

[129] See, eg, *Heatley v Tasmanian Racing and Gaming Commission* (1977) 137 CLR 487.

[130] *Corporations Act 2001* (Cth), ss 761A (definitions of 'AFCA', 'AFCA scheme'), 1050–1055D. AFCA has a statutory duty to comply with specific decision-making standards, including fairness.

374 *Margaret Allars*

Fourth, an existing company may be engaged by a statutory power holder to carry out some of its functions. Whether it operates as a delegate, or as an agent under the *Carltona* principle,[131] or as a provider of a service under contract, the company escapes judicial review unless its decisions are carried out as the alter ego of government, relying upon *Master Builders*, or are directed to, or have some kind of proximity to, a possible exercise of statutory power, as in the *Offshore Processing case*.

In each of these four examples, as the decision-maker's distance from the statute increases, the prospect of establishing justiciability diminishes. Categorisation of an entity as a domestic body does not offer a simple answer to a question as to its justiciability. Tests of justiciability look first to whether the source of power is statute, and increasingly recognise looser connections with statute or less formal delegations of governmental power.

B. Breach of Contract

Failing the justiciability test is not the end of the matter in connection with the applicability of administrative law standards. A private law action for breach of contract, seeking a declaration or injunction, may be brought against a domestic body that acts in breach of a contract with its member. The rules of a domestic body may expressly require that it make decisions fairly, or in conformity with procedural fairness.[132] A contractual term to the same effect may be implied.

In *Ridge v Baldwin*,[133] Lord Reid affirmed the authority of cases dating back to the 1870s where disciplinary decisions made by professional and social bodies, including mutual insurances societies and associations,[134] clubs[135] and trade unions,[136] in relation to their members, were declared void for denial of procedural fairness. In an early decision in Australia, *Dickason v Edwards*,[137] the High Court described the basis for intervention by equity in a disciplinary decision of a friendly society that had exceeded its power as being 'entirely a question of the construction of the contract'.[138] In interpreting its rules giving it jurisdiction over its members, an underlying condition was to be read in, that the proceedings for the expulsion of a member be carried on in accordance with procedural fairness, subject to its express or implied exclusion.[139]

Australian courts have continued to intervene by granting equitable relief in cases where a domestic body disciplines or expels a member whose livelihood or occupation depends

---

[131] *Carltona Ltd v Commissioners of Works* [1943] 2 All ER 560.
[132] *Trivett v Nivison* [1976] 1 WLR 312; *Lawlor v Union of Post Office Workers* [1965] Ch 712.
[133] *Ridge v Baldwin* [1964] AC 40, 70–71.
[134] *Wood v Woad* (1874) LR 9 Ex 190, 196; *Lapointe v L'Association de Bienfaisance et de Retraite de la Police de Montreal* [1906] AC 535, 539.
[135] Referring to *Fisher v Keane* (1878) 11 Ch D 353; *Dawkins v Antrobus* (1879) 17 Ch D 615; *Weinberger v Inglis* [1919] AC 606, 615.
[136] An example is *Annamunthodo v Oilfields Workers' Trade Union* [1961] AC 945, referred to by Lord Evershed: *Ridge v Baldwin* (n 133) 88.
[137] *Dickason v Edwards* (1910) 10 CLR 243.
[138] ibid 250 (Griffiths CJ), 255 (O'Connor J). See also 258 (Isaacs J).
[139] ibid 250 (Griffiths CJ), 255 (O'Connor J). See also *Australian Workers' Union v Bowen (No 2)* (1948) 77 CLR 601, 603.

upon membership, without affording the member procedural fairness.[140] *Cameron v Hogan*[141] was a confining influence, holding that some consensual arrangements do not amount to a contract because there is no intention to create legal relations, and that a member must be injured with regard to his property or a civil right.[142] The decision has in some respects been overtaken by the development of more general principles, including with regard to the availability of equitable relief.[143] The overwhelming contemporary tendency is to find that the rules of the domestic body do constitute a contract,[144] that property rights or livelihood are affected by the relevant decision, and that damage to reputation may suffice because of its indirect effect upon livelihood.[145]

In *Dickason v Edwards*,[146] Isaacs J described the terms implied in the rules of a domestic body expansively, stating that the Court would interfere if the decision was not in accordance with the rules, involved a denial of natural justice, a failure to act bona fide or was 'a decision at which no reasonable man could honestly arrive', a ground later known as *Wednesbury* unreasonableness.[147] Thus, in *Agricultural Societies Council*, the Court was clearly prepared to accept that equitable relief may be available in relation to a decision of a domestic body like the ASC if contractual or other private law rights were affected. However, the plaintiff had brought a judicial review action, and failed to present a case that there was a breach of an implied contractual term that the ASC was to proceed in accordance with procedural fairness.[148] By contrast, in *CECA* the applicant for membership of

---

[140] *Field v NSW Greyhound Breeders Owners and Trainers Association Ltd* [1972] 2 NSWLR 948; *Trivett v Nivison* (n 132); *Hall v NSW Trotting Club Ltd* [1977] 1 NSWLR 378; *Forbes v NSW Trotting Club Ltd* (n 81); *Malone v Marr* [1981] 2 NSWLR 984; *Scandrett v Dowling* (1992) 27 NSWLR 483, 503–04; *Australian Football League v Carlton Football Club Ltd* [1998] 2 VR 546, 548, 561, 576; *Mitchell v Royal NSW Canine Council Ltd* (2001) 52 NSWLR 242, 248, [34]–[36]; *McClelland v Burning Palms Surf Life Saving Club* (n 127) 779–91, [81]–[117]; *Minister for Local Government v South Sydney City Council* (2002) 55 NSWLR 381, 416; *Hall v University of New South Wales* [2003] NSWSC 669, [116]; *Viskovic v Vulela* [2005] WASC 92, [33]; *Sydney United Football Club v Soccer NSW* [2005] NSWSC 474; *Wilson v RSL of Australia (Qld Branch)* [2006] QSC 376, [45]–[46]; *David Love v AFL Canberra Ltd* [2009] ACTSC 135, [10].

[141] *Cameron v Hogan* (1934) 51 CLR 358, 370 (Rich, Dixon, Evatt and McTiernan JJ); cf 383 (Starke J).

[142] eg the compact between adherents to the faith of a church: *Scandrett v Dowling* (n 140) 513, 562.

[143] *McKinnon v Grogan* [1974] 1 NSWLR 295; *Cardile v Led Builders Pty Ltd* (1999) 198 CLR 380, 395.

[144] Statute may provide that the rules of an incorporated association or of a cooperative are a contract: eg *Associations Incorporation Act 2009* (NSW), s 26(1); *Co-operatives (Adoption of National Law) Act 2012* (NSW), s 4, Appendix (*Co-operatives National Law*, s 55).

[145] *Plenty v Seventh-Day Adventists Church of Port Pirie* (1986) 43 SASR 121, 123–25, 139, 143–44; *Australian Football League v Carlton Football Club Ltd* (n 140) 550; *Carter v NSW Netball Association* [2004] NSWSC 737, [100]–[109]; *Islamic Council of South Australia Inc v Australian Federation of Islamic Councils Inc* [2009] NSWSC 211, [31], [49]; *Fitzpatrick v Lithgow and District Workmens' Club Ltd* [2012] NSWSC 265, [101]–[108]; *Sturt v The Right Reverend Dr Brian Farran, Bishop of Newcastle* [2012] NSWSC 400, [162]–[163]; *Harrington v Coote* (2013) 119 SASR 152, [19]; *Abela v Royal New South Wales Canine Council Ltd t/as Dogs New South Wales* [2015] NSWSC 242, [45]–[46]; cf *Rush v WA Amateur Football League (Inc)* (2007) 35 WAR 102, [30], [37]; *Liverpool Touch Football Association v New South Wales Touch Association Incorporated* [2014] NSWSC 1553, [12]–[13]; *DEF v Trappett* [2016] NSWSC 1698, [119], [175].

[146] *Dickason v Edwards* (n 137).

[147] ibid 258. Similar implied terms based on administrative law standards drawn from a number of grounds of review were accepted in *Australian Football League v Carlton Football Club Ltd* (n 140) 551–52 (Tadgell JA), 567–68 (Hayne JA), 578–80 (Ashley JA). Here and in Australian case law generally, '*Wednesbury* unreasonableness' does not denote the collection of abuse of power grounds described by Lord Greene MR in *Associated Provincial Picture Houses Ltd v Wednesbury Corporation* [1948] 1 KB 223, 229, but only denotes the single ground established where a decision is so unreasonable that no reasonable decision-maker could have come to it: at 230.

[148] *Agricultural Societies Council of NSW v Christie* (n 121) 568–69, [35], [40]–[41] (Meagher JA) (Ward JA agreeing). In any event the Court concluded that there was no apprehended bias.

ACPET failed to establish justiciability on the basis of *Datafin*, but was granted a declaration that ACPET breached an implied contractual term that it was to afford procedural fairness in refusing membership.[149]

Challenges to decisions of FOS have tended to focus on establishing justiciability in a judicial review action as the entrée to arguing failure to meet administrative law standards as grounds of review. In *Mickovski*, the plaintiff failed to persuade the Court that FOS's decision was justiciable on the basis of *Datafin*. However, the plaintiff also sought equitable relief for breach of contract, by an erroneous determination that the rules did not give FOS jurisdiction over the complaint. The Court agreed that a declaration could be sought, that a decision of domestic body is invalid for restraint of trade, or because it is plainly contrary to the contract or made in bad faith, with bias or dishonesty, or in breach of procedural fairness, or because it was a decision to which no reasonable tribunal could properly come on the evidence.[150] The hurdle that proved insurmountable in the contract claim was a rule providing that decisions of FOS were final. On the authorities, this meant that FOS's decisions were not subject to review in a contract claim unless affected by fraud, dishonesty or lack of good faith, or that it was otherwise apparent that the determination had not been carried out in accordance with the agreement.[151] FOS had erred in interpreting the rules, but the error was not of a kind that fell within that window.[152]

Breach of contract was the exclusive claim directed at FOS in *Cromwell Property Securities Ltd v Financial Ombudsman Service Ltd*.[153] Attention turned to terms implied into FOS's rules.[154] The parties did not dispute the implication in the rules of a domestic body of implied terms as to bad faith, *Wednesbury* unreasonableness and procedural fairness as a matter of law, breach of these terms being subject to equitable intervention.[155] *Cromwell Property* extended the list of administrative law standards identified in *Dickason* as implied terms, to include the principle that policy should not be applied inflexibly without consideration of the merits of a case.[156] Argument centred on whether the implied term

---

[149] *CECA Institute Pty Ltd v Australian Council of Private Education and Training* (n 105) 111–15, [114]–[133].

[150] *Mickovski v Financial Ombudsman Service Ltd* (n 86) 468, [38]–[40], fn 26.

[151] ibid 468, [38]–[41], referring to *Legal & General Life of Australia Ltd v A Hudson Pty Ltd* (1985) 1 NSWLR 314, 336 (McHugh JA); *Holt v Cox* (1994) 15 ACSR 590, 597 (Mason P); *AGL Victoria Pty Ltd v SPI Networks (Gas) Pty Ltd* [2006] VSCA 173, [51]–[52].

[152] cf *R (on the application of Oxford Study Centre Ltd) v British Council* (n 91), where the British Council did not fall within *R v Panel on Take-overs and Mergers, ex parte Datafin Plc* (n 84) and so was not subject to judicial review, but was declared to have breached its contractual obligation to act fairly when it withdrew the accreditation of a language school.

[153] *Cromwell Property Securities Ltd v Financial Ombudsman Service Ltd* (2014) 288 FLR 374. The plaintiff abandoned its initial concurrent invocation of judicial review jurisdiction and relied solely on a claim for declaratory and injunctive relief for breach of contract: *Cromwell Property Securities Ltd v Financial Ombudsman Service Ltd* [2013] VSC 333, [5]–[6]. See also *Bilaczenko v Financial Ombudsman Service Ltd* [2013] FCA 1268 (Mansfield J), where the issue of the application of *Datafin* (ibid) was left open.

[154] The Court did not discuss the rule providing that decisions of FOS were final, presumably because the breach of contract was alleged to have occurred in making a ruling that a dispute was not excepted from FOS's jurisdiction, rather than in the making of a recommendation resolving the dispute.

[155] *Cromwell Property Securities Ltd v Financial Ombudsman Service Ltd* (2014) (n 153) [257]–[258].

[156] ibid 408–09, [137]–[147] (Warren CJ and Osborne JA); 451–53, [294]–[300] (Tate JA). This principle has been expressed as a requirement to give 'genuine, proper and realistic consideration to the merits' of the case, a formula that has attracted judicial disquiet lest it encourage a slide into review of the merits: *Minister for Immigration and Citizenship v SZJSS* (2010) 243 CLR 164, 175–76, [30]. The Victorian Court of Appeal accepted that this was an implied term, but it was not breached.

as to reasonableness involved the *Wednesbury* test or a lower standard of an objective test of reasonableness.[157] Consistently with the authorities traced back to *Dickason v Edwards*, the applicable test was the *Wednesbury* test.[158] By majority the Court concluded that in the circumstances FOS did not act *Wednesbury* unreasonably in refusing to except a particular dispute from its jurisdiction so as to enable the member to bring proceedings in a court.[159] The breach of contract claim failed.

FOS itself has brought a breach of contract claim against a former member, in *Financial Ombudsman Service Ltd v Pioneer Credit Acquisition Services Pty Ltd*,[160] seeking damages for outstanding fees, with its former member counter-claiming breach of contract. FOS accepted that its decision-making must be in accordance with an implied term that it must not act *Wednesbury* unreasonably. The Court concluded that in refusing the former member consent to commence legal proceedings in relation to the dispute, FOS did not act in breach of an implied term not to act unreasonably. The standard of reasonableness appeared to be broader than the *Wednesbury* test.[161] It was the standard of reasonableness, in place since the High Court's decision in *Minister for Immigration and Citizenship v Li*,[162] based on an interpretive presumption that any statutory power is to be exercised reasonably. *Li* unreasonableness is established where the decision-maker makes a decision that lacks an evident and intelligible justification.[163]

Administrative law standards of procedural fairness and reasonableness have been applicable to FOS, not because it was shown to be a public body or exercising a regulatory function for government, but because at common law these standards have been implied in relation to contracts governing the members of private domestic bodies. Two difficulties have arisen in extending the boundaries of administrative law via a contract action.

The first is that the rules of the domestic body may expressly exclude the standards,[164] or include a finality clause making the relevant decision final and not subject to challenge, unless it is beyond the realm of contractual contemplation.[165] The latter kind of rule precluded relief for breach of contract in *Mickovski*.[166] The second limitation is that a person whose rights or interests are affected by a breach of the rules or failure to observe implied terms embodying administrative law standards, and who seeks equitable relief, may not be a member of the domestic body. Upon further examination the second limitation, a private law counterpart to the problem of standing to seek review in administrative law, may have little practical operation.

In the case of conventional domestic bodies, the absence of privity of contract tends often to be somehow overcome. It is common in the sporting world that a disciplinary decision is made by an overarching state or national association with which a member of an

---

[157] *Cromwell Property Securities Ltd v Financial Ombudsman Service Ltd* (2014) (n 153) [62]–[63].
[158] ibid 401, [93] (Warren CJ and Osborne JA); 412, [163]; 433, [231] (Tate JA).
[159] ibid 410, [154] (Warren CJ and Osborne JA) (Tate JA dissenting on the question of breach of the terms).
[160] *Financial Ombudsman Service Ltd v Pioneer Credit Acquisition Services Pty Ltd* [2014] VSC 172 (Ferguson J).
[161] ibid [50]. The Court rejected as implied terms alleged obligations to decide a question of law correctly, and not to determine the dispute as if it were a legal proceeding in a court.
[162] *Minister for Immigration and Citizenship v Li* (2013) 249 CLR 332.
[163] ibid 367, [76] (Hayne, Kiefel and Bell JJ).
[164] eg a rule may exclude procedural fairness: *Australian Workers' Union v Bowen (No 2)* (n 139) 617.
[165] See n 151 above.
[166] *Mickovski v Financial Ombudsman Service Ltd* (n 86) [41]. See text accompanying n 151 above.

affiliated local association has no direct contractual relationship. The member of the affiliated association has been treated as having a contractual relationship with the overarching association, via the latter's direct contractual relationship with the affiliated association.[167]

The issue of privity of contract was inconspicuous in *Forbes*. The non-statutory Rules of Trotting, which operated as a self-regulatory scheme in the trotting industry, were made by a domestic body, the Australian Trotting Council (ATC), whose members were trotting clubs in Australia. The NSW Trotting Club Ltd ('Club') was the controlling body responsible for administering the rules in NSW. The rules empowered a committee of the Club to exclude any person from any racecourse in NSW where the rules operated. Applying the rules, the Club's committee resolved to exclude Forbes, a racegoer and professional punter, from all racecourses it occupied or controlled. Forbes sought a declaration and injunction on the ground that he had not been heard before the committee made its resolution. As noted in the earlier discussion of the obiter dicta in *Forbes* proposing that public power may be exercised by a private landowner, the Club owned two of the racecourses. The High Court identified implied terms in the rules: that the Club would not exclude him except (i) in accordance with the rules and (ii) observing procedural fairness.[168] The Court made a declaration that the warning-off notice was ultra vires and void.

Although Forbes was a member of his own local club, he was not a member of the Club, nor a party to the contract between the ATC and the Club and local clubs.[169] The Club had applied its rules to a person who was not its member. Justice Gibbs overcame the privity problem by identifying another contract, between Forbes and the Club, which was formed when Forbes entered the racecourse and impliedly agreed to be bound by those of the rules that were applicable.[170] This included an implied term that the applicable rules be applied in accordance with procedural fairness.[171] Other Justices in *Forbes* simply held that the Club was required to act in accordance with procedural fairness in administering the rules, without paying regard to the fact that Forbes was not a member of the Club bound by the rules. The implied term cast an obligation on the Club, responsible for administering the rules, that was owed not just to the other parties to the contract but to any individual whose interests were affected by the application of the rules.[172] This view was influenced by the fact that the issue of a warning-off notice had further consequences under the rules, including loss of the right as a member of a local club to enter a horse in any race, and indeed loss of membership of that local club.

There was of course another contract, the revocable licence to enter granted by the Club (as a local club) to Forbes upon entry. Justice Gibbs adopted, and the other Justices implicitly accepted, the submission made by counsel for *Forbes* that the rules, express or implied,

---

[167] *Rose v Boxing NSW Inc* [2007] NSWSC 20, [45], [55] (Brereton J), relying on *Hawick v Flegg* (1858) WN (NSW) 255 and *Finnigan v New Zealand Rugby Football Union Inc* [1985] 2 NZLR 159 (granting a declaration that the state boxing association denied a member of a local club procedural fairness in breach of an implied term of that contract).

[168] *Forbes v NSW Trotting Club Ltd* (n 81) 271–72 (Gibbs J).

[169] ibid 279 (Aickin J) (Stephen J agreeing at 272).

[170] ibid 271.

[171] ibid 272.

[172] There is a suggestion of this kind in the judgment of Stephen J (ibid 272), who observed that the 'tenuous' nature of the relationship between Forbes and the Club and the nature of the injury Forbes suffered became irrelevant once the parties accepted that the exercise of the warning-off power by the Club called for the observance of procedural fairness.

displaced the implied terms of the revocable licence to enter.[173] What is interesting is the unarticulated dictum, of Justices other than Gibbs J, that under its contract with the ATC and the local clubs, the Club owed contractual obligations directly to individuals who were not its members but whose interests were affected by its application of the rules, and that they could obtain declaratory relief to enforce them.

In the case of domestic bodies of the regulatory or complaint-handling kind, privity of contract may be a more difficult issue. In *Cromwell Property* there was no problem of privity of contract because FOS's rules made a complainant a party to the contract.[174] The constitution of a complaint-handling body may not in every case contain such a provision. The plaintiffs in *Datafin* probably could not have brought an action for breach of contract.[175] The unexpressed and neglected dictum in *Forbes* suggests that in such cases attention be given to the nature of the contract and its implied terms before privity of contract is assumed to impede the enforcement via contract of administrative law standards.

VII. Implying Terms in Other Contracts

The basis for equitable intervention for breach by domestic bodies of implied contractual terms has sometimes been thinly identified. In *Dickason v Edwards*, although breach of contract was identified as the basis for intervention, O'Connor J suggested that equitable relief is available because the domestic body's decision 'results in injury to property or to civil rights'.[176] Occasionally the basis for intervention has been expressed in sweeping terms, encouraging the impression that equitable relief is available against a domestic tribunal purely in order to protect a property or other common law right, or out of the necessity to attain justice.[177] Any assumption that equitable relief is based on a vague unidentified right is misconceived, as was demonstrated in *Agricultural Societies Council*, where the plaintiff horse trainer failed to establish, or even argue, the proper basis for relief, which was breach of contract. The only basis for equitable intervention is breach of the contract between the

---

[173] ibid 244 (counsel being MH McHugh QC, later a Justice of the High Court), 268–69 (Gibbs J).

[174] cf *CECA Institute Pty Ltd v Australian Council of Private Education and Training* (n 105) 115, [133], where the training organisation sought relief for the very reason that it was refused membership of ACPET. In the absence of any direct supporting authority, the problem of privity was overcome by reference to the duty of ACPET to notify its refusal decision to the Minister and other bodies that could make related decisions with respect to the organisation, noting the reputational damage that may be done by the decision.

[175] The Panel in *R v Panel on Take-overs and Mergers, ex parte Datafin Plc* (n 84) had 12 members, including representatives of associations concerned with financial markets, along with the Stock Exchange and the Bank of England. The Panel had no contractual relationship with those who dealt in the market and were subject to its determinations applying the non-statutory City Code on Take-overs and Mergers. The plaintiffs, a company making a take-over bid and its financial backer, alleging that the Panel should have found a breach of the Code, were not members of the Panel. A determination by the Panel could have indirect consequences when certain statutory powers were exercised by the Bank of England and delegates of the Secretary of State for Trade and Industry. In argument the plaintiffs sought to establish that the Panel had public duties, unlike domestic bodies that were accountable via contract. The Panel contended that the plaintiffs should have sought relief in private law: *Datafin* (n 84) 818, 820. No consideration was given in argument or in the judgments to administrative law standards as implied terms of any contract. That is not surprising, as the plaintiffs only sought leave to bring judicial review proceedings and had no contractual relationship with the Panel.

[176] *Dickason v Edwards* (n 137) 255.

[177] *Australian Football League v Carlton Football Club Ltd* (n 140) 550 (Tadgell JA).

member and the domestic body, or some other entitlement recognised at law or in equity, including restraint of trade, as discussed in *Cromwell Property* and *Agricultural Societies Council*. In most cases a contract will be established, and the critical question will then be whether there is a breach of an implied term requiring the body to comply with procedural fairness or some other administrative law standard.

The implication of such terms does not seem to have generated great controversy. Scant attention has been given to whether the implication is in accordance with general principles governing the implication of terms into a contract. If the implication of terms requiring conformity to administrative law standards is to be extrapolated to bodies that are not conventional domestic bodies, it will be necessary to grapple with general tests for the implication of contractual terms.

A term may be implied in a contract in fact in order to give it business efficacy, as a matter of construction.[178] Implication in fact occurs if the term: is reasonable and equitable; is necessary to give business efficacy to the contract (and is not implied if the contract is effective without it); is so obvious that it goes without saying; is capable of clear expression; and does not contradict any express terms of the contract.[179] A term may be implied by law in particular classes of contract, or by law in all classes of contract, as a matter of the common law or by statute. Implication of a term by law at common law is based on more general considerations, but the implication must be a matter of 'necessity', such that rights conferred by the contract would otherwise be rendered worthless.[180]

The issue of implication in fact or law is a familiar one in the case of the implied obligation of good faith. At least in the context of a contractual clause that empowers a party to act to the detriment of another, the obligation of good faith requires a party to act honestly and with fidelity to the bargain; not to act dishonestly or to undermine the bargain entered into or the substance of the contractual benefit; and to act reasonably and with fair dealing, having regard to the interests of the parties and the provisions, aims and purposes of the contract, objectively ascertained.[181] The High Court has yet to determine whether an obligation of good faith is implied in law in a particular class of contracts.[182] An implied term of mutual trust and confidence in employment contracts has been decisively rejected,[183] in contrast to its acceptance in the United Kingdom.[184] On the other hand, a duty to cooperate is a term implied by law in employment contracts.[185] The High Court has expressed

---

[178] *Codelfa Construction Pty Ltd v State Rail Authority (NSW)* (1982) 149 CLR 337, 347.

[179] *BP Refinery (Westernport) Pty Ltd v President, Councillors and Ratepayers of the Shire of Hastings* (1977) 180 CLR 266. A term may also be implied by custom in particular classes of contract, the custom or usage being notorious, certain, legal and reasonable: *Byrne v Australian Airlines Ltd* (1995) 185 CLR 410, 423–24.

[180] *Byrne v Australian Airlines Ltd* (n 179) 450; *Commonwealth Bank of Australia v Barker* (2014) 253 CLR 169, 189, [28]–[29]; 199, [56]; 215 [113].

[181] *Macquarie International Health Clinic Pty Ltd v Sydney South West Area Health Service* [2010] NSWCA 268, [12] (Allsop P) and *Paciocco v Australia and New Zealand Banking Group Ltd* (2015) 236 FCR 199, 273, [288] (Allsop CJ), summarising the content of good faith derived from *Renard Constructions, Hughes Bros Pty Ltd v Trustees of Roman Catholic Church (Archdiocese of Sydney)* (1993) 31 NSWLR 91; *Burger King Corporation v Hungry Jack's Pty Ltd* (2001) 69 NSWLR 558; *Alcatel Australia Ltd v Scarcella* (1998) 44 NSWLR 349. See also *Mineralogy Pty Ltd v Sino Air Iron Pty Ltd (No 6)* (2015) 329 ALR 1, 161 [1010] (Edelman J).

[182] *Royal Botanic Gardens and Domain Trust v South Sydney City Council* (2002) 240 CLR 45, 63, [40]; 94, [156]; *Commonwealth Bank of Australia v Barker* (n 180) 214, [107].

[183] *Commonwealth Bank of Australia v Barker* (n 180) (nor was the term implied in fact in that case).

[184] *Malik v Bank of Credit & Commerce International SA (In liq)* [1998] AC 20.

[185] *Concrete Pty Ltd v Parramatta Design & Developments Pty Ltd* (2006) 229 CLR 577, 596, [59].

wariness lest it go beyond its proper function in imposing broadly normative standards reflected by terms implied by law.[186] Intermediate appellate courts have accepted that an obligation of good faith should not be implied indiscriminately into all contracts, because implication requires close attention to the terms of the contract, and the content of the good faith obligation may differ according to the contractual context. An obligation to act in good faith is implied in fact in a written contract between commercial entities of equivalent bargaining power that meets the general test for implication in fact.[187]

The content of the private law obligation of good faith varies, as does the content of an obligation to afford procedural fairness, according to the context. The conception of fair dealing contained within good faith is a more fluid and less precise obligation than procedural fairness, and may include more than just an obligation of each party to deal with the other honestly.[188] Good faith most likely includes an element similar to procedural fairness where that is raised by the context.[189] The High Court has hinted that the undecided question is whether contractual powers are limited by 'good faith and rationality requirements analogous to those applicable in the sphere of public law'.[190]

In *Hughes Aircraft Systems International v Airservices Australia*,[191] Finn J held that a term requiring good faith was implied by law in a pre-award contract governing a competitive tendering process operated by a statutory authority, the former Civil Aviation Authority (CAA). That conclusion was in part driven by Finn J's view that the CAA was a public body.[192] The content of good faith was informed by the administrative law standard of procedural fairness.[193] Its essential requirement is giving the other party a reasonable opportunity to present its case. The familiar aspects of the content of procedural fairness include giving reasonable time to prepare a case, giving notice of allegations, disclosing issues or adverse material, allowing for written or oral submissions, or ensuring a decision is made by a person who does not have an appearance of bias. In a particular context good faith may require conduct that is not analogous to any of these matters. The relationship between good faith and procedural fairness has yet to evolve.

Whether reasonableness or rationality could be a contractual term implied at law depends upon considerations similar to those affecting the implication of a good faith term. As noted, good faith may itself include a requirement to act reasonably.[194] In the United Kingdom it was confirmed in *Braganza v BP Shipping Ltd*[195] that in a contract containing

---

[186] *Commonwealth Bank of Australia v Barker* (n 180) 185, [20]; 189, [29].
[187] *Specialist Diagnostic Services Pty Ltd v Healthscope Ltd* (2012) 41 VR 1, 20, [87]; *Androvisaneas v Members First Broker Network Pty Ltd* [2013] VSCA 212, [108].
[188] *Mineralogy Pty Ltd v Sino Air Iron Pty Ltd (No 6)* (n 181) 161, [1008] (Edelman J). cf *Strzelecki Holdings Pty Ltd v Cable Sands Pty Ltd* (2010) 41 WAR 318, 339, [61] (Pullin JA) (Newnes JA agreeing).
[189] *Commonwealth Bank of Australia v Barker* (n 180) 213, [104] (Kiefel J).
[190] ibid 195–96, [42] (French CJ, Bell and Keane JJ).
[191] *Hughes Aircraft Systems International v Airservices Australia* (1997) 76 FCR 151.
[192] ibid 195–97.
[193] ibid 196. This was a contract action rather than a judicial review action. Even as a statutory authority, the CAA's decisions had been held not to be justiciable under the *ADJR Act*: *CEA Technologies Pty Ltd v Civil Aviation Authority* (1994) 51 FCR 329. This was an application of the approach taken in *General Newspapers Pty Ltd v Telstra* (n 78) 172–73 (discussed in text accompanying n 78 above), of treating a general statutory capacity to enter contracts as not giving force or effect to a contractual decision, which was therefore not made 'under an enactment'.
[194] Text accompanying n 181 above; *Virk Pty Ltd (in liq) v YUM! Restaurants Australia Pty Ltd* [2017] FCAFC 190, [149], [156]–[176].
[195] *Braganza v BP Shipping Ltd* [2015] 1 WLR 1661.

a contractual clause empowering a party to act to the detriment of another, a term is implied that the power not be exercised arbitrarily, capriciously or unreasonably.[196] This implied term sounds like the administrative law standard of *Wednesbury* unreasonableness. *Li* unreasonableness, requiring that conduct not lack an evident and intelligible justification, is a less rigorous standard. It also comes close to a requirement to act on the basis of evidence, and to give adequate reasons for a decision. *Braganza* went further, accepting as implied terms, at least in an employment contract, the administrative law standards requiring that the decision-maker take into account relevant considerations it is bound to take into account, and not take into account irrelevant considerations it is bound not to take into account.[197]

Braganza frankly embraced the prospect of implied terms as to the manner of exercise of a contractual discretionary power as 'drawing closer and closer to the principles applicable in judicial review',[198] with the prospect that in connection with the relevant power (at least of an employer under an employment contract) 'decision-making should be subject to scrutiny that is [no] less intense than that which the court applies to the decision of a public authority which is charged with making a finding of fact'.[199]

The view adopted in *Braganza* finds support in authorities such as *Dickason v Edwards* and *Cromwell Property*, and may gain support in Australia. A suggestion of this possibility is found in *Mineralogy Pty Ltd v Sino Iron Pty Ltd (No 6)*,[200] where Edelman J considered that any implication of a term that a contractual discretionary power be exercised reasonably should mirror the administrative law standard of *Li* reasonableness.[201]

VIII. Conclusions

Tests of justiciability have drawn the boundaries of judicial review. The settled principle that an exercise of statutory power is justiciable has been expanded and eroded. Invocation of public power or a public law element to justify either development has been unhelpful. The fate of the *Forbes* dicta and of *Datafin* demonstrates that point, having perhaps done more to contract the boundaries of administrative law than to expand them.

The revisionist approach to justiciability that emerged in *Probuild* may be attributable to a mistaken perception that the adjudicator was akin to a private arbitrator who is not

---

[196] ibid 1669–72, [20]–[30] (Baroness Hale DPSC) (Lord Kerr JSC agreeing), referring to Lord Sumption JSC's conclusions in *British Telecommunications plc v Telefonica O2 UK Ltd* [2014] Bus LR 765, [37] and *Hayes v Willoughby* [2013] 1 WLR 935, [14].

[197] *Braganza v BP Shipping Ltd* (n 195) 1672, [29]–[30] (Baroness Hale DPSC) (Lord Kerr JSC agreeing); 1677, [53]–[54] (Lord Hodge JSC) (Lord Kerr JSC agreeing).

[198] ibid 1672, [28].

[199] ibid 1678, [57] (Lord Hodge JSC) (Lord Kerr agreeing). See also at 1688, [103] (Lord Neuberger PSC) (Lord Wilson JSC agreeing).

[200] *Mineralogy Pty Ltd v Sino Iron Pty Ltd (No 6)* (n 181) 162, [1013]–[1014].

[201] ibid 162–63, [1014]–[1015]. In *Mineralogy Pty Ltd v Sino Air Iron Pty Ltd (No 6)* (n 181), a term requiring a termination power to be exercised reasonably was not implied, because the contract contained express provisions governing the manner and basis for exercise of the power: at 164, [1020]–[1025]. See also *Minister for Immigration and Border Protection v SZVFW* (2018) 357 ALR 408, 436–37, [132]–[135] (Edelman J); and the similar observations of Lee J in *Bupa HI Pty Ltd v Andrew Chang Services Pty Ltd* [2018] FCA 2033, [119]–[124]. cf *Metro Investments Holdings Pty Ltd v GM Holden Ltd* [2017] FCA 1523, [47] (White J).

amenable to review simply for legal error. This is consistent with the idea that since domestic bodies operate consensually they should not be subject to judicial review. Similar reasoning is found in conclusions that *Datafin* could not apply to a domestic body performing a regulatory function because it is a consensual body. This is not to disapprove *Datafin* but to unwind it. Although its membership was limited to representative associations, the Panel in *Datafin* operated on a consensual basis. The thinking in *Datafin* was that it is important to look not just at the source of the decision-making power but at the nature of the power or duty.[202] This is not to say that identifying public power is a helpful test of justiciability.

The boundaries of administrative law are not exclusively set by tests of justiciability. The grounds of review, with their evolving content, also operate as a boundary. In the form of implied contractual terms, administrative law standards are being extended to apply to decision-makers in the private sphere. This is no new idea, as *Dickason v Edwards* demonstrates. Ironically, the contractual source of a domestic body's power has justified the non-justiciability of its decisions, but is also the foundation for the implantation of administrative law standards. The view adopted in *Braganza* may gain support in Australia. The implication of terms requiring fairness and reasonableness in contracts between members of domestic bodies may be replicated for other kinds of contracts. That would call for justification.

The requirements of procedural fairness and reasonableness in administrative decision-making are the product of a process of interpretation. Common law procedural fairness is implied in order to 'supply the omission of the legislature'.[203] *Wednesbury* unreasonableness and *Li* unreasonableness have been described as a matter of statutory implication.[204]

The implication of contractual terms also emerges from a process of interpretation. In private law interpretation of the contract is a search for the intention of the parties, while in public law the interpretation of the statute is a search for the legislative intention. Each search is premised upon a fiction that the relevant intention existed. In both interpretive exercises it is the intention manifested by the written words that must be identified, with some resort to the context at the relevant time. To this extent the interpretive exercises match.[205]

On one view, called the ultra vires theory, the application of administrative law standards in judicial review is legitimised on the basis that the function of the judicial branch is to ensure the executive branch conforms to the will of the legislature. Interpreting the statute as requiring a power holder to act fairly and reasonably is a matter of identifying with greater precision the legislative will. The judicial branch is impliedly authorised by the legislature to do so.[206] The old debate sparked by the ultra vires theory, as to whether the implication of procedural fairness is a matter of statutory interpretation or required by the common law, has understandably led to a degree of ennui.[207] In implying procedural fairness, statute and fundamental common law rights and principles both play a part. However, when procedural

---

[202] *R v Panel on Take-overs and Mergers, ex parte Datafin Plc* (n 84) 847–48 (Lloyd LJ).
[203] *Cooper v Board of Works for the Wandsworth District* (1863) 143 ER 414.
[204] *Minister for Immigration and Citizenship v Li* (n 162) 351, [29] (French CJ); 363–64, [67] (Hayne, Kiefel and Bell JJ); 370–71, [88]–[92] (Gageler J).
[205] *Byrnes v Kendle* (2011) 243 CLR 253, 284, [98] (Heydon and Crennan JJ).
[206] C Forsyth, 'Of Fig Leaves and Fairy Tales: The Ultra Vires Doctrine, Sovereignty of Parliament and Judicial Review' (1996) 55 *Cambridge Law Journal* 122, 135.
[207] *Plaintiff S10-2011 v Minister for Immigration and Citizenship* (n 81) 666, [97] (Gummow, Hayne, Crennan and Bell JJ).

fairness and reasonableness are implied in relation to the exercise of non-statutory power,[208] the ultra vires theory crumbles.

The ultra vires theory cannot explain the basis on which standards of procedural fairness and reasonableness become implied contractual terms, and has never attempted to do so. The legitimacy of the implied terms importing administrative law standards has been sought in private law principles governing the implication of terms in fact and at law. Since the implied terms extend the boundaries of administrative law, such justifications may be enriched by reference to rationales or theories known to public law, unless they prove inadequate or inimical to the task.

---

[208] *R v Criminal Injuries Compensation Board, ex parte Lain* (n 127); *Ainsworth v Criminal Justice Commission* (1992) 175 CLR 564, 580; *Minister for Local Government v South Sydney City Council* (n 140) 384–86, [6]–[15] (Spigelman CJ).

PART 4

Public Law and Public Administration

17

The Nature and Bounds of Executive Power: Keeping Pace with Change

KM HAYNE

A subject as large as the frontiers of executive power demands attention to basic questions. The most basic question is whether public law doctrines have kept pace with changes in the ways in which executive power is used. There are at least three, and probably more, changes in the way in which executive power is used in Australia, which require asking whether public law doctrines have kept pace. First, the political branches of government have looked more and more to the market economy as a model for providing services to society. Second, legislation has been enacted to establish numerous authorities (more or less independent of the political branches of government) to regulate particular industries or activities. Third, governments and regulators have sought to modify behaviour by promulgating 'soft law' – 'guidelines', 'codes of conduct' and the like – rather than black-letter regulation.

All three of these areas merit closer attention. This chapter, however, looks only at some issues that arise from the political branches' looking to the market economy as the model for providing public services. And for the most part, this has been done by making a contract that obliges a private counterparty to supply services to the public generally (like a toll road) or to a section of the public (like a private prison).

When a contract of this kind is made, there are at least three kinds of issue that should be considered. First, which organs of government must be engaged to create the obligations? Second, how transparent is the process for negotiating and then administering the arrangement that is made? Third, who is to be accountable for the arrangements that have been made and for their performance?

How these issues intersect with accepted notions of governmental structures and judicial review of administrative action depend upon what those notions are. Whether, and to what extent, these developments suggest that public law doctrines should change necessarily leads into consideration of questions about standing to sue, about grounds for challenge and about what relief may be given, to whom it may be given and when it may be given.

I. Private Parties Providing Public Services

More and more public services are provided by private parties. Many of those private parties are commercial enterprises conducted for private profit.[1] Some of those enterprises are entities whose shares or other securities are traded on a stock exchange. Other private parties are, or are associated with, charitable bodies and are not conducted for private profit.[2] But all of them deal with government at more or less arm's length.

How do the dealings between entities of these kinds and government intersect with accepted notions of governmental structures?

A. Governmental Structures

The making and administration of a contract with a private counterparty for provision of public services intersects with basic questions about governmental structures, because it is necessary to consider which organs of government must participate in its making and administration, as well as what power there is to make the contract.

Australian public lawyers are well used to notions of separation of powers and drawing distinctions, at least at the national level of government, between legislative, executive and judicial power. They are well used to thinking of the duty and jurisdiction of courts to review administrative action as not going beyond the declaration and enforcement of the law that determines the limits and governs the exercise of the repository's power.[3] The chief focus of Australian notions of the separation of powers has been upon the distinctive features of the judicial power of the Commonwealth dealt with in Chapter III of the Constitution. Behind the conclusions that have been reached about judicial power lie conceptions of separation of powers that find their roots in the observation that the Australian Constitution (like the United States (US) Constitution) deals separately with the legislative power of the Commonwealth, the executive power of the Commonwealth and the judicial power of the Commonwealth.[4] Yet, unlike the US Constitution, the Australian Constitution establishes a system of responsible and representative democracy. Hence the separation of legislative and executive powers effected by the Australian Constitution permits and requires that some who exercise executive power (Ministers of State) will participate in the exercise of legislative power and are answerable to the Parliament.

---

[1] See, eg, the tollroad operator considered in *Commissioner of Taxation v Citylink Melbourne Ltd* (2006) 228 CLR 1.
[2] See, eg, the provider of school chaplaincy services considered in *Williams v The Commonwealth* (2012) 248 CLR 156; *Williams v The Commonwealth [No 2]* (2014) 252 CLR 416.
[3] *Attorney-General (NSW) v Quin* (1990) 170 CLR 1, 35–36 (Brennan J).
[4] Chapter I deals with the legislative power of the Commonwealth, which s 1 vests in 'a Federal Parliament, which shall consist of the Queen, a Senate, and a House of Representatives'. Chapter II deals with the executive power of the Commonwealth, which s 61 provides ' is vested in the Queen and is exercisable by the Governor-General as the Queen's representative'. Chapter III deals with the judicial power of the Commonwealth, which s 71 vests in 'a Federal Supreme Court, to be called the High Court of Australia, and in such other federal courts as the Parliament creates, and in such other courts as it invests with federal jurisdiction'.

The Australian separation of powers may appear, then, to present a conundrum. If it does, the solution has two parts. First, the division effected between the three species of power is a division of powers whose character is determined according to traditional British conceptions.[5] Second, the division does not depend upon fundamental functional differences so much as upon distinctions generally accepted at the time the Constitution was framed, between classes of powers requiring different professional skills and habits in the authorities entrusted with their exercise.[6]

Considered against this background, it may not be surprising that, for many years, little attention was given to charting the bounds of executive power. More particularly, little attention was given to considering which organs of government must participate in the making and administration of a contract by which a private party agreed to provide public services, or to considering what power there is to make contracts of that kind. By contrast, judicial review of executive action demands attention to those boundaries.

B. Judicial Review

The Australian Constitution gives the High Court an entrenched jurisdiction to grant certain kinds of relief against an 'officer of the Commonwealth'.[7] The relevant section of the Constitution, section 75(v), is treated as providing an entrenched minimum provision of judicial review. But the central concern of judicial review of administrative action, whether under section 75(v) or more generally, is seen as being to enforce the legal limits on the exercise of public power. Inevitably, then, the focus of proceedings brought under section 75(v), and non-statutory judicial review more generally, is upon the identification of those limits: constitutional limits to power and express or implicit limits on the exercise of statutory power.

Despite familiarity with these ideas about judicial review, Australian lawyers have not often engaged in fundamental examination of the nature or extent of executive power. Judicial review of administrative action has predominantly focused upon constitutional or statutory limits on power, rather than on any consideration of limits deriving from constitutional or governmental structure. That is, for the most part, the question arising on judicial review of administrative action has been about the constitutional or statutory limits on the decision-maker's powers rather than upon more fundamental issues of whether the appropriate organs of government have participated in the steps said to give rights to or impose duties on a private counterparty.

With a few exceptions, most notably the consideration in *Dignan's* case of the delegation of legislative power,[8] debates about the constitutional separation of powers have focused upon the negative implications drawn from Chapter III of the Constitution that preclude conferral of judicial power on bodies other than Chapter III courts, and which preclude conferral on Chapter III courts of powers that are foreign to judicial power.

---

[5] *R v Kirby, ex parte Boilermakers' Society of Australia* (1956) 94 CLR 254, 276.
[6] *R v Davison* (1954) 90 CLR 353, 382.
[7] Matters in which a writ of mandamus or prohibition or injunction is sought against an officer of the Commonwealth. Section 75(v) was included to deal expressly with issues of the kind that had emerged in the US in *Marbury v Madison*, 5 US (1 Cranch) 137 (1803).
[8] *Victorian Stevedoring and General Contracting Co Pty Ltd and Meakes v Dignan* (1931) 46 CLR 73.

Analyses of these kinds are incomplete if they proceed from unstated premises about the nature and extent of executive power. And, as is apparent from what has already been said about Ministers' being legislators as well as the repository of executive power, if attention has been given to the nature of executive power, it has usually been by reference only to traditional conceptions of that power. But those traditional conceptions were formed in other times, before the more recent and more novel exercises of executive power. It is important to say something about the extent to which conceptions of executive power have developed.

II. The Nature and Extent of Executive Power

No doubt the executive is responsible for defence of the nation. The executive conducts foreign affairs. The executive must, and does, execute the law by maintaining and supporting the courts and executing the judgments of the courts. But, as Harrison Moore pointed out, soon after federation, there is much more to government than mere execution of the law:

> The State is a going concern; it has affairs which must be managed with prudence and judgment and which are not necessarily related to law in any sense other than that in which all conduct may be bounded by legal restraints.[9]

Or, as Arthur Berriedale Keith put it, when writing in the middle of the twentieth century about the English constitution, the executive administers the law of the land through the departments of state, 'preserving internal order as the first condition of progress' while looking to expand trade and 'improve in every way the social and economic conditions of the realm'.[10]

The management of the affairs of the body politic has changed in recent decades both in Australia and elsewhere. At the national level, conducting foreign affairs by the sending and receiving of embassies, securing protection of the nation and executing the law remain central to the exercise of executive power. But what has changed is the extent to which, and the means by which, other aspects of the affairs of the Australian polities, national and State, are managed. More and more, the governments of Australia have looked to trading and financial corporations as the model for management of those affairs. And there has followed the blizzard of corporatisation and privatisation with which we are all familiar.

Disposing of the rights and assets associated with provision of services to the public was driven by maximising return to government while shifting responsibility for the quality of service provided from government to the private sector operators.

The terms on which private sector operators acquired the right to provide such services have often been kept confidential. In some cases, government has sought to increase its return by giving the private counterparty a preferred position in the relevant market for a period extending well beyond the life of the administration that made the arrangement. And in some cases – most notably what have come to be called 'market-led proposals' or 'unsolicited offers to government' – the processes by which private sector operators

---

[9] WH Moore, *The Constitution of the Commonwealth of Australia* (London, Murray, 1902) 211.
[10] AB Keith, *The Constitution of England: Queen Victoria to George VI*, vol 2 (London, Macmillan, 1940) 44.

acquire rights or assets from government are kept confidential. The phrase 'commercial-in-confidence' has increasingly been treated as a complete answer to any call for public revelation of, or debate about, the terms on which transactions are effected.

All three features of these changes – outsourcing, maximisation of returns and opacity – provoke consideration of what is the role of executive government. More particularly, they invite attention to whether, and when, arrangements which the political executive conclude are for the better arrangement of the affairs of the polity, can be effected by the exercise of executive power alone, or require some express legislative authority. That is, they are issues that direct attention to consideration of structures of government and which organs of government must be engaged to effect certain arrangements.

For the most part, the arrangements that require particular attention either are expressed as contracts between a private counterparty and the polity (or an officer entering the contract 'for and on behalf of the Crown in right' of a particular polity), or otherwise call for the expenditure of public moneys.

Too often, I think, the answer that is made to any attempt to raise questions about the transactions is to say no more than that the contracts in issue either are 'Crown contracts' or are contracts made in the exercise of some 'non-statutory executive power'.

Neither form of answer grapples with the real issues. Each is little more than the ritual incantation of a slogan.

A. Government Contracts

As I have sought to explain elsewhere, references to the Crown and its capacities distract attention from the issues that arise when a body politic makes a contract.[11] To answer those issues by saying only that 'the contract is made by or in the name of the Crown and is to be enforced in accordance with Crown Suits Acts; the Crown has the powers and capacities of a natural person; *therefore* the contract is valid' slides over fundamental issues. It does that in at least two ways.

First and foremost, the 'Crown' is an ambiguous metaphor. In Australian constitutional law, the relevant right- and duty-bearing entity is the polity called into being by the Constitution (the Commonwealth of Australia) or one of the States identified in covering clause 6 of the Constitution as distinct bodies politic. The 'Executive', whether referred to as the Crown or otherwise, is not a right- and duty-bearing entity.

Second, observing that a polity (or 'the Crown') has capacity to make *a* contract does not show that the Executive of that polity has power to make *all* kinds of contract on behalf of the polity. The observation about capacity says only that there is capacity to contract. It says nothing about whether any particular contract is made within power.[12] The question about power requires consideration of not only any subject matter limits on power but also what organs of government must be engaged to make an enforceable contract. The question about organs of government too often goes unasked and unanswered. The issue is allowed

---

[11] KM Hayne, 'Government Contracts and Public Law' (2017) 41 *Melbourne University Law Review* 155, 162–63.
[12] In the Australian context, federal considerations necessarily deny that the executive government of the Commonwealth has power to make any and every kind of contract. See *Williams v The Commonwealth* (n 2); *Williams v The Commonwealth [No 2]* (n 2).

to hide behind an unelaborated assertion that the Executive has exercised some form of 'non-statutory executive power'.

The third point to be made is that references to royal 'prerogative' are equally unhelpful and misleading. Even if the definitional debate about 'prerogatives' is resolved, the fundamental question about which organs of government must be engaged to subject the polity to a binding obligation is not assisted by reference to prerogative.

Nor do I think that these issues are resolved by observing, as the Supreme Court of the United Kingdom has, that 'the Crown possesses some general administrative powers to carry on the ordinary business of government which are not exercises of the royal prerogative and do not require statutory authority'.[13] As the Supreme Court also said, both the extent and the 'exact juridical basis of the powers are controversial'.[14]

At least three different accounts have been given of these 'general administrative powers'.[15] The first is founded in a notion that what is not prohibited is permitted.[16] The second seeks to root the powers in the common law.[17] The third seeks to divide general administrative powers into legal and non-legal powers: those that have an effect on legal rights, duties or status; and those (like powers to circulate written material or consult officials) that do not have any immediate effect on rights, duties or status. The former kinds of power are said to be limited to incidental matters and have their source in the common law; the latter are said to have their source in community acceptance.[18] And all three accounts of 'general administrative powers' appear to treat those powers as different from implied statutory powers, identified as being necessary for the administration of a statutory scheme.

Lying behind any account of the so-called 'general administrative powers' of the Crown is a more basic question. Does the rule of law require that the executive be able to point to some source for any exercise of power, whether that source be statute, the prerogative (strictly so called) or the common law?[19]

To treat the executive government as having power to do anything that is not positively forbidden cannot sit with the rule of law. At least for an Australian lawyer, the executive government of the polity has no separate legal personality. It is not itself a right- and duty-bearing entity. To equate its powers (whatever 'it' is regarded as being) with a natural person ignores the real and radical distinctions between the individual member of society and the executive government of the polity in which that individual lives. I think that the equation both provokes and depends upon asking the wrong question.

---

[13] *R (New London College) v Secretary of State for the Home Department* [2013] 1 WLR 2358, 2371, [28] (Lord Sumption JSC). See also BV Harris, 'The "Third Source" of Authority for Government Action' (1992) 108 *LQR* 626; BV Harris, 'The "Third Source" of Authority for Government Action Revisited' (2007) 123 *LQR* 225.

[14] *New London College* (n 13) 2371, [28].

[15] A Perry, 'The Crown's Administrative Powers' (2015) 131 *LQR* 652.

[16] *Malone v Metropolitan Police Commissioner* [1979] Ch 244, 366–67 (Sir Robert Megarry V-C).

[17] *R v Secretary of State for Health, ex parte C* [2000] 1 FLR 627; *R (Shrewsbury and Atcham Borough Council) v Secretary of State for Communities and Local Government* [2008] 3 All ER 548; cf *R (Hooper) v Secretary of State for Work and Pensions* [2005] 1 WLR 1681.

[18] Perry, 'The Crown's Administrative Powers' (n 15) 667.

[19] *R v Somerset County Council, ex parte Fewings* [1995] 1 All ER 513, 524 (Laws J). See also P Craig, 'The Rule of Law', written evidence to the House of Lords Select Committee on the Constitution, *Relations between the Executive, Judiciary and Parliament*, HL 151 (2006–2007) 98; A Tomkins, 'The Authority of *Entick v Carrington*' in A Tomkins and P Scott (eds), *Entick v Carrington: 250 Years of the Rule of Law* (Oxford, Hart Publishing, 2015) 164–69.

When considering what an individual may do, the legal system rightly asks 'why not?' But when considering the exercise of public power, the critical question must always be 'why?' The rule of law requires no less.

What has been said in Britain about general administrative powers of the Crown must be seen, in Australia, through the prism of section 64 of the Constitution and its provisions that the 'Governor-General may appoint officers to administer the departments of State of the Commonwealth' and that such officers 'shall be the Queen's Ministers of State for the Commonwealth'. Appointment 'to administer the departments of State' carries with it all of the powers that are necessary for and incidental to the administration of a department of State. Those powers have since been amplified and regulated by legislation made under section 51(xxxix) of the Constitution (as well as under applicable specific heads of legislative power). But powers to consult (within and beyond the public service and government more generally), powers to adopt policies and guidelines for the internal administration of the department, as well as the exercise of statutory authorities given to Ministers or departmental officers, and powers to engage staff, make contracts to procure use of premises, furniture and consumable supplies, all find their ultimate roots in section 64 of the Constitution. This list of powers is not exhaustive.

But government contracts that are not made for the administration of a department of State are not supported by section 64. They must find their support elsewhere. So in those cases the question remains: can officers of the executive create rights and duties binding the polity without legislative authority or approval?

At some time after 1945, it came to be asserted in Whitehall that a Minister may do anything that a natural person can do, unless limited by legislation. This view was said to be based on a memorandum written in 1945 by the then First Parliamentary Counsel, Sir Granville Ram, and it came to be known as 'The Ram doctrine'. As Adam Tomkins has demonstrated, Ram's memorandum neither asserted nor supported the view attributed to it, and the so-called doctrine has now been discredited.[20]

Although that is so, I mention the so-called Ram doctrine because, if a Minister standing at the apex of administration of a department of State does not have general power of the kind asserted by the Ram doctrine, why would it be supposed that the permanent head of the department, or some more junior officer in the executive, would? Yet it is an assertion of the kind made by the Ram doctrine that lies beneath any proposition that the executive has general power, without statutory authority or approval, to make contracts that are not for the administration of a department of State but which nonetheless bind the polity.

III. Government Contracts – Consequences

If a contract that is not for the administration of a department of State binds the polity, two matters arise for consideration: one political; the other financial. First, what are the political

---

[20] Tomkins, 'The Authority of *Entick v Carrington*' (n 19) 169–72. See also House of Lords Select Committee on the Constitution, *The Pre-Emption of Parliament*, HL 165 (2012–2013) 17, [55]; HM Government (UK), *House of Lords Select Committee on the Constitution Report on the Pre-Emption of Parliament: Government Response* (14 October 2013) [9]–[10].

consequences that follow if the contract is to endure beyond the term of the political administration that makes it? Second, what are the financial consequences that will follow from performing the contract or breaching it?

A. Political Consequences

In order to maximise the amount a private counterparty will pay for the privilege of building or operating infrastructure or providing a service to the public, governments may make long-term contracts that in effect give the counterparty a privileged position. If there is a change of government, or the government wishes to follow some different policy, seeking to vary or terminate the contract will have adverse political consequences. Variation will likely come only at a price. Termination will likely lead to claims for damages. Compelling variation or termination will be said to be the realisation of a form of sovereign risk and may be reflected in the pricing of future transactions.

What power has the executive government to commit the polity to consequences of this kind? Does the nature of the consequences that will follow, or the period during which those consequences may be realised, require the conclusion that contractual obligations of this kind may be undertaken only with legislative authority or approval? How specific must that authority or approval be? Must the particular agreement be approved, or would it be enough to give general authority for a Minister to make contracts relating to particular subject matters where the outlays to be made by government do not exceed a stated sum and the contract is not to endure for more than a stated period?

Or can doctrines of public law develop to the point of recognising the essentially political dimension of some kinds of contract to which a polity is party by holding, as in France, that certain contracts with government can be varied or terminated at any time when the public interest so requires (albeit on terms that the polity indemnifies the private party for resulting loss and lost gains)?[21]

In that much criticised decision, *Rederiaktiebolaget Amphitrite v The King*, Rowlatt J embraced the first of these ideas (but not the proviso for compensation).[22] He said that

> it is not competent for the Government to fetter its future executive action, which must necessarily be determined by the needs of the community when the question arises. It cannot by contract hamper its freedom of action in matters which concern the welfare of the State.[23]

This has rightly been criticised as being expressed too generally, because 'it would be detrimental to the public interest to deny to the government or a statutory authority power to

---

[21] J Bell, 'Administrative Law' in J Bell, S Boyron and S Whittaker (eds), *Principles of French Law* (New York, Oxford University Press, 2008) 195–98.
[22] *Rederiaktiebolaget Amphitrite v The King* [1921] 3 KB 500.
[23] ibid 503.

enter a valid contract merely because the contract affects the public welfare'.[24] Yet, as was also said,

> the public interest requires that neither the government nor a public authority can by a contract disable itself or its officer from performing a statutory duty or from exercising a statutory discretion conferred by or under a statute by binding itself or its officer not to perform the duty or to exercise the discretion in a particular way in the future.[25]

The implications of these observations remain largely unexplored by Australian public lawyers.

B. Financial Consequences

Public moneys cannot be applied except under appropriation made by law.[26] The making of a valid appropriation of public moneys to satisfy performance of obligations undertaken by contract is not a condition of the validity of a government contract.[27] But payments under the contract cannot be made except out of moneys lawfully available for the purpose under parliamentary appropriation.[28]

Australian parliamentary appropriation practice, and government accounting more generally, has changed over time. In the 1990s, the Commonwealth decided to have government accounts and the annual Budget prepared on an accruals basis rather than by reference to cash receipts and expenditures.[29] More recently, appropriations have been specified by reference to generally expressed 'outcomes' rather than more particularly identified purposes. At least since the 1980s, the chief means of limiting expenditures made by departments of State that has been adopted in the annual Appropriation Acts has been to specify the *amount* that may be spent rather than further define purposes or activities for which it may be spent.[30]

All this being so, there is no little difficulty in demonstrating that expenditure to be made in satisfaction of contractual obligations is not available from moneys lawfully appropriated. The nature and extent of those difficulties can be seen from the arguments and reasons for judgment in *Combet v The Commonwealth*.[31] There the High Court held that government expenditure on advertising its 'workplace reforms package' was validly applied for departmental expenditures authorised by the relevant Appropriation Act, and that it need not be shown to answer one or more of the stipulated outcomes identified in respect of 'administered items'.

---

[24] *Ansett Transport Industries (Operations) Pty Ltd v The Commonwealth* (1977) 139 CLR 54, 74 (Mason J). See also PW Hogg, 'The Doctrine of Executive Necessity in the Law of Contract' (1970) 44 *Australian Law Journal* 154; JDB Mitchell, *The Contracts of Public Authorities: A Comparative Study* (London, G Bell & Sons, 1954) 27–32, 62.
[25] *Ansett* (n 24) 74–75.
[26] Constitution, ss 81 and 83.
[27] *State of New South Wales v Bardolph* (1934) 52 CLR 455.
[28] ibid.
[29] *Combet v The Commonwealth* (2005) 224 CLR 494, 574, [154].
[30] ibid 577, [161].
[31] *Combet* (n 29).

The argument in *Combet* also reveals a further, supervening difficulty: standing to sue. Who has standing to complain that public moneys are being misapplied if the test for standing is special interest in the subject matter of the action?[32] The question of standing was not resolved in *Combet* or in the more recent decision about the postal survey relating to same-sex marriage: *Wilkie v The Commonwealth*.[33]

In *Combet*, the Commonwealth did not assert that the complaints the plaintiffs made about application of moneys under an Appropriation Act raised no justiciable issue.[34] By contrast, that issue was raised in *Wilkie*. A central question in *Wilkie* was whether a provision of an annual Appropriation Act had permitted a particular application of funds appropriated as an advance to the Finance Minister, when the provision required that the Finance Minister be satisfied that there was an urgent need for expenditure that was not provided for because the expenditure was unforeseen until after a specified day. The High Court held that the construction of that provision raised a justiciable issue; and further held that, on its proper construction, the provision authorised the particular determination that had been made.

It follows that questions about the *application* of moneys under an Appropriation Act may raise a justiciable issue. Questions of that kind are not the sole preserve of the Parliament. By contrast, questions about the validity of an appropriation (as distinct from an application) of public moneys may not raise any justiciable issue. The appropriation of moneys may be a matter wholly for the Parliament.

It is not yet clear who has standing to bring an action raising an issue about the validity of a particular application of public moneys. And, if the party seeking relief is found to have standing, there may remain issues about whether injunctive relief would be granted if the statutes regulating use of public moneys provide civil or criminal consequences where public moneys are misapplied.[35] These issues are further obscured when it is recognised that the Executive can waive payment of debts otherwise due to the polity, and that powers of this kind have been used to waive repayment of sums paid by the Commonwealth under arrangements found by the High Court to be beyond power.[36]

IV. Conclusion

The question overarching the political, financial and other issues that have been touched on is how, if at all, do doctrines of public law intersect with those issues? The answers that are given will depend upon and affect basic ideas. They depend upon and will affect basic notions about structures of government. They will entail consideration of issues about

---

[32] *Australian Conservation Foundation v The Commonwealth* (1980) 146 CLR 493; *Onus v Alcoa of Australia Ltd* (1981) 149 CLR 27.
[33] *Wilkie v The Commonwealth* [2017] HCA 40.
[34] *Combet* (n 29) 505.
[35] ibid 499; cf *Financial Management and Accountability Act 1997* (Cth), s 15 and *Public Governance, Performance and Accountability Act 2013* (Cth), ss 68–70.
[36] See, eg, *Public Governance, Performance and Accountability Act 2013* (Cth), s 63. Repayment of sums paid under the arrangements considered and held to be invalid in *Williams v The Commonwealth [No 2]* (n 2) was waived.

standing and relief. The answers that are given will affect, may even determine, questions of transparency and accountability.

So I return to where I began. Are our ideas about executive power keeping up with the new and different ways in which executive power is being used? More and more often, governments are resorting to the executive power to make contracts for provision of services to the public. Too often lawyers look at these arrangements only through the lens of the law of contract. If we look at them through the lens of public law principles, do we ask whether public law has kept pace with this change? Or is our thinking confined by habits of thought and argument that were formed in other times and in other circumstances? Too often we are creatures of habit. Too often we apply old rules to new circumstances, without pausing to examine whether that is right.

18

Peering into the Black Box of Executive Power: Cabinet Manuals, Secrecy and the Identification of Convention

ANNE TWOMEY

I. Introduction

Executive power in Westminster-style systems tends to straddle the frontier between constitutional law and politics. On one side there is legal clarity, with executive power being conferred and limited by statute and its exercise being subject to judicial review by the courts. On the other side, non-statutory executive power relies on uncertain historical usage of prerogative powers, the exercise of which may often be non-justiciable[1] and the limits of which are frequently unclear. Constraints upon the exercise of such power tend to be imposed by convention, rather than law, but the terms of the convention may also be unsettled and the precedent upon which it rests may be shrouded in secrecy.

This chapter is directed at the non-statutory remnant prerogatives, such as the power to enter into or withdraw from treaties and the power to declare war and deploy troops. In particular, it considers that sub-set of prerogatives that in some circumstances reserve discretion to the Sovereign or his or her vice-regal representative, such as the power to commission a chief minister to form a government, the power to dismiss a government, the power to assent or refuse assent to legislation, and the power to prorogue, summon or dissolve the Houses of Parliament. For present purposes, these will be described as 'high prerogative' powers.

Rather than consider the scope of such powers and the conventions that govern their exercise,[2] this chapter instead addresses the tension between secrecy and transparency, and

---

[1] In *Council for Civil Service Unions v Minister for the Civil Service* [1985] AC 374, Lord Roskill noted (at 418) that prerogative powers such as the making of treaties, the defence of the realm, the grant of honours, the dissolution of Parliament and the appointment of Ministers are not susceptible to judicial review because 'their nature and subject matter are such as not to be amenable to the judicial process'. He added that the 'courts are not the place wherein to determine whether a treaty should be concluded or the armed forces disposed in a particular manner or Parliament dissolved on one date rather than another'. Sedley LJ has sought to qualify this statement by observing that 'the grant of honours for reward, the waging of a war of manifest aggression, or a refusal to dissolve Parliament at all' might call in question any immunity from judicial review: *R (Bancoult) v Secretary of State for Foreign and Commonwealth Affairs (No 2)* [2008] QB 365, [46].

[2] This is addressed in A Twomey, *The Veiled Sceptre – Reserve Powers of Heads of State in Westminster Systems* (Cambridge, Cambridge University Press, 2018).

how it has affected the development and effectiveness of these constitutional conventions. After first discussing the nature of constitutional conventions and how they are recognised, the chapter goes on to consider the rise of both transparency and secrecy in relation to public access to government documents through archival releases and freedom of information. Its focus here is on documents concerning the acts of the Sovereign and his or her vice-regal representatives and their communications with government, as this is the field in which convention may be identified but is more often than not hidden. Examples are drawn from the United Kingdom (UK) and Australia.

The chapter then goes on to consider the recent trend towards a different kind of transparency by the formalisation of conventions in Cabinet Manuals. Here, it draws on examples from New Zealand and the UK, comparing them with Australia and Canada. It considers the difficulty of identifying conventions in the absence of free public access to the relevant precedents, and the problem of potential distortion of convention or the creation of self-serving conventions if the executive both holds confidential all the primary material concerning past practice and precedent and controls the contents of the Cabinet Manual. It also addresses the status of such conventions and the possibility that their formalisation in a Cabinet Manual might place them on a trajectory towards becoming law.

II. Constitutional Conventions

To understand the impact of secrecy and transparency on constitutional conventions, one first needs to explain what is meant by the term. The most famous definition is that by Jennings. He set out three questions that must be asked to identify whether a practice has been transformed into a convention:

> [First], what are the precedents; secondly, did the actors in the precedents believe that they were bound by a rule; and thirdly, is there a reason for the rule? A single precedent with a good reason may be enough to establish a rule. A whole string of precedents without such a reason will be of no avail, unless it is perfectly certain that the persons concerned regarded them as bound by it.[3]

Jennings' definition needs qualification. As discussed below, not every convention requires precedent and a history of practice. New conventions may be created to deal with changed circumstances, if those who participate in the exercise of constitutional power reach a solemn agreement as to its future exercise.

The use of convention, rather than law, in governing the exercise of executive power has distinct advantages. Convention both permits the reconciliation of legal form with practice[4] and provides the bridge between legal rules and constitutional principles.[5] As those

---

[3] I Jennings, *The Law and the Constitution*, 2nd edn (London, University of London Press, 1938) 131.

[4] A Blick, *The Codes of the Constitution* (Oxford, Hart Publishing, 2016) 91. Note Heard's observation that much of the Constitution does not match reality without the intervention of convention: A Heard, 'Constitutional Conventions and Written Constitutions: The Rule of Law Implications in Canada' (2015) 38(2) *Dublin University Law Journal* 331, 333–39.

[5] On the relationship between constitutional conventions and constitutional principles, see J Bowden and N MacDonald, 'Cabinet Manuals and the Crown' in DM Jackson and P Lagassé (eds), *Canada and the Crown – Essays on Constitutional Monarchy* (Montreal, McGill-Queen's University Press, 2013) 180–81; Heard, 'Constitutional Conventions' (n 4) 354–55; Twomey, *The Veiled Sceptre* (n 2) 26–30.

principles, such as the separation of powers, the rule of law, and representative and responsible government evolve over time, convention is sufficiently flexible to accommodate this evolution. Hence, the British Constitution has become more democratic over the centuries without any great fracture or disruption in the system of government. No revolution was required to give effect to the increasingly democratic spirit of the people.

Similarly, the decolonisation process for many British colonies, including those with written entrenched federal Constitutions, such as Australia and Canada, was primarily given effect through changes in convention. For example, while the Commonwealth of Australia, at the time it was established in 1901, had no power to enter into treaties on its own behalf or declare war, it acquired such powers, without a word of its Constitution being amended, by virtue of changed conventions concerning the source of ministerial advice to the Sovereign and the divisibility of the Crown.[6]

But a distinct disadvantage of conventions that are not set out in a formal agreement is the difficulty in identifying what the convention is at any particular time, and on what basis that convention may change. This will often require knowledge of precedent, including the actions of the Sovereign, vice-regal officers and Ministers in relation to the exercise of high prerogative powers. Despite other forms of liberalisation of access to government documents, the secrecy concerning regal and vice-regal matters has in recent times increased, rather than reduced. This secrecy gives rise to a significant risk that there will be a divergence of understanding both amongst constitutional actors and between them and the people (as informed by academics and the media) as to what the relevant convention is and how it applies in particular circumstances. The resulting mismatch of expectations as to acceptable behaviour can be a factor contributing to a constitutional crisis, or magnify the disruptive effects of such a crisis.

An example is the controversy that arose in 1926 from the refusal by the Canadian Governor-General, Lord Byng, to grant a dissolution to his Prime Minister, Mackenzie King, when King was about to face a no confidence motion in the House and another government was capable of being formed. Berriedale Keith argued strongly that Lord Byng should have exercised the British practice of immediate acceptance of the advice of the Prime Minister in relation to a request for a dissolution. He identified a convention as arising from the precedent of His Majesty's grant of a dissolution to Ramsay MacDonald two years earlier in 1924.[7] Keith argued:

> There is no answer to Mr King's arguments; the precedent of the King's immediate grant to Mr Ramsay MacDonald of a dissolution in 1924, without even considering whether the Government could be carried on without a dissolution, ought to have been conclusive, for it put an end at once to whatever value might have attached to the dictum of Lord Oxford and Asquith that the King still preserved an independent judgement in matters of dissolution ...[8]

---

[6] See generally L Zines, 'The Growth of Australian Nationhood and its Effect on the Powers of the Commonwealth' in L Zines (ed), *Commentaries on the Australian Constitution* (Sydney, Butterworths, 1977) 30–35; A Twomey, 'Federal Parliament's Changing Role in Treaty Making and External Affairs' in G Lindell and R Bennett (eds), *Parliament – The Vision in Hindsight* (Sydney, The Federation Press, 2001) 37. For the equivalent Canadian experience, see *Reference re Weekly Rest in Industrial Undertakings Act* [1936] SCR 461, 476–77.

[7] AB Keith, *Responsible Government in the Dominions*, vol 1, 2nd edn (Oxford, Clarendon Press, 1928) 147–48.

[8] ibid. Note, however, Forsey's rejection of the relevance of this precedent, as MacDonald did not ask for a dissolution while a motion of censure was under debate and MacDonald had not had the previous dissolution: E Forsey, *The Royal Power of Dissolution of Parliament in the British Commonwealth* (Toronto, Oxford University Press, 1968) 160.

It was not until 16 years after the King's death that his biographer, Harold Nicolson, who was given access to the documents in the Royal Archives, revealed that Keith was wrong in his assessment of the relevant convention. George V in fact only dissolved Parliament in 1924 with extreme reluctance, after ascertaining from party leaders that they were not able to form a ministry.[9] Hence, the precedent upon which Keith relied for his convention instead showed that the opposite was the case. The King regarded himself as holding the power to reject a dissolution and considered exercising it, but ultimately granted the dissolution because no other government could be formed. Lack of public knowledge of what had occurred, however, distorted understanding of both convention and the continued existence of an important prerogative. This misunderstanding then fuelled the controversy concerning the King/Byng affair in Canada.

Similarly, the social upheaval that resulted from the dismissal of the Whitlam Government in Australia in 1975 was exacerbated by a lack of understanding in the public and the media about the existence of the reserve powers of the Governor-General and the conventions concerning their exercise. Indeed, the disagreement between constitutional actors, including the Governor-General, the Chief Justice, the Prime Minister and the Leader of the Opposition, as to the nature of the applicable conventions was a critical component and trigger of the constitutional crisis. In a febrile political atmosphere and in the absence of previously published and accepted rules, conventions were misconstrued or alleged to have been recently invented for political purposes, and conspiracy theories festered. Much of the public angst could have been allayed and the entire controversy could probably have been averted if all the constitutional actors, the media and the public were working from the same understanding of the applicable conventions.

This raises the question of how conventions can be better understood to avert such problems in the future. One approach is to increase transparency about precedents, including access to primary documents concerning what has occurred in the past, in order to found a better understanding of current conventions. The other approach is to formalise the conventions in an authoritative document, while seeking to maintain their characteristics of flexibility and non-justiciability.

III. Access to Royal and Vice-Regal Official Records

The UK Royal Commission on Public Records noted that from the earliest times, the Royal archives of the UK have been 'accessible to native or foreign scholars under such conditions and restrictions as might from time to time be imposed by the Government or the officials in whose custody they were preserved'.[10] There are reports as early as the ninth century of an 'Anglo-Saxon noble searching the Royal archives'.[11] By the mid-sixteenth century, it was noted that 'records were searched for historical purposes by legal antiquaries, and no attempt seems to have been made by the Crown to withhold constitutional precedents on the score of public policy'.[12] Yet over time, as access was broadened to a wider group of

---

[9] H Nicolson, *King George the Fifth – His Life and Reign* (London, Constable & Co Ltd, 1952) 400.
[10] *Royal Commission on Public Records, Appendices, Vol I (Part II)*, Cd 6395 (London 1919) 56.
[11] ibid 57.
[12] ibid.

people, greater restrictions came to be imposed, via a permit system, upon what could be viewed or copied.

The existence of a separate, private Royal Archives only occurred in 1914, primarily to deal with the vast official and private correspondence of Queen Victoria.[13] From then, the correspondence of the monarch, both official and private, was collected and preserved in the Royal Archives at Windsor Castle. Nonetheless, the other end of official correspondence remained on government files and became available through government archives upon the relevant date for public access.

In the UK, although the Public Record Office was established in 1838, the general public only gained access to government archives from the 1850s. Different government departments, such as the Home Office, the Foreign Office and the Treasury, initially had different dates for public access, often limiting it to documents created more than 100 years earlier, with more recent material released only to those who obtained permits.[14] One consequence was a general lack of understanding of the internal workings of government and, in particular, the changing constitutional role of the monarch as performed largely behind closed doors.

A classic British example is the work of Walter Bagehot. His much lauded 1867 book, *The English Constitution*, is most famous for its description of the Sovereign as having but 'three rights – the right to be consulted, the right to encourage, the right to warn'.[15] This was a completely inaccurate description of the role of Queen Victoria, who most certainly exercised far greater power and influence than Bagehot's book suggested. Bagehot readily conceded that the courtiers of both King George III and Queen Victoria were agreed as to the 'magnitude of the royal influence' and that it is 'an accepted secret doctrine that the Crown does more than it seems'.[16] He concluded that the influence of Queen Victoria and Prince Albert would not be known until the history books were written by future generations.

The publication in 1907 of edited copies of the first three volumes of Queen Victoria's letters[17] and extracts from her journals revealed a far more active and politically involved Sovereign than had been publicly understood in her lifetime, particularly after her retirement from public appearances following the death of Prince Albert. The early publication of her letters, before government departments released relevant government documents, caused some departments to speed up the release of their documents, to deal with the anomaly that only part of the record had been revealed.[18] Another spur to action by the Foreign Office was the problem that in the absence of authentic English sources, historians had come to accept the 'assertions of somewhat imaginative foreign publicists'.[19]

---

[13] The Royal Archives has also been given or acquired some earlier royal correspondence. For example, the papers of George III and George IV were 'discovered' in Apsley House in 1912. They had been preserved by the Duke of Wellington, who was the chief executor of the will of King George IV.

[14] For a more detailed discussion of the relevant periods and different rules for different departments, see TG Otte, '"More Liberal Facilities for the Purposes of Historical Research": Whitehall and Public Records in the Early Twentieth Century' (2008) 33 *Archives* 162; *Royal Commission on Public Records, Appendices*, Vol I (Part II) (n 10) 60–61.

[15] W Bagehot, *The English Constitution* (London, Chapman and Hall, 1867) 103.

[16] ibid 86–87.

[17] See A Benson and Viscount Esher (eds), *The Letters of Queen Victoria*, vols 1–3 (London, John Murray, 1907).

[18] Otte, '"More Liberal Facilities"' (n 14) 174–75.

[19] ibid 178.

Misconceptions, once created and fed by a lack of available authoritative sources, become very hard to shift. By locking up its primary sources for so long, the British Government found that it was damaging its representation in history.

The early publication of Queen Victoria's letters after her death in 1901, while an improvement on the haphazard past practice, still did not necessarily fully reveal precedents relevant to conventions. Her letters were closely edited, as were her journals, which were re-written by her daughter Princess Beatrice after having been purged of any material that might cause embarrassment, with the originals being burnt.[20] Royal records have continued to be tightly controlled ever since, with very limited access being granted and with content control being imposed upon what can be published.

As for the royal correspondence contained in government files, it was not until 1958, after the Report of the Grigg Committee,[21] that a statutory right of public access to government documents was given 50 years after they were created, unless subject to additional protection.[22] The rationale behind the choice of '50 years' was that it comprised the working life of most public servants and would avoid their acting in a self-conscious manner when advising the Government.[23]

In 1965 the newly elected Wilson Government decided to reduce the 50-year period to 30 years as a step towards a more open government.[24] The Public Records Act was amended to this effect in 1967.[25] Applications to the Lord Chancellor to defer opening access to records for longer than 30 years had to meet particular criteria. The Lord Chancellor was advised on such matters by the Advisory Council on Public Records.

Correspondence between the Queen's Private Secretary, acting on the Queen's behalf, and Ministers or government officials, was routinely found on government files when they reached the open access point, 30 years after their creation. Examples on the files of the National Archives of the UK include Palace correspondence concerning the constitutional turmoil in Western Nigeria in 1962,[26] the attempt to remove the Governor-General of Ceylon in 1962,[27] the coup in Sierra Leone in 1967[28] and the petition to remove the Queensland Governor in 1975.[29]

Correspondence showing the Sovereign's role in domestic UK affairs also appears in government files released by the National Archives. For example, in 1964, the Queen's Private Secretary, Sir Michael Adeane, commenting on a press release for the announcement of the 1964 election, wrote to the Prime Minister's Principal Private Secretary '[f]rom the Queen's point of view the important point on these occasions is that the

---

[20] See generally Y Ward, *Unsuitable for Publication: Editing Queen Victoria* (Melbourne, Black Inc, 2013).

[21] Committee on Departmental Records, *Report*, Cmd 9163 (July 1954). The Committee had apparently been established after the Prime Minister, Winston Churchill, objected to the cost of extra filing cabinets to hold government documents and suggested that some old documents should be destroyed: P Rock, 'A Brief History of Record Management at the National Archives', available at http://sas-space.sas.ac.uk/6233/1/Paul_Rock_Brief_history_of_record_management_at_the_National_Archives_LIM.pdf.

[22] Public Records Act 1958 (UK), s 5.

[23] Committee on Departmental Records, *Report* (n 21) 57.

[24] 'Records show 30 years of the 30-year rule' *The Independent* (London) (1 January 1996), available at https://www.independent.co.uk/news/records-show-30-years-of-the-30-year-rule-1321932.html.

[25] Public Records Act 1967 (UK), s 1, which came into effect on 1 January 1968.

[26] The National Archives of the United Kingdom (TNA): DO 195/89 and 195/90.

[27] TNA: DO 196/98.

[28] TNA: FCO 49/88.

[29] TNA: FCO 24/2224 and 24/2225.

Prime Minister asks for a dissolution rather than that he advises one because this makes clear the Royal Prerogative in such matters'.[30] Despite Keith's view in 1926 that the King had no discretion in relation to dissolution, the Queen clearly regarded herself as continuing to hold such a discretion in 1964 – a fact only publicly known due to the presence of this correspondence on a government file released by the Archives under the 30-year rule.

Correspondence with the Sovereign or the Sovereign's Private Secretary can also be found on the files of other countries, such as New Zealand[31] and Australia,[32] including correspondence with Australian State Governors.[33]

A. UK Freedom of Information Legislation

In the UK, the enactment of the Freedom of Information Act 2000 had an impact upon the application of the 30-year rule. It both facilitated access to government documents before they were 30 years old and imposed exemptions and restrictions, which in some cases continued to apply after the 30 years had ended. Like the Public Records Act, it did not extend in its application to documents held in the Royal Archives. However, this Act did address communications with the Palace that are found on government files.

Section 37(1)(a) exempted from access information relating to 'communications with Her Majesty, with other members of the Royal Family or with the Royal Household'. This was not an absolute exemption – a public interest test applied. The relevant public authority had to decide whether in all the circumstances the public interest in maintaining the exemption outweighed the public interest in disclosing the information.[34] Once the relevant documents became 'historical records', which was 30 years after their creation,[35] the exemption in section 37(1)(a) ceased to apply.[36] At this stage, therefore, all official correspondence with the Queen on government files was released at least 30 years after its creation (subject to other applicable ongoing exemptions), and earlier if requested and in the public interest.

The commencement of the Freedom of Information Act 2000 in 2005 led to two significant developments, which in turn resulted in changes that both widened and limited access to documents. The first was the establishment in 2007 of the Dacre Committee to review the continuing relevance of the 30-year rule, which had been undermined

---

[30] Letter by Sir Michael Adeane to Derek Mitchell, Principal Private Secretary to the Prime Minister, 6 September 1964: TNA: PREM 11/4756.

[31] See, eg, Memorandum of Governor-General to the King's Private Secretary, Sir AF Lascelles, 6 November 1945, regarding the grant of royal assent to a constitutionally controversial Bill: Archives of New Zealand (ANZ) R19162234. See also telegram by Sir Martin Charteris, 25 October 1973, stating that the Queen's approval must be sought both to the introduction of a Bill concerning her royal style and titles and the exact wording of the proposed new style and title: ANZ R18230308.

[32] See, eg, Letter by the Queen's Private Secretary to the Governor-General, 25 October 1974, regarding the 'Queen of Queensland' petition, stating that Her Majesty is grateful for the advice and will take full note of it when the reference is made: National Archives of Australia (NAA) 1209 1974/6962.

[33] See, eg, the correspondence between the NSW Governor, Sir Philip Game, and King George V and his Private Secretary, in the State Library of New South Wales: CY3269: MLMSS 2166/2.

[34] Freedom of Information Act 2000, s 2.

[35] Freedom of Information Act 2000, s 62.

[36] Note, in contrast, that communications concerning honours, under s 37(1)(b), remained exempt for 60 years after their creation: Freedom of Information Act 2000, s 63(3).

by the earlier access rights made available under freedom of information. The Dacre Committee concluded in 2009 that the 30-year rule should be reduced to 15 years.[37] In consideration of this proposed significant reduction in the period of confidentiality, it also recommended that the Government consider whether there was a case for enhanced protection of certain categories of information.[38] In discussing the reasons for reducing the period of confidentiality, the Committee noted the view of historians that 'knowledge of past public affairs can help us to learn and apply beneficial lessons for today and the future, thereby improving governance and democracy', and that it would 'enhance public understanding and improve the development and implementation of government policy'.[39]

B. The Black-spider Letters

The second development was the application in 2005, under the Freedom of Information Act 2000, by a journalist from *The Guardian*, for access to letters by the Prince of Wales that lobbied government ministers, known as the 'black-spider letters'.[40] Under the Act, such letters had to be made available if their release met the public interest test. The Government declined to release the letters, arguing that they fell within a convention regarding the training of the Prince of Wales to be Sovereign and must therefore be exempt. The Upper Tribunal rejected this argument. It found that the lobbying of Ministers falls outside the traditional rights of the monarch, as described by Bagehot, to be consulted, to encourage and to warn, and therefore did not fall within any 'education convention', as the apprentice is not trained in skills different from those required of the master.[41] Here, the belief of judges concerning the constitutional rights and powers of the Sovereign, based upon Bagehot, was used as justification for supporting transparency rather than secrecy. It was also used to reject a dubious manufactured 'convention' that the training of the Prince of Wales includes the Prince's pressuring and lobbying Ministers to change policy to meet his personal views when this would, at least according to the Bagehot approach, fall outside what is conventionally permitted of the Sovereign.

The British Government did not appeal the Upper Tribunal's decision. Instead the then Attorney-General, Dominic Grieve, sought to impose secrecy by issuing a certificate under section 53(2) of the Freedom of Information Act 2000 that denied access to the documents, overriding the decision of the Upper Tribunal. In the certificate, Grieve also referred to the 'tripartite convention' identified by Bagehot, and contended that the Prince's involvement in lobbying Ministers would assist him in fulfilling his future duties as King. He stated that 'urging views' upon Ministers falls within the ambit of 'advising' and 'warning' about the Government's actions. He concluded that if this were done by the Monarch, it would 'fall squarely within the tripartite convention'. He considered that

---

[37] P Dacre, *Review of the 30 Year Rule* (London, The Stationery Office, 2009) 30.
[38] ibid 36.
[39] ibid 22.
[40] This was a reference to the spidery hand-writing in black ink.
[41] *Evans v Information Commissioner* [2012] UKUT 313 (AAC), [105], [111]–[112], [170]. Note that by the time this case was heard, the law had been amended to provide an absolute exemption for such communications, but it did not apply with retrospective effect to applications made before its commencement.

'advocacy correspondence', in which the Prince advocated changes to government policy to suit his own personal views, enabled him to 'make points which he would have a right (and indeed arguably a duty) to make as Monarch'.[42]

This view that it is the Sovereign's right and duty to advocate and urge ministers to change government policy to suit the personal wishes of the Sovereign appears to go much further than Bagehot ever suggested, and certainly extends beyond what the public and the judiciary believe to be the conventional rights and duties of the Sovereign. The fact that such a statement was made by the Attorney-General, a Minister of the Crown and the First Law Officer, suggests that in practice there remains a significant gap between the perception and reality of the constitutional role of the Sovereign and the applicable conventions founded on precedents. While the courts relied upon a public understanding of the relevant convention, based upon Bagehot, the Attorney-General, who might be presumed to have a better knowledge of actual practice, took a much broader view of the Sovereign's conventional 'rights and duties'.

In this case, the Government's efforts at secrecy failed, with the Attorney-General's certificate being quashed, in litigation that was finally determined by the Supreme Court of the United Kingdom.[43] The relevant letters were later released, revealing little more than views that were already well known. Far more damage was caused to the monarchy by the efforts to maintain secrecy than by the publication of the letters. Most damaging of all was the apparent acceptance by the Attorney-General that it is the right and duty of the Sovereign to urge personal views upon Ministers.

C. Reforms to the UK Freedom of Information Act

In response to both the Dacre Committee report and the initiation by *The Guardian* of its freedom of information requests concerning the correspondence between the Prince of Wales and Ministers, the British Government announced in February 2010 that it proposed to change the law. The access period for government documents would be reduced from 30 years to 20 years (rather than the 15 years recommended by the Dacre Committee). This would also be the point at which exemptions expire in relation to 'historical' documents.

The Government also addressed whether special categories of information required additional protection. It considered the importance of collective Cabinet responsibility, but concluded that 'the principle of openness means that greater protection should only be introduced if it is essential to maintaining the constitutional position of collective responsibility'. In contrast, it recommended increased secrecy in relation to royal correspondence. It stated:

> The Government believes it is important to protect the constitutional conventions surrounding the Monarchy and its records. Of particular importance are the political impartiality of the Monarchy, the Sovereign's right and duty to counsel, to encourage and to warn her Government, as well as the right of the Heir to the Throne to be instructed in the business of Government in preparation for the time when he will be King. These rely on well-established conventions of confidentiality.

---

[42] D Grieve, UK Attorney-General, 'Statement of Reasons under s 53(6) of the Freedom of Information Act', 16 October 2012. A copy is attached as Annex A to *R (Evans) v Attorney-General and Information Commissioner* [2013] 3 WLR 1631.

[43] *R (Evans) v Attorney-General* [2015] AC 1787. See also *R (Evans) v Attorney-General and Information Commissioner* [2014] 1 QB 855.

In order to ensure that the constitutional position of the Monarchy is not undermined, information relating to communications with the Sovereign, the Heir to the Throne and the second in line to the Throne, and those acting on their behalf, will be covered by an absolute exemption for a period of 20 years. If the Member of the Royal Family to whom the information relates is not deceased after the end of this 20-year period the absolute exemption will continue to apply until five years after their death.[44]

These changes were made by the Constitutional Reform and Governance Act 2010. Section 37(1) of the Freedom of Information Act now imposes an absolute exemption on 'information … if it relates to' communications with the Sovereign and the next two persons in line to the throne and any member of the Royal Household acting on their behalf.[45] That exemption extends for the life of the member of the royal family, plus five years, and it is only then that the 20-year rule becomes relevant. In the case of a long-lived monarch or heirs, nothing can be known about their constitutional role for possibly 80 years or longer, taking us back to the type of secrecy imposed at the beginning of the twentieth century.

The Information Commissioner has interpreted the term 'relates to' broadly, so that it includes not only correspondence between the Sovereign and Ministers or officials, but also any information that refers to such communications or is derived from them,[46] and information about proposals to send correspondence or draft letters or speeches.[47] Where a public interest test is applied in relation to communications with other members of the Royal Family, the Information Commissioner has concluded that there 'is an inherent public interest in preserving the political neutrality of the Royal Family, as this is key to the stability of our constitutional democracy, and cannot be restored once lost'.[48] Authorities are therefore advised to place weight on this factor if disclosure could compromise the political neutrality of the Royal Family.

D. Access to Government Documents in Australia

In Australia, the development of a separate archives institution for the preservation of government documents and general access by the public to those documents was slower than in the UK. Initially archives were to be found in different institutions, such as the War Memorial and the National Library. A Commonwealth Archives Office was established in the Prime Minister's Department in 1961, becoming the Australian Archives in 1974 with its own repositories and finally formally established by legislation in 1983.[49] Public access to government records was granted by Cabinet (rather than legislation) in 1966, with a 50-year

---

[44] Ministry of Justice, *Government Response to 30-Year Rule Review* (February 2010) 16, [50]–[51].
[45] Note that a qualified exemption, requiring the application of a public interest test, applies to communications with other members of the Royal Family.
[46] Information Commissioner's Office, 'Communicating with Her Majesty and the awarding of honours (section 37)' para 15, available at https://ico.org.uk/media/for-organisations/documents/1194/communications_with_her_majesty_and_the_awarding_of_honours.pdf.
[47] ibid para 16.
[48] ibid para 59.
[49] *Archives Act 1983* (Cth).

rule imposed. It was shortly afterwards reduced to 30 years in 1970 (except for Cabinet records, which were not reduced to 30 years until 1972).[50] Cabinet notebooks, which record the actual deliberations of individuals at Cabinet meetings, were completely exempt from access until 1994, when they were subjected to a 50-year period of confidentiality.[51]

The Archives Act 1983 (Cth) did not exclude from its application the documents of the Governor-General.[52] On the contrary, it included 'the official establishment of the Governor-General' within the definition of 'Commonwealth institution'. The Act applied to 'Commonwealth records', being records that are the property of the Commonwealth or of a Commonwealth institution. It also stipulated that when Commonwealth records are included within private papers deposited with the Archives, the Commonwealth records are subject to the access periods applicable in the Act – not the terms of any arrangement relating to those private records.[53]

In 2010, the access period was reduced from 30 years to 20 years for government records, and from 50 years to 30 years for Cabinet notebooks.[54] In practice, however, even though documents are formally available once in the access period, an application must be made for them to be 'opened', which involves officials checking for exemptions. This can take years for the National Archives to complete, meaning that access for scholars remains unreliable and often impracticable to meet publishing deadlines.

E. The Kerr–Palace letters

The most controversial exercise of the reserve powers of a vice-regal officer in Australia was the dismissal of the Whitlam Government by the Governor-General, Sir John Kerr, in 1975. While official government records and Kerr's personal records have been released concerning those events, the one missing piece of the primary records is Kerr's correspondence with the Queen, commenting on events as they unfolded and justifying his actions. In particular, there has been speculation in some quarters as to what the Queen knew in advance, and the extent of her involvement or support in relation to Kerr's actions.[55]

While copies of the correspondence are held in the National Archives of Australia, they are not treated as 'Commonwealth records' by the Archives but as private papers of Sir John, on the ground that the documents comprise 'personal and private correspondence' between Sir John and the Queen. The Archives concluded that it did not have the power to give public access to these documents, even though they are more than 30 years old, except in accordance with the conditions set out in the instrument of deposit.

These conditions originally provided that the documents were to remain closed for 60 years after Sir John's term as Governor-General ended in 1977, and then only

---

[50] Australian Law Reform Commission, *Australia's Federal Record: A Review of Archives Act 1983*, Report No 85 (1998) paras 2.11–2.16.
[51] ibid para 20.99.
[52] This was despite proposals in an earlier bill to do so. See *Hocking v Director-General of National Archives of Australia* [2018] FCA 340, [42].
[53] *Archives Act 1983* (Cth), s 6(3).
[54] *Freedom of Information Amendment (Reform) Act 2010* (Cth), sch 3.
[55] J Hocking, *The Dismissal Dossier* (Melbourne, Melbourne University Press, 2017).

opened after consultation with the 'Sovereign's Private Secretary of the day and with the Governor-General's Official Secretary of the day'.[56] In 1991 the Queen instructed that the release date be amended to 8 December 2027 (ie 50 years after Sir John's resignation as Governor-General, rather than 60 years as previously stipulated).[57] In doing so, it appears that the requirement for 'consultation' before their release has hardened into one requiring the 'approval' of the Sovereign's Private Secretary and the Official Secretary to the Governor-General.[58]

In 2018 it was held by the Federal Court that the 'correspondence between a Governor-General and the Queen arising from the performance of the duties and functions of the office of Governor-General' was different from correspondence between the Governor-General and others arising from the performance of those duties and functions.[59] The correspondence with the Sovereign, even though it concerned the Governor-General's functions as the Sovereign's representative, was treated as private and personal correspondence, which did not fall within the description of a 'Commonwealth record' and was therefore not subject to the open access period applicable to Commonwealth records.[60]

This finding seemed to be based primarily upon a belief on the part of Governors-General, as instructed by the Palace, that such correspondence falls outside government records and an assertion that it was a 'convention' that it was treated as such. It is difficult to see how the correspondence between the Queen of Australia and her official representative concerning the exercise by that official representative of powers in the Queen's name could possibly be regarded as something that is private and personal. Manifestly, it is official correspondence and an important part of the country's historical records.

As for there being a convention that the correspondence between the Governor-General and the Queen is excluded from government records, this is difficult to substantiate. First, Commonwealth record-keeping was at best haphazard and little regulated until the enactment of the *Archives Act* in 1983. Many vice-regal records appear to have been destroyed or lost. Some have been kept by family members and later handed to institutions such as the National Library. Some remain in private hands. Others remain on government files in archives.[61] It is therefore very difficult to ascribe a convention in relation to the handling of such records.

Second, the precedents in relation to the handling of such records are thin. It would appear that the earliest example of the application of similar conditions to vice-regal correspondence occurred in 1968 when Lord Stonehaven's papers were deposited in the National Library and given a 60-year embargo. This was at a time when a 50-year rule still

---

[56] *Hocking* (n 52) [4], [18].

[57] ibid [12], [22]–[23]. At the same time, it was agreed that the release dates for Sir Zelman Cowen's correspondence with the Queen would be 29 July 2032 and for Sir Ninian Stephen's would be 16 February 2039. Sir Paul Hasluck's papers are to be released after 11 July 2024, and Lord Casey's papers are to be released after 30 April 2019. In all cases access is only to be given with the 'approval' of the Sovereign's Private Secretary and the Official Secretary of the Governor-General.

[58] *Hocking* (n 52) [22].

[59] ibid [132].

[60] ibid [133]. The Full Federal Court dismissed an appeal: *Hocking v Director-General of National Archives of Australia* [2019] FCAFC 12. At the time of writing an application for special leave to appeal to the High Court of Australia had been lodged but not determined.

[61] See, eg, the extensive collection of vice-regal records in the Public Records Office of Victoria, including VPRS 7571 P001 18 and VPRS 7571/P1/1.

applied in Australia to government documents, so that an extra 10 years no doubt did not appear to be of particular significance. When the correspondence between Sir Philip Game, the Governor of New South Wales, and the King was deposited in the State Library of New South Wales in 1971, it too was given a 60-year embargo from its creation.

It appears that these two precedents were applied in relation to Kerr's correspondence in 1977, when again the Palace sought to impose a 60-year embargo on their release. This did not take into account the change in Australia to the 30-year rule.

Precedents, as Jennings said, do not necessarily give rise to a convention. There must also be a reason for it. So far no adequate reason has been given for keeping confidential such correspondence for 60 years, or 50 years, or any period longer than the embargo on all the other government documents concerning the same events.

It also appears that the Director-General of the National Archives of Australia, Professor Neale, was under the misconception that in Britain it was a convention that royal documents were not made available until 60 years from the date of their creation. He gave evidence of this supposed British convention to a Senate Committee shortly afterwards in 1978.[62] But, as discussed previously, this does not appear to be the case. While the Royal Archives was excluded altogether from the application of the Public Records Act, there was no exemption from release for royal correspondence held on UK government files under the ordinary 30-year rule until the Freedom of Information Act 2000 was amended in 2010 as a consequence of the black-spider letters controversy. The only 60-year embargo was for correspondence concerning 'honours' under section 37(1)(b) of the Freedom of Information Act 2000.

Even if a convention does exist, the critical question is how it could affect the application of the law. Conventions, as discussed in section IV.C, are generally regarded as non-justiciable in nature and cannot be used to override rights of access granted by statute. In this case section 6 of the *Archives Act* provides that the ordinary access period applies to Commonwealth records in collections of personal papers deposited with the Archives. A Commonwealth record is defined as a record that is the 'property of the Commonwealth or of a Commonwealth institution', which includes the 'official establishment of the Governor-General'. In the *Hocking* case, the Federal Court relied upon an alleged convention to interpret 'Commonwealth record' so as to exclude official communications between the Governor-General of Australia and the Queen of Australia. This would appear to fall outside the plain meaning of the term in the Act.

In 2015, the then Australian Prime Minister, Malcolm Turnbull, stated that he intended to advise the Queen to approve the release of the correspondence between Sir John Kerr and the Queen.[63] When asked in Parliament in 2017 whether he had given such advice to the Queen, the Prime Minister responded that discussions and communications 'between the Prime Minister and Her Majesty The Queen are confidential'.[64] On 8 November 2016,

---

[62] Senate Standing Committee on Constitutional and Legal Affairs, *Report on the Freedom of Information Bill 1978 and aspects of the Archives Bill 1978* (Canberra, AGPS, 1979) 339, para 33.22.

[63] P Kelly and T Bramston, 'Malcolm Turnbull's bid to unlock John Kerr's letters' *The Australian* (9 November 2015); P Kelly, 'Malcolm Turnbull to try recovering John Kerr's letters to Queen' *The Australian* (11 November 2015).

[64] Australia Cth, House of Representatives, Questions in Writing, Question No 641, 5 September 2017, vol 45, 9393.

William Summers applied under freedom of information for access to 'all letters sent from the Prime Minister of Australia to Queen Elizabeth II or her representatives since 1 January 2013'. If released, this would inform the Australian public of the type of matters in relation to which the Prime Minister advises the Queen, including whether any advice was given to release the correspondence between Kerr and the Queen.

The Department of the Prime Minister and Cabinet refused to release the documents, arguing that they were exempt because their release would cause damage to the international relations of the Commonwealth and the deliberative processes of the Government.[65] This decision was reversed by the Australian Information Commissioner (AIC).[66] The AIC pointed out that the communications were made to the Queen in her capacity as Queen of Australia, not a foreign head of state. He did not accept that the release of such correspondence would diminish the confidence of the authorities of other countries in Australia as a reliable recipient of confidential communications.[67] While the AIC accepted that the documents were deliberative in nature, this provides only a qualified exemption, meaning that a public interest test must apply. The AIC took into account the public interest in informing debate on a matter of public importance, being the operation of the Australian system of government and its relationship with the Queen of Australia, as well as the risk to the frankness and candour of the relationship between the Prime Minister and the Queen. He concluded that he was not persuaded that the public interest factors against disclosure outweighed those in favour of disclosure. The Department has since taken the matter to the Administrative Appeals Tribunal.[68]

The excessive secrecy concerning the Kerr–Palace letters, extending even to any advice that the Prime Minister may have given to the Queen about the release of these letters, would appear to be more damaging to the system of government than their release. It is the secrecy that stirs distrust and conspiracy theories. While the release of the correspondence is unlikely to shed much light on events that have already been subject to extreme scrutiny, it may provide closure, and even aid the rebuilding of trust in the institutions of government. Greater transparency in relation to the precedents that provide the foundations for constitutional conventions may also build a consensus as to the nature of those conventions, helping to avert future constitutional crises.

IV. Cabinet Manuals

Another means of creating consistent expectations as to the content and application of constitutional conventions is to record them in an authoritative work and for the Government to commit to their observance. This has been done in recent decades through the creation and publication of Cabinet Manuals, which record practices, rules and conventions concerning the operation of government and its relationships with other institutions, including conventions concerning high prerogative powers. A Cabinet Manual is essentially

---

[65] *Freedom of Information Act 1982* (Cth), ss 33(a)(iii) and 47C.
[66] William Summers and Department of the Prime Minister and Cabinet (Freedom of Information) [2018] AICmr 9 (16 January 2018).
[67] ibid [19], [25].
[68] At the time of writing the proceedings before the Administrative Appeals Tribunal had not been determined.

a manual by government and for government, which outlines how the Government operates and proposes to continue to operate.[69] It therefore does not purport to bind others, such as the Sovereign, Governor-General or Parliament. As Duncan has observed, it is 'not up to Cabinet to say what the Sovereign may do'.[70]

Cabinet Manuals are primarily directed at describing or explaining practices and conventions, often leaving room for the exercise of discretion and judgement.[71] In some cases, as discussed below, the Cabinet Manual may make or alter existing conventions. By setting out an authoritative set of practices[72] and conventions, the Cabinet Manual aids stable government by creating expectations as to how certain constitutional actors will behave, potentially averting constitutional crises due to consistent understandings across relevant parties of the basic rules.[73]

A. Reasons for the Publication of a Cabinet Manual

One driving factor behind the development of Cabinet Manuals has been the loss of internal memory within government due to the corporatisation of the senior echelons of the public sector, with officials being placed upon contracts or brought in from outside the public sector. The greater fluidity of movement in and out of public service may have added broader experience to the public sector, but has also reduced the kind of long-term knowledge and experience that was previously held by senior public servants who had spent many decades in public service, through multiple changes of government. It is quite obvious from reading government files over a long period of time that the level of institutional memory and consequential understanding of convention and its sources has dramatically diminished over the last 30 years. Accordingly, there needs to be a way for incoming people to understand the conventional rules, if they cannot rely on instruction from 'old hands' or the experience of long tenure and exposure to such issues from the beginning of their careers.[74]

Another factor has been the break-down of the two-party system, resulting in the splintering of political support amongst a number of small parties whose members have little experience or institutional memory, and the consequential increased likelihood of minority governments and coalitions.[75] The introduction of a proportional electoral system

---

[69] G O'Donnell, 'The New Cabinet Manual', UCL Constitution Unit's Public Seminar (24 February 2011).
[70] G Duncan, 'New Zealand's Cabinet Manual: How Does It Shape Constitutional Conventions?' (2015) 68 *Parliamentary Affairs* 737, 750.
[71] PH Russell, 'The Principles, Rules and Practices of Parliamentary Government: Time for a Written Constitution' (2012) 6 *Journal of Parliamentary and Political Law* 353, 356.
[72] Note the observation by McGrath that most of the New Zealand Cabinet Manual comprises 'usages in relation to government practices', rather than constitutional conventions: J McGrath, 'The Harkness Henry Lecture: The Crown, the Parliament and the Government' (1999) 7 *Waikato Law Review* 1, 18.
[73] Russell, 'Principles, Rules and Practices' (n 71) 363; F Harland, 'Constitutional Convention and Cabinet Manuals' (2011) *Canadian Parliamentary Review* 25, 30.
[74] Note that in the UK a 'Precedent Book' was kept for this purpose but was discontinued in 1992, with reliance instead being placed upon 'unwritten corporate memory': House of Commons Political and Constitutional Reform Committee, *Revisiting the Cabinet Manual* (January 2015) 13.
[75] For example, interest in the creation of a modern Cabinet Manual for Canada was sparked by a cycle of minority government in Canada: J Bowden and N MacDonald, 'Writing the Unwritten: The Officialization of Constitutional Convention in Canada, the United Kingdom, New Zealand and Australia' (2012) 6 *Journal of Parliamentary and Political Law* 365, 366.

may have a similar effect. The political, social and economic disruption that can arise from the election of a hung parliament may be allayed if there are consistent expectations and understanding both within and outside Parliament of how a government is to be formed and operate.

Other factors that have been regarded as supporting the need for a Cabinet Manual have included the move towards greater transparency and openness in government action,[76] as indicated by the spread of freedom of information legislation across the Commonwealth of nations, and the fact that there is no longer a small homogeneous political class that can conduct government on the basis of gentlemen's agreements.[77] The diversity of origins and backgrounds of the population, the limited teaching about the system of government in schools and the general public ignorance of how the nation is governed have also been regarded as reasons for the publication of a Cabinet Manual to provide an accessible overview.[78]

B. The Development of Cabinet Manuals in New Zealand, Australia, Canada and the UK

Although the origins of the New Zealand Cabinet Manual can be traced back to a set of records first kept by the Cabinet Secretary from 1948,[79] its modern form as a consolidation of 'rules, precedents, conventions and procedures' appeared in 1979 as a confidential document that could only be accessed from within the public service.[80] In 1996, however, it was published and placed on sale in bookshops.[81] This was because the new electoral system was expected to result in hung parliaments and longer periods of negotiation to form governments. The Cabinet Manual was employed to manage public and political expectations as to how the new system of forming governments would operate.

The practice in New Zealand is for the Cabinet of a new government, at its first meeting, to endorse the Cabinet Manual, as it plays a key role in the orderly change of governments and commencement of business for a new government.[82] Blick has described this as a form of 'self-sustaining legitimacy that arises simply by virtue of its being well-established'.[83] It has even been suggested that this practice might now have become a convention in its own right.[84]

Australia has long had a Cabinet Handbook at the national level, which can be traced back to 1927. But it is much more narrowly confined in its scope. Its treatment of constitutional conventions is primarily directed at those relating to individual and collective

---

[76] Blick, *Codes of the Constitution* (n 4) 88.
[77] Russell, 'Principles, Rules and Practices' (n 71) 354–55.
[78] ibid 355.
[79] E McLeay, 'What is the Constitutional Status of the New Zealand Cabinet Office Manual?' (1999) 10 *Public Law Review* 11.
[80] R Kitteridge, 'The Cabinet Manual: Evolution with Time', Paper delivered at the Eighth Annual Public Law Forum (20 March 2006) (copy on file with author). It was not until 1991 that it was distributed more widely to public servants. See further: Blick, *Codes of the Constitution* (n 4) 87.
[81] In 1998 it was also published online: Duncan, 'New Zealand's Cabinet Manual' (n 70) 741.
[82] McLeay, 'Constitutional Status' (n 79) 13; Blick, *Codes of the Constitution* (n 4) 87.
[83] Blick, *Codes of the Constitution* (n 4) 88.
[84] Duncan, 'New Zealand's Cabinet Manual' (n 70) 743; Blick, *Codes of the Constitution* (n 4) 89.

ministerial responsibility.[85] There is a short discussion of the caretaker conventions, but they are primarily dealt with in separate guidelines.[86] The Cabinet Handbook does not address other constitutional conventions, such as those on the formation of government in a hung parliament.[87] One reason for the absence of a comprehensive Cabinet Manual is that unlike that of New Zealand and the UK, Australia's Constitution is largely entrenched in statutory form. While conventions still apply, particularly to the formation of government and the grant of prorogation and dissolution of Parliament, the formal source of these powers is express constitutional provisions.[88]

In Canada, a *Manual of Official Procedure of the Government of Canada* was produced between 1964 and 1968. Despite Canada's also having a written entrenched Constitution, the *Manual* was a very detailed document that set out technical forms and procedures as well as conventions. It had a second volume of appendices that included templates and historical documents. The *Manual* went beyond Cabinet and governmental matters to include those concerning Parliament, judges, the Sovereign and protocol matters such as funerals and memorial services and visits by foreign dignitaries. It was a confidential document that was directed solely at official use. It was not, however, updated and fell into disuse, as subsequent governments focused on trying to achieve constitutional change.[89] In more recent times, it has been supplanted by a number of separate documents, such as *Open and Accountable Government*,[90] and caretaker government guidelines,[91] which partially fill the role of a Cabinet Manual.

In the UK, the spur for a formal written Cabinet Manual was the likelihood of a hung parliament at the 2010 election[92] and the perceived need to protect the Queen from political controversy,[93] calm the markets and the media, and provide an ordered process for the formation of a government.[94] A draft chapter was produced and subjected to scrutiny before the election. It was also regarded as important for setting community expectations about the period of time this would take, so that a sense of crisis or panic did not result from the uncertainty. In this, it was highly successful.[95] It was followed by a completed Manual under the new Government.

While the usefulness of Cabinet Manuals has generally been accepted, it does lead to difficult questions about the status of a Cabinet Manual – whether it is simply recording

---

[85] Department of the Prime Minister and Cabinet, *Cabinet Handbook*, 10th edn (2017).
[86] Department of the Prime Minister and Cabinet, 'Guidance on Caretaker Conventions' (2016), available at https://www.pmc.gov.au/resource-centre/government/guidance-caretaker-conventions.
[87] It does, however, mention that the Prime Minister advises the Governor-General on the appointment of ministers: *Cabinet Handbook* (n 85) 6.
[88] See ss 5 and 64 of the Australian Constitution.
[89] See also Bowden and MacDonald, 'Cabinet Manuals' (n 5) 183–86.
[90] Government of Canada, *Open and Accountable Government* (2015), available at http://publications.gc.ca/collections/collection_2016/bcp-pco/CP1-11-2015-eng.pdf. It is not clear whether this document continues to apply since the election of the Trudeau Government later in 2015.
[91] Privy Council Office, 'Guidelines on the Conduct of Ministers, Ministers of State, Exempt Staff and Public Servants During an Election' (August 2015), available at https://www.canada.ca/en/privy-council/services/publications/guidelines-conduct-ministers-state-exempt-staff-public-servants-election.html.
[92] For a discussion of the process for its adoption, see Russell, 'Principles, Rules and Practices' (n 71) 356–57.
[93] V Bogdanor, *The Coalition and the Constitution* (Oxford, Hart Publishing, 2011) 17–18.
[94] B Hicks, 'Advice to the Minister of Democratic Reform' (2013) 21(2) *Constitutional Forum* 23, 33; Blick, *Codes of the Constitution* (n 4) 191.
[95] Russell, 'Principles, Rules and Practices' (n 71) 364.

existing conventions, or creating or qualifying them, its standing if the incoming government does not support the conventions it describes, how it is changed, and what relevance it should have for the courts and in legal proceedings.

Former British Prime Minister David Cameron, in his introduction to the first edition of the UK Cabinet Manual, gave some mixed messages. On the one hand he described it as 'an authoritative guide for ministers and officials', and stated that he expected 'everyone working in government to be mindful of the guidance it contains'. This may be contrasted with his earlier reference to it as 'the internal rules and procedures under which the Government operates' and his reference to the codification of those rules. He did not acknowledge or develop any distinction between 'guidance' and codified 'rules'.

So what is the status of a Cabinet Manual? Is it a code comprised of rules, or simply guidance? Who controls its content and how it is amended?

C. The Legal Status of Cabinet Manuals

Cabinet Manuals are not intended to be legally binding or enforceable by the courts. This is usually made clear by those who write and approve them. Sir Gus O'Donnell, in his Preface to the first edition of the UK Cabinet Manual, stated that it 'is not intended to be legally binding'.[96] He later observed that its purpose is 'to guide but not to direct' and that it 'will have no legal status'.[97] Rebecca Kitteridge, a former New Zealand Cabinet Secretary, also asserted that the New Zealand Cabinet Manual is 'not a legal document'.[98]

Apart from the intention behind Cabinet Manuals, the nature of their contents also suggest that they are not legally enforceable. They are comprised generally of practices and conventions. In New Zealand, Sir Kenneth Keith in an introductory essay to the Cabinet Manual, observed that constitutional conventions, while of critical importance to the working of the Constitution, 'are not enforceable by the courts'.[99] Indeed many definitions of the term 'constitutional convention' expressly identify conventions by reference to the fact that they are not enforceable by courts of law.[100] Courts, too, have frequently described constitutional conventions as unenforceable by the courts. Such a view has been taken by both the Supreme Court of Canada[101] and the Supreme Court of the United Kingdom.[102] In New Zealand, Ellis J of the High Court considered that the Cabinet Manual was 'informative, rather than directive' and that 'it is not, and never could be, independently justiciable'.[103]

---

[96] Cabinet Office, *The Cabinet Manual* (2011) iv.
[97] O'Donnell, 'The New Cabinet Manual' (n 69).
[98] Kitteridge, 'The Cabinet Manual' (n 80).
[99] K Keith, 'On the Constitution of New Zealand: An Introduction to the Foundations of the Current Form of Government' in New Zealand Cabinet Office, *Cabinet Manual* (2017) 1, 2.
[100] See, eg, G Marshall and GC Moodie, *Some Problems of the Constitution*, 5th edn (London, Hutchinson University Library, 1971) 23–24; P Hogg, *Constitutional Law of Canada* (Scarborough, Carswell, 2014) para 1.10(a); and the discussion in R Brazier and St John Robilliard, 'Constitutional Conventions: The Canadian Supreme Court's Views Reviewed' [1982] *PL* 28, 30.
[101] *Re Resolution to Amend the Constitution* [1981] 1 SCR 753, 774–75 (Laskin CJ, Dickson, Beetz, Estey, McIntyre, Chouinard and Lamer JJ).
[102] *R (on the application of Miller) v Secretary of State for Exiting the European Union* [2018] AC 61, [146]. See also the view of the Judicial Committee of the Privy Council in: *Madzimbamuto v Lardner-Burke* [1969] 1 AC 645, 723 (Lord Reid).
[103] *Rabson v Attorney-General* [2016] NZHC 2876 (Ellis J). See also *Rabson v Attorney-General* [2017] NZSC 22.

If a government wishes to codify a convention in law then it may invite Parliament to do so by the enactment of a statute. If it has instead included a convention in a Cabinet Manual, it intends for it to be a political, not a legal, matter. If the executive could legislate without the need for Parliament, simply by publishing rules in a Manual, this would be a serious breach of constitutional principle.

Political enforcement may be just as effective as legal enforcement, or even more so, but the institutions engaged in interpretation and enforcement, and the methods of doing so, are different. The courts are often unsuited to assessing and enforcing conventions.[104] Conventions are primarily enforced by political and public pressure. In New Zealand, when there was a clash between the operation of the Cabinet Manual and a Coalition Agreement between governing parties, the Cabinet Manual prevailed – but as a political, rather than a legal, outcome.[105]

Attempts to achieve judicial enforcement of conventions outlined in executive codes or manuals have tended to fail. An example in the UK is *R (Hemming) v Prime Minister*. In that case a Member of Parliament sought judicial review of the Prime Minister's failure to answer questions, on the ground that it breached conventions set out in the Ministerial Code of Conduct. The proceeding was dismissed as 'unarguable': the Prime Minister was not under any legal duty to answer questions and the Ministerial Code was regarded as a matter for political enforcement, not judicial review.[106] On appeal, the Court of Appeal also accepted that the Ministerial Code provides 'guidelines' to Ministers, but that compliance with such guidance is 'a matter in the first instance for resolution through the procedures of Parliament'.[107] Lord Justice Auld concluded that 'there is no basis for any respectable argument that the guidance contained in the ministerial Code creates any obligation of law on a Minister in responding to correspondence from Members of Parliament'.[108] In New Zealand, the Court of Appeal also dismissed an attempt to enforce the caretaker government conventions.[109]

If conventions are not transformed into law by statute or incorporated in written Constitutions (as many are), is it possible that at some stage they may become so fundamental that they crystallise into law and are upheld by the courts? This is a highly contentious issue.[110] Marshall, for example, was sceptical about the possibility of conventions crystallising, congealing or hardening into law. He noted that while courts may need to recognise the existence of a convention as a matter of fact, or consider convention for the purpose of

---

[104] *Adegbenro v Akintola* [1963] AC 614, 630–31 (Viscount Radcliffe); Russell, 'Principles, Rules and Practices' (n 71) 360. See examples of the unsuitability of courts for this role in J Jaconelli, 'The Proper Roles for Constitutional Conventions' (2015) 38(2) *Dublin University Law Journal* 363, 376–77.
[105] McLeay, 'Constitutional Status' (n 79) 14–16.
[106] *R (Hemming) v Prime Minister* [2006] EWHC 2831 (Admin), [4].
[107] *R (Hemming) v Prime Minister* [2007] EWCA Civ 206, [13] (Auld LJ, with Chadwick LJ and Carnwath LJ agreeing). In reaching that conclusion the Court referred to a report of the Select Committee on Public Administration and a joint resolution of the Houses of Parliament concerning the status of the Code.
[108] *R (Hemming) v Prime Minister* (n 107) [15].
[109] *Te Waka Hi Ika O Te Arawa v Graham* (NZCA, 27 November 1996).
[110] See also F Ahmed, R Albert and A Perry, 'Judging Constitutional Conventions' *International Journal of Constitutional Law* (forthcoming); L Sirota, 'Towards a Jurisprudence of Constitutional Conventions' (2011) 11(1) *Oxford University Commonwealth Law Journal* 29; TRS Allan, *Law, Liberty, and Justice: The Legal Foundations of British Constitutionalism* (Oxford, Clarendon Press, 1994) 237–63.

statutory interpretation, it is difficult to find modern examples of the direct conversion of convention into enforceable laws.[111]

Barber has gone further, describing the identification of a convention that has crystallised into law as 'one of the holy grails of Commonwealth constitutional scholarship'.[112] He postulated, however, that the inclusion of conventions in formal codes or manuals may satisfy the criteria laid down by HLA Hart for the establishment of law, as one can identify the primary and secondary rules that Hart saw as the core of a legal system.[113] He considered that the Ministerial Code, for example, 'has become steadily more law-like over recent years' and 'now possesses many of the characteristic features of a legal system'.[114] The same could be said for the conventions contained in Cabinet Manuals.[115] Other objections to the crystallisation of convention into law – that conventions lack sufficient precision, that evidence of their ambit is lacking and that one cannot know whether constitutional actors regarded themselves as bound by the convention[116] – are countered to some extent by an authoritative and precise identification of conventions and their ambit in a Cabinet Manual that is accepted by the executive government as binding upon it. But it must nonetheless be recognised that matters are often included in a Cabinet Manual precisely because the Government wishes to prevent their becoming justiciable.[117]

In Canada, the Supreme Court was prepared to recognise the existence of a constitutional convention and outline its terms,[118] as a matter of fact,[119] but did not consider that convention could crystallise into law, no matter how long established it may be. Their Honours observed:

> The proposition was advanced ... that a convention may crystallize into law ... In our view this is not so. No instance of an explicit recognition of a convention as having matured into a rule of law was produced. The very nature of a convention as political in inception and as depending on a consistent course of political recognition by those for whose benefit and to whose detriment (if any) the convention developed over a considerable period of time is inconsistent with its legal enforcement.[120]

---

[111] G Marshall, *Constitutional Conventions* (Oxford, Clarendon Press, 1984) 14–17. See also the observation by Brazier and Robilliard that 'it is beyond argument that a convention cannot, without the intervention of statute, crystallise into a rule of law, and the breach of it therefore cannot be visited by legal consequences': Brazier and Robilliard, 'Constitutional Conventions' (n 100) 34.

[112] N Barber, *The Constitutional State* (Oxford, Oxford University Press, 2010) 97. Note Barber's distinction between a court's turning a convention into law and a convention that 'crystallises' into law by a gradual process without a defining intervention by a law-making body.

[113] ibid 100–01.

[114] ibid 103. See also Sirota, 'Towards a Jurisprudence' (n 110) 43.

[115] Heard, 'Constitutional Conventions' (n 4) 353.

[116] Brazier and Robilliard, 'Constitutional Conventions' (n 100) 33.

[117] See, eg, the 'war convention' concerning votes by the House of Commons authorising military deployments. Efforts to include it in statute have failed because of government concerns regarding justiciability. See further T Chowdhury, 'Statutorising UK Military Deployments and Assessing Anxieties of Their Justiciability' UK Const L Blog (17 September 2018), available at https://ukconstitutionallaw.org/2018/09/17/tanzil-chowdhury-statutorising-uk-military-deployments-and-assessing-anxieties-of-their-justiciability/.

[118] *Re Resolution to Amend the Constitution* (n 101) 884–86, 904–05 (Martland, Ritchie, Dickson, Beetz, Chouinard and Lamer JJ). For other Canadian examples, see *Wells v Newfoundland* [1999] 2 SCR 199; *Black v Canada (Prime Minister)* (2001) 199 DLR (4th) 228; *Reference re Senate Reform* [2014] 1 SCR 704. Compare Dicey's view that courts cannot recognise conventions: AV Dicey, *Introduction to the Study of the Law of the Constitution*, 7th edn (London, Macmillan, 1908) 435.

[119] 'Recognition is a fact-finding activity; the judge engages with the convention on a factual basis': Ahmed, Albert and Perry, 'Judging Constitutional Conventions' (n 110).

[120] *Re Resolution to Amend the Constitution* (n 101) 774–75 (Laskin CJ, Dickson, Beetz, Estey, McIntyre, Chouinard and Lamer JJ).

There are numerous other ways in which conventions have been used by the courts in legal proceedings. Barber has best summarised the position, stating:

> Judges can use conventions as an interpretative aid to clarify the meaning of statutes. Sometimes statutes make reference to conventions, an interpretation of the statute requires an interpretation of the convention. Sometimes statutes are passed in the context of conventions; the structure of the statute presupposes the parallel operation of these rules. A court which ignored conventions in this context would risk producing an impractical interpretation of the statute. Conventions can also form part of the background set of facts which are relied upon to make out a legal right.[121]

The primary way in which constitutional conventions are used by the courts is in the course of statutory interpretation.[122] This may be because the statute codifies or alters an aspect of an existing convention, so that recognition of the underlying convention is necessary in order to be able to interpret and apply the statutory provision.[123] References to the Cabinet Manual in judgments may also be made to provide the context in which a law operates,[124] particularly as to the role and conduct of Ministers,[125] and the relationship between the institutions of government.[126]

The recognition of convention may also be relevant to the application of a public interest test. This proved relevant in relation to the publication of the Crossman Diaries in the UK,[127] when it was argued that confidentiality was required by the convention of collective ministerial responsibility, and in the case of the black-spider letters, where it was argued that an alleged convention[128] concerning the education of the heir should affect the application of the public interest test under freedom of information.[129]

Conventions and practices set out in a Cabinet Manual may also give rise to legitimate expectations about how the executive government will behave in certain circumstances.[130] The New Zealand Cabinet Manual has also been referred to in criminal proceedings against a Member of Parliament, as it supported inferences concerning the state of mind of the Member and his awareness of wrongdoing.[131]

Most significantly, there is the potential for constitutional conventions to form part of a constitutional implication that may in some constitutional systems constrain legislative or executive power. In Canada this may occur through the application of constitutional

---

[121] Barber, *Constitutional State* (n 112) 90.

[122] See, eg, *British Coal Corporation v The King* [1935] AC 500; *Liversidge v Anderson* [1942] AC 206; *Ontario (Attorney-General) v OPSEU* [1987] 2 SCR 2.

[123] Marshall, *Constitutional Conventions* (n 111) 13. See the example given by Waldron of the convention that royal assent is required for a bill to become a law. That convention may be altered or regulated by statute, but acceptance of the convention is necessary for such a statute to make any sense: J Waldron, 'Are Constitutional Norms Legal Norms?' (2006) 75 *Fordham Law Review* 1697, 1703.

[124] *Boscawen v Attorney-General* [2009] 2 NZLR 229, [14], [17], [29].

[125] *Prasad v Minister for Immigration* [2011] NZHC 700; *Field v The Queen* [2011] 1 NZLR 784, [23]–[26], [192].

[126] *Attorney-General v Taylor* [2017] 3 NZLR 24, [74]; *Criminal Bar Association of New Zealand Inc v Attorney-General* [2013] NZCA 176, [93].

[127] *Attorney-General v Jonathan Cape Ltd* [1976] QB 752, 770.

[128] See the discussion of this case and doubt as to whether such a convention existed in Jaconelli, 'Proper Roles' (n 104) 372–74.

[129] *Evans v Information Commissioner* (n 41).

[130] *R v Secretary of State for the Home Department, ex parte Ruddock* [1987] 2 All ER 518; Duncan, 'New Zealand's Cabinet Manual' (n 70) 745; Allan, *Law, Liberty* (n 110) 259; TRS Allan, 'Law, Convention, Prerogative: Reflections Prompted by the Canadian Constitutional Case' (1986) 45 *CLJ* 305, 314. Note that conventions and practices may also have this effect even if they are not codified in a Manual: *Council of Civil Service Unions* (n 1).

[131] *Field v The Queen* (n 125) [192]. See also ibid [23]–[27].

preambles. For example, the preamble to the Constitution Act 1867 refers to the uniting of Canadian provinces with 'a Constitution similar in Principle to that of the United Kingdom'. This has resulted in the Canadian courts concluding that there is a constitutional guarantee of the unwritten principles (to which conventions give effect) of parliamentary governance,[132] including parliamentary privilege and judicial independence. These principles can be resorted to for 'the filling of gaps in the express terms of the constitutional text'.[133] While this approach has been the subject of significant criticism,[134] it continues to be a means by which constitutional principles can be transformed into law by the Canadian courts, potentially importing the application of conventions in giving those principles effect.[135] Hence the formalisation of conventions in a Cabinet Manual in Canada could provide further support for their constitutionalisation through the channel of the preamble.

In Australia, constitutional principle has also been given the effect of law by the High Court of Australia, at least to the extent that it forms part of a constitutional implication derived from the system of representative and responsible government.[136] While the focus of the courts has been on the constitutional principle, rather than on the conventions that give effect to it, there has been some suggestion in Australia that this may be regarded as a means by which convention is transformed by the courts into law.[137] Australian courts have also relied upon convention and practice to inform the interpretation of the common law[138] and statute, particularly in matters relating to parliamentary proceedings and appropriations. Hence, even if the conventions set out in a Cabinet Manual are not directly enforced at law, they may still potentially have a significant impact upon the application of law. The formalisation of them in a more comprehensive Cabinet Manual would increase that likelihood.

---

[132] *New Brunswick Broadcasting Co v Nova Scotia* [1993] 1 SCR 319; *Reference re Remuneration of Judges* [1997] 3 SCR 3, [102]–[103] (Lamer CJ).

[133] *Reference re Remuneration of Judges* (n 132) [104]. See also *Reference re Secession of Quebec* [1998] 2 SCR 217, [49]–[54].

[134] See, eg, SM Corbett, 'Reading the Preamble to the British North America Act, 1867' (1998) 9(2) *Constitutional Forum* 42, 43–44; J Goldsworthy, 'The Preamble, Judicial Independence and Judicial Integrity' (2000) 11(2) *Constitutional Forum* 60; and MD Walters, 'The Common Law Constitution in Canada: Return of *Lex Non Scripta* as Fundamental Law' (2001) 51 *University of Toronto Law Journal* 91, 103.

[135] Heard, 'Constitutional Conventions' (n 4) 356.

[136] See the constitutional implications drawn from ss 7 and 24 of the Australian Constitution, which give effect to the constitutional principles of representative and responsible government, including an implication of freedom of political communication and implications concerning voting: *Australian Capital Television Pty Ltd v Commonwealth* (1992) 177 CLR 106; *Lange v Australian Broadcasting Corporation* (1997) 189 CLR 520; *Roach v Electoral Commissioner* (2007) 233 CLR 162; *Rowe v Electoral Commissioner* (2010) 243 CLR 1; *Murphy v Electoral Commissioner* (2016) 334 ALR 369; *Brown v Tasmania* (2017) 349 ALR 398.

[137] See, eg, G Lindell, *Responsible Government and the Australian Constitution – Conventions Transformed into Law?* (Annandale, NSW, Federation Press, 2004); P Gerangelos, 'Of Laws, Conventions and Hung Parliaments' (2010) 12(3) *Constitutional Law and Policy Review* 39.

[138] See *Egan v Willis* (1998) 195 CLR 424, [50] (Gaudron, Gummow and Hayne JJ), where their Honours relied upon convention to determine what is 'reasonably necessary' for the proper exercise of the functions of the Legislative Council.

D. Do Cabinet Manuals Merely Record Conventions or Create and Alter Them?

There is significant controversy as to whether a Cabinet Manual merely records existing conventions or, by virtue of its authoritative status, has a role in altering or creating conventions. Jaconelli, for one, has rejected the notion that convention can be created or altered simply by recording it in writing in an authoritative work. He observed:

> Constitutional conventions, like all conventions, are based on social practice, to which written forms are very largely irrelevant. For as Atiyah has observed correctly: 'Customs and conventions arise from what people do, not from what they agree or promise' – nor, we should add, from what they write down, or what others write down on their behalf. The idea that written forms can promulgate conventions is misconceived since the latter are rooted in what the relevant actors actually do – not in what they say that they do, still less in what others say that they do. Written forms, certainly, may have a role to play after a pattern of social practice has emerged, in that they may purport to record that practice. But once again the idea that the written form possesses any independent 'enactment' force is mistaken. Like the dictionary of a living language it may record, with varying degrees of accuracy, what are taken to be the norms of usage (linguistic in the one case, constitutional in the other).[139]

Cabinet Manuals are therefore often characterised as descriptive, rather than prescriptive.[140] It is claimed that they act as a form of dictionary,[141] transcribing and recording information but not establishing or altering it. The then New Zealand Prime Minister, Helen Clark, in her Foreword to the 2008 edition of the New Zealand Cabinet Manual, stated that the Cabinet Manual 'does not effect change but, rather, records incremental changes in the administrative and constitutional arrangements of executive government'.[142]

It has been contended that it is only once a 'critical mass' is reached in terms of practice and support for a convention that it is included in the Cabinet Manual.[143] The Cabinet Manual therefore 'lags behind' constitutional developments.[144] McLeay has argued that the conventions set down in the Cabinet Manual find their importance in their status as constitutional conventions that 'have acquired legitimacy through tradition and utility', not in their inclusion in the Manual.[145] John McGrath, the then Solicitor-General of New Zealand, asserted that amendment of the terms of the Cabinet Manual 'does not necessarily alter existing conventions in any way'.[146]

While these claims may be comforting, they do not appear to be accurate for a number of reasons. First, due to the secrecy concerning the actions of high constitutional actors, it

---

[139] Jaconelli, 'Proper Roles' (n 104) 365 (footnotes excluded).
[140] McGrath, 'Harkness Henry Lecture' (n 72) 18; Bowden and MacDonald, 'Writing the Unwritten' (n 75) 367.
[141] Kitteridge, 'The Cabinet Manual' (n 80); D Morcom, 'Preface' in New Zealand, Cabinet Office, *Cabinet Manual* (2008) xvii.
[142] New Zealand Cabinet Office, *Cabinet Manual* (2008) xv.
[143] Hicks, 'Advice' (n 94) 32; Kitteridge, 'The Cabinet Manual' (n 80).
[144] Kitteridge, 'The Cabinet Manual' (n 80).
[145] McLeay, 'Constitutional Status' (n 79) 13.
[146] McGrath, 'Harkness Henry Lecture' (n 72) 19.

can take decades, or now even a lifetime, before sufficient information is revealed to know what the practice is that supports a convention. Public perception of a precedent may be incorrect, and it is also possible that some of those involved have made 'self-serving or deceptive statements' to explain their actions.[147] A study of primary records, many decades after the relevant constitutional events occurred, often shows that contemporary works were inaccurate in their understanding of what occurred.[148] Bagehot's work, as discussed in section III, was later shown to be an inaccurate and misleading portrayal of the conventions of the British Constitution, but has nonetheless taken on the mantle of orthodoxy verging on scripture. Secrecy often means that the source of 'convention' is a misunderstanding of the past, but one that is regarded as authoritative in the present. Conventions may therefore be based not on what the relevant actors actually do, but on what writers mistakenly believe them to have done.

As Bowden and MacDonald have observed, 'constitutional actors cannot bind themselves to rules or precedents of which they remain ignorant, even if they *should* know of them'.[149] When institutional memory is degraded, personnel change frequently and official secrecy is maintained for long periods in relation to constitutional acts, it is more than likely that constitutional actors will rely upon and regard themselves bound by 'conventions' articulated in secondary sources that do not reflect actual past practice. Hence, recording conventions in writing, whether in an academic work or in a Cabinet Manual, does have the effect of creating new conventions when it is not fully informed due to lack of access to historical records and loss of institutional memory.

Second, changes in laws and constitutional arrangements will demand the creation of new conventions that are not backed by practice. For example, when the Crown became divisible and a number of self-governing colonies achieved constitutional autonomy in the 1920s, new conventions were needed concerning the source of advice to the Sovereign. These conventions were recorded in the Imperial Conferences and in part in the preamble to, and section 4 of, the Statute of Westminster 1931. Latham suggested that while this method of establishing new conventions may occur in the field of relations amongst Commonwealth nations, it is more problematic to establish convention by agreement in domestic affairs, because Ministers and Members of Parliament do not have the 'moral authority to bind their successors by mere agreement apart from precedent'.[150] Nonetheless, despite the lack of authority to bind successors, there have in more recent times been domestic examples of the creation of convention by agreement. They include in the UK the Sewel Convention concerning devolution,[151] and in Australia the convention agreed at the time of the enactment of the Australia Acts 1986 that the Queen will only

---

[147] Heard, 'Constitutional Conventions' (n 4) 355; A Twomey, 'Constitutional Convention and Constitutional Reality' (2004) 78(12) *Australian Law Journal* 798, 809–10.
[148] For a detailed example, see Twomey, 'Constitutional Convention' (n 147) 798.
[149] Bowden and MacDonald, 'Writing the Unwritten' (n 75) 367–68.
[150] RTE Latham, *The Law and the Commonwealth* (Oxford, Oxford University Press, 1949) 610. See also Hogg, *Constitutional Law* (n 100) para 1.10(d).
[151] The Sewel Convention was recorded, but not given the force of law, in Scotland Act 1998 (UK), s 28(7) and (8). The UK Supreme Court recognised it as a political convention, rather than as a legal rule that could be enforced by the courts: *R (on the application of Miller) v Secretary of State for Exiting the European Union* (n 102) [148]. Note Jaconelli's concern about the form of such a legislative record of a convention: Jaconelli, 'Proper Roles' (n 104) 379.

perform acts within the Australian States if there has been prior and mutual agreement to do so.[152]

One reason why alterations in law and constitutional institutions may require a change in convention is because the existing convention may no longer serve the relevant constitutional principle. Jaconelli has given as an example the Salisbury Convention,[153] which was arguably affected by the removal of most hereditary peers from the House[154] and would certainly be affected if the House instead became an elected body.

A stark example of the creation of new convention to accommodate changed constitutional circumstances arose in New Zealand when there was a shift to a proportional electoral system. While the mantra was still recited that this did not result in changes to constitutional conventions,[155] the reality was that the conventions recorded in the Cabinet Manual concerning the formation of government from a hung parliament and the role of the Governor-General were significantly different from what they had been in the past.[156] Quentin-Baxter and McLean have observed that the chapter in the Cabinet Manual on the formation of government 'was almost entirely rewritten' prior to the implementation of the voting system.[157] New convention was made, based largely on public speeches by the then Governor-General, Sir Michael Hardie Boys. He drew on experiences in other countries that had voting systems based on proportional representation. The Cabinet Manual described these new practices as 'convention',[158] and they have since been applied as such, despite lacking any prior history of precedent.

Third, as noted by Heard, precedents can be 'hopelessly outdated' and 'are often non-existent for the most problematic of constitutional crises as novel circumstances can be at play'.[159] The New Zealand Cabinet Manual illustrates the difficulty of claiming to describe conventions derived from past practice, when the most recent precedent may have occurred more than half a century ago and in completely different constitutional circumstances. Prior to the introduction of a proportional electoral system, hung parliaments were rare, and a mid-term loss of confidence and change of government had not occurred in New Zealand since 1912. Duncan has observed that the 'fact that such a mid-term change has not happened in New Zealand in the last 100 years makes the idea that the Manual only ever records, rather than leads, convention seem a little strained'.[160]

---

[152] This convention was agreed upon by all State Premiers and included in the second reading speeches on the relevant Bills in the States: A Twomey, *The Australia Acts 1986 – Australia's Statutes of Independence* (Sydney, The Federation Press, 2010) 169–76.

[153] This is a convention that the House of Lords will pass government bills that had been proposed in the governing party's election manifesto. It was based upon the premise that the House of Lords was a hereditary, not a democratically elected, House. Note the problems with its application where there is a coalition government or a minority government: N Newson, 'Salisbury Convention in a Hung Parliament', House of Lords Library Briefing (20 June 2017), available at http://researchbriefings.files.parliament.uk/documents/LLN-2017-0030/LLN-2017-0030.pdf.

[154] Jaconelli, 'Proper Roles' (n 104) 380.

[155] Duncan, 'New Zealand's Cabinet Manual' (n 70) 746.

[156] Compare, eg, Memorandum by Sir Cecil Day, Official Secretary to the Governor-General, Government House, November 1928: ANZ R19162235.

[157] A Quentin-Baxter and J McLean, *This Realm of New Zealand – The Sovereign, The Governor-General, The Crown* (Auckland, Auckland University Press, 2017) 171.

[158] New Zealand Cabinet Office, *Cabinet Manual* (n 99) 94, para 6.44. See also Quentin-Baxter and McLean, *This Realm of New Zealand* (n 157) 177.

[159] Heard, 'Constitutional Conventions' (n 4) 355.

[160] Duncan, 'New Zealand's Cabinet Manual' (n 70) 748.

The immense power of a Cabinet Manual lies in the fact that not only can it be used to establish new conventions, but it can do so while convincing people that it is only describing conventions that already exist, simply by asserting that this is the case. This is because the Government is assumed to have greater information about past practice and may therefore more authoritatively declare the existence of precedents and conventions. It may also, by excluding reference to conventions, lead to an implication that they no longer apply or result in their neglect. Once conventions are codified in a Manual, it is unlikely that people will look beyond it to discern the applicable conventions.

One way of getting around the problem of the creation of new conventions without existing precedent or formal agreement of all the constitutional actors, is to argue that the Cabinet Manual merely establishes new practices, which will eventually take on the status of convention once they have been given effect on a number of occasions. An example in the UK is the use of the Civil Service, with the authorisation of the Prime Minister, to aid negotiations for the formation of government after the election of a hung parliament. The relevant chapter of the draft Cabinet Manual permitted this in 2010, and it was given effect, creating a precedent. There has been speculation that this precedent might transform into a convention in future.[161] This is, nonetheless, a weak way of avoiding the underlying truth that Cabinet Manuals do have the effect of changing convention. The key test is whether any new 'practice' set out in the Cabinet Manual is overridden by pre-existing contrary conventions, or whether the new practice displaces or alters existing convention.[162] If the latter then it is a new or altered convention that is being created by the Cabinet Manual, contrary to the frequently recited dogma.

Another way of dealing with the problem is to assert that it is not the Cabinet Manual that is making the change in convention but the Cabinet itself in approving that change, or the other bodies that caused the constitutional alteration to which the new convention is a response. Kitteridge put it this way:

> The key point is that although amendments to the Manual may reflect and promulgate change, they do not, in themselves, effect change. Change is effected by new legislation, or Cabinet minutes, or judicial decisions, or amendments to the Standing Orders. Even rules on the processes of executive government, which may not be recorded anywhere except in the Manual, are approved by Cabinet at the time the Manual is issued. Their authority derives from Cabinet.
>
> The fact that the Manual cannot, by itself, effect change is even more significant in respect of those provisions that articulate elements of the constitution. Clearly the constitutional conventions exist independently of the Manual, although they are authoritatively expressed there. So, for example, changing the provisions of the Manual relating to the constitutional powers of the Prime Minister, in the absence of separate constitutional developments, will not have any effect on the conventions themselves.[163]

Clearly, however, where there have been constitutional developments, such as a change of the electoral system, and there is a need for new conventions to accommodate that change, the determination of the nature and scope of the new conventions, and their

---

[161] Hicks, 'Advice' (n 94) 33; Blick, *Codes of the Constitution* (n 4) 195.
[162] See the discussion by Blick of whether this new practice is inconsistent with conventions requiring Civil Service impartiality and ministerial responsibility: Blick, *Codes of the Constitution* (n 4) 196–98.
[163] Kitteridge, 'The Cabinet Manual' (n 80).

'promulgation'[164] in the Cabinet Manual, does give effect to that change. In such circumstances the Cabinet Manual does indeed give effect to a new convention, even though it may be in response to some other constitutional change and the new convention is approved by the Cabinet.

Finally, a Cabinet Manual is a promise with regard to future behaviour. While it may seek to bolster its authority by reference to past behaviour, its primary role is to assert that this is how the Government intends to behave now and into the future, until such time as the Manual is amended. A Cabinet Manual is not a history of past behaviour – although its successive endorsement by different governments does enhance its status. It is a commitment to future behaviour. It therefore regularly makes convention by providing a solemn commitment to behave in a particular way in the future.

E. Control Over the Content of the Cabinet Manual

One of the difficulties with Cabinet Manuals and their authoritative status is that they represent only one perspective on the prevailing conventions. There is a significant likelihood that the conventions recorded will arrogate power to the constitutional actors who control the process – usually the Chief Minister and sometimes senior bureaucrats.

An example is the Canadian *Manual of Official Procedure of the Government of Canada*. It provided, amongst other things, that 'the Governor General accepts the Prime Minister's advice on summoning and proroguing Parliament', and that the Governor-General 'does not retain any discretion' with regard to these matters.[165] While some may accept this as correct,[166] many have regarded it as both wrong and self-serving because it enhances the power of the Prime Minister.[167] It has been pointed out that even at the time it was written, the 1968 Manual's description of the Governor-General's lack of discretionary power in relation to the summoning and prorogation of Parliament was contrary to the leading academic works of the day by Dawson and Forsey.[168] The Harper Government's reliance on this passage from the Manual in 2008 in circumstances where prorogation was sought to defer a vote of no confidence in the Government has been regarded as contrary to the principle of responsible government, because it was being relied upon as a means of avoiding responsibility to Parliament.[169]

On the other hand, it has also been argued that in the absence of an authoritative summary of constitutional conventions, the executive can 'distort and misrepresent them

---

[164] Compare the use of 'promulgation' by Kitteridge, above, with the rejection by Jaconelli, also above, of the proposition that a Cabinet Manual can promulgate conventions. Note also that promulgation by courts or legislatures is an essential step in the identification of law.
[165] *Manual of Official Procedure of the Government of Canada* (Ottawa, 1968) 150.
[166] Bowden and MacDonald, 'Cabinet Manuals' (n 5) 186.
[167] RP Alford, 'Two Cheers for a Cabinet Manual (And a Note of Caution)' (2017) 11 *Journal of Parliamentary and Political Law* 41, 48; Hicks, 'Advice' (n 94) 32; Harland, 'Constitutional Convention' (n 73) 26–27. See further the survey of views of constitutional scholars in Canada on whether the Governor-General has discretion in relation to prorogation: J Wheeldon, 'Constitutional Peace, Political Order or Good Government? Organizing Scholarly Views on the 2008 Prorogation' (2014) 8(1) *Canadian Political Science Review* 102.
[168] Alford, 'Two Cheers' (n 167) 46.
[169] ibid.

to the government's advantage' in dealing with a particular crisis.[170] On this basis, it is preferable to have an authoritative document, such as a Cabinet Manual, which is established outside the hurly-burly of a political crisis, so that there is a more objective record of precedent and convention that may be called upon when needed. The question then is who prepares and amends the Cabinet Manual so it can fulfil that objective and impartial role.

In New Zealand it was the Cabinet Office that was substantially involved in developing the Cabinet Manual. Russell has pointed out that there are advantages in this, as it is prepared by experienced public servants who have access to relevant (confidential) records and have direct knowledge of the relationships and practices covered by the Manual. They are also 'non-partisan' and are the ones to whom the Manual is largely directed.[171] But Russell argued that it is important for academics and Parliament to have a role so that the Manual may be acceptable to all parliamentary parties as a non-partisan document.[172] Alford has criticised the method of creating and approving the New Zealand Cabinet Manual, noting that it 'has never been subjected to any procedures that would suggest that it has obtained Parliamentary or academic *imprimatur*'.[173] While it has been cited in the New Zealand Parliament, it has not been the subject of debate or parliamentary inquiry.[174]

Hicks has praised the UK method of developing a Cabinet Manual, which involved not only the Cabinet Office but also parliamentary committees in both Houses of Parliament[175] and no doubt significant consultation with the Queen's Private Secretary. A small number of academics were also privately consulted during its drafting.[176] Alford, however, cautioned that the Manual was written by officials working under the authority of Ministers, and that consultation with scholars was 'conducted informally and in private with experts chosen by the executive'.[177] The British Cabinet Manual has certainly been the subject of greater scrutiny by parliamentary committees, which involved public and academic input through the making of submissions and the giving of oral evidence.

One issue that has arisen is how to accommodate the fact that there are different views about the scope or application of some conventions. The House of Commons Political and Constitutional Reform Committee was critical in 2011 of the failure of the Cabinet Manual to signal the existence of uncertainty in some cases. It observed that the Manual must 'avoid presenting as unchallengeable fact a statement that the Government knows to be disputed'.[178] The Government responded that the Cabinet Manual represents the executive's understanding of the conventions, but that it is not binding and 'others are entitled to take a different view on the operation or extent of a particular convention'.[179] It would be difficult,

---

[170] ibid 42.
[171] Russell, 'Principles, Rules and Practices' (n 71) 362.
[172] ibid.
[173] Alford, 'Two Cheers' (n 167) 47.
[174] Duncan, 'New Zealand's Cabinet Manual' (n 70) 740.
[175] Hicks, 'Advice' (n 94) 32. See also Russell, 'Principles, Rules and Practices' (n 71) 356–57.
[176] Bogdanor, *Coalition* (n 93) 24.
[177] Alford, 'Two Cheers' (n 167) 50.
[178] House of Commons Political and Constitutional Reform Committee, *Constitutional Implications of the Cabinet Manual*, HC 734 (March 2011) para 21.
[179] *Government Response to the House of Lords Constitution Committee, Political and Constitutional Reform Committee and Public Administration Select Committee on the Cabinet Manual*, Cm 8213 (October 2011) 18.

however, for other views to prevail against an authoritative document such as a Cabinet Manual. By setting it down in writing, the executive does privilege its own interpretation of conventions, to the detriment of any other interpretation.

Another issue is the absence of specific accountability for the content of the UK Cabinet Manual. The then UK Cabinet Secretary, Sir Jeremy Heywood, told a UK parliamentary committee that it is the Cabinet that takes collective responsibility for the Cabinet Manual. Yet this meant that the Committee was unable to find an individual Minister who would appear before it to explain the Government's policy on the Manual.[180] While collective responsibility is all well and good, it may have the effect of clouding individual responsibility and thwarting methods of obtaining accountability.

Debate has also arisen as to the method of amendment, its frequency and the role of Parliament in raising matters that should be altered or updated in the Cabinet Manual.[181] It is understandable that the executive sees the Cabinet Manual as its own guide, and therefore as something it controls in terms of content and presentation. Yet in those countries with substantial Cabinet Manuals, it plays a more significant role than a mere guide for the executive. It is also an authoritative source of understanding of the constitution of the nation and a source of civic education. The manner in which its contents are determined and updated is therefore important.

V. Conclusion

One of the virtues of convention is its flexibility and its capacity to give effect to evolving constitutional principles. But a concomitant defect is the difficulty of determining the existence and ambit of conventions so that some kind of consensus can develop concerning their operation. As long as precedents, which are the primary (but not exclusive) basis for conventions, are kept locked in a black box of secrecy, there will be misunderstanding, distortion and misrepresentation of conventions. This can lead to constitutional crises when constitutional actors rely on different understandings of convention, and such crises can be exacerbated when the public understanding of the operation of the system of government differs substantially from the practice.

There remain good reasons for keeping government documents confidential for a period of time. While the length of that period – whether it be 30, 20 or 15 years – is a matter for debate, it is important that there be public access to primary documents that show how the system of government has operated in practice in the relatively recent past, so that a fair assessment can be made of the conventions that govern its operation in the present. Without such knowledge, the people are denied the capacity to assess, criticise and seek to reform the operation of government, which is fundamental to a healthy representative democracy. The 2010 changes in the UK, which locked away all royal correspondence for beyond the lifetime of the relevant monarch, not only affected the ability of the people of the UK to understand how their system of government works and make an accurate appraisal

---

[180] House of Commons Political and Constitutional Reform Committee, *Revisiting the Cabinet Manual* (n 74) 9.
[181] ibid ch 4.

of their own history, but also prevented people from other countries, such as Australia, New Zealand and Canada, from having access to fundamentally important aspects of their own history and governance.

Recent efforts to increase transparency through recording conventions in Cabinet Manuals aid transparency in the workings of government. Yet without independent knowledge of the precedents that underlie asserted conventions, there remains a risk that these authoritative works may well distort conventions in a way that increases the power of the executive government. The greater transparency provided by a Cabinet Manual must be supported by greater transparency in access to the documents that support the practices and conventions set out in the Manual. This will allow such Manuals to be the subject of independent scrutiny and criticism when it is warranted.

19
Fomenting Authoritarianism Through Rules About Rulemaking

KATHRYN E KOVACS

I. Introduction

In recent years, the President of the United States (US) has assumed increasing power. Among other things, the President now makes decisions that federal administrative agencies previously would have made. This trend is not new, but it has reached a new height in the Trump Administration. Some of the reasons for this development are obvious: over the course of many years and for various reasons, Congress's lawmaking ability has atrophied, and technology and the media encourage the President to take credit for federal policy decisions. Just as Congress's inaction contributes to this trend, so too does agency inaction. When agencies cannot make or change policy in a timely and efficient manner, the President is more inclined to do it himself.

Agency rulemaking has become extremely resource-intensive, making agencies increasingly unable to respond to changing circumstances in a timely fashion. That is due in part to requirements imposed by Congress, the President and the courts. Though well-intentioned, the judicial rules about rulemaking are particularly problematic. Many of those rules conflict with the Administrative Procedure Act (APA), the primary statute governing federal agency procedure and judicial review. That conflict is of great concern, because the passage of the APA in 1946 marked a significant moment in deliberative democracy: after years of debate among Congress, the Executive Branch and the public, Congress passed the APA unanimously, and the President signed it into law. The APA balanced multiple values, concerns and variables. When the courts disturb that balance, they raise exceptional separation of powers and political accountability concerns.

The judicial rules governing agency rulemaking also are problematic because they have unanticipated consequences. Of the three branches of the US Government, the courts are the least capable of considering various positions and proposals and predicting which approach to administrative policymaking will be most effective. Thus, their rules seeking to enhance transparency, accountability and public participation in administrative processes yield other results as well. Among other things, the courts' rules about rulemaking have fomented the growth of authoritarianism by making agency rulemaking more difficult.

Changing times require changing policy. Congress's policymaking ability, however, is severely compromised, and federal agencies are overburdened by procedural requirements.

Thus, the President has stepped into the policymaking breach. The courts should recognise their role in the changing power structure of the US Government and adhere to the careful balance achieved in the APA. They should require agencies to fulfil the APA's requirements without overburdening them.

II. Agencies in the US Government

A. The Original Design

The US Constitution assigns the powers of government to three different branches: legislative powers are vested in a Congress; judicial powers are vested in a Supreme Court and whatever other courts Congress creates; and executive powers are vested in a President.[1] Along with that separation of governmental powers, the US Constitution provides for each branch of the Government to be able to check the power of the other branches. For example, Congress may enact a statute only with the President's agreement or a supermajority vote to override his veto.[2]

This model of government was intended to protect liberty and avoid tyranny.[3] No single branch can exercise all of the powers of government, and no single branch can act without limit. As James Madison explained, 'The accumulation of all powers, legislative, executive, and judiciary, in the same hands, whether of one, a few, or many, and whether hereditary, self appointed, or elective, may justly be pronounced the very definition of tyranny.'[4]

The US Constitution also anticipated that the President would not execute all of the law on his own. It recognised that governmental powers might be vested in a 'Department or Officer'.[5] It provided for principal officers to be appointed by the President with the advice and consent of the Senate.[6] It authorised the President to request a written opinion from 'the principal Officer in each of the executive Departments'.[7] And it delegated to Congress the responsibility for specifying which officer would act as President if the President and Vice President could not act.[8] The Departments of War, Treasury and State came first, followed by the Post Office.

Over the years, Congress increasingly has delegated both rulemaking and adjudicatory authority to agencies. This trend picked up steam in the New Deal period of the 1930s, and again with the enactment of broad social and environmental legislation in the 1970s. Now

---

[1] US Constitution, Art I, s 1; Art II, s 1; Art III, s 1.
[2] US Constitution, Art I, s 7.
[3] See *Boumediene v Bush*, 553 US 723, 742 (2008); TB Olson, 'Tex Lezar Memorial Lecture' (2004) 9 *Texas Review of Law and Policy* 1, 2.
[4] *The Federalist*, Number 47. The Federalist Papers are 85 essays written by Alexander Hamilton, James Madison, and John Jay in 1787 and 1788 urging ratification of the US Constitution. Madison wrote a series of essays on the separation of powers that 'were then, and still are today, considered a seminal work on the nature of the Constitution and its structure': V Nourse, 'Toward a "Due Foundation" for the Separation of Powers: The Federalist Papers as Political Narrative' (1996) 74 *Texas Law Review* 447, 521.
[5] US Constitution, Art I, s 8, cl 18.
[6] US Constitution, Art II, s 2, cl 2.
[7] US Constitution, Art II, s 2, cl 1.
[8] US Constitution, Art II, s 1, cl 6.

Congress typically enacts broad statutory outlines, leaving gaps for agencies to fill. These broad statutory delegations have become an entrenched part of the US's constitutional structure, making the federal bureaucracy a necessary element of the US Government.[9]

There are multiple, overlapping means for controlling federal agencies. The Constitution authorises the President to control agencies through his power to appoint their leaders (with the advice and consent of the Senate);[10] Congress appropriates agency funds and writes the statutes that delineate agency authority;[11] and the federal courts review the legality of agency actions.[12] Many other mechanisms for controlling agencies have arisen over the years as well. For example, the President can remove most of his appointees at will.[13] He can issue Executive Orders to direct agency action.[14] Agency budget requests filter through the President's office.[15] Congress can investigate and hold hearings on agencies,[16] and it can invalidate agency rules using a fast-track procedure.[17]

B. Recent Changes

Over the past 50 years, the structure of the US Government has shifted dramatically. Among other things, the President has increasingly made policy decisions himself that previously would have been made either by Congress or by a government agency. This phenomenon began decades ago, but it has reached a frightening crescendo in the Trump Administration.[18]

For example, when President Reagan wanted a change in immigration policy, he left the matter to Congress.[19] In the Obama Administration, the policy change came from the Secretary of Homeland Security, but the President held a press conference to announce it.[20] President Trump, by contrast, simply issued a Proclamation banning immigration from certain countries.[21] Other recent examples of the President's taking on the role of an agency include his order directing the Secretary of the Interior to expand broadband in

---

[9] See GE Metzger, 'Foreword: 1930s Redux: The Administrative State Under Siege' (2017) 131 *Harvard Law Review* 2, 95.
[10] US Constitution, Art II, s 2, cl 2.
[11] US Constitution, Art I, s 8, cls 1 and 18.
[12] See US Constitution, Art III, s 2, cl 1 (extending the Judicial Power 'to Controversies to which the United States shall be a Party').
[13] See *Free Enterprise Fund v Public Company Accounting Oversight Board*, 561 US 477, 483 (2010).
[14] See KM Stack, 'The Statutory President' (2005) 90 *Iowa Law Review* 539, 546–57.
[15] See E Pasachoff, 'The President's Budget as a Source of Agency Policy Control' (2016) 125 *Yale Law Journal* 2182.
[16] See JM Beermann, 'Congressional Administration' (2006) 43 *San Diego Law Review* 61, 124–27.
[17] Congressional Review Act, Public Law Number 104–121, title II, s 251 (1996), codified at 5 US Code, ss 801–808.
[18] See DA Farber, 'Presidential Administration Under Trump' UC Berkeley Public Law Research Papers (2017) 4, 30, available at papers.ssrn.com/sol3/papers.cfm?abstract_id=3015591.
[19] Immigration Reform and Control Act, Public Law Number 99–603, 100 Statutes at Large 3445 (1986).
[20] See J Napolitano, 'Exercising Prosecutorial Discretion with Respect to Individuals Who Came to the United States as Children' (15 June 2012), available at www.dhs.gov/xlibrary/assets/s1-exercising-prosecutorial-discretion-individuals-who-came-to-us-as-children.pdf; see also JL Mashaw and D Berke, 'Presidential Administration in a Regime of Separated Powers: An Analysis of Recent American Experience' (2018) 35 *Yale Journal on Regulation* 549, 563.
[21] Executive Order 13,769 (2017) s 3(c).

rural areas;[22] his order establishing a policy regarding mental healthcare for veterans;[23] the memorandum dictating timing and testing requirements under the Clean Air Act;[24] and the memorandum establishing a new policy regarding arms transfers.[25] Years ago, such policy changes would have come from an agency exercising power delegated by Congress. Now, the President makes the policy himself.

There are of course many reasons for this development. First, Congress is increasingly unable to enact legislation.[26] Congress has not even enacted a federal budget on time since the 1990s.[27] Teter has noted that 'Scholars point to a variety of factors contributing to gridlock: divided government, increased party polarization, interest groups, the congressional committee system, Senate rules, the health of the economy, electoral pressures and strategies, and even the national mood'.[28]

If Congress does not make policy to address new problems and circumstances as they arise, doing so is left to the executive branch. Congress has largely abdicated its central role in policy making and acquiesced in the transfer of that power to the President.[29] Justice Jackson's prediction has come to pass that Congress's power would slip through its fingers if it was 'not wise and timely in meeting its problems'.[30] Moreover, even when Congress does act, the President cannot rely on it to make the policy he desires unless his party controls both houses. That sort of governmental unity has been scarce since the administration of Franklin Delano Roosevelt ended in the 1940s.[31] Thus, legislative atrophy has fostered presidential unilateral action.

Another reason for this development is technology and the media. Everything the Government does is promptly splashed across the Internet, and Americans do not tend to distinguish between the President and federal agencies. In this atmosphere, the President is inclined to take the credit for and control policy decisions, particularly because he is likely

---

[22] Executive Order 13,821 (2018).
[23] Executive Order 13,822 (2018).
[24] Presidential Memorandum for the Administrator of the Environmental Protection Agency, 12 April 2018, available at www.whitehouse.gov/presidential-actions/presidential-memorandum-administrator-environmental-protection-agency/.
[25] National Security Presidential Memorandum Regarding US Conventional Arms Transfer Policy, 19 April 2018, available at www.whitehouse.gov/presidential-actions/national-security-presidential-memorandum-regarding-u-s-conventional-arms-transfer-policy/.
[26] See MJ Teter, 'Congressional Gridlock's Threat to Separation of Powers' (2013) *Wisconsin Law Review* 1097, 1103.
[27] J Dickerson, 'The Hardest Job in the World' *The Atlantic* (May 2018), available at www.theatlantic.com/magazine/archive/2018/05/a-broken-office/556883/. 'In fact, in the four decades since the current system for budgeting and spending tax dollars has been in effect, Congress has managed to pass all its required appropriations measures on time only four times: in fiscal 1977 (the first full fiscal year under the current system), 1989, 1995 and 1997': D Desilver, 'Congress Has Long Struggled to Pass Spending Bills on Time' *Pew Research Center Fact Tank* (16 January 2018), available at www.pewresearch.org/fact-tank/2018/01/16/congress-has-long-struggled-to-pass-spending-bills-on-time/. A sizeable portion of the US Government shut down for lack of funding early in 2019.
[28] Teter, 'Congressional Gridlock's Threat to Separation of Powers' (n 26) 1108.
[29] ibid.
[30] *Youngstown Sheet & Tube Co v Sawyer*, 343 US 579, 654 (1952) (Jackson J concurring). The 'problem' at issue in *Youngstown* was a labour strike that threatened to shut down the nation's steel mills at a time when the military required steel. The Court held (at 589) that the President's effort to seize the steel mills to keep them operating was unconstitutional. Justice Jackson's concurrence discussing the relationship between congressional and presidential power is 'one of the most influential concurring opinions in [US] history': JC Eastman, 'Live by the Executive Pen, Die by the Executive Pen?' (2017) 65 *Drake Law Review* 997, 1001.
[31] E Kagan, 'Presidential Administration' (2001) 114 *Harvard Law Review* 2245, 2311.

to be blamed for them if they go wrong regardless of whether the decision was actually his or not.[32]

Federal agencies' inability to act is another reason why the President has increasingly stepped into their shoes. It is commonly accepted that Congress's inaction is one of the primary reasons for increasing presidential power. By the same token, agencies' inaction creates a power vacuum for the President to fill. Just as Congress's ineptitude inspires the President to make policy himself, so too does agency sloth increase the tendency towards presidential power.[33] Governmental power in the US may be seen as a hydraulic system. The Supreme Court observed that each of the three branches of the Government applies pressure 'to exceed the outer limits of its power'.[34] On the other hand, if one branch contracts its activity and reduces that outward pressure, another branch will expand to fill the void. Like water, governmental power 'expands where it meets no check from other sources of authority'.[35]

Gillian Metzger argued recently that bureaucracy is essential for constraining presidential power.[36] Federal agencies combine expert, professional, civil service personnel with multiple oversight and accountability mechanisms, public participation and procedural requirements.[37] That complexity makes them 'the key to an accountable, constrained, and effective executive branch'.[38] A necessary corollary to Metzger's argument is that without functioning agencies, the executive branch would be less accountable, constrained and effective.[39]

In short, if agencies cannot make policy in a timely fashion, the President will. Presidential policymaking, however, entails less transparency, public participation and accountability than agency rulemaking. The President's actions often are insulated from judicial review.[40] A plaintiff may challenge a federal agency's action under the APA.[41] In 1992, however, the

---

[32] Farber, 'Presidential Administration Under Trump' (n 18) 23. Other motivations for the President to act unilaterally include 'paying political debts, demonstrating action for a constituency, responding to political adversaries, or sending political signals': PJ Cooper, *By Order of the President: The Use and Abuse of Executive Direct Action*, 2nd edn (Lawrence, KS, University Press of Kansas, 2014) 66.

[33] Cooper, *By Order of the President* (n 32) 85.

[34] *INS v Chadha* 462 US 919, 951 (1983).

[35] TW Merrill, 'Presidential Administration and the Traditions of Administrative Law' (2015) 115 *Columbia Law Review* 1953, 1976; see also S Issacharoff and PS Karlan, 'The Hydraulics of Campaign Finance Reform' (1999) 77 *Texas Law Review* 1705, 1708.

[36] Metzger, 'Foreword: 1930s Redux: The Administrative State Under Siege' (n 9) 7, 51.

[37] ibid 72, 78–87.

[38] ibid 72.

[39] Jon Michaels propounds a theory of administrative separation of powers: presidentially appointed agency heads, civil servants and members of the public work with and against each other and the three constitutional branches of government, making the federal bureaucracy 'a self-regulating, constitutionally sound ecosystem unto itself': JD Michaels, 'Of Constitutional Custodians and Regulatory Rivals: An Account of the Old and New Separation of Powers' (2016) 91 *New York University Law Review* 227, 232. Interference by one of the constitutional branches disturbs that balance and may inspire civil servants and the public might to team up against it: ibid 259, 268. Specifically, 'presidential efforts to direct a particular agency result … directly weaken the administrative separation of powers': ibid 269.

[40] CA Bradley and TW Morrison, 'Presidential Power, Historical Practice, and Legal Constraint' (2013) 113 *Columbia Law Review* 1097, 1111 ('The bottom line is that many issues of presidential power are resolved, if at all, outside the courts').

[41] 5 US Code, s 702 ('A person suffering legal wrong because of agency action, or adversely affected or aggrieved by agency action within the meaning of a relevant statute, is entitled to judicial review thereof').

Supreme Court held that the President is not an 'agency' under the APA.[42] Rather than suing the President directly, then, plaintiffs typically challenge the agency's implementation of the President's order.

Even where a claim against the President himself is available, the courts' review is quite deferential. For example, in the State of Hawaii's suit challenging President Trump's proclamation restricting entry into the US from eight foreign states, the Supreme Court assumed without deciding that judicial review was available, but went on to hold that the proclamation violated neither the relevant statute nor the Establishment Clause of US Constitution.[43]

Moreover, because the President is not constrained by the APA, he need not solicit input from effected interests to hone his policy,[44] and he is not subject to the Freedom of Information Act, which allows public access to many government records.[45] Finally, unlike agency officers, the President can only be removed from office in quadrennial elections, through impeachment,[46] or by the written declaration of the Vice President and a majority of the President's principal officers that he is 'unable to discharge the powers and duties of his office'.[47]

III. Agency Inertia

The Administrative Procedure Act of 1946 fills in the gaps in the US Constitution regarding agency procedure and judicial review of agency action. It has effectively become the constitution for the fourth branch of the US Government.[48] It took many years of deliberation, discussion and compromise for Congress to pass the APA, which it did unanimously, in a form that President Truman would endorse.[49]

A brief history of the APA will set the stage.[50] In 1933, Franklin Delano Roosevelt became President and kicked off the New Deal, which entailed a vast expansion of the US Government to combat the Great Depression. At the same time, fascism was taking hold in Europe, and government agencies were tools of those administrations. Many people in the US feared that President Roosevelt would go down the same road.[51] The desire to avoid

---

[42] *Franklin v Massachusetts*, 505 US 788 (1992).
[43] *Trump v Hawaii*, 138 Supreme Court 2392 (2018).
[44] See 5 US Code, s 553 (requiring agencies to seek and consider public comments before publishing final rules).
[45] 5 US Code, s 552(f)(1).
[46] US Constitution, Art I, ss 2 and 3. Removal through impeachment requires a majority vote in the House of Representatives followed by a trial and conviction by a supermajority in the Senate.
[47] US Constitution, amendment XXV.
[48] See KE Kovacs, 'Superstatute Theory and Administrative Common Law' (2015) 90 *Indiana Law Journal* 1207, 1208.
[49] See GB Shepherd, 'Fierce Compromise: The Administrative Procedure Act Emerges from New Deal Politics' (1996) 90 *Northwestern University Law Review* 1557. A Bill becomes law only if the President signs it or Congress overrides his veto with a supermajority of both houses: US Constitution, Art I, s 7.
[50] For a more complete history of the APA, see Shepherd, 'Fierce Compromise' (n 49); and KE Kovacs, 'Rules About Rulemaking and the Rise of the Unitary Executive' (2018) 70 *Administrative Law Review* 515, 519–33.
[51] See RE Schiller, 'Reining in the Administrative State: World War II and the Decline of Expert Administration' in DR Ernst and V Jews (eds), *Total War and the Law: The American Home Front in World War II* (Westport, CT, Praeger, 2002) 188; see also RE Schiller, 'Free Speech and Expertise: Administrative Censorship and the Birth of the Modern First Amendment' (2000) 86 *Virginia Law Review* 1, 77.

totalitarianism became one of the driving forces behind the conservative drive for administrative reform.[52] During World War II, the federal bureaucracy expanded further and increasingly affected people's everyday lives through rationing and price controls. The belief that administrative agencies could pave the way for totalitarianism went mainstream.[53] That concern infused the entire debate on the APA from 1933 until its passage in 1946.

That deliberation underlying the APA was unusually robust and public. The historic record includes numerous public hearings, committee reports and floor debates, as well as a lengthy report from a bipartisan committee President Roosevelt asked the Attorney General to form.[54] Members of Congress conferred regularly not just with dozens of federal agencies, but also with state and local governments and bar associations, the American Bar Association, chambers of commerce, law firms, companies, trade associations, lawyers, businessmen, engineers, consultants and laypersons.[55]

When Congress first codified requirements for agency policymaking in the APA, it agreed on a process for rulemaking that was simple and left much to agency discretion.[56] When an agency proposes a rule, it must publish a notice including the time, place and nature of any public proceedings; the authority for the proposed rule; and 'either the terms or substance of the proposed rule or a description of the subjects and issues involved'.[57] Any interested person may submit comments on the proposal in writing, and the agency may allow oral presentations as well. The agency then must consider 'all relevant matter presented' and 'incorporate in any rules adopted a concise general statement of their basis and purpose'.[58] This process is known as 'notice-and-comment rulemaking'.

Despite that unanimous agreement in 1946, agency policymaking in the US has become increasingly difficult.[59] Congress has piled requirements for rulemaking on agencies without providing adequate resources to meet those requirements. Agencies must examine the potential impacts of their proposals on the environment and on small businesses; minimise the burden of paperwork; and analyse the financial impact on state, local and tribal governments,[60] among many other mandates.[61]

The President also has piled on requirements for rulemaking. Most notably, Executive Order 12,866, signed by President Clinton in 1993, requires agencies to send their proposed rules, some of which must be accompanied by a cost–benefit analysis, to the Executive Office of the President for review. Agencies must retrospectively review rules as well to determine

---

[52] See Kovacs, 'Rules About Rulemaking and the Rise of the Unitary Executive' (n 50) 520–21.
[53] ibid 528.
[54] Committee on Administrative Procedure, *Administrative Procedure in Government Agencies*, Senate Document Number 77-8 (1941) 103.
[55] KE Kovacs, 'A Day in the Life of an Administrative Law Nerd' *Notice & Comment* (29 October 2018), available at yalejreg.com/nc/a-day-in-the-life-of-an-administrative-law-nerd-by-kathryn-e-kovacs/.
[56] See Kovacs, 'Rules About Rulemaking and the Rise of the Unitary Executive' (n 50) 528–31.
[57] Administrative Procedure Act, Public Law Number 79-404 § 4, 60 Statutes at Large 237 (1946), codified at 5 US Code, s 553(b).
[58] 5 US Code, s 553(c).
[59] US Government agencies also may make policy through case-by-case adjudication: *SEC v Chenery Corp*, 332 US 194, 209 (1947).
[60] JS Lubbers, *A Guide to Federal Agency Rulemaking*, 5th edn (Chicago, IL, American Bar Association, 2012) 130–71.
[61] M Seidenfeld, 'A Table of Requirements for Federal Administrative Rulemaking' (2000) 27 *Florida State Law Review* 533.

which may be modified or repealed.[62] In the Trump Administration, agencies must repeal two rules for every one they promulgate.[63]

The courts have added to the burden of rulemaking as well. In the 1960s and 1970s, Congress enacted statutes that gave agencies the authority to issue rules that could have an enormous impact on the economy and on people's lives. The courts responded to that development with legal doctrines that they believed would support judicial review of agency actions and enhance accountability, fairness and accuracy in agency rulemaking.[64] For example, agency actions are now subject to so-called 'hard look' review: the Supreme Court moved away from its traditional deference to agency determinations and instead subjected them to 'thorough, probing, in-depth' review.[65] In addition, the Supreme Court opened the door for challenges to rules before the agency seeks to enforce them; previously, rules would be challenged in enforcement actions initiated by the agency.[66] Moreover, the courts must review agency actions based on the agency's contemporaneous explanation for its decision, not on a *post-hoc* justification.[67]

Those doctrines necessitated changes to the rulemaking process. To enable hard-look review before enforcement, the courts required agencies to keep a record of their rulemaking processes and provide an elaborate explanation for the final rule, including a discussion of why it rejected alternatives and reacted to policy issues the way it did, as well as a response to all significant comments on the proposed rule.[68] Courts also require agencies, when giving notice of a proposed rule, to include in the notice the information the agency considered in drafting the rule[69] and to document *ex parte* contacts during the rulemaking process.[70]

While these myriad rules about rulemaking were well-intentioned to maintain a proper balance of power in the US Government, ensure transparency and public participation, and advance other laudable goals, they have made it difficult for agencies to publish rules in a timely and efficient manner. Rulemaking has become 'a complex, time-consuming, resource-intensive procedural maze'.[71] None of the judicial rules about rulemaking appears

---

[62] Executive Order 13,563 (2011).

[63] Executive Order 13,771 (2017); see also Executive Office of the President, *Guidance Implementing Executive Order 13771* (5 April 2017), available at www.whitehouse.gov/sites/whitehouse.gov/files/omb/memoranda/2017/M-17-21-OMB.pdf (this Order was challenged promptly). See BCE Dooling, 'Update: Litigation Challenging Trump's Regulatory "Two-for-One" EO' *Notice & Comment* (4 September 2018), available at yalejreg.com/nc/update-litigation-challenging-trumps-regulatory-two-for-one-eo/.

[64] Kovacs, 'Rules About Rulemaking and the Rise of the Unitary Executive' (n 50) 549–50.

[65] *Citizens to Preserve Overton Park v Volpe*, 401 US 402, 415 (1971).

[66] RJ Pierce, Jr, 'Rulemaking and the Administrative Procedure Act' (1996) 32 *Tulsa Law Journal* 185, 192; PR Verkuil, 'Judicial Review of Informal Rulemaking' (1974) 60 *Virginia Law Review* 185, 198, 205.

[67] *Motor Vehicles Manufacturers Ass'n v State Farm Mutual Automobile Insurance Co*, 463 US 29, 43, 50 (applying *SEC v Chenery Corp* (n 59), to notice-and-comment rulemaking).

[68] Lubbers, *A Guide to Federal Agency Rulemaking* (n 60) 287, 341; see also Section of Administrative Law and Regulatory Practice, *A Blackletter Statement of Federal Administrative Law*, 2nd edn (Chicago, IL, American Bar Association, 2013) 28 (explaining that the rulemaking record includes all notices, materials the agency relied on and public comments).

[69] Lubbers, *A Guide to Federal Agency Rulemaking* (n 60) 277.

[70] JM Beermann and G Lawson, 'Reprocessing *Vermont Yankee*' (2007) 75 *George Washington Law Review* 856, 885.

[71] R Murphy, 'Enhancing the Role of Public Interest Organizations in Rulemaking Via Pre-Notice Transparency' (2012) 47 *Wake Forest Law Review* 681, 687–88; see also TO McGarity, 'Some Thoughts on "Deossifying" the Rulemaking Process' (1992) 41 *Duke Law Journal* 1385, 1400–01; AL Nielson, 'Sticky Regulations' (2018) 85 *University of Chicago Law Review* 85, 89; RJ Pierce, Jr, 'Rulemaking Ossification Is Real: A Response to Testing the Ossification Thesis' (2012) 80 *George Washington Law Review* 1493, 1494.

to be all that burdensome standing alone, but taken together they increase the difficulty of rulemaking considerably. In particular, writing preambles to rules has become increasingly onerous, given the need to explain rules in more depth and respond to a rising number of public comments.[72] Creating a rulemaking record requires staff time and external contractors,[73] and all of the judicial rules about rulemaking increase the risk of litigation, which also demands agency resources.[74]

Rulemaking is now sufficiently difficult that agencies avoid it and presidents do not rely on it. Thus, agencies have become increasingly unable to respond to changing circumstances and elections.[75] At the same time, congressional policymaking also has atrophied, leaving a power vacuum for the President to fill.

IV. The Trouble With Judicially-created Rules about Rulemaking

A. Conflict with Precedent

The judicially-created rules about rulemaking are particularly problematic for a number of reasons. First, the judicially-imposed requirements for rulemaking are contrary to Supreme Court precedent. In *Vermont Yankee Nuclear Power Corp v NRDC*, the Supreme Court held that courts may not impose procedural requirements on rulemaking beyond those codified in the APA, unless the Constitution requires it.[76] Leaving procedure to agency discretion, the Court said, was not only consistent with Congress's intent, but also normatively preferable because it would make judicial review less subjective.[77]

Yet each of the judicial rules about rulemaking highlighted in the previous section is directly contrary to the text and history of the APA. Congress deliberated about whether to require agencies to keep a record in rulemakings and decided not to require such records in notice-and-comment rulemaking. Rulemaking records are required only when another

---

[72] See McGarity, 'Some Thoughts on "Deossifying" the Rulemaking Process' (n 71) 1400; Nielson, 'Sticky Regulations' (n 71) 11. Ironically, lengthy and dense preambles are less accessible to the public: AA Webley, 'Seeing through a Preamble, Darkly: Administrative Verbosity in an Age of Populism and "Fake News"' (2018) 70 *Administrative Law Review* 1, 10.
[73] See PR Verkuil, 'The Wait Is Over: *Chevron* as the Stealth *Vermont Yankee* II' (2007) 75 *George Washington Law Review* 921, 928: 'The use of consultants to prepare rules for review has become a common practice.'
[74] See McGarity, 'Some Thoughts on "Deossifying" the Rulemaking Process' (n 71) 1400.
[75] Kovacs, 'Rules About Rulemaking and the Rise of the Unitary Executive' (n 50) 554. The courts have invalidated many of the Trump Administration's rushed policy changes. See, eg, *Natural Resources Defense Council v National Highway Traffic Safety Administration*, No 17-2780 (2d Cir, 23 April 2018); *Clean Air Council v Pruitt*, 862 F 3d 1, 4 (DC Cir, 2017); *Pineros y Campesinos Unidos del Noroeste v Pruitt*, 293 F Supp 3d 1062 (ND Cal, 2018); *California v Bureau of Land Management*, 286 F Supp 3d 1054 (ND Cal, 2018); *Natural Resources Defense Council, Inc v Perry*, No 17-CV-03404-VC, 2018 WL 922032 (ND Cal, 15 February 2018).
[76] *Vermont Yankee Nuclear Power Corp v NRDC* 435 US 519, 524, 542 (1978).
[77] ibid 546: 'If courts continually review agency proceedings to determine whether the agency employed procedures which were, in the court's opinion, perfectly tailored to reach what the court perceives to be the "best" or "correct" result, judicial review would be totally unpredictable.' See generally KE Kovacs, 'Pixelating Administrative Common Law in *Perez v Mortgage Bankers Association*' (2015) 125 *Yale Law Journal Forum* 31.

statute requires the rulemaking to be 'on the record'.[78] Such so-called 'formal' rulemakings must adhere to a host of other requirements that resemble a full trial.[79] For example, in formal rulemakings, agencies may not rely on *ex parte* communications but must limit their consideration to the public record.[80] Prohibiting *ex parte* communications in notice-and-comment rulemaking exceeds the terms of the statute.[81]

Similarly, Congress decided to require a notice of a proposed rulemaking to include 'either the terms or substance of the proposed rule or a description of the subjects or issues involved'.[82] Requiring agencies to include information they considered in drafting a proposed rule exceeds the terms of the statute.[83] Finally, the APA requires agencies to provide 'a concise general statement' of each rule's 'basis and purpose'.[84] Pre-enforcement judicial review of rules necessitates far more robust explanations than Congress judged would be sufficient.[85]

B. Structural Concerns

In the US, courts often exceed the terms of statutes, bending and stretching them to keep up with new and changing circumstances.[86] The APA, in particular, has long been considered a 'common law statute'.[87] Congress has not updated the law significantly since 1976; hence few people complain when the courts keep the law in step with changing times.[88] While 'dynamic' statutory interpretations are often criticised,[89] in administrative law they are typically accepted, if not welcomed.[90]

That traditional view extends back to 1946. As already mentioned, the APA reflects a compromise between liberals and conservatives. Though the Act passed unanimously, neither side was fully satisfied. Thus, after President Truman signed the APA, the two sides tried to influence the courts' view of the law. Conservatives pitched the APA as imposing new constraints on agencies. Liberals sold it as restating pre-existing common law. For the

---

[78] 5 US Code, s 553(c); see also Kovacs, 'Rules About Rulemaking and the Rise of the Unitary Executive' (n 50) 537.

[79] See 5 US Code, ss 556 and 557.

[80] 5 US Code, s 557(d)(1).

[81] See Beermann and Lawson, 'Reprocessing *Vermont Yankee*' (n 70) 883–88.

[82] 5 US Code, s 553.

[83] *American Radio Relay League v FCC*, 524 F3d 227, 246 (DC Cir, 2008) (Kavanaugh J concurring in part and dissenting in part: 'One searches the text of APA § 553 in vain for a requirement that an agency disclose other agency information as part of the notice or later in the rulemaking process'). See also Beermann and Lawson, 'Reprocessing *Vermont Yankee*' (n 70) 894–95.

[84] 5 US Code, s 553(c).

[85] See Kovacs, 'Rules About Rulemaking and the Rise of the Unitary Executive' (n 50) 543.

[86] See WN Eskridge, Jr, *Dynamic Statutory Interpretation* (Cambridge, MA, Harvard, 1994); AJ Mikva and E Lane, *An Introduction to Statutory Interpretation and the Legislative Process* (New York, Aspen Law & Business, 1997); CR Sunstein, 'Interpreting Statutes in the Regulatory State' (1989) 103 *Harvard Law Review* 405, 426.

[87] See D Zaring, 'Rule by Reasonableness' (2011) 63 *Administrative Law Review* 525, 536.

[88] But see, eg, JF Duffy, 'Administrative Common Law in Judicial Review' (1998) 77 *Texas Law Review* 113; Kovacs, 'Superstatute Theory and Administrative Common Law' (n 48).

[89] eg A Scalia and BA Garner, *Reading Law: The Interpretation of Legal Texts* (St Paul, MN, Thomson/West, 2012).

[90] See, eg, KC Davis, *Administrative Law Treatise*, 2nd edn (San Diego, CA, KC Davis Publishing Company, 1978) ss 2.17, 2.18, 6.37, 7.19, 14.10; GE Metzger, 'Ordinary Administrative Law as Constitutional Common Law' (2010) 110 *Columbia Law Review* 479.

most part, the liberals won the debate.[91] Courts not only interpret the terms of the APA loosely, but they also continue to apply doctrines that contradict the statute or exceed its boundaries entirely.[92]

In my view, and as I have explicated fully elsewhere,[93] that method of interpretation, while appropriate in other contexts, is not appropriate in US administrative law. Adhering to the terms of the APA is particularly important because it grew out of an epic legislative battle spanning 17 years and codified one of the most monumental legislative compromises of the twentieth century. No single view of the administrative state prevailed. Instead, Congress balanced multiple views and values: 'the APA settlement reflects a particular effort to balance a range of variables, including stability, constraints on executive power, accountability, and the need for expedition and energy – for vigorous government'.[94] That legislative compromise mandates respect from the courts.[95] Failure to focus on the terms of the statute, as well as its context and history, risks undermining the legislative bargain.[96]

The deep deliberation underlying the APA also warrants judicial respect. Courts' discounting of the results of civic republican discourse in the most democratically accountable branch of government raises serious concerns. First, while courts certainly deliberate, they do not involve the public in their deliberation: 'Courts have neither the motivation nor the means to obtain information about the values of the general polity, on which civic republicanism's common good depends'.[97] William Eskridge and John Ferejohn established that, when a statute arises from unusually robust public deliberation and becomes entrenched in our law, the courts should take 'the deliberative process seriously, as having significant normative force,' and defer to 'the deliberated views of Congress and the President'.[98] Congressional deliberation is often flawed or entirely absent. When Congress does deliberate in a meaningful way, as it did with the APA, the courts should pay close attention to the results of that process.[99]

Second, the US Constitution assigns to the Congress the duty to make policy decisions so as to avoid tyranny, safeguard liberty and ensure political accountability.[100] Whenever a court makes a policy decision, instead of simply interpreting and applying the law, separation of powers concerns arise.[101]

---

[91] See KE Kovacs, 'A History of the Military Authority Exception in the APA' (2010) 62 *Administrative Law Review* 673, 706–07.
[92] See Kovacs, 'Superstatute Theory and Administrative Common Law' (n 48) 1208.
[93] ibid.
[94] CR Sunstein and A Vermeule, 'The New Coke: On the Plural Aims of Administrative Law' (2015) 2015 *Supreme Court Review* 41, 82.
[95] Federal judges in the US enjoy life tenure: US Constitution, Art III, s 1.
[96] See WN Eskridge, Jr, 'No Frills Textualism' (2006) 119 *Harvard Law Review* 2041, 2053; JF Manning, 'Second-Generation Textualism' (2010) 98 *California Law Review* 1287, 1290; VF Nourse, 'A Decision Theory of Statutory Interpretation: Legislative History by the Rules' (2012) 122 *Yale Law Journal* 70, 119.
[97] M Seidenfeld, 'A Civic Republican Justification for the Bureaucratic State' (1992) 105 *Harvard Law Review* 1511, 1543.
[98] WN Eskridge, Jr and J Ferejohn, *A Republic of Statutes: The New American Constitution* (New Haven, CT, Yale University Press, 2010) 435–36.
[99] See Kovacs, 'Superstatute Theory and Administrative Common Law' (n 48) 1250–54; see also G Staszewski, 'Statutory Interpretation as Contestatory Democracy' (2013) 55 *William and Mary Law Review* 221, 252.
[100] See KE Kovacs, 'Scalia's Bargain' (2016) 77 *Ohio State Law Journal* 1155, 1191.
[101] See TW Merrill, 'The Common Law Powers of Federal Courts' (1985) 52 *University of Chicago Law Review* 1, 23, 27.

Third, and relatedly, court decisions that do not respect the terms of the APA lack political accountability and thus democratic legitimacy.[102] The separation of powers and political-accountability objections must answer to current legal doctrine, which recognises that courts often 'create law'.[103] Those concerns are particularly salient, however, in this context where the statute at issue resulted from a lengthy and deep debate between Congress, the Executive Branch and the public. The APA's text concluded that debate. The courts' decisions contradicting that text provide particularly noteworthy examples of the unelected judiciary trespassing on the representative legislature's territory.[104]

C. Unanticipated Consequences

Finally, the judicially-created rules about rulemaking are problematic because they yield unanticipated consequences. Courts consider solely the views of the parties to a particular case, which typically includes only one federal agency. They do not have the institutional capacity to weigh competing policy considerations or predict the results of their decisions. Congress, on the other hand, can consider the views and insights of multiple parties and debate numerous proposals simultaneously.[105] Therefore, Congress is better suited than the courts to determine which rules of administrative procedure will be best.[106] In the APA, Congress balanced multiple values: 'The courts have no constitutional authority to revise that judgment and no epistemic basis for thinking they can make a better one.'[107]

The judicially-created rules about rulemaking have had many consequences that the courts did not anticipate. Among them is the fomenting of authoritarianism, already described. Notably, Congress recognised the possibility that a growing administrative state might undermine the US's representative democracy when it started contemplating the APA in the 1930s. As explained, Congress designed the APA to avoid the danger that agencies would become tools of a dictatorial president.[108] Among other things, it provided that agencies would be able to flesh out statutes in rules following a quite simple procedure. Congress recognised that agency rulemaking gives regulated entities and the public notice of the agency's position and avoids the need for courts to fill the gaps that Congress leaves in statutes.[109] The federal courts should not disturb the careful balance the APA achieved.

That said, the APA, the fundamental charter for the US's vast federal bureaucracy, has not been updated significantly in 40 years.[110] Congress has often considered updating the statute, but it has not had the political wherewithal to pass an amendment. Many academics

---

[102] ibid 24–25, 27.
[103] GE Metzger, 'Foreword: Embracing Administrative Common Law' (2012) 80 *George Washington Law Review* 1293, 1347–48.
[104] Kovacs, 'Superstatute Theory and Administrative Common Law' (n 48) 1255–57; see also N Bagley, 'The Puzzling Presumption of Reviewability' (2014) 127 *Harvard Law Review* 1285, 1320–21.
[105] See Bagley, 'The Puzzling Presumption of Reviewability' (n 104) 1322.
[106] Kovacs, 'Scalia's Bargain' (n 100) 1193.
[107] Bagley, 'The Puzzling Presumption of Reviewability' (n 104) 1330.
[108] See text accompanying nn 50–55.
[109] See, eg, Senate Report 76-442 (1939) 11.
[110] See CJ Walker, 'Modernizing the Administrative Procedure Act' (2017) 69 *Administrative Law Review* 629, 635.

thank the courts for intervening to keep the APA up to date.[111] The courts' interventions, however, enable Congress's dysfunction. It is past time for Congress to do its job and for the courts to encourage that.

V. Conclusion

Avoiding authoritarianism in the US requires agencies that are empowered to be effective partners in governance. The federal courts must ensure that agencies play by the rules of the APA, but they should take a step back and recognise that every time they create a new rule of administrative procedure, that rule may have consequences that the courts cannot anticipate. Congress should enable agencies to do their jobs and not burden them beyond their capacity. Clearly, removing some of the obstacles to efficient and effective agency rulemaking will not solve all of the US Government's problems and will not reverse the trend toward authoritarianism. But it is a step in the right direction. Without effective agency policymaking, we cannot avoid falling into the trap the APA was designed to avoid.

---

[111] eg Metzger, 'Ordinary Administrative Law as Constitutional Common Law' (n 90).

20
Non-fettering, Legitimate Expectations and Consistency of Policy: Separate Compartments or Single Principle?

SHONA WILSON STARK*

In *Nadarajah*, Sir John Laws said 'it is all too easy to make separate compartments of the law where, in truth, different applications represent a single principle or at least interlocking principles'.[1] In this chapter, I argue that separate compartments (ie separate grounds of review) can play a useful function, even where those grounds share certain underlying principles. The particular focus of my inquiry is: (i) how to distinguish meaningfully between the emergent consistency of policy ground of review confirmed in *Mandalia*[2] (although called into question in *Gallaher*)[3] and its progenitor, legitimate expectations; and (ii) how to reconcile any ostensible tension between those grounds of review on the one hand and the non-fettering principle on the other. Such tension may be perceived because whereas non-fettering allows decision-makers to act with considerable freedom, legitimate expectations and consistency of policy may bind them to their decisions or policies.

After comparative neglect, the apparent non-fettering/consistency paradox has been subjected to increasing academic scrutiny. In 2017, Adam Perry wrote in defence of the non-fettering principle.[4] Perry's defence is based primarily on flexible policies' ability to afford the claimant a hearing – something he argues rigid policies do not allow. Later that same year, Aileen McHarg, in contrast, advocated abandoning the non-fettering principle, which she sees as being in 'considerable tension' with the modern drive for greater consistency.[5]

---

*I am grateful to participants in the Third Biennial Public Law Conference, *The Frontiers of Public Law*, Melbourne Law School, July 2018, and in the Centre for Public Law Seminar Series, October 2018, for useful discussions. My particular thanks to Joanna Bell, Mark Elliott and Alison Young for their extremely helpful comments on earlier drafts of this chapter.

[1] *R (on the application of Nadarajah and Abdi) v Secretary of State for the Home Department* [2005] EWCA Civ 1363, [49].
[2] *Mandalia v Secretary of State for the Home Department* [2015] 1 WLR 4546.
[3] *R (on the application of Gallaher Group Ltd) v Competition and Markets Authority* [2019] AC 96.
[4] A Perry, 'The Flexibility Rule in Administrative Law' (2017) 76 *CLJ* 375.
[5] A McHarg, 'Administrative Discretion, Administrative Rule-making, and Judicial Review' (2017) 70 *Current Legal Problems* 267, 291.

In this chapter, I propose a third option. As others have contended, non-fettering and consistency are in fact two sides of the same coin.[6] My argument is that this contention can survive developments such as *Mandalia*. In order to substantiate this argument, I first demonstrate that the non-fettering principle continues to have a vital place in the judicial review toolbox, distinct from substantive review. I then show how legitimate expectations and consistency of policy can be meaningfully distinguished. Calls have been made for legitimate expectations to be restricted to cases where direct promises have been made to the claimant.[7] If such calls were heeded, that ground of review would be better able to perform a distinct function, separate from cases of changes of, or departures from, policy where claimant knowledge is less relevant. I then demonstrate how both of those grounds of review can exist alongside the non-fettering principle, showing that consistency is not a novel innovation but has co-existed with non-fettering for some time as part of rationality review. I then analyse how the courts can decide whether a decision-maker has acted properly, assessing the different factors that indicate whether application of, or departure from, a policy is warranted. This analysis demonstrates that the central principle underpinning this area of law is that policies should be applied unless there is good reason to depart from them. At the same time as demonstrating the coherence of non-fettering, legitimate expectations and consistency inter se, I argue that it is useful to separate these grounds of review, and to carve them out from broader categories such as unfairness or unreasonableness. Those separate compartments allow the courts' assessments to operate with optimum transparency, but also send clearer messages to decision-makers about how they are expected to act.

I. The Non-fettering Principle

One potential advantage of the well-established non-fettering principle is that it should encourage all features of every individual case to be taken into account.[8] Initially, therefore, courts were apparently sceptical of policies because 'discretion must be brought to bear on every case'.[9] In law, parties have to be treated alike, but administrators were traditionally thought to act in a more individualised manner, looking at each case on its merits and not slavishly aiming for consistency.[10] The non-fettering principle also allows decision-makers to replace an existing policy with a new policy if that seems necessary or desirable for good administration.

The non-fettering principle appears, however, to be threatened by developments around it. The erosion of the judicial/administrative dichotomy has made it less clear why administrators should not also strive for consistency and predictability.[11] Furthermore, the

---

[6] DJ Galligan, 'The Nature and Function of Policies Within Discretionary Power' [1976] *PL* 332; C Hilson, 'Policies, the Non-fetter Principle and the Principle of Substantive Legitimate Expectations: Between a Rock and a Hard Place?' [2006] *Judicial Review* 289.

[7] R Clayton, 'Legitimate Expectations, Policy, and the Principle of Consistency' (2003) 62 *CLJ* 93, 95; JNE Varuhas, 'In Search of a Doctrine: Mapping the Law of Legitimate Expectations' in M Groves and G Weeks (eds), *Legitimate Expectations in the Common Law World* (Oxford, Hart Publishing, 2017) 40.

[8] C Hilson, 'Judicial Review, Policies and the Fettering of Discretion' [2002] *PL* 111, 113.

[9] HWR Wade and CF Forsyth, *Administrative Law*, 11th edn (Oxford, Oxford University Press, 2014) 272.

[10] ibid.

[11] *British Oxygen Co Ltd v Minister of Technology* [1971] AC 610, 620.

emergence of grounds of review such as legitimate expectations and consistency of policy give administrators less freedom to depart from, or change, their policies than they enjoyed in the past. And the sheer size of the modern administrative state makes individual consideration seem more like a drawback than a benefit.

In *British Oxygen*, Lord Reid set out the acid test for non-fettering, which may be viewed as a compromise between those benefits and drawbacks – a policy can be devised, but the decision-maker must be willing to listen to someone with something new to say and to depart from the policy if appropriate. In accordance with the non-fettering principle, due consideration had in this case been given to the appellants' claim – they just had not convinced the decision-maker that an exception should be made for them.

A. Non-fettering and Common Law Powers

My view is that, despite developments around it, non-fettering continues to play an important role and should not be collapsed into substantive review as others have argued.[12] In order to substantiate that view, this section analyses judicial review of common law powers, to which the non-fettering rule does not traditionally apply, to show what we lose when non-fettering is off the table.

Policies that set out how common law powers will be exercised can be challenged as being irrational[13] or disproportionate.[14] The orthodox view has been that non-fettering does not apply to common law powers because, unlike statutory powers, 'there is no external originator who could have imposed any obligation to exercise them in one sense, rather than another. They are intrinsic to the Crown and it is for the Crown to determine whether and how to exercise them in its discretion.'[15] But, contrary to the prevailing judicial view, it does not automatically follow that '[t]here is no necessary implication that a blanket policy is inappropriate, or that there must always be room for exceptions, when a policy is formulated for the exercise of a prerogative power'.[16] A blanket policy may be unfair, and common law powers need to be exercised fairly.[17]

Traditionally, however, the non-fettering principle is thought to apply only to statutory powers. In *Elias*, for example, a common law compensation scheme for those who had been interned during the Japanese occupation of Hong Kong in 1941–45 could not be challenged on the ground that the decision-maker had fettered her discretion (by having a policy that those born abroad would not receive compensation). But non-statutory powers have to be exercised lawfully.[18] In this case, the criteria were held to be disproportionate and indirectly discriminatory. The same scheme had, however, passed a rationality test when no discrimination argument was advanced in *ABCIFER*.[19] Non-fettering therefore would provide a

---

[12] eg McHarg, 'Administrative Discretion' (n 5) 267.
[13] eg *R v Ministry of Defence, ex parte Smith* [1996] QB 517.
[14] eg *R (on the application of Elias) v Secretary of State for Defence* [2006] 1 WLR 3213.
[15] *R (on the application of Sandiford) v Secretary of State for Foreign and Commonwealth Affairs* [2014] 1 WLR 2697, [61].
[16] ibid [62].
[17] ibid [83].
[18] *Council of Civil Service Unions v Minister for the Civil Service* [1985] AC 374.
[19] *R (on the application of ABCIFER) v Secretary of State for Defence* [2003] QB 1397.

vital ground of review that is currently lacking for those who face the 'uphill struggle' of challenging a non-statutory scheme on rationality, as opposed to proportionality, grounds.[20]

One case, however, suggests both a relaxation of the rationality test and the application of the non-fettering principle to certain common law powers. *Adath Yisroel* concerned a coroner's policy that she would not prioritise any death on religious grounds (speedy burial of the dead being very important for the Muslim and Jewish faiths).[21] The Court found the policy to be irrational because it was discriminatory, which is perhaps unsurprising.[22] But the Court went on to say that the policy would have been irrational even without the discriminatory element, because it prevented any individual circumstances from being taken into account.[23] This extreme conclusion threatens to collapse non-fettering into rationality review. Strict policies have often passed the rationality test before,[24] and it is not necessarily irrational to apply a policy strictly. Indeed, it may be irrational *not* to apply certain policies strictly.[25] It may appear that non-fettering plays a less useful role where irrationality is applied robustly, or where proportionality can be applied. But rationality review should not be seen as being substitutable for non-fettering – as will be argued in this chapter, the latter plays a distinct and important role. Furthermore, it is evident that rationality itself is a 'highly malleable' concept that can produce unpredictable results.[26]

As Perry has argued, the good reasons for the non-fettering principle justify its application whatever the source of the power.[27] Those good reasons can benefit both the claimant (to challenge an overly rigid policy) and the decision-maker (to defend a well-thought-through policy, or a change of policy). Legitimate expectations can of course arise from the exercise of common law powers.[28] The offshoot, consistent application of policy, should apply to common law powers too.[29] And if consistency applies, so too should non-fettering, since it is its necessary corollary. To avoid unfairness (and common law powers must be exercised fairly) common law powers should be exercised consistently.[30] But since inflexible policies can also be unfair, the non-fettering principle must apply too.[31] Non-fettering and consistency are two sides of the same coin and thus cannot be severed.

B. Substantive Review and Non-fettering Distinguished

Non-fettering ought to remain distinct from substantive review. For one thing, non-fettering can serve a different purpose than substantive review. Substantive review will be appropriate

---

[20] ibid [87]. See also *Sandiford* (n 15) [62].
[21] *R (on the application of Adath Yisroel Burial Society and Cymerman) v HM Senior Coroner for Inner North London* [2019] QB 251.
[22] ibid [91].
[23] ibid [92].
[24] eg *Smith* (n 13); *Elias* (n 14).
[25] eg *Mandalia* (n 2). See section II.A.ii.
[26] M Elliott, 'Consistency as a Free-Standing Principle of Administrative Law?' Public Law for Everyone Blog (15 June 2018), available at https://publiclawforeveryone.com.
[27] Perry, 'The Flexibility Rule' (n 4) 386–87.
[28] *Sandiford* (n 15) [83].
[29] If it survives *Gallaher* (n 3): see section II.A.ii.
[30] *Sandiford* (n 15) [85].
[31] K Costello, 'The Scope of Application of the Rule Against Fettering in Administrative Law' (2015) 131 *LQR* 354, 357.

if a policy is so misguided, or based on an irrelevancy, that having a more flexible policy of the same nature will not do. In *Smith*, for example, a blanket policy banning gay men and lesbians from serving in the British military was rational under domestic law but held to be disproportionate by Strasbourg.[32] Non-fettering was not on the table since there was no statutory power being exercised; the policy concerned the exercise of the prerogative power of defence of the realm. But non-fettering would not have been an appropriate ground of review in any event. The tempering of a discriminatory policy such that exceptions could be made was not what the claimants sought.[33] Inflexibility was not what lay at the root of the claimants' objection to the policy.

On the other hand, it is arguable that *Elias*, discussed in section I.A, concerned an overly rigid rather than an irrational policy.[34] For example, those born abroad may have been compensated for their internment by their birth country, and exceptions could have been made for those who were not. Non-fettering thus has the potential to be more deferential than substantive review. Either ground of review could be used to argue, for example, for the addition of a new exception to a policy – the absence of the exception could be seen as either irrational or as a fetter. But whereas non-fettering is always so limited, substantive review can strike at the very substance of a policy, rendering it unlawful.

Smith also shows that although challenging a policy on rationality grounds can be difficult, blanket policies are more likely to fail a proportionality assessment.[35] Indeed the European Court of Human Rights in *Smith* found the 'absolute and general character' of the policy to be 'striking'.[36] The rise of proportionality review may suggest that the non-fettering principle is less vital than it once was. But non-fettering still has an important role to play. For one thing, proportionality will not always apply, and we have seen that overly rigid policies may not necessarily be irrational. But the main point of distinction between non-fettering and substantive review is that non-fettering should encourage high standards of policy *making*, policy *changes* and policy *application*.

In terms of policy making, decision-makers who are under a duty to establish merely rational or proportionate policies have little guidance as to what constitutes 'good' policy. Those with a duty to formulate proportionate policies at least have to give careful thought to tailoring their policy in a way that avoids setting down any blanket rule, whereas the instruction that rationality sends to decision-makers is exceptionally vague. The non-fettering principle, by contrast, encourages detailed policies to be set out and reminds decision-makers about the importance of treating people as individuals. Making exceptions to policies runs the risk of inconsistency and arbitrariness. But if the policy itself sets out the circumstances in which exceptions will be made, it can mitigate that risk, as well as facilitating close consideration of the relevant issues and careful tailoring of the policy. Non-fettering can thus incentivise careful and nuanced policy formulation, as opposed to broad policies that may admit of more ad hoc exceptions. In turn, nuanced policies will be more likely to withstand judicial review on non-fettering grounds since they are indicative of a decision-maker's careful policy formulation and willingness to make exceptions.

---

[32] *Smith* (n 13); *Smith and Grady v United Kingdom* (2000) 29 EHRR 493.
[33] *Smith* (n 13) 525.
[34] See also *Sandiford* (n 15).
[35] See also *R v Secretary of State for the Home Department, ex parte Simms* [2000] 2 AC 115; *R (on the application of Daly) v Secretary of State for the Home Department* [2001] 2 AC 532.
[36] *Smith and Grady v United Kingdom* (n 32) [93].

Decision-makers must be allowed to change their policies, and non-fettering allows them this freedom. As we shall see below, only in rare cases will individuals be entitled to argue for anything but the current policy to be applied to them when the unfairness to them outweighs the administrator's freedom. Wild fluctuations in policy are, however, undesirable. They indicate potentially poor administration, and threaten rule-of-law values such as clarity and certainty. Thus it is important for decision-makers to be clear that consistency is also an important value to be balanced against non-fettering.

In terms of application of policies, non-fettering again plays an important role. Failure to apply a policy may be irrational, but we can be clearer on what precise species of irrationality this is – namely, that the decision-maker has reneged on her own policy. Reneging on a policy risks treating claimant X inconsistently from claimant Y. Where, however, there is good reason to treat X and Y differently, an exception should be considered. Rationality review provides little protection for the claimant who seeks departure from, rather than adherence to, the policy. As we have seen, overly rigid policies may well be rational,[37] and application of a rational policy may only rarely be irrational. Non-fettering provides for ongoing reconsideration of policies, because decision-makers have a constant duty to consider making an exception to their policy. The non-fettering principle should encourage better policy making, but a policy may still be imperfect. Consideration of an individual's case might reveal something that had not been considered. An exception to the policy may be made, and perhaps that exception might lead to the policy's being revised (or even abandoned).[38] In that way, making an exception can in fact be reconciled with consistency, because the same exception will then be made in similar, future cases. Proportionality, where it applies, may play a similar reconsideration role, but it does not *necessitate* it, nor does it send a clear instruction about what optimal policy application entails. Decision-makers operating under the shadow of proportionality review may disapply or revise a policy where its application seems disproportionate. But exceptions can be made under non-fettering where application of the policy would be unfair, not just where it would be disproportionate. It is only through invocations of fairness (especially compared to mere rationality) that there can be 'a measure of external justice between citizen and state'.[39] The imbalance of power between citizen and state is often at its greatest in cases concerning policies that cover, for example, asylum seekers,[40] those seeking allocation of benefits or benefits in kind,[41] or those otherwise in a vulnerable position with fundamental rights at stake.[42] Non-fettering is therefore an important way to protect the most vulnerable from being excluded from very basic safety nets.

The Windrush scandal in the UK has given a good reason for retaining the non-fettering principle, albeit that it shows it is not working as one might hope. Indeed, the former Home Secretary, Amber Rudd, said in Parliament in 2018 'I am concerned that the Home

---

[37] Unless the reasoning in *Adath Yisroel* (n 21) takes root.

[38] Galligan, 'The Nature and Function of Policies' (n 6) 334.

[39] S Sedley, 'Policy and Law' in S Sedley, *Ashes and Sparks: Essays on Law and Justice* (Cambridge, Cambridge University Press, 2011) 261.

[40] P Reynolds, 'Legitimate Expectations and the Protection of Trust in Public Officials' [2011] *PL* 330, 334; eg *R (on the application of Rashid) v Secretary of State for the Home Department* [2005] EWCA Civ 744; *Nadarajah* (n 1).

[41] eg *R v Warwickshire County Council, ex parte Collymore* [1995] ELR 217; *Attorney-General ex rel Tilley v Wandsworth London Borough Council* [1981] 1 WLR 854.

[42] eg *Mandalia* (n 2), and the Windrush scandal.

Office has become too concerned with policy and strategy and sometimes loses sight of the individual.'[43] In this case, a policy to make the UK a 'hostile environment' for illegal immigrants was applied rigidly to those who could not produce the relevant documents, including those who came to the UK as British citizens when they were children and had no documents to produce, sometimes due to the destruction of their landing cards by the Home Office. Such decisions could, if nothing else, be irrational. But the non-fettering principle, properly used, could have provided greater protection against such decisions' being made in the first place by encouraging decision-makers to always be alert to the specific possibility of making an exception, rather than being under a vague duty to act rationally. The Windrush scandal suggests that non-fettering has fallen by the wayside as consistency has risen to prominence. As Galligan has said, policies in fact necessitate individual consideration to see if the policy should be departed from.[44] But this benefit could be lost without the non-fettering principle. For those reasons, Perry's thesis on this issue[45] is to be preferred to McHarg's proposed abolition of the doctrine. Non-fettering and consistency in fact complement one another to give us the general rule that a policy should be applied unless good reason is shown for departure.

II. Legitimate Expectations and Consistency of Policy

Since emerging 'out of [Lord Denning's] head' in the 1960s,[46] the doctrine of legitimate expectations has existed in apparent tension with the long-established non-fettering principle. Whereas non-fettering allows decision-makers to adjust, depart from or completely change their policies, the doctrine of legitimate expectations aims to hold them to their previous promises, policies or practices. In recent years, the apparent tension between the different grounds has been exacerbated by legitimate expectations' offshoot – the freestanding ground of consistent application of policy, although its continued existence is in question following *Gallaher*.

A. The Unaware Claimant

i. Legitimate Expectations: The Knowledge Requirement

Historically, it has been unclear whether a claimant could have a legitimate expectation where she was not aware of the policy that would otherwise give rise to the expectation. The Australian case of *Teoh* provided a turning point – although it was perceived by many to be a wrong turn.[47] The Court held that it was not necessary for a claimant to be aware of the source of the potential expectation in order for a legitimate expectation to arise.[48] McHugh J

---

[43] *Hansard*, HC Deb 16 April 2018, vol 639, col 28.
[44] Galligan, 'The Nature and Function of Policies' (n 6) 350.
[45] See also Costello, 'The Scope of Application of the Rule Against Fettering' (n 31) 357.
[46] *Schmidt v Secretary of State for Home Affairs* [1969] 2 Ch 149; CF Forsyth, 'The Provenance and Protection of Legitimate Expectations' (1988) 47 *CLJ* 238, 241.
[47] *Minister of State for Immigration and Ethnic Affairs v Ah Hin Teoh* (1995) 183 CLR 273.
[48] ibid [34] (Mason CJ and Deane J).

dissented strongly, arguing that a lack of knowledge requirement renders legitimate expectations 'a fiction'.[49]

Teoh was retreated from in *Lam*. In fact, in *Lam* the Court did not simply retreat by adding a knowledge requirement back into legitimate expectations, instead it collapsed the doctrine back into a general unfairness test.[50] Groves has stated that after a 'chequered' past, legitimate expectations has now 'passed into history' in Australia, having 'declined to the point of extinction'.[51] Retreating to unfairness is, however, a retrograde step, for one reason because someone who does not have knowledge of a policy will have a harder time demonstrating unfairness.[52] Thus we fall into the trap *Teoh* sought to avoid – disadvantaging the uninformed. Although it may be true that there has been more subjective unfairness to the claimant who knew of and relied on the policy, we are (or should be) concerned with something more than subjective unfairness in such cases. We should focus our attention on the decision-maker, assessing whether she ought to be allowed to renege on a policy, regardless of who saw it. This argument can be supported by using *Khan* as an example. A legitimate expectation had arisen from a circular issued to the claimant at an Advice Bureau, but the decision (as to whether the claimant could adopt his brother's child from Pakistan) was taken based on a different policy. The 'grossly misleading' circular[53] was 'positively cruel' in getting potential adoptive parents' hopes up.[54] But misleading circulars should not be published by public bodies because they indicate 'bad and grossly unfair administration',[55] regardless of who sees them. Routinely reneging from, or changing, policies could be indicative of bad administration, and in particular a need for more careful consideration of policy formulation in the first place.

In England, a similar approach to that in *Teoh* was taken in *Rashid*,[56] where the Court held that the unfairness was so great as to amount to an abuse of power given 'startling and prolonged' Home Office failures.[57] When unfairness 'leaps up from the page', the Court indicated that it would not hesitate to intervene.[58] It was therefore held that a legitimate expectation 'plainly' arose that the Minister would apply his policy, regardless of the claimant's lack of knowledge.[59] To demand knowledge from claimants would, the Court said, be 'grossly unfair'.[60] The Court noted, however, that the decision did not exactly sit comfortably within the legitimate expectations doctrine.[61] The decision was nevertheless rationalised on the basis that abuse of power was the 'root concept' from which legitimate expectations grew,[62] and because there had been an abuse of power in this case, intervention was justified.[63]

---

[49] ibid [31] (McHugh J dissenting).

[50] *Re Minister for Immigration and Multicultural Affairs, ex parte Lam* (2003) 214 CLR 1, [34] (Gleeson CJ).

[51] M Groves, 'Legitimate Expectations in Australia: Overtaken by Formalism and Pragmatism' in M Groves and G Weeks (eds), *Legitimate Expectations in the Common Law World* (Oxford, Hart Publishing, 2017) 319.

[52] M Groves, 'Treaties and Legitimate Expectations – The Rise and Fall of *Teoh* in Australia' [2010] *Judicial Review* 323, 333–34.

[53] *R v Secretary of State for the Home Department, ex parte Khan* [1984] 1 WLR 1337, 1343.

[54] ibid 1348.

[55] ibid.

[56] *Rashid* (n 40) does not cite *Teoh* (n 47).

[57] *Rashid* (n 40) [11], [13], [50], [53].

[58] ibid [23].

[59] ibid [25].

[60] ibid.

[61] ibid [26].

[62] ibid [28].

[63] ibid [34].

No explanation had been given for the policy's not being applied to the claimant; rather, the administrator had demonstrated 'flagrant and prolonged incompetence'.[64]

Rashid and Teoh have been heavily criticised on the basis that there is an 'inherent contradiction' in allowing unaware claimants to avail themselves of a doctrine designed to honour expectations.[65] Although citizens may frequently rely on rules of which they were earlier unaware, this particular doctrine is labelled according to 'expectations', so that relying on it where in fact no expectation arose is apparently 'artificial' and 'tenuous'.[66] The lack of knowledge requirement has been said to render a legitimate expectations ground of review 'a complete misnomer'.[67] Similarly, Varuhas has argued that it is 'perplexing' to talk of legitimate expectations without knowledge.[68] In his analysis of Rashid, Elliott argues that abuse of power allows for the modification of existing grounds of review where the circumstances are closely analogous to, but not quite within the remit of, an existing ground, but a 'super-added element of unfairness' justifies intervention over strict legalism.[69] In the Court's view, the level of unfairness in Rashid met that threshold. By contrast, a failure to apply a policy in ZK was not unlawful, because it was 'far removed from the cumulative errors' amounting to an abuse of power in Rashid.[70] Such cases prove Lord Carnwath's candid admission that the court intervenes if it thinks it should, adapting a ground of review if necessary, then trusting the academics to do some post hoc reasoning.[71] Unsurprisingly, Elliott does not endorse such an approach. He states that although abuse of power ensures a fair outcome, the Court went too far in Rashid, because the norms of the case were not consistent with the norms underpinning legitimate expectations.[72] He argues that the rationale for legitimate expectations is to honour the dashed hopes of people who have planned their lives by placing trust in governmental statements or practices.[73] There were no dashed hopes in Rashid.[74] In Rashid, the issue was one of equality of treatment (applying the same policy to the claimant that others in his situation had enjoyed), which is different from the norms underpinning legitimate expectations (which may in fact justify treating people differently).

But there is some normative connection between Rashid and legitimate expectations as commonly understood. This connection is not that the public generally have an 'expectation' that the Government will act lawfully and fairly. As others have argued, such a notion is very 'general and vague',[75] and indeed it underestimates the cynicism of much of the

---

[64] ibid [53].
[65] Groves, 'Treaties and Legitimate Expectations' (n 52) 335.
[66] ibid.
[67] Lam (n 50) [140] (Callinan J). See also Reynolds, 'Legitimate Expectations and the Protection of Trust' (n 40) 336.
[68] Varuhas, 'In Search of a Doctrine' (n 7) 30.
[69] M Elliott, 'Legitimate Expectation, Consistency and Abuse of Power: the Rashid Case' [2005] Judicial Review 281, 285.
[70] R (on the application of ZK) v Secretary of State for the Home Department [2007] EWCA Civ 615, [26]. The claimant also gave no explanation as to why the case was brought 'hopelessly out of time': ibid [23], [25].
[71] Lord Carnwath, 'From Judicial Outrage to Sliding Scales – Where Next for Wednesbury?', The ALBA Annual Lecture (12 November 2013) 19–20, available at https://www.supremecourt.uk/docs/speech-131112-lord-carnwath.pdf.
[72] Elliott, 'Legitimate Expectation, Consistency and Abuse of Power' (n 69) 285–86.
[73] ibid 283. See also Reynolds, 'Legitimate Expectations and the Protection of Trust' (n 40) 330.
[74] Elliott, 'Legitimate Expectation, Consistency and Abuse of Power' (n 69) 283.
[75] Reynolds, 'Legitimate Expectations and the Protection of Trust' (n 40) 343. See also I Steele, 'Substantive Legitimate Expectations: Striking the Right Balance?' (2005) 121 LQR 300, 309, fn 43; and Elliott, 'Legitimate Expectation, Consistency and Abuse of Power' (n 69) 282–83.

population when it comes to public bodies. Instead, the connection is that public authorities should do what they have indicated they will. As Sir John Laws said in *Nadarajah*, 'public bodies ought to deal straightforwardly and consistently with the public'.[76] A non-reneging principle underpins both *Rashid* and legitimate expectations as commonly understood. Non-reneging may be seen as the opposite of non-fettering. Decision-makers should be free to change or depart from their policies or promises. But too many changes or departures are unsatisfactory, because they send out confusing messages to the public and may undermine public confidence in, or even the legitimacy of, administrators. Even where the public is not aware of the previous position, too many changes of heart may be indicative of poor administration – of a decision-maker who has not thought through her policy carefully enough, or is too focused on the short-term, or who makes capricious decisions. Consistency of policy and legitimate expectations are both invocations of a non-reneging principle. Their separate compartments are useful, however, in clarifying whether claimant knowledge is required.

ii. Consistent Application of Policy

The apparent paradox of a claimant who in fact expected nothing invoking the ground of review of legitimate expectations seemed, until recently, to have been resolved in English law. The cases of *Lumba* and *Mandalia* suggested that knowledge *is* a requirement to found a legitimate expectation, and that cases with an 'unaware' claimant are better argued on the basis that a policy has been applied inconsistently.[77]

In *Lumba*, an unpublished policy regarding detention pending deportation of foreigners leaving UK prisons was being applied in preference to a different, published policy, but caseworkers were under orders to give reasons for their decisions that were consistent with the published policy.[78] As Lady Hale rightly observed, it was 'disturbing' that bogus reasons might be given so as not to draw attention to the secret policy.[79] In *Mandalia*, the UK Border Agency did not apply its policy that it would ask for missing documentation, and the claimant's application for renewal of his visa was rejected.

In *Mandalia*, the Supreme Court noted that the doctrine of legitimate expectations is 'strained' where the claimant is not aware of the policy.[80] The Court therefore invoked a free-standing 'principle' of consistent application of policy.[81] By 'principle' I take the Court to mean 'ground of review'. One central theme of this chapter is whether we create new grounds of review or allow broader grounds of review to be animated by multiple underlying principles. I favour the former approach, and also endorse more careful enunciation of what a 'ground of review' is, and what comprises a 'principle' underpinning that ground of review. A decision to turn down Mandalia's application rather than simply ask for the correct documents in order to give his application proper consideration (especially when he

---

[76] *Nadarajah* (n 1) [68].
[77] *R (on the application of Lumba) v Secretary of State for the Home Department* [2012] 1 AC 245; *Mandalia* (n 2).
[78] *Lumba* (n 77) [163].
[79] ibid [205].
[80] *Mandalia* (n 2) [29].
[81] ibid. Although Mandalia received a letter from the Agency stating that if there was a problem with his application, 'such as missing documentation', he would be contacted to give him the opportunity to rectify the problem ([10]), the case was decided on the process instructions issued by the Agency to caseworkers ([36]).

had already spent four years in the UK and his application revealed nothing unfavourable) was, if nothing else, potentially *Wednesbury* unreasonable. It is arguable that no reasonable decision-maker would have acted as the UK Border Agency did. Thus we can see that rigidly applied policies will not always be irrational[82] – sometimes *not* applying a policy rigidly will be irrational. But although *Mandalia* could potentially have been decided on the basis of rationality, we should scratch beneath the surface to honour the specific norms at play here. It is not that the decision-maker has merely acted unreasonably. She has devised an official policy. She had no good reason not to apply it in this case. She has therefore reneged on the policy she devised and promulgated. Or more precisely, and even more worryingly, a caseworker has reneged on an official policy distributed by a delegator to ensure consistent decision-making across her delegates.[83] Where a policy has been adopted, applications of it must not be arbitrary.[84] *Mandalia* makes it very clear that the non-fettering principle survives but that there was simply no good reason to depart from the established policy in the instant case,[85] just as *British Oxygen* did not convince the Board of Trade that there was good reason to depart from its policy.[86] The only difference between the cases is that the decision-maker applied his policy correctly in *British Oxygen* and did not apply it (but should have) in *Mandalia*, thus indicating that there may be less tension between non-fettering and consistency than has sometimes been supposed. Policies should be applied unless there is good reason to depart from them. That message is better conveyed to administrators via consistency and non-fettering grounds of review rather than a simple message to act rationally.

The emerging consistency ground of review has, however, been thrown into some doubt by *Gallaher*, which concerned allegations of price-fixing by several tobacco manufacturers and retailers. The question for the Court was whether Gallaher were entitled to the same penalty refund as TM Retail (TMR), despite only TMR receiving a direct assurance from an Office of Fair Trading (OFT) agent that they could benefit from another party's appeal. Lord Carnwath (with whom the other four Justices agreed) held that Gallaher were not so entitled. Indeed he said that domestic administrative law recognised no 'distinct principle' of equal treatment – although consistency was 'generally desirable', it was not an 'absolute rule'.[87] Again, the word 'principle' seems to be to be used to mean 'ground of review'. This meaning is clearest when the Court goes on to note that 'the ordinary principles of judicial review' include irrationality and legitimate expectations.[88] Again, the recommendation in this chapter is for greater clarity between grounds of review and underlying principles. This clarity is beneficial not only for justifying judicial intervention, but also for giving clearer advice to administrators about the bases on which their decisions may be challenged (and thus what to strive for to avoid such challenge). It may be true that the decision in *Gallaher* may not signal a change in judicial approach,[89] at least as far as outcome is concerned. But we should be concerned with judicial reasoning as well as outcomes. Retreating from

---

[82] See section I.A.
[83] See section III.A.
[84] Wade and Forsyth, *Administrative Law* (n 9) 272–73.
[85] *Mandalia* (n 2) [31].
[86] See section I.
[87] *Gallaher* (n 3) [24].
[88] ibid [41].
[89] S Daly and J Tomlinson, 'Administrative Inconsistency in the Courts' [2018] *Judicial Review* 190, 192.

Mandalia risks returning to the distortion of legitimate expectations seen in *Rashid* and *Teoh*, as well as relying unduly on rationality review.

Mandalia is not cited in *Gallaher*. It would not have availed the claimant because there was no good reason not to treat Mandalia according to the policy, whereas in fact the policy was being applied to Gallaher – an exception was made for TMR because there was a good reason to depart from it in TMR's case. There was therefore no need for the *Gallaher* Court to state that consistency was not a ground of review – there was a good reason to treat TMR differently and in fact no inconsistent treatment. As Lords Sumption and Briggs noted, the assurance made to TMR was made in error,[90] and so the decision whether to replicate that mistake was for the decision-maker.[91] As Lord Sumption observed, there was no reason to assume that the OFT would have repeated its mistake had Gallaher asked the same question TMR had asked.[92] There was no misleading information promulgated by the OFT other than the representation to TMR, and therefore no reason to depart from the policy other than in their case. As we already know, policies are to be applied unless there is good reason to depart from them.

B. Separate Compartments

As we saw earlier, the Australian courts have collapsed legitimate expectations back into a general fairness assessment. By contrast, English law carved a new consistency of policy ground of review out of legitimate expectations. The separate English compartments are preferable to the single Australian principle of fairness, and so the *Gallaher* decision is to be lamented. We must try to be more precise as to what is distinct about the grounds of review under consideration.[93]

Various justifications have been put forward for legitimate expectations, including abuse of power,[94] reasonableness,[95] fairness[96] and good administration.[97] As has been pointed out elsewhere, such concepts, although certainly 'relevant', are also a little 'abstract'.[98] The problem with relying on such terms is that they are 'imprecise' but also 'difficult to disagree with', letting us know nothing of the deeper normative reasons for judicial intervention.[99]

---

[90] *Gallaher* (n 3) [48], [52], [59].
[91] ibid [62].
[92] ibid [54].
[93] Reynolds, 'Legitimate Expectations and the Protection of Trust' (n 40) 332; F Ahmed and A Perry, 'The Coherence of the Doctrine of Legitimate Expectations' (2014) 73 *CLJ* 61, 69.
[94] *R v North and East Devon Health Authority, ex parte Coughlan* [2001] QB 213, [71]; *R v Secretary of State for Education and Employment, ex parte Begbie* [2000] 1 WLR 1115, [76]; P Sales and K Steyn, 'Legitimate Expectations in English Public Law: An Analysis' [2004] *PL* 564, 580.
[95] *R v Inland Revenue Commissioners, ex parte Unilever Plc* [1996] STC 681, for example, can be better understood as an irrational decision, rather than as a legitimate expectations case: Sales and Steyn, 'Legitimate Expectations' (n 94) 574–75. See also Clayton, 'Legitimate Expectations, Policy, and the Principle of Consistency' (n 7) 94.
[96] eg *R v Secretary of State for the Home Department, ex parte Ruddock* [1987] 1 WLR 1482, 1497 (Taylor J).
[97] eg *Nadarajah* (n 1) [68]; Reynolds, 'Legitimate Expectations and the Protection of Trust' (n 40) 330.
[98] Reynolds, 'Legitimate Expectations and the Protection of Trust' (n 40) 330.
[99] M Groves, 'The Surrogacy Principle and Motherhood Statements in Administrative Law' in L Pearson, C Harlow and M Taggart (eds), *Administrative Law in a Changing State: Essays in Honour of Mark Aronson* (Oxford, Hart Publishing, 2008) 93.

These 'motherhood statements', as Groves terms them, are vague and platitudinous, demonstrating cases as 'result in search of a principle'.[100] The *Gallaher* Court's desire not 'unnecessarily to multiply categories', but to collapse consistency back into rationality is regrettable.[101] As Elliott has commented, compartmentalising is not 'taxonomical fetishism'[102] but may help us to drill down to find the precise norms at play, rather than relying on such 'amorphous concepts as rationality'.[103] The *Gallaher* Court singled out abuse of power and substantive unfairness for criticism (confirming that they are not distinct grounds of review).[104] It is unfortunate they did not realise that rationality (although certainly a ground of review) can be subject to similar objections in 'conferring a thin veneer of respectability upon a form of gut-instinct adjudication'.[105] To those compelling arguments I would add that the grounds of judicial review should also guide administrators' decision-making, to help them avoid their decisions being challenged. The more specific those grounds are, the more precise the message they send to administrators.

As Varuhas has pointed out, there is a distinction between legitimate expectations and its offshoot (consistent application of policy), because the latter requires a policy to be applied, whereas the former may require it to be departed from in favour of a previous policy or promise.[106] To honour a claimant's legitimate expectation, a decision-maker may have to act consistently, but with her *previous* guarantee rather than her current one. The claimant's legitimate expectation may be a reason for her to be treated differently from other people who do not share the same expectation. Varuhas therefore argues that legitimate expectation cases are about being treated differently, not being treated the same. Being the 'polar opposite' of consistency cases, it is 'utterly incoherent' to include policy and promise cases under one umbrella doctrine of legitimate expectations.[107] As Varuhas goes on to note, the rationale for legitimate expectations is that a decision-maker should 'stand by its word'.[108] My argument is that both legitimate expectations and consistency of policy have an underlying principle of non-reneging. The rationale of both grounds of review is a presumption that public bodies should do what they indicated they would do.[109]

Calls have been heard for legitimate expectations to be rationalised by restricting the doctrine to only those cases that concern promises made directly to the claimant, rather than those that concern changes to, or departures from, policies.[110] Despite the link between legitimate expectations and consistency, that body of scholarship is one that I support. As Clayton has argued, it is difficult to see how a claimant would not know of a promise made directly to her, but it is 'not so obvious' why knowledge would be required in policy cases

---

[100] ibid 92. See too Elliott, 'Consistency as a Free-Standing Principle of Administrative Law?' (n 26).
[101] *Gallaher* (n 3) [26], [50].
[102] M Elliott, 'A "Principle" of Consistency? The Doctrinal Configuration of the Law of Judicial Review' (2018) 77 CLJ 444, 447.
[103] Elliott, 'Consistency as a Free-Standing Principle of Administrative Law?' (n 26).
[104] *Gallaher* (n 3) [40], [41].
[105] Elliott, 'Consistency as a Free-Standing Principle of Administrative Law?' (n 26).
[106] Varuhas, 'In Search of a Doctrine' (n 7) 43.
[107] ibid.
[108] ibid.
[109] Ahmed and Perry, 'The Coherence of the Doctrine of Legitimate Expectations' (n 93) 67.
[110] Clayton, 'Legitimate Expectations, Policy, and the Principle of Consistency' (n 7) 95; Varuhas, 'In Search of a Doctrine' (n 7) 40.

rather than promise cases.[111] Restricting legitimate expectations to promise cases allows all other (policy) cases to be dealt with regardless of claimant knowledge. Legitimate expectations and consistency partly share a normative base, but their separation respects their differences and optimises the clarity of their application.

C. Reconciliation with Non-fettering

Both legitimate expectations and consistent application of policy aim to bind a decision-maker to her promise or policy,[112] whereas the non-fettering principle allows her the freedom to make exceptions or change her mind. Some potential tension exists and the relationship between the grounds of review 'remains fully to be worked out'.[113] But there is less tension than is sometimes supposed. Take, for example, the very first recognised legitimate expectations case, *Schmidt*.[114] *Schmidt* concerned the question of whether a policy not to renew the visas of any Scientology students was overly rigid, and cited *Kynoch*, the key non-fettering authority at the time.[115] There was no reason to treat the claimants as exceptional and so no exception to the policy had to be made. Thus *Schmidt*, a legitimate expectation case, stands for the same principle as *Kynoch*, a non-fettering case. Where a promise (giving rise to a legitimate expectation) and a policy clash, the decision-maker has to renege from either her policy or her promise if she cannot honour both.[116] In other words, a legitimate expectation may invoke both the principle that a decision-maker should not renege on her promise *and* the non-fettering principle because the promisee has established a reason that the policy should not apply to her.

As Forsyth has argued, it would be 'monstrous' if public bodies could freely renege on their undertakings.[117] The principle of non-reneging is simply the other side of the coin from non-fettering, which suggests that the decision-maker ought to keep an open mind about departing from, or changing, her policy. There is nothing paradoxical about having both non-reneging and non-fettering principles. Instead it simply shows the balance decision-makers must strike in devising policies that must adapt to individual circumstances, or which may be revised completely. We ought also to move our focus from what the citizen 'legitimately expects' to encouraging good administration. The terminology of legitimate expectations is rather odd because it is described from the claimant's perspective – it is she who has the legitimate expectation. Other grounds of review tend to tell the decision-maker how to act – for example reasonably, proportionately, taking all relevant considerations into

---

[111] Clayton, 'Legitimate Expectations, Policy, and the Principle of Consistency' (n 7) 102. See also R Williams, 'The Multiple Doctrines of Legitimate Expectations' (2016) 132 *LQR* 639. It is possible to imagine, however, a situation where a claimant may not know about a direct promise made to her. Say, for example, a letter is sent to C promising a departure from a policy, but the letter goes astray and only comes to light after a decision is taken to apply the policy. In such circumstances, C can rely neither on legitimate expectations (were it to require knowledge, because she has none) nor on the consistency ground of review (because the policy has been applied). She could, however, rely on the non-fettering ground of review to argue that the letter justifies a departure from the policy.

[112] See section II.B, where it was explained that legitimate expectations may involve a decision-maker in honouring a *previous* promise/policy where it conflicts with a later position.

[113] M Elliott, 'Legitimate Expectations: Procedure, Substance, Policy and Proportionality' (2006) 65 *CLJ* 254, 255.

[114] *Schmidt* (n 46).

[115] *R v Port of London Authority, ex parte Kynoch* [1919] 1 KB 176.

[116] A case could also concern a clash between an old policy and a new policy.

[117] Forsyth, 'The Provenance and Protection of Legitimate Expectations' (n 46) 239.

account and discarding all irrelevant considerations, etc. Its label has caused the unease with legitimate expectations cases where the claimant has no knowledge. But rather than recommend an impractical rebranding exercise, limitation of legitimate expectations to promise cases, as has already been endorsed, would resolve the issue of whether knowledge is required. In any event, the citizen's state of mind is less important than encouraging careful deliberation as to what decision-makers promise, and their careful deliberation before breaking those promises. That balance can be achieved through a combination of legitimate expectations, consistency of policy and non-fettering. As we saw earlier, non-fettering allows decision-makers to change their policies. Legitimate expectations and consistency of policy preserve that freedom but merely allow a remedy for those who would be most harshly affected by the change.

III. Judicial Attitudes to Policies

In 1976, based on *British Oxygen*, Galligan predicted an era of judicial encouragement, rather than scepticism, of policies.[118] That prediction has unsurprisingly come true. Policies have several advantages. They allow fairness and consistency by guiding decision-making – decision-makers are placed behind a 'Rawlsian veil of ignorance',[119] thus making it harder for them to take irrelevant considerations into account. They promote efficiency. They allow citizens to plan their affairs. And they can be examined and thus the decision-maker held to account.[120] There are of course corresponding disadvantages. If a policy is too rigid, decision-makers will be unable to respond to individual circumstances. Although policies may prevent the taking into account of irrelevant considerations, they may exclude relevant considerations too.[121] Decision-makers may also be reluctant to expose their policies to increased scrutiny and potential challenge. It has therefore been argued that decision-makers will be less willing to have policies if they will be bound by them.[122] But such a result seems unlikely given that it may be difficult, or even impossible, for decision-makers to function without policies. Decision-makers benefit from policies too for efficient decision-making, including facilitating delegation. A policy may in fact insulate a decision-maker from judicial review if a court is satisfied that it has been carefully thought out and ought not therefore to be called into question. In any event, the courts might find a lack of policy to be irrational,[123] and may even order a decision-maker to devise one.[124] Decision-makers who attempt to conceal their policies may also be ordered by the courts to publish them.[125] Although the courts can be said to have tolerated policies for the

---

[118] Galligan, 'The Nature and Function of Policies' (n 6) 343.
[119] Y Dotan, 'Why Administrators Should be Bound by their Policies' (1997) 17 *OJLS* 23, 29.
[120] *Nicholds v Security Industry Authority* [2007] 1 WLR 2067, [56]; Hilson, 'Judicial Review, Policies and the Fettering of Discretion' (n 8) 112; Dotan, 'Why Administrators Should be Bound by their Policies' (n 119).
[121] *Adath Yisroel* (n 21) [87].
[122] Sales and Steyn, 'Legitimate Expectations' (n 94) 582.
[123] *R v North West Lancashire Health Authority, ex parte A* [2000] 1 WLR 977, 991 (Auld LJ). See too, in less strong terms, *In Re Findlay* [1985] AC 318, 335 (Lord Scarman).
[124] For discussion see McHarg, 'Administrative Discretion' (n 5) 288–90.
[125] *Lumba* (n 77). As far back as *R v Torquay Licensing Justice, ex parte Brockman* [1951] 2 KB 784, the Court indicated that if a decision-maker has decided on a policy, it is 'only fair' that is it published: 788 (Goddard CJ). See also *Nicholds* (n 120), where it was observed that the courts tend to encourage publication of policies: [57].

greater part of the twentieth century, judicial endorsement of policy creation and publication is a more recent development.[126]

A. Reasons for Endorsing Policies

Policies are both realistic (they are inevitable) and conceptually attractive.[127] Two main reasons for greater judicial recognition of the role of policies can be discerned: one pragmatic, the other principled.

First, the pragmatic reason. The increased burden on administrators necessitates policies to process large numbers of applications with speed and efficiency. Because of the 'increasing scale and complexity of modern government', policies are not only tolerated but also welcomed.[128] West, additionally, has made the insightful point that policymaking has increased because of the need to allocate increasingly scarce resources.[129] Policy 'has prospered' as a need for efficiency and filtered-down expertise has increased.[130] Where it is inevitable, a policy can facilitate delegation by ensuring delegates act in accordance with the delegator's wishes.[131] Policies can aid error-avoidance, by providing a framework for decision-makers to follow.[132] Where there are multiple decision-makers, policies prevent decisions from being 'wildly inconsistent'.[133] But, given both the presumption against delegation and the non-fettering principle, policies must be carefully drafted to allow delegates to know when to depart from the policy (or, more likely, to know when to refer a case back to the delegator for her to consider whether or not to make an exception, and to revise the policy in the light of that case if necessary). Setting out when an exception might be warranted also alleviates the risk of introducing uncertainty and arbitrariness through departures from the policy,[134] especially if undertaken inconsistently across multiple decision-makers. Treating like cases alike also means treating different cases differently.[135] So if an exception is made, it is not arbitrary provided that that person had something different to say. Lord Scarman once said that '[i]nconsistency is not necessarily unfair'.[136] But if two cases are not the same, there is no inconsistency. Again, we can see how policies and non-fettering can go hand-in-hand to ensure not only individualised decision-making, but also detailed policies. As we saw earlier, nuanced policies that can be applied fairly rigidly are preferable to ad

---

[126] Sedley, 'Policy and Law' (n 39) 256.
[127] Galligan, 'The Nature and Function of Policies' (n 6) 351–52.
[128] McHarg, 'Administrative Discretion' (n 5) 268. See also R Creyke and J McMillan, 'Soft Law v Hard Law' in L Pearson, C Harlow and M Taggart (eds), *Administrative Law in a Changing State: Essays in Honour of Mark Aronson* (Oxford, Hart Publishing, 2008) 383–87.
[129] W West, 'Administrative Rulemaking: An Old and Emerging Literature' (2005) 65 *Public Administration Review* 655, 657. We can see this in, for example, *British Oxygen* (n 11) and *Collymore* (n 41).
[130] HL Molot, 'The Self-Created Rule of Policy and other ways of Exercising Administrative Discretion' (1972) 18 *McGill Law Journal* 310, 335.
[131] C Harlow and R Rawlings, *Law and Administration*, 3rd edn (Cambridge, Cambridge University Press, 2009) 195–96. See also *Lumba* (n 77) [190]. Hence why it was particularly troubling that the *Mandalia* (n 2) caseworker did not follow the stated policy: see section II.A.ii above.
[132] *cf* Perry, 'The Flexibility Rule' (n 4), who argues that they can cause errors if they are overly rigid.
[133] G Weeks, *Soft Law and Public Authorities: Remedies and Reform* (Oxford, Hart Publishing, 2016) 156.
[134] *R v Ministry of Agriculture, Fisheries and Food, ex parte Hamble (Offshore) Fisheries Ltd* [1995] 2 All ER 714, [22].
[135] As can be seen in *Gallaher* (n 3): see section II.A.ii above.
[136] *HTV Ltd v Price Commission* [1976] ICR 170, 192.

hoc exceptions to blanket policies, because the latter encourage inconsistency – the former encourage thoughtfully drafted and consistently applied policies.

The second, principled, reason for favouring policies is that society is now less tolerant of arbitrariness. We demand transparency, equality and certainty. There is not only a demand for more 'open and fair administrative procedures',[137] but also a demand for more 'professionalism'.[138] Blanket policies in the human rights context will be unlikely to pass a proportionality test. At the same time, our human rights culture has instilled more of a desire for equality, which exercises of discretion are unlikely to provide unless carefully structured.[139] The emerging duty to give reasons for administrative decisions is a similar consequence of our increasing desire for transparency, which goes hand-in-hand with an increased role for policy.[140] We have long known that reasons will be needed if a decision is aberrant,[141] and a decision that departs from a policy will likely fit that description.[142] Policies can also assist busy decision-makers by providing a source of reasons. The unsuccessful claimant may be able to discern reasons from the policy (eg because she was not 'exceptional', or because she did not argue persuasively that the policy should be departed from), if necessary together with the decision-maker's explanation of how the policy was applied.[143] Indeed, as Sedley LJ noted in *Begbie*, departure from policy can be arbitrary or inconsistent, and refusal to depart can be overly rigid, therefore reasons might be needed in either case.[144] Policies therefore aid ultimate transparency.

B. A Long History of Consistency

It is unsurprising that judicial attitudes to policies softened in line with the administrative law revolution of the 1960s. Since a duty to act fairly is no longer contingent on a decision-maker's fulfilling a judicial rather than an administrative function,[145] 'in our modern approach' decision-makers must generally act fairly.[146] Sometimes fairness will demand departure from a policy.[147] But fairness would be increasingly difficult to achieve without policies to achieve consistency. What is perhaps more surprising is that judicial appreciation for policies started much earlier than the 1960s. In 1919, the Court in *Kynoch* set out the basis of the test later adopted in *British Oxygen* – that policies are permissible provided that the decision-maker listens to each applicant and considers making an exception to the policy.

Stringer is commonly cited as a case that shows the court taking a more sceptical view of policies.[148] It stands, it is said, for the authority that a policy can be but one relevant

---

[137] Galligan, 'The Nature and Function of Policies' (n 6) 357.
[138] Creyke and McMillan, 'Soft Law v Hard Law' (n 128) 384–86.
[139] McHarg, 'Administrative Discretion' (n 5) 268; Harlow and Rawlings, *Law and Administration* (n 131) 218.
[140] Dotan, 'Why Administrators Should be Bound by their Policies' (n 119) 24.
[141] eg *R v Civil Service Appeal Board, ex parte Cunningham* [1991] 4 All ER 310.
[142] *Oakley v South Cambridge District Council* [2017] 1 WLR 3765.
[143] L Sossin and CW Smith, 'Hard Choices and Soft Law: Ethical Codes, Policy Guidelines and the Role of the Courts in Regulating Government' (2003) 40 *Alberta LR* 867, 887.
[144] *Begbie* (n 94) [93].
[145] *Ridge v Baldwin* [1964] AC 40.
[146] *R v Liverpool Corporation, ex parte Liverpool Taxi Fleet Operators' Association* [1972] 2 QB 299, 308 (Denning MR) and see also 310 (Roskill LJ).
[147] Such as in the Windrush scandal (see section I.B), or for TMR in *Gallaher* (n 3) (see section II.A.ii).
[148] *Stringer v Minister of Housing and Local Government* [1970] 1 WLR 1281.

consideration a decision-maker takes into account.[149] Having a policy as merely one relevant consideration would vastly reduce its role, since decision-makers can choose how much weight to give to a relevant consideration (including giving it no weight whatsoever, provided it is at least considered, and subject of course to rationality review).[150] Coming between the fairly consistent cases of *Kynoch* (1919) and *British Oxygen* (1971),[151] both of which took a more permissive view of policies, *Stringer* seems like a surprising anomaly. My reading of *Stringer*, however, suggests that it in fact says much the same as those more permissive cases. The ambiguous passage is Cooke J's assertion that the policy was not 'to be pursued to the disregard of other relevant considerations'.[152] But that statement need not be read to connote that the policy itself was merely a relevant consideration. It could be read to mean the same as *Kynoch* and *British Oxygen* – that, despite the policy, the decision-maker must still take all relevant considerations into account in order to consider making an exception to the policy. It is my view that since at least *Kynoch* in 1919, the courts have looked favourably on policies, provided that they admit of exceptions.

Consistent application of policy as a separate ground of review is a modern development. But its roots within other grounds of review stretch back further than *Nadarajah* in 2005, which was cited as the inspiration for recognising a free-standing 'principle' of consistent application of policy in *Mandalia* in 2015.[153] For example, in *ex parte Chaudhary* in 1995, the Court chose to exercise its 'sparingly' used power to review the Director of Public Prosecution's decision not to prosecute.[154] The decision was unreasonable, because the Code for Crown Prosecutors had not been followed. In 1996, in *Urmaza*, Sedley J went a step further, 'bypassing *Wednesbury*'[155] and noting that '[t]he legal principle of consistency ... creates a presumption that [a decision-maker] will follow his own policy'.[156] But in fact we can go back much further. As Karen Steyn has argued, the requirement of consistency is deeply rooted in English law. Our whole system of precedent is based on it and equality is a component of the rule of law.[157] A duty to treat people in an equal manner can be seen in *Kruse v Johnson* as far back as 1898. Although *Kruse* did not deal with someone's being treated contrary to a policy, it stands for the unsurprising proposition that discretionary power must not be exercised arbitrarily. It shows that rationality review is grounded in avoiding discrimination or partiality. Thus it can be said that equality (the opposite of discrimination or partiality) is a component of rationality review, and equality demands consistency. This discovery is unsurprising since we have already seen that the ground of legitimate expectations has sometimes been justified in terms of rationality, and consistency grew out of legitimate expectations. But what is worth realising is that consistency has always been a sub-set of rationality because, fairly axiomatically, the courts will not tolerate inequality, and will assume that Parliament did not intend it without explicit authorisation.[158] For the

---

[149] Galligan, 'The Nature and Function of Policies' (n 6) 348–50.
[150] *Tesco Stores Ltd v Secretary of State or the Environment* [1995] 1 WLR 759.
[151] See also *H Lavender and Son Ltd v Minister of Housing and Local Government* [1970] 1 WLR 1231.
[152] *Stringer* (n 148) 1297.
[153] *Mandalia* (n 2) [29].
[154] *R v Director of Public Prosecutions, ex parte Chaudhary* [1995] 1 Cr App R 136, 140.
[155] Sedley, 'Policy and Law' (n 39) 257.
[156] *R v Secretary of State for the Home Department, ex parte Urmaza* [1996] COD 479.
[157] K Steyn, 'Consistency – A Principle of Public Law?' [1997] *Judicial Review* 22, 22. See also *R (on the application of Kambadzi) v Secretary of State for the Home Department* [2011] 1 WLR 1299, [73] (Lady Hale).
[158] *Kruse v Johnson* [1898] 2 QB 91, 99–100.

reasons advanced earlier, we should not collapse consistency back into rationality, but rather embrace the free-standing ground of review carved out in *Mandalia*.

The foregoing discussion reveals no tension with the non-fettering principle. The non-fettering principle says that exceptions have to be considered; the consistency rule clarifies that there must be good reasons for those exceptions to be made. The bigger challenge is to work out when such exceptions are justified. To do so, we need to consider how rigid or flexible a policy should be.

IV. How Consistent is Too Consistent?

The central question for decision-makers is how to meet the 'perennial challenge' of achieving consistency while dealing appropriately with individual cases.[159] The solution, it has been said, is to have a policy but not to shut one's ears to exceptional or unpredicted cases.[160] But in fact that is only the beginning of the solution, in particular because we need to know how flexible that policy should be and when exceptions should be made. Perry has argued that sometimes a flexible policy will be superior, sometimes a rigid policy will be superior, and he doubted that 'we can say anything much more general than that'.[161] Similarly, Cane has expressed sympathy for administrators who have to decide how flexibly their policies should be applied.[162] Knight has described this area as a 'tightrope' for decision-makers to walk.[163] A good starting point is to devise a policy that tells people what to expect and decision-makers how to act. Application of a policy should be easier with a detailed policy that sets out when exceptions will be made (as endorsed in this chapter) but which can be adapted when unforeseen circumstances arise. Beyond that, various factors can help us to determine how consistently a policy may – or must – apply.

A. Statutory Purpose

As ever, our starting point has to be the statutory purpose. It is axiomatic that a policy cannot cut across a statutory purpose. For example, in *Tilley*, a local authority's policy that intentionally homeless families would not be given housing even if they had young children was contrary to a statutory duty to promote the welfare of children.

Where a policy is not contrary to a statutory purpose, how rigidly it may apply also depends on the empowering statute.[164] The terms of a statutory power will tell us the extent to which a decision-maker can choose her policy.[165] A statute that deals with a 'vague and variable concept' such as 'need' can be defined (and redefined according to supply and demand) by the decision-maker.[166] For example, the terms of the statute in *British Oxygen*

---

[159] *Hesham Ali v Secretary of State for the Home Department* [2016] 1 WLR 4799, [15] (Lord Reed).
[160] ibid.
[161] Perry, 'The Flexibility Rule' (n 4) 390.
[162] P Cane, *Administrative Law*, 5th edn (Oxford, Oxford University Press, 2011) 154, fn 34.
[163] CJS Knight, 'A Framework for Fettering' [2009] *Judicial Review* 73, 77.
[164] *Findlay* (n 123) 334–35.
[165] Galligan, 'The Nature and Function of Policies' (n 6) 333.
[166] ibid.

gave the decision-maker a lot of discretion as to how to distribute its money. The statutory purpose in fact necessitated that not everyone eligible for a grant would get one. Until the Industrial Development Act 1966, applicants could claim investment allowances as of right. But the 1966 Act made awards discretionary.[167] The permissive statutory wording specifically set out that grants 'may' be made.[168] In other words, demand would outstrip supply, and a policy to structure who would receive preference was not only acceptable but also desirable. But a completely rigid policy would have frustrated the statutory purpose because claimants such as British Oxygen were not excluded by the terms of the statute. The policy therefore had to be flexible enough to allow the claimants to be heard, although it is clear that there was a high burden on them to prove they were an exceptional case. Statutory purpose will also influence whether to allow a policy departure because of a legitimate expectation – purported expectations cannot be honoured if they thwart a statutory purpose.[169]

Sometimes, however, a policy can admit of no exceptions whatsoever if the statutory purpose demands it. For example, in *Nicholds*, a policy that those with certain criminal records could not get a door supervisor's ('bouncer's') licence was better applied rigidly in order to meet the statutory purpose of driving criminality out of that industry. To do otherwise would have '[made] a mockery' out of the statutory purpose.[170] Notably the statute specifically required criteria to be published. Thus what Parliament had conferred was 'a rule or policy making power', rather than a broad discretion as in the legislation under consideration in *British Oxygen*.[171]

If the non-fettering principle were extended to common law powers, policy rigidity could be determined by the nature and purpose of a common law power, as well as the following other features, which will apply regardless of the source of the power.

B. Aim and Content of Policy and Nature of Right

It has been suggested that the legality of a policy will depend on how many applications the decision-maker has to process (which itself may be closely related to the statutory scheme).[172] More rigid policies may be legitimate when large numbers of applications indicate a need for efficiency, and even delegation.[173] In *British Oxygen*, for example, the main aim of the policy was to manage a large number of applications of a similar nature, and so the policy was allowed to be fairly rigid.[174] If, however, applications are fewer in number and differ more in their content, a more flexible policy might be required.[175] Even policies concerning a large number of applications need to have some flexibility, however.[176] The problem with this consideration is that it does not say anything about the importance of the issue or right at stake. For example,

---

[167] *British Oxygen* (n 11) 621.
[168] See also the permissive language in *Kynoch* (n 115).
[169] eg *Hamble (Offshore) Fisheries* (n 134).
[170] *Nicholds* (n 120) [45].
[171] ibid [53].
[172] Molot, 'The Self-Created Rule of Policy' (n 130) 321–22.
[173] ibid 335. See section III.A.
[174] Hilson, 'Judicial Review, Policies and the Fettering of Discretion' (n 8) 120.
[175] Wade and Forsyth, *Administrative Law* (n 9) 276; McHarg, 'Administrative Discretion' (n 5) 274.
[176] *Sagnata Investments Ltd v Norwich Corporation* [1971] 2 QB 614, 626–27.

a Minister might have to deal with a huge number of asylum applications. Pragmatism is certainly one reason to have a policy, but there will be certain circumstances where the fundamentality of the right at stake requires a more individualised approach.

Tilley is again a good example. The local authority's policy not to rehome intentionally homeless families was overly rigid. The ruling here is undoubtedly concerned with the nature of the right, that is accommodation for homeless children. But what if the policy were reversed so that it in fact provided that families with young children would be given *priority*, even if they were intentionally homeless? In *Daly*, the Court found a blanket policy excluding prisoners during cell searches to be disproportionate. The Court added that a reverse general policy in Scotland (that the prisoner should be present during searches unless there was good reason to exclude her) was more desirable.[177] It is therefore not only the *right* involved that is relevant but also the *content* of the policy, and particularly whether the policy promises to *benefit* the claimant or to *disadvantage* her. In any event, however, a completely blanket policy is unacceptable. In the *Daly* scenario, prison discipline would be compromised were it not possible to make an exception to a general policy that prisoners should be present for cell searches. In the *Tilley* scenario, a policy prioritising homeless families with children would operate harshly against those without children unless exceptions were possible.[178] Again, we can see the benefit of the non-fettering principle's working in tandem with policies.

In *Tilley*, each case had to be considered individually, to the extent that Templeman LJ doubted that even a policy hedged with exceptions could survive. But like Adam Perry, Templeman LJ does not consider policies that are designed to give more individualised treatment rather than less. Perry has argued that rigid policies are objectionable because they prevent the claimant from participating in the decision-making process. 'Rigid policies', he argues, 'do not allow a person affected by a decision to participate in the process by which that decision is made. Flexible policies do.'[179] But his argument needs to incorporate policies regarding procedure (rather than substantive outcomes) that may actually be designed to facilitate participation. *Mandalia* is one example – it was the departure from the UK Border Agency's policy that prevented the claimant's application from being properly considered, not its consistent application. For example, a policy that every homeless family with a child would be met in person rather than having their application decided on paper would need to be more rigid than flexible for maximum participation.[180] Even then, it may be prudent to allow the decision-maker flexibility to make an exception for a case that is very obviously doomed to fail. Under Perry's theory, the key test should surely be whether the claimant was given the opportunity to present her case.

Even policies as to substantive outcomes on fundamental issues can be dealt with by strict policies on occasion.[181] For example, in *Hesham Ali*, the immigration rules for

---

[177] *Daly* (n 35) [20], [22].

[178] See also *Adath Yisroel* (n 21) [70], where it was observed that it would be equally problematic to reverse a policy that the coroner would not take religious reasons into account in prioritising any death (ie giving automatic priority to those for whom speedy burial was important because of their religion).

[179] Perry, 'The Flexibility Rule' (n 4) 376.

[180] I am aware that Perry does not use 'hearing' in the literal, oral sense. The same point may be made with other procedural examples, eg a policy that all such families would have a right of appeal.

[181] See, for example, the 'right to hope' saga: *R v Secretary of State for the Home Department, ex parte Hindley* [2001] 1 AC 410; *Hutchinson v United Kingdom* (2017) 43 BHRC 667; HM Prison and Probation Service, *PSO 4700 Indeterminate Sentences Manual* (the 'Lifer Manual') (last updated 2017).

foreigners with certain criminal records were extremely prescriptive.[182] But they had been approved by Parliament, and there was still an exceptional circumstances 'get out' clause. So long as there is some ability to depart from the policy, that may suffice. Arguably the fundamentality of the issue at stake for the claimant here was offset by countervailing public interest concerns that justified few exceptions being made. The purpose of the scheme is therefore an important consideration.

C. Apply Policies unless Good Reason to Depart

A claimant who seeks to benefit from the consistent application of a policy is usually in a stronger position than the claimant who seeks to challenge a policy.[183] Existing policies should generally be followed because citizens are entitled to rely on them.[184] Consistent application of policies (particularly if they are published) adheres to Fullerian or Razian conceptions of the rule of law, that is as a formal, conduct-guiding concept that allows people to plan their lives.[185] But conduct-guiding cannot be the only rationale for consistency, because otherwise knowledge of the policy would be a requirement,[186] and I have outlined reasons why it ought not to be.[187] We have seen that consistent application of policies also promotes equality and generality, and encourages good administration. The biggest 'challenge for the modern legal system' is to balance equality and discretion – and policies can help.[188] Most of the time, application of a policy will promote equality. Where a claimant seeks an exception to the policy, or to have an old policy applied, equality appears to be threatened rather than promoted. But that claimant may have relied on a promise that an exception would be made, or may have benefited from a previous policy.[189] Equality requires not only like cases to be treated alike but also different cases to be treated differently, and a claimant who points to a 'difference' may establish a good reason to depart from the policy. One such reason may be that she can point to a previous promise, practice or policy.[190]

The court will assume that policies should be followed. The burden will lie on the individual to prove that she should be treated as exceptional,[191] and this can be a 'very considerable onus'.[192] Conversely, if a policy is departed from, the burden will be on the decision-maker to show why an exception was made. This is quite proper.[193] There is less risk of the court's usurping the decision-maker's role by ordering it to follow its own policy than if the court orders that a policy be departed from or changed.[194] If the decision-maker seeks to depart

---

[182] *Hesham Ali* (n 159) [15]–[16]; cf Lord Kerr's dissent, where he argued that the cases should have had more individualised consideration: ibid [115].
[183] eg *Nadarajah* (n 1) [61].
[184] Dotan, 'Why Administrators Should be Bound by their Policies' (n 119) 27.
[185] Sales and Steyn, 'Legitimate Expectations' (n 94) 582.
[186] Dotan, 'Why Administrators Should be Bound by their Policies' (n 119) 28.
[187] See section II.A.i.
[188] Dotan, 'Why Administrators Should be Bound by their Policies' (n 119) 28.
[189] ibid 34.
[190] Such as TMR in *Gallaher* (n 3).
[191] Molot, 'The Self-Created Rule of Policy' (n 130) 321.
[192] *Brockman* (n 125) 792.
[193] Knight, 'A Framework for Fettering' (n 163) 79.
[194] Dotan, 'Why Administrators Should be Bound by their Policies' (n 119) 34.

from that policy then reasons should be given and scrutinised for those dangers the policy sought to remove, for example inequality, bias and irrelevant considerations.[195]

In determining whether a decision-maker has genuinely considered if there is a good reason to depart from a policy, or whether she has fettered her discretion, the court will look behind the form of a policy to its operation in substance.[196] For example, in *Collymore*, the policy technically allowed for exceptions in 'most extraordinary' cases, but no exceptions had been made in around 300 applications over three years. Looking at the substance behind the form, the Court was satisfied that the policy was overly rigid. Likewise, in *Sagnata*, the local authority's policy to not permit amusement arcades to be established in its area was overly rigid. Although the claimants had been given the opportunity to be heard, the same reasons for the refusal of the application could have been given in any case, suggesting that the decision had been made solely on the basis of the policy.[197] Such hearings are a 'sham or pretence' and benefit no one.[198] By contrast, *Adath Yisroel* shows the dangers of prioritising substance over form. In *Adath Yisroel*, the defendant stated that she did not in fact apply her policy rigidly, but the court noted the 'difficulty ... that the policy ... says what it says on its face'.[199] We have seen that policies have benefits for a conduct-guiding conception of the rule of law. Such benefits are lost if the policy is misleading on its face, regardless of how it operates in practice.[200]

D. Changing Policies

A distinction should be drawn between departing from an existing policy and changing from one policy to a new policy.[201] As Steele has argued, it is worse for the claimant to have a policy not applied to her than to lose out when a policy is changed, because equality is only threatened in the former case.[202] The courts will invariably allow a decision-maker the freedom to reformulate her policy, but may need to decide whether a particular claimant should benefit from a previous policy. There is a risk that the courts can become too interventionist, considering that a decision-maker may have decided, for example, that her old policy is no longer affordable, or is not in the public interest.[203] Administrative policies cannot be ossified.[204]

But, as we have seen, sometimes equality necessitates treating people differently, and those who have relied on something other than the new policy may be in a sufficiently different position. The courts, therefore, may intervene if the claimant can rebut the presumption

---

[195] ibid 37.
[196] Knight, 'A Framework for Fettering' (n 163) 78.
[197] *Sagnata* (n 176) 638–39.
[198] Perry, 'The Flexibility Rule' (n 4) 392.
[199] *Adath Yisroel* (n 21) [46].
[200] ibid [46], [48]. See also *Tilley* (n 41), where the local authority pleaded that they were prepared to listen to exceptions in practice and indeed exceptions did appear to have been made – but were not provided for on the face of the policy.
[201] Dotan, 'Why Administrators Should be Bound by their Policies' (n 119) 33–35.
[202] Steele, 'Substantive Legitimate Expectations' (n 75) 303.
[203] eg *R (on the application of Abbassi) v Secretary of State for the Home Department* [2011] EWCA Civ 814.
[204] eg *Findlay* (n 123); Varuhas, 'In Search of a Doctrine' (n 7) 21.

that the new policy should be applied to her.[205] The court can weigh the reason for changing the policy against the reliance on the old policy. Where a promise is personalised, the scales may tip in favour of applying a previous policy. Absent such a promise, the claimant may be protected by transitional arrangements, or may be able to argue that the change in her treatment is irrational or procedurally unfair.[206] In this way, we can see that there is not necessarily tension between legitimate expectations and non-fettering – both may indicate that a departure from a policy is warranted.

E. Different Scenarios

In determining whether a policy should be applied or whether an exception should be made, it is helpful to identify the five most common scenarios in this area. Every scenario involves an assessment weighing the decision-maker's freedom against the benefits of holding her to her word, both for the individual claimant and to encourage good administration. Where the balance is to be struck will be determined according to the various issues we have already considered, but also according to which scenario is engaged (where C = claimant):

(i) C is treated differently on Occasion 2 than she was on previous Occasion 1;[207]
(ii) C is treated differently on Occasion 2 than she was *promised* on previous Occasion 1;[208]
(iii) C is treated inconsistently with the current policy;[209]
(iv) C is treated consistently with Current Policy 2 but inconsistently with Previous Policy 1/Person B;[210]
(v) C seeks to challenge the current policy that has been applied to her.[211]

Scenario (i) could be a change of policy case. At present, the claimant could argue a legitimate expectation case established by practice. If legitimate expectations were restricted to explicit promises, the claimant could argue that her previous reliance on the old policy outweighs the decision-maker's freedom to apply the new policy to her. The ground of consistent application of policy ought therefore to accommodate cases where an old policy has to be applied consistently to a person, even if that means applying a current policy inconsistently.

Alternatively, in scenario (i), Occasion 1 could have occurred before any policy was devised, or an exception to a policy may have been made on Occasion 1 but the policy applied on Occasion 2. The *Flintshire* case is a good example. Theatre A was allowed (as an exception to the usual policy) to sell alcohol; but when Theatre B was not allowed an alcohol licence, Theatre A's licence was revoked. There was an admirable desire to achieve consistency between the two theatres, but the Court held that it was wrong to '[pursue] consistency

---

[205] Dotan, 'Why Administrators Should be Bound by their Policies' (n 119) 34, 40.
[206] Varuhas, 'In Search of a Doctrine' (n 7) 20.
[207] eg *R v Flintshire County Council County Licensing (Stage Plays) Committee, ex parte Barrett* [1957] 1 QB 350; *HTV Ltd* (n 136); *Unilever* (n 95).
[208] eg *Coughlan* (n 94); *Begbie* (n 94).
[209] eg *Rashid* (n 40); *Nadarajah* (n 1); *Mandalia* (n 2).
[210] eg *Hamble (Offshore) Fisheries Ltd* (n 134); *Gallaher* (n 3).
[211] eg *British Oxygen* (n 11); *Sagnata* (n 176); *Tilley* (n 41); *Collymore* (n 41); *Adath Yisroel* (n 21).

at the expense of the merits of individual cases'.[212] But what the decision-maker actually did was to pursue consistency *between venues* at the expense of consistency *over time* for Theatre A. In other words, it was not the consistency per se that was the problem but the fact that there was good reason to treat the two venues differently (remembering that treating like cases alike means treating different cases differently). Theatre A had set up first, had held a licence for over 50 years and had invested money in installing bar facilities; and the reason for Theatre B's not being granted a licence was that there was now ample provision in the area. This case also shows that the distinction between application and revocation made in *McInnes v Onslow-Fane*,[213] although not as sharply drawn as it once was,[214] should not be completely discarded. The unfairness Theatre A suffered by having its licence revoked was greater because of its reliance on previous decisions than any unfairness suffered by Theatre B, who had no such reliance, in not obtaining its licence. In short, the scales may tip in favour of the claimant in scenario (i). As Steyn has argued, public law has traditionally provided more protection for the individual who is treated differently over time than for the claimant who is treated differently from others.[215]

Scenario (ii) is legitimate expectation established by a promise – the type of case that, it has been argued elsewhere and agreed with here, should be the only type of legitimate expectations case. In legitimate expectations cases, the 'sliding scale of review'[216] the court uses is essentially a balance between when acting consistently with the promise will trump the freedom to renege from it and vice versa.

Scenario (iii) throws the burden onto the decision-maker to rebut a presumption against non-reneging using the non-fettering principle. The claimant might have been treated differently from others (which she may or may not be aware of), or a confusing message may have been promulgated by the decision-maker. The decision-maker is free to devise her own policy. Having devised her policy, she should follow it, unless there is good reason not to. If she fails to follow that policy, she will need to demonstrate the good reason for departure.

In scenario (iv), a policy or practice may have changed, and the burden is placed on the claimant to argue against the non-fettering principle, or to argue that the policy change is (or its transitional arrangements are), for example, irrational.[217] This burden will be difficult to shift in the absence of the features of scenarios (i) or (ii), that is where the claimant has neither benefited from nor been promised that she will benefit from something other than the current policy. Scenario (iv), although disappointing for the claimant, demonstrates less unfairness than scenarios (i) or (ii), where the decision-maker has reneged on her previous treatment of, or promise to, the claimant, or scenario (iii), where there is potential inequality or potential poor administration. Even where a legitimate expectation exists, it can be 'shatter[ed]' by changes of policy.[218] Claimants can only expect application of an existing policy, because a decision-maker must be able to change her policy.[219] Transitional

---

[212] *Flintshire County Council County Licensing (Stage Plays) Committee* (n 207) 368 (Jenkins LJ).
[213] *McInnes v Onslow-Fane* [1978] 1 WLR 1520.
[214] *R v Secretary of State for the Home Department, ex parte al Fayed (No 1)* [1998] 1 WLR 763; P Craig, *Administrative Law*, 8th edn (London, Sweet & Maxwell, 2016) [12–024].
[215] Steyn, 'Consistency' (n 157) 22.
[216] *Begbie* (n 94) [78].
[217] For discussion, see Varuhas, 'In Search of a Doctrine' (n 7) 27–28.
[218] *Findlay* (n 123) 325.
[219] ibid 338.

arrangements will be made for 'those who are caught in the pipeline', and legitimate expectations can operate 'as a kind of court-ordered transitional provision',[220] but everyone else should, prima facie, have the new policy applied to them. Thus a balance can be struck between allowing decision-makers the freedom to formulate and reformulate policy, and protecting people who would be affected particularly harshly by the policy change.[221]

Alternatively, scenario (iv) might entail a policy's being applied as normal (ie no change of policy) but a claimant may become aware that an exception has been made for someone else whose circumstances are different. Thus we can see how the *Gallaher* case should have been rationalised – Gallaher were treated according to the policy. TMR were able to argue for a departure from the usual policy as an example of scenario (ii), but nothing justified a departure in Gallaher's case (scenario (iv)).

In scenario (v), a claimant could invoke the non-fettering principle to argue that the policy is overly rigid if it concerns a statutory power. Alternatively, regardless of the source of the power but depending on the nature of the right involved, she could argue that the policy is irrational or disproportionate. As we have already seen, overly rigid policies are likely to be disproportionate, but they may well be rational. Substantive review will be the better choice where the policy should be completely revised rather than just softened.

V. Conclusions

The grounds of judicial review are not entirely distinct from each other, nor can they be. But care must be taken for them to have their own points of distinction (otherwise what is the point in having them) and not contradict each other in a way that sends a confusing message to administrators and the public. By requiring knowledge from the claimant, the boundary is being set more clearly around legitimate expectations. The distinctiveness of its role could be further improved by limiting it to 'promise' cases, as others have convincingly argued. The ground of consistency of policy could then take over in all policy cases in a way that does not discriminate against uninformed claimants. Thus any unnecessary overlap between those grounds of review can be prevented, and consistency's place in the judicial toolbox could be confirmed. The separate compartments of legitimate expectations and consistency of policy put the knowledge requirement controversy to bed.

The next challenge is to resolve any apparent clash between legitimate expectations/consistency of policy, on the one hand, and the non-fettering principle, on the other. The purpose of this chapter has been to argue that we need not see the non-fettering principle as being in 'considerable tension' with developments around it.[222] Legitimate expectations/consistency of policy and the non-fettering principle can co-exist, and in fact are complementary. Where the balance is struck will depend on the statutory purpose, the aim and content of the policy (including in particular whether it is a policy regarding process or substance), the nature of the right involved and whether the claimant seeks adherence to, or departure from, the policy. In short, a policy should be applied unless there are good

---

[220] Williams, 'The Multiple Doctrines of Legitimate Expectations' (n 111) 654.
[221] *Hamble (Offshore) Fisheries* (n 134) [47].
[222] McHarg, 'Administrative Discretion' (n 5) 291.

reasons to depart from it, and such reasons can only be ascertained by considering each individual case. In addition, we need to consider change of policy cases, where non-fettering/non-reneging can be invoked to decide whether to protect the administrator's freedom or the consistency of the claimant's treatment.

Both the English and Australian courts have backed away from the *Rashid/Teoh* approach, but in different ways. The Australian courts have collapsed legitimate expectations back into fairness, whereas the English courts by contrast have carved out a new ground of review. This new ground might be useful for other jurisdictions. Australian administrative law, for example, already recognises that policies must be applied flexibly,[223] but consistency is not currently a freestanding ground of review.[224] Instead, inconsistent decisions are challenged on other grounds,[225] such as relevance or rationality. But despite the Supreme Court's concern in *Gallaher* not 'unnecessarily to multiply' the grounds of review,[226] compartmentalising vaguer notions such as 'fairness' and 'reasonableness' helps us to better identify and honour the precise values we seek to uphold, and which we wish decision-makers to be guided by. The public interest can be benefitted by flexibility, which aids careful policy-making, individualised decision-making and policy changes that respond to changing circumstances.[227] But it is also in the public interest that decision-makers should honour their undertakings, promote equality, not promulgate misleading information and not change their policies too frequently. Policies have 'virtues of flexibility which rules lack, and virtues of consistency which discretion lacks'.[228] We can have the best of both worlds.

---

[223] Creyke and McMillan, 'Soft Law v Hard Law' (n 128) 393.
[224] Weeks, *Soft Law and Public Authorities* (n 133) 156.
[225] ibid.
[226] *Gallaher* (n 3) [50] (Lord Sumption).
[227] Sales and Steyn, 'Legitimate Expectations' (n 94) 582.
[228] *Begbie* (n 94) [94] (Sedley LJ). See also Sedley, 'Policy and Law' (n 39) 262.

21
The In-between Space of Administrative Justice: Reconciling Norms at the Front Lines of Social Assistance Agencies

JENNIFER RASO*

I. Introduction

Two spaces exist within the field of public law: the well-mapped and traversed terrain of external constraints on administrative actors; and the lesser-known, but much broader, landscape of decision-making practices within administrative agencies. Much conventional public law literature examines the first space, looking to external constraints on administrative agencies as the primary mechanism for holding executive power to account.[1] Though this work is significant, it represents only a limited range of the possibilities for executive branch accountability and government according to law. Legislative bodies and courts are often conceived of as the main mechanisms for holding administrative actors to account for their actions, because of a broader sentiment that administrators cannot be trusted to subject themselves to the rule of law.[2] Yet the largest set of decisions that affect individuals' rights are made by administrative officials at and behind the front lines of executive agencies. These decisions are explored by socio-legal scholars and legal scholars in street-level bureaucrat and administrative justice literatures, respectively. Though it may lie at the fringes of doctrinal scholarship, administrative justice has recently been the subject of

---

*This chapter has benefited from the critical comments of Denise Réaume, Audrey Macklin, Simon Halliday, David Dyzenhaus and Richard Stacey, as well as the editors of this collection. I also owe a debt of gratitude to my research participants, all of whom must remain anonymous. The findings reported here would have been impossible if not for their generous participation. This research was funded by the Social Sciences and Humanities Research Council (Canada) and the Endeavour Fellowship Program (Australia).

[1] cf C Harlow and R Rawlings, *Law and Administration*, 3rd edn (Cambridge, Cambridge University Press, 2009).

[2] NR Parillo, 'Jerry Mashaw's Creative Tension with the Field of Administrative Law' in NR Parillo (ed), *Administrative Justice from the Inside Out: Essays on Themes in the Work of Jerry Mashaw* (Cambridge, Cambridge University Press, 2017) 2.

renewed interest in the United Kingdom (UK),[3] the United States (US)[4] and Canada.[5] Yet the space *behind* the front desks of administrative institutions is relatively unknown to legal scholars, who largely remain outsiders to the world of street-level decision-making.

Empirical socio-legal literature has long suggested that administrative institutions' capacity to govern themselves depends on the models of justice operating within these institutions. Much of this literature uses Mashaw's theory of administrative justice – in which three distinct justice models exist in tension, with one dominating over the others – as its analytical starting point.[6] Yet administrative justice scholars rarely explore front-line practices. Street-level bureaucrat scholarship, meanwhile, focuses on workers' professional identities. Studies in this field commonly find that officials in benefits-delivering agencies tend to polarise into social workers and efficiency engineers, which roughly map onto two of Mashaw's justice models.[7] This work suggests ongoing tension between norms, rather than one dominating others, but rarely considers how workers' practices interact with the legal and managerial principles operating within a given institutional setting.

Front-line decision-making practices are not only significant for empirical researchers, but they also raise important public law questions given the growth of the administrative state and the consequent need for delegated authority. Chief among these are questions about how decision-making unfolds in practice, and how we might best assess these front-line practices against normative standards. As a preliminary step towards answering these questions, this chapter draws on a qualitative empirical study of front-line decision-making practices in Ontario Works, a last-resort social assistance programme.[8] This study focused specifically on how caseworkers in a notoriously rule-bound programme performed operational discretion. By 'operational discretion' I mean how front-line

---

[3] eg M Adler (ed), *Administrative Justice in Context* (Oxford, Hart Publishing, 2010); R Thomas, *Administrative Justice and Asylum Appeals: A Study of Tribunal Adjudication* (Oxford, Hart Publishing, 2011); the UK Administrative Justice Institute, available at https://ukaji.org/.

[4] eg Parillo (ed), *Administrative Justice from the Inside Out* (n 2); GE Metzger and KM Stack, 'Internal Administrative Law' (2017) 115 *Michigan Law Review* 1239.

[5] Administrative justice is less commonly interrogated by legal academics in Canada, though it is discussed in C Flood and L Sossin (eds), *Administrative Law in Context*, 3rd edn (Toronto, Emond, 2017). For a classic study (albeit of British administrative justice arrangements), see HW Arthurs, *Without the Law: Administrative Justice and Legal Pluralism in Nineteenth-Century England* (Toronto, University of Toronto Press, 1985).

[6] M Adler, 'Fairness in Context' (2006) 33 *Journal of Law & Society* 615; RA Kagan, 'The Organisation of Administrative Justice Systems: The Role of Political Mistrust' in Adler (ed), *Administrative Justice in Context* (n 3); R Sainsbury, 'Administrative Justice, Discretion, and the "Welfare to Work" Project' (2008) 30 *Journal of Social Welfare & Family Law* 323.

[7] More recently, see C Watkins-Hayes, *The New Welfare Bureaucrats: Entanglements of Race, Class, and Policy Reform* (Chicago, IL, University of Chicago Press, 2009); S Maynard-Moody and M Musheno, 'State Agent or Citizen Agent: Two Narratives of Discretion' (2000) 10 *Journal of Public Administration Research & Theory: J-PART* 329.

[8] This research includes semi-structured interviews with 25 front-line workers averaging two hours in length, which were audio recorded and transcribed with participants' consent. Research participants varied in age, citizenship status and ethnicity. Their experience as caseworkers ranged from two to 26 years. The majority of participants self-identified as women, but my sample size is too small to identify significant gender-based differences in interpretive approaches to Ontario Works rules. Nonetheless, even this small sample included a range of male and female caseworkers who spanned the professional identity spectrum from 'pro-client' rule benders to 'black-and-white' rule-enforcers. My qualitative study also included on-site observation and one-on-one and group meetings with management staff, which provided contextual information about my research sites. In addition, I analysed internal policies, decision-making tools and government reports, such as Auditor-General reports, provincially commissioned reviews of the Ontario Works programme and the Social Assistance Management System (SAMS), and public-sector union reports on SAMS' effects on front-line workers.

workers locate and animate flexibility within legislative frameworks during routine interactions with benefits applicants and recipients, and how they balance competing program norms in the process.[9]

Ontario Works offers a rich context for examining this balancing act. While the provincial legislature creates and amends Ontario Works legislation, routine benefits and services are delivered by caseworkers in hundreds of municipal social services offices. To be eligible for benefits, individuals must have income and assets that fall below provincially set thresholds, meet regularly with their caseworker, and complete and periodically update a Participation Agreement (a document that states their commitment to engage in vocational training and employment-seeking activities). Ontario Works benefits are divisible into core and supplementary benefits. Core benefits include fixed monthly allowances intended to cover basic needs such as shelter, food and clothing, and are calculated based on the number of individuals living in one household. Supplementary benefits, by contrast, include funds to help cover expenses related to seeking employment, such as the cost of public transit, training programmes, uniforms and grooming.[10] In addition to cash assistance, in-kind supplementary benefits are also available, such as vocational workshops, local recreation and support programmes, and so on. Supplementary benefits are often crucial for Ontario Works recipients because, as many caseworkers acknowledge, core benefits simply do not cover the actual cost of living in Ontario.[11]

Ontario Works, like similar programmes elsewhere, affects many individuals.[12] Yet few caseworker decisions are ever reviewed by external tribunals,[13] and virtually none are judicially reviewed.[14] Front-line workers, then, are both gatekeepers and final decision-makers; their interpretation of Ontario Works' flexible and complex legislative framework is practically, if not formally, 'the law'. As I argue, however, the finality of caseworkers' discretionary decisions does not mean that caseworkers reach these decisions in a law-free

---

[9] While front-line workers also strive for consistency as they perform operational discretion, their chief concern is consistency among their decisions that affect one client. That is, caseworkers try to ensure that they each respond to the same client's requests in more or less the same manner. They are less concerned with ensuring that they treat requests for the same benefit, made by different clients, in the same way. For further detail about what 'consistency' means in Ontario Works, see J Raso, 'Unity in the Eye of the Beholder? Reasons for Decision in Theory and Practice in the Ontario Works Program' *University of Toronto Law Journal* (forthcoming, 2019).

[10] Ontario Works Act 1997 (OWA 1997), SO 1997, c 25, sch A. I use the term 'core benefits' to include income assistance and other benefits that the OWA 1997 identifies as mandatory benefits, and 'supplementary benefits' to include the panoply of other supports that exist within the Ontario Works programme.

[11] At the time of my research, core benefits for a single person in Ontario were $681/month; for a sole-support parent with one child they were $951/month: O Reg 134/98, pt VI. A recent report by the Canadian Centre for Policy Alternatives notes that Ontario Works recipients live in deeper poverty today than they did after benefits rates were cut in the 1990s, as rates have not kept pace with inflation and cost-of-living increases: K Tiessen, *Ontario's Social Assistance Poverty Gap* (May 2016), available at www.policyalternatives.ca/publications/reports.

[12] Ontario Works remains a crucial support, providing benefits to almost 450,000 people each year: Office of the Auditor-General of Ontario, *2015 Annual Report of the Office of the Auditor General* (Toronto, A-G Ontario, 2015) ch 3, s 3.12.

[13] Ontario, *Social Justice Tribunal Ontario Annual Report 2016–2017* (Toronto, SJTO, 2017); J Raso, 'Tranchemontagne Revisited: Lessons from the Game of Jurisdiction' (2017) 13 *Journal of Law & Equality* 31.

[14] A recent search of CanLii's reported decisions shows only eight instances in which decisions in the Ontario Works programme were the subject of a judicial review application. Similarly low appeal rates have been found by V Lens, 'Bureaucratic Disentitlement After Welfare Reform: Are Fair Hearings the Cure?' (2005) 12 *Georgetown Journal on Poverty Law & Policy* 13.

space. Rather, workers' everyday performance of discretion is regulated by their common method of accommodating seemingly divergent programme norms. This balancing act, I claim, constitutes a space between Mashaw's justice models where norms are reconciled between and accommodated to one another.

This chapter thus has two purposes. Its central aim is to further develop administrative justice theory. To that end, it asks how we might evaluate the justice of decision-making in contexts where front-line workers essentially determine access to last-resort benefits and services. Rather than rely on public law doctrines or managerial initiatives, I use front-line workers' practices to enrich administrative justice theory. Mashaw's core insight, taken up by others, is that while many justice models may operate within a given institutional context, one will tend to dominate and thus serve as the standard against which the acceptability of that agency's decisions are to be measured. Ultimately, I argue that Mashaw's theory needs fine-tuning to account for the normative balancing practices evident at administrative agencies' front lines. Drawing on my empirical research, I demonstrate that, rather than one justice model prevailing in Ontario Works, two justice models – professional treatment and bureaucratic rationality – are *accommodated between*. This accommodation is apparent as front-line workers navigate the multiple norms governing Ontario Works, suggesting that these micro-level practices have institution-wide impacts.

This chapter's second goal is to demonstrate the ongoing relevance of administrative justice theory for public law. It achieves this goal by adapting administrative justice theory to the rich normative practices evident behind the front-lines of benefits-delivering agencies. Ultimately, it suggests that we may evaluate a decision's acceptability according to how well front-line workers have balanced the norms operating within a given administrative agency. This approach might be viewed as a practice of reasonableness, producing outcomes that fall within an acceptable range.

My argument proceeds in three sections. First, I review Mashaw's theory of administrative justice, showing how the theory assumes that one justice model will dominate over others. I then turn to the underexplored area of front-line decision-making practices. Drawing on my empirical research, section III demonstrates that front-line workers in the Ontario Works programme identify with two professional identity categories – pro-client social workers and black-and-white efficiency engineers – that correspond with Mashaw's professional treatment and bureaucratic rationality models of justice. Building on street-level bureaucrat literature, I claim that these two categories persist rather than subsume one another. Section IV then illustrates how front-line workers navigate the space in between justice models through a common process of accommodating competing programme norms. I close by offering some thoughts on administrative justice as an in-between space.

II. Administrative Justice Theory: Tension and Domination

Though administrative justice theory may be less familiar to legal academics, just administration has been examined in one form or another since at least the mid-twentieth century. Between the late 1950s and the 1970s, government-commissioned studies scrutinised the activities of administrative agencies in the UK[15] and Canada.[16] During the same period, administrative lawyers addressed the proliferation of broad discretion within American administrative agencies,[17] and regulatory scholars considered how agencies develop internal decision-making standards.[18] This work shared a common concern: how the design and function of administrative agencies, and the relationships between agency actors, impacted administrative decision-making. Today, administrative justice research has grown so wide that the term 'administrative justice' means many different things. Instrumentalist proposals about access to appellate tribunals,[19] empirical analyses of how rules are applied in public programmes[20] and normative claims about the justice standards that decision-makers ought to meet:[21] all of these matters fit under the rubric of administrative justice.

Despite their diverse pursuits, scholars in the field of administrative justice continue to draw on and expand the foundational theory first advanced by Jerry Mashaw in *Bureaucratic Justice*.[22] Since its articulation in the early 1980s, this theory has been further developed by scholars in the UK,[23] the US[24] and elsewhere.[25] Two elements of Mashaw's theory are particularly significant: the nature and source of internal administrative law; and the relationship between administrative justice models.

First, Mashaw proposes that we should look to an agency's internal law, rather than externally developed standards, as a central source for decision-making norms. This internal approach to law responded to the times; today, administrative law scholars continue to rely heavily on external mechanisms (legislative rules, judicial decisions) when subjecting administrative agencies to the rule of law.[26] Yet Mashaw recognised that administrative

---

[15] In the UK, see the *Report of the Committee on Administrative Tribunals and Public Inquiries (Franks Report)*, Cmnd 218 (1957), which led to the passing of the Tribunals and Inquiries Act 1958. See also the later report, commissioned by the Social Sciences and the Law Committee of the Economic and Social Research Council, by R Rawlings, *The Complaints Industry* (London, ESRC, 1985).

[16] In Canada, see the *McRuer Report*: Ontario, Lieutenant Governor of the Province of Ontario, *Royal Commission Inquiry into Civil Rights: Report Number One*, vol 1 (Toronto, Queen's Printer, 1968); other volumes published between 1968–71. See also the Law Reform Commission of Canada's Working Paper 25, *Administrative Law: Independent Administrative Agencies* (Ottawa, Minister of Supply and Services Canada, 1980).

[17] KC Davis, *Discretionary Justice: A Preliminary Inquiry* (Baton Rouge, LA, Louisiana State University Press, 1969).

[18] RA Kagan, *Regulatory Justice: Implementing a Wage-Price Freeze* (New York, Russel Sage, 1978).

[19] eg A Grant and L Sossin, 'Fairness in Context: Achieving Fairness Through Access to Administrative Justice' in Flood and Sossin (eds), *Administrative Law in Context* (n 5); L Sossin and A Hill, 'Social Rights and Administrative Justice' in M Jackman and B Porter (eds), *Advancing Social Rights in Canada* (Toronto, Irwin Law, 2014).

[20] Kagan, 'Political Mistrust' (n 6).

[21] M Harris and M Partington, 'Introduction' in M Harris and M Partington (eds), *Administrative Justice in the 21st Century* (Oxford, Hart Publishing, 1999) 2. Some propose that administrative justice can be normatively plural, and that determining what is 'just' in a particular administrative agency requires balancing between procedural and substantive justice: R Baldwin and K Hawkins, 'Discretionary Justice: Davis Reconsidered' (1984) *PL* 570, 573–77.

[22] JL Mashaw, *Bureaucratic Justice: Managing Social Security Disability Claims* (New Haven, CT, Yale University Press, 1983).

[23] Adler 'Fairness in Context' (n 6); S Halliday, J Ilan and C Scott, 'Street-Level Tort Law: The Bureaucratic Justice of Liability Decision-Making' (2012) 75 *MLR* 347.

[24] eg most recently, Metzger and Stack, 'Internal Administrative Law' (n 4); Kagan, 'Political Mistrust' (n 6).

[25] eg in the Netherlands, M Hertogh, 'Through the Eyes of Bureaucrats: How Front-Line Officials Understand Administrative Justice' in Adler (ed), *Administrative Justice in Context* (n 3).

[26] Parillo, 'Creative Tension' (n 2).

agencies, too, could generate law, and that they might do so better than legislatures or courts. The challenge, as Mashaw framed it,

> is to admit to the limitations of an externally oriented administrative law and yet to affirm a vision of administration that is subject to the normative evaluation and improvement that is the promise of legal discourse; to view the administrative process, like the judicial and legislative processes, as somehow in pursuit of justice and the general welfare; to see 'administration', like 'democracy' and 'the rule of law', as a motivating ideal.[27]

We can meet this challenge, according to Mashaw, by identifying the 'internal' administrative law operating within an agency's everyday decision-making practices. This proposal presents a normative and empirical dilemma, however. How do we investigate the internal law of administration at work within a particular institution while maintaining a stance on the kind of administrative law that *ought* to operate within that agency?[28] Internal administrative law is inadequate without an ideal notion of the type of justice that an agency should produce.[29] Mashaw's concept of administrative justice solves this dilemma by offering a pluralist, process-focused definition of justice. For Mashaw, administrative justice is 'those qualities of a decision process that provide arguments for the acceptability of its decisions'.[30] 'Acceptability', in this model, is evaluated using an agency's internal law, which comprises multiple norms or models of justice. Though these norms are plural, Parillo explains that they nonetheless 'serve law's purposes: to constrain official action, serve as workable focal points for reform, and foster legitimacy'.[31] How do we determine which norms are acceptable in a given situation, though? Mashaw answers this question by proposing that the tension between justice models is resolved through a process of competition and eventual domination of one model over others.

This relationship between plural internal norms is thus a second key feature of Mashaw's theory. While multiple justice models will exist within a given administrative agency, one will nevertheless prevail over others.[32] In the American social security disability insurance programme, which was the subject of his study, Mashaw found three justice models in operation: professional treatment, bureaucratic rationality, and moral judgment. Drawing from critical studies of disability insurance administration, he concluded that these three models represented decision-making characteristics – professional, managerial and judicial – each with its own value. In an agency governed by bureaucratic rationality, such as the American disability insurance programme, an acceptable decision would be one that was made efficiently and consistently with other decisions. Efficiency and consistency required easily available information, clear rules and hierarchical institutional organisation.[33] In settings where professional treatment rules, decisions must meet a client's individual needs. Front-line workers must provide appropriate, individualised support to those whom they serve, and will function together as a lateral network of experts governed by a common set of professional standards.[34] In agencies dominated by moral judgment, administratively just

---

[27] Mashaw, *Bureaucratic Justice* (n 22) 14.
[28] ibid 15.
[29] ibid 15–16.
[30] ibid 24–25.
[31] Parillo, 'Creative Tension' (n 2) 4.
[32] Mashaw, *Bureaucratic Justice* (n 22) 23–31.
[33] ibid 25–26.
[34] ibid 26–29.

outcomes are reached using a 'fair' method. This model centres on procedural justice, with just decisions reached through adversarial processes that give each party an opportunity to present its position. Such decisions are made by neutral, arm's-length officials responsible for fleshing out vague statutory texts.[35]

Although often described as pluralist, this theory relies on one justice model's prevailing over others. While we can expect competing justice models to exist within any given administrative agency, one of these norms will tend to dominate, as 'the internal logic of any one of them tends to drive the characteristics of the others from the field as it works itself out in concrete situations'.[36] This dominant justice model is the standard against which the acceptability of administrative decisions is ultimately assessed.[37] Others have elaborated Mashaw's original theory, but the notion that one justice model will necessarily supersede endures. For instance, though Adler proposes additional justice models to account for new public management's effects on administration, he nonetheless maintains that we can identify one overarching model in a given institutional setting.[38] Similarly, Kagan's recent analysis uses decision-making spectrums to expand Mashaw's typologies from three to four models, but does not challenge the relation between justice models.[39] While these developments have enriched administrative justice theory, the domination thesis remains intact.[40]

As the next section will explore, socio-legal studies of 'street-level' decision-makers and my empirical research both suggest that the relationship between plural justice models may not be so easily resolved by a dominant justice model thesis. Rather, we may need a more nuanced theory of how competing justice norms are balanced by the different actors who collectively constitute an administrative agency.

III. From Administrative Justice to Street-level Bureaucracy: Pro-client Social Workers and Black-and-White Efficiency Engineers

Compared to administrative justice theorists, who identify a range of justice models, scholars who study front-line decision-makers commonly identify two stylised professional identity types in benefits-delivering agencies: efficiency engineers and social workers.[41] These two types roughly correspond with Mashaw's bureaucratic rationality and professional treatment justice models. Yet although they may share features with these two models, their relationship *to* one another is distinguishable. As this section demonstrates, street-level

---

[35] ibid 29–31.
[36] ibid 31.
[37] ibid 23–31.
[38] Adler, 'Fairness in Context' (n 6).
[39] Kagan, 'Political Mistrust' (n 6).
[40] Other recent work does not challenge this thesis: Halliday, Ilan and Scott, 'Street-Level Tort Law' (n 23); Metzger and Stack, 'Internal Administrative Law' (n 4).
[41] eg Watkins-Hayes, *New Welfare Bureaucrats* (n 7); ZW Oberfield, *Becoming Bureaucrats: Socialization at the Front Lines of Government Service* (Philadelphia, PA, University of Pennsylvania Press, 2014); CJ Jewell, *Agents of the Welfare State: How Caseworkers Respond to Need in the United States, Germany, and Sweden* (New York, Palgrave Macmillan, 2007).

bureaucracy scholars typically dichotomise between these two professional identity types, assessing how front-line workers operate in relation to each category. Rather than suggesting that one prevails over the other, these scholars anticipate that both identity types may coexist, and that front-line workers will cluster within each identity type.

Why do administrative justice theory and street-level bureaucracy studies diverge on this point? Their contrasting methods offer some insight. Research into front-line practices conducted in the early 1980s,[42] and more recently,[43] demonstrates that officials respond *to* and interact *with* managerial and legislative initiatives. Many of these authors trace a range of front-line responses to normative frameworks, showing how workers make policy rather than merely implement what is given to them. Studying front-line practices, these authors illustrate how plural notions of justice may survive within agencies through workers' divergent approaches, which undermines the possibility that one justice model will necessarily drive all others to the margins.[44] These distinct findings are likely the result of different methods. Street-level studies typically examine front-line workers' practices through qualitative empirical studies, while administrative justice theory tends to centre on statutory and policy reforms, managerial strategies and structural changes, which are one or more steps removed from front-line practices. It would be disingenuous to conclude, then, that this divergence suggests that front-line workers are acting roguishly. Rather, the persistent pluralism evident at an agency's front lines indicates that something complex is occurring as workers navigate the many justice models underlying a given programme. This phenomenon may escape most administrative justice theories.

The two stylised professional identity types – social workers and efficiency engineers – arise from the institutional contexts in which front-line workers operate. These contexts typically present front-line workers with a consistency versus responsiveness trade-off: should they make decisions that are internally consistent en masse, or should they respond to the unique needs of those seeking assistance?[45] The stakes of this trade-off intensify when it occurs in what Watkins-Hayes describes as a 'catch-all' bureaucracy. Catch-all bureaucracies, she suggests, are those agencies that implement targeted public programmes. Because these programmes serve marginalised clients, they function as a safety net that 'catches' all of those who have few alternative supports available to them.[46] Though the programmes delivered by catch-all bureaucracies are typically rule-saturated, front-line workers in such environments develop styles of delivering messages and navigating legal rules based on their beliefs about what they should accomplish, their group membership

---

[42] M Lipsky, *Street-Level Bureaucracy: Dilemmas of the Individual in Public Services* (New York, Russell Sage Foundation, 1980); JM Prottas, *People Processing: The Street-Level Bureaucrat in Public Service Bureaucracies* (Lexington, VA, Lexington Books, 1979).

[43] Jewell, *Agents* (n 41); M Diller, 'The Revolution in Welfare Administration: Rules, Discretion, and Entrepreneurial Government' (2000) 75 *New York University Law Review* 1121; EZ Brodkin, 'Inside the Welfare Contract: Discretion and Accountability in State Welfare Administration' (1997) 71 *Social Service Review* 1; S Maynard-Moody and M Musheno, *Cops, Teachers, Counsellors* (Ann Arbor, MI, University of Michigan Press, 2003).

[44] eg Lipsky, *Street-Level Bureaucracy* (n 42); Prottas, *People Processing* (n 42); J Braithwaite and V Braithwaite, 'The Politics of Legalism: Rules Versus Standards in Nursing Home Regulation' (1995) 4 *Social & Legal Studies* 307; J Raso, 'Displacement as Regulation: New Regulatory Technologies and Front-Line Decision-Making in Ontario Works' (2017) 32 *Canadian Journal of Law & Society* 75.

[45] Jewell, *Agents* (n 41).

[46] Watkins-Hayes, *New Welfare Bureaucrats* (n 7) 30–32. Watkins-Hayes' study centres on caseworkers in the Temporary Assistance for Needy Families programme, an American last-resort cash assistance programme.

and their perception of administrative cues.[47] As workers become socialised within a catch-all bureaucracy, Watkins-Hayes suggests that two professional identity types emerge: the first is efficiency engineers – a rules-observant, efficient bureaucrat role; the second is social workers – a client counselling, rules-bending role. These identities shape how workers navigate programme rules and deliver benefits and services to the public.[48] While she positions these professional identities at either end of a continuum, Watkins-Hayes analyses how they intersect with front-line workers' social identities (ie class, race, gender) and shape caseworkers' understanding and performance of their roles.

Other research suggests that similar professional identities exist within catch-all bureaucracies that correspond with Mashaw's bureaucratic justice and professional treatment models. For example, in her study of municipal service providers, DeHart-Davis proposes that workers can generally be categorised as having bureaucratic or unbureaucratic personalities. Bureaucratic personalities adhere closely to rules, similar to bureaucratically rational efficiency engineers. Unbureaucratic personalities, meanwhile, bend rules to meet broader programme goals, akin to Watkins-Hayes' social workers and Mashaw's professional treatment model.[49] Maynard-Moody and Musheno, by contrast, claim that front-line workers in a variety of catch-all bureaucracies strategically bounce between state-agent and citizen-agent roles. State-agents, they argue, conceive of their role in relation to rules, self-interest and bureaucratic efficiency, while citizen-agents make decisions in response to their interactions with citizens rather than programme rules or norms.[50] Based on their qualitative study of police officers, teachers and employment counsellors, Maynard-Moody and Musheno suggest that most front-line workers identify as citizen-agents rather than state-agents, but may strategically act as state-agents depending on their individual interactions. While these studies offer insights into how front-line workers ascribe to professional identity types, they conceive of workers as falling and more or less remaining at one of two ends of a continuum.[51] Just as one administrative justice model becomes dominant within an agency in this theory, in street-level bureaucrat literature workers settle into and maintain a professional identity: either as bureaucratic efficiency engineers who apply rules consistently, or as professionally minded social workers who bend rules to meet individuals' unique needs.

Like the officials in these studies, my research participants explicitly described themselves and their colleagues as ascribing to two professional identities,[52] with efficient 'black-and-white' rule-enforcers in one group and 'pro-client' rule-benders in the other. These categories helped caseworkers rationalise how they performed operational discretion and to articulate how their approaches converged or diverged from those of their colleagues.

---

[47] Maynard-Moody and Musheno, 'State Agent' (n 7); Brodkin, 'Inside the Welfare Contract' (n 43); Oberfield, *Becoming Bureaucrats* (n 41).
[48] Watkins-Hayes, *New Welfare Bureaucrats* (n 7) 10–12, 14–16.
[49] L DeHart-Davis, 'The Unbureaucratic Personality' (2007) 67 *Public Administration Review* 892.
[50] Maynard-Moody and Musheno, *Cops* (n 43).
[51] Longitudinal research suggests that front-line workers' professional identities become set over time, and that they remain more settled than Maynard-Moody and Musheno suggest: ZW Oberfield, 'Rule-Following and Discretion at Government's Frontlines: Continuity and Change During Organization Socialization' (2009) 20 *Journal of Public Administration Research & Theory: JPART* 735.
[52] This positioning came through consistently in my research across sites, and without prompting. Similar distinctions appear in social work studies of Ontario Works delivery: S Baker Collins, 'The Space *in* the Rules: Bureaucratic Discretion in the Administration of Ontario Works' (2016) 15 *Social Policy & Society* 221.

Some workers explicitly identified themselves as 'pro-client' decision-makers who would locate and operationalise discretion wherever they could find it, even if it required 'bending' programme rules. A number of these individuals had experience working with very marginalised benefits recipients with histories of chronic homelessness or alcohol and drug dependencies. Others described themselves as risk-takers who were not afraid to advocate to management staff for an exceptional legislative or policy interpretation so that a particularly needy or sympathetic client received benefits. These workers linked their approach to a different 'mindset' or disposition. The following participant, for instance, described herself as a rule-bender who sought the best outcomes for her clients within the confines of anticipated managerial review:

> How much discretion you feel you have really has to do with workers' personality. It's a matter of what is your level of fear or concern about management coming to you. And my practice has always been – my coworkers laugh at me for it – 'cause I always say, 'I *bend* rules. I don't break them.' So, *I* feel that as long as I just bend the rule, I didn't *break* it, I shouldn't be able to get in trouble for it, right? And just measuring things by best outcome for the client within guidelines. So, if you have to *bend* the rule a little bit to support a client, how much trouble will I actually get into for maybe bending the rule or stretching it a little bit too far?

By contrast, other workers positioned themselves as 'black-and-white' rule-enforcers, echoing the commitments of both efficiency engineers and bureaucratic rationality. These workers took a clear-cut approach to performing operational discretion, so that they could quickly justify their decisions as rooted in 'the legislation' should a client complain to a supervisor or office manager. One front-line worker noted:

> I'm also very black-and-white: 'Yes I can. No I can't.' And it's not personal. I can justify every answer I give to anybody because I may have to. So, I think about, 'Ok, if I say no, what does this look like? Is my supervisor gonna support me, and does the legislation support my answer?' If it's yes, then that's how I move forward. If I believe it, that's how I move forward.

However, this worker also tempered her black-and-white approach. She noted that she might find 'grey area' within the rules, provided that she could justify her decision to avoid future conflicts with clients:

> I'm a black-and-white person. I can work in a grey area, but I have to be able to justify it in a way that actually agrees with me, right? And I have a means of operating where I think – like, I'm very careful not to make promises I can't keep to my clients.

Although each group contrasted their approach with that of colleagues in a different camp, they did not condemn one another. Black-and-white caseworkers may have expressed frustration with their pro-client coworkers, and vice versa, but each group appeared to accept that they needed to reach outcomes that would be agreeable to workers from across the professional identity spectrum. This behaviour was likely encouraged by the fact that each group was more or less equally represented among the caseworkers in the offices I studied. Furthermore, the supervisors who provided advice on difficult cases and office managers also seemed evenly dispersed between both professional identity models.

While these two stylised identity types operate within the Ontario Works programme, the bureaucratic efficiency versus individualised treatment dichotomy oversimplifies how even the staunchest rule-enforcers and rule-benders perform operational discretion in practice. Caseworkers who identified themselves as 'black-and-white' decision-makers recalled instances where they broadly interpreted narrow rules to reconcile conflicting programme norms. Likewise, those participants who identified as 'pro-client' social workers described situations where they were unable to bend the rules far enough to provide a client with a particular benefit because one programme norm weighed heavily in their decision (ie promoting self-sufficiency over preventing hardship). This heterogeneity will be familiar to socio-legal scholars, who have long recognised that individuals tend to shift between cognitive structures and previously constructed interpretations of rules.[53] Yet my research also suggests that the divergence we might expect to find among workers with polarised professional identities is tempered by the normative balancing act that all decision-makers, regardless of their professional identity, described undertaking. Many front-line workers perform discretion in the space between these poles, where workers' professional identities operate more ambiguously than street-level bureaucracy literature has previously suggested.

The remainder of this chapter thus explores this space in between professional treatment, or pro-client social work, and bureaucratic rationality, or black-and-white efficiency engineering. As I go on to demonstrate, caseworkers commonly reconcile overlapping and conflicting norms rather than simply adhering to a subset of principles that reinforce their professional identity.

IV. Administrative Justice as a Middle Ground: Accommodating Divergent Norms

Ontario Works caseworkers routinely make decisions in which they have multiple options available to them. In these circumstances, caseworkers must perform operational discretion. While they may consult with colleagues and supervisors on such issues, their practices also suggest that they reconcile competing programme norms in the process. As this section will demonstrate, regardless of a front-line worker's professional identity, this normative balancing ultimately engages decision-makers within a mid-space between bureaucratic rationality and professional treatment models. This process has micro- and macro-level effects. Not only does it mitigate the potential polarising effects of workers' individual professional identities, but, at an institutional level, normative balancing also suggests that administrative justice may require accommodating and balancing between models rather than evaluating outcomes based on a (purportedly) dominant model of justice. The possibilities of balancing between justice models are further bolstered by, and perhaps depend upon, the fact that Ontario Works is governed by multiple norms that engage both professional treatment and bureaucratic rationality values.

---

[53] These observations about social and cognitive heterogeneity, in which individuals invoke alternative meanings in a single utterance and switch between 'different registers of voice', stem from Bakhtin's concept of 'heteroglossia', which is rooted in the specific literary form of the novel: MM Bakhtin, *The Dialogic Imagination: Four Essays*, ed M Holquist, trs C Emerson and M Holquist (Austin, TX, University of Texas Press, 1981). Despite these origins, Bakhtin's concept of heteroglossia has influenced how socio-legal scholars approach apparent disunity and incoherence in a variety of individual and institutional settings: P Ewick and SS Silbey, *The Common Place of Law: Stories from Everyday Life* (Chicago, IL, University of Chicago Press, 1998) 50–51; M Valverde, *Chronotopes of Law: Jurisdiction, Scale, and Governance* (Abingdon, Routledge, 2015).

This section unpacks and substantiates these claims. Using my empirical data, I articulate a series of six norms operating within the Ontario Works programme and illustrate how caseworkers engage in individual normative balancing, with institutional effects. Though front-line workers may indicate that they are guided by only one norm, I show that this is rarely, if ever, the case. Rather, by engaging in a shared process of balancing divergent norms, workers moderate how they perform operational discretion so that their decisions fall within a band of possible outcomes somewhere between bureaucratic rationality and professional treatment. Because of the confluence of professional identity types and programme norms, this band of institutionally acceptable outcomes may be narrower than the range of 'reasonable' outcomes that a court might identify as acceptable on merits review. Thus, we may regard caseworkers as regulating themselves more closely, but quite differently, than a court would through judicial review proceedings.

My fieldwork suggests that Ontario Works caseworkers balance between the following six principles. As they perform operational discretion, these workers strive:

(a) not to create undue hardship;
(b) to act in a client's best interests;
(c) to safeguard taxpayer-funded benefits;
(d) to promote self-sufficiency;
(e) to efficiently manage their overall workload; and
(f) to move clients from Ontario Works to an alternative means of support.

While these norms intersect, front-line workers distinguish between them and suggest that they function in different ways. For this reason, I articulate each one as a distinct principle. The first four norms require caseworkers to consider the effect of their decisions on a particular benefit applicant or recipient, but of course have wider implications for taxpayer-funded benefits. Though connected to new public management initiatives, these four have stronger ties to the purposes of the OWA 1997. The last two norms are more managerial than legal, as they mandate caseworkers to evaluate how a particular decision will affect their overall workplace, such as their ability to manage their caseload, while also impacting individual clients insofar as moving a client into paid employment is understood to be in a client's interests. While traceable to the goals of the OWA 1997, these two norms cleave closely to new public management strategies.

At the outset, it is necessary to address some preliminary concerns about the uniqueness, origin and function of these six programme norms. First, in terms of their novelty, competing principles are not exclusive to Ontario Works; rather, they are a common feature of legal-managerial regimes governing other administrative agencies.[54] Because they tend to serve particularly divisive goals, however, welfare and other last-resort programmes may be subject to an even wider range of guiding principles.[55] The tensions that arise as workers balance between these principles do not suggest a deficit in the Ontario Works programme

---

[54] Mashaw, *Bureaucratic Justice* (n 22); Brodkin, 'Inside the Welfare Contract' (n 43); Baldwin and Hawkins, 'Davis Reconsidered' (n 21).

[55] V Eubanks, *Automating Inequality: How High-Tech Tools Profile, Police, and Punish the Poor* (New York, St Martin's Press, 2017); N Harris, *Law in a Complex State: Complexity in the Law & Structure of Welfare* (Oxford, Hart Publishing, 2013); P Henman, *Governing Electronically: E-Government and the Reconfiguration of Public Administration, Policy and Power* (London, Palgrave Macmillan, 2010).

or its legal architecture; if anything, they show that front-line workers are doing the difficult job delegated to them by provincial legislators. Most importantly, as this chapter demonstrates, caseworkers feel bound by conflicting norms and perform sophisticated balancing acts that might diverge from (but are no less reasonable than) the weighing and balancing hinted at in conventional legal analyses of discretion and reasonableness.

As for their origin, these six norms have both managerial and legal sources. They mirror the 'new public management' strategies that have transformed public service delivery since the 1990s, as well as the stated legislative objectives of the OWA 1997. New public management is, admittedly, a slippery term.[56] However, its most uncontroversial features are evident in Ontario Works, including commitments to individualised customer service, operational efficiency and horizontal disaggregation of public services.[57] These values are embodied in the managerial initiatives and regulatory mechanisms common to my research sites, such as performance-based employee reviews, regular randomised audits and customer service initiatives. They also echo throughout Ontario Works' legislative framework, which has a number of intersecting and diverging principles embedded within it.[58] The purpose section of the OWA 1997, for instance, reflects these tensions:

1. The purpose of this Act is to establish a program that,
   (a) recognizes individual responsibility and promotes self-reliance through employment;
   (b) provides temporary financial assistance to those most in need while they satisfy obligations to become and stay employed;
   (c) effectively serves people needing assistance; and
   (d) is accountable to the taxpayers of Ontario.

These combined principles are traceable throughout the norms that caseworkers describe as guiding their routine discretionary decisions.

Finally, in terms of their function, the six programme norms are constantly balanced by front-line workers. Thus, while I tease out their distinct features, I also show how they are often all at work. While research participants may describe how a particular decision was influenced by one principle, other norms are subtly operating. What is significant is their effect: front-line workers feel bound, to some degree, by these norms; and, by negotiating between them, workers ultimately accommodate, at an institutional scale, both bureaucratic rationality and professional treatment justice models.

The theoretical conflicts that legal scholars might identify between these six norms may not arise in practice; if they do, caseworkers appear to resolve such conflicts in novel ways. For instance, the norm of not creating undue hardship might hypothetically conflict with the norm of advancing a client towards self-sufficiency, particularly if we accept that some

---

[56] M Barzelay, *The New Public Management: Improving Research and Policy Dialogue* (Berkeley, CA, University of California Press, 2000); P Dunleavy and C Hood, 'From Old Public Administration to New Public Management' (1994) 14 *Public Money & Management* 9.

[57] eg P Dunleavy et al, 'New Public Management is Dead – Long Live Digital-Era Governance' (2006) 16 *Journal of Public Administration Research and Theory: J-PART* 467.

[58] Socio-legal scholars recognise that managerial and legal standards may cross-pollinate over time, which might partially explain the synergy between new public management goals and the objectives of the OWA 1997, eg most recently, LB Edelman, *Working Law: Courts, Corporations, and Symbolic Civil Rights* (Chicago, IL, University of Chicago Press, 2016).

amount of hardship is necessary for promoting self-reliance or disciplining clients who disregard programme rules. In practice, however, front-line workers may find both norms to be complementary, noting that clients must be supported if they are to exit the Ontario Works programme. Thus, the in-between space that front-line workers evidently engage in through their everyday practices may offer useful insights for administrative justice theory.

In what follows, I connect these norms to legislative and managerial principles and show how they arise in my research data. I also illustrate how navigating this normative landscape not only regulates caseworkers' operational discretion, but also balances administrative justice models.

A. Do not Create Undue Hardship

When describing how they performed operational discretion, front-line workers explicitly indicated that they aimed to not create hardship for their clients (which they sometimes described as 'preventing' hardship). This norm reflects two of the four stated objectives of the OWA 1997: to 'provid[e] temporary financial assistance to those most in need'; and to 'effectively serv[e] people needing assistance'.[59] Intentionally creating hardship for Ontario Works recipients is, of course, an *in*effective means of serving those who need assistance. A desire to not create hardship also parallels new public management's goal of reorienting public services from a hierarchical bureaucratic model to one that values individualised 'customer service'.[60]

Most front-line workers appear to consider whether a particular decision will create undue hardship for a client before performing operational discretion. Where written rules were flexible, some stated that they must 'err on the side of the client' because they 'didn't want to cause any hardship'. Not creating hardship influenced even those workers who did not describe themselves as being particularly 'pro-client'.[61] One caseworker who self-identified as a black-and-white efficiency engineer explained this norm's strength as follows: 'People scream bloody murder and we just generate those funds for them. The legislation is often bypassed, as we, as they say, try to avoid hardship or however it's justified, right?'

This norm is so ingrained that many caseworkers recounted using 'hardship' as a code word when they needed supervisory approval before turning to exceptional emergency assistance rules to provide assistance. One of my research participants frankly explained the power of 'hardship' when seeking a supervisor's support for an extraordinary decision to replace a lost cheque:

> Before issuing additional benefits, you have to have spoken to a supervisor to say, 'Listen, my client lost their money and I need a double issuance this month.' Or 'I've already issued this, but

---

[59] OWA 1997, ss 1(b)–(c).

[60] C Pollitt, *Managerialism and the Public Service*, 2nd edn (Oxford, Blackwell, 1993); J Soss, RC Fording and SF Schram, *Disciplining the Poor: Neoliberal Paternalism and the Persistent Power of Race* (Chicago, IL, University of Chicago Press, 2011) ch 10, note how 'customer' terminology has infiltrated Florida's TANF programme and other social services. See also D Cowan and S Halliday, *The Appeal of Internal Review: Law, Administrative Justice, and the (non-)Emergence of Disputes* (Oxford, Hart Publishing, 2003) ch 4.

[61] This norm appeared to be a particularly strong guide for caseworkers. It may be connected to the pull of 'humanitarian reason,' which Fassin identifies as the central value underlying contemporary international politics: D Fassin, *Humanitarian Reason: A Moral History of the Present*, tr R Gomme (Berkeley, CA, University of California Press, 2012).

they need it. I can't get the cheque back from the landlord but they need it today. They swear that the money went this place.' And you just run that word 'hardship' and supervisors get frightened. They do! [laughs ... imitating supervisor] 'Ohhh! Don't say the word "hardship"! Give it to them!'.

While this norm closely aligns with notions of professional treatment and pro-client social work, front-line workers also harmonise it with principles, such as efficient case management and promoting self-sufficiency, that align more closely with bureaucratic rationality. For instance, participants noted that granting clients benefits could make volatile clients easier to work with and encourage them to meet programme requirements. This accommodating between norms comes through in the following passage, where a caseworker describes how she uses operational discretion to both prevent hardship and more efficiently manage high-needs clients:

> So, if it says, 'they may be eligible if they are in an activity,' or whatever, I feed on that word 'may' because it's not absolute. And I think if a client is experiencing hardship I just really try – if I can hear they're struggling, I don't care. I'll just do whatever I can. I don't like to hear clients struggling because they're harder to work with when they are in crisis. And they can be at risk of so many things.[62]

Thus, the pro-client norm of preventing client hardship may converge with principles, such as efficiently managing one's caseload and even promoting self-sufficiency, that cleave more closely to bureaucratic rationality. Of course, promoting self-sufficiency may also be pro-client, in that it may support self-determination among clients. This practice of reconciling divergent norms was demonstrated not only by social work-oriented caseworkers who served clients with histories of homelessness or substance abuse, but also by front-line workers who used supplementary benefits to entice clients to return to their next appointment. Research participants might explicitly identify these decisions as preventing hardship for particularly desperate clients, but distributing additional benefits also enabled them to reward responsible clients and to oversee large caseloads, especially as they were under management-imposed pressure to meet their clients more frequently. These norms thus interact in ways that are more sophisticated than simply being either in harmony or in conflict.

B. Act in a Client's Best Interests

In addition to not creating hardship, many participants also indicated that their operational discretion was guided by a commitment to act in a client's best interests, or 'erring on the side of the client'. Of course, what might be in a client's 'best interests' is flexible. Consequently, this norm can be linked to three of the legislative objectives of the OWA 1997: the two objectives noted in the previous section (providing temporary assistance to those most in need and effectively serving people needing assistance) and a third objective, 'recogniz[ing] individual responsibility and promot[ing] self-reliance through employment'.[63] Acting in a client's best

---

[62] This participant's account echoes Prottas's finding decades earlier that front-line workers use discretion not only to bend rules to fit their clients, but also to bend clients' circumstances to fit within the rules: Prottas, *People Processing* (n 42). Prottas claimed that front-line workers engage in this dual bending to assert their own professional autonomy, but my findings suggest that more is at play.
[63] OWA 1997, s 1(a).

interests also echoes the 'customer service' focus of new public management strategies.[64] It may seem bizarre to conflate 'customers' with the marginalised individuals who seek assistance from last-resort benefits. Nonetheless, 'customer satisfaction' has motivated welfare delivery reforms in both the UK[65] and the US,[66] and it spurred some of the policy initiatives at my research sites.[67]

Acting in a client's best interest clearly overlaps with the norm of not creating undue hardship and others, such as promoting self-sufficiency. While they share common normative ground, I distinguish between them because front-line workers explicitly referenced each principle during my fieldwork. Further, each of these principles appears to perform different work. Acting in a client's best interests seemed foundational; like efficiently managing one's caseload, it is almost always operating in the background. Preventing hardship and promoting self-sufficiency, by contrast, are more concentrated variations of acting in a client's best interest. Where a particular discretionary decision would clearly create hardship for an individual, the norm of preventing hardship might exercise strong pull (a distinctive, stronger pull than acting in a client's best interests) as workers balanced it against other programme norms. The same can be said about the relationship between the principles of acting in a client's best interests and promoting self-sufficiency. Thus, despite their common elements, I consider these norms separately from one another because all three had varied effects on my research participants.

While the term 'best interests' may be vague, this norm was frequently referred to by research participants as an influential rule of thumb. Front-line workers described how this principle led them to locate 'grey area' in legal rules to respond to Ontario Works recipients' unique needs. One front-line worker explained this principle's force, noting that it would encourage her to 'go around' policies via creatively relying on *other* policies to support clients:

> There's an overlying policy that we have to *adhere* to, but if you're creative enough to get around that in your procedures, to support the people that you're serving, then every office will do things differently. And I know I have in my own work, for sure. If it benefits the client at the end of the day, I will do what I have to do to go around that policy and make sure that we're assisting them.

This norm might seem to polarise between pro-client workers, who strive to act in their clients' best interests, and black-and-white workers, who efficiently manage their large caseloads, but workers instead reconciled acting in a client's best interests with other principles, such as managing their caseloads efficiently and preventing hardship. This balancing was evident when front-line workers explained how they determined benefits start dates for recently unemployed Ontario Works applicants. Though outsiders might expect such a question to be clearly regulated by the OWA 1997, it was an area in which caseworkers had

---

[64] Dunleavy and Hood, 'From Old Public Administration' (n 56).

[65] S Halliday, 'Institutional Racism in Bureaucratic Decision-Making: A Case Study in the Administration of Homelessness Law' (2000) 27 *Journal of Law & Society* 449, 457, noting that in some offices, UK homeless persons applying for housing support were referred to as 'customers'.

[66] Diller, 'Revolution in Welfare Administration' (n 43); J Soss, RC Fording and SF Schram, 'The Organization of Discipline: From Performance Management to Perversity and Punishment' (2011) 21 *Journal of Public Administration Research and Theory: J-PART* 203.

[67] One such initiative was a new policy that caseworkers must acknowledge clients who dropped into their offices, unscheduled, within 15 minutes. Failure to do so could result in their name's being announced over the office intercom system.

broad flexibility. For instance, a front-line worker explained how she might find flexibility in income-reporting deadlines and effective eligibility dates out of a concern for an applicant's best interests. By doing so, she would ensure that a newly unemployed individual who had earned a small income in the same month that he or she applied for assistance (which might render that individual ineligible for benefits during that month and potentially the next) would become eligible for Ontario Works benefits starting in his or her first month without income. Ultimately, this decision would prevent the shortfall in this individual's finances that would otherwise occur if he or she had to return to the office the following month, when he or she had no income whatsoever, and reapply for Ontario Works:

> So, income received from the 16th of October until the 15th of November will affect the December entitlement, okay? So, we don't deduct up front. It's sort of a month later. So, if someone applying now at this time in October, like today, and they lost their job last week, we would look at all of the income that they had received in the month of grant. So, there is a bit of a different way that we look at it. It depends on what are the expenses that they had, and what happened. We may *not* do the deduction based on the income statement period, or we look at maybe not issuing for the month of October anymore but looking at November and trying to support them. So, *those* are the cases that sometimes the caseworker checks with the supervisor as to what would be the best approach to take, not to be punitive towards the applicant, to see if there's a way that we can support them.

In these circumstances, the law does not specify a particular outcome. When an individual applies for Ontario Works assistance shortly after losing his or her job, Ontario Works legislation and regulations are silent on how front-line workers should treat that applicant's recent employment earnings; these details are left to a provincial policy.[68] Likewise, though the Regulation states that front-line workers 'shall' make certain inquiries into an applicant's circumstances, the details of these inquiries are left to provincial policies and local office practices.[69] The Regulation gives caseworkers freedom to set an effective date for benefits eligibility decisions and flexibility in how to treat income from a recently lost job. In terms of a decision date, front-line workers are empowered to set the date on which their decisions take effect, which may include the day on which they met with an applicant or a previous or future point in time.[70] Front-line workers cannot, practically speaking, make decisions that would take effect too far into the future. However, if they receive evidence from an applicant showing a recent job loss, as well as other supporting documents (ie, bank

---

[68] The OWA 1997 does include some eligibility requirements for benefits applications. For instance, applicants must be residents of Ontario, their budgetary expenses must exceed their income, the value of their assets must fall below amounts set out in the Regulation (which vary according to family size) and they must provide a municipal caseworker with all of the information needed to determine eligibility: OWA 1997, s 7(3), which is negatively worded to read, 'No person is eligible for income assistance unless …' and then lists a series of conditions. Details about the amount, timing and manner of providing both income assistance (core benefits) and employment assistance (supplementary benefits) are left to the Regulation: OWA 1997, s 16.
[69] O Reg 134/98, s 22 states, 'In determining the eligibility of an applicant who applies for basic financial assistance, the administrator shall make or cause to be made an enquiry into the living conditions and the financial, employment and other circumstances of the members of the benefit unit.'
[70] O Reg 134/98, s 25(1) states, 'A decision of the administrator shall be effective from the date fixed by the administrator, whether it is before, on or after the date of the decision.' Section 25(2) then sets out a series of rules for calculating budgetary requirements (shelter, basic needs), which allow front-line workers some ability to calculate shelter costs to be lower than an applicant's actual shelter costs and that require basic needs costs be prorated for those applicants who apply for benefits mid-month.

account statements, proof of residence, housing costs, etc), workers are empowered (but not required) to look to the next month in which the benefits applicant will have no income and grant Ontario Works benefits beginning in that month. If the applicant had any earned but unpaid wages, he or she would have to report that income, once it is actually received, to the local Ontario Works office, which may lead to an overpayment being calculated and gradually recovered from any future Ontario Works benefits payments.[71]

While the caseworker above describes being guided by a desire to support her clients' best interests, her discretion is shaped by other norms, such as efficient case management and preventing hardship. Requiring an applicant to return the following month and reapply for Ontario Works almost certainly creates undue hardship, which caseworkers may construe flexibly to respond to clients' unique circumstances. However, this outcome is also highly inefficient. A delay in receiving Ontario Works benefits could threaten an individual's housing, as well as the ability to pay utility bills or to purchase groceries. Moreover, rejecting a newly unemployed person's benefits application simply creates future work, requiring a caseworker to meet this applicant again the following month and review the same documents with a client who may then be in crisis. Thus, acting in a client's best interest, which echoes the professional treatment model, is balanced together with a range of other norms, such as preventing hardship and managing one's caseload efficiently.

C. Safeguard Taxpayer-funded Benefits

While my research participants indicated that they were guided by 'pro-client' principles such as preventing hardship or supporting a client's best interests, many were steered by a need to conserve publicly funded benefits. When evaluating available options, participants explained that they had to consider that they were spending government funds. They would also indicate that they must be 'accountable' – that is, able to explain why they issued funds – through a combination of recorded reasons and documented evidence. This norm reflects one of the stated aims of the OWA 1997: to establish a programme that 'is accountable to the taxpayers of Ontario'.[72] This preoccupation with 'accountability' also mirrors new public management strategies, which strive to decrease programme spending through a combination of performance targets, incentives to ensure workers achieve those targets, and intensive auditing as a primary means of tracking the performance of front-line workers and their managers.[73]

---

[71] Though the Regulation includes asset ceilings and formulas for calculating eligibility, it is silent on how to treat income from a recently lost job. Instead, provincial policies clarify that unspent employment income received before an individual makes an Ontario Works application should be treated as an asset. Meanwhile, income that is earned, but not received, during the month of application should not be considered income until it has been received by a benefits applicant: Ontario Works Policy Directive 5.1: *Income and Exemptions* (last updated June 2018). Because front-line workers can (but are not required to) make eligibility decisions that take effect in the future, a front-line worker may decide that someone is eligible for assistance at a specific point in time that falls *after* the date on which the worker and the benefits applicant met in person. Such a decision would be based on information that the benefits applicant provides to the caseworker at this meeting: OWA 1997, ss 19, 25.

[72] OWA 1997, s 1(d).

[73] M Barzelay, *Breaking Through Bureaucracy: A New Vision for Managing in Government* (Berkeley, CA, University of California Press, 1992); M Power, *The Audit Society: Rituals of Verification* (Oxford, Oxford University Press, 1997).

As with the principle of acting in a client's best interests, safeguarding taxpayer-funded benefits has ambiguous normative content. This ambiguity is reflected in my interviews, where some participants referred to a rule of thumb that they should 'err on the side of caution', rather than 'on the side of clients', when performing discretion, so as to judiciously conserve taxpayer-funded benefits. Others would indicate that this norm required them to carefully weigh all of the relevant factors in a particular decision because they were spending tax dollars:

> In terms of issuing, it's not my money. Just like I say to the other workers too, it's not – it's the Province's money. I have to really think, I *do*, or else I wouldn't be in this specialised role if the supervisors thought I wasn't being responsible.

Some pro-client caseworkers critiqued this norm's ability to sway colleagues who may be more inclined to 'err on the side of caution' and refuse to grant benefits where the legislative framework was ambiguous. Yet this norm also encourages front-line workers in situations where they have the discretion to inquire into clients' personal lives but are uncomfortable doing so. For instance, a pro-client social worker described how conserving taxpayer-funded benefits helped her justify the decision to investigate the case of two roommates who received Ontario Works benefits as single persons, and consider whether they were actually co-dependent members of one 'benefit unit'. These inquiries are tricky: they require caseworkers to invasively scrutinise people's private lives, and if certain facts are discovered during the process, workers may have little choice but to reduce a client's already low monthly benefits payments. This caseworker explained:

> When couples live together and say, 'Oh, we're just roommates.' And we need to investigate a little bit further whether they have joint bank accounts, whether they're perceived by their friends as a couple, or are they on the lease together as a family unit, or just – like, there are different things where we need to look at things together to make the best possible decision. And it's not always about really penalising the client, making them ineligible. It's just us being the stewards, applying the assistance or assessing the eligibility. We need to make sure we do it the best way possible so that it's equitable to anybody else who applies being in similar circumstances. Because we're accountable for what we do. It's the taxpayers' money that we assign, so there *has* to be compliance with the policies and guidelines and with the Act. We're accountable for every benefit that we issue. So there has to be justification for any of that.

Because monthly benefits are so low, adult benefit recipients commonly live with roommates. In these cases, Ontario Works' legislative framework permits a range of outcomes, depending on how a caseworker interprets a particular client's circumstances. Some options may be foreclosed to a caseworker. For instance, if a worker discovers that a client is legally married to a roommate, or if a client and his or her roommate are parties to a court order requiring one to support the other, they must be considered members of the same benefit unit.[74] However, many shared living situations are unclear. In these instances, caseworkers must evaluate whether 'the extent of the social and familial aspects of the relationship between the two persons' and 'the extent of the financial support provided by one person to the other or the degree of financial interdependence between the two persons' are 'consistent with cohabitation'.[75] The OWA 1997 and the Regulation offer no guidance as to what

---

[74] Definition of 'spouse', O Reg 135/98, s 1(1).
[75] ibid para (d).

'consistent with cohabitation' means. While policy tools, including a provincial questionnaire, guide how front-line workers perform operational discretion,[76] norms such as conserving taxpayer-funded benefits also steer workers towards a particular outcome.

As with other norms, safeguarding public benefits overlaps with and tempers other guiding principles, such as not creating undue hardship by 'penalising' a client. As the above-quoted participant explains, she reconciles contrasting norms so that she can 'look at things together to make the best possible decision'. In the process, this normative balancing act also tempers the result that she might reach if her professional identity as a pro-client social worker was the sole guide of her operational discretion. The flexibility of this balancing process may suggest that any decision can be rationalised as supporting many norms simultaneously, but this process nonetheless imposes some basic constraints on how front-line workers perform operational discretion. While they may weigh things differently from case to case, reconciling between norms mitigates against the most egregious outcomes that outsiders might fear will result in a programme shot through with formal discretion.

D. Promote Self-sufficiency

A fourth distinct norm, promoting clients' self-sufficiency or responsibility, also guides Ontario Works caseworkers. Participants explained how, as they used discretion, they would consider whether a particular outcome would support a client who was taking steps to become self-sufficient or whether it might encourage responsibility. This norm is linked to the legislative purpose of the OWA 1997 of 'recogniz[ing] individual responsibility and promot[ing] self-reliance through employment',[77] as well as its goal of assisting individuals who are taking steps to obtain paid employment.[78] Promoting self-sufficiency is also traceable to new public management principles, though perhaps less so than the other norms discussed here. New public management-inspired reforms to social service agencies have arguably reinforced the view that receiving public benefits, especially from catch-all programmes like Ontario Works, is a temporary state of affairs and that such programmes will eventually transform benefits recipients into self-sufficient, stably employed individuals.[79] These reforms indirectly promote client self-sufficiency through measurable performance targets and audits, which may evaluate front-line workers' performance according to whether they produce reformed, self-sufficient clients.[80] This evaluative strategy has a normative trickle-down effect, as it encourages front-line workers to teach their clients lessons by paying or withholding benefits.[81]

---

[76] The 'Questionnaire', or 'Form 2764,' discussed in Ontario Works Policy Directive 3.3: *Co-Residency* (last updated July 2008).
[77] OWA 1997, s 1(a).
[78] OWA 1997, s 1(b).
[79] Eubanks, *Automating Inequality* (n 55); MK Meyers, NM Riccucci and I Lurie, 'Achieving Goal Congruence in Complex Environments: The Case of Welfare Reform' (2001) 11 *Journal of Public Administration Research & Theory: J-PART* 165; V Lens, 'Work Sanctions Under Welfare Reform: Are They Helping Women Achieve Self-Sufficiency?' (2006) 13 *Duke Journal of Gender Law & Policy* 255.
[80] Barzelay, *The New Public Management* (n 56); P Aucoin, *The New Public Management: Canada in Comparative Perspective* (Ottawa, Institute for Research on Public Policy, 1990).
[81] Soss, Fording and Schram, *Disciplining the Poor* (n 60).

As with the other principles identified here, this norm's content is somewhat fluid. Promoting self-sufficiency may guide caseworkers to reward or punish clients for behaviours that enhance or detract from their ability to become self-sufficient. Believing that this approach will ultimately help clients to achieve self-sufficiency, front-line workers describe themselves as teaching clients 'soft' and 'hard' lessons. Thus, front-line workers may grant clients access to benefits or services in exchange for responsibility-demonstrating behaviour, such as keeping commitments identified in their Participation Agreements or attending appointments. This norm may also direct workers to withdraw benefits or services to teach a 'lesson' to a client who does not behave responsibly.

Promoting self-sufficiency may justify decisions to provide, delay or withdraw assistance from benefits recipients. Caseworkers who otherwise identify as black-and-white efficiency engineers may gesture towards this norm as supporting a discretionary decision to *provide* clients with supplementary funds to cover public transit passes and cell phones. The written legal framework governing these 'employment-related expense' benefits flexibly permits caseworkers to issue such benefits if clients demonstrate that they are participating in or about to begin an employment assistance activity.[82] As research participants explained, these funds give clients a chance to learn self-sufficiency lessons on their own time. If clients use these funds wisely then they will be better equipped to search for a job, attend vocational training sessions and ultimately (or hopefully) become self-sufficient. However, if clients 'blow' their benefits on something else, they learn the value of responsibility the hard way by having to walk all month or losing telephone access. A self-identified efficiency engineer explained:

> I would *never* deny someone a public transit pass, because if they call the supervisor they're getting a public transit pass, you know what I'm saying? And the thing is, if you blow your public transit pass money, I don't *care*. That just means you're walking all month, 'cause you're not getting another one. So, the thing, with the benefits, is that I'm very inclined to support – so my $250 Employment-Related Expenses (ERE), I rarely give the full ERE. Most of my clients get in the neighbourhood of about $140 a month for a public transit pass and cell phone money. I like to leave the other $100 for wiggle room in case they'd like to take CPR or other courses, forklift training, that type of stuff. Whether or not you actually bought the public transit pass is irrelevant. I gave you your transportation money. If you make a shitty choice, now you're walking all month and that *sucks*, you know what I'm saying? So, honestly, that's where I'm at with that. If they tell me that they're job searching, they're never going to be denied from me a public transit pass or cell phone money, ever. Those are the staples in my opinion.

Though she identified as a black-and-white rule enforcer, this caseworker applies flexible programme rules in a pro-client manner to promote self-sufficiency. Her decision appears to balance this principle with a number of other programme norms. It safeguards taxpayer-funded benefits by withholding some of the total ERE benefit amount this client might otherwise receive. It is in a client's best interests because it creates a reserve of available funds in case future opportunities arise. Further, it efficiently manages this worker's caseload, as setting aside these reserve funds obviates the additional approvals she might need if a client requests additional funds in the same month, while granting transit pass funds reduces the potential for conflict with her clients and with management staff who may take a more pro-client approach.

---

[82] O Reg 134/98, ss 25–26; Ontario Works Policy Directive 7.4: *Employment and Participation Benefits* (last updated May 2016); Ontario Works Policy Directive 7.7: *Other Benefits* (last updated November 2015).

As with the other norms analysed here, workers reconcile the principle of fostering self-sufficiency with others as they perform operational discretion. The following passage illustrates how front-line workers' commitment to other norms – preventing undue hardship or acting in a client's best interests, for example – may be balanced against and moderate the effect of a promoting self-sufficiency principle. At the time of our interview, the participant quoted below worked in a 'customer service' role and was responsible for drop-in clients who were unable to meet with their assigned caseworkers. Here, she contrasts her approach to responsibility and accountability with her colleagues' practices, describing a situation in which a client's monthly benefits payment was delayed after failing to submit documents to the caseworker before the payment processing deadline:

> If someone comes in, say there's been a long weekend and it's August 4th or what have you, you're already into the month and a client comes in about his cheque or her cheque. What I'll often do is I'll take away, I'll remove the direct deposit for that day and request an instant cheque. That's so they can have it today, so they don't have to wait two days for the cheque to be deposited into their bank account. At the same time, I'm educating and informing: 'You know, really you should try to clear this up before the end of the month, before cutoff. You need to have better communication with your worker if possible but because you're saying that it's urgent, you need to pay your rent, your landlord's asking for rent, I'm going to issue it today in a paper cheque to prevent hardship.' I find that there's some workers who like to teach lessons and who will leave it for direct deposit. So that's where the teaching of lessons isn't really, it doesn't sit well with me 'cause it's not our role. But it comes up and I've had conflict with workers about that. I've actually said, 'What are you trying to do?' and they've said, 'Well, they need to learn.' Ok, so you want to teach them a lesson? That I don't, I just don't understand. Like, I *guess* I understand but I don't like it, you know?

Ontario Works' legislative scheme is silent on this matter. This front-line worker describes balancing between the needs to promote self-sufficiency, prevent hardship and act in a client's best interests as she locates and performs operational discretion. Issuing same-day benefits prevents immediate hardship (and possibly crisis) while teaching this client a lesson about how to avoid receiving late Ontario Works payments the following month. Her 'educating and informing' approach is both in the client's best interests and promotes self-sufficiency. By contrast, her stricter colleagues may be more strongly guided by the norm of efficient caseload management, especially at the very busy start of the month. Not only is it less time-consuming for caseworkers to leave benefits payments to be made by direct deposit, but also, because it delays payment, this option teaches clients the importance of meeting documentation deadlines and promotes behaviour (ie, timely document submission) that may make it easier for caseworkers to manage their caseloads in the future.

Thus, even where no written rules guide workers' operational discretion, their decisions remain regulated by a normative balancing process. The relation between these norms remains dynamic, and the in-between space of administrative justice is constituted as these principles are weighed and reconciled with one another.

E. Efficiently Manage the Workload

A fifth norm of efficient workload management informs how front-line decision-makers perform operational discretion. This norm combines the consistent treatment of individual benefits recipients with other elements, such as timesaving decision-making practices, continuous improvement strategies and individually focused customer service. Though efficient case management reflects the normative commitments underlying the OWA 1997, it is primarily linked to new public management goals. Because efficient workload management would ideally lead caseworkers to review and respond to their clients' requests in a fair and timely manner, it arguably furthers two of the four stated purposes of the OWA 1997: effectively serving people who need assistance; and remaining accountable to taxpayers.[83] This principle is more strongly linked to new public management's goals of improving administrative efficiency and increasing agencies' responsiveness to service-users' concerns. These goals are typically pursued through managerial tools, such as output indicators and performance incentives, and quasi-legal instruments, such as internal review mechanisms and agencies' mission statements. All of these tools embed an efficiency ethos within Ontario Works offices.[84]

Efficiency concerns recur throughout my research data and appear to be ubiquitous in local offices. Efficient caseload management is a practical necessity in Ontario Works, where each caseworker is typically responsible for between 100 and 140 'benefit units', with a benefit unit ranging from a single client to a primary client plus his or her dependants (ie spouse/partner, children, other family members). Recent policy and technological developments have intensified the pressure to meet clients frequently, return telephone calls, review new policies, cover the files of vacationing or ill co-workers, and promptly meet with those clients who drop into the office unannounced.

The principle of efficient case management is enriched by other programme norms. As a result, it does not mandate addressing clients' requests in the shortest time possible, nor does it require similar requests to be treated alike (even though, in an ideal world, we might expect that it would include both of these things). Rather, this norm is shaded by the other principles that front-line workers balance as they perform operational discretion. We might assume that black-and-white rule-enforcers would use this norm to justify interpreting Ontario Works rules strictly, in line with a bureaucratic justice model. Yet self-identified black-and-white caseworkers noted that such an approach was impossible, given their large caseloads and performance targets. One participant bluntly stated:

> I think that if you stay true to your role and true to the legislation, you're not going to have a hard time doing your job. But it's the people who think it's their job to, as a taxpayer, to ensure that every dollar going out the door's legitimate: what the hell you going to do with that? To the tune of $250 a month? Do you think you're impacting anything? [...] All of my clients are adults and the reality is that I'm mandated to see them only once every three months. I am not – it's delusional to think that I am going to change the course of any of these peoples' lives. How I approach every day is that I'm at work today, I'm getting paid to service these people essentially, and I can make life harder or easier for 120 people. That's my reach. Nothing greater than that. I can't fix OW [Ontario Works]. I can't fix the Province. I can't fix these peoples' lives. I can make life harder or easier for 120 people. That's it. And the thing is, is that whole 'catch more flies with honey' thing, man I *live* by it. Easy on you, easy on me.

One meaning of efficiency, then, can be characterised as keeping things 'easy on you, easy on me': workers strategically perform operational discretion to keep their clients happy,

---

[83] OWA 1997, ss 1(c)–(d).
[84] Dunleavy and Hood, 'From Old Public Administration' (n 56); Barzelay, *The New Public Management* (n 56).

minimise potential conflicts and encourage clients to comply with programme requirements. As one caseworker noted:

> I'm not able to provide them with a lot of money. If someone is trying to get on their feet or is trying to live with dignity, they need funds in order to be able to do so because things aren't that cheap, even in this city. And in turn, my clients have shown me nothing but respect – they're *lovely*. They will submit forms and receipts on time, because I ask them for things that they need.

Similarly, others explained that if they acknowledged their clients' hardships, this approach would foster a respectful relationship that, ultimately, helped them keep their files up to date. In one participant's words, clients then 'think you understand them and they're more open to coming back to see you'. These caseworkers may take a social work approach, but they do so knowing that their performances are continuously monitored through case management software and assessed against quantified indicators. For instance, workers are expected to meet with clients and update their clients' Participation Agreements every three to six months,[85] and experience pressure to move clients into paid employment. They regularly receive reports about how their individual performances and those of their local office compare with other offices in the same municipal social services department. Thus, even some pro-client social workers noted that they may target their efforts at those clients who seem most employable. Here, efficient case management functions together with other norms – moving clients to alternative means of support, safeguarding taxpayer-funded benefits, acting in a client's best interests – to influence how front-line workers perform operational discretion for differently situated clients. Balancing between these norms, caseworkers aim to reduce their overall workload (however temporarily) and achieve some sense of satisfaction, as they feel that they are positively impacting their clients' lives while keeping the auditors at bay. As a result, these caseworkers may remain motivated to address their more challenging clients and to meet managerial performance targets.

Efficient case management may also bolster caseworkers who proactively suspend or reduce clients' benefits as a means of incentivising them to attend appointments. Some pro-client participants explained that they might have to penalise clients whose behaviour impeded their ability, as caseworkers, to meet performance targets.[86] One front-line worker articulated being sandwiched between serving his clients and meeting efficiency targets:

> We're supposed to see our clients once every three months but they don't respond to the appointment letters, so sometimes we have to put the cheques on hold if they're not showing up for appointments. And, of course, some of them get nasty about it, but the department has to be accountable. […] For me, personally, if you don't show up for the appointment, I put your cheque on hold, then you call. Clients are aware that they're not keeping the appointments. They'll give you a lot of excuses: they didn't get the appointment letter, or the letters come but they didn't open the letters. They become very apathetic about life. They don't even open the letters to read them. So, even if *gold* came in the letters! They tell you, 'Oh yeah, I saw the letter.' You know? But if the *cheque* doesn't come and they have to pay the rent, they'll call. So, I'll say, 'Ok, you'll come?' I don't get any arguments from them. Unfortunately, I have to hold the cheques, but if they don't show up so I can review the file, then *I* hear it. Everything is computerised, and the managers of the offices, they're challenged by *their* managers, so it's like you have 100 cases and 98% of them are outdated,

---

[85] Ontario Works Policy Directive 9.1: *Reviewing Eligibility* (last updated: December 2016).
[86] OWA, s 14; O Reg 134/98, ss 28, 29, 33.

so *they* have to meet their bosses' mandate and we have to try and meet the clients' needs and the clients are not responding! So, sometimes we, as front-line workers, are caught in the middle.

This caseworker explicitly connects efficiency with the managerial pressures common across Ontario Works. Efficiency here is weighed with other norms, such as promoting self-sufficiency, but it strongly guides this caseworker's operational discretion when clients fail to attend scheduled meetings. Workers whose professional identity may incline them towards being more generous or strict rule interpreters all consider how their approach would stand up to efficiency principles. Yet flexibly addressing individual clients' needs and strictly applying programme rules can both be justified as efficient: both approaches may help caseworkers manage their larger caseloads more easily in the future; and efficiency's content is coloured by the range of other principles that guide caseworkers in particular performances of discretion.

F. Move Clients to Alternative Means of Support

Finally, front-line workers are guided by the norm of moving clients from Ontario Works to an alternative means of support. Like efficient caseload management, this norm reflects managerial concerns. It appears to be strongest when aligned with other norms in opposition to rules that may counterproductively bar a client from exiting Ontario Works. This principle connects to some of the stated legislative goals of the OWA 1997, such as 'promot[ing] self-reliance through employment' and assisting people 'while they satisfy obligations to become and stay employed'.[87] Because Ontario Works purports to provide temporary, last-resort benefits, rather than ongoing support, the entire legislative scheme seems focused on moving people *off* Ontario Works benefits, though particular rules may suggest otherwise.[88] This norm relates to many of the new public management principles already articulated. Performance assessments, for example, emphasise the importance of moving clients from Ontario Works to paid employment or other income supplements as appropriate (ie disability benefits, pension schemes). As just noted, these indicators influence routine audits, which quantify individuals' ability to 'exit' clients from the Ontario Works programme.

When it complements other guiding principles, this norm is strongly influential. It guides front-line workers most noticeably when they encounter programme rules or office practices that may trap a client within Ontario Works. Typically, these rules or practices are understood as impeding caseworkers from granting that one final benefit a client may need to obtain paid employment. Research participants recalled how they creatively performed discretion, bending legal rules or departing from local practices, to get clients off of Ontario Works. However, the rules that workers assumed to be black-and-white were rarely inflexible. Many of them contained explicit, tacit or nested grants of discretion; instead, it was workers' repeat performances of operational discretion that appeared to transform flexibly written rules into practices that workers felt bound to replicate.

---

[87] OWA 1997, ss 1(a)–(b).
[88] Some note that Ontario Works rules and the programme's administration appear designed to discourage people from using it as a last-resort source of support: D Herd, A Mitchell and E Lightman, 'Rituals of Degradation: Administration as Policy in the Ontario Works Program' (2005) 39 *Social Policy & Administration* 65, 70–71, 74. Yet the multiple rules that make Ontario Works so unattractive can also trap people within the programme.

Transportation benefits provide the clearest example of how the norm of moving clients to alternative supports interacted with other principles. These benefits are one of many flexible supplementary benefits, and front-line workers have at least six discrete options for granting transportation funds.[89] Nonetheless, many caseworkers perceive limited formal discretion to exist for certain requests for transportation funding. For instance, if a client asks for financial assistance to secure a driver's licence that could be used for both paid employment activities and to meet personal needs (ie a car or motorcycle licence rather than a specialised transport truck or bus licence), caseworkers commonly read (or overlook) Ontario Works' rules to bar this sort of assistance. As a result, this belief in a blanket prohibition on funding the cost of standard drivers' licences has coalesced into an office practice that is essentially more binding than the legislative framework governing Ontario Works. This practice only seems to be challenged when caseworkers recognise an opportunity to help a client exit Ontario Works. In such instances, the norm of moving clients to alternative means of support, balanced with others, encourages caseworkers to depart from office practices and perform operational discretion.

When a driver's licence is the only thing preventing a client from obtaining paid employment, workers might find a way to grant funds so that a client can secure the necessary licence. One caseworker described a situation where a client's access to a well-paying job hinged on his ability to renew his driver's licence. His low monthly benefits were insufficient to cover his licence renewal fees, which included some unpaid traffic tickets. Here, the worker mobilised others in her office to activate the flexibility embedded within supposedly black-and-white rules so that this client could secure his licence, leave Ontario Works and start a new job:

> We don't pay for drivers' licences, that's not something that we do. But when we had a client come with an employment letter that he was going to be hired earning $50,000 a year which, for him, was ... unbelievable, he had tickets that needed to be paid and needed to renew his licence. We don't do that: we *did* it. The manager approved it and we paid for it, because we're not going to stand in the way of that. [...] We're not going to pay for someone to relocate, but a $150 fee to pay for a licence, I understand that we don't *do* that but – like, and the guy is working and he's financially independent, so ...

Unbeknownst to this caseworker, Ontario Works' layered legal framework permits caseworkers to provide clients with the funds needed to renew a driver's licence, especially if the licence is a prerequisite for a specific job. Depending on the client's particular circumstances, this supplementary benefit could be provided as a once-a-year part-time or full-time employment benefit.[90] If these benefits have already been exhausted, funds can be

---

[89] Six mechanisms are traceable throughout my study: (1) the *ad hoc* distribution of in-kind public transit funding by customer service representatives or receptionists, which seems to be an unwritten local policy in many offices; (2) the 'mandatory' transportation benefit (identified as 'Transportation-Medical' in SAMS); (3) the 'discretionary' transportation benefits ('ERE-Transportation' in SAMS) for out-of-pocket transportation costs, regulated by Ontario Works Policy Directive 7.4 (n 82); (4) the 'mandatory' Employment Assistance Activity Benefit, also referred to as the 'Part-Time Employment Benefit', which provides $253 once every 12 months to clients who require assistance covering the costs of employment assistance activities, and which provincial policies indicate must be exhausted first before workers provide clients with ERE-Transportation; (5) other 'discretionary' benefits to assist benefits recipients who need to leave Ontario for work or to be reunited with family members, which Ontario Works Policy Directive 7.7 (n 82) distinguishes from the above benefits; and (6) the 'mandatory' Full-Time Employment Benefit, which provides Ontario Works recipients with $500 once in a 12-month period for the costs associated with beginning a full-time job, which may include transportation costs.

[90] OWA 1997, ss 3, 4; O Reg 134/98, s 55(1), paras 5.1, 6.

provided as an employment-related expense benefit to help offset the costs of participating in vocational training programmes or meeting the licensing requirements of a new employment opportunity.[91] Provincial policies confirm the breadth of this formal discretion,[92] but it is not uncommon for front-line workers to perceive this assistance to be an exception to a general rule against paying for licensing fees. In such cases, a confluence of norms – preventing hardship, acting in a client's best interests, promoting self-sufficiency, even efficient case management – are balanced with moving clients off of Ontario Works to inspire workers to locate and activate discretion.

This norm also guides even black-and-white efficiency engineers, who are less likely to go out of their way to grant benefits. For instance, one such caseworker recalled how this norm encouraged him to provide a client with funding for a motorcycle licence so that he could drive to British Columbia (BC) and take up agricultural work:

> I had one client just two weeks ago, he's going to BC. He wants to go to BC picking fruits for the summer. And many clients wanting to go to another province will come to us and ask us if we can pay their transportation to get there. We can't *do* that. We can't do that. And sometimes, in this client's case, he wanted to go to BC, he wanted transportation money, but he knew that I couldn't give him transportation. He has a motorbike and he was riding out there. He didn't have his M, they're supposed to have an M1 licence, and we don't pay for licences, right? We don't pay for a G licence. Only if you're doing a DZ, AZ or BZ for the bus driving, we'll send you to one of our contracts and we'll pay for that, but your basic driver's licence, we don't pay for that. So M1, we couldn't. But to get his M1, it only cost $100 or $100-and-something. So, I made a decision around giving him $120 for ERE-Transportation costs because he's looking for work, technically, so I give him $120 so that he can use it to – I usually tell them, 'Look, I'm giving you this money for transportation. Don't use that for another worker to say my worker gave me that' – because they like to develop patterns quickly to get what they want, you know? [laughs] So, you have those leeways, you know?

This front-line worker anticipated that the rules regarding driver's licence funding were strict; his initial response to his client's request was, 'We can't *do* that'. However, his performance of discretion is key, because the written legal framework governing Ontario Works enables (but does not require) caseworkers and supervisors to provide funding to help a client cover the costs of travelling to a new place of employment.[93] The norm of moving clients to alternative means of support had a strong pull here because, as he weighed it with other norms falling between bureaucratic rationality and professional treatment, it aligned with so many of them. Providing this client with driver's licence funds prevented hardship and promoted self-sufficiency, as he could take up paid employment instead of having to continue to rely on Ontario Works. It was also in this client's best interests not just because it allowed him to

---

[91] Participants commonly referred to 'ERE' or the 'Employment-Related Expense' benefit. This reference encompasses the benefits listed in the 'Discretionary Benefits' provision of O Reg 134/98. On the issue of funding drivers' licences, s 59(1) and (2) state: '(1) A delivery agent may pay or provide one or more of the benefits set out in subsection (2) to or on behalf of a person referred to in section 8 of the Act in the amount determined by the administrator. (2) For the purposes of subsection (1), the benefits are the following: … 3. The cost of vocational training and retraining. 4. The cost of travel and transportation.'

[92] Ontario Works Policy Directive 7.4 (n 82).

[93] The same OWA 1997 and O Reg 134/98 provisions, cited in n 90 and n 91, support this funding. In addition, Ontario Works Policy Directive 7.7 (n 82), indicates that s 59 'discretionary' benefits may be provided 'when the Administrator considers travel and transportation reasonable and appropriate'. It then uses the example of travelling to a new place of employment as a situation where an administrator may find it reasonable and appropriate to provide a client with financial assistance.

work in a job that he wanted to pursue but also because, as this caseworker noted elsewhere, participating in employment boosts one's self-esteem. While paying for a motorcycle licence may appear to be a poor short-term use of taxpayer-funded benefits, particularly if we are unconvinced that this client would ultimately pursue employment, it arguably safeguards taxpayer funds long-term if this client continues to be employed or becomes eligible for other privately funded assistance programmes.[94] Finally, and perhaps most important for this particular caseworker, this use of operational discretion efficiently reduced his workload, at least for the short term, and improved his file management statistics.

V. Conclusion: The In-between Space of Administrative Justice

This chapter demonstrates how administrative justice becomes instantiated, at an institutional level, in the space between justice models. When idealised, models of justice, such as bureaucratic rationality and professional treatment, may appear to be in conflict. Yet when they are embellished through front-line practices of normative balancing, these same models may not only shade into one another but even be reconcilable. The findings set out throughout the chapter have at least two lessons for administrative justice theory.

The first lesson is that legislative purposes, together with managerial standards, may have significant impacts within administrative agencies. Mashaw acknowledged that the laws governing disability insurance were plural and complex. However, he suggested that administrators would often face decisions 'for which external standards provide no binding, perhaps no relevant, guidelines'.[95] My research suggests otherwise. As I have shown, front-line workers in Ontario Works reconcile between a range of norms that can be traced to a combination of external legal and 'internal' managerial sources. The conflicting statutory purposes of the OWA 1997 repeated themselves throughout my fieldwork, often without explicit references to the legislation itself. This phenomenon suggests that these external standards have somehow become internal, as they are accommodated in workers' everyday decisions. Further study of how such norms become internalised and blended with managerial and professional norms would thus enrich administrative justice theory.

A second lesson from my study is that front-line practices are essential for fully realising the promise of administrative justice theory. The assumption that one justice model will necessarily win out over others, necessitating trade-offs between models,[96] has itself dominated administrative justice theory since it was first proposed. But my research suggests that reconciliation and accommodation between models is the norm, not the exception, at least within Ontario Works. If we are to further theorise how the internal law of administration functions, or how administrative justice may guide administrative action and foster legitimacy, then we must better grasp how front-line practices are engaged in generating and maintaining principles of administrative justice.

---

[94] By 'privately funded', I mean programmes that provide benefits based on funds collected from employer and employee contributions, such as Canada's federal Employment Insurance programme.
[95] Mashaw, *Bureaucratic Justice* (n 22) 16.
[96] M Adler, 'Understanding and Analysing Administrative Justice' in Adler (ed), *Administrative Justice in Context* (n 3) 152.

22

A 'Culture of Justification'? Police Interpretation and Application of the Human Rights Act 1998

RICHARD MARTIN*

I. Introduction

As Roger Cotterrell remarked over two decades ago, engagement with, and application of, the law is no longer, if it ever was, the sole preserve of lawyers and judges: 'Law's community of interpretation is not one but many. Legal theory must explore ... the possibilities for rational interpretation within such communities'.[1] The domestication of the Convention for the Protection of Human Rights and Fundamental Freedoms (ECHR) in the UK through the Human Rights Act 1998 (HRA 1998) has expanded the scope and significance of human rights law's interpretive community in the UK. Beyond equipping the courts with a new interpretive tool to smooth out incompatibilities in primary and subordinate legislation (section 3) and a power to declare legislation incompatible with a Convention right (section 4), the HRA 1998 also requires public authorities to play they their part in domestic human rights protection. The Act makes it 'unlawful for a public authority to act in a way which is incompatible with a Convention right' (section 6(1)). Leading proponents of the HRA 1998 championed the impact this provision could have in fostering within public authorities what has become known as a 'culture of justification': the purposeful and well-reasoned consideration of human rights principles in everyday decision-making.[2]

The near-exclusive focus of public law scholarship on judges as *the* interpreters and appliers of the HRA 1998 is entirely understandable given the judiciary's constitutional role of authoritatively determining the scope of human rights law. But what I want to suggest in

---

* The chapter benefited from the feedback of participants of the third biennial Public Law Conference, Melbourne, July 2018. I am particularly grateful to Shona Wilson Stark, Sandra Fredman, Meghan Campbell, Helen Taylor and Jason Brickhall for their helpful comments on earlier drafts.
[1] R Cotterrell, *Law's Community: Legal Theory in Sociological Perspective* (Oxford, Clarendon Press, 1997) 289.
[2] See especially Lord Irvine, 'The Development of Human Rights in Britain under an Incorporated Convention on Human Rights' [1998] PL 221; F Klug and K Starmer, 'Standing Back from the Human Rights Act: How Effective is it Five Years on?' [2005] PL 716.

this chapter is that if we extend our gaze just a bit further, into the realm of public administration, there are parallel communities of interpretation whose understandings and applications of human rights are well worthy of examination in their own right. As Poole rightly observes, '[t]he reality of interpreting and applying law within the administrative context is that it is public authorities themselves who are the principal actors'.[3] This is made more complex by the open texture of human rights, which 'are by nature vague, imprecise and open to competing interpretations even by those who are fully committed to them'.[4] How do public authorities learn about, accept, reject, interpret or appropriate human rights? Indeed, do they think much about human rights at all? If so, how do they compare with the judicial community we know so well?

These are pertinent questions that we, as public lawyers, remain poorly resourced to answer with any great insight or confidence given the paucity of research on public authorities as 'interpretive communities'. They beckon us towards a more empirical analysis of public law – towards a new frontier. A better understanding of how and why public authorities apply human rights in the way they do is important because of the considerable power, discretion and resources authorities have, with their potential to protect, but also to undermine, the rights the HRA 1998 proudly 'brought home'. The skills, judgement and motivation of authorities in conducting rights-based decision-making tells us something about how the 1998 Act has fared beyond the courts; perhaps even a litmus of the ethical credentials of public administration if we accept Francesca Klug's memorable description of human rights as 'values for a godless age'.[5] So too is it relevant to judicial decision-making, because of the deference the courts accord to public authorities out of respect for their institutional competence.

In the spirit of socio-legal inquiry, this chapter charts a less familiar course in public law by examining non-judicial interpreters and appliers of the HRA 1998. It presents a case study of an 'interpretive community' that, I argue, offers meaningful insights into what a 'culture of justification' might look like: the public order commanders of the Police Service of Northern Ireland (PSNI), tasked with policing contentious parades and protests. These senior officers work in a police service that has spent much of the last decade striving to achieve a technical and cultural commitment to human rights in the wake of landmark police reform.[6] Section II introduces a 'culture of justification' as an aspirational vision of public administration and the merits of an empirically-grounded inquiry. The case study of the PSNI is explained further in the section III. Marshalling data from my qualitative research with the PSNI, section IV examines the legal training and advice police commanders are given to promote a rights-based approach to public order policing. Section V explores in greater detail how human rights law is practised by commanders, revealing how they use human rights to manage positive human rights law duties, as well as 'trouble' from police oversight bodies.

---

[3] T Poole, 'The Reformation of English Administrative Law' (2009) 68 *CLJ* 157.
[4] S Greer, 'Being "Realistic" About Human Rights' (2009) 60 *NILQ* 147, 155.
[5] F Klug, *Values for a Godless Age: The Story of the United Kingdom's New Bill of Rights* (London, Penguin, 2000).
[6] Independent Commission on Policing for Northern Ireland, *A New Beginning: Policing in Northern Ireland* (September 1999); D Bayley, 'Post-conflict Police Reform: Is Northern Ireland a Model?' (2008) 2 *Policing: A Journal of Policy and Practice* 233.

II. A 'Culture of Justification'

The domestic codification of international human rights law standards raised hopes of fostering within public authorities what has been referred to as a 'culture of justification'. Expressed in its strong form by Mureinik in the South African context, a culture of justification is the opposite of a 'culture of authority', in that it requires every exercise of public power to be fully justified, with cogent arguments and powers of persuasion replacing fear and coercion.[7] When applied to societies with a tradition of civil liberties like the UK,[8] a culture of justification is perhaps better understood as distinct from rationality review of administration.[9] Public authorities, in exercising their power, should not merely refrain from *Wednesbury* unreasonable decisions;[10] they should reflect upon, consider and account for how their decisions impact on individuals' legally recognised rights – and where an interference with rights arises, authorities ought to provide a legitimate basis and proportionate means for such interference. As articulated by Lord Irvine, a leading architect of the HRA 1998:

> [I]f there are to be differences or departures from the principles of the Convention they should be conscious and reasoned, and not the product of rashness, muddle or ignorance ... Ministers and administrators will be obliged to do all their work keeping clearly and directly in mind its impact on human rights.[11]

There are, I think, four dimensions lurking within Lord Irvine's authoritative formulation of a culture of justification in the UK context. The first is a constitutional outworking of the HRA 1998: individuals are no longer to be seen as subjects of executive power reliant on a cluster of residual liberties or mere service-users of the administrative state, but as holders of distinct claim-rights that the state must respect. The second, and closely related, is the substantive basis in which 'justifications' of administrative power must be grounded: the ECHR and its principle of proportionality that guides the balancing of competing rights. Rash, muddled or ignorant decisions will not do; authorities must offer reasoned and rational arguments, capable of persuading relevant audiences of their justification.[12] Whether authorities' reasoning ought to incorporate more demanding court-determined standards of the ECHR is, as we shall see, a matter of debate. The third

---

[7] E Mureinik, 'A Bridge to Where? Introducing the Interim Bill of Rights' (1994) 10 *South African Journal on Human Rights* 31. See also K Moller, 'Justifying the Culture of Justification' *International Journal of Constitutional Law* (forthcoming) on the moral appeal and institutional implications of a culture of justification.

[8] On the chequered history of the protection of civil liberties in the UK, see K Ewing and C Gearty, *The Struggle for Civil Liberties* (Oxford, Oxford University Press, 2000).

[9] H Woolf et al, *De Smith's Judicial Review*, 8th edn (London, Sweet and Maxwell, 2018) 11–102.

[10] Traditional grounds of review still require public authorities to justify the legality of their decisions, albeit not to the same extent: Poole, 'The Reformation of English Administrative Law' (n 3) 147. Indeed, in the decade prior to the HRA 1998, the courts required the executive to provide public interest justifications for interference with common law constitutional rights: see especially *R v Secretary of State for the Home Department, ex parte Brind* [1991] AC 696; *R v Ministry of Defence, ex parte Smith* [1996] QB 517.

[11] D Irvine, *Human Rights, Constitutional Law and the Development of the English Legal System: Selected Essays* (Oxford, Hart Publishing, 2003) 23.

[12] M Cohen-Eliya and I Porat, 'Proportionality and the Culture of Justification' (2011) 59 *American Journal of Comparative Law* 463. See also S Fredman, 'From Dialogue to Deliberation: Human Rights Adjudication and Prisoners' Rights to Vote' [2013] *PL* 292.

concerns the institutional actors to whom such 'justifications' ought to be made, scrutinised and validated. The judiciary is the obvious candidate, but as this chapter will reveal, non-judicial oversight bodies and accountability arrangements hold great potential in scrutinising authorities' justifications prior to, or in the absence of, litigation. The fourth is the cultural dimension – the idea of embedding a justificatory mindset within authorities as a routine part of how they 'think'. This alerts us to culture as the 'general environment of social practices, traditions, understandings and values in which law exists'.[13]

Just how far this four-dimensional vision of a culture of justification has been realised in the UK remains deeply questionable. Early studies on the impact of the HRA 1998 suggest limited change in institutional mindsets due to inadequate training and internal reform, as well as cultural resistance within public authorities.[14] Some legal commentators suggest responsibility also lies with the style of judicial review under the HRA 1998 adopted by the House of Lords in the landmark judgments of *R (SB) v Governors of Denbigh High School*[15] and *Belfast City Council v Miss Behavin' Ltd*.[16] In both cases, the House of Lords held that the sole concern of the courts is whether the decision the public authority arrives at violates the Convention: what matters is the 'practical outcome, not the quality of the decision-making that led to it'.[17] An authority's failure to reason its way to a conclusion using the Convention is no basis for unlawfulness under section 6(1) of the HRA 1998. Where an authority is conscious of, or addresses its mind to, the Convention in arriving at its decision, the court 'will give due weight to such judgments'.[18] Indeed, the court will be 'inherently less likely' to disagree with the public authority's decision where there has been 'proper consideration' of the Convention,[19] and 'a challenger's task will be the harder' where the authority has 'conscientiously paid attention to all human rights considerations'.[20]

The House of Lords' approach to review has provoked lively debate. Some consider it a nuanced, pragmatic response to the realities of public administration. For Poole, it incentivises authorities to think in rights terms because of the court's deference to such assessments, without forcing a strained, artificial translation of policy matters into human rights terminology.[21] This will enable the 'polyglot patchwork of institutions and players', operating in 'a multiplicity of contexts and structures', to establish their own respective human rights discourses.[22] Similarly, Kavanagh argues that the House of Lords' approach gives public authorities a 'steer in the direction of a culture of rights', without requiring an overly

---

[13] R Cotterrell, *Law, Culture and Society: Legal Ideas in the Mirror of Social Theory* (Aldershot, Ashgate, 2006) 88.
[14] Department for Constitutional Affairs, 'Review of the Implementation of the Human Rights Act' (2006); A Donald et al, 'Human Rights in Britain since the Human Rights Act 1998: A Critical Review', Equality and Human Rights Commission Research Report No 28 (April 2008). For an analysis of the challenges of mainstreaming human rights in light of the Northern Ireland equality-mainstreaming model, see C McCrudden, 'Mainstreaming Human Rights' in C Harvey (ed) *Human Rights in the Community: Rights as Agents for Change* (Oxford, Hart Publishing, 2005).
[15] *R (SB) v Governors of Denbigh High School* [2007] 1 AC 100.
[16] *Belfast City Council v Miss Behavin' Ltd* [2007] 1 WLR 1420.
[17] *Denbigh* (n 15) [31] (Lord Bingham).
[18] *Miss Behavin'* (n 16) [47] (Baroness Hale).
[19] ibid [91] (Lord Neuberger).
[20] *Denbigh* (n 15) [31] (Lord Bingham).
[21] Poole, 'The Reformation of English Administrative Law' (n 3).
[22] ibid 155.

prescriptive, legalistic decision-making process.[23] Others lament what they consider to be a missed opportunity to commit public authorities to a culture of justification. Hickman accepts that whilst a strict, legalistic assessment of proportionality[24] may be undesirable, some procedural obligation on authorities to weigh competing interests and consider less intrusive means would promote greater rights protection.[25] In its absence, Hickman predicts public authorities will be reluctant to consider Convention rights for fear of making actionable errors or precluding post hoc rationales in a future appeal.[26]

There is, however, only so far a doctrinal analysis can take us in advancing this debate. It is best enriched by bringing the ECHR with us into the realm of public administration, to ask how well authorities are equipped to perform this interpretive role and how they do, in fact, make sense of and apply human rights law. The questions we might begin to ask take several forms. Most elementary are ones of legal learning and consciousness: how do public authorities become aware of human rights standards and principles? A series of interpretive questions then arise: how are these concepts translated and understood by public authorities? What kinds of organisational attitudes or agendas impact on the delivery and reception of human rights law? These, in turn, lead to questions of impact on decision-making and rights realisation: do human rights resonate with policy concerns and routine practices decision-makers routinely face? Do they promote the kind of reflexivity at the heart of a culture of justification, or are they merely a bureaucratic exercise? This chapter offers some preliminary answers by focusing on an instructive case study where a form of a 'culture of justification' has begun to emerge: the public order commanders responsible for policing Northern Ireland's contentious parades and protests.

III. The Case Study of the PSNI

The HRA 1998 has been described as producing a 'new agenda in policing',[27] even as 'the most important development in law for policing',[28] yet 'we know little about how the police understand human rights, how the police's institutional and working cultures shape individuals' responses to those rights'.[29] Such space provides fertile ground for empirical exploration and analysis. This chapter draws on findings from a larger research project conducted by the author with the PSNI, which explored how officers of varying rank, role

---

[23] A Kavanagh, 'Reasoning About Proportionality under the Human Rights Act 1998: Outcomes, Substance and Process' (2014) 130 *LQR* 235, 258.
[24] As proposed by Brooke LJ in *R (Begum (Shabana)) v Headteacher and Governors of Denbigh High School* [2005] 1 WLR 3372, [75].
[25] See especially T Hickman, *Public Law after the Human Rights Act* (Oxford, Hart Publishing, 2010) ch 8; D Mead, 'Outcomes Aren't All: Defending Process-based Review of Public Authority Decisions under the Human Rights Act' [2012] *PL* 61.
[26] Hickman, *Public Law after the Human Rights Act* (n 25) 239.
[27] P Neyroud and A Beckley, *Policing, Ethics and Human Rights* (Abingdon, Routledge, 2013).
[28] D Dixon, 'Changing Law, Changing Policing' in M Mitchell and J Casey (eds), *Police Leadership and Management* (Sydney, The Federation Press, 2007) 32.
[29] B Goold, 'Policing and Human Rights' in B Bradford et al (eds), *The SAGE Handbook of Global Policing* (London, Sage, 2016) 236.

and responsibility understand, interpret and apply human rights in their daily work.[30] The primary data marshalled here are based on: semi-structured interviews with 12 public order commanders; four interviews with public order trainers/tactical advisers; and observations of three public order training days and a week-long Bronze Command course. The average interview with commanders lasted 55 minutes. To protect anonymity, pseudonyms are used and geographical identifiers removed. The chapter's analysis shines a rare light on how commanders, in receipt of bespoke training, knowledge and resources, seek to manage public order operations under the mantra of a 'human rights approach' to policing.

Organisationally, the PSNI is an instructive case study because of its landmark reform programme to embed human rights into its organisational culture and routine practices following the Independent Commission on Policing's seminal report in 1999. It was precisely a 'culture of justification' that the Commission had in mind when it spoke of human rights as the 'philosophy of policing' for post-conflict Northern Ireland: officers should not just master the basics of the ECHR but also internalise it: '[Officers] should perceive their jobs in terms of the protection of human rights'.[31] The reforms included a new police oath and code of ethics incorporating the ECHR; training in principles and standards of human rights; a statutory duty on the Northern Ireland Policing Board (NIPB) to monitor police compliance with the HRA 1998;[32] a bespoke oversight regime established by Sir Keir Starmer; and the recruitment of a human rights lawyer within the PSNI. Brevity precludes further discussion of the socio-political context of parades and protests in Northern Ireland,[33] but it should be noted that the PSNI enforces the determinations of the Parades Commission, a quasi-judicial body responsible for regulating public processions.[34]

Legally, events that prompt a police public order response – protests, parades, marches and demonstrations – require commanders to plan and conduct operations in a way that respects the participants' closely associated Convention rights to freedom of expression (Article 10) and peacefully assembly (Article 11).[35] To secure the effective enjoyment of these rights, police are under a positive duty to take reasonable and appropriate measures to enable lawful demonstrations to proceed peacefully.[36] In recent years, the policing of public order events in the UK has been the subject of high-profile human rights law challenges concerning the use of police containment tactics,[37] pre-emptive measures[38] and the appropriate balancing of the competing rights, including positive duties.[39] The implications

---

[30] R Martin, *Policing Human Rights: Law, Politics and Practice in Northern Ireland* (Oxford, Oxford University Press, forthcoming 2020). See also R Martin, 'Ethno-Political Tenors of Human Rights: The Case of the Northern Irish Policing Board' (forthcoming, *Modern Law Review*).
[31] Independent Commission on Policing for Northern Ireland, *A New Beginning* (n 6) 21.
[32] Police (Northern Ireland) Act 2000, s 3(b)(ii).
[33] See generally M Hamilton, 'Processions, Protests and Other Meetings' in B Dickson and B Gormally (eds), *Human Rights in Northern Ireland: The CAJ Handbook* (Oxford, Hart Publishing, 2015).
[34] The PSNI must respect Arts 10 and 11 ECHR when enforcing the Commission's determinations, as well as in situations where parade/protest organisers fail to notify the Commission: see M Hamilton, 'Freedom of Assembly, Consequential Harms and the Rule of Law: Liberty-limiting Principles in the Context of Transition' (2007) 27 *OJLS* 75.
[35] *Christian Democratic People's Party v Moldova* (2007) 45 EHRR 13.
[36] *Plattform 'Ärzte für das Leben' v Austria* (1988) 13 EHRR 204.
[37] *Austin and Another v Commissioner of Police of the Metropolis* [2009] 1 AC 564.
[38] *R (Laporte) v Chief Constable of Gloucestershire Constabulary* [2007] 2 AC 105; *R (Hicks) v Commissioner of Police of the Metropolis* [2017] AC 256.
[39] *Re DB's Application* [2014] NICA 56.

of the ECHR for public order policing remain a live issue following Her Majesty's Chief Inspector of Constabulary's (HMCIC) nationwide review, which was highly critical of police awareness of, and training in, ECHR standards.[40]

The operational response of police to public order events has particular salience for our analysis of a 'culture of justification'. First, there are dicta that suggest some form of procedural duty may, in fact, arise under the HRA 1998 in protest scenarios. Lord Rodger in *R (Laporte) v Chief Constable of Gloucestershire Constabulary*[41] stated:

> Under the Human Rights Act 1998 the police *must have regard* to the rights to freedom of expression and freedom of assembly which protesters, such as the claimant, are entitled to assert under articles 10 and 11 of the Convention.[42]

Just how demanding a duty to 'have regard' is remains to be determined. By analogy, 'have regard' would, linguistically, appear to impose a less onerous obligation than the public sector equality duty's '*due* regard' standard,[43] which has been interpreted as requiring authorities to undertake specific procedural steps.[44] In *R(A) v Chief Constable of Kent Constabulary*, Beatson LJ suggested *Laporte* might belong to a select category of cases in which 'substance and procedure are difficult to disentangle'.[45] In *Laporte*, the apparent 'entanglement' might be said to have arisen because the Court's assessment of the claimants' right to demonstrate at a lawful assembly (the substance of the decision) ran in conjunction with its assessment of whether the police commander had reasonable apprehension of an imminent breach of the peace (the decision-making process). Analysing the coherency of this apparent category of case and its compatibility with the weighty authorities of *Denbigh* and *Miss Behavin'*[46] is an important task, albeit one best left for elsewhere.[47] What it does serve to emphasise, though, is the value of this chapter's empirical exploration of how police might respond to, and seek to fulfil, the kind of procedural duty alluded to by Lord Rodger.

Second is the courts' willingness to defer to the operational expertise of police commanders when assessing Convention rights. Deference is the weight the court will give police decision-makers when conducting its own proportionality assessment of Convention rights. In *E v Chief Constable of Northern Ireland*, Lord Carswell stated the police in Northern Ireland were 'uniquely placed', by virtue of their experience and intelligence, 'to make a judgment on the wisest course to take' in dealing with serious riotous situations.[48] Quoting Lord Bingham in *Huang*,[49] Lord Carswell described deference as part

---

[40] HMCIC, *Adapting to Protest – Nurturing the British Model of Policing* (London, HMCIC, 2009).
[41] *Laporte* (n 38).
[42] ibid [85] (emphasis added).
[43] Equality Act 2010, s 149.
[44] For a helpful overview, see A McColgan, 'Litigating the Public Sector Equality Duty: The Story So Far' (2015) 35 *OJLS* 453.
[45] *R(A) v Chief Constable of Kent Constabulary* [2013] EWCA Civ 1706, [52]–[53]. See also *B v Chief Constable of Hampshire Constabulary* [2015] 1 WLR 5250, [86].
[46] For further endorsement of these cases in *R (Nasseri) v Secretary of State for the Home Department* [2010] 1 AC 1, [13]–[14].
[47] It would seem significant that Lord Hoffmann stated in *Miss Behavin'* (n 16) [15] that even where Convention rights have what Lord Bingham referred to in *Denbigh* as 'procedural content', the question remains exclusively one of the substantive violation, not procedural neglect, of the right. For an earlier discussion of this issue, see Hickman, *Public Law after the Human Rights Act* (n 25) ch 8.
[48] *E v Chief Constable of the Police Service of Northern Ireland* [2009] 1 AC 536.
[49] *Huang v Secretary of State for the Home Department* [2007] 2 AC 167.

of the 'ordinary judicial task of weighing up the competing considerations on each side and according appropriate weight to the judgment of a person with responsibility for a given subject matter and access to special sources of knowledge and advice'.[50] But deference to the police in Northern Ireland has also been formulated in spatial terms as an 'area of discretionary judgment' within which courts will be sympathetic to the situational exigencies facing decision-makers:

> A definite area of discretionary judgment must be allowed the police. And a judgment on what is proportionate should not be informed by hindsight. Difficulties in making policing decisions should not be underestimated, especially since these frequently require to be made in fraught circumstances.[51]

Regardless of its precise formulation, the principle of deference underscores the importance of understanding how police arrive at decisions and form judgements that have the potential to influence the court's own assessment of proportionality. Let us now embark on this empirical analysis, exploring how commanders become familiar with the ECHR, before considering how they interpret and apply it.

IV. Learning Rights

Public order policing is regulated by a distinct operational command structure, based on the College of Policing's guidelines. Officers have defined command roles, reflecting their rank and training/accreditation: the 'Gold Commander' (Assistant Chief Constable) sets the strategic parameters for public order operations; the 'Silver Commander' (Superintendent) has primary operational responsibility for deployments and use of tactics; and the 'Bronze Commander' (Inspector) oversees the implementation of the tactics. I want to look closely at three ways in which commanders come to learn about and understand human rights law, and how these might relate to a 'culture of justification'.

A. Public Order Command Training

Certified public order commanders must pass specialist command courses based on the College of Policing's standardised curriculum and assessment. In the wake of critical findings by HMCIC, efforts have been made to remedy the knowledge deficit identified amongst commanders in England and Wales.[52] Key learning outcomes for courses now include consideration of powers and policies relating to human rights, alongside an understanding of the human rights framework.[53] In the trainers' guidance, the ECHR is described as

---

[50] *E* (n 48) [58] (Lord Carswell).
[51] *Re DB's Application* [2017] NI 301 [76] (Lord Kerr). For contrasting assessments of police decision-making, see the High Court ([2011] HRLR 24, [57]–[61]) and the Court of Appeal ([2012] EWCA Civ 12, [78]–[88]) in *R (McClure and Moos) v Commissioner of Police of the Metropolis*.
[52] *Adapting to Protest – Nurturing the British Model of Policing* (n 40).
[53] College of Policing, 'National Policing Curriculum, C2 Public Order: Silver Commander, Version 2.01' (Coventry, College of Policing, 2014).

'an overarching theme' that must be 'delivered throughout all aspects of the public order training curriculum' as part of a 'pragmatic and lawful approach to human rights'.[54] With command training emerging as a key site of human rights law translation by the police for the police, I eagerly took up the PSNI's offer to observe a Bronze Commander Course in early summer 2015.

Equipped with PowerPoint, a whiteboard and the College of Policing lesson plans, a five-person team of accredited public order trainers delivered the course across six days. The nine aspiring Bronze Commanders, drawn from police departments across the country, assembled in a well air-conditioned, windowless training room. The prospective commanders were instructed by trainers, much like undergraduate law students are by tutors, to select and cite relevant authorities, rather than 'just listing a whole load of cases' from the training material.[55] Commanders were taught to cite the principle for which the case was an authority and how it might apply to a police operation:

> TRAINER: Don't just give us [in the operational orders commanders would have to produce for specific public order events] *McCann and Others*[56] but what you're going to do to make sure *McCann and Others* is covered – we're looking for the 'wheres' and the 'hows' … Can anyone give me a stated case?
>
> INSP: Is *Osman* one?[57]
>
> TRAINER: Yep, some info that could have brought to arrest, you need to know it.[58]

One trainer remarked: 'there are loads of cases and you should be familiar with them, they're in [operational] orders now and again'. In choosing which cases to reference in their deployment plans, the training team helped by identifying the leading European Court of Human Rights (ECtHR) cases in their presentations, such as *Bukta and Others v Hungary*[59] and *Handyside v UK*[60] for Article 11, as well as the domestic authorities under the HRA 1998, for example *Wood v Commissioner of Police for the Metropolis*[61] (retention of photographic evidence).

In most instances, trainers managed to summarise the law accurately. The ambit of the right to peaceful protest (discussed below) – comprising clear core principles – proved straightforward to convey to trainee commanders:

> After the right to freedom of assembly, the next slide was freedom of expression. The trainer was explaining how it applies to opinions and ideas. Speaking through rhetorical questions again, he asked '*Handyside v UK*, tell me about it? I think he was an artist – anyway, the point is that freedom of expression includes ideas that offend, shock or disturb. If I hold an opinion that you find offensive, unlucky! If I'm not being obstructive or breaking the law, then we should be tolerant'.[62]

---

[54] College of Policing, 'National Police Public Order Training Curriculum, Guidance for Trainers, Module A2 – Underpinning Public Order Knowledge Version 1.2' (Coventry, College of Policing, 2016) 17.
[55] Fieldnotes (11 June 2015).
[56] *McCann and Others v United Kingdom* (1996) 21 EHRR 97.
[57] Referring to *Osman v United Kingdom* (2000) 29 EHRR 245.
[58] Fieldnotes (11 June 2015).
[59] *Bukta and Others v Hungary* (2010) 51 EHRR 25.
[60] *Handyside v United Kingdom* (1979–80) 1 EHRR 737.
[61] *Wood v Commissioner of Police for the Metropolis* [2010] 1 WLR 123.
[62] Fieldnotes (11 June 2015).

For more technical aspects of the law, like the formula to be applied for qualified rights, trainers seemed less comfortable and relied heavily on the College of Policing curriculum. On the concept of proportionality, for instance, trainers explained the need for a link between the measures and the legitimate aim, reading out the considerations verbatim from the public order manual and bluntly telling the commanders: 'You must be cognisant of these when planning. It's in APP [Authorised Professional Practice]. Look for it.'[63] In an effort to make this policy meaningful, officers were shown short video clips of public order scenarios. Clarity of understanding was not helped, however, by encouraging trainees to make impressionistic judgements based on the police actions and decision-making they could glean from the short video clips. The responses of the aspiring commanders suggested that the structured thinking and precise terminology recited to them by trainers had already faded.

Most interesting was how trainers presented cases that were both trickier to grasp and more contested. It is in these situations that we might think more deeply about what it means to translate human rights law for police as practitioners, applying principles 'on the ground'. Take, for example, the case of *Austin v Commissioner of the Metropolis*.[64] The issue was whether the police containment of thousands of protestors and bystanders in a confined urban area for up to seven hours in cold conditions in order to prevent an imminent breach of the peace amounted to an unlawful deprivation of liberty under Article 5. The House of Lords held that the right to liberty was not engaged by this so-called 'kettling' of protestors. In command training, the points deduced were practical ones, stated plainly and without controversy by trainers: 'Containment is a Gold consideration. Provided the tactic is used in good faith, proportionate to the necessary situation and enforced no longer than necessary it's lawful'; 'the Bronze will have to be working with the Silver for this to work properly'; 'you should be thinking about things like access to toilets or the weather, it's a hot July, will there be water for them?'[65]

In the case of *Laporte*, anti-war protestors were intercepted by police en route to a military air base. Rigorously applying the standards of Article 11(2), the House of Lords held that the police use of breach of the peace to send protestors back to London failed the standards of 'prescribed by law', 'necessity' and 'proportionality'. Central to the reasoning was temporal proximity. The breach of the peace had to be 'imminent' at the point of police intervention: the violence had to be 'about to happen' and not just 'anticipated to be a real possibility'.[66] Yet no clear view emerged from the judgment as to what these terms really meant.[67] The trainers turned to the expertise of the PSNI's human rights lawyer, showing the trainees a copy of the lawyer's email, which identified the factors police ought to consider in light of the House of Lord's discussion of 'imminence' (eg whether it was the last opportunity police had to take preventative action). Officers were told to write down the lawyer's number: 'If you have any questions phone him and he'll get back to you, he's been very supportive in putting together the training. The advice of our legal adviser takes

---

[63] ibid.
[64] *Austin and Another v Commissioner of Police of the Metropolis* (n 37).
[65] Fieldnotes (11 June 2015).
[66] ibid.
[67] See especially R Glover, 'Keeping the Peace and Preventive Justice – A New Test for Breach of the Peace?' [2018] *PL* 444.

precedence over the cases we've mentioned'.[68] A further case mentioned briefly by trainers was *R (McClure and Moos) v Commissioner of Police of the Metropolis*,[69] where the issue was whether a police commander had reasonably apprehended an imminent breach of peace. This case was summed up briefly by the trainer: 'The Met are at fault. Met appealed. All these fancy barristers paid loads of money to make the police look awful. But it was upheld on appeal that it was an honestly held belief by the police officer and that it was proportionate and in line with human rights'.[70]

In translating these leading authorities, trainers deemed finer points of law and broader concerns of constitutional principle academic (in both senses of the word). In the legal scholarship, the *Austin* judgment provoked discussion over the Court's premature assessment of proportionality and the purpose of the interference to determine the very ambit of the right to liberty.[71] Criticism has also been levelled at the excessive deference to the executive resulting from the Court's reasoning. As argued by Fenwick, '[t]he impression given by all the judges involved in *Austin* is that they were seeking, after the event, and in reliance on doubtful and convoluted reasoning, to find a justification for the police action'.[72] Similarly, in *McClure and Moos*, the Court of Appeal can be criticised for its reluctance to meaningfully scrutinise decision-making, based as it was on an overly subjective assessment of police decision-making that relied on what the officer knew and perceived at the time, provided the evidence seemed honest and accurate.[73]

But does it matter that finer issues of law and broader points of principle were lost in translation? One police trainer acknowledged 'on a command course we're saying … we could spend days debating, and I'm sure if you went to Strasbourg you could spend the rest of your life discussing it, but when it comes down to the basics, for operational people, this is what you need to know'. Although such pedagogy undoubtedly has merit – most obviously, it makes rights meaningful and practically applicable for police as practitioners on the ground[74] – from my short observations, a more contextualised account (debated for minutes, not days) might be important for further promoting a positive culture of human rights. If a typical fear amongst officers is that human rights limit their ability to police effectively and firmly then, if presented in terms of the role and extent of the court's oversight role, cases like *Austin* and *McClure and Moos* are an opportunity to reassure officers that the courts are interpreting human rights in a way that is sensitive to operational discretion. Conversely, *Laporte* could be taught as a reminder that breach of the peace, as the go-to police power of choice and as wide-ranging as it is, should be used with greater precision.[75]

More critically, in the absence of a closer analysis of the substantive scope of human rights, the aspiring commanders seemed to be left relying on a 'gut feeling' of the ambit of

---

[68] Fieldnotes (11 June 2015).
[69] *R (McClure and Moos) v Commissioner of Police of the Metropolis* (n 51).
[70] Fieldnotes (11 June 2015).
[71] See H Fenwick, 'Marginalising Human Rights: Breach of the Peace, "Kettling", the Human Rights Act and Public Protest' [2009] *PL* 737; M James and G Pearson, 'Public Order and the Rebalancing of Football Fans' Rights: Legal Problems with Pre-emptive Policing Strategies and Banning Orders' [2015] *PL* 458.
[72] Fenwick, 'Marginalising Human Rights' (n 71) 757.
[73] See especially *McClure* [2012] EWCA Civ 12 (n 51) [89].
[74] See, eg, NIPB, *Human Rights Annual Report 2009* (Belfast, NIPB, 2010) 111; NIPB, *Human Rights Annual Report 2010* (Belfast, NIPB, 2011) 57.
[75] Fenwick, 'Marginalising Human Rights' (n 71).

the Convention. In one scenario, for example, officers were grappling with what to do about football supporters' misbehaving on the way to the football stadium:

> Officers were told that supporters were urinating and throwing litter in gardens of local residents. They were trying to decide whether or not to deploy uniform officers in the area to try and do something about it. Having decided to do so, they were faced with typing up the rationale for their decision on the computer. The officer typing explained he was going to record it as 'protecting human rights of the residents' and in an easy manner spoke aloud 'Their right to private life ... that's Article 8. Oh, and Freedom of Movement – the rights of both sets of football supporters too'.[76]

This kind of headline reading of the ECHR was apparent again in another group, when one officer got out his mobile phone out to search the HRA 1998 online. In an effort to impress the trainers, and slightly in jest, the inspector told his fellow trainees 'Aye, articles 9, 10, 11, put them down!' Although it is encouraging to see aspiring commanders aware of the Convention, the detachment from legal standards in these instances tended to result in a superficial, if not inappropriate, application of broadly worded articles of the ECHR to the facts, which undermined the likelihood of human rights law's informing police planning in a more precise manner.

B. The 'Bridgers'

The course I observed was just the very beginning of aspiring commanders' professional development. With formal exams to pass, refresher courses to attend and prolonged operational exposure, commanders' more commonsense understandings were set to mature. Crucially, Commanders would benefit from the human rights expertise of what one Silver Commander referred to as the PSNI's 'bridgers' – those with knowledge and expertise of both human rights law and police practice, who were able, therefore, to bridge the two. The most significant bridger is the PSNI's human rights lawyer, who acts as the authoritative voice of translation of human rights law within the PSNI. Legal departments are a crucial source of knowledge and a conduit for informing officers of updates in case law and legislation.[77] The PSNI's lawyer has provided training programmes rolled out for all officers involved in operational planning and command of public order events, outlining the legislative framework for parades and protests and the relevant human rights law standards from the case law.[78] Notably, the lawyer's legal translation has been incorporated into police planning documents, which replicate the course material in the Gold Commanders' strategy.[79] Such courses illustrate what Chayes and Chayes refer to as 'preventative law', whereby in-house lawyers attempt to insert legal standards and considerations into the earliest stages of decision-making.[80]

When it came to the Gold and Silver Commanders' planning meetings, commanders stressed how the human rights lawyer would be 'a part of the furniture, part of the team – a

---

[76] Fieldnotes (12 June 2015).
[77] D Dixon, *Law in Policing: Legal Regulation and Policing Practice* (Oxford, Clarendon Press, 1997) 278–80.
[78] NIPB, *Human Rights Annual Report 2008* (Belfast, NIPB, 2009) 119.
[79] ibid 120.
[80] A Chayes and AH Chayes 'Corporate Counsel and the Elite Law Firm' (1985) 37 *Stanford Law Review* 277, 280.

trusted and well-liked member of the team, who's known to give sound advice regularly' (Bronze Commander Cliff).[81] Although commanders took the final operational decisions, their human rights lawyer was described as an 'active player' whose advice 'certainly goes a long way' to informing the approach taken (Silver Commander Andrew). Commanders expressed the usefulness of having someone who could help them get a sense of issues like the level of tolerance police were expected to show in facilitating protest activity, or the legal powers they had to restrict protestors' movement (eg, whether breach of the peace could be used, or whether more specific legislation was more appropriate): 'We've used him very practically. What is the terminology? What does it mean by imminence? [see *Laporte* in section IV.A]' (Bronze Commander Cliff); and 'they would tell you the kind of out workings of case law, give you their interpretation … there's certainly room within that if you needed to go back and further debate the point or expand upon it' (Bronze Commander Daniel). This accessible human rights legal advice, available 'on demand' throughout the strategic planning stages of operations, was heavily encouraged by the NIPB's legal advisers as good practice.[82]

In-house lawyers' familiarity with, and responsiveness to, their organisations enables them to inject legal standards and opinion into decision-making, promoting the knowledge base for a culture of justification to emerge.[83] Commanders emphasised that in planning meetings there was time and space to 'throw ideas round a bit' and seek clarification on ECHR standards:

> Say we're going to put a block in at the exit of a roundabout or street, we're going to put a barrier in – we're thinking about the right to privacy of the nearby residents, blocking access to road users: Are we blocking access to arterial route? Are there other routes that we could block instead? What other options and alternatives are there to that barrier? In the slower time of planning meeting we can think about all of this, we don't have the split-second decisions to make. (Silver Commander Brian)

With a select group of senior officers regularly performing Silver Command roles for major events in recent years, their continued exposure to legal advice led them to believe they had improved their understanding far beyond that taught in command courses. Commanders described having had to confront many scenarios that required discussions with their human rights lawyer: 'we've been round the cycle in Northern Ireland, we've been right from that low-level sight and sound piece[84] all the way round to serious disorder and all the way back round again, and we understand what each phase looks like and what the priorities are' (Silver Commander Brian). Consequently, although commanders admitted they would 'never feel entirely comfortable talking to anybody whose specific focus is human rights legislation' (Silver Commander Andrew), they were accustomed to, and comfortable with, hearing case law and ECHR standards from their lawyer.

---

[81] The presence of PSNI's human rights lawyer at meetings was also reported in the NIPB's Annual Reports (see, eg, NIPB, *Human Rights Annual Report 2007* (Belfast, NIPB, 2007) 123).

[82] NIPB, *Human Rights Annual Report 2006* (Belfast, NIPB, 2006) 61.

[83] L Edelman and M Suchman, 'When the "Haves" Hold Court: Speculations on the Organizational Internalization of Law' (1999) 33 *Law and Society Review* 970.

[84] This is a reference to the Organization for Security and Cooperation in Europe, *Guidelines on Freedom of Peaceful Assembly*, 2nd edn (Warsaw, OSCE, 2010) 17: 'as a general rule, assemblies should be facilitated within "sight and sound" of their target audience'.

The particular skill that commanders thought their lawyer had was the ability to take a 'pragmatic approach' that identified the legitimate police objective and guided officers through how they could reach it, bearing in mind potential challenges. As explained by Silver Commander Brian:

> I have become increasingly aware that perhaps the policing approach to human rights is very pragmatically based and that's where we would tend to differ from others in the legal profession who are much about a paper-based exercise and that's where the likes of [NIPB legal adviser] and [PSNI human rights lawyer], who can inhabit both sides of the world, are of such benefit, because they can translate both. I think the key element is that interaction.

Such interaction was necessary, Silver Commander Andrew suggested, because 'we're cops, and cops have a broad knowledge of legislation, but we're not trained like lawyers'. Being 'trained like a lawyer', commanders thought, brought with it unique knowledge and expertise. Commanders referred, for instance, to documents sent by their lawyer, offering specific commentary on the interpretation of 'lawful' and 'peaceful' protest under Article 11 and a condensed version of case law and legal opinion that was 'really effective, practical guidance'.

The working relationship between in-house legal teams and their organisations has been identified as an area of concern. Edelman and Suchman argue that organisations are powerful engines of socialisation. As lawyers become more embedded in them, the more likely they are to use their legal expertise to secure, rather than challenge, organisational goals.[85] Lawyers can use their talents to make organisations more skilfully evasive, and can equip them with legal justifications that are skewed to satisfy the exigencies of the organisation.[86] Suspicions of such co-option have been voiced by outside observers of the PSNI, and commanders themselves did suggest, albeit in coded fashion, that they could draw upon legal advice to inform, if not realise, police goals. One example involved the assessment of proportionality made in the context of qualified rights. A commander explained how they had learnt from their lawyer to emphasise the seriousness of the police objective for big parading events. By suggesting, for instance, that 'the whole rule of law in Northern Ireland is at stake and if that falls to the wayside, here are the potential consequences, even demonstrating that rationale immediately changes the proportionality discussion and debate and lifts it up', police tactics could appear more proportionate, and therefore defensible, in the context provided by police. This links to the management of 'trouble', a theme discussed in section V.B.

C. Organisational Processes

Commanders have made a determined effort to write human rights standards into the police 'script' to manage contentious parades and protests. In its material form, the script comprises the strategic and operational plans devised by commanders, the content of which is an amalgamation of policies, law, information about the event and 'community intelligence'. The Gold Commander's strategy document, devised months in advance of major

---

[85] Edelman and Suchman, 'When the "Haves" Hold Court: Speculations on the Organizational Internalization of Law' (n 83).
[86] ibid.

protests and parades, sits at the apex of public order operations. As described by one former PSNI Deputy Chief Constable:

> This document is a comprehensive resource, containing detailed references to the HRA 1998 and other human rights standards, and addressing a range of potential operational scenarios ... A detailed analysis of the European Convention rights engaged is provided in relation to each scenario ...[87]

In writing their operational and deployment plans, Silver and Bronze Commanders were expected to embed the relevant aspects of the PSNI's Policy Directives and Service Procedures, as well as the College of Policing's Authorised Professional Practice, each of which contained references to the HRA 1998. The format and language of Commanders' plans were heavily dictated by these pre-written policies, first encountered as part of their command training. By referencing these documents, specifically the sections on ECHR standards, commanders' plans formed part of the bureaucratic bind that embedded the discourse of human rights into the policing operation.

Further efforts to foster a culture of justification have been advanced through the reports the PSNI must submit to the Parades Commission following notice of a sensitive parade/protest. Using a standardised form, Silver Commanders must make a 'judged assessment' of how police strategies might impact the rights of the individuals involved, by filling in a series of boxes assigned to Convention rights. Commanders are instructed to pay special regard to

> the effects police tactics have had in the past and may have in the future upon individual human rights. The author should in particular note the circumstances under which a human right can be restricted in furtherance of a legitimate aim by a public authority.[88]

The guide makes clear that such reports may also be disclosable to public audiences and should be written with this in mind. Accurate completion of the form was made easier by a detailed sample report issued to commanders, which stated the broad ECHR principles to be applied. It is easy to dismiss these reports as merely a bureaucratic exercise, but commanders keenly described it as an 'added element' to the planning process that underscored the organisation's focus on rights. As hinted at by Silver Commander Andrew, through this process of repetition, rights become a normal part of the process: 'Yeah it's a template and that doesn't mean it's embedded in our culture and stuff but actually over a period of time it is, so you know we report our evidence to the parades commission along that spine of key human rights.' Observational research on how such administrative tasks are undertaken would be a fruitful avenue for further study.

The NIPB's human rights legal adviser – an independent position held by three barristers over the past 15 years – has become a principal audience responsible for receiving and reporting on the 'justification' offered by Commanders in operational policing contexts. The NIPB first recruited Sir Keir Starmer as its adviser in 2003, shortly after which the PSNI granted Starmer extensive access to police training, policies and operations. This approach was guided by a positive vision of oversight that would encourage a dialogue with the PSNI,

---

[87] D McCausland, 'Policing Parades and Protest in Northern Ireland' (2007) 3 *EHRLR* 211, 216.
[88] PSNI, 'Service Procedure: Public Processions (Northern Ireland) Act 1998 and the Parades Commission' (SP 14/2008) 10, available at http://library.college.police.uk/docs/APPref/service-procedures-processions-2008.pdf.

addressing issues as they arose.[89] For contentious parades and protests, the advisers actively monitor the PSNI's operations, observing the early stages of planning through to the post-event de-briefs, and writing up their findings in the NIPB's Annual Human Rights Report. Attendance at these events, particularly planning sessions, has been described by an adviser as 'the most critical element of what I do', because it provides an insight into how police are planning, with their positive duties under the HRA 1998 in mind[90] – most notably Article 2, which requires the police to plan in such a way that minimises the likelihood of recourse to potentially lethal force.[91]

Starmer's presence at police planning meetings and command rooms was something commanders found unnerving at first. In 2004 and 2005, for example, Starmer undertook post-event reviews of decision-making, working through video footage and breaking down incidents frame by frame, asking commanders to account for their decision-making.[92] Silver Commander Edwin recalled staffing the Gold Command room during one of the worst periods of disorder:

> That was first time anyone of us had really seen a QC [Starmer] in a command room. I mean, lawyers and police command rooms don't always go together ... and this one wasn't working for us, I mean, he was employed by the Board, he was there in an oversight capacity and he was able to see and listen to everything the Gold Commander is seeing and listening to. And sometimes that got really ugly, you had Commanders showing less than perfect composure at times, you had stuff said on the radio that makes your toes curl a little bit and yet we exposed ourselves completely and utterly to someone of Keir Starmer's quality ...

The 'exposure' to outside lawyers is anathema to the police – an occupation with a culture of secrecy and defensiveness, best-defined by its 'common-sense' knowledge.[93] The threat the NIPB's legal advisers posed, however, was overcome by a mixture of Starmer's charisma and constructivism and commanders' astute awareness that the adviser could help improve their decision-making at a time when the PSNI was keen to convince sceptics that the Police Service was adopting a new-style of public order policing distinct from its predecessor, the Royal Ulster Constabulary. In the years since, the NIPB's legal advisers have continued to enjoy access to public order planning, briefings and command rooms.[94]

V. Practising Rights

Having now identified and examined how and to whom commanders learn to 'justify' their decisions using human rights law and principles, I want to explore more fully some of the cultural features accompanying commanders' routine practice of human rights. The

---

[89] K Starmer, 'Monitoring the Performance of the Police Service in Northern Ireland in complying with the Human Rights Act 1998' (2007) 1 *Policing* 94.

[90] A Kilpatrick, Freedom of Information Request 44/2015, 33, available at https://www.nipolicingboard.org.uk/sites/nipb/files/media-files/foi-442015.pdf.

[91] *McCann* (n 56).

[92] NIPB, *Report on the Policing of the Ardoyne Parades 12th July 2005 and the Whiterock Parade 10th September 2005* (Belfast, NIPB, 2005).

[93] See especially R Reiner, *The Politics of Policing* (Oxford, Oxford University Press, 2010) ch 4.

[94] A Kilpatrick, Speech, Launch of Human Rights Annual Report, Crumlin Road Gaol, Belfast (7 September 2016) (author's attendance notes).

NIPB's legal advisers have consistently praised the operational performance of public order commanders,[95] which resonates with my own findings that commanders had come to grasp human rights as an important and constructive aspect of decision-making. This section focuses on how commanders used human rights law to manage both positive obligations and the potential for 'trouble' that arose from exacting oversight.

A. Managing Positive Obligations

The most challenging situation for commanders in Northern Ireland has arisen where protestors take part in un-notified, and thus unlawful, parades that have a significant impact on residents and businesses situated along protest/parade routes. How commanders balance competing rights became a live issue recently in the case of *Re DB*, which reached the UK Supreme Court in 2017.[96] The applicant was a resident of the Short Strand (a Nationalist enclave in predominantly Loyalist east Belfast) whose house was attacked by a Loyalist group involved in un-notified protests. Because these protests were un-notified, the Parades Commission was powerless to issue a determination to regulate the protest; the responsibility fell solely on the PSNI. Commanders opted to allow the Loyalist protestors to travel in and out of the city centre via the Short Strand. Hundreds of officers were deployed to manage the protests and record evidence of offences taking place. The protest lasted three months, and over the course of several weekends protestors threw missiles at homes in the Short Strand as they returned from the City Hall. The applicant claimed, inter alia, that the failure of the police to actively intervene and stop the illegal protests violated his Article 8 right to respect for private and family life, which the PSNI had a positive duty to protect.

The case threw into sharp relief how the PSNI balances competing rights, specifically whether it can justify a non-interventionist/defensive approach to disorder notwithstanding its positive duty to protect the rights of those in the vicinity who may be affected by parades/protests.[97] The PSNI responded that its non-intervention, and thus interference with the applicant's Article 8 rights, was justified by competing Article 2 duties to protect the lives of those in the vicinity.[98] If the PSNI had acted more assertively (eg, halting protestors or making arrests), it submitted there was a real risk this would have sparked serious disorder, capable of threatening the lives of those in the vicinity and the wider community. This mindset, couched in 'justificatory' terms of the ECHR, was explained by Silver Commander Brian:

> They [Loyalist protestors] did it last week, they marched into the city centre and back out again and nothing happened and there was some disruption to the community in the city centre, so

---

[95] This is reflected in one of many similar statements found in the NIPB's Annual Reports: '[T]he Silver Commander showed exemplary knowledge, understanding and practical application of human rights principles ... During what was a long and extremely challenging process he ... demonstrated that he clearly understood not simply what the Human Rights Act required of him, but how that knowledge needed to be translated into practice.' (*Human Rights Annual Report* 2009 (n 74) 98).
[96] *Re DB v Chief Constable of Northern Ireland* (n 51).
[97] See also *E v Chief Constable of the Police Service of Northern Ireland* (n 48) on whether police were entitled to consider risks to those in the wider community, as well as in the immediate vicinity, when deciding how to protect school children from illegal protests that interfered with the applicant's right to freedom from inhuman or degrading treatment or punishment (Art 3).
[98] *McCann* (n 56).

back to *Bukta*,[99] back to *Plattform*[100] – minor inconvenience has been tolerated and will continue to be tolerated, okay, so what are our alternatives? Well, it is an illegal parade and there is an argument to say look we can, we can stop it … Essentially your two options are: facilitate this march in the city centre or stop the march somewhere on the route. The primary place to stop it [is before it reaches the Short Strand], bearing in mind your most likely conflict is likely to be around the Short Strand … the resources necessary to stop a march such as that – and I would suggest the likelihood of force – meant that we would have had to have significant justification to do that, because we would have ended up fighting … arresting a lot of people, including police officers would have ended up getting injured …

The illegal protests were thus initially facilitated with Article 11 in mind (the right to peaceful assembly, even in the absence of notification) but they were ultimately allowed by police to continue due to a fear of the potentially lethal consequences of stopping the protest, raising the issue of Article 2 ECHR.

The High Court held that the PSNI violated the applicant's Article 8 rights, and was critical of the PSNI's handling of the protest.[101] The un-notified parades were unlawful and outside the protections of Article 11, and thus required of the PSNI 'the clearest possible explanation and justification for not taking appropriate measures'.[102] Treacy J was sceptical that fear of serious disorder was the true rationale for the PSNI's reluctance to intervene, suspecting that the PSNI had really preferred to sit back and allow protestors to 'vent anger' outside the City Hall. Treacy J questioned whether there was sufficient evidence to substantiate the claim of an Article 2 risk at the time of the protests affecting the residents of the Short Strand, given that these particular protests took place a month after the worst disorder.[103] In short, Treacy J found the PSNI's human rights 'justification' unpersuasive. The judgment of the High Court provoked concern amongst chief officers. The then PSNI Chief Constable stated publicly:

> We have to appeal this. I cannot have the expectation or implication that the police will always be able to take immediate and forceful action. It would require a far greater reliance on force and an uplift of resources to deal, there and then, with large crowds – it's not a merely technical matter.[104]

Revealing of the police mindset, the PSNI was wary of the resource implications if Commanders would be required, by law, to forcefully intervene, disperse crowds and make arrests in future situations where rights of local residents were engaged by those taking part in un-notified protests. Here we see a keenness to avoid confrontation with demonstrators – or what Waddington has previously referred to as 'on-the-job trouble'[105] – aligning with a human rights-based justification for non-intervention grounded in Article 2.

The Northern Ireland Court of Appeal went on to allow the PSNI's appeal and accepted its Article 2 justification for not forcefully intervening.[106] Lord Morgan CJ affirmed the

---

[99] *Bukta and Others v Hungary* (n 59).
[100] *Plattform* (n 36).
[101] *Re DB's Application* [2014] NIQB 55.
[102] ibid [137].
[103] ibid [122].
[104] M Baggott, oral response to question, Northern Ireland Policing Board, Public Session (29 May 2014) 11.16–11.53 mins, available at https://www.facebook.com/policingboard/videos/703911832989005/.
[105] PAJ Waddington, *Liberty and Order: Public Order Policing in a Capital City* (London, UCL Press, 1994).
[106] *Re DB's Application* (n 39).

discretionary judgement the courts are prepared to grant the police in trying operational situations. Accepting that Article 2 considerations to the wider community fell within this realm, Lord Morgan CJ reviewed the PSNI's criminal justice strategy and held that in this 'difficult situation', which 'left the police to manage such parades using public order powers rather than providing a tailored legislative scheme',[107] the PSNI had taken proportionate steps to protect the applicant's Article 8 rights. The judgment was handed down shortly before I began fieldwork and was still fresh in commanders' minds. In commanders' eyes, the Court of Appeal had rightly endorsed a pragmatic approach, 'dictated by operational resilience and the realities' (Bronze Commander Daniel). This supports Waddington's earlier finding that commanders' sub-culture is often one animated by fear of legal challenges that might result in judicial constraint on their operational discretion.[108] Commanders emphasised the importance of protecting operational discretion, and expressed the importance of the successful appeal in protecting police discretion: 'Ultimately had we lost that appeal it would have put us in a very difficult position, practically in all sorts of ways' (Silver Commander Andrew) and '[w]e'll appeal it all the way to Europe if we have to, it's that important to us' (Silver Commander Edwin).

In the end, the applicant successfully appealed to the UK Supreme Court. The argument before the Supreme Court shifted away from the Article 2 issue to an earlier issue concerning whether or not the PSNI had properly grasped its power to intervene in un-notified protests under provisions of the Police (Northern Ireland) Act 2000. Giving judgment, Lord Kerr deemed there to be 'something of an air of unreality' about discussing the PSNI's operational decision-making and balancing of Articles 2 and 8, given that the PSNI had wrongly construed its powers under the Police (Northern Ireland) Act 2000.[109] Lord Kerr did, however, correct the Gold Commander's inaccurate interpretation of the scope of Article 11 (reflected in the words of Silver Commander Brian, above). Article 11 only requires police to facilitate un-notified protests in 'exceptional circumstances' like spontaneous events – a description the two-month period of protests and parades in Belfast clearly did not meet.[110] Lord Kerr did, however, remain sympathetic to the struggles the PSNI faced in managing positive duties to protect the rights of nearby residents, business owners and the public, all the while being cognisant of the potentially lethal effect that forceful removal of volatile protestors might have in confined urban spaces where paramilitary groups remain active.[111]

What *Re DB* reveals is how competing human rights duties, owed to different parties, in fraught situations, have come to animate how public order events are managed by PSNI Commanders. In approaching the operational difficulties alluded to by Lord Kerr, commanders were in no doubt that the framework of the ECHR aided them in their decision-making. Being able to compute policing strategies in terms of their impact on individuals' rights was a part of the planning process: 'It's the touchtone you come back to, to make sure your decision is justifiable, proportionate and isn't gonna have adverse reactions in terms of the rights that are there for people' (Silver Commander Andrew). Commanders' discussion

---

[107] ibid [54].
[108] Waddington (n 105).
[109] *Re DB* (n 51) [74].
[110] ibid [58]–[61].
[111] ibid [76].

of human rights in our interviews was part of an eagerness to exhibit to me how they could work between human rights law, operational realities and the tactical options available in planning events. Indeed, a number of commanders have taken part-time LLM courses (sponsored by the PSNI), honing their knowledge of the case law related to their policing specialism.[112] This rights-inspired planning and management of public order events was, however, animated by a sub-culture that was wary of the community fallout from heavy police intervention in politically-sensitive demonstrations and protests. Where such intervention might lead to potentially lethal tactics being used, or even to those deemed 'heavy-handed' by some communities, Commanders seemed to find Article 2 ECHR a useful basis for justifying their less interventionist approach, albeit – as the High Court held – that this can have deleterious consequences for the rights of nearby residents affected by sustained protests.

Ultimately, a culture of justification requires public authorities to carefully and persuasively reason their way through the decisions they make, using the principles of the ECHR. The persuasiveness of such reasoning is the constitutional task of the courts to determine. Commanders in the PSNI have embarked on a more detailed, substantive engagement with, and application of, specific Convention standards, derived from the case law of the ECtHR. This fuller 'justification' can, I think, serve two functions crucial to promoting a 'culture of justification', which *Re DB* illustrates. First, the court is better equipped to conduct a detailed and constructive review of any errors that occur in the 'justification', serving as a useful guide for future decision-making. In *Re DB*, the PSNI's misunderstanding of Article 11 was detected and rectified. Second, the contrasting judgments of the courts in *Re DB* demonstrate how determining the lawful balancing competing rights can be a fraught task, with room for reasoned disagreement. When Commanders conduct their own, carefully recorded assessment of what *they* think a proportionate balance is between competing rights, based on their unique operational expertise, the reviewing court can usefully draw upon this assessment, making it better placed, in terms of its institutional competence, to conduct its own, authoritative proportionality assessment.[113]

B. Managing Trouble

As observed by Waddington in his seminal study of policing protest in London in the early 1990s, public disorder and the use of force can create considerable 'on the job' legal challenges and political pressure for commanders.[114] Commanders in the PSNI were acutely aware of the present-day sensitivities that surrounded public order policing in Northern Ireland, and spent much of the year with one eye on high-profile parades and protests. It was the avoidance of the 'trouble' these events could provoke that further animated commanders' practice of human rights.

Breaking with our discussion of *Re DB*, the primary source of 'trouble' commanders sensed was not in fact the court but rather the non-judicial oversight bodies they

---

[112] A PSNI Gold Commander even penned an article describing the PSNI's rights-inspired approach in the *EHRLR* (n 87).
[113] See especially *Miss Behavin'* (n 16) [37] (Baroness Hale).
[114] Waddington (n 105).

encountered routinely in conducting public order operations. The first of these bodies is the Police Ombudsman. Commanders knew that the use of force tactics, like Attenuated Energy Projectiles (AEP)[115] or water cannon, automatically triggered an Ombudsman investigation, regardless of whether or not a complaint was made.[116] Commanders described handing over their policy and decision logs to the Ombudsman after they clocked off in the command room; and they could be interviewed months later about the justifications they made when authorising the deployment of use-of-force tactics. The second body viewed as a source of 'trouble' was the NIPB, specifically the close involvement of its own legal adviser in overseeing the PSNI's planning and briefing sessions. As Silver Commander Edwin explained:

> Lots in policing say 'Oh, it's a lonely place when you're in the witness box at the public inquiry' and of course very few of us get near a public fucking inquiry, they're that rare! But the reality is we have quasi-judicial interventions almost all the time, and it's not worrying about the public inquiry, it's worrying about what the Policing Board lawyers will say because they have unfettered access.

These 'quasi-judicial' interventions of the Ombudsman and NIPB meant these bodies had become the primary audiences to whom 'justifications' had to be made, with practical ramifications arising from unpersuasive justifications. Far from being perceived as soft options, these non-judicial bodies have proved to be key allies in encouraging, even pressuring, the PSNI to visibly commit to compliance with the ECHR. If AEP were to be discharged, the commander would have to submit a use of force form to the NIPB, alongside a public disorder incident form providing an overview of the relevant details. This was not purely an academic exercise. In 2011, an increase in the use of AEP (in the face of widespread disorder in Belfast and surrounding areas) provoked concern from some members of the NIPB. Notwithstanding the positive reports from the Ombudsman's investigations, the NIPB determined that the need remained for a 'discrete and careful analysis', with a renewed focus on the training and briefing on the legal test for the lawful deployment and use of AEP.[117]

The wariness of this kind of external scrutiny was clear in the commander course I observed – and it is here where a culture of justification moved closest to the kind of 'formulaic incantations' of the ECHR warned of by Lord Hoffmann in *Miss Behavin'*.[118] Trainers asked officers to think about whether or not their decisions would 'look good in court', that is to say, 'will that option stand up to scrutiny if examined?'.[119] A stark warning came when a qualified commander arrived to share their experiences of being subject to a lengthy Health and Safety Executive investigation after a rioter had been injured following police use of force. Commanders were told to anticipate and negotiate this sort of legal accountability during a session devoted to decision logs and audit trails, during which they were trained in producing clear, thorough rationales for decision-making, making

---

[115] These are projectiles fired from a gun. They replaced plastic baton rounds as a less lethal option for managing hostile crowds.
[116] Police (Northern Ireland) Act 1998, s 55.
[117] NIPB, *Human Rights Annual Report 2011* (Belfast, NIPB, 2012) 64.
[118] *Miss Behavin'* (n 16) [13].
[119] Fieldnotes (12 June 2015).

specific reference to relevant case law, as outlined in section IV.A. Commanders could then rely on such references, should they be subject to judicial scrutiny. In earlier courses, trainers went as far as to hire barristers to cross-examine commanders in a mock court scenarios.

The explicit framing of decision-making using Convention language was further embedded in the formal record of events through the live decision-making logs of Silver and Gold Commanders. Silver Commander Charley gave an example: 'Say I need to move the crowd from A to B that will be recorded as a decision. I will then say to the loggist "That's because –" and then I'll rattle off articles 9, 10, 11.' Likewise, Silver Commander Andre described how human rights offered an objective standard that he and his colleagues could reference in accounting for the decision they made:

> Because of the scrutiny and accountability we're under, for a large part of this we understand we need to be able to show, audit and reflect on our decision-making and thinking, so waiting for the challenge after the fact, not least the legal challenge, are you with me? So all that sort of [human rights] language, we capture that and we document it. As I say, my log, I can show you where I've taken legal advice from [human rights lawyer] and factored that in, but that's there in many respects for the safety net after the fact.

The strategic deployment of ECHR verbiage was a technique used by commanders to manage 'trouble' emanating from their intensely-scrutinised working environment; it was deemed prudent to 'copper fasten' decisions in case legal challenges arose. But, as revealed in the preceding analysis and evidenced by the NIPB's legal advisers' own reports, it would be inaccurate to cast commanders' engagement with the ECHR as amounting to no more than 'formulaic incantations'. Commanders used human rights to reason their way to a decision, not merely to rationalise it to appeal to oversight bodies. Given what is at stake for protestors, residents, business owners and police officers themselves, PSNI commanders – equipped with bespoke training and legal advice – saw the Convention principles and standards as offering a practical guide that made such difficult decisions more, not less, manageable. This reflects in practice what Lord Reed has noted from the bench: 'There is no doubt that one of the virtues of procedurally fair decision-making is that it is liable to result in better decisions, by ensuring that the decision-maker receives all relevant information and that it is properly tested'.[120] That commanders have stepped closer towards the ECHR, rather than further away from it – as Hickman feared might be the case with some public authorities[121] – perhaps reflects the extensive human rights reform programme the PSNI has undertaken, as well as the internal processes, described in section IV, designed to instil routine practices orientated towards rights consciousness and equip commanders with greater legal understanding.

VI. Conclusion

I want to pull together the strands of the chapter's analysis by returning to the debate over whether public authorities ought to have a procedural obligation to respect Convention

---

[120] *Osborn v Parole Board* [2014] AC 1115, [67].
[121] Hickman, *Public Law after the Human Rights Act* (n 25).

rights under section 6(1) of the HRA 1998. A core rationale for precluding procedural review from section 6(1) rests on an empirical claim that it would result in an administratively burdensome and costly exercise for public authorities that would be unduly legalistic in nature.[122] The empirical findings in this chapter demonstrate that the technical grasp of the Convention, with which seasoned Commanders became familiar through their training, legal advice and operational experience, did not, in fact, produce either a thoughtless 'tick-box' exercise or excessive judicialisation of decision-making. Commanders were mindful of the need to give rationales for each decision made, and considered the application of the Convention in devising and conducting operations to be an effective means of managing 'trouble', especially from oversight bodies. Most positively, Commanders were highly conscious of the ramifications their decisions had for the rights of parties involved, and of the need to address whether specific operational plans and tactical options would likely comply with more specific Convention standards. Doing so empowered Commanders to police Northern Ireland's deeply divisive, and at times violent, parades and counter-protests, which continue to animate the country's imperfect peace. This positive outlook was encouraged by an occupational sub-culture of senior officers, which valued a sound grasp of the law as a mark of professionalism and savvy means of managing oversight.

The case study further reveals that any procedural duty placed on public authorities – perhaps to 'have regard'[123] or give 'proper consideration'[124] to human rights – must form a part of a much bolder commitment to cultural reform and regulatory oversight of public authorities. The chapter alludes to the types of human rights training, legal advice and organisational processes likely to be required in order to foster a culture of justification within public authorities. But equally significant is that such internal reform is aligned to a regulatory regime attuned to the specific formats, operational dynamics and cultural settings within which authorities routinely make decisions affecting human rights. The mainstreaming of a culture of justification requires non-judicial bodies capable of encouraging, challenging and pressurising authorities to better deliver on their obligations to protect and fulfil human rights long before litigation arises.[125] In this respect, the pioneering police oversight mechanisms in Northern Ireland, especially the work of the NIPB's legal advisors, have proved instrumental in both introducing and maintaining an emphasis on human rights law in PSNI training, processes and practices. It is noteworthy that the NIPB's oversight regime is itself born out of its own unique statutory duty to monitor the performance of the police in complying with the HRA 1998.[126]

There is no doubt that the efforts of the PSNI to foster a human rights-inspired culture of justification in public order policing have been extensive, expensive and propelled by a

---

[122] See *Denbigh* (n 15) and *Miss Behavin'* (n 16) and Poole, 'The Reformation of English Administrative Law' (n 3). Whether the language of HRA 1998, s 6(1) permits a broader interpretation of 'acts' to include the process by which a decision is made is open to debate. See R Masterman, 'Process and Substance in Judicial Review in the United Kingdom and at Strasbourg: Proportionality, Subsidiarity, Complementarity?' in J Gerards and E Brems (eds), *Procedural Review in European Fundamental Rights Cases* (Cambridge, Cambridge University Press, 2017).
[123] *Laporte* (n 38) (Lord Rodger).
[124] See Victoria's *Charter of Human Rights and Responsibilities Act 2006*, s 38(1).
[125] McCrudden, 'Mainstreaming Human Rights' (n 14) 13.
[126] Police (Northern Ireland) Act 2000, s 3(b)(ii); see especially Martin, 'Policing Human Rights' (n 30).

wider human-rights consciousness that animates public and political life in post-conflict Northern Ireland.[127] If a culture of justification is going to take root in public authorities across the UK, those authorities must be sufficiently eager and well-resourced to embark on the institutional and cultural commitment this vision demands. Whether the Convention offers a meaningful or attractive legal resource for decision-makers in schools, hospitals, leisure centres or city councils, and how human rights interact with, and are shaped by, other working cultures, is the task for future research, here at this frontier of public law.

---

[127] See J Curtis, *Human Rights as War by Other Means* (Pennsylvania, PA, University of Pennsylvania Press, 2014); C Harvey, 'Bringing Humanity Home: A Transformational Human Rights Culture for Northern Ireland?' in AM McAlinden and C Dwyer (eds), *Criminal Justice in Transition: The Northern Ireland Context* (Oxford, Hart Publishing, 2015).

INDEX

Introductory Note

References such as '178–79' indicate (not necessarily continuous) discussion of a topic across a range of pages. Wherever possible in the case of topics with many references, these have either been divided into sub-topics or only the most significant discussions of the topic are listed. Because the entire work is about 'public law', the use of this term (and certain others which occur constantly throughout the book) as an entry point has been minimised. Information will be found under the corresponding detailed topics.

30-year rule   405–6, 411

Aarhus Convention   43
Aboriginal and Torres Strait Islander Commission   9, 229, 242–51
Aboriginal and Torres Strait Islander peoples   8–9, 157–77, 182, 207–8, 211, 215–17, 228–29, 237–38, 242–44, 247–49, 251–53
Aboriginal communities   160–61, 221, 243, 248
Aboriginal land   157, 160–61, 165
Aboriginal rights   135, 177, 198, 216–17
absolute exemption   405, 408
academy schools   344, 347
accommodation   182, 232–33, 240, 463, 474, 498
accountability   48–49, 53, 56, 243, 245, 324–25, 327–30, 427, 429
   executive branch   471
   legal   54, 112–13, 519
   political   112–13, 429, 439–40
accreditation   60, 62
active hostilities   72, 80–81, 84
active protection   136, 141–42
active support   52, 236, 239, 247, 251
activists   228–29, 231–32, 295
actors   20, 43, 45, 68, 87–88, 195, 316
   administrative   471
   international   27–29, 31–32
   non-governmental   325
   private   43, 54, 324, 349
adjudication   19, 52, 202, 293, 313, 363
   constitutional   6, 33–35, 40
   and interpretation   33–39
adjudicators   113, 359–61, 382
administration   5–6, 53–55, 86–88, 295, 297, 388–90, 392–93, 432, 476–77
   and administrative action   53–56
   of criminal justice   303, 307, 310

   distributed   6, 43–44, 54, 60–64
   good   96, 444, 454, 456, 464, 466
administrative action   13, 53, 55, 282, 296, 353, 387–89
administrative agencies   11, 13, 227, 435, 471, 474–77, 482
administrative courts   318, 320
administrative decision-makers   192, 199, 301, 361
administrative decisions   43, 55, 157, 362, 459, 477
Administrative Decisions (Judicial Review) Act 1977   157, 362–63, 365
administrative discretion   300–301, 310
administrative justice   13, 471–98
   as middle ground   481–98
   models   475, 479, 484
   theory   13, 474–78, 484, 498
administrative law   4–8, 10–12, 178–80, 190–92, 199–203, 298–301, 330, 332, 353–54, 364, 366–68, 380–84
   baselines   194, 196, 199
   boundaries   364, 366, 368, 377, 382–84
   decolonisation   177–203
   principles   11, 187, 355
   public and private boundaries   353–83
   remedies   362
   review   191, 197
   standards   353–55, 357, 359–60, 362, 366, 369, 372–74, 376–77, 379–80, 382–84
administrative power   43, 300, 501
administrative procedure   440–41
Administrative Procedure Act, *see* **APA**
administrative processes   300, 429, 476
administrative state   315, 317, 431, 439–40, 445, 472, 501
administrative tort liability   318, 323
administrators   444–45, 451–53, 455, 458, 461, 468, 471, 498, 501

advice and consent   430–31
advisers, legal   508, 511–15, 519–20
AEP (Attenuated Energy Projectiles)   519
affirmative action   221, 223, 225
AFI (Athletics Federation of India)   65
agencies   51, 332, 335, 337, 346–48, 429–38, 440–41, 475–76, 478–79
　administrative   11, 13, 227, 435, 471, 474–77, 482
　benefits-delivering   472, 474, 477
agency policy making   435
agency rulemaking   12, 429, 433, 436, 440
Al Qaeda   71–72, 76–77
alcohol   220–22, 466, 480
Alcohol Management Plans, *see* AMP
ambiguity   78–79, 82–83, 489
Amoonguna   157, 162–64
AMP (Alcohol Management Plans)   221–23
anthropologists   163–65, 176
anti-discrimination principles   225
Aotearoa New Zealand   124, 255–59, 263, 270, 272, 274
APA (Administrative Procedure Act)   12, 429–30, 433–35, 437–41
appeal   133, 135–36, 138–43, 289, 297–99, 302–7, 309–10, 312–13, 340–41, 366, 417, 516–17
　criminal   298, 306–7
　sentence   298, 304
　tribunals   196, 198–200
appellate bodies   48, 195–96, 199
appellate courts   130, 147, 302, 305, 311, 366, 381
appellate review   298, 308
applications for judicial review   282, 288, 344–46, 350
appointments   124, 283, 361, 393, 485, 491, 494
appropriateness   94, 302, 308, 312, 355
appropriations   395–96, 420
arbitrariness   447, 458–59
archives   179, 405, 408–11
Archives Act   409–11
armed conflict   71–72, 74–75, 77–79, 81–82, 84, 88
　international   75–76
　ongoing   77
armed forces   75, 290, 321
arrests   283–84, 507, 516
aspirations   57, 196, 207, 211, 214, 228–29, 277
assessment   74–76, 81, 163, 165, 309, 311, 502, 505–6
assets   47, 136–38, 152, 302, 390–91, 473
assimilation   183, 185–86
assistance   308, 313, 478, 483–87, 489, 491, 493, 496–97
associations, unincorporated   165, 366, 371–73
assurances   134, 140, 454
asylum seekers   38, 357, 448
ATC (Australian Trotting Council)   366, 378–79

athletes   64–66
Athletics Federation of India, *see* AFI
ATSIC (Aboriginal and Torres Strait Island Commission)   210, 229–30, 242–43, 245–51, 253
Attenuated Energy Projectiles (AEP)   519
Austin   509
Australia   7–8, 36, 38, 159, 164–66, 173–74, 209–13, 217–20, 250–53, 368–70, 400–402, 408–12
　and communal, land-related decision-making   157–76
　Constitution   38, 207, 209, 217, 229, 388–89, 415
　constitutional recognition debate   206–9
　courts   165, 175, 205, 366, 374, 420, 469
　executive power   387–96
　governmental structures   388–89
　governments   38, 169, 205–6, 208, 213, 218–20, 225
　High Court   2, 297, 302, 304, 306, 308, 311
　Indigenous challenge to public law   8–9, 205–25
　judicial review   389–90
　law   158, 160, 162, 166, 210, 225
　Maloney   206, 219–26
　nature and extent of executive power   390–93
　New South Wales (NSW)   172, 359, 361, 365–66, 371, 378, 411
　Northern Territory   157, 159–62, 208, 262
　official responses to proposals for Indigenous representation   209–13
　public law of Indigenous state relationships   213–19
　Queensland   166–67, 220–23, 248–49
　Referendum Council   207–8, 237–38
　representative and majority decision-making   165–75
　Uluru Statement from the Heart   8, 205–9, 211, 213, 215, 219, 226, 228
　Victoria   2, 237–38, 252, 297, 307–8, 313, 368–70
Australian Trotting Council (ATC)   366, 378–79
Australians   8, 36–37, 209, 323, 388, 449
authorisation   8, 170, 173–74, 272, 424
authoritarianism   280, 429–41
authoritative documents   402, 426–27
availability of judicial review   341, 350, 370
Awa Tupua Act   266–67, 271

Bagehot, W.   403, 406–7
balance   94, 306, 309, 429–30, 436, 439–40, 466–68, 482, 484
band chiefs   183–85, 198
band councils   183, 189, 199–200
band governments   199–200
bargaining power   347–48, 350, 381
Barnet   345–46
barristers   10, 280, 295, 513, 520

Index 525

battlefields 71, 73, 76–77, 83, 86
BC (British Columbia) 179–80, 186, 497
Beetham, D. 235–36
behaviour 13, 193, 324, 328, 425, 491–92, 494
beliefs 30, 235, 239, 264, 318, 406, 410
beneficiaries 195, 220, 222–25
benefits 144, 224–25, 264–65, 274, 317–18, 445–46, 448–49, 463–67, 479–80, 484–87, 491–92, 496
   public 345, 490
   taxpayer-funded 482, 488–91, 494, 498
benefits-delivering agencies 472, 474, 477
best interests 172, 225, 482, 485–89, 491–92, 494, 497
bias 197, 200, 330–31, 376, 381, 465
bills of rights 3, 97–99, 126, 328
bipartisan support 229, 237, 250
black-and-white efficiency engineers 474, 481, 484, 491, 497
black-and-white rule-enforcers 479–80, 493
black-spider letters 406, 419
blanket policies 445, 447, 459, 463
Boards of Visitors 290–92
body politic 130, 186, 210, 390–91
boundaries
   of administrative law 364, 366, 368, 377, 382–84
   of judicial review 11, 353, 382
Braganza 382–83
branches of government 7, 123, 131, 146, 330
breach of contract 374–79
Brexit 6–7, 91–119
   and constitutional law generally 102–19
   and grounds for judicial review 91–102
   and proportionality 92–99
   and rights 99–102
      under Charter 99
   scope of inquiry 91
bridgers 510–12
British Columbia, *see* BC
Bronze Commanders 506–7, 511, 513
bureaucracies 211, 433, 478–79
bureaucratic efficiency 479–80
by-laws 187, 192–96, 198–99, 202, 270

Cabinet Manuals 12, 213–14, 399–428
   control over content 425–27
   development 414–16
   legal status 416–20
   reasons for publication 413–14
   recording or creating/altering 421–25
Canada 7–8, 125–27, 177–203, 205–6, 215–18, 400–402, 414–16, 418–20, 425, 471–72
   administrative decision-makers 187–95
   BC (British Columbia) 179–80, 186, 497
   Charter of Rights and Freedoms 97, 190, 319
   Constitution 206, 215, 217

   decolonisation of administrative law 200–202
   extension or reclamation of jurisdiction 195–200
   Indigenous peoples before Indian Act 179–87
   Ontario Works programme 13, 472–74, 480–84, 486–90, 492–93, 495–98
   postcolonial public law 177–79
Canadian state 8, 178–79, 187, 197
capacity 64, 142, 153, 225, 227, 252–53, 363–66, 391, 427
   common law 11, 363–64, 368
   to contract 347, 391
care homes 328, 342
careers 283, 315, 413
Carillion 324, 337–38, 348–49, 351
case management, efficient 485, 488, 493–94, 497
case studies 9, 12, 72, 101, 500, 503–4
caseloads 482, 485–86, 488, 492–93, 495
   management 492–93, 495
caseworkers 13, 452–53, 472–73, 479–89, 491–98
casinos 61, 363–64, 372
Caster Semenya 60, 66–67
catalysts 19, 22, 25, 27, 34, 105, 230
CDM (Clean Development Mechanism) 63
central government 317, 338, 347
Central Land Council (CLC) 157, 161–64
certification 62–63
certiorari 287, 289, 291, 293, 360, 367, 373
change, and constitution-making 27–32
charges 69, 74, 139, 288, 290, 292–93, 295
   criminal 289, 293, 295
   disciplinary 290, 292–93, 295
charging decisions 277–78, 288
chiefs 181, 184–85, 188–89, 193, 209, 286–87, 395
   band 183–85, 198
China 24, 26, 46, 49, 51, 68
choices 83, 85, 88, 192, 198, 247, 328–29, 343–44
citizens 36–37, 108–9, 212–13, 334, 336, 343–47, 351, 448, 456–57
   Australia 37, 209, 251
   and government 343–46
citizenship 37, 94, 188, 209
   multiple 36–37
civil jurisdiction 98, 289
civil liberties 280, 331, 501
civilian lawyers 82, 89
civilians 74–76, 81–82, 84
claim groups 167–75
claimant knowledge 444, 452, 456
claimants 138, 140, 173–74, 340–42, 443–44, 446–52, 454–57, 462–68, 505
claims 19–20, 27–28, 31–34, 56–59, 133–34, 138–40, 154–55, 166–70, 173, 262–63, 343, 345–46
   contract 349, 376–77
   overlapping 168–69

clans   173, 175, 180, 184
CLC, *see* Central Land Council
Clean Development Mechanism (CDM)   63
clients   350, 476, 480–86, 488–98
climate change   25, 327
clubs, local   378–79
Coal case   137, 151–52
coalitions   46, 413
coercive powers   59, 135, 222, 232, 299
collective responsibilities   407, 427
Combet   396
commanders   181, 500, 504, 506–8, 510–21
   aspiring   508–10
Commanders
   Bronze   506–7, 511, 513
   Gold   506, 510, 512, 514, 517, 520
   Silver   506, 510–15, 517, 519–20
commentators   73, 105, 366–67
Commercial radio assets case   137, 151
commitments   32, 50, 473, 480, 483, 485, 491–92
common law   92–97, 99–103, 108–11, 114, 292–93, 296, 302, 315–17, 379–80, 383, 392
   capacity   11, 363–64, 368
   jurisdictions   33, 54, 97, 125, 319–20
   legitimacy of development of rights inspired by EU Charter   101
   powers   445–46, 462
   rights   95, 98–101, 110, 115, 336
     of a constitutional or fundamental nature   99–100
     origins   99–100
common lawyers   315–16
communal decision-making   158–59, 161, 163, 165, 167, 169, 171, 173, 175–76
communications   400, 405, 408, 411–12, 438
communities   162–63, 176, 183–84, 186–94, 221–25, 228–29, 233–35, 237–39, 244–50, 252, 304–5, 515
   political   212–13, 236
companies   196, 324, 328–29, 356, 358, 362–63, 371–73
compensation   166–68, 170, 222, 283, 321, 394, 445
competence   58, 103, 115–18
competencies   116–18
competing interests   55, 93, 285, 503
competing rights   501, 504, 515, 518
complaint-handling bodies   370–71, 379
complaints   172, 298, 301, 305, 344, 370–71, 376
complexity   4, 10, 89, 91, 158, 168–69, 174
compliance   29, 34, 40, 56–57, 62, 85, 89
compromise
   legislative   166, 439
   principled   257, 265, 273
conduct of hostilities   77–78
conferences   1–2, 33, 240

confidence, public   224, 301, 303–4, 307–8, 452
confidentiality   110, 406–7, 409, 419
conflict   25, 27, 32, 72–73, 78, 84, 86, 483, 491–92
   intrastate   22, 24, 28
Congress   173, 429–32, 434–41
congressional policy making   12, 437
congruence   237, 239–40
consensus   84, 89, 115, 174, 207, 239, 270
consent   115, 117, 158, 161–66, 176, 217, 235–36, 430–31
   as a group   159–65
   informed   223–24
   resource   142, 269, 271
conservation   137, 140, 153, 257, 259–60, 264–66, 270
   estate   259–60, 265
consistency   10, 12–13, 164–65, 297–305, 307–11, 443–46, 448–49, 453–57, 459–61, 466–69
   of approach   297, 308
   and discretionary power   297–313
   ground of review   12, 443, 453
   of policy   12, 443–45, 449, 452, 454–55, 457, 468
   reasonable   297, 300, 305, 307, 309–10
   in sentencing   303, 308–9
   tools for   299, 314
consistent application of policy   446, 449, 452–56, 460, 464, 466
consistent expectations   412, 414
Constitution Act   177–78, 182, 420
constitutional actors   105, 401–2, 413, 418, 422, 424–25, 427
constitutional adjudication   6, 33–35, 40
constitutional arrangements   19, 21–24, 103–5, 108, 113, 127, 421–22
constitutional change   22, 32, 124, 208, 415, 425
constitutional conventions   400–402, 407, 412, 414–16, 418–19, 421, 423–25
constitutional crises   12, 401–2, 412–13, 423, 427
constitutional design   123, 125
constitutional dialogue   7, 123–24, 126, 129–34, 150
constitutional jurisdiction   34, 354
constitutional law   3, 6, 8, 19–20, 24, 26, 29–30, 36
   domestic   6, 20, 24
   United Kingdom   102–19
constitutional legitimacy   28–29, 31
constitutional monarchy   40, 200
constitutional norms   23, 125, 128
constitutional powers   207, 400, 424
constitutional principles   21, 107, 213, 216, 354, 417, 420, 423
constitutional protection   7, 123, 128, 353–54
constitutional recognition   206–10, 212, 237
constitutional rights   108, 110–11, 406
constitutional roles   115, 123, 403, 407–8, 499

Index 527

constitutional status   32, 104, 108–9, 132, 182, 213
constitutional statutory provisions   107–11
constitutional structures   9, 37, 91, 110, 119, 125, 274
constitutional systems   7, 23, 123, 419
constitutionalism, global   6, 19–40
constitution-making   6, 19, 24, 36, 40
  and change   27–32
constitutions, *see also under individual countries*
  interpretation and adjudication   33–39
  national   20–21, 23–24, 32, 34, 39–40, 328
  political   103, 112, 114, 118, 125, 129, 134
constraints, external   272, 471
consultation   141–42, 147, 152–55, 214–17, 219, 222–25, 237–39, 244–45, 410
  duty of   216–18
  expectation of   154–55
  processes   67, 141, 244–45
consultative obligations   206, 218–19
contentious parades and protests   500, 503, 512, 514
contract   10–12, 316–17, 323–24, 337, 339–43, 345–50, 358–59, 363–66, 371–83, 387–89, 391, 393–95
  breach of   374–79
  implying terms   379–82
  law   5, 135, 323, 353–54
contract claims   349, 376–77
contracted-out services   339, 342–43
contracting, processes   343, 345, 348
contractors   11, 38, 335–39, 341–43, 358, 368
  and government   346–51
contracts, government   336, 339, 343, 346–50, 391, 393, 395
  consequences   393–96
contractual obligations   379, 394–95
contractual relationships   335–37, 341, 378
  direct   324, 378
contractual terms   374, 380–81, 383
  implied   353, 366, 369, 375–80, 382–84
control   51, 63, 182–84, 186–87, 283–85, 321, 325, 425
  of land and resources   182, 216
  over content of Cabinet Manuals   425–27
control of discretion   286–89
Convention rights   100, 112, 278, 328, 503–5, 513
Convention standards   518, 521
conventions   11–12, 93–94, 99–100, 112, 115, 356, 399–407, 409–27, 499, 501–2, 510, 521–22
  constitutional   400–402, 407, 412, 414–16, 418–19, 421, 423–25
convergence   21, 28, 34, 332
convictions   222, 283, 286, 298
cooperation games   43–44, 60
corporations   331, 365, 373

Corporations Act   370–71, 373
corrupt practices   193, 368
costs   43–44, 194, 338–39, 349, 435, 473, 496–97
councils, band   183, 189, 199–200
counter-terror operations   6, 72, 89
Court of Arbitration for Sport   60, 62, 64
Court of Justice of the European Union (CJEU)   97–98, 118
courts   33–39, 91–103, 112–16, 132–36, 138–40, 192–95, 286–96, 305–9, 339–46, 436–41, 449–55, 463–67
  administrative   318, 320
  appellate   130, 147, 302, 305, 311, 366, 381
  Australia   165, 175, 205, 366, 374, 420, 469
  criminal   287, 293, 303
  inferior/lower   198, 287, 298, 354–55, 361
  intermediate   309, 366, 381
  regional   33–35, 64
  supranational   33, 88
CPS (Crown Prosecution Service)   287–89
crime   76, 277–97, 311
criminal charges   289, 293, 295
criminal courts   287, 293, 303
criminal justice   277–80, 282, 289–90, 295–96, 303–4, 307, 310, 313
  administration of   303, 307, 310
  systems   277, 282, 296, 299, 303–4, 308
criminal law   2–5, 9–10, 279, 287, 293, 297–99, 309
  as public law   298–300
criminal proceedings   293, 298–99, 319, 419
criminal records   221, 462, 464
crises, constitutional   12, 401–2, 412–13, 423, 427
Cromwell Property   376, 379–80, 382
Crown land   128, 136, 259
Crown Prosecution Service, *see* CPS
culture   3–4, 7, 137–38, 228, 231, 238, 502, 513–14
  of justification   13, 499–522
customary elections   188–89, 191–93, 200
customary international law   79, 85–87
customary laws   89, 177, 189, 191–92, 198–99, 201
customary practices   187, 199, 260
customary title   135, 140, 151
customer service   345, 483–84, 486, 492–93
customs   8, 166–67, 175, 185, 190–91, 198, 201–2

Daly   99, 463
Datafin   341, 366–73, 376, 379, 382–83
Daugherty, W.   186
decision-makers   158–59, 199, 269, 271–72, 300–301, 356, 358–62, 382–83, 443–50, 452–62, 464–65, 467–69
  administrative   192, 199, 301, 361
  independent   191, 196
  Indigenous   8, 177, 179–80, 187, 191, 196–98, 200
  public   273, 288

528 Index

decision-making 7–8, 43–45, 134–36, 157–59, 164–65, 167–68, 175–76, 233–34, 300–302, 508–11, 514–15, 517–21
  authority 227, 231, 243
  bodies 192, 200, 227–30, 236, 239, 251–53, 368
  communal 158–59, 161, 163, 165, 167, 169, 171, 173, 175–76
  institutions 9, 228–30, 232, 235, 239, 241–42, 251
  methods 173, 175
  models 158–59
  power 270–71, 274, 321, 383
  practices 471–72, 474, 476, 492
  processes 164–65, 170, 172–73, 175–76, 269, 274, 503, 505
decisions
  administrative 43, 55, 157, 362, 459, 477
  best possible 489–90
  caseworker 13, 473
  charging 277–78, 288
  disciplinary 289, 291, 293, 372, 374, 377
  discretionary 473, 483, 491
  judicial 159, 282, 323, 424, 475
  justiciability 359, 367, 369
  policy 86, 88, 429, 431, 439
  reasoned 41, 53
  sentencing 10, 297, 299, 303–4, 309, 313
  tendering 364–65
declarations of inconsistency 126, 130
declaratory relief 155, 379
deference 8, 10, 192–94, 196, 199, 201, 278, 505–6
delegated authority 193, 231, 472
delegated legislation 106, 192, 356
delegated powers 183, 201
delegates 2, 207, 228, 301, 374, 453, 458
  statutory 190–91, 196, 201
delegation 54, 389, 457–58, 462
delegators 453, 458
deliberative democracy 429
deliberative processes 207, 412, 439
democracy 25, 28–29, 51, 179–80, 200, 209, 212
  deliberative 429
  representative 388, 427, 440
democratic governance 40, 56, 252
democratic institutions 192, 211, 241
democratic legitimacy 21, 46, 211, 240, 440
democratic processes 8, 206, 211
denial of procedural fairness 360, 364, 374
design 8, 32–33, 61, 238–39, 242, 247, 252–53
  constitutional 123, 125
  institutional 227–28, 230, 232, 236, 244, 246, 251–52
detainees 38, 74, 76, 79–80
detention 38–39, 72–74, 76, 284, 289, 357, 452
deterrence 38, 305
devolution 109, 115–19, 422

devolved legislatures 102, 105, 115, 117
dialogue 3, 7, 66, 129, 232, 234, 513
  constitutional 7, 123–24, 126, 129–34, 150
  institutional 129
  metaphor 129–30, 132
differential treatment 220, 304
digitisation 52–53, 331
direct action 80–81, 84, 86–87
Director of Public Prosecutions, *see* **DPP**
disciplinary decisions 289, 291, 293, 372, 374, 377
discipline, prison 278, 290, 293, 295, 463
disclosure 408, 412
discretion 285–86, 288–89, 291–92, 298–300, 302–4, 312, 444–45, 462, 464–65, 480–81, 488–90, 495
  administrative 300–301, 310
  control of 286–89
  exercise of 306, 413, 459
  fettered 10, 314
  formal 490, 496–97
  judicial 198, 299, 302–3, 310, 312, 319
  operational 286, 472, 479–82, 484–85, 490, 492–96, 498, 517
  prosecutorial 10, 287, 431
  sentencing 10, 297–314
  structured 10, 314
discretionary decisions 473, 483, 491
discretionary power 182, 184, 188, 201, 266, 299, 304
  and consistency 297–313
discrimination 66, 219, 331, 445, 460
discriminatory laws 219, 225
disorder 279, 290, 511, 514–16, 519
  public 285, 518–19
dispute resolution 26, 359, 373
disputes 73, 82, 84, 100, 102, 359, 361, 363, 376–77
dissolution of Parliament 401–2, 405, 415
distributed administration 6, 43–44, 54, 60–64
divergent norms 474, 481, 485
documents 181, 400, 402–3, 405–6, 408–9, 412, 415, 487–88, 512–13
  authoritative 402, 426–27
  confidential 414–15
  government 400–401, 403–5, 407–8, 411, 427
  historical 407, 415
  primary 402, 427
domestic authorities 43, 45, 62, 289, 507
domestic bodies 11, 354, 366–67, 369, 371–80, 383
domestic constitutional law 6, 20, 24
domestic law 3, 6, 72, 92–93, 95, 98–101, 103–4, 106–8
domestic public law 6, 19–20
double jeopardy 293
DPP (Director of Public Prosecutions) 287–89
dual jurisdiction 320, 331

Index

due process 74, 199, 277–78, 324, 330
duties 201–2, 216–17, 268–69, 273–74, 291–92, 340–41, 353–55, 364–65, 388–89, 392, 406–7, 447
  fiduciary 135, 181, 216–18
  free-standing 216–17
  general 296, 322
  positive 214, 500, 504, 514–15, 517
  public 342, 368, 371

ECHR (European Convention on Human Rights) 92–102, 112, 278, 288, 295, 501, 503–4, 506, 510, 515–20
economic governance 48
economic inequality 51
ECtHR (European Court of Human Rights) 23, 35, 92, 97–98, 286, 295, 507
education 107, 143–44, 173, 249, 333, 419
  civic 427
effective delivery of public services 11, 336
effectiveness 21, 24, 29, 62, 68, 101, 249–50
efficiency 328, 330, 339, 457–58, 462, 493, 495
  bureaucratic 479–80
efficiency engineers 472, 477–80
  black-and-white 474, 481, 484, 491, 497
  bureaucratic 479
efficient case management 485, 488, 493–94, 497
elected representatives 118, 193, 269
elections 37, 187–88, 190, 194, 198–200, 248, 251, 414–15
  customary 188–89, 191–93, 200
electoral models 190, 248
electoral processes 8, 187–88, 191, 248
electoral systems 106, 127, 184, 187, 211, 414, 424
  proportional 413, 423
Ellis 157, 161–62, 164
empirical research 13, 279, 284, 474, 477
employment 473, 482–83, 485, 487, 490, 494–98
  contracts 380, 382
employment-related expense benefits 491, 497
empowerment 28, 176
enforcement 23, 43, 52, 62, 333, 379, 388
  actions 57, 436
  legal 417–18
  political 32, 417
entrenched minimum provision for judicial review 354–55, 360, 367, 389
equality 209–10, 212, 300–301, 304–5, 324, 328, 459–60, 464–65
  political 212, 227
equitable intervention 376, 379
equitable relief 366, 374–77, 379
errors 135–36, 138, 142, 303, 308, 312, 358, 360–61
  jurisdictional 354–55, 358–61, 363
  non-jurisdictional 354–55, 359–61, 363

ethical standards 324, 327, 334
European Communities Act 103, 109
European Convention on Human Rights, *see* ECHR
European Court of Human Rights, *see* ECtHR
European Union 22–23, 25, 27, 36, 46, 91–92, 102
eviction 341–42
evidence 25, 66–67, 85–86, 162–63, 175–76, 194, 235–36, 283–84, 286–87, 291–92, 298–99
executive branch 77, 80–85, 87–88, 354, 356, 363–64, 429, 432–33
  accountability 471
executive government 127, 391–92, 394, 418–19, 421, 424, 428
executive power 12, 354–55, 357, 387–91, 393, 395, 397, 399–400
  as black box 399–427
  exercise of 12, 357, 389–91, 400
    non-statutory 11, 301
  nature and bounds 387–96
  non-statutory 11, 301, 357, 391–92, 399
exemptions 370, 405, 408–9, 411
  absolute 405, 408
  qualified 412
exercise
  of discretion 306, 413, 459
  of executive power 12, 357, 389–91, 400
  of judicial discretion 198, 310
  of prerogative powers 107, 111
  of public power 158, 235, 299, 332, 366, 389, 393
  of statutory power 11, 353, 355–57, 359–61, 369, 382, 389
expectations 154–55, 251, 271, 333, 401, 449–51, 455
  consistent 412, 414
  legislative 271
  legitimate, *see* legitimate expectations
experience 35, 131, 229, 240, 248, 303, 413
expertise 192–94, 199, 201, 347, 508, 510, 512
  legal 13, 512
experts 49, 198, 201, 360–61, 426, 433, 476
external constraints 272, 471
external influence 22, 27–30
external involvement 28–30
external review 290, 353, 358
external sovereignty 36, 40
extinguishment of title 166, 168–69, 174

fair hearing 277, 290, 292
fairness 191–92, 196–97, 199, 289–92, 296, 327–28, 454, 459, 469
  procedural, *see* procedural fairness
federal governments 183–85, 188–89, 197, 203, 228, 246, 250
fees 63, 95–96, 101–2, 143, 377, 496–97
fiduciary duty 135, 181, 216–18

Financial Ombudsman Service Ltd (FOS)   369–71, 373, 376–77
First Nations   178, 183–84, 187–91, 193, 201, 203, 205, 228, 251
First Nations Elections Act (FNEA)   188–90
fishing, rights   142, 154, 273
flexibility   308–10
FNEA, *see* First Nations Elections Act
foreign affairs   113, 115, 390
formal discretion   490, 496–97
formalisation   400, 420
FOS, *see* Financial Ombudsman Service Ltd
France   72, 281, 317–18, 320–21, 394
Freedom of Information Act   405–8, 411, 434
freedom(s)   182–83, 215, 302, 349–50, 443, 445, 456–57, 465, 467–68
   of expression   93, 504–5, 507
   fundamental   220, 222, 225, 499
   of information   12, 331, 400, 405–8, 411–12, 414, 419
free-standing duties   216–17
front-line workers   473–74, 476, 478–98
functions, transnational governance   53, 332
fundamental freedoms   220, 222, 225, 499
fundamental principles   75, 109, 209, 306, 309, 360
fundamental rights   7, 64, 92–93, 96–97, 99–101, 109–11, 333
funding   52, 60, 63, 143, 244, 296, 496–97

GAL, *see* global administrative law
Gallaher   443, 449, 453–55, 468–69
games, cooperation   43–44, 60
GCHQ   321, 356
general law   4, 272, 355–56, 359–60, 363–65, 367–68, 373
general principles   92, 98, 131, 375, 380
global administrative law (GAL)   6, 20, 41–69, 332
   and changes in global political, economic and social orders   45–53
   concepts and methods   53–64
   future   50–53
   and law   56–59
   practices informing development as analytic field   42–45
   principles   48, 64, 69
   procedures   43–44, 60
   reasons for rise   46–49
global constitutionalism   6, 19–40
global governance   46, 49–51, 56, 58, 60, 67–68, 332
global institutions   57, 60, 62–64, 332
global regulators   43, 45, 62, 64
global regulatory bodies   41, 43, 45, 58, 62, 69
global regulatory governance   46, 60, 67–68

globalisation   6, 19–28, 33–40, 45, 50–51, 69, 332
   and global governance   50–51
   impact   20, 23, 33
good administration   96, 444, 454, 456, 464, 466
good faith   147, 149, 156, 214–15, 217, 219, 376, 380–81
good reason to depart from policy   444, 453–54, 464–65
goods   22, 62, 212, 287, 324, 335, 337–39
   public   324, 333
   and services   324, 335, 338–39
governance   42, 44, 173, 191–92, 200–202, 229–30, 233–34, 250–51, 263
   arrangements   169, 241, 269–70
   democratic   40, 56, 252
   economic   48
   global   46, 49–51, 56, 58, 60, 67–68, 332
   Indigenous   180–82, 187, 189–90, 196, 200–201, 234
   institutions   60, 228, 233
   powers   47, 183
   private   6, 42, 46, 64–68
   structures   46, 58, 60, 68, 257
   transnational   52–53, 59, 332
government
   and citizens   343–46
   and contractors   346–51
   contracts   336, 339, 343, 346–50, 391, 393, 393–96
   departments   262, 318, 346–48, 403
   documents   400–401, 403–5, 407–8, 411, 427
   policy   211, 242, 250–51, 368, 406–7
   records   408–10, 434
governmental power   212, 367, 374, 430, 433
governmental structures   387–89
governments   1–5, 7–11, 126–32, 243–47, 249–53, 328–31, 334–39, 346–51, 387–97, 399–404, 412–19, 423–28
   band   199–200
   federal   183–85, 188–89, 197, 203, 228, 246, 250
   local   128, 187, 191, 263, 337–38, 347, 435
   minority   106, 413
   settler   213, 218, 227, 231
   state   64, 168, 221
   United Kingdom   91, 102, 114, 116–18, 317, 323, 404, 406–7
   United States   48, 71–72, 429–31, 434, 436
governors   126, 181, 279, 289–93, 295
Governors-General   393, 402, 404, 409–11, 413, 423, 425
grounds of review   7, 12–13, 164, 350, 353, 443–47, 451–56, 468–69
guardianship structures   266, 269–70
guidance/guidelines   108, 286, 288–89, 300–303, 306–8, 310, 416–17, 489
   and consistency   300–308

hardship   484–86, 492, 494
  prevention   481, 484–86, 488, 497
  undue   482–84, 486, 488, 490, 492
health   143–44, 249, 263, 266–68, 271, 432
  services   144, 152, 155
hearings   117, 129, 140–41, 271, 287, 291–92, 431
  substantive   140, 142, 153
Hinkley   363–64, 366, 369, 372
historical records   405, 410, 422, 435
homeless families   461, 463
honesty   194, 327–28
hospitals   337–38, 340, 348, 522
hostilities   75–78, 258
  active   72, 80–81, 84
  conduct of   77–78
House of Lords   93, 98, 288, 292, 328–29, 342, 502, 508
HRA, *see* Human Rights Act
human rights   20–21, 88–89, 92–93, 177, 286, 499–501, 503–4, 506–7, 509, 512–16, 518, 520–22
  community   6, 82, 87–89
  law   332–33, 499–500, 503, 506, 508, 510, 514–15, 518, 521
  lawyers   504, 508, 510–12, 520
Human Rights Act   13, 92, 97–98, 100–101, 108–9, 112, 328–29, 335–36, 341–43, 499–522
hung parliaments   414–15, 423–24
Hydro-electric Dams case   137, 151–52
Hyperandrogenism Regulations   65–66

identification   8, 160, 306, 389, 418
identity   69, 139, 188, 264, 266–67, 304, 307
  professional, *see* professional identity
  types   477–80, 482
IHL/LOAC (international humanitarian law/law of armed conflict)   6, 71–72, 74–80, 82–84, 86, 88–89
  minimum requirements   82, 84
  obligations   76, 79
  paradigm   74, 78
IHRL, *see* international human rights law
illegal protests   515–16
illegality   136, 145–47, 149–50
  ground of   146–47
ILUAs (Indigenous Land Use Agreements)   158, 168–75
imminent threats   74–75, 80–82, 508, 511
impartiality   33, 197, 298, 313, 327, 407, 426
implied contractual terms   353, 366, 369, 375–80, 382–84
imprisonment   283, 293, 295, 304, 309
  false   100
IMR (Independent Merits Review)   358
incomes   473, 487–88

inconsistency   126, 136, 143, 146, 300–301, 303–4, 307, 458–59
  declarations of   126, 130
inconsistent legislation   107, 125–26
in-country reform   49
incursions   189, 217, 314, 326, 353–54
independence   197, 249–50
  institutional   198, 201
  judicial   33, 420
Independent Adjudicators   293, 295
Independent Merits Review, *see* IMR
Indian Act   178–80, 182–93, 195–96, 198–200, 202
Indian Advancement Act   185–86
Indigenous authorities   8, 177, 179, 187, 193–95, 199, 201–2
Indigenous decision-makers   8, 177, 179–80, 187, 191, 196–98, 200
Indigenous governance   180–82, 187, 189–90, 196, 200–201, 234
Indigenous institutions   9, 201–2, 227–53
  and the state   230–34
Indigenous interests   4–5, 181–82, 213, 217, 231, 234, 236, 239
Indigenous Land Use Agreements, *see* ILUAs
Indigenous peoples   1–5, 7–9, 121–274
  consultation   9, 206, 218
  interests   4, 176, 234
  and public law   7–9
  rights   123, 134, 149–50, 159, 177, 215, 224
Indigenous rights   4, 7, 203, 212–14, 220, 243, 249
  New Zealand   123–55
  political protection   127–29
  protection   7, 123–24, 129
Indigenous self-governance   179, 228
Indigenous sovereignty   8, 205–6, 230–31
Indigenous values   192, 234, 239, 253
individual responsibility   427, 483, 485, 490
individualised justice   10, 297, 309, 313
inequality   49, 67–68, 347, 460
  economic   51
inferior courts   287, 298, 354–55, 361
influence, external   22, 27–30
information   22, 60, 62, 311–12, 405–8, 422, 424, 436, 438–39
  freedom of   12, 331, 400, 405–8, 411–12, 414, 419
informed consent   223–24
in-house lawyers   13, 510–11
injunctions   282, 287, 294, 354–55, 367, 369, 374, 378
injustice   69, 233, 300, 303–5, 307, 311
inquiries   10, 156, 160, 245, 279, 487, 489
  public   279, 295, 519
instinctive synthesis   297, 306, 310–12
institutional design   227–28, 230, 232, 236, 244, 246, 252
  future   251–53

institutional independence 198, 201
institutionalised governance 67–68
institutions 9–10, 22, 28–29, 47–49, 54, 56–58, 60, 109, 228–29, 234–39, 241–42, 251–53
   decision-making 9, 228–30, 232, 235, 239, 241–42, 251
   democratic 192, 211, 241
   global 57, 60, 62–64, 332
   of government 21, 131, 237, 412, 419
   Indigenous 9, 201–2, 227–53
   international 22, 47, 51, 61–62, 332
   legitimacy 236–37
   penal 277, 289–95
   political 234, 241
   public 212, 235, 237, 279, 299
   public law 231–32, 234–35
   state 102, 110, 230, 232, 282
insurers 322–23, 371
intelligible justification 377, 382
interdependence 6, 12, 19, 21–22, 25, 68, 233
interests
   best 172, 225, 482, 485–89, 491–92, 494, 497
   competing 55, 93, 285, 503
   Indigenous 4–5, 181–82, 213, 217, 231, 234, 236, 239
   in land 160, 165–66
   Māori 128, 143, 153
   private 265, 362
   public, *see* public interest
   special 259, 396
interference 93, 97, 501, 509, 515
interim relief 138, 140
intermediate courts 309, 366, 381
International Criminal Court 34, 50
international human rights law (IHRL) 6, 71–76, 78–80, 82–84, 86, 94
international humanitarian law, *see* IHL
international institutions 22, 47, 51, 61–62, 332
international law 17–19, 223
   and national security policy making 71–89
   public 19, 46, 58
   and public law 5–7
International Monetary Fund (IMF) 48, 332
interoperability 62, 72, 84, 86
interpretation 13, 72, 83, 174–75, 383, 419–20, 427, 499–500, 511–12
   and adjudication 33–39
   statutory 3, 8, 146, 159, 193–94, 198, 201, 418–19
intersections 3–5, 9, 11–12, 73, 79–80, 203, 211
intervention 42, 64, 189, 374, 379, 441, 450–51
   equitable 376, 379
   judicial 453–54
   legislative 10, 283
   police 508, 518
   rule 144, 151

Inuit 178, 239–40
ISIS 76–77
iwi 136, 138–43, 151, 255–56, 260, 264–65, 267–68, 270–71, 274
   authority 139, 151

Jackson v Piikani Nation 194–95
Japan 30–31, 46, 68
judges 2–3, 145–46, 223–25, 280–83, 286, 294–300, 307–9, 311–14, 316, 319–20, 322–23, 344–46
   sentencing 293, 297–98, 303, 305–9, 311–12, 314
   single 361, 369–70
   surrogate 312–13
judicial attitudes to policies 457–61
judicial branch 7, 123, 129, 131, 354–55, 357, 383
judicial decisions 159, 282, 323, 424, 475
judicial discretion 198, 299, 302–8, 310, 312, 319
judicial independence 33, 420
judicial intervention 453–54
judicial power 38–39, 125–26, 354, 388–89, 430–31
judicial review 11–13, 96–98, 124–25, 135–37, 145–47, 149–51, 189–96, 198–99, 335–36, 339–47, 349–51, 353–55
   actions 359, 369, 375–76
   of administrative action 282, 387, 389
   applications for 282, 288, 344–46, 350
   Australia 389–90
   availability 341, 350, 370
   boundaries of 11, 353, 382
   doctrines of 336, 343, 348
   entrenched minimum provision for 354–55, 360, 367, 389
   freestanding grounds of 93, 97–98
   grounds of 6, 12, 91, 93, 98, 145–46, 149–50
   intensity of 193, 199
   law 4, 12, 135, 145, 147, 149–50, 194
   New Zealand 123–55
   proceedings 135, 137, 149, 329, 482
   scope of 11, 91, 336, 341
   and Treaty of Waitangi 134–49
Judiciary Act 157–58, 362–63, 367, 373
jurisdiction 1, 8–9, 33, 125–26, 179–80, 193–94, 196–202, 293, 354–55, 358–59
   civil 98, 289
   constitutional 34, 354
   dual 320, 331
   separate 315–16, 318–19, 321
   supervisory 299, 354, 360
jurisdictional error 354–55, 358–61, 363
jurisprudence 92, 94, 98, 100–101, 187, 193–95, 216, 220
jus ad bellum 78–80

jus in bello 71
justice 95, 102, 125–26, 199–200, 284, 294, 300–304, 310, 378–79, 474, 476
 administrative, *see* administrative justice
 individualised 10, 297, 309, 313
 models 474–79, 481, 484, 498
  competing 477
  Mashaw's 472, 474
 natural, *see* natural justice
justiciability 114, 353–57, 359–63, 366–69, 372–74, 376, 382
 of decisions 359, 367, 369
 and executive capacities 363–66
 general law test of 355–56, 358, 362–63, 365, 373
 test of 354, 356, 358, 361–63, 365–66, 369, 373–74, 382–83
justification 93, 212–13, 383–84, 501–2, 513, 516, 518–19, 521
 culture of 499–507, 509, 511, 513, 515, 517–19, 521–22
 intelligible 377, 382

kāwanatanga 124–25
Kennedy 95–96, 100
Klug, F. 500
knowledge 295–96, 450–52, 455, 457, 504, 506, 510, 512
 claimant 444, 452, 456
 requirement 449–51, 468
 traditional 240, 264

Lam 450
land 123–25, 132–33, 136–38, 141–44, 154–55, 158–62, 165–67, 169–70, 181–82, 258–60, 265–66, 272–74
 Aboriginal 157, 160–61, 165
 Crown 128, 136, 259
 interests in 160, 165–66
Land Rights Act 157, 159–62, 164–65, 170
Land Trusts 160–62
language 130–31, 147, 149, 206–7, 227, 229, 233, 267
 Māori 124, 128, 148, 153, 258
law of armed conflict, *see* IHL/LOAC
lawyers 12–13, 71, 73–74, 89, 148, 151, 285–86, 510–12, 514
 civilian 82, 89
 common 315–16
 human rights 504, 508, 510–12, 520
 public 1–4, 11, 315–16, 323–24, 335, 337, 500
leaders 40, 68, 128, 190–91, 195, 209, 213
leadership 63, 174, 176, 183–84, 186, 250, 252
legal advice 82, 284, 511–12, 520–21
legal advisers 508, 511–15, 519–20
legal enforcement 417–18

legal expertise 13, 512
legal norms 4, 6, 11–12, 23, 235, 334
legal obligations 72, 79, 85–87, 89, 201
legal orders 20, 64, 178–79, 182, 202, 304, 318
legal personality 256–57, 260–61, 264–65, 274, 392
 as bridging concept 263–65
legal persons 9, 255, 257, 268, 274
legal principles 131, 134, 181, 305, 308–10, 313, 329
legal recognition 5, 257, 263, 273
legal rights 4, 95, 111–12, 181, 269, 273, 291
legal systems 4–5, 45, 189, 196, 199, 201, 418
legal validity 126, 234–35
legalised policies 6, 72, 80–82, 84
legalistic policies 72–73, 82–84, 87–88
legislation 8–9, 109–10, 115–16, 126, 130, 138–40, 146–47, 182–83, 265–68, 272–74, 284–86, 510–12
 delegated 106, 192, 356
 inconsistent 107, 125–26
 subordinate 109, 499
legislative authority 391, 393–94
legislative branch 61, 353–55
legislative frameworks 134, 265, 473, 483, 489, 496, 510
legislative power 354, 388–89, 393, 430
legislative reform 131, 284
legislative schemes 158–61, 165, 168, 176, 492, 495, 517
legislatures 91, 110, 112–14, 129–30, 302, 315, 317, 383, 473
legitimacy 32, 34, 212, 214, 217, 228–29, 234–42, 247, 250–52
 constitutional 28–29, 31
 democratic 21, 46, 211, 240, 440
 of institutions 236–37
 sociological 234–35, 242, 250
legitimate expectations 146–47, 149, 154–55, 443–46, 449–57, 460, 462, 466–68
 knowledge requirement 449–52
lethal force 74–76, 79, 81–84, 514
liability 54, 255, 268, 272, 286, 321–23
 administrative tort 318, 323
 private 323
 public 321–23
 vicarious 322
liberty 279, 286–87, 293–95, 304, 329, 430, 508–9
licences 44, 141, 364, 371, 462, 466–67, 496–98
litigation 113–14, 133–34, 174, 176, 279–80, 284–86, 292, 341, 343
 strategic 280, 351
local authorities 265–66, 269, 271–73, 286–87, 340–41, 461, 463, 465

Index

local clubs 378–79
local government 128, 187, 191, 263, 337–38, 347, 435

McClure and Moos 509
MacDonald, Ramsay 401
McGlade 157–58, 165, 167–75
MacNeil-Brown 312–13
Madill, D. 186
magistrates 222, 282, 286–87, 290, 295, 299
Maloney 206, 219–26
management 25, 51, 55, 59, 260, 262–63, 266, 390
 caseload 492–93, 495
 plans 270, 274, 356
 staff 480, 491
 water 142, 153
managers 340, 488, 494, 496
Mandalia 443–44, 452–54, 460–61, 463
Māori 9, 124–28, 132–36, 142–44, 146–48, 150–51, 153, 213–15, 255–74
 claims 132–34
 interests 128, 143, 153
 land 125, 128, 133, 135, 137–38
 language 124, 128, 148, 153, 258
 seats 128, 215
 understandings 264, 269, 271–72
Māori Appellate Court 139–40, 155
market economy 12, 387
market values 63, 133, 327
markets 68, 325, 329, 337, 339, 346–48, 350
 internal 116, 349
Mashaw, JL 13, 431, 472, 474–77, 479, 498
Master Builders 368–70, 374
Maynard-Moody, S. 479
media 256, 401–2, 415, 429, 432
 social 296
medicines 61–62
Melbourne Law School 1–2, 123, 157, 177, 205, 443
Members of Parliament, see MPs
Meneling Station 160
Métis peoples 178
military operations 48, 72–74, 89
Miller 7, 36, 91, 99, 102–19
mining 141, 151–52, 155, 161, 272, 356
minority governments 106, 413
mixed member proportional (MMP) representation 127, 130
models 212, 262, 264, 387, 390, 472, 476–77, 498
 electoral 190, 248
 justice 474–79, 481, 484, 498
 private law 317, 322, 324
 professional treatment 479, 481, 488
monarchs 403, 406–8, 427
monarchy 317, 407–8
 constitutional 40, 200

mountains 259, 263, 267
MPs (Members of Parliament) 128, 213, 215, 284, 417, 419, 422
multijural state 177–203
multi-national enterprises 332–33
multi-people states 206, 211–12
multiple citizenships 36–37
municipalities 185, 187, 192–93, 196, 202
Murphy, L. 56–57
Musheno, M. 479

national security 72, 85, 89, 356
 policy making 71–90
native title 158, 165–70, 174, 176, 218, 220, 249
 holders 167–68, 220
 rights 165, 167–68, 171, 173, 218
natural justice 140, 146–47, 149, 155, 189, 192, 291–92, 298
 principles 140, 147, 155, 189, 192, 298
natural persons 272, 274, 363, 391–93
natural resources 128, 267, 274
Nauru 38, 357
necessity 4, 94, 96, 108, 310, 313, 379–80
negotiations 127–28, 130–31, 133–34, 137, 139, 244, 249, 260–62
networks 46, 49, 53, 60–62, 295–96, 325, 332
New South Wales (NSW) 172, 359, 361, 365–66, 371, 378, 411
 Court of Appeal 360, 364, 366
New Zealand 7, 9, 12, 205–6, 212–15, 218, 414–17, 421, 423
 Cabinet Manual 414, 416, 419, 421, 423, 426
 Indigenous rights 123–55
 judicial review 123–55
 legislative framework for recognising personhood 265–73
 Māori 255–74
 Parliament 9, 126, 128, 215, 426
 political constitution 125–27
 political protection of Indigenous rights 127–29
 recognising personhood in the context of sovereignty 258–65
 Supreme Court 130
 Treaty of Waitangi, see Treaty of Waitangi
New Zealanders 126, 129, 262, 265, 267
Ngāi Tahu 133, 140–41, 143, 153, 264
Ngati Apa ki te Waipounamu Trust v Attorney-General 140–41, 147, 155
NGOs (non-governmental organisations) 43–44, 82, 87–88, 90, 279–80, 288, 294–95
 transnational 46, 52
NIACs (non-international armed conflicts) 75, 78–80
non-fettering principle 12, 301, 443–49, 452–53, 456–58, 461–63, 466–69

Index   535

non-governmental organisations, *see* NGOs
non-Indigenous peoples   159, 219, 233, 245
non-interference   52, 138–39
non-international armed conflicts, *see* NIACs
non-jurisdictional error   354–55, 359–61, 363
non-justiciability   152, 383, 402
non-reneging principle   452, 455–56, 467, 469
non-statutory executive power   11, 301, 357, 391–92, 399
non-statutory powers   10–11, 355, 357, 359, 362–63, 365, 369
non-statutory regulators   366–72
Noongar   169–71, 174
normative orders   9, 56–57, 211, 228–29, 246
norms   39, 42–43, 45, 54, 56–58, 235–37, 303–4, 474, 476–77, 481–86, 488–95, 497–98
  constitutional   23, 125, 128
  divergent   474, 481, 485
  legal   4, 6, 11–12, 23, 235, 334
  programme   13, 474, 481–83, 486, 491, 493
Northern Ireland   13, 115, 504–6, 511–13, 515, 517–18, 521
Northern Territory   157, 159–62, 208, 262
notice-and-comment rulemaking   435, 437–38
NSW, *see* New South Wales
Nunavut   239–40

obligations   74–76, 142–43, 148, 155–56, 213–14, 218, 288–89, 300, 381
  legal   72, 79, 85–87, 89, 201
  procedural   76, 147, 155, 503, 520
  Treaty   138, 141, 143, 148–49, 151, 214
offences   280, 285, 288, 290, 293, 303, 305–8, 310–11
offenders   280, 294, 303–7, 309–10, 338, 344
Office of Fair Trading (OFT)   453–54
official records, Royal and Vice-Regal   402–12
Offshore Processing case   358–59, 363, 367, 369, 374
OFT (Office of Fair Trading)   453–54
Ontario Works programme   13, 472–74, 480–84, 486–90, 492–93, 495–98
operational discretion   286, 472, 479–82, 484–85, 490, 492–96, 498, 517
organs of government   387–89, 391–92
organs of state   34
outcomes   94, 236, 241, 248–49, 304–5, 307, 318, 344–45, 453, 488–89
outsourcing   323, 336–39, 343, 345–46, 351, 366–67, 391
owners, traditional   1, 123, 157, 160–65, 169, 174, 220
ownership   61, 183, 260–63, 265, 273
  national   31–32

Palm Island   221–22
parades   504, 510, 513, 515, 517, 521
  contentious   500, 503, 512, 514

parliamentary sovereignty   104–5, 112, 114–15, 119, 131, 146
Parole Board   281, 289, 293, 344
partial privatisation   134, 137
partnership   133, 149, 214, 219, 260, 338, 340
peace   22, 32, 285–86, 505, 508–9, 511
peaceful protests   507, 512
penal institutions   277, 289–95
performance targets   488, 490, 493–94
Perry, A.   107, 109–10, 443, 446, 449, 461, 463
personal data   99, 331
personality, legal   256–57, 260–61, 263–65, 274, 392
personhood   5, 9, 255, 257–58, 266, 268–69, 271
  legislative framework for recognising   265–73
  recognition in the context of sovereignty   258–65
petitions   262, 290–91, 404
PFI (Private Finance Initiative)   335, 338, 351
Pham   95–96, 297, 309–10
piikanissini   193–94
places-as-persons   255–74
police   10, 13, 222, 277–86, 288–89, 291, 499–522
  actions   285, 508–9
  forces   279–80, 284, 286
  intervention   508, 518
  learning rights   506–14
  malpractice   282–83
  officers   277, 282–87, 479, 509, 516, 520
  organisational processes   512–14, 521
  powers   277, 279, 283
  practising rights   514–20
  stations   222, 284
Police Service of Northern Ireland (PSNI)   13, 500, 503–8, 510, 512–21
policies
  advantages of policy solutions   83–85
  blanket   445, 447, 459, 463
  bridging gaps in legal interpretation   83–84
  changing   429, 465–66
  consistent application of   446, 449, 452–56, 460, 464, 466
  disadvantages of policy solutions   85–87
  flexibility   83
  good reason to depart from   444, 453–54, 464–65
  government   211, 242, 250–51, 368, 406–7
  legalised   6, 72, 80, 82, 84
  legalistic   72–73, 82–84, 87–88
  and resolution of legal interpretation differences within a government   84–85
policing   278–80, 282, 284, 286, 294, 296, 500, 503–4, 506
  and public law   282–86
policy decisions   86, 88, 429, 431, 439

policy making
  agency   435
  congressional   12, 437
  national security   71–90
political accountability   112–13, 429, 439–40
political authority   236, 239, 251, 332
political branch of government   7, 12, 124, 130, 387
political communities   212–13, 236
political constitutions   103, 112, 114, 118, 125, 129, 134
political enforcement   32, 417
political equality   212, 227
political institutions   234, 241
political participation   219, 240
political pressure   124, 134, 284, 518
political process   37, 138–39
political systems   127, 179, 183
politicians   10, 131, 211, 288, 294, 326
politics   4, 6–7, 28, 123, 127, 131, 253
popular sovereignty   29, 206, 212
positive duties   214, 500, 504, 514–15, 517
postcolonial public law   177–79
post-Washington Consensus   48–49
power
  administrative   43, 300, 501
  bargaining   347–48, 350, 381
  decision-making   270–71, 274, 321, 383
  executive, *see* executive power
  presidential   12, 433
  private   324, 329–30, 363
  public   131, 298–99, 332, 341–42, 355–56, 363, 365–67, 382–83
  race   207–8, 225
  shifts   51–52, 67
  territories   207
  vacuum   12, 433, 437
powerlessness   69, 212, 226
powers   53–54, 127, 270–73, 282–85, 353–59, 361–65, 367–69, 388–94, 399, 401–3, 428–33, 450–51
  common law   445–46, 462
  delegated   183, 201
  governance   47, 183
  governmental   212, 367, 374, 430, 433
  judicial   38–39, 125–26, 354, 388–89, 430–31
  legislative   354, 388–89, 393, 430
  non-statutory   10–11, 355, 357, 359, 362–63, 365, 369
  police   277, 279, 283
  prerogative   104, 107, 111, 113, 321, 356–57, 399, 401, 445
  separation of   21, 28, 131, 388–89, 401, 429, 439–40
  statutory   271–72, 287, 340, 356–57, 359, 362–66, 368–69, 372–73, 445

PPG (Presidential Policy Guidance)   71–90
precedents   399–402, 404, 407, 410–12, 414, 422–24, 426–28
prerogative powers   104, 107, 111, 113, 321, 356–57, 399, 401, 445
  and legal rights   111–12
prerogative remedies   361–62
prerogative writs   287, 289
Presidential Policy Guidance, *see* PPG
presidential power   12, 433
pressure, political   124, 134, 284, 518
primary documents   402, 427
Prime Ministers   260, 401–2, 405, 411–12, 417, 424–25
principled compromise   257, 265, 273
prison boards of visitors   290, 292–93, 295
prison discipline   278, 290, 293, 295, 463
prison officers   279, 290–91
Prison Rules   289–90, 293–94
prisoners   76, 279–81, 289–94, 463
prisons   277, 279–82, 289–92, 294, 296, 335, 337
  private   347, 387
Private Finance Initiative, *see* PFI
private governance   6, 42, 46, 64–68
private interests   265, 362
private international law   58
private law   2–5, 9–11, 315, 317, 321, 323–25, 327–29, 331, 336, 353
  model   317, 322, 324
private liability   323
private life   288, 326, 328, 350, 510
private ordering   52
private power   324, 329–30, 363
private prisons   347, 387
private sector decision-makers   363, 372
privatisation   134, 316, 323–25, 390
  partial   134, 137
privative clauses   194, 199, 202, 354–55, 359–60
privileges   125, 290–91, 331, 394, 427
privity of contract   351, 377–79
Probuild   359–61, 363, 382
procedural duties   505, 521
procedural fairness   191–92, 195–97, 199, 201, 364–66, 373–78, 380–81, 383–84
  denial of   360, 364, 374
procedural obligations   76, 147, 155, 503, 520
procedural requirements   81, 219, 429, 433, 437
procurement process   345, 349
professional identity   472, 474, 479, 481, 490, 495
professional treatment models   479, 481, 488
profit   62–63, 316, 328, 339, 350, 388
programme norms   13, 474, 481–83, 486, 491, 493
programme rules   479–80, 484, 491, 495
promise cases   455–57, 468

Index 537

property 5, 124–25, 212, 258, 375, 379, 409, 411
  rights 43, 64, 213, 273, 283, 375
proportional electoral system 413, 423
proportionality 7, 34–35, 64, 66–67, 75–76,
    446–48, 501, 503, 508–9
  analysis 93, 97–98
  assessment 447, 505–6, 512, 518
  and Brexit 92–99
  development 93–97
  doctrinal basis 97–98
  future 98–99
  principle 76, 91–98, 119, 501
  review 447–48
  role 96–97
  test 93–94, 96, 98, 459
prorogation 415, 425
prosecution decisions 286–89
prosecutions 277, 279, 282, 286–88, 312–13
prosecutorial discretion 10, 287, 431
prosecutors 286–88, 312–14
protection
  active 136, 141–42
  rights 64, 96, 99–101, 114–15, 241, 503
protestors 508, 511, 515–17, 520
protests 51, 241, 262, 500, 503–4, 510, 512–18
  illegal 515–16
  peaceful 507, 512
  un-notified 515–17
provincial legislators 192, 483
PSNI, *see* **Police Service of Northern Ireland**
public access 12, 260, 400, 403–4, 408–9, 427, 434
public administration 2–5, 11–12, 299, 301, 330,
    332, 500, 502–3
  and public law 11–13
public authorities 234–35, 322–23, 331, 333, 341,
    343–44, 346, 499–503, 520–22
public bodies 337, 340–42, 347–48, 350–51, 377,
    450, 452, 455–56
public confidence 224, 301, 303–4, 307–8, 452
public disorder 285, 518–19
public duties 342, 368, 371
public goods 324, 333
public inquiries 279, 295, 519
public institutions 212, 235, 237, 279, 299
public interest 285–87, 319, 322, 325, 368, 394–95,
    405, 464–65, 469
  goals 330, 334
  test 405–6, 408, 412, 419
public international law 19, 46, 58
public law, *see also* **Introductory Note**
  apparatus 9, 228, 242, 250
  architecture 232, 250
  Australia 8–9, 205–6, 210, 213, 218, 220
  context 157–58, 165, 175–76, 198, 351
  doctrines 12, 387, 394, 474

  domestic 6, 19–20
  frameworks 9, 228–30, 232, 236, 242, 253
  institutions 231–32, 234–35
  and international law 5–7
  and policing 282–86
  principles 8, 10, 293, 295, 298–99, 315, 328–29
  and public administration 11–13
  remedies 299, 316
  values 323, 327
public lawyers 1–4, 11, 315–16, 323–24, 335, 337, 500
public liability 321–23
public life 223, 315, 328, 333
public moneys 335, 391, 395–96
public order 13, 284–85
  commanders 500, 503–4, 506–10, 515
  events 504–5, 507, 510, 517–18
  policing 285–86, 500, 505–6, 514, 518, 521
public power 131, 298–99, 332, 341–42, 355–56,
    363, 365–67, 382–83
  exercise of 158, 235, 299, 332, 366, 389, 393
public scrutiny 130, 326
public services 11–12, 130–31, 246–47, 336–39,
    343, 347–48, 387–89, 413–14, 483–84
  outsourced 336–37, 351
public/private distinction/divide 11, 315–34,
    336–37, 339, 341, 343, 345, 347, 349
  and contracting state 335–51
punishment 277, 280, 293, 298–99, 304–5, 307–8,
    310–11

qualified exemptions 412
qualified rights 508, 512
Queensland 166–67, 220–23, 248–49

race 205–6, 211, 213, 219–20, 222, 225, 479
  power 207–8, 225
racial groups 220, 224–25
Radio Frequencies case 137, 152
Radio Spectrum case 137, 151, 155
rangatira 124–25, 213
rangatiratanga 124–25, 258
rank 185, 281, 503, 506
Rashid 450–52, 454
rationality 93, 95–98, 301, 324, 327, 446–48, 453,
    455, 460–61
  requirements 67, 381
  review 93–94, 97, 444, 446, 448, 454, 460
  test 445–46
reasonable actions 152–53, 156
reasonable apprehension 200, 505
reasonable consistency 297, 300, 305, 307, 309–10
reasonableness 143, 147–49, 193–94, 198, 201, 377,
    381–84, 469
  review 94, 198
  test of 94, 148

recognition   8–9, 56, 58–59, 105, 177–79, 184, 230–31, 274, 419
  constitutional   206–10, 212, 237
  explicit   99, 418
  of Indigenous rights   159, 243
  legal   5, 257, 263, 273
reconciliation   176, 179, 182, 202–3, 210, 216, 219
records   354–55, 359–61, 363, 402–4, 407, 409–12, 414, 421, 436–37
  government   408–10, 434
  historical   405, 410, 422, 435
  of understanding   255, 262–63
redress   133–34, 138, 148, 273
  cultural   260
referenda   112–13, 127, 207–9, 225, 228, 237, 251
Referendum Council   207–8, 237–38
reforms   45, 47, 279, 281, 284, 287, 296
  in-country   49
  legislative   131, 284
regional courts   33–35, 64
regional plans   243, 249
regional structures   243, 247, 249
regulators
  global   43, 45, 62, 64
  non-statutory   366–72
regulatory bodies   44, 53, 60–63, 269, 341
  global   41, 43, 45, 58, 62, 69
  hybrid   68
  national   53, 61
regulatory governance   54, 68
  global   46, 60, 67–68
regulatory regimes   42, 44–45, 68, 266, 521
relationships, contractual, *see* contractual relationships
reliance   135, 176, 361–62, 369, 466–67, 509, 516
relief   141, 289, 353, 379, 387, 389, 396–97
  declaratory   155, 379
  equitable   366, 374–77, 379
  interim   138, 140
remedies   8, 202, 282, 295–96, 317, 353, 355
  administrative law   362
  prerogative   361–62
  public law   299, 316
  special   349
remission   290–91
representation   127, 192, 280, 404, 454
representative and majority decision-making   165–75
representative bodies   173, 176, 207, 210, 227–29, 238, 240, 242–44, 250–51
representative democracy   388, 427, 440
representatives   126–27, 169, 171, 173, 187, 241, 244, 270–71
  elected   118, 193, 269

research   13, 42, 471, 478–79, 481, 498, 500
  empirical   13, 279, 284, 474, 477
  participants   471, 479, 483–86, 488, 491, 495
reserve lands   178, 183, 195
reserves   182, 184, 195, 221, 491
residential schools   177, 184
residents   208, 340, 342, 350, 510–11, 515–18, 520
  local   510, 516
resilience   6, 20, 105, 517
resource consent   142, 269, 271
resource management   137, 140, 266, 271
Resource Management Act (RMA)   135–36, 265, 269, 271
resources   26, 58, 61, 141–42, 238, 244, 516
  natural   128, 267, 274
responsibilities   32, 113–14, 181–82, 242–43, 246, 248–49, 333, 335, 490–92
  collective   407, 427
  individual   427, 483, 485, 490
  primary   114, 181, 506
responsible government   401, 420, 425
restraint   217, 346–47, 349, 376, 380
review   11–13, 42–44, 54–56, 93–94, 191–92, 335–36, 345–46, 359–61, 443–47, 451–56, 460–61, 468–69; *see also* judicial review
  administrative law   191, 197
  appellate   298, 308
  effective   41, 53
  emergent consistency ground of   12, 443, 453
  external   290, 353, 358
  grounds of   7, 12–13, 164, 350, 353, 443–47, 451–56, 468–69
  processes   48, 66–67, 80
  proportionality   447–48
  rationality   93–94, 97, 444, 446, 448, 454, 460
  reasonableness   94, 198
  substantive   8, 67, 93, 187, 191–92, 194, 444–47
rights   103–4, 107–12, 124–26, 159–60, 166–67, 201–2, 212–20, 268–69, 389–93, 500–505, 513, 515–18
  Aboriginal   135, 177, 198, 216–17
  bills of   3, 97–99, 126, 328
  and Brexit   99–102
  common law   95, 98–101, 110, 115, 336
  competing   501, 504, 515, 518
  to an effective remedy   99, 101–2
  equal   209, 223, 251
  fishing   142, 154, 273
  fundamental   7, 64, 92–93, 96–97, 99–101, 109–11, 333
  Indigenous   4, 7, 123–24, 126–29, 134–35, 203, 212–14, 220
  of Indigenous peoples   123, 134, 149–50, 159, 177, 215, 224
  learning   506–14

legal   4, 95, 111–12, 181, 269, 273, 291
native title   165, 167–68, 171, 173, 218
practising   514–20
protection   64, 96, 99–101, 114–15, 241, 503
qualified   508, 512
risk   87, 278, 280, 282–83, 286, 293, 323, 447, 464–65
rivers   9, 138, 255, 259, 262–63, 266–69, 271
RMA, *see* Resource Management Act
roles   7, 82, 89, 91, 101–3, 112–16, 118, 130–31, 134, 146–47, 313, 445–48
  constitutional   115, 123, 403, 407–8, 499
Royal and Vice-Regal official records   402–12
Royal Proclamation   180–82, 185, 201
rule of law   20–21, 47, 97–98, 296, 300, 327–28, 355, 392–93, 464–65
rule-benders   480
rule-enforcers, black-and-white   479–80, 493
rulemaking   55, 429–41
  agency   12, 429, 433, 436, 440
  formal   438
  notice-and-comment   435, 437–38

scandals   10, 283–84, 448–49
schools   107, 144, 151, 337, 347–48, 414, 522
  residential   177, 184
Scotland   102, 108, 117–18, 287, 338, 463
scrutiny   10, 94, 106, 147, 304, 313, 519–20
  judicial   193, 223, 277, 280, 285, 520
  public   130, 326
secrecy   399–401, 403, 405–9, 411–13, 415, 417, 419, 421–23, 427
sector decision-makers, private   363, 372
securitisation   47–48
security   28, 31–32, 43, 50, 68, 180, 331
Security Council   24, 26, 47, 79, 333
self-defence   78–80
self-determination   203, 230, 237, 245–46, 250, 264
self-governance   179, 200, 225, 228, 230
self-government   179, 184, 187, 192, 196–99, 202, 227, 232
  agreements   189–90
self-interest   22, 234, 327, 479
self-reliance   483–85, 490, 495
self-rule   230–31
self-sufficiency   242, 481–83, 485–86, 490–92, 495, 497
sentence appeals   298, 304
sentences   240, 289–90, 293, 295, 297–98, 303–9, 311–12
sentencing
  consistency in   303, 308–9
  courts   304, 307–8
  decisions   10, 297, 299, 303–4, 309, 313
  discretion   10, 297–314

guidelines   10, 297, 303, 306, 308, 314
judges   293, 297–98, 303, 305–9, 311–12, 314
principles   305–6, 312
separate jurisdictions   315–16, 318–19, 321
separation of powers   21, 28, 131, 388–89, 401, 429, 439–40
service delivery   163, 242, 330, 347
service users   326, 336, 343, 347
services, contracted-out   339, 342–43
settler governments   213, 218, 227, 231
settler societies   211–12, 219
settler states   2–3, 7, 9, 210, 212–13, 218, 227
Silver Commanders   506, 510–15, 517, 519–20
Singh   143–44, 153
social and legal attitudes   251, 278–82
social assistance agencies   471–98
social life   4, 326, 329
social media   296
social services   128, 137, 143, 152, 326
social workers   13, 472, 474, 477–79, 481, 489–90, 494
sociological legitimacy   234–35, 242, 250
SOEs (State-Owned Enterprises)   59, 128–30, 132–38, 146–47, 149–50, 152, 154
soft law   3, 5–6, 11, 20, 326–27, 387
solicitors   10, 280, 286, 349–50
sovereignty   124, 196, 205, 214, 216, 257–58, 264
  external   36, 40
  Indigenous   8, 205–6, 230–31
  parliamentary   104–5, 112, 114–15, 119, 131, 146
  popular   29, 206, 212
special interest   259, 396
special measures   61, 166, 220, 222–25
spiritual values   146, 266
sports   42–43, 59–60, 62–65, 335, 341, 372
standards   61–63, 72, 74, 76, 83–86, 327–29, 353–54, 377, 508
  administrative law   353–55, 357, 359–60, 362, 366, 369, 372–74, 376–77, 379–80, 382–84
  Convention   518, 521
  ethical   324, 327, 334
  minimum   74, 199
  normative   381, 472
Starmer, Sir Keir   504, 513–14
state governments   64, 168, 221
state institutions   102, 110, 230, 232, 282
statehood   21, 24
State-Owned Enterprises, *see* SOEs
states, distinctiveness   320–21
statutory authority   190, 245, 355, 362, 373, 381, 392–94
statutory interpretation   3, 8, 146, 159, 193–94, 198, 201, 418–19
statutory power, exercise of   11, 353, 355–57, 359–61, 369, 382, 389

540 Index

statutory powers   271–72, 287, 340, 356–57, 359, 362–66, 368–69, 372–73, 445
statutory purpose   461–62, 468, 498
strategic litigation   280, 351
structured discretion   10, 314
structures
   constitutional   9, 37, 91, 110, 119, 125, 274
   governmental   387–89
   guardianship   266, 269–70
   hierarchical   290, 347
   regional   243, 247, 249
subjective unfairness   450
subordinate legislation   109, 499
subsidiarity principle   332
substantive hearings   140, 142, 153
substantive law   97, 145, 147, 149
substantive review   8, 67, 93, 187, 191–92, 194, 444–47
suicide   114, 288
supervision   43, 63, 139, 182, 295
supervisors   462, 480–81, 484–85, 487, 491, 497
supervisory jurisdiction   299, 354, 360
support   44–46, 67–69, 86, 174–75, 208–10, 236–37, 247–48, 290–91, 382–83, 420–21, 486–91, 494–97
   active   52, 236, 239, 247, 251
   financial   61, 489
supranational courts   33, 88
supreme courts   93–95, 97–98, 100–102, 106–8, 116, 118, 137–39, 216–17, 369–70, 416, 433–34, 436–37
surrogate judges   312–13
synthesis   98, 312
   instinctive   297, 306, 310–12

tangata whenua   142, 152–53, 258, 267
taonga   125, 141–42, 148
Taranaki, Mt   9, 257, 259, 265
targets
   legitimate   75
   performance   488, 490, 493–94
   terrorist   74, 80–82
taxpayer-funded benefits   482, 488–91, 494, 498
taxpayers   322, 349, 483, 488–89, 493, 498
Te Awa Tupua   263, 265–73
Te Urewera negotiations   260–62
Technical Barriers to Trade (TBT)   67
technology   4, 53, 330, 429, 432
tendering decisions   364–65
Teoh   449–51, 454
terms, implied contractual   353, 366, 369, 375–80, 382–84
territories   21, 32, 36, 78–81, 84, 239, 249
territories power   207
terrorism suspects   73–74

terrorist groups   71, 76–78, 84
terrorist organisations   75, 77–78, 80
terrorist targets   74, 80–82
terrorists   72–73, 80, 87
tests
   justiciability   354, 356, 358, 361–63, 365–66, 369, 373–74, 382–83
   proportionality   93–94, 96, 98, 459
   rationality   445–46
   reasonableness   94, 148
Thoburn   108–9
threats   74–75, 79, 81, 83, 280, 283–84, 329, 331
   imminent   74–75, 80–82, 508, 511
Tilley   461, 463
title   201, 217, 273
   customary   135, 140, 151
   extinguishment of   166, 168–69, 174
   native   158, 165–70, 174, 176, 218, 220, 249
TMR (TM Retail)   453–54, 468
Torres Strait Islanders, *see* Aboriginal and Torres Strait Islander peoples
tort law and government liability   321–23
TPP (Trans-Pacific Partnership)   25, 43, 46, 50, 68
traditional knowledge   240, 264
traditional laws   8, 166–68, 175, 221, 264
traditional owners   1, 123, 157, 160–65, 169, 174, 220
trainers   506–10, 519–20
training   326, 331, 406, 504–5, 508, 519, 521
   bespoke   504, 520
   command   507–8, 513
translation   33, 158, 228, 233, 252, 509–10
transnational governance   52–53, 59, 332
transnational NGOs   46, 52
Trans-Pacific Partnership, *see* TPP
transparency   12, 41–44, 52–54, 56, 324–25, 327–29, 399–400, 428–29, 459
TRC (Truth and Reconciliation Commission)   177–78
treaties   2, 5, 103–4, 210, 215–16, 218–19, 399, 401
treatment, differential   220, 304
treaty law   56, 79, 149–50
Treaty of Waitangi   124, 126, 128–29, 147, 149–50, 213, 215, 257, 271
   and constitutional dialogue   129–34
   and judicial review   134–49
   obligations   138, 141, 143, 148–49, 151, 214
   principles   136, 141–42, 144, 147, 149–50, 152–53, 214
tribunals   43, 64, 66, 133–34, 192, 196, 320, 354–55, 361
trust   144, 148, 151, 156, 241, 247–48, 412
trustees   269, 271
truth   8, 203, 205, 212, 228, 313, 323

Truth and Reconciliation Commission, see TRC
Tūhoe   259–62, 264, 267, 270

UK, see United Kingdom
Uluru   8–9, 206–7, 212
Uluru Statement from the Heart   8, 205–9, 211, 213, 215, 219, 226, 228
unanimity   113, 162–63, 270
unaware claimants   449–54
undue hardship   482–84, 486, 488, 490, 492
unfairness   287, 304, 444, 446, 448, 450–51, 467
  subjective   450
  substantive   455
unincorporated associations   165, 366, 371–73
UNISON   95, 101
United Kingdom   91, 93–95, 97–99, 101–13, 115–17, 316, 335–38, 400, 402–5, 414–17, 427, 448–49
  after Brexit   91–119
  Constitution   104–5
  constitutional law   102–19
  executive and Parliament   106–7
  governments   91, 102, 114, 116–18, 317, 323, 404, 406–7
  House of Lords   93, 98, 288, 292, 328–29, 342, 502, 508
  Human Rights Act   13, 92, 97–98, 100–101, 108–9, 112, 328–29, 335–36, 341–43, 499–522
  Parliament   106–7, 115, 118
  Police Service of Northern Ireland (PSNI)   13, 500, 503–8, 510, 512–21
  policing   499–522
  role of courts   112–15
  Supreme Court   2, 110, 117, 515, 517
United Nations   28, 31–32, 47, 250, 333
  Security Council   24, 26, 47, 79, 333
United States   6, 27–28, 45–46, 49–51, 71–73, 75–82, 84–86, 323–24, 429, 431, 433–35, 438–41
  approach to use of force   76–77
  Constitution   71, 388, 430–31, 434, 439
  executive branch   83–87
  governments   48, 71–72, 429–31, 434, 436, 441
un-notified protests   515–17
unreasonableness   145–50, 156, 285, 298, 301, 375–77, 382–83
Urewera   9, 255–57, 259–68, 270, 272–74
US, see United States

use of force   71–74, 79, 85–86, 88, 518–19
  ambiguity and overlap in approach   78–80
  approach of some US allies   78
  international humanitarian law/law of armed conflict model   75–76
  legal paradigms   73–80
  strict law-enforcement model   73–74
  United States approach   76–77

validity   37–38, 43, 168, 216, 229, 395–96
values   9–10, 131, 203, 227–28, 234, 236–40, 251–52, 327–28, 439, 483–84
  Indigenous   192, 234, 239, 253
  market   63, 133, 327
  public law   323, 327
  rule-of-law   300, 448
  social   235, 239
  spiritual   146, 266
  and tenets   327–34
vicarious liability   322
victims   251, 288, 305, 322, 344
Victoria   2, 237–38, 252, 297, 307–8, 313, 368–70
  Court of Appeal   297, 303–4, 309, 312, 370
visas   358, 362, 452, 456
voter turnout   240, 247–48, 251
voters   209, 215, 247–48

Waitangi
  Fisheries Commission   140, 143–44, 151
  Treaty of   124, 126, 128–29, 132–37, 145, 147, 149–50, 257, 271
  Tribunal   128–29, 132–34, 139–40, 143, 149–52, 154–56, 262–63
Wales   102, 282, 287, 290, 296, 319, 406–7
water, management   142, 153
welfare   49, 68–69, 243, 394, 461, 482
  benefits   326, 338
wellbeing   263, 266, 271
Whanganui Iwi   255, 259, 262–63, 269, 271
Whanganui River   9, 255–57, 259, 262–63, 265–74
  negotiations   262–63
Williscroft   311–12
Windrush scandal   448–49
withdrawal   25, 91, 94, 102–3, 112–13, 117
witnesses   291–92
workload   482, 492–94, 498
WTO (World Trade Organization)   43, 46, 48, 50–51, 67

CPSIA information can be obtained
at www.ICGtesting.com
Printed in the USA
LVHW081531101221
705865LV00017B/1711